Nanjing
and the
Lower Yangzi

Text and Photos by
Eric N Danielson

Text and photographs by: Eric N. Danielson
Editor: Patricia Ng
Designer: Jean Tan

© 2004 Marshall Cavendish International (Asia) Private Limited

Published by **Times Editions** – Marshall Cavendish
An imprint of Marshall Cavendish International (Asia) Private Limited
A member of Times Publishing Limited
Times Centre, 1 New Industrial Road, Singapore 536196
Tel: (65) 6213 9288   Fax: (65) 6285 4871
E-mail: te@sg.marshallcavendish.com
Online Bookstore: www.marshallcavendish.com/genref

Malaysian Office:
Federal Publications Sdn Berhad (General & Reference Publishing) (3024-D)
Times Subang
Lot 46, Persiaran Teknologi Subang
Subang Hi-Tech Industrial Park
Batu Tiga, 40000 Shah Alam
Selangor Darul Ehsan, Malaysia
Tel: (603) 5635 2191   Fax: (603) 5635 2706
E-mail: cchong@tpg.com.my

All rights reserved. No part of this publication may be reproduced, stored in a retrieval system or transmitted, in any form or by any means, electronic, mechanical, photocopying, recording or otherwise, without the prior permission of the copyright owner.

Limits of Liability/Disclaimer of Warranty: The author and publisher of this book have used their best efforts in preparing this book. The publisher makes no representation or warranties with respect to the contents of this book, and specifically disclaims any implied warranties or merchantability or fitness for any particular purpose, and shall in no events be liable for any loss of profit or any other commercial damage, including but not limited to special, incidental, consequential, or other damages.

National Library Board Singapore Cataloguing in Publication Data

Danielson, Eric N.
Nanjing and the lower Yangzi :- from the past to present / text and photos by Eric N. Danielson. – Singapore :- Times Editions-Marshall Cavendish,- 2004.
p. cm. – (The new Yangzi River trilogy ;- vol. 2)
Includes bibliographical references and index.
ISBN : 981-232-598-0

1. Historic sites- - China- - Nanjing Shi- - Guidebooks. 2. Historic sites – China- - Jiangsu Sheng – Guidebooks. 3. Historic sites- - China- - Anhui Sheng – Guidebooks. 4. Historic sites – China- - Jiangxi Sheng – Guidebooks.
5. Nanjing Shi (China)- - Guidebooks. 6. Jiangsu Sheng (China) – Guidebooks.
7. Anhui Sheng (China)- - Guidebooks. 8. Jiangxi Sheng (China)- - Guidebooks.
9. Yangtze River Delta (China)- - Guidebooks.
I. Title. II. Series: The new Yangzi River trilogy ;- vol. 2

DS793   915.1 — dc21   SLS2004042494

Printed in Singapore by Times Printers Pte Ltd

Contents

Vol. 2 Nanjing and the Lower Yangzi

Series Introduction	iv
Volume 2 Introduction	vi

Part 1

The Yangzi Estuary — 1
Jiangsu Province

a. Zhenjiang	5
b. Nanjing	37

Anhui Province

a. Ma An Shan	181
b. Wuhu	193
c. Jiuhua Shan	223
d. Anqing	249

Jiangxi Province

a. Hukou	281
b. Jiujiang	301
c. Lushan	327

Part 2

Topics of Interest

a. The Treaty Ports	419
b. Navigation of the Lower Yangzi River	428
c. Buddhism in China	430

Bilbiography — 445
Appendices:

Appendix A: Notes on Chinese Nomenclature	456
Appendix B: Survival Travel Chinese	458
Appendix C: Transportation in China	463

Index	466
About the Author	472

Series Introduction

he history of China is, in many ways, the story of three inland waterways: the Yellow River (Huang He), the Grand Canal (Da Yun He), and the Yangzi River (Chang Jiang). Although each of these has played a dominant role in China's historical development, this series of three books is about the Yangzi River (sometimes Yangtze or even Yangtsze), which is known to the Chinese as Chang Jiang or "Long River." The Chinese name is appropriate as the Yangzi is the world's third longest river, after the Nile River and the Amazon River. Although it flows 6,276.4 kilometers (3,900 miles) from the Qinghai-Tibetan Plateau to the East China Sea, only the 2,735.9-km (1,700-mile) section east of Yibin in Sichuan Province has, historically, been navigable by ships. The section west of Yibin was once referred to by a different name, Jinsha Jiang or "River of Golden Sands." This series focuses on the navigable section of the Yangzi River from Shanghai to Chongqing, a total distance of 2,365.7 km (1,470 miles).

China's most ancient imperial capital cities were built along the Yellow River (Huang He). Later, it was the Grand Canal (Da Yun He) that became China's main economic artery, transporting rice and manufactured goods from the south and the east to the imperial capital in Beijing in the north. The Grand Canal gave rise to culturally and economically important cities such as Yangzhou, Suzhou and Hangzhou.

The Yangzi River (Chang Jiang) began playing an important role in China's history during the era of the Three Kingdoms (San Guo; 220–280AD), when two of the three rival regimes had territory along the river, and most of the significant battles were fought for control of Yangzi River towns such as Jingzhou and Jinling (Nanjing). The Yangzi again became a power center during the five Southern Dynasties (317–589AD), which ruled southern China between the fall of the Western Jin Dynasty and the reunification of the whole country under the Sui Dynasty.

It is in the last 1,000 years, however, that the Yangzi River has truly dominated China's history. Military defeats in northern China saw the retreat of the Southern Tang and Southern Song to southeastern China, where the Yangzi served as their frontline of defense against the advancing barbarians. The Yangzi became the lifeblood of China especially after Zhu Yuanzhang (Hong Wu) established the first Ming Dynasty (1368–1644) capital in Nanjing.

In a dramatic reversal of fortunes, the Yangzi River provided barbarians from the west access to the ancient Ming capital in the 19th century. The First Opium War ended in August 1842 with the signing of the Treaty of Nanking. For the next 100 years, until the unequal treaties were abolished in 1943, the Yangzi served as a highway into central China for foreign businessmen, missionaries and diplomats, together with the foreign gunboats that protected them. During this period, foreign domination of the Yangzi served as a symbol of China's humiliation by Western powers. Regaining full autonomy was one of the first steps taken by the New China in 1949, as witnessed by the HMS Amethyst Incident in May of that year.

This series is meant to serve as a historical guide to the cities, towns, and sights of interest along the stretch of river from Shanghai to Chongqing. It identifies for the reader the sites of historical significance that still remain amid China's current explosion of economic development, to explain the roles these sites played in China's history, and to provide practical guidance on finding them. All too often, travelers visit historic sights without truly understanding their significance and may, therefore, be unable to truly appreciate them. At other times, visitors fail to find these sites because they are ignorant of them, or wish to visit a site but are unable to locate it. This series hopes to help the foreign traveler to China overcome these pitfalls.

This trilogy also provides a wealth of practical information for the traveler. This includes:
- contact information for the main hotels in every city described;
- recommended restaurants for all but the smaller towns;
- local transportation guides;
- precise street addresses and directions;
- useful telephone numbers; and
- Pinyin phonetic transliterations of all Chinese place names and individuals mentioned.

After more than 1,000 years of dominating China's culture, economy, and politics, the Yangzi River today is in the midst of major changes. These come in the form of urban development, hydroelectric projects, and transportation infrastructure, which will result in an entirely new Yangzi River. Yet, together with modernization comes a trend for preservation, restoration, and reconstruction of China's key historic relics. This sees China actively rediscovering and embracing its previously lost heritage while moving forward into the 21st century.

After the Communist victory of 1949, today known in China somewhat one-sidedly as the "Liberation" (Jiefang), all structures remotely related to the defeated Guomindang regime and the capitalist class were occupied by the Communist Party (Gong Chang Dang), the People's Republic government (Renmin Zheng Fu), and the People's Liberation Army (Renmin Jiefang Jun). For over 50 years, these sites remained closed to the public. Currently, many historic mansions and estates are being turned into hotels, restaurants, and public museums. This series assists readers in discovering these formerly forbidden places.

Preface

his second volume in our series takes us up the Yangzi River through the three provinces of Jiangsu, Anhui, and Jiangxi. In comparison to the much better known Three Gorges (San Xia) on the upper Yangzi, few foreigners visit the areas described in this volume. Nonetheless, this is a region rich in historical sights and natural wonders. It is the heartland of Buddhism in China, with a revival in temple reconstruction and renovation under way. It is the home of impressive mountains such as Jiuhua Shan and Lushan. A whole series of fascinating temple islands dot this section of the river, from Jiao Shan and Jin Shan in Zhenjiang, to Xiao Gu Shan mid-way between Anqing and Hukou, and Da Gu Shan in Poyang Hu. Ancient brick and stone pagodas line both sides of the river, from Ma An Shan's Jin Zhu Ta and Huang Shan Bao Ta, to Wuhu's Zhong Jiang Ta, Anqing's Zhen Feng Ta, Shi Zhong Shan's Lin Jiang Ta , and Jiujiang's Suo Jiang Ta. Rock promontories are dotted with traditional pavilions, such as Zhenjiang's Bei Gu Shan, Nanjing's Yanzi Ji, Ma An Shan's Cai Shi Ji, and Hukou's Shi Zhong Shan. Relics of western imperialism still stand in the form of the former treaty ports' British consulates, Christian churches, and missionary schools. The lower Yangzi awaits rediscovery.

Our guide to these sights will help us understand their significance by showing them through the eyes of Tang and Song dynasty poets, Buddhist monks, Confucian scholars, Christian missionaries, European explorers, Western diplomats, rebels against regimes as well as dynastic supporters, conquerors and the conquered, Nationalists and Communists, revolutionaries and reactionaries, modern-day scholars, and the author himself.

Visiting these sights is becoming easier by the day with the completion of a growing network of modern highways. Places once reachable only by river steamer can now be visited by motor vehicle much faster and more conveniently than by boat. North and south banks of the river, separated for thousands of years, are now being joined together as never before by an increasing series of bridges. Less than five years ago, this lower section of the Yangzi below Wuhan could only be crossed by bridge at Nanjing. By October 2003, three new bridges had already crossed the Yangzi at Jiangyin, Wuhu, and Jiujiang, with a second bridge added at Nanjing. Two more bridges were under construction at Zhenjiang and Anqing. Future plans call for a whole network of bridges to connect Shanghai with Nantong in northern Jiangsu, via the islands of Changxing, Hengsha, and Chongming which is located at the mouth of the Yangzi, just before it flows into the East China Sea.

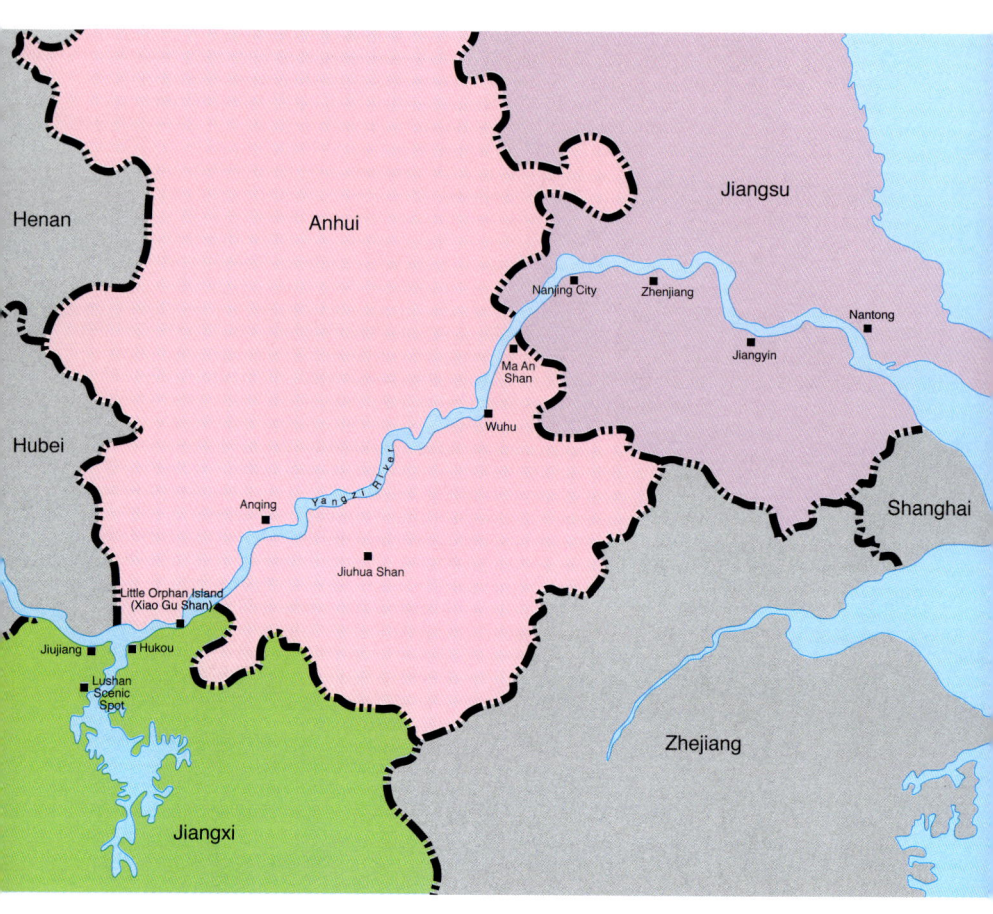

An Overview of the Yangzi River, with the provinces and places covered in this book highlighted.

Part 1:

The Yangzi Estuary

Sailing up the Yangzi River from its 25-km-wide (15.5-mile-wide) mouth, you take the southern of two channels past **Chongming Island** (Chongming Dao) — the third largest island in China after Hainan and Taiwan — which covers a total area of 1,041 sq km (402 sq mmiles). Formed by centuries of silt washed down the river from its upper reaches, the island has grown dramatically over 100 years, as evidenced by historic maps. In 1947, G.R.G. Worcester measured it as being 60 km (37 miles) long and 8 to 16 km (5 to 10 miles) wide, but estimated it was only 500 years old.

The completion of the Three Gorges Dam in 2003 will stop the downward flow of silt, causing Chongming to stop growing and possibly even contract in size. Chongming's other connection with the Three Gorges (San Xia) is its role as the new home for thousands of resettled migrants from the area of the new dam reservoir. Established as a county (*xian*) in 1369, the island is now part of the Shanghai municipality (*shi*). Few Shanghainese from the city center have visited this rural county that currently can only be reached by a one-hour boat ride from Baoshan.

Lying in between Chongming Island and the south bank of the Yangzi estuary are the two much smaller islands of Hengsha Dao and Changxing Dao. Even more isolated than Chongming, these islands also belong to the Shanghai municipality, and can also only be reached by boat from Baoshan. The islands are inhabited, but until now have largely been the secluded home of quiet temples and restful holiday resorts. All that is set to change in the near future, with the construction of China's largest shipbuilding yard on Changxing Dao. Eight km (5 miles) of its coastline have been designated for the project. Several existing shipbuilding companies will move their operations there from the Shanghai city center, including the famous Jiangnan Shipyard. Furthermore, it was announced in November 2003 that a 9-km-long (5.6-mile-long) tunnel would be built from the south bank of the Yangzi estuary to Changxing Dao, followed by a 10-km-long (6.2-mile-long) bridge connecting the island of Changxing to that of Chongming.

The Huangpu River empties into the Yangzi from the south about 51 km (32 miles) from the mouth of the latter, at Wusong Kou. From here, the Shanghai city center is 25km (15 miles) up the Huangpu. It is sometimes said you can see three different colors of water at this spot where the Yangzi, Huangpu, and East China Sea all meet.

On the north side of the Yangzi estuary — in the northern Jiangsu province, 60 km (37 miles) upriver from Wusong — is the town of **Nantong**, known before 1949 as Tong Zhou (Tungchow). Until now, the absence of direct road or rail connections between Shanghai and Nantong has meant that the town received few visitors. The Yangzi River is 18 km (11.2 miles) wide at this point and crossing it by boat can be a time consuming process. The nearest highway bridge spanning the Yangzi to the north side is now at Jiangyin, but plans are in motion to integrate Nantong much more closely into the Shanghai transportation hub. As part of the Changxing Dao project, it is expected that the western tip of Chongming Dao will be connected with Nantong. These changes may make it much easier to visit the sights at these places, but it may also cause their natural charms to be destroyed by development.

Nantong is known for its five hills of Lang Shan, Jian Shan, Jun Shan, Huang Ni Shan, and Ma An Shan. Lang Shan is by far the highest of the five at 107 m (351.1 ft) in height. It is located in the north of Nantong city, overlooking the Yangzi River. Sights on Lang Shan include two temples, the Guang Jiao Si Buddhist Temple and the Fa Ru Temple, as well as two pagodas, Huan Gong Ta and Zhi Yun Ta.

Although Lang Shan has the most numerous sights, the other four hills are also worth visiting. Before 1949, the summit of Jian Shan was also home to another Buddhist temple, which has only recently been rebuilt. At the foot of Ma An Shan and Huang Ni Shan is a causeway extending out into the Yangzi River where stands the Jia Zhen Memorial Tower (Jia Zhen Ji Nian Bei) which commemorates the many attempts the Buddhist monk Jia Zhen made to sail from Yangzhou to Japan during the Tang Dynasty. On at least two failed attempts, his boat capsized and sank in the treacherous ocean-like waters off the coast of Nantong's Five Hills (Wu Shan).

Jun Shan was the site of an astronomical observatory founded by the local industrialist Zhang Jian (1853–1926) over one hundred years ago. The Jun Shan Observatory used to collect weather data and send it to the Zikawei Observatory run by the Roman Catholic Jesuit priests in Shanghai. Today, the newly reopened Zikawei Library still has copies of the some of the reports sent by the Jun Shan Observatory. In fact, the observatory building still stands on Jun Shan and is open to visitors. Although it is no longer a functioning observatory and all its equipment has been removed, it does contain some fascinating exhibits. Next door is the newly rebuilt Pu Tuo Si Buddhist Temple with its Jade Buddha (Yu Fo).

It is also said that Nantong has three notable pagodas. The square Wen Feng Ta is located in Wu Fu Temple and dates from the Ming Dynasty (1368–1644). The hexagonal Guang Xiao Ta was built in the Tang Dynasty (618–907 AD) and stands in the north of Nantong City. The octagonal Zhi Yun Ta was built in the Song Dynasty (960–1279) and stands on the summit of Lang Shan.

The small Jiangsu town of Taicang, on the south bank across from Nantong, is a major oil import center. Multinational oil companies such as ExxonMobil, British Petroleum, and Shell have enormous tank farm and refinery facilities here. In order for oil tankers to unload their cargo safely, piers have been built as far as 1.6 km (1 mile) out into the middle of the Yangzi River.

Jiangyin, 176 km (105 miles) from the mouth of the Yangzi River, has always impressed travelers as the spot where the wide Yangzi estuary suddenly closes into a narrow neck marking the beginning of the river proper. In 1842, the British fleet anchored at Jiangyin for several days before proceeding onward to Zhenjiang and Nanjing. In November 1858, the Earl of Elgin's secretary Laurence Oliphant described Jiangyin as being a narrows sandwiched between two high hills topped by fortresses, temples, and pagodas. Thomas W. Blakiston described Jiangyin as "the gate of the Yangtsze" after sailing upriver to Zhenjiang in February 1861. In fact, the Yangzi is only 1.2 km (0.75 mile) wide at Jiangyin.

Due to the natural defenses of its topography, Jiangyin has always been the site of fortifications designed to stop either the advance of invaders sailing upriver, or northern barbarians trying to cross the Yangzi River to southeastern China (Jiangnan). After the fall of the Southern Ming regime in Nanjing on 8 June 1645, Jiangyin was the last city of the Jiangnan region to finally fall to the Manchu invaders of the new Qing Dynasty. Ming loyalists in Jiangying held out against an 80-day siege until 9 October 1645. When Commander F.H.E. Skyrme published his guide to the Yangzi in April 1937, he described forts as being strategically placed on the top of hills on the south bank. At that time, the town of Jiangyin was still surrounded by a 6.4-km-long (4-mile-long) square wall. After the November 1937 fall of Shanghai to the Japanese, a last-ditch attempt to stop the invader's advance on Nanjing was made at Jiangyin, where a boom was placed across the river to stop ships from sailing upstream. Later, during the Chinese civil war, the sudden surrender of the Guomindang garrison at the Jiangyin fort on 21 April 1949 allowed the Communist army to cross the Yangzi River to the south bank. This in turn caused the fall of the Guomindang capital in Nanjing two days later on 23 April.

Today, Jiangyin is a highly industrialized area with investments from 1,600 foreign companies. Since it opened on 28 September 1999, this has also been the site of the lowest highway bridge crossing the Yangzi River, providing a land route for vehicles driving from Shanghai to Yangzhou in Jiangbei. At 3,071 m (10,075.5 ft) in length, it was the longest bridge in China when it was completed. It is 196 m (643 ft) high, about the same as a 70-story building.

Jiangsu Province

Zhenjiang

Historical Introduction

Zhenjiang has had ten names, including Dantu County (Dantu Xian) in Qin Shi Huang Di's reign (221–220 BC), and Jingkou during the Three Kingdoms (San Guo) (220–280 AD) when Sun Quan, the King of Wu, built a city here. It received its current name in the year 1113, near the end of the Northern Song (Bei Song) Dynasty (960–1126), when it was declared a prefecture named Zhenjiang Fu. The name Zhenjiang (Chinkiang) means, appropriately, "guard the river."

Zhenjiang has been an important Chinese naval base since the time of the Southern Song (Nan Song) Dynasty (1127–1279), when the Yangzi served as the Song northern line of defense against the invading Jin barbarians from the North. In later years, this town played a key strategic role in defending the much larger city of Nanjing from fleets of foreign invaders traveling up the river. Much evidence remains of the town's defensive role, with gun battery emplacements and underground tunnels left over from World War II dotting the landscape, as well as fortifications from as early as the First Opium War of 1839–1842.

Zhenjiang's strategic importance was derived largely from its location at the crossroads of two of China's most important transportation waterways: the east-west transport link of the Yangzi River and the north-south line of the **Grand Canal** (Da Yun He) connecting Beijing with the rich Jiangnan region of the south. Typically the Jiangnan region provided the rice, silk, fish, and taxes required to support the capital city and imperial court in the barren north of China. During the Qing Dynasty (1644–1911), the emperors **Qian Long** and **Kang Xi** both made six inspection tours of southeastern China, each time visiting Zhenjiang on their way down the Grand Canal from Beijing. Their visits were so frequent that temporary imperial palaces were established for them to stay in during their visits.

In addition to its transportation and military importance, Zhenjiang has, for centuries, been one of the most important centers of Buddhism in China. Its three picturesque riverside hills of Jin Shan, Bei Gu Shan, and Jiao Shan have traditionally been home to some of the largest, most respected, and devout Buddhist communities in the whole country.

Zhenjiang was once home to a special pavilion housing one of only seven sets of the Complete Library of the Four Branches (Si Ku Quan Shu) which was compiled during the Qian Long reign (1736–1796) of the Qing Dynasty. This compilation took a team of scholars 15 years — beginning in 1722 — to complete, and included 3,500 selections from four categories of books: classics (*jing*), history (*shi*), philosophy (*zi*), and literature (*ji*). It was partly based on the earlier Yong Le Encyclopedia (Yong Le Da Dian), completed in 1408. The final version of the Si Ku Quan Shu was estimated to be 2.3 million pages long. Unfortunately, the pavilion was burned down and its contents lost during the British occupation of the city in 1842.

Zhenjiang was captured in the **First Opium War** of 1839–1842 by a British naval expedition led by Sir Henry Pottinger and Admiral Sir William Parker. Sailing upriver from Shanghai, which they had already captured, the British fleet first attacked the Chinese forts on **Jiao Shan**, an island 4.8 km (3 miles) east of Zhenjiang. The remains of the primitive gun emplacements and earthen barricades of these forts can still be seen today. After the fall of Jiao Shan, the British fleet anchored in the river off Zhenjiang on 17 July 1842 and their troops camped on **Bei Gu Shan**, from where they could look down on the walled city of Zhenjiang below.

At the time, Zhenjiang still had a city wall approximately 6.4 km (4 miles) in circumference, 9 m (30 ft) high, and 1.5 m (5 feet) thick, with four gates. According to R.A. Villard's map, and a similar one in the *Jingkou Qu Zhi*, the walled city lay roughly in the area between Bei Gu Shan to the north and the Grand Canal (Da Yun He) to the west and south. The walls were repaired in 1841, making them a formidable barrier to the final British assault on 21 July 1842. A breach was ultimately made in the Western Gate, allowing the city to be captured by the British the same day. However, the British lost more troops in the battle for Zhenjiang than during any other incident of the First Opium War, suffering 168 casualties out of a force of 9,000 men. After the city's capture, additional sections of the city wall were later torn down by the British on July 26th and 27th.

The capture of Zhenjiang was crucial in the subsequent surrender of Nanjing, further up the Yangzi River, as it meant that the Qing forces in Nanjing were cut off from any reinforcements or supplies that might have been sent down the

Grand Canal (Da Yu He) from Beijing. Although most of the naval expedition force left Zhenjiang on 29 July 1842 headed for Nanjing, a small occupation force remained camped on Bei Gu Shan until 4 October 1842.

Twelve days after the Taiping rebels established the capital of their Taiping Heavenly Kingdom (Taiping Tian Guo) in Nanjing on 19 March 1853, Zhenjiang was also occupied by them for the first time on 31 March 1853. It continued to serve as the eastern defense of Nanjing for nearly five years until it was recaptured by Qing forces on 27 December 1857. The Taipings' occupation of Zhenjiang also gave them control over the Grand Canal (Da Yun He), preventing the Qing from using this important waterway to ship men, materials, or supplies either north or south.

Despite its previous capture and two-month occupation by the British in 1842, Zhenjiang did not actually become a treaty port until April 1861, in accordance with the 1858 **Treaty of Tientsin** (Tianjin) between Britain and China. The delay of several years in opening Zhenjiang as a port was caused by the outbreak of the Second Opium War and the subsequent need for the foreign powers to occupy the capital city of Beijing in 1860 before the terms of the Treaty of Tientsin could be implemented.

After the port's opening as a treaty port on 10 May 1861, British and American diplomats, businessmen, and missionaries began arriving to take up residence. Zhenjiang's new resident foreign community constructed a Bund along the Yangzi River, and established a concession area separate from the Chinese part of the city. A self-governing municipal council elected by the foreign leasers of the land administered the concession, which was protected by a private police force that included the dreaded Sikhs from British India. The foreign concession was centered around what is today **Bo Xian Park** (Bo Xian Gongyuan).

By 1877, Zhenjiang had 42 foreign residents, of whom 31 were British, not counting a floating population of Protestant and Catholic missionaries. In the early 1890s, this number had actually dropped to less than 40 foreign residents. Nonetheless, the port was considered important enough for the British firm of Butterfield & Swire to open an office there in 1890 for their steamship line, the China Navigation Co.

Relations between the foreigners and the local population were not good. On 5 February 1889, after British Sikh policemen in the concession had mistreated some Chinese, riots broke out and a mob angrily destroyed the offices of foreign companies and concession police stations, as well as the British and American Consulates. The entire foreign population fled to the safety of a river steamer anchored in the Yangzi. By the time the unrest was over, both the British and American consulates had been looted of their contents, wrecked, and burned down, as had several missionary houses. The rebuilt British Consulate was a palatial Victorian-era edifice, which later became the **Zhenjiang Museum** (Zhenjiang Bowuguan) and still stands today.

One dramatic change to Zhenjiang's natural environment was the silting up of the former riverside bund along the British Concession, a process that was started in 1879 and completed by 1908. The result was that a new area of land was created, almost equal in size to the former concession, and the town's riverside waterfront had moved considerably to the north. A street named Xiao Matou Jie (Ferry Dock Road), near the former British Consulate, testifies to this change.

Immediately after the infamous **May 30 Incident** of 1925, which sparked anti-foreign protests in all the major cities of China, the British consulate in Zhenjiang was again under siege by protesters. The concession's police station was also attacked and set on fire, causing the concession police to fire volleys over the heads of the protesters. Many foreign civilians were evacuated by river boat to the safety of Shanghai.

Despite this incident, life for the resident foreign community returned somewhat to normal for several more years until the Guomindang's Northern Expedition (Bei Fa) of 1926–1927 caused its final demise. The British Concession was occupied in 1927, but not formally returned to China until 15 November 1929, following an exchange of diplomatic notes on 31 October that year. The former British Waterworks and British Power Station were both taken over by the local authorities. The British Consul was withdrawn, and the former Consulate abandoned.

After Nanjing became the national capital in 1927, Zhenjiang became the provincial capital of Jiangsu Province. In 1929, the Guomindang formally moved the capital of Jiangsu province (Jiangsu Sheng Zhen Fu) from Nanjing to Zhenjiang. In the same year, part of the city wall was torn down to make way for the new Zhongshan Road, which crossed the whole city by 1931.

By 1931, there were only half a dozen resident foreigners left. The Zhenjiang Club continued to function in the old Customs Club Building, but consisted of nothing more than a small library and billiard room. The former Victoria Park had been surrendered and converted into today's Bo Xian Park (Bo Xian Gongyuan).

Zhenjiang was considered a key strategic point in both the Sino-Japanese War (1937–1945) and the Chinese Civil War (1946–1949) that followed. In December 1937, the Guomindang army mounted a desperate last-ditch effort in Zhenjiang to stop the Japanese advance up the Yangzi River from Shanghai, towards the national capital at Nanjing. Concrete gun emplacements, pillboxes, and tunnels left over from this defense can still be found at Bei Gu Shan, Elephant Hill (Xiang Shan), Jiao Shan, and even along city streets such as Bo Xian Lu and Changjiang Lu.

During the Chinese Civil War of 1946–1949, the Communists crossed the Yangzi River from Jiang Bei to Jiang Nan at Zhenjiang, cutting the railway from Nanjing to Shanghai and thus depriving the Guomindang capital city of supplies, reinforcements, or an escape route. It was in the waters off Zhenjiang that the British warship, HMS Amethyst, was shelled and immobililzed in April 1949 by Communist artillery as it tried to reach Nanjing with supplies.

Nowadays, Zhenjiang is a relaxing riverside town at the junction of the Yangzi River and the Grand Canal (Da Yun He). The latter actually runs through the middle of town and is lined with well-manicured greenbelts, featuring pedestrian promenades and willow trees along both sides. This is a sleepy town full of tree-lined streets, friendly residents, and small old *longtang* houses. So far, it has largely been bypassed by the ravages of economic development, urban renewal, and foreign investment currently taking their toll on Nanjing and Shanghai. The natural beauty of its three riverside hills still survives, and several of its former Buddhist communities have experienced a healthy revival in recent years.

Urban Development

Located 291 km (182 miles) from the mouth of the Yangzi, the Zhenjiang Municipality (Zhenjiang Shi) now covers an area of 3,843 sq km (1,483.8 sq miles) and shares a western border with the eastern boundary of Nanjing. In 1987, the port was opened to foreign ships for the first time since 1949. Although it had previously avoided both the benefits and destruction of the economic development that had earlier hit Shanghai and Nanjing, by 2003, some large scale urban development had begun to take place.

Changjiang Lu is a new six-lane boulevard running along the town's Yangzi River waterfront, connecting Jiao Shan to Jin Shan. This new road is 3 km (1.9 miles) long and 40 m (131.2 ft) wide. Construction started in 2001 and was completed in the fall of 2003. The building of this new boulevard from one end of town to the other has caused some previous street names to disappear, such as Jin Shan Xi Lu and Bin Jiang Lu. Along the section of Changjiang Lu, formerly known as Bin Jiang Da Dao, a waterfront pedestrian promenade has been built. This section lies roughly between Bei Gu Shan and Jin Shan. Here you can walk along the river's edge, past a boat dock (*matou*) and a floating restaurant.

Yangzi River Runyang Highway Bridge (Runyang Changjiang Gonglu Da Qiao)

Construction of this highway bridge that will cross over the Yangzi River from Zhenjiang to Yangzhou began in October 2000 and its estimated completion date is October 2005. It will be 23.56 km (14.6 miles) long when completed. This bridge will connect Zhenjiang with Yangzhou by road for the first time in history.

About 8 km (5 miles) from the city center, out in the western suburbs of town, a new **Economic Development District** was under construction in October 2003.

Zhenjiang Yangzi Dolphin Nature Reserve

In October 2003, a nature reserve for the endangered White Flag Dolphin was established in a 57-sq-km (22-sq-mile) section of the Yangzi River, off the coast of Zhenjiang. Although experts estimate that in 1949, there were between 5,000 and 6,000 Yangzi dolphins. By 1986, their numbers had been reduced to only 300, and by 1997, just 100 were thought to remain. Today, it is estimated that only 50 wild dolphins continue to survive in the Yangzi River, making them one of the 12 most endangered species in the world. Four dolphins were spotted swimming in the Zhenjiang section of the Yangzi River in 1997, and this is the site of the only film footage ever recorded of them in their natural habitat. Three other nature reserves already exist for the dolphins in other sections of the river, including one in Tongling, Anhui, and another in Wuhan, Hubei. The Wuhan reserve had been the only one to successfully capture a live dolphin in 1980 but after 23 years in captivity, this dolphin, named Qi Qi, passed away in August 2002 without producing any offspring.

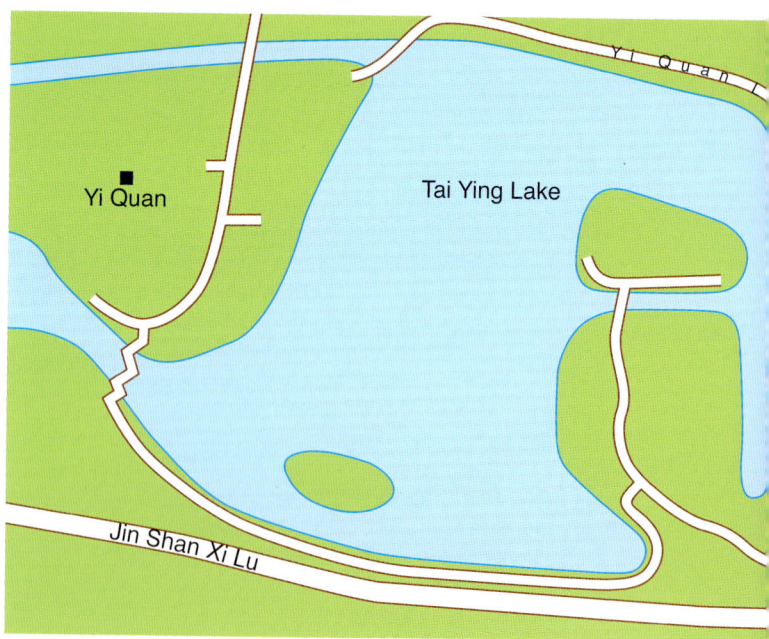

Map of Jin Shan

Zhenjiang Sights

Zhenjiang is most famous for its three riverside temple hills of Jin Shan, Bei Gu Shan, and Jiao Shan. However, out in the surrounding countryside of the Zhenjiang municipality are the mountain top temple complexes of Mao Shan (Taoist), Bao Hua Shan (Buddhist), Bao Ta Shan, the Nan Shan Scenic Area, and the Hermit's Hill. In Zhenjiang's Danyang County, one can find the tombs of emperors from the Qi Dynasty (479–502 AD) and Liang Dynasty (502–557 AD), leaders who once ruled Southern China from their capital in Nanjing. The tomb of Liang Emperor Wu Di's son Xiao Ji (d. 529AD), with its impressive stone sculptures of mythical winged Bixie animals, can be found in Zhenjiang's Ju Rong County. Relics of Western imperialism survive in the form of the British Consulate and other buildings along Bo Xian Lu in the former British Concession, as well as the home of American missionary Pearl S. Buck.

Golden Island (Jin Shan)

This temple hill northwest of downtown Zhenjiang was originally an island in the middle of the Yangzi River. During the Dao Guang reign (1821–1850) of the Qing Dynasty, the island began to move closer to the southern shore of the Yangzi river as the main channel shifted northward. According to Chinese sources, from the fifth year of the Guang Xu reign (1879), the island began to be connected to the south bank by a narrow neck of

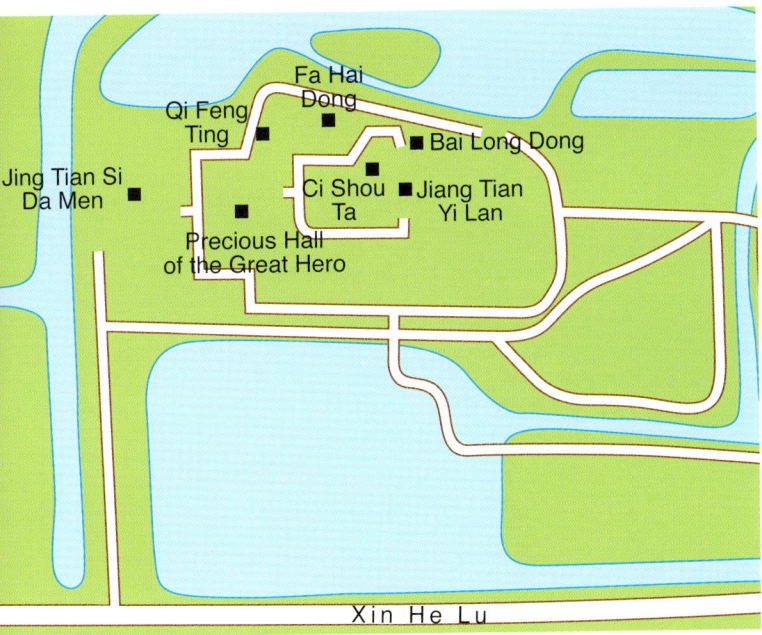

The Jin Shan Ci Shou Ta pagoda in Zhenjiang.

land. By the last year of the Guang Xu reign (1908), it was completely surrounded by land on all sides. Commander F.H.E. Skyrme gives a slightly different account in his 1937 guide to the Yangzi. He states that Jin Shan was on the north bank of the river in 1823. In 1842, it became an island in the middle of the river, then was joined to the south bank of the river by a narrow sand spit in 1862. By 1862, Jin Shan arrived at its present position a mile inland from the southern bank. However, Skyrme was probably relying on the record of infrequent Western travelers rather than more precise Chinese sources. Although no longer an island in the Yangzi, the hill is still framed by water on all sides in the form of several large lakes and a network of canals. To the north is Ying Shan Lake and to the west is Tai Ying Lake.

This western area is a newly developed green park featuring several traditional style pavilions

 POINT OF INTEREST

Jin Shan's Buddhist temple has had many names throughout its long history. It was first built more than 1,500 years ago in the Eastern Jin (Dong Jin) Dynasty (317–419 AD) and known as Ze Xin Si. Later, in the Tang Dynasty (618–907), it was called Jin Shan Si. During the the Northern Song (Bei Song) Dynasty (960–1126), the temple's name was repeatedly changed by various emperors. In the Zhen Zong reign (997–1022), the emperor Zhao Heng dreamt he visited Jin Shan and renamed it Long You Si (Dragon Visit Temple). Although the name was briefly changed back to Jin Shan Si, it was changed again during the Hui Zong reign (1101–1125) because this emperor believed in Taoism and had Jin Shan converted into a Taoist temple. Later in the Song Dynasty (960–1279), Hui Qing Er Di converted Jin Shan back to a Buddhist temple under the name Long You Si. From the Yuan Dynasty (1279–1368) through the Ming Dynasty (1368–1644), it was once again named Jin Shan Si. Wood block printed pictures of the island appeared in a 1610 edition of the Ming novel, Water Margin (Shui Hu Zhuan) under its previous name of Jin Shan. However, later in the Qing Dynasty (1644–1911), it was renamed again in the Kang Xi reign (1661–1722) when the emperor gave the temple its present name of River-Heaven Buddhist Temple (Jiang Tian Si) during a visit to Zhenjiang on one of his six southern inspection tours.

around the shores of Tai Ying Lake, such as the Lotus Flower Building. Among the local residents, this is a popular place for kite flying and early morning exercises. Moreover, it provides the best vantage point for views of the entire 63-m-high (206.7-ft-high) Jin Shan hill. It is said that the upside-down image of the Ci Shou Ta atop Jin Shan can be seen reflected in the lake, so Tai Ying Hu is sometimes called Pagoda Shadow Lake. A site, traditionally known as the Number One Spring in China (Yi Quan), was rebuilt in 1992. The circuitous Yi Quan Lu makes a loop around the lake, providing access to the two newly built hotels, the Bamboo Hotel (Zhu Xuan Binguan) and the First Spring Hotel (Yi Quan Binguan). Both these hotels offer beautiful views of Jin Shan, but they seem to be frequently booked up by large groups of party officials for meetings and conferences, so it's best to phone ahead if you plan on staying there. Located west of the lake is the Jin Shan hotel (phone: (0511) 562-3888). Except for its mysteriously abandoned garden complex, this hotel would provide a convenient location to stay at.

When Captain Arthur Cunnynghame visited the island of Jin Shan in July 1842 during the British naval expedition up the Yangzi River, he recorded that the pagoda which existed then had a spiral flight of 238 steps leading to the top. At that time, there was also a very large library of woodblock printed books on the island.

Jiang Tian Si had 350 resident monks in the 1940s, but soon after the 1949 revolution, this number dropped by more than two-thirds to 100 in 1952. This sharp drop was undoubtedly related to the Agrarian Reform Law of June 1950, which eliminated the temple's source of financial support and food. Before 1950, the temple owned 4,800 *mu* of land, but afterwards, its holdings were reduced to only 60 *mu* of land. By 1963, the number of resident monks had fallen precipitously to only 47, less than one-eighth of the population that had lived there before 1950. In 1966, it was closed for at least ten years and not reopened until after the Cultural Revolution ended in 1976.

Holmes Welch used Jin Shan as one of his main case studies in his 1967 work, *The Practice of Chinese Buddhism, 1900–1950*. He describes Jin Shan in the Min Guo era, before 1949, as having had at least 14 main halls, including a Dragon King Shrine (Long Wang Dian), Guan Di Shrine (Guandi Dian), Heavenly

A map of the Jin Shan scenic area in Zhenjiang.

Kings Hall (Tian Wang Dian), Meditation Hall (Chan Tang), Wei Tuo Hall (Wei Tuo Dian), Guest Hall (Ke Tang), Buddha Recitation Hall (Nian Fo Dian), Ancestors Hall (Zu Tang), Great Shrine Hall (Da Xiong Bao Dian), Dharma Law Hall (Fa Tang Shuo Fa), Abbot's Quarters (Fang Zhang Shi), Liu Yu Pavilion (Liu Yu Ting), and Miao Gao Terrace (Miao Gao Tai). A permanent work force of ten carpenters was employed to maintain the buildings all year round. The Wandering Monks Hall (Yun Shui Tang) could hold more than a hundred visiting monks, who were called "cloud water monks." A huge wooden fish (*kai pang*) hung outside the Dining Hall (Kuo Tang), also known as the Five Reflections Hall (Wu Guan Tang), along with a heart-shaped bronze disc (*huo tian*). Both of these were struck to announce meal times. In Welch's opinion Jin Shan's Meditation Hall (Chan Tang) was 'the most illustrious in China'. One of its main tools was the round hollow wooden fish (*mu yu*) with an open slot in its side which was struck with a stick to keep the rhythm of chanting.

A closer look at the Jin Shan Ci Shou Ta pagoda in Zhenjiang.

The official history of the temple *Qi Li De Jin Shan* published in 1990, and the larger history of the city *Zhongguo Zhenjiang Fengjing Mingsheng* issued in 2001, both claim that a fire in 1948 destroyed the entire temple, including the Da Xiong Bao Dian and Cang Jing Lou. However, as Holmes Welch did not mention this incident in his well-researched history of Jin Shan, it seems likely that the destruction actually took place during the Cultural Revolution. Either way, today's visitor will notice that none of the pre-1949 buildings have survived to the present. A 1992 history of Zhenjiang, *Jingkou Quzhi*, shows a photograph of the present-day Precious Hall of the Great Hero (Da Xiong Bao Dian) under construction, but still surrounded by somewhat older buildings, both on the flat plateau at the foot of the hill and on the western hillside. Modern reproductions of the other buildings have only recently been rebuilt, which explains their brand new appearance. The official name of the site is now **Jin Shan Park** (Jin Shan Gongyuan), although the temple itself continues to be known as Jiang Tian Si.

A new three portal red cement gate (*pai lou*) now marks the entrance to Tian Jiang Si. Immediately outside the gate are incense burners where visitors can pray, and a few steps further up the road is the Fo Yin Ju vegetarian restaurant. After entering the new gate, the first hall you encounter is the Heavenly Kings Hall (Tian Wang Dian). Inside are four statues of the Heavenly Kings, two at either end, and a Maitreya Buddha (Mi Le Fo) in the center.

Exiting this hall, visitors will step into a courtyard that leads straight ahead up several short flights of steps to the Precious Hall of the Great Hero (Da Xiong Bao Dian). Inside are three large gilded Buddha statues (San Fo), with Amitabha (O-Mi-Tuo-Fo) on the left, Sakyamuni (Shijiamouni) in the center, and Yao Shi Fo on the right. Along the side walls are gilded statues of the 18 Arhats (Shi Ba Luohan) with nine on each side. Behind the San Fo is a statue of Guanyin facing the exit, divided from the rest of the hall by a partition.

Around the central courtyard are side halls that appear brand new and, in most cases, are completely empty. There seems to be no sign of any genuine historic relics in the temple compound at the foot of the hill. Several old monks encountered by the author were not able to shed much light on the temple's recent history. The temple now has about 60 resident monks who practice both Chan Zong and Jing Tu Zong.

The hillside begins behind the Da Xiong Bao Dian, with flights of 620 steps leading up the western slopes to stone block terraces and halls higher up the hill. One of the first sights is the one-story, octagonal, open-air **Seven Peak Pavilion** (Qi Feng Ting), which in comparison seems a bit older than the rest of the buildings. From its terrace, you can enjoy a view of the surrounding landscape — the canals and lakes below and pagoda above.

About halfway up the hillside, you reach another ticket booth where you must pay 4 Rmb to enter the upper half of the hill containing the following sights: Fa Hai Cave (Fa Hai Dong), 500 Arhat Hall (Wu Bai Luohan Tang), Ci Shou Pagoda (Ci Shou Ta), Kang Xi Imperial Tablet (Yu Bei), River Heaven Viewing Terrace (Jiang Tian Tai), and Guanyin Pavilion. The Kang Xi Imperial Tablet (Yu Bei) and River Heaven Viewing Terrace (Jiang Tian Tai) are reached by following a trail to your right, while

Buddhist monks at the Jiang Tian Si Buddhist Temple at the foot of Jin Shan.

The entrance to Fa Hai Cave (Fa Hai Dong) on Jin Shan in Zhenjiang.

all the other sights are found in succession along a separate trail to your left. The Kangxi stele bears the four characters for Jiang Tian Yi Lan, and is housed inside the small open air Liu Yun Ting pavilion.

Walking to your left from the ticket booth, you will encounter the brand new Wu Bai Luohan Tang. At the far end of this hall, near the exit, is the Relics Hall, which is a kind of Buddhist museum with a few genuine historical items in glass cases. One of the relics is supposedly the jade belt of the Northern Song Dynasty poet Su Dong Po (Su Shi) (1037–1102), surrendered by him to the temple after failing to win a philosophical debate with the monks there. Exiting out the far end takes you to the foot of the Ci Shou Ta.

The 36-m-high (118-ft-high), seven-story, octagonal **Ci Shou Ta** may be a survivor from an earlier age. If so, it is the only such structure remaining on the hill. Its architecture features wooden roof eaves on each level, yellow-painted stucco-covered brick walls, and wooden roof beams with carvings of animals, including a recurring pattern of elephant heads. Unfortunately, the view of this artwork is somewhat obstructed by an exterior wall surrounding the whole ground floor. Two ground floor entrances allow visitors to enter and ascend a flight of wooden steps all the way to the top.

The ground floor entrance to the Jin Shan Ci Shou Ta pagoda in Zhenjiang.

According to the official history of the Ci Shou Ta, posted on a sign near its entrance, a pagoda was first built on this spot 1,400 years ago during the Liang Dynasty (502–558). Between the Tang and Qing dynasties, it was destroyed and rebuilt several times. During the Song Dynasty (960–1279), there were two pagodas on Jin Shan, one at the southern end of the summit known as the Jian Ci Ta, and another at the northern summit called the Jian Shou Ta. Both were later destroyed. During the third year of the Long Qing reign of the Ming Dynasty, the Buddhist monk Liao Ming had one new pagoda built on the hill's northern summit and combined the names of the two earlier pagodas by calling it the Ci Shou Ta. The pagoda that exists today was built on the same site as Liao Ming's pagoda by the Abbot Yin Ru in August 1900, during the 26th year of the Guang Xu reign (1875–1908) of the Qing Dynasty. This would make the present day Ci Shou Ta approximately 104 years old.

Below the pagoda, perched on the northern slope of the hill's summit facing the river, is a cave known as the **Fa Hai Dong**, which can only be reached via steps that lead down from the Ci Shou Ta. A small enclosed pavilion covers the entrance to the cave, which seems to be at least partly man-made from stones cemented together. The pavilion is inhabited by one attendant monk, and inside the deepest recess of the cave is a white statue of the monk Fa Hai.

Fa Hai was a Buddhist monk who lived sometime in the Tang Dynasty (618–907). His father, Pei Xie, had been the Prime Minister in the central government, which is why Fa Hai is sometimes known as Pei Gong. Fa Hai studied Buddhism at Dong Lin Si on Mount Lushan before coming to Jin Shan. Sometime after arriving here, he discovered a cache of gold buried at the foot of the hill beside the Yangzi River. Fa Hai offered the gold to the government, but they returned it to him, and it was these funds that paid for the founding of Tian Jiang Si. Another result of Fa Hai's discovery was that the hill was given its present name, Jin Shan (Gold Hill).

At the foot of the hill, walk the circuit counterclockwise around its base and you will find a series of lesser sights. First is a collection of red brick buildings, apparently dating from the Min Guo era, which are probably the oldest existing structures after the hilltop pagoda. At the northern foot of the hill is the White Dragon Cave (Bai Long Dong). Legend has it that a fearsome white snake once lived inside this cave but was chased away by the powerful piety of a meditating Buddhist monk who dared to venture inside one day. Like the Fa Hai Dong, this one also seems to have been man-made by cementing rocks together.

The main entrance gate (Da Men) of Jiang Tian Si Buddhist Temple at the foot of Jin Shan in Zhenjiang.

Address: The old address was 62 Jin Shan Xi Lu, but the street has been widened into a six lane boulevard and renamed as part of the new road Changjiang Lu
Phone: 527-2992, 522-3479, 562-6220
Admission Ticket: 45 Rmb

The front of Gan Lu Si Buddhist Temple on Bei Gu Shan in Zhenjiang.

Bei Gu Shan

This large hilltop park overlooking the Yangzi River actually contains three small peaks, with some very steep trails ascending them. From the pavilions on top of the mountain, one can have a good view of the river, the marshes, and Jiao Shan island in the distance. The park is traversed by a network of foot trails that pass by a collection of Qing era pavilions, former temples, and houses. At the summit stands **Bei Gu Lou**, a two-story

A waterfall on Bei Gu Shan in Zhenjiang.

A pavilion on Bei Gu Shan in Zhenjiang.

The summit-top, two-story, Qing Dynasty, Bei Gu Lou pavilion with views of the Yangzi River from its second floor.

wooden Qing Dynasty house with incredible views from its second floor balcony facing the river. Behind Bei Gu Lou is a complex of Qing courtyard houses.

The **Iron Pagoda** (Tie Ta) supposedly dates from the early Tang Dynasty (618–907 AD). Other accounts dates it from 960AD, the first year of the Northern Song Dynasty (960–1126), making it over 1,000 years old at least. It was last repaired in the Ming Dynasty (1368–1644) when it was blown down by a typhoon. It is an ornamental cast iron pagoda with fascinating Buddhist images cast on its sides. Only four levels remain of what was originally a seven-story pagoda. It was never meant to be ascended and can only be viewed from the ground. This is the same pagoda that the British tried unsuccessfully to steal as a war trophy during their two-month occupation of Zhenjiang in 1842. At the time, it was estimated to be 9.1 m (30 ft) high, but at least another 3 m (10 ft) of its base was later found to be buried underground. Although the British failed to remove the pagoda, some parts were apparently removed from its pinnacle as souvenirs.

The Tang Dynasty Iron Pagoda (Tie Ta) on Bei Gu Shan in Zhenjiang.

Gan Lu Buddhist Temple (Gan Lu Si) has a long history but its present condition is a bit disappointing. One tiny chapel with three brand new plastic Buddhas that automatically blink their eyes open and shut if you bow down and pray on your knees. Currently, it is not a functioning temple and has no resident monks.

The Emperor Liang Wu Di (502–549 *ad*) once called Bei Gu Shan the first hill on the Yangzi River (Tian Xia Di Yi Jiang Shan). Today, unfortunately, its natural beauty is somewhat marred by the unpleasant smells coming from the factories located on either side.

A close up of the Buddhist images embedded in one side of the Tang Dynasty Iron Pagoda (Tie Ta) on Bei Gu Shan in Zhenjiang.

POINT OF INTEREST

Historically, Bei Gu Shan has had great military importance to the defense of Zhenjiang. In July 1842, the British established their military headquarters here, where they could look down on the walled city below. The foot of hill is still honeycombed with underground tunnels cutting through the middle of it from all sides. Walk along the river front promenade encircling the foot of the hill and you will see the gated entrances to these tunnels, some of which bear evidence of railroad tracks. There are also World War II concrete pillboxes for gun emplacements, and a Guomindang radar installation on one peak.

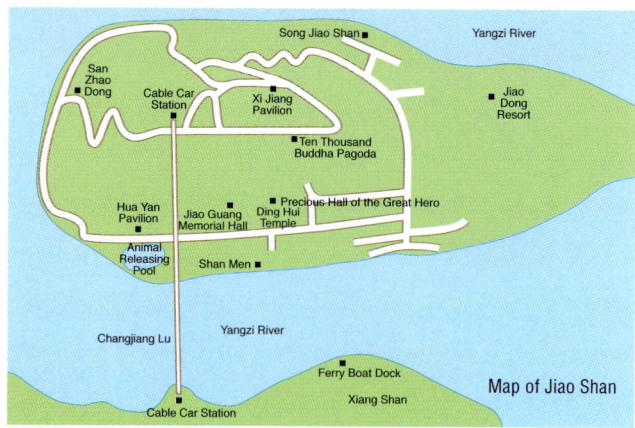

Jiao Shan (Silver Island)

This is a small island in the Yangzi River, 4.8 km (3 miles) northeast of the Zhenjiang city center. The island is dominated by a steep hilltop upon which stands a tall pagoda of recent construction. The island has been home to an important Buddhist temple since the Eastern Han Dynasty.

The name Jiao Shan comes from a man named Jiao Guang, who at the end of the Han Dynasty left his home in Shanxi Province to escape the warfare there and came to live on this peaceful island as a reclusive hermit. According to legend, Liu Xie, the last Eastern Han Emperor Xian Di (189–220) offered Jiao Guang official posts three times, but each time he refused. Instead he chose to live alone on this island, sleeping in stone caves and thatched grass huts, eating wild plants, and earning a meager income from chopping firewood for nearby villagers. In 194AD, Jiao Guang founded the Pu Ji Buddhist Temple

The new entrance gate (Shan Men) for Ding Hui Si Buddhist Temple on Jiao Shan island in Zhenjiang, with the temple's halls visible behind it.

POINT OF INTEREST

Jiao Shan was also the place where the Qing Dynasty emperors — Kang Xi (1661–1722) and Qian Long (1736–1795) — stayed at when they each made six imperial journeys to the south during their reigns. Kang Xi first stayed here in 1684, and his last visit was in 1707. Later, Qian Long felt the need to match Kang Xi's six southern journeys, and also stayed here six times, starting in 1761. Each emperor began his journey at Beijing then floated down the Grand Canal (Da Yun He) to Yangzhou in northern Jiangsu (Jiang Bei), from where they crossed the Yangzi River to Zhenjiang. Qian Long's temporary imperial palace, supposedly dating from 1761, can still be seen here. Inside the compound is the Imperial Stele Pavilion (Yu Bei Ting).

(Pu Ji Si) here. He supposedly lived to be more than 100 years old before he finally died a natural death on this island, after a long and tranquil life. In the Zhen Zong reign (997–1022) of the Northern Song (Bei Song) Dynasty (960–1126), Emperor Zhao Heng had a dream in which Jiao Guang appeared to him and gave him some medicinal pills. After the emperor took the pills, he recovered from his previously incurable illness. As a result, he began the practice of establishing ancestral temples devoted to Jiao Guang (Jiao Guang Ci). A Memorial Hall (Ji Nian Guan) devoted to him still stands on the island today.

Despite its role as a tranquil retreat for hermits, Buddhist monks, and traveling emperors, Jiao Shan has also played a role as the fortress guarding the gates to the upper Yangzi River. In July 1842, Chinese forts on the island tried unsuccessfully to stop the advance of the British fleet headed towards Zhenjiang and Nanjing. The earthen walled remains of the forts and their gun emplacements can still be seen at the base of the hill today. The half-circle mud wall fort has nine gun emplacements preserved. A wall map of 16–21 June 1842 river battles shows the old walled city of Zhenjiang between Bei Gu Shan and the Grand Canal. In Chinese, the site is known as *Jiaoshan Kang Ying Pao Tai Jie Shao*.

Although the Chinese named the island after Jiao Guang, 19th Century European descriptions of Zhenjiang referred to Jiao Shan by the name of **Silver Island**, in order to distinguish it from Gold Island (Jin Shan). English books and maps printed before 1949 all tend to use the name Silver Island.

When H.G.W. Woodhead visited in 1931, the island had already been refortified by the Guomindang, and the top of the hill turned into an off-limits military zone. Chiang Kai Shek (Jiang Jieshi) himself had visited the island. In December 1937, the Japanese shelled the island, damaging some of its buildings, during their advance from Shanghai to Nanjing.

Beautiful botanical gardens now cover a large flat plain east of the Opium War forts and temple. The **Jiao Dong Resort** at the east end of the island seems abandoned and closed, although

the exterior of the buildings has been finished, the interiors are bare and unfurnished. Work has completely stopped as if the investors ran out of money.

Out in the northern wetlands past the old Opium War fort stands **Song Jiao Shan**, a single lone giant rock formation surrounded by marsh and reeds, with a natural cave inside. A dirt trail leads up to it. The tall reeds are higher than a 1.8-m-tall (6-ft-tall) man.

The forested slopes of Jiao Shan island in Zhenjiang, with the waters of the Yangzi River visible through the trees down below.

Ding Hui Temple (Ding Hui Si)

Upon disembarking on Jiao Shan, visitors are greeted by the new **Shan Men**, a three-portal stone gate (*pai lou*) completed in September 2002. It replaced an earlier gate thought to be 300 years old, as it was supposedly built in the year 1709, the 48th year of the Kang Xi reign. Following this is a new screen wall, then a Bell Tower (Zhong Lou), Drum Tower (Gu Lou), and two sets of three stone footbridges (Fang Sheng Qiao) over several Animal Releasing Pools (Fang Sheng Chi), all of which were completed at the same time as the new gate. Photos taken before the 2002 construction show the natural coastline of the island still intact here, with much more vegetation, and a tree-lined avenue leading from the boat dock to the temple.

The new entrance gate (Shan Men) for Ding Hui Si Buddhist Temple on Jiao Shan island in Zhenjiang.

The front entrance to the Precious Hall of the Great Hero (Da Xiong Bao Dian) of Ding Hui Si Buddhist Temple on Jiao Shan island in Zhenjiang.

There are three main temple halls along the central axis. The first is the Heavenly Kings Hall (Tian Wang Dian), followed by the Precious Hall of the Great Hero (Da Xiong Bao Dian). Finally, there is a two-story Scripture Pavilion (Cang Jing Ge). Despite its name, the third hall seems to contain no books or scrolls, but simply has some tables and chairs set up like a reception lobby, with ash trays provided. The Da Xiong Bao Dian has three very large gilded golden Buddhas (San Fo) in front, and golden statues of the 18 Arhats (Shi Ba Luohan), nine along each side. This second hall is quite active with laymen in black robes chanting. In this sense, the temple seems more spiritually alive than the one at Jin Shan. All three of the main halls are brand new. Reconstruction of the site had started by 2001 and was completed by the fall of 2003. Despite its newness, it is an impressive and actively functioning temple with resident monks in yellow and green robes, as well as many faithful layman worshippers clad in black robes.

To the west of the Tian Wang Dian is the **Jiao Guang Memorial Hall** (Jiao Guang Ji Nian Guan) with a new three-portal stone gate of its own in front. Inside is a seated white statue of the island's patron saint, Jiao Guang, with a long beard and flowing robes like a Confucian scholar. This hall seems to have taken the place of an earlier Ancestor Hall (Zu Tang).

There seems to be little sign of any authentic historic relics until you wander off the beaten track into a construction yard where you find stacks of aged wooden beams and broken inscribed stone tablets piled up carelessly on the dirt ground. These are obviously the remaining pieces of the temple's original halls torn down to make way for the current new buildings. Towards the Hua Yan Pavilion, which is now being used as a temporary home by construction workers, is a cave in the hillside, with a faded three-character inscription over the top of its entrance. Strangely, the cave does not seem to appear on maps of the island.

The statue of Jiao Shan island's namesake patron saint Jiao Guang. It sits inside the San Zhao Dong cave on the island.

The remains of the Chinese fortresss used to defend Jiao Shan island against the British fleet's invasion of the Yangzi River during the First Opium War (1839–1842). Today, it is known to Chinese as the Jiao Shan Kang Ying Pao Tai or Jiao Shan Anti-British Gun Terrace.

The entrance to a Buddhist hall on Jiao Shan island in Zhenjiang.

Although, the current buildings and statues appear new, the temple does have a long history. It was originally called **Pu Ji Si** when it was built by the official Jiao Guang in 194–195 AD during the reign of the the last Eastern Han Emperor Xian Di (189–220 AD). During the Song Dynasty (960–1279), the name was changed to **Pu Ji Chan Si** to reflect the dominance of the Chan (Zen) Buddhist sect amongst the monks at the temple. In the Yuan Dynasty (1297–1368), the name was changed to **Jiao Shan Si**, in honor of its original founder Jiao Guang. After it was destroyed by a fire, the temple was rebuilt in the Ming Dynasty during the Xuan De reign (1426–1435) of Zhu Zhan Ji. Later, Qing Dynasty Emperor Kang Xi (1661–1722) renamed the temple **Ding Hui Si** in 1703, the forty-second year of his reign, and it is this name which has lasted until today.

At the end of the Qing Dynasty, Ding Hui Si was still considered as belonging to the Chan (Zen) sect, but during the Min Guo period, it followed the anti-sectarian trend of unifying all schools of thought. The joint practice of both Chan and Pure Land doctrines (Chan-Jing Shuang Xiu) became common in the Min Guo era. Nonetheless, the temple maintained a Meditation Hall (Chan Tang) common to the Chan sect.

H.G.W. Woodhead observed the Meditation Hall (Chan Tang) in use when he visited the Buddhist temple here in 1931. He says the monks there spent most ot their time day and night in the Meditation Hall, being allowed to sleep only from 10:00PM to 1:30AM. Discipline was strict, but the temple was considered quite wealthy. According to Woodhead, the Master or Abbot of the temple (Fang Zhang) sat on a throne donated by Emperor Qian Long.

In 1934, a Buddhist college was established on the grounds beside the temple. During the 12 years it functioned, the Buddhist college had 300 graduates. The original red brick buildings of the college still stand beside the temple complex.

The layout of Ding Hui Si in 2003 is remarkably similar to Johannes Prip-Moller's 1937 map of the temple, although the current structures have been recently rebuilt. The most notable difference is that the first floor of the Library (Cang Jing Lou) is now no longer designated as a Meditation Hall (Chan Tang). Other halls which are now absent include the Wandering Monks Hall (Yun Shui Tang), Hall of the Buddhist Law (Fa Tang), and Guest House (Ke Tang). New additions that did not appear on the 1937 map include a Pi Lu Hall (Pi Lu Dian) located east of the central axis near the buildings of the former Buddhist College, a Jiao Guang Memorial Hall (Jiao Guang Ji Nian Guan) west of the main temple buildings, and a Hua Yan Pavilion (Hua Yan Ting) along the western trail up the hillside.

The former site of Emperor Qian Long's temporary imperial palace on Jiao Shan island in Zhenjiang.

Nowadays, Ding Hui Temple has about 40 resident monks who still practice the Chan school (Chan Zong) of Chinese Buddhist thought. The temple is very popular with lay Buddhists and hosts conferences where participants study the scriptures.
Phone: 523-1372.

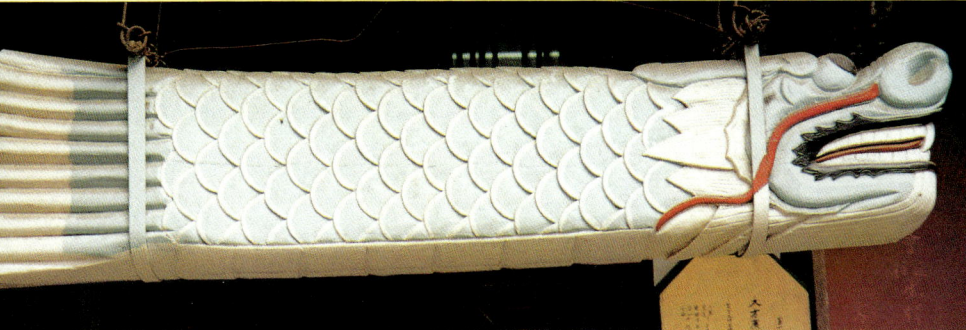

Ten Thousand Buddha Pagoda (Qian Fo Ta)

Located at top of Jiao Shan peak is a fairly new structure built between May 1998 and September 1999. The **Ten Thousand Buddha Pagoda** (Qian Fo Ta) is an octagonal seven-story reinforced concrete structure, which one can ascend all the way to the top. A cable car, which stops at the foot of the pagoda, takes visitors up the hill. Photos of Jiao Shan in the 1992 *Jingkou Qu Zhi*

A wooden fish (*kai pang*) used by the Buddhist monks at Ding Hui Si on Jiao Shan island as a dinner bell. To announce meal times, they beat it with a stick. It hangs from a rafter outside the temple's dining hall.

A distant view of the Qian Fo Ta standing atop the summit of Jiao Shan island in Zhenjiang, viewed from the foot of the hill.

A close up view of the Qian Fo Ta standing atop the summit of Jiao Shan island in Zhenjiang, viewed from the base of the pagoda.

show the island looking considerably different, with no pagoda or cable car installation on the summit, and much more natural vegetation. Just below the new pagoda is a smaller and slightly older two-story **Xi Jiang Pavilion** (Xi Jiang Ting), which offers splendid views of the Yangzi River and the marshes below.

Jiao Shan Trail

The best part of the island is probably the winding foot path which leads to the top of the peak. The path circles round and round the mountain slopes, offering increasingly better views of the surrounding Yangzi River as you climb slowly, higher and higher, in a corkscrew fashion. Many calligraphic carvings can be found on the rocks along the path. Some of these may be quite old, as 19th century visitors have commented on the many inscribed rocks they saw on the island then, including some with names such as the Stone Screen (Shi Ping) and Arhat Rock (Luohan Yan). Views downward from the trail take in the marshes which are dotted with small wooden boats on which the families of boat people still live. The occasional World War II concrete bunker also appears along the way. A cave beside the trail known as Jiao Gong Dong or **San Zhao Dong** has a white statue of a bearded, robed Jiao Guang inside.

Getting To Jiao Shan

The new Changjiang Lu now extends all the way to Jiao Shan island in the northeast corner of the city. Ticket prices are 35 Rmb, but this includes the cost of the ferry ride across the river channel to the island.

The island can also be reached by a ferry boat ride from the shore, or by a cable car directly to the top of the peak. The boat leaves once every 20 minutes. The ferry boat dock sits at the foot of **Elephant Hill** (Xiang Shan), which is honeycombed with long deep tunnels left over from former defensive fortifications, some of which are open to visitors.

Shuang Jing Lu

Located just off of Zhongshan Dong Lu, this is a nice old neighborhood of tree-lined streets that follows the **Grand Canal** (Da Yun He). Sidewalk restaurants sell the local version of Niu Ruo Huo Guo (Beef Hot Pot). The trees are so thick that they form a canopy overhead. *Longtang* and *shikumen* houses, with wooden double doors pasted with New Year couplets, occupy the edge of the canal, which can be reached by following cobblestone pathways in between the houses.

Bo Xian Park (Bo Xian Gongyuan)

This park is located in the center of the former foreign concession. It covers an area of 8.6 hectares (212.5 acres), including a hill, and contains specimens of 150 kinds of plants. Construction started in 1926 and was completed in June 1931. In 1953, a greenhouse and zoo were added. A stone tablet outside the gate has the date "1981" which seems to note the park's reopening to the public that year.

Bo Xian Park's original purpose was to commemmorate the "democratic revolutionary martyr" Zhao Shen, known by his posthumous honorific title Bo Xian. Just inside the entrance gate stand two stone dragons. Just beyond this, at the foot of the hill, is a bronze statue of Bo Xian known as the **Martyr's Statue** (Lieshi Xiang). It shows Bo Xian on a pedestal, dressed in a military officer's uniform from the World War I era. He has a sword hanging from his waist belt, holds a pair of binoculars, and wears knee-high boots with horse spurs attached to the

The new Bo Xian Memorial Hall (Bo Xian Ji Nian Guan), inside Bo Xian Park (Bo Xian Gongyuan) on Bo Xian Street (Bo Xian Lu) in Zhenjiang.

The bronze Bo Xian Martyr's Statue (Bo Xian Lieshi Xiang) that stands immediately inside the entrance gates of Bo Xian Park (Bo Xian Gongyuan) on Bo Xian Street (Bo Xian Lu) in Zhenjiang.

heels. On the pedestal are the characters for "Zhao Gong Bo Xian Zhi Xiang". To the right of the statue is a new **Memorial Hall** (Ji Nian Guan) devoted to Bo Xian. The Hall contains some black and white photos and artists' simulations of scenes from his life. In glass cases are some relics believed to be genuine. From these exhibits, one learns that Bo Xian was a follower of Sun Yat Sun (Sun Zhongshan) who participated in some of the early failed uprisings against the Qing Dynasty in Guangdong province before the 1911 Revolution. Bo Xian died in Hong Kong at the age of 31, and this park was dedicated to him because he was a native son of Zhenjiang.

The ruins of the original Bo Xian Memorial Hall stand on the hill's summit. Also on the summit is the site of Emperor Shao Zong's Library (Cang Shu Lou). About midway up the hillside stands the 30 May Lecture Hall (Wu Sa Yan Jiang Ting) and the Jade Green Tea House (Cui Lu Cha Lou). The summit of the hill has a view of Jin Shan in the distance, but there is no trace left of the original Bo Xian Memorial Hall except for three flights of stone steps leading up several terraces to a stone walled platform on the flat summit. How or when the original hall was destroyed is a mystery.

A short distance away, but hidden in the midst a forest of trees behind an encircling chain link fence, stands an incredibly impressive French colonial mansion on the southern end of the summit. This weathered, two-story authentic Min Guo structure has yellow walls, a second floor veranda, first floor porch, and two Greco-Roman columns in the center front. A four-post monumental gateway with inscriptions stands a few yards from the building itself. Stone pedestals and pieces of other monuments have been used in the steps leading up to the house. A modern day inscribed tablet stands in the front yard. According to the inscriptions, this was once the **Shao Zong National Library** (Shao Zong Guo Xue Cang Shu Lou), and was built in March 1934, the 22nd year of the Republic (Min Guo Er Shi Er Nian San Yue). Surprisingly, people are visibly living inside the house today, even though the only access is via the foot trail up the hill from the Bo Xian Park gate. Unfortunately, the inhabitants seem reluctant to open the locked gate to let visitors inside.

Halfway down the hill, beside a children's playground stands a two-story traditional-style hall with red brick walls, red wooden pillars, and upturned roof eaves covered with ceramic tiles. Two corner stones at both ends have original inscriptions, while a

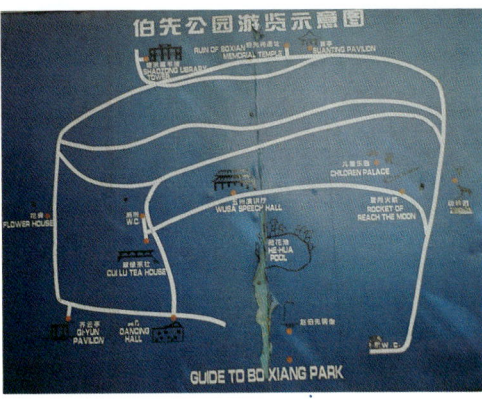

A Chinese language map of Bo Xian Park (Bo Xian Gongyuan) on Bo Xian Street (Bo Xian Lu) in Zhenjiang.

The main entrance gate (Da Men) of Bo Xian Park (Bo Xian Gongyuan) on Bo Xian Street (Bo Xian Lu) in Zhenjiang.

modern day inscribed tablet stands in front of the building with the date "August 1925." According to the inscriptions, this was originally the **30 May Speech Hall** (Wu Sa Yan Jiang Ting) built in August 1925 (Min Guo Shi Si Nian Ba Yue). However, figurines of Confucian scholars and fish on the roof ridges give it the appearance of a traditional temple rather than a revolutionary shrine. Closed doors prevent a closer inspection of the interior.

Address: Bo Xian Lu

POINT OF INTEREST

Just off Bo Xian Lu stands the Zhenjiang Shang Hui. This is an authentic and impressive guild hall, complete with an inscribed stone façade.

Royal Hotel (Da Huang Jia)

Dating from treaty port days, this old European-style building is now more of a historic relic than a functioning hotel. After being briefly renamed the Ming Du Hotel, it was closed in 2001 and was still padlocked shut as of October 2003. The rooms on the two upper floors of this three-story structure are decorated with French double doors opening out onto iron veranda balconies. Viewed through the ground floor windows, the interior is still impressive, with marble fireplaces, crystal chandeliers, and ornate plaster moldings on the ceilings. Local residents still tell the story of how this is where Chiang Kai Shek (Jiang Jieshi) stayed when he was in town. Since Zhenjiang was the provincial capital from 1929 to 1937 and the site of important military defenses, the stories of Jiang's visits are plausibly true.

Address: 35 Bo Xian Lu
Phone: 527-1438

Zhenjiang Museum (Zhenjiang Bowuguan)

The Museum is located inside the grounds of the old British Consulate, which itself is a complex of five impressive 19th century European buildings. The date on one building states that it was constructed in 1890.

At the moment, only one of the buildings is open to the public, and this displays ancient period bronzes. The museum's most famous artifact is the anchor of the HMS Amethyst, the British ship which was held hostage on the nearby Yangzi River by Communist military forces in May 1949. Although you would expect this to be their most prized trophy, it was nowhere to be seen on the author's visit in 2001. A second visit in October 2003 was foiled by a gatekeeper who refused entry to visitors, claiming the facility was closed for lunch at 2:30PM. Despite the vast modernization of China since 1979, this small museum still seems to be a die-hard bastion of 1980s style Communist cadre customer service. According to Simon Winchester's account, museum staff were not very polite to him during his 1996 visit, and completely ignorant about the anchor's existence. He was, however, later able to find the neglected anchor hidden in some overgrown bushes on the hillside behind the buildings.

Address: Bo Xian Lu

The former British Consulate building in Zhenjiang.

Xi Jing Ferry Lane (Xi Jing Du Jie)

This pedestrian lane begins next door to the former British Consulate, below an arched brick gateway over the lane. Shops along the lane and vendors in the street spread out a motley collection of antiques for sale at inflated prices. Further up, some broken fragments of authentic carved stone blocks and an old iron cannon lie at the side of the alley, beside a flight of steps. High red brick walls frame the lane on either side. At a second arched brick gate over the lane, several iron incense burners and two octagonal brick pavilions with burning incense mark the approach to a Buddhist site. Shortly after this second gate is a Tibetan-style stone Buddhist stupa, balanced on top of a square stone gate over the street. This stupa was apparently built in 1311, and later rebuilt in 1582. It is named **Xi Jing Du Jiao Guan Shi Ta**.

The former British Consulate building in Zhenjiang on the left, with the main entrance gate to Xi Jing Ferry Lane (Xi Jing Du Jie) visible on the right.

The outdoor antique street market on Xi Jing Ferry Lane (Xi Jing Du Jie) in Zhenjiang.

Two more of the many arched brick gates over the long pedestrian lane of Xi Jing Ferry lane (Xi Jing Du Jie) in Zhenjiang.

A long side-view of the historic buildings lining Xi Jing Ferry Lane (Xi Jing Du Jie) in Zhenjiang.

The stupa's name requires some explanation. Xi Jing Du Jie (Xi Jing Ferry Lane) is the present name of the street, known at one time as Jing Ling Du (Jing Ling Ferry), and at another as Xiao Matou Jie (Small Ferry Dock Lane). All three of the street's names originate from the fact that this was once the location of the town's port and ferry dock, before silting up of the Yangzi River, that began in 1879, had by 1908 moved the southern shore far to the north. Jiao Guan was the Buddhist patron saint of Jiao Shan island, and the term "shi ta" refers to a stone pagoda.

Nearby are several shops selling Buddhist trinkets, and one Buddhist chapel built right into the natural rock of the hillside. However, this does not seem to be a functioning temple. The lane continues for a considerable distance beyond the stupa beneath several more brick archways and past old houses along both sides. Three of the arched gates over the lane are known as **San Dao Juan Men.**

Some intricately carved stone relics lying abandoned in the dust along the side of the historic pedestrian lane of Xi Jing Ferry Lane (Xi Jing Du Jie) in Zhenjiang.

The Tibetan-style stone Buddhist stupa gate known as the Xi Jing Du Jiao Guan Shi Ta, covering the historic pedestrian lane of Xi Jing Du Jie in Zhenjiang.

Zhenjiang Lieshi Lingyuan

The main sights here are a memorial hall with a glass pyramid over the top and an enormous socialist realist stone statue of ideal Communist heroes. The hilltop cemetery offers spectacular views of sites such as Gan Lu Si and other pavilions on the summit of Bei Gu Shan, as well as the Yangzi River in the distance. In 1998, a monument was added to the martyrs of 1842 and 1937, illustrating the party's widening reinterpretation of Chinese history to include non-Communist martyrs as heroes who defended the national interest.

Another one of the many arched brick gates over the long pedestrian lane of Xi Jing Ferry Lane (Xi Jing Du Jie) in Zhenjiang.

A historic stone guild hall on a short side street off of Bo Xian Lu in Zhenjiang.

Zhenjiang Practical Information

Zhenjiang Area Code: (0511)

Transportation
Zhenjiang is not a major transportation hub. There is no airport and long distance buses have avoided the town as it is not on the main highway from Shanghai to Nanjing. Nor has there been a bridge over the Yangzi River providing connections with cities in Jiangbei. This leaves the train as the only viable option. However, the slow train from Shanghai can be a frustrating four-hour ride that stops at every village along the way. Boarding the train in Zhenjiang usually means getting a ticket without a reserved seat number. This causes a mass stampede as passengers scramble for unoccupied seats, leaving the unlucky ones to stand for the whole ride. The T-trains are much faster and comfortable, but Zhenjiang is too small a town for most of them to stop at as they rush on towards Nanjing or Shanghai. The train station is on Zhongshan Lu.

Restaurants
Yan Chun Can Guan

Phone: 523-1615

Zhenjiang Hotels
Most of Zhenjiiang's hotels are located along the Zhongshan Lu main street through the city center. However, several new hotels have recently been built near the base of Jin Shan. Travelers should note that several older hotels advertised by other guidebooks have been closed for several years, including the Royal Hotel and Jin Shan Hotel. Furthermore, the Jiao Dong Resort on Jiao Shan had not yet opened for business in October 2003 and seemed to be abandoned.

Zhenjiang International Hotel
(Zhenjiang Guoji Fandian) ****
The newest and most upscale hotel in town.

Address: 218 Jie Fang Lu
Phone: 502-1888
Fax: 502-1777
Prices: 388–598 Rmb

Zhenjiang Hotel (Zhenjiang Binguan) *** & ****
The new No. 1 building is a four-star hotel while the older No. 2 building is a three-star hotel.

>Address: 92 Zhongshan Xi Lu
>Phone: 523-3888
>Fax: 523-1055
>Prices: 308–408 Rmb for No. 1 Bldg,
>228 Rmb for No. 2 Bldg

Bamboo Hotel (Zhu Xuan Binguan) ***
Located at the northwestern foot of Jin Shan.

>Address: 8 Yi Quan Lu
>Phone: 551-1618

First Spring Hotel (Yi Quan Binguan)
Located at the northwestern foot of Jin Shan. The hotel is unrated but it is a hotel with three to four-star quality.

>Address: 1 Yi Quan Lu
>Phone: 551-1666

Jing Kou Hotel (Jing Kou Fandian) **
Located in the city center, south of Zhongshan Lu and just east of the Grand Canal.

>Address: 407 Zhongshan Dong Lu and Bin He Lu
>Phone: 522-4866
>Fax: 523-0056
>Prices: 500 Rmb for rooms in the new wing,
>120 Rmb for the old wing

Zhenjiang Dajiudian

>Address: Zhongshan Xi Lu
>Phone: 523-5290
>Prices: 200–300 Rmb

Jiangsu Province

Nanjing

Historical Introduction

Nanjing has been the capital city of many dynasties and political regimes throughout its long history. With the rise and fall of dynasties, the city's name has been changed many times: from Jinling to Jianye under the Wu Kingdom, Jiankang in the Eastern Jin, Jinling in the Southern Tang, Jiangning in the Song dynasties, Nanjing under the Ming Dynasty, back to Jiangning in the Qing Dynasty, Tianjing under the Taipings, and back to Nanjing again under the Min Guo and the People's Republic of China. For convenience, we will refer to it as Nanjing in this account of its history.

Over a period of four hundred years, from the 3rd to 6th century, Nanjing was the capital of six successive Southern Dynasties, so called because they only governed South China. A seventh southern dynasty was briefly established there once again in the 10th century. These southern dynasties included the Wu Kingdom (220–280 AD), the Eastern Jin (317–420 AD), the Liu Song (420–479 AD), Southern Qi (479–502 AD), Liang (502–557 AD), the Chen Dynasty (557–589 AD), and the Southern Tang Dynasty (937–975 AD). Despite the brief life span of these ephemeral dynasties, a brief outline of their chronology is worth knowing because of the hundreds of remarkable imperial tombs and stone monuments they left scattered about Nanjing's surrounding countryside, many of which have lasted much longer than the dynasties themselves.

Sun Quan, the founding ruler of the Wu Kingdom (220–280 AD), one of the three rival states in the Yangzi River valley during the **Three Kingdoms** (San Guo) period, was the first to choose Nanjing as his capital city in 229 AD. After Sun Quan's death in 252 AD, his heirs proved less able rulers than he, and the Wu Kingdom was defeated by the Western Jin in 280 AD.

After the capture of the Western Jin capital at Luoyang in 316 AD, a surviving Jin prince established the Eastern Jin Dynasty (317–420 AD) in Nanjing, giving himself the title of Emperor Yuan Di. The Eastern Jin were great supporters of the new Buddhist faith, which was then still in its early stages. In 414AD, the Buddhist monk **Fa Xian** returned to China from India with Buddhist scriptures after a journey which began in 399AD. He decided to make Nanjing his new home and the center for his translations work.

The Eastern Jin Dynasty was finally overthrown by a palace coup led by one of their own generals, **Liu Yu**, who in 420AD declared himself Emperor Wu Di (420–422 AD) of the Liu Song Dynasty (420–479 AD). After Liu Yu's death in 422AD, a string of seven more rulers followed over the next 60 years. The Liu Song suffered a similar fate as the previous Eastern Jin Dynasty, when the regent, Xiao Dao Cheng, led a palace coup in 479AD and later established himself as Emperor Gao Di of the new Qi Dynasty (479–502 AD). After seven emperors and countless court intrigues and assassinations, the Qi Dynasty was finally overthrown in 502AD by one of its own generals, Xiao Yan, who then established the new Liang Dynasty (502–557 AD) and proclaimed himself Emperor Wu Di.

Liang Wu Di reigned for a remarkable 48 years (502–549 AD), longer than any previous emperor had ruled in Nanjing, and nearly

POINT OF INTEREST

During the Tang Dynasty (618–907 AD), poets began to romanticize the ancient city of Nanjing that the Sui had destroyed. On one of his many visits to Nanjing, the poet Li Bai (Li Tai Po) (701–762 AD) wrote a short verse called, "Climbing Phoenix Terrace at Jinling." Here are two variant translations of what he said:

"The phoenix birds (*fenghuang*) once frolicked on Phoenix Terrace (Fenghuang Tai),
The birds are gone, the terrace empty, and the river flows on.
Flourishing waters of Wu palace are buried beneath dark trails;
Caps and gowns of Jin times all lie in ancient mounds.
The three-peaked mountain (Zijin Shan) half visible under the blue sky,
The two-forked stream (Qinhuai He) separated by White Egret Isle (Bai Lu Zhou).
It's always the clouds that block the sun.
I do not see Changan (Xian) and I grieve."
Liu Wu Chi and Lo Yu Cheng, 1975

"Phoenixes (*fenghuang*) that played here once, so that the place was named for them,
Have abandoned it now to this desolate river;
The paths of Wu Palace are crooked with weeds;
The garments of Jin are ancient dust.
Like this green horizon halving the Three Peaks (Zijin Shan),
Like this Island of White Egrets (Bai Lu Zhou) dividing the river (Qinhuai He),
A cloud has arisen between the Light of Heaven and me,
To hide his city from my melancholy heart."
Witter Bynner, 1929

as long as some of the prior dynasties had lasted. He was devoted to the Buddhist faith, so much so that he had a complete set of the Buddhist Tripitaka (San Zang) scriptures printed. On four occasions, he tried to become a Buddhist monk but his ministers hauled him back to the secular world of politics. Liang Wu Di's most trusted advisor was the Buddhist monk **Bao Zhi Gong** (436–514 AD), whose commemmorative stupa can be seen today near Ling Gu Temple. After the death of the 86-year-old Emperor Liang Wu Di in 549AD, his heirs were mere puppets of generals and ministers. Finally in 557AD, after much court intrigue and numerous assassinations of Liang princes, the Liang general Chen Ba Xian founded the new Chen Dynasty (557–589 AD) and named himself Emperor Chen Wu Di.

With the capture of Nanjing in 589AD by troops of the Sui Dynasty (581–618AD), the Chen Dynasty was overthrown, and Nanjing's 400-year reign as the political center of six southern dynasties came to an end. China was reunited under, first, the Sui and then the Tang, both of which had their capital in the northern city of Xian, on the headwaters of the Yellow River (Huang He). Thus political power shifted once again from the Yangzi River valley, where it had been since the start of the Three Kingdoms (San Guo) period, back to the Yellow River (Huang

POINT OF INTEREST

Liu Yu Xi (772–842 AD) continued the romanticization of Nanjing's past begun by Li Bai. This accumulated body of poems eventually created a mystique about the city that was so powerful that it later guided the first Ming emperor in his choice of capital. Liu's poem was the classic example of this genre, so much so that Luo Guanzhong later incorporated it into the final chapter of his Ming Dynasty novel about the Three Kingdoms (San Guo). Here are two variant translations of what Liu wrote:

"When the towered galleys of Wang Jun came down from Yizhou,
The royal air of Jinling (Nanjing) retreated dull and dim.
A thousand leagues of iron links sank to the river's bed;
Flags of surrender rose in a file over the Wall of Stone (Shitou Cheng).
So many times in human life we grieve for bygone things;
The mountains' form, as long ago, lies pillowed on the cold flow.
Now all within the four seas has come under a single house,
And the old battlements sigh forlornly in an autumn of reeds."
                                    Liu Wu Chi and Lo Yu Cheng, 1975

"Jin's tall ships subdued the Riverlands;
The kingly air of Jinling ebbed away.
The thousand links sank to the riverbed;
One flag of surrender rose above the stone city.
How often man must grieve for what has passed;
The cold streams run below the changeless hills.
Today the king has no home but the world,
His battlements forlorn in a reed-bare autumn."
                                                    Moss Roberts, 1995.

He) valley, where it had originally been during the earlier Han Dynasty. Nanjing's demise as a political center was made even more complete by the Sui army's intentional total destruction of the city, which left no structures standing save for those made of stone, such as city walls and tombs.

Nanjing briefly resumed its central prominence in the 10th century when the remnants of the Tang Dynasty established themselves here after fleeing to the South. The Southern Tang (Nan Tang) Dynasty had three emperors over a period of nearly 40 years (937–975 AD). The limits of their authority only covered the provinces of Jiangsu, Anhui, Jiangxi, and Hunan. Nonetheless, it was by all accounts a peaceful and prosperous time for Nanjing, during which literature and the arts flourished here. The two beautiful tombs, and their contents, built to commemmorate their emperors Li Bian and Li Jing at **Nan Tang Er Ling** bear witness to this dynasty's high cultural development. However, it came to an end in 975AD when the recently established Northern Song Dynasty (960–1126) kidnapped the third Nan Tang emperor and took him back to their capital at Kaifeng on the Yellow River (Huang He). Nanjing thus slipped out of the political limelight and back into the shadows for another 400 years, during which the Yellow River reasserted its predominance over the Yangzi and North China ruled over the South.

During the Northern Song (Bei Song) (960–1126) and Southern Song (Nan Song) (1127–1279) dynasties, palaces for the emperors were maintained in Nanjing, although the capitals were elsewhere. The second to last Northern Song emperor, Hui Zong (1101–1126), chose to retire in Nanjing after his abdication. In 1127, Emperor Gao Zong declared the start of his reign and the establishment of the Southern Song Dynasty in Nanjing, after the Song capital at Kaifeng had been captured. Later the Nan Song capital was moved to Hangzhou. Nonetheless, Nanjing played an important role in the Nan Song defense system, as the Yangzi River was considered their front line of defense against invasion from the North. The famous Nan Song general **Yue Fei** (1103–1141) spent quite a lot of time in Nanjing and built defensive ramparts in the hills south of the City, remnants of which can still be seen today.

Nanjing as Ming Capital

The city resumed its central role in China's political history when it was captured in March 1356 by Zhu Yuanzhang, who was then a rebel against the Mongol Yuan Dynasty, which had its capital in Beijing. Zhu apparently chose Nanjing as his new capital at the recommendation of his adviser, Feng Sheng. In the summer of 1353, when Zhu and his entourage were still based in the small town of Chuzhou, in a part of Anhui province north of the Yangzi River, Feng Sheng had told Zhu, "Jinling (Nanjing) is at the place where the dragon coils and the tiger crouches, a past capital of kings and emperors. If you capture it as your base, you can then go forth in conquest from it in all directions…" In the Chinese mind, Nanjing has, for centuries, been seen as a place characterized by "a coiling dragon" (*long pan*) and "crouching tiger" (*hu ju*), and having an atmosphere filled with "royal air" (*wang qi*). Today, this legend is kept alive in Nanjing in the name of one of the city's main north-south avenues, Long Pan Lu.

Twelve years after he had actually captured the city, Zhu founded the Ming Dynasty (1368–1644) here in 1368. He became the new dynasty's first Emperor, taking the reign title Hong Wu. It was during his reign that the impressive city wall, which still stands today, was first built. The entire city experienced a massive construction boom of public works during this time, including palaces, temples, pagodas, and monuments. When Nanjing's residents reflect on their city's history, it is undoubtedly the reign of Hong Wu which stirs their pride the most. Much of the Ming city has either survived intact or is being restored and reconstructed today.

The second Ming emperor, Jian Wen (1399–1402), kept the capital in Nanjing. However, within four years he was overthrown by Zhu Di, the rival Prince of Yan who became known as the Yong Le emperor (1403–1425). Since Yong Le had previously been based in Beijing, he preferred to live there and began preparations for moving the capital in 1403 when he renamed Beiping (Northern Peace) as Beijing (Northern Capital). This in itself was not unusual as it had become customary since the Tang Dynasty to have dual capitals. Yongle continued to live in Nanjing until 1409, after which he spent half his time in Beijing and half in Nanjing for another eight years. In 1417, he made his final move to Beijing, after which he began construction of his new palace there. It was finally completed in 1421. However, Nanjing maintained its status as the second capital and six central government ministries continued to have their offices there. Four years later, the Yong Le reign ended. The fourth Ming emperor, Hong Xi, decided to move the capital back to Nanjing. He issued orders to this effect on 16 April 1425. However, the Hong Xi reign (1425–1426) was cut short with the emperor's unexpected death on 29 May 1425 and his successor, the Xuan De emperor (1426–1436), canceled the planned move, keeping the capital in Beijing instead. If either the Jian Wen or Hong Xi emperors had lived longer, Nanjing would likely have maintained its position as the national capital. Even so, Beijing was not formally designated the permanent capital until 1441.

On occasion, the Italian Jesuit Matteo Ricci (1552–1616) made Nanjing his base of operations from 1595 to 1600, while attempting to gain admission to the capital in Beijing. Ricci's diary, first published in Latin by Nicola Trigault in 1615 and later translated into English by Louis J. Gallagher in 1953 under the title *China in the Sixteenth Century*, provides valuable information on Nanjing in the late Ming Dynasty.

Ricci paints a picture of Nanjing as a city that is full of lively cultural activities and impressive monuments. He opens his account with the bold assertion that "this city surpasses all other cities in the world in beauty and in grandeur." Even though it is no longer the capital, it has "lost none of its splendor" and that "in the whole kingdom of China ... Nanjing is rated as the first city." He describes the city as "filled with palaces and temples, and towers and bridges" that are "scarcely surpassed by similar structures in Europe." He witnessed the Lantern Festival celebrating the first full moon of the new lunar year, complete with displays of fireworks, and concluded that "Nanjing surpasses the rest of the kingdom in pyrotechnic display, and perhaps the rest of the world."

Ricci describes Nanjing as a city "surrounded by three circles of walls," including the Palace Wall, the Inner City Wall (Nei Cheng Qiang) with twelve gates, and the Outer City Wall (Wai Cheng Qiang). In fact, there were four sets of walls, if one counted the old Ming Palace (Ming Gu Gong) and Imperial City (Huang Cheng) separately, plus the Inner City Wall had 13 gates, not 12. Ricci said the Outer City Wall had such a large circumference that if two men on horseback left from the same spot along the wall in opposite directions, it would take them a full day before they could meet again. The Ming Palace (Ming Gu Gong) was apparently still maintained in good condition, as Ricci glowingly asserts that "there is probably no king in the world with a palace surpassing this one." In addition to its fixed defenses, the city was protected by an army of 40,000 soldiers.

The city's natural beauty also impressed Ricci, who raved about its "expansive parks, mountains, and forests interspersed with lakes." On the top of one mountain, either Zijin Shan or Beijige, he discovered a collection of four cast iron astronomical instruments used to "observe the heavens and to record celestial phenomena" such as comets and shooting stars. Although the instruments were nearly 250 years old, they were still used every night, and in his judgment they "surpassed anything of the kind as yet seen or read about in Europe." Replicas of these instruments can now be seen at the Zijin Shan Observatory.

Early Qing Nanjing

The Jiangnan region continued to be a center of passionate Ming loyalism for several years after the fall of the capital in Beijing in April 1644 and the establishment of the Qing Dynasty by the Manchus. Remnants of the old regime established the Southern Ming Dynasty in Nanjing, placing the Prince of Fu, Zhu You Song, on the throne as the Hong Guang emperor on

19 June 1644. When the Manchus finally captured Nanjing a year later on 8 June 1645, the Hong Guang emperor fled westward to Wuhu. His capture on the hill of Zhe Shan about ten days later effectively ended Ming resistance on the Yangzi.

During the Qing Dynasty (1644–1911), the national capital was in Beijing. However, Nanjing was still the important seat of a Viceroy and from where he governed the Liangjiang region, which included the three provinces of Jiangsu, Jiangxi, and Anhui. The Jiangnan Gongyuan continued to be the most important testing center in east China for the imperial civil service examinations, hosting as many as 20,000 candidates at one time. This made the city a major center of learning, education, culture, and the arts. Despite its importance, the city's name was changed from Nanjing (Southern Capital) to Jiang Ning.

In 1724, the revocation of the former religious toleration policy of the Ming Dynasty by the Qing Dynasty's Yong Zheng emperor (1723–1735) spelt an end to the Jesuit presence that had existed in Nanjing since Matteo Ricci's first visits in the 16th century, and effectively closed it to foreign visitors until 1842.

In August 1842, foreigners returned to Nanjing in the form of a British fleet sent to forcibly open China's doors to Western commerce. The three-month stay of the British occupation force left many more eyewitness accounts of the city. However, the 1842 Treaty of Nanking did not open Nanjing itself as a treaty port so this window to the outside world was soon closed ant it stayed that way until the Taiping Heavenly Kingdom (Taiping Tian Guo) made the city its capital and invited foreign diplomats, military advisors, and missionaries to visit.

Nanjing as Taiping Capital

After marching overland from Guangdong to Lake Dongting Hu in Hunan, and then using a captured Qing fleet of sailing vessels to sail down the Yangzi River from Wuhan, Taiping rebels arrived outside the city walls of Nanjing on 8 March 1853. They captured the city on 19 March 1853, after a brief siege of only 11 days, and renamed it Tianjing, making it the new capital of the Taiping Heavenly Kindgom (Taiping Tian Guo). By that time, their followers had grown to over a million, of whom only 20,000 were original members from Guangdong.

One Taiping writer described Nanjing this way, "Jinling's city walls are strong and thick; Jinling's granaries are full and sufficient; Jinling's topographical conditions are like a crouching tiger and a coiling dragon; and Jinling's customs are elegant, simple, and generous."

Another contemporary observer described Nanjing as it was in 1853, when the Taipings captured it, in this way, "Nanjing is the residence of the literati, the men of science, the dancers, the painters, the antiquaries, the jugglers, the physicians, and the courtesans of celebrity. In this charming city are held schools of science, art, and pleasure…."

The Taiping treasury at Nanjing amounted to 18 million taels, six times the amount the Qing central government then had at their disposal in Beijing. These funds, along with the region's ample natural resources, and their control of the Yangzi River, would allow the Taipings to maintain their position in Nanjing for 11 years.

In November 1851, the Taipings had established a leadership structure consisting of five kings (*wang*) below the supreme ruler the Heavenly King (Tian Wang). These five leaders included the East King (Dong Wang) Yang Siu Ching, the West King (Xi Wang) Xiao Chao Kwei, the South King (Nan Wang) Feng Yun Shan, the North King (Bei Wang) Wei Chang Hui, and the Assistant King (Yi Wang) Shi Da Kai. The Xi Wang and Nan Wang both fell in battle before the capture of Nanjing in 1853. After the capture of Nanjing, the Dong Wang increasingly dominated the government.

Contrary to the Communist view of the Taipings as a popular peasant movement, Franz Michael depicts it as a "totalitarian" regime, with "a system of total control of all life by the state." Michael argues that "the Taiping movement did not have as its goal an agrarian revolution that would give the peasant the use of his land," and "was not … a peasant rebellion…" All surplus agricultural produce was to be deposited in the "common treasury" or "public granary." He says it was "a system of military discipline" and "control of all economic, social, and intellectual life."

The Qing Dynasty had been slow to organize an effective military response to the Taiping threat, allowing the rebels to seize control of the entire Yangzi River from Yuezhou (Yueyang) in the west to Zhenjiang in the east within a time span of only three and a half months, from mid-December 1852 to 1 April 1853. On 29 January 1853, dismayed at the emperor's inaction, the Hanlin Academy scholar and *chin-shih* degree-holder Zeng Guofan (1811–1872) decided on his own initiative to begin organizing a new loyalist Qing fighting force in his home province of Hunan. This provincial militia later became known as the Hunan Army (Xiang Jun). By 25 February 1854, Zeng had assembled a fleet of 240 ships and 5,000 marines which were able to challenge the Taipings for control of Lake Dongting Hu and finally succeed in recapturing Hunan's important Yangzi River port city of Yuezhou (Yueyang) on 25 July 1854. This first Qing victory against the Taipings was the beginning of a long ten-year military campaign in which Zeng's forces slowly moved down the Yangzi River towards their final goal of recapturing the Taiping capital of Nanjing.

Foreign Visitors to the Taiping Capital at Nanjing

Many foreign visitors sailed up the Yangzi River from Shanghai to the capital of Nanjing during the Taiping's early occupation of the city. The first two years of their rule in Nanjing saw many opportunities to make a favorable impression on foreign public opinion and to establish diplomatic relations with foreign governments. Foreign powers were officially neutral during this period, but were initially interested in the possibility of diplomatic negotiations with the Taipings. Unfortunately, the Taipings never fully took advantage of this opportunity and failed to reach any definite agreements with the foreign powers.

In April 1853, Sir George Bonham, representing the British government, sailed to Nanjing on HMS Hermes, stopping to meet Taiping officials in Zhenjiang on the way. Those on board included the British Consul Thomas Taylor Meadows, W.H. Medhurst, and the ship's Captain Edmund G. Fishbourne. All four left detailed written accounts of the visit, and Medhurst was responsible for producing a valuable volume of translations of Taiping documents.

In May 1854, U.S. Commissioner **Robert McLane**, joined by the missionary E.C. Bridgman, visited Nanjing on board the USS Susquehanna. McLane and Bridgman reported that because the Taipings controlled the Yangzi River and its trade, they could keep Nanjing well supplied with provisions. However, they noted ominously that the Taiping leadership had banned all unauthorized books, including the classics of Confucius and Mencius. Their visit was followed in June 1854 by the British representative Sir John Bowring, who sailed to Nanjing on HMS Rattler.

After the signing of the 1858 Treaty of Tientsin between China and Britain, **Lord Elgin** commanded a flotilla of British ships that sailed up the Yangzi River to Hankou in November 1858 and came back down the river in December of the same year. Elgin passed Nanjing without stopping, going upstream on 20 November 1858, during which time gunfire was exchanged with the Taiping defenders. However, on their way back down the river, the Elgin Mission stopped at Nanjing on 29 December 1858 and disembarked a landing party. Although Lord Elgin himself seems to have stayed safely on board his ship, he sent his secretary Laurence Oliphant and his interpreter Alexander Wylie into the city to meet with Taiping leaders and explore the city.

In addition to these diplomatic visitors, a number of foreigners journeyed to Nanjing in order to join the Taiping cause and participate in the movement, motivated either by romantic notions of a just cause, mercenary profit, or dreams of converting them to Christianity. In the fall of 1860, two American missionaries, **I.J. Roberts** and **Griffith John**, each paid separate visits to Nanjing. One British adventurer, **A. F. Lindley** (Lin Li), served as a military officer in the Taiping army and lived with the Taipings in Nanjing for several years. **Thomas W. Blakiston** made two visits to Nanjing in 1861, along with his interpreter the Reverend Samuel Isaac Schereschewsky. This five-month journey up the Yangzi River to Chongqing and back is described in Schereschewsky's 1862 travel account, *Five Months on the Yang-Tse*.

1856 Taiping Civil War

Internal fighting among the Taiping Kings (wangs) between September and November 1856 left the original leadership decimated, and the Heavenly King (Tian Wang), Hong Xiu Quan, in a rather isolated position. The ever-growing pretensions of the East King (Dong Wang) led to a plot by the North King (Bei Wang) and the Assistant King (Yi Wang), Shi Da Kai, to eliminate him. After the Dong Wang's elimination, the Bei Wang turned his focus to eliminating the Yi Wang. Although the Yi Wang escaped, his entire family perished at the hands of his rival. The Tian Wang was finally alerted to the danger, and after eliminating the Bei Wang himself, invited the Yi Wang to return to the capital. Although Shi Da Kai returned briefly to the capital, he soon left for good. As the original conqueror of Anqing and Wuhu in 1853, this was a great loss to the Taiping cause. It was sometime during this internal civil war of 1856 that the far-famed Porcelain Pagoda (Bao En Ta) was intentionally destroyed by rival combatants who saw it as a strategic prize.

The self-inflicted decimation of the Taiping's original leadership was followed by a year of successive military defeats. Wuchang fell to a Qing army on 19 December 1856 after being occupied by the Taipings for 18 months and besieged for an entire year. Jiujiang was besieged by Qing forces on 13 January 1857. The Taiping garrison at Jiujiang continued to hold out, but Hukou, strategically located downriver at the mouth of Poyang Hu, was captured on 18 October 1857. Zhenjiang fell to the Qing in December 1857. The Taiping movement was collapsing from within and being defeated from without.

The New Taiping Leadership of 1858

In March 1858, the Taiping Heavenly King (Tian Wang) appointed seven new kings (*wang*) in an attempt to replace the earlier five who had all died in battle or been decimated in internicine fighting. Of the original leaders, only the Assistant King Shi Da Kai still lived and he had departed Nanjing on a wandering odyssey, never to return. Among this new group of leaders the two most important would prove to be the Heroic King (Ying Wang) Cheng Yu Chen and the Loyal King (Zhong Wang) Li Xiu Cheng. Before this new leadership could have any impact, the Taiping stronghold of Jiujiang fell on 19 May 1858 to a Qing land and water force led by Peng Yu Lin, after having been in Taiping hands for three years.

In the aftermath of this disaster, the Taiping's new leadership held an important strategy council in October 1858 at the town of Zong Yang, in the Anqing prefecture of Anhui province. The Ying Wang and Zhong Wang took the lead in forming a new military strategy that would prove successful in reviving the Taiping movement for another six years. In 1859, a final addition was made to the Taiping leadership when the Tian Wang's brother Hong Ren Kan arrived and assumed the role of prime minister of the civil government, the other kings being primarily military leaders.

After years of operating under unimpressive titles that failed to get the cooperation of local officials, Zeng Guofan was finally appointed Viceroy of the three Liangjiang provinces of Jiangxi, Anhui, and Jiangsu on 10 June 1860. Soon after, he received the added title of Imperial Commissioner for Jiangnan on 10 August 1860.

After nearly two years of siege, Anqing finally fell to Zeng Guoquan's forces on 5 September 1861. After the recapture of Anqing, Peng Yu Lin was appointed Governor of Anhui province, and Anqing became Zeng Guofan's new headquarters. Wuhu remained the last Western defense of Nanjing still in Taiping hands, along with a spot on the Yangzi known as "the Two Pillars," a place where two hills framed both sides of the river.

With Peng Yu Lin in command of the Qing river fleet, Zeng Guoquan slowly moved down the Yangzi from Anqing until he arrived outside the city walls of Nanjing on 31 May 1862 and occupied the commanding heights of the Yuhua Tai outside the South Gate (Jubao Men). On 13 October 1862, the Zhong Wang besieged Zeng Guoquan on the Yuhua Tai for 46 days, until the Taiping's lifted the siege on 26 November 1862. In March 1863, Zeng Guofan left his headquarters at Anqing for a tour of the front lines around Nanjing, visiting his field commander Peng Yu Lin in Wuhu, and his brother Zeng Guoquan on the Yuhua Tai.

The Fall of Taiping Nanjing, 1863–1864

On 13 June 1863, Zeng Guoquan captured the Taiping trenches that had surrounded his camp on the Yuhua Tai, and Peng Yu Lin captured the Xiaguan district along the Yangzi River. The Taiping capital was now surrounded from the south, east, and west. On 18 December 1863, the Qing besiegers exploded a mine near the South Gate (Jubao Men) and succeeded in blowing up part of the city wall. Although the Qinhuai River still served as a natural defense, the tightening encirclement caused the Zhong Wang to recommend to the Tian Wang on 20 December 1863 that the city be abandoned in favor of a withdrawal to the mountains of Jiangxi.

The front lines held until 3 July 1864 when the Qing forces captured the strategic heights of Dragon Shoulder Peak (Long Wei Feng), now known as Fu Gui Shan. From this position, they were able to place a mine against the city wall and blow a hole in it 200 feet wide on 19 July 1864. It was through this hole that the Qing forces poured into the walled city, laid siege to the inner walls of the imperial city, and then captured it later the same night. The Zhong Wang had led the doomed defense at the Taiping Men city gate. He abandoned his position only to help the Taiping heir apparent, Hong Fu Tian, successfully escape the city by giving him his horse, only to be captured himself. Fighting within the city continued for three days and nights until an estimated 100,000 Taiping residents had been massacred.

The Taiping Impact on Nanjing

During the Taipings occupation of Nanjing from March 1853 to July 1864, they destroyed nearly all the historic buildings and temples within the city, including the famous Porcelain Pagoda (Bao En Ta) and the Confucius Temple (Fuzi Miao) on the banks of the Qinhuai River, which had been the city's social center. The only structures left standing were the Ming Dynasty city walls, which the Taipings had needed to defend the city against the Qing armies attempts to recapture it, and the palaces where the Taipings own leaders lived. Even the palaces of the Taipings' kings were destroyed during Zeng Guofan's 1864 recapture of the city, when all the wooden structures in Nanjing were burnt to the ground in a furious firestorm. Virtually none of Nanjing's Taiping defenders chose to surrender, making destructive house-to-house combat necessary.

Post-Taiping Reconstruction

Zeng Guofan arrived in Nanjing on 28 July 1864, not having personally participated in its capture. He later made amends for his contribution to the city's destruction when he served three terms as the Governor-General of the Liangjiang provinces with his headquarters in Nanjing. During his terms in office, Zeng was personally responsible for massive reconstruction efforts, including the rebuilding of Fuzi Miao, Chao Tian Gong, and the Viceroy's residence at the present-day Tushuo Zongtongfu. On 20 December 1864, he resumed the provincial imperial civil service examinations, which had not been held for over 11 years.

However, Zeng's services were repeatedly needed elsewhere by the Qing Dynasty in its efforts to quell other uprisings. His first period of administration in Nanjing lasted from Juy 1864 to June 1865, before he was called away to Shandong. During his nearly two-year absence from Nanjing, Zeng was temporarily replaced as Governor-General by Li Hong Zhang, governor of Jiangsu province. Zeng returned to Nanjing in mid-December 1866. In September 1868, he was again called away from Nanjing to take over as Governor-General of Chihli province. In August 1870, Zeng was reappointed Viceroy of Liangjiang, but did not arrive in Nanjing until 14 December 1870. He died in March 1872 and was given the posthumous title of Weng Cheng, with a memorial temple erected in Nanjing in his honor.

Zeng Guofan was followed in the post of Liangjiang Viceroy by several other Qing heroes of the Taiping defeat, including Zuo Zong Tang in 1881 and his brother Zeng Guoquan (1824–1890), who served from April 1884 until his death in November 1890.

For several years in the 1890s, Nanjing was governed by another enlightened reformer when **Zhang Zhi Dong** (1837–1909), better known for his 18 years as the Governor-General at Wuhan, served as Viceroy of the Liangjiang provinces. Zhang arrived in Nanjing in November 1894 and stayed there until he was sent back to Wuhan in February 1896. During 1894, Zhang constructed the first asphalt road in Nanjing, cutting across the city from the Xiaguan plain on the Yangzi River, entering the city at Yi Feng Men, passing through the Drum Tower (Gu Lou), and exiting the east end of the city at Tong Ji Men. This modern road replaced a stone paved trail that had passed through the Gu Lou before. He was once again briefly appointed Viceroy of the Liangjiang provinces on 8 October 1902. His brief tenure only lasted five months this time, but he made good use of it by organizing the first modern Chinese-run university in Nanjing. Late in 1902, Zhang founded **Sanjiang Normal College**, later known as Liangjiang Normal College, and the predecessor to the Guomindang's National Central University established in May 1928. This school still exists today, and is now known as Southeast University.

Nanjing had been listed as a treaty port in the 1858 Treaty of Tianjin, but its occupation by the Taipings had made opening the port to trade impossible. Christian missionaries began arriving in Nanjing after the signing of the 1876 Chefoo (Yantai) Convention. Some of the first Christian colleges in the city were established in the 1880s. However, the city was not actually opened to foreign trade until a Customs House was established in 1899. This combination of religious, educational, and economic interests led to the establishment of British, American, and Japanese Consulates in the city by 1910. Nonetheless, Nanjing never had a demarcated foreign settlement or concession area the way that most of the other Yangzi River treaty ports did.

The aftermath of the Taiping Rebellion also saw the first construction of facilities by the Christian missionaries who had settled here. Several of these facilities still survive today. The **Hui Wen Academy**, built by Jesuits in 1888, is now the Jinling Middle School (Jinling Zhong Xue), while **Marlin Hospital**, built by the Jesuits in 1892, still serves as part of the Gu Lou Hospital (Gu Lou Yiyuan) today.

Revolutionary Nanjing, 1911–1927

When the 1911 Revolution (Xin Hai Geming) against the Qing Dynasty started with the 10 October military uprising in Wuhan, Nanjing remained under the control of Qing loyalist Zhang Xun. An attack by the Ninth Brigade of the New Army under Xu Shao Zhen failed to capture the city on 8 November 1911. After this, a Republican army of 10,000 volunteers from Jiangsu and

Zhejiang was formed under Xu's command. On 24 November 1911, the Republicans began their second attack on the city. On 1 December 1911, the Republicans occupied the fortress of Tian Bao Cheng on the western peak of Zijin Shan, from where they were able to shell Taiping Men and the city below with cannon fire. Zhang Xun's Qing loyalists continued to hold a cannon fort equipped with modern artillery gun emplacements on western Zijin Shan's Dragon Shoulder Peak (Long Wei Feng), now known as Fu Gui Shan. However, on the night of 1 December, Zhang Xun abandoned his headquarters on Bei Ji Ge Hill and his troops surrendered the next day. Nonetheless, Zhang would later return to crush the Republicans in 1913, and also be responsible for the brief restoration of the last Qing Emperor Pu Yi in Beijing in July 1917.

This military victory led to the formation of a provisional republican national government in Nanjing. An assembly of 44 delegates representing 17 provinces of China convened in Nanjing for the first time on 14 December 1911, meeting in the **Jiangsu Provincial Assembly** (Jiangsu Zi Yi Ju). This impressive Baroque-style hall still stands on the north side of Hunan Lu at its intersection with Yunnan Lu, in an area once known as Ding Jia Qiao, a few blocks west of Zhongyang Lu. On 29 December 1911, the assembly elected Sun Yat Sen (Sun Zhongshan) as the first President of the newly declared Republic of China. Sun arrived in Nanjing for his inauguration on 1 January 1912. His government included civilian scholar officials such as Hu Han Min and Cai Yuan Pei, while Huang Xing served as the Commander in Chief of his military forces. However, Sun's presidency was short-lived. On 1 April 1912, he resigned the presidency in favor of Yuan Shi Kai. On 3 April, he left the presidential compound in Nanjing and headed for Shanghai. Yuan demanded that the national capital be in Beijing, so the assembly members moved there.

By July 1913, Sun Yat Sen (Sun Zhongshan) realized that Yuan Shi Kai was not keeping the promises he had made when Sun agreed to resign in April 1912. Sun chose to launch a Second Revolution in the form of a militray uprising by his supporters in Jiangxi, Jiangsu, and Guangdong. Nanjing was one of Sun's main centers of support in this episode.

On 15 July 1913, Huang Xing, Sun's former commander-in chief in the 1912 provisional government, raised a revolutionary army in Nanjing to oppose Yuan Shi Kai as part of the Second Revolution, and Jiangsu province proclaimed its independence from the Beijing government. However, Huang Xing fled from Nanjing on 29 July 1913, and the anti-Yuan resistance in Nanjing continued under new leadership. It was not until a full month later that the monarchist general, **Zhang Xun**, recaptured Nanjing on 1 September 1913, in the face of determined resistance from its revolutionary defenders. After its capture, the city suffered three days of chaotic looting, in which three Japanese residents were killed. As a reward for his loyalty, Yuan appointed Zhang Xun Governor of Jiangsu province on 3 September 1913.

During the 1920s Nanjing was governed by a succession of warlords, the most significant being **Sun Chuan Fang**. By 1926, Sun had reunited the Liangjiang provinces of Jiangsu, Anhui, and Jiangxi under his rule, and had added Zhejiang province to his domain.

As part of their 1926-1927 Northern Expedition (Bei Fa) from Guangzhou, the Guomindang captured Nanjing from Sun Chuan Fang's forces on 24 March 1927. During the first days of their occupation of the city, the large resident foreign community of Nanjing was subjected to a seemingly orchestrated campaign of terror, pillaging, rape, and assassination. The Vice-President of the University of Nanking, John E. Williams, was executed by Guomindang soldiers. Even the diplomatic community was not immune, as the Japanese Consul was executed and the British Consul severely wounded. A large group of foreign residents gathered together on Ding Shan from where they climbed over the city wall and ran across the flat plain of Xiaguan to the safety of gunboats anchored in the Yangzi River. Later investigation into the incident failed to offer an adequate explanation other than to pin the blame on supposed Communist elements in the Guomindang army.

Nanjing as Guomindang Capital, 1927-1937

Nanjing was chosen as the Guomindang capital on 18 April 1927 and remained so for 22 years until April 1949. In the beginning, the new national regime established in Nanjing by Chiang Kai Shek (Jiang Jieshi) had little support from civilian members of the moderate center or left wing of the Guomindang party. Although Chiang (Jiang) had the guns and the generals, his political support was limited to a small circle of conservative traditonal scholars, including **Cai Yuan Pei** (1868-1940), **Lin Sen** (1868-1943), and **Hu Han Min** (1879-1936). These men still dressed in Mandarin robes and probably would have felt more comfortable in the company of Li Hong Zhang and Zeng Guofan, Qing Dynasty scholar officials who had governed Nanjing 50 years before. Lin Sen had been a member of the Guomindang's ultra conservative **Western Hills Clique** since it was formed at the Bi Yun Temple in Beijing on 23 November 1925. This group was considered so extremely right wing that it had been proscribed by the Guomindang party's Second National Congress held in Guangzhou in January 1926. The more famous celebrities of the party leadership, such as Song Qingling (1893-1981) and Wang Jingwei (1883-1944), initially stayed away in protest. In order to compensate for this paucity of political support, Jiang needed another way to gain legitimacy for his regime. His solution was to launch a massive wave of public construction, building impressive edifices comparable only to that under Emperor Hong Wu in the 14th century. This completely changed the face of Nanjing during the first decade that it served as the Guomindang capital from 1927 to 1937.

The Guomindang regime was determined to make Nanjing as impressive a national capital as Washington DC in the United States. American architects such as **Henry K. Murphy** (1877–1954) were even brought in to help design the new capital city. Murphy served as the chief architectural adviser to the National Capital Reconstruction Planning Committee (Shoudu Jianshe Wei Yuan Hui) from 1928 to 1930. Most of their plans had just been completed when the city was captured by the Japanese in December 1937.

Although Western scholars such as Lloyd E. Eastman have tended to villify the Guomindang as politically repressive and militarily inept, more recent reappraisals have emphasized the great improvements made to urban living conditions in all the cities the Guomindang governed during the so-called Nanjing Decade between 1927 and 1937. For example, when the Guomindang captured Nanjing in March 1927, large parts of the city within the walls were still open fields, most roads were unpaved narrow lanes, homes and buildings had neither clean water supply nor electricity. In many ways, the city still had not recovered from the devastation it suffered during the 1853–1864 Taiping occupation. However, by January 1937, the city was ready to boast of major transformations when Mayor **Ma Chao Jun** (Ma Chao Chun) published his decennial report on Nanjing's urban development. The city now had public parks, electric lights, a clean drinking water supply, public mass transportation, and a network of wide paved avenues and boulevards.

As part of their national capital plan, the Guomindang built many of what are still the main avenues of the city, including Zhongshan Dong Lu, Zhongshan Bei Lu, Zhongshan Lu, Taiping Nan Lu, Taiping Bei Lu, Zhongyang Lu, and Hanzhong Lu. Zhongshan Road was built bisecting the city from Northwest to East, with its first purpose being to provide passage through the city for Sun Yat Sen's (Sun Zhongshan's) 1929 funeral procession.

It was primarily along the newly constructed main street of Zhongshan Road that the Guomindang erected new buildings for the various departments of their national government. Many of these government buildings were located on North Zhongshan Road (Zhongshan Bei Lu), running between the Drum Tower (Gu Lou) and the Yi Jiang Men city gate, and are so distinctive in their architecture that they are distinguishable as Min Guo buildings.

A new style of architecture was developed for these government buildings, one which was a combination of 1930s modern Art-Deco borrowed from the West and neo-classical Chinese style. They adopted many cultural symbols from the Ming Dynasty in order to give government structures a kind of imperial authority. This was an attempt to boost the regime's legitimacy and provide people with a sense of historical continuity. Typically, the buildings featured massive tiled roofs with upturned eaves placed atop concrete or brick walls, decorated with red pillars, and characterized by arched windows and doorways. Public buildings were set back from streets, within walled compounds entered through monumental gateways (*pai lou*). This style is sometimes referred to as a kind of Chinese Renaissance architecture, and it makes Guomindang era buildings easy to detect wherever they still stand in China.

Top: Former Guomindang Foreign Affairs Ministry (Wai Jiao Bu), now Communist party offices.

The first pair of Min Guo government buildings can be found northwest of the intersection of Zhongshan Bei Lu and Yunnan Lu, near the present day Ramada Plaza near the present day Ramada Plaza Hotel at 45 Zhongshan Bei Lu. The **Ministry of Foreign Affairs** (Wai Jiao Bu) was built in 1933 on the north side of the street at 32 Zhongshan Bei Lu. Along with a modern building next door, it now serves as the headquarters of the Jiangsu Provincial Communist Party and Provincial Peoples' Congress. As such its gates are guarded by armed soldiers, and public visitors are not allowed. The **Supreme Court** (Zuigao Fayuan) was housed in the Nanjing Theological Seminary on Hanzhong Lu for six years, until its new quarters were finished in 1933 at 101 Zhongshan Bei Lu, across the street from the Foreign Affairs Ministry. This building still stands, but is one of the few Guomindang government buildings now open to the public.

Farther northwest on Zhongshan Bei Lu, near its intersection with Chahar Lu and Guangdong Lu, stood another cluster of important Guomindang buildings. The **Ministry of Railways** (Tie Dao Bu) was built in 1930 at 252–254 Zhongshan Bei Lu. The **Ministry of Communications** (Jiaotong Bu) building across the street, at 303–305 Zhongshan Bei Lu, took four years to construct, between 1930 and 1934. These two buildings still stand today but are occupied by the Chinese military and are off limits to public visitors.

Center: Former Guomindang Ministry of Railways (Tie Dao Bu), now a military base.

Bottom: Former Guomindang Ministry of Communications (Jiaotong Bu), now a military base.

Another important government building on Zhongshan Bei Lu, standing within sight of Yi Jiang Men, was the **Ministry of the Navy** (Hai Jun Bu). The Navy Ministry was housed in an old Qing Dynasty compound of traditional courthouse halls that had previously served as a Naval College (Jiangnan Shui Shi Xue Tang) since 1890. China's most famous 20th century writer, **Lu Xun** (1881–1936), received his first higher education here at this Naval College in 1898. In 1927, it was converted into the Navy Ministry and had an impressive new monumental façade added facing the street, much like the monumental gate placed in front of the old Qing Dynasty yamens initially used for the Presidential Palace (Zongtong Fu). The new façade made it look like a French Catholic cathedral, although behind this Potempkin wall stood the same old Qing Dynasty halls that had served the college. It still stands today, next door to the Hai Zhi Yuan restaurant at 346 Zhongshan Bei Lu. Unfortunately it is kept closed and seems abandoned. There are no armed soldiers at this site, but one unarmed security guard (*bao an*) says visits are not permitted.

Former Republican (Min Guo) Ministry of the Navy (Hai Jun Bu), which is now closed.

A number of important Guomindang buildings were also constructed along East Zhongshan Road (Zhongshan Dong Lu). At the far eastern end stood the National Central Museum within sight of Zhongshan Men. A few blocks west, on the other side of the Qing Xi River is the former offices of the **Guomindang Central Supervisory Committee** (Zhongyang Jian Cha Wei Yuan Hui) at 311 Zhongshan Dong Lu. Designed in 1934 by the architect Yang Ting Bao (1901–1982) in traditional Chinese style with modern construction techniques, it was sometimes called the Eastern Palace (Tai Xue Dong Gong). It still stands on the north side of Zhongshan Dong Lu, near its intersection with Qing Xi Lu. It is now the **Military Archives** (Jun Shi Dang An Guan) and is off limits to public visitors. From the vantage point of its impressive monumental gateway (*pai lou*), you can enjoy looking at the building from a respectful distance.

Former Guomindang Central Supervisory Committee Zhongyang Jian Cha Wei Yuan Hui), now the PLA Military Archives (Junshi Dang An Guan).

Farther west, on the same side of the street at 309 Zhongshan Dong Lu, is another impressive traditional Chinese style building once used as the **Guomindang Historical Relics Exhibition Building** (Dang Shi Shi Liao Chen Lie Guan) and offices of the Guomindang Party History Compilation Committee. This building was also designed by the architect Yang Ting Bao, and as the

Former Guomindang Historical Relics Exhibition Building (Dang Shi Shi Liao Chen Lie Guan) and offices of the Guomindang Party History Committee (Guomindang Lishi Hui), now the China Second National History Archives (Zhongguo Di Er Lishi Dang An Guan).

sister building of the East Palace, it was sometimes called the Western Palace (Xi Gong). The designs for the building were drawn up in 1934, but the building itself was not completed until July 1935. In 1977, two modern side halls were added to the west of the original building. The Min Guo structure still stands today, and the whole complex now serves as China's **Second National History Archives** (Zhongguo Di Er Lishi Dang An Guan). Like its sister building, its entrance is marked by an imposing traditional Chinese style gateway (*pai lou*), but once again armed soldiers standing watch in the two guardhouses on either side prevent public visitors from entering. If you would really like to visit this site, try calling ahead (phone: 8480-9328) for an appointment.

On the west side of the National History Archives flows the Yu Dai River. Across the river stands a complex of three historic Min Guo buildings, also designed by architect Yang Ting Bao, once collectively known as the **Lizhi Association of Huangpu Classmates Society** (Huangpu Tongxue Hui Li Zhi She). The Huangpu Classmates were those who had graduated from the Whampoa Military Academy in Guangzhou, once under the directorship of Chiang Kai Shek (Jiang Jieshi) from 1924–1926. As a result, this acted as a military officers club for the highest ranking commanders in the Guomindang army. The Lizhi Association was founded in January 1929 with Chiang (Jiang) as its head. The Lizhi Association complex now stands on the grounds of the modern day Zhongshan Hotel, its highrise skyscraper towering over it, at 307 Zhongshan Dong Lu, near its intersection with Huangpu Lu.

The western building is a three-story red brick structure known as the Grand Hall (Da Li Tang). Inside, it contains an Assembly Hall (Da Hui Tang) or theater with stone balconies around three sides, looking down on a stage at the east end of

New commemorative sign outside the Lizhi Association of the Huangpu Classmates Society (Huangpu Tongxue Hui Li Zhi She).

the ground floor. It was designed by the architect Yang Ting Bao and constructed in 1931. In 1947, Chinese members of the Wang Jingwei regime who had collaborated with the Japanese were put on trial here. After 1949, it was used by the Jiangsu provincial government for party conferences, and several Communist propaganda films were shot here.

Another Yang Ting Bao designed building is the two-story red brick structure central building, now known simply as Building No.1 (Yi Hao Lou). Completed in 1929, it served as the headquarters of the Lizhi Association. The cedar tree out in front of the hall was planted in 1929 by Lin Sen, chairman of the national government, to commemorate the founding of the Lizhi Association. A jade tablet, inlaid in the southeastern cornerstone of the building's exterior foundation, bears eight Chinese characters — written by Chiang Kai Shek (Jiang Jieshi) himself — which reads, "Li Ren Li Ji Ge Min Ge Xin." Cloud patterns decorate the stone railings leading up the steps to the front entrance. Inside, the central lobby is decorated with colorful coffered ceilings supported by round red pillars, while a marble fireplace stands along the north wall. In recent times, historic photos have been on display here, including many of Chiang (Jiang). At the east end of the hall's second floor was Chiang's (Jiang's) own office and bedroom. For six months in 1947, his son, Jiang Jing Guo, lived in room No. 301 of the same hall, after returning from Russia. From 1949 to 1955, the Sino-Russian Friendship Association was based here. After 1955, it was used by the Jiangsu provincial government.

The eastern building is a three-story red brick structure known as Building No. 2 (Er Hao Lou). Constructed in 1929, it was also designed by Yang Ting Bao, the architect. The purpose of this building was to serve as a guest house for honored visitors to Nanjing. The American architect Henry K. Murphy lived here when he served for several years as an advisor to the Capitol Planning Committee.

The original corner stone of the Lizhi Association's Building No. 1 (Yi Hao Lou) bearing a jade tablet inscribed by Chiang Kai Shek (Jiang Jieshi) himself in 1929. It reads, "Li Ren Li Ji Ge Min Ge Xin."

Impressive original entrance gate of the former Guomindang Examination Yuan (Kaoshi Yuan), now the offices of the Nanjing Municipal People's Government (Nanjing Shi Renmin Zhengfu).

Other government offices were housed in exisiting buildings with a historic aura that might lend them legitimacy. The Guomindang **Central Party Headquarters**, where the Central Committee met, was in the old Qing Dynasty **Jiangsu Provincial Assembly** (Jiangsu Zi Yi Ju), the same place where Sun Yat Sen (Sun Zhongshan) had been proclaimed President of the Republic in 1912. The **Examination Yuan** (Kaoshi Yuan) was built near Jiming Si in 1931 on the site of the former **War God Temple** (Guandi Miao), and incorporated some of the remaining temple buildings, which were themselves of Qing era construction dating from 1868. The Ming Yuan Tower was built in May 1931 and the Pao Chang Pavilion was added in March 1934. Other parts of the complex included the Ming Chih Tower, the Da Zhong Lou, and the Ning Yuan Tower. Meanwhile, the Nanjing City Government was housed in the old Qing Dynasty imperial civil service **Examination Halls** (Jiangnan Gong Yuan) and the three-story **Ming Yuan Tower** (Ming Yuan Lou), built during the Ming Dynasty in the Yong Le reign (1403–1424), located on the east side of the **Confucius Temple** (Fuzi Miao), at the southend of the city near the Qinhuai River.

A side view of the rows of traditional style halls of the former Guomindang Examination Yuan (Kaoshi Yuan).

The commercial center at Xin Jie Kou started to take shape in 1933 with the completion of the Nanjing branch of the **Bank of Communications** (Jiaotong Yinhang). Designed by Liao Kai Bo, the building features an impressive Roman-style façade with a row of Ionic columns and a peculiar two-story separate structure on its roof. The building still stands at 1 Zhongshan Dong Lu and continues to dominate the Xin Jie Kou traffic circle. It was recently restored and now houses a branch of the Industrial and Commerical Bank of China (ICBC). Next door at 3 Zhongshan Dong Lu was the **Xin Ye Bank** of Zhejiang, completed in 1937. It is now a branch of the Bank of China (Zhongguo Yinhang).

The former Overseas Chinese Hotel, now the Jiangsu Yishi Yuan Jiudian.

By 1937, a new **Overseas Chinese Hotel** had been completed in palace-style architecture to welcome returning supporters of the regime to the new capital. This three-story hotel still stands today at 81 Zhongshan Bei Lu, but has been renamed the Jiangsu Yishi Yuan Jiudian. Its red-columned exterior walls, upturned roof eaves, and marble column ballroom clearly mark it as a Min Guo building.

With the urban development of the city came migrants seeking to participate in and benefit from the building boom. Many new jobs were available in the expanding government civil service, the military, the construction, engineering and architectural industries, the growing university faculties, as well as cultural and scientific institutions that were located here because it was the national capital. A population estimated at only 330,000 in 1910 had grown to over 1 million by December 1935. Unfortunately, this only meant that more would suffer during the devasation that was soon to come.

Japanese Occupied Nanjing, 1937–1945

The first Japanese air raid on Nanjing occurred on Sunday, 15 August 1937. However, it was not until 22 September 1937 that the Japanese began bombing Nanjing indiscriminately in massive waves, with the first day's air raid consisting of 65 Japanese war planes. In November 1937, some Soviet Russian fighter planes and pilots arrived to help defend the city. With their assistance, it was estimated that 300 Japanese planes were shot down over Nanjing before the city was finally captured.

When Shanghai fell on 12 November, Japanese troops quickly began moving westward towards the Chinese capital at Nanjing, capturing the Yangzi port of Liuhe on 14 November, and Kunshan on 15 November. Moving westward up the Yangzi River, the Japanese captured the town of Jiangyin, where a defensive boom had been placed across the river to block their advance. However, some Chinese fortifications in the area apparently continued to hold out longer.

After the fall of Shanghai, the defense of Nanjing was placed in the hands of General Tang Sheng Zhi and an army of 100,000 Chinese troops. Although the Chinese central government announced on 20 November that the capital would be moved to Chongqing, with some functions moving to Wuhan, General Tang vowed to stay behind with his army to defend Nanjing.

On 7 December 1937, Japanese military forces occupied the heights of Purple and Gold Mountain (Zijin Shan) just outside Nanjing, after arriving at the outskirts of the Chinese capital the day before. From this vantage point, they were able to rain artillery shells down on the city. Shortly thereafter, a second Japanese armored column occupied the heights of Yuhua Tai, south of Zhonghuamen. From a military history standpoint, the Japanese strategy was eerily reminscent of previous conquests of the city by Zeng Guoquan in 1864 and the Republican army in 1911.

At that time, the 600 year-old Ming Dynasty city wall was still sufficiently intact to temporarily provide a successful defense of the city, even against the modern 20th century weapons of the Japanese. The Guomindang had, in recent months, fortified this wall with some modern modifications, including concrete machine gun pillboxes, deep concrete bunkers, and other concrete gun emplacements, designed with the advice of German military advisers. The city gates were all closed in early December and their portals filled up with earth and timber, except for two that were left partially open. The suburbs outside the city wall were intentionally set ablaze to eliminate any cover for the attackers.

When the Japanese finally arrived, much of the fighting was centered around the invaders' attempts to seize control of key city gates that would allow them entrance into the walled city's urban center. The southeastern city gate, Guang Hua Men, at the end of Yu Dao Jie, was reportedly captured by the Japanese on 10 December. The capture of this city gate precipitated the final fall of the city three days later. On 13 December, the Guomindang commander General Tang Sheng Zhi fled the city just before Japanese troops poured through Guang Hua Men, and an armored column of Japanese tanks drove through Zhong Hua Men into the southern city.

On 17 December 1937, the Japanese commander, General Iwane Matsui, rode a horse through the Zhongshan City Gate (Zhongshan Men). He headed a Japanese victory parade that proceeded down the full length of the city's main street, Zhongshan East Road (Zhongshan Dong Lu) and Zhongshan North Road (Zhongshan Bei Lu). Photos of the event show that all three of Zhongshan Men's arched portals were still intact, although some of the parapets on top had been blasted away by gunfire. Eight years of occupation by the Japanese started in mid-December 1937 with the infamous Nanjing Massacre (Da Tu Sha). Chinese sources have estimated that 300,000 civilians perished in the weeks after the city was captured, even though the Japanese have continued to deny that any human rights violations took place during that time. In recent years, a growing body of Western publications has sought to document the exact details and statistics. What is certain is that during the first five and a half months after local Chinese military resistance had completely ceased, there was a great numbers of casualties among innocent Chinese civilians and wanton destruction of Chinese property. From mid-December 1937 to the end of May 1938, the campuses of the two schools run by foreign missionaries — Ginling College and the University of Nanking — served as an internationally recognized safe haven for an estimated 250,000 Chinese civilian refugees seeking to flee the carnage happening elsewhere in the city.

This period of unrestrained destruction and slaughter was followed by the emergence of the collaborationist Chinese puppet regime led by Wang Jingwei (1883–1944). Understanding Wang's motives in cooperating with the Japanese is difficult if seen in the light of their brutal occupation of the city. It does, however, appear more logical in light of Wang's whole political career.

Wang was born on 4 May 1883 in Guangdong and when he was 19, went to Japan where he later graduated from the Tokyo Law College. While living in Japan, he joined the Tongmenhui, an early predecessor to the Guomindang founded by Sun Yat Sen (Sun Zhongshan).

After attempting to assassinate the Prince Regent Zai Feng, father of Emperor Pu Yi, he was arrested on 16 April 1910 and sentenced to life in prison, but was released after the 1911 Revolution. This incident made him famous, but he did not assume any leadership positions for quite some time. Wang's political star began to rise on 30 January 1924 when he was elected a member of the party's Central Executive Committee by the Guomindang First National Congress. His star hit its zenith when it became known that he had drafted Sun Yat Sen's (Sun Zhongshan's) will and political testament while the latter lay on his deathbed at Beijing in March 1925. After this, he was seen by most party members as the heir apparent to the Guomindang's political leadership.

On 1 July 1925, his leadership of the party seemed secure when he was elected to all three of the top party and government posts in the Guomindang's Guangzhou regime: Chairman of the National Government, Chairman of the Military Affairs Commission, and Chairman of the Political Council of the Party Central Executive Committee. This was probably the height of his political career. Although he was reelected to all his positions by the Guomindang Second National Congress in January 1926, he resigned all his posts on March 22 in a dispute with Chiang Kai Shek (Jiang Jieshi) and fled Guangzhou to temporary exile in France. This began a downward slide in his career and a six-year-period in which he wandered on the fringes of political power.

He returned to Shanghai on 2 April 1927 and became the titular head of the left Guomindang regime in Wuhan. Unfortunately, when the Wuhan regime fell in August 1927, he fled to France in exile once again. He only returned to China in September 1929, having missed the Guomindang Third National Congress in March, and Sun Yat Sen's (Sun Zhongshan's) funeral in July, both of which were held in Nanjing that year.

On 1 September 1930, after his second return from exile, Wang joined an ephemeral opposition Guomindang regime in Beijing, with the warlords Feng Yu Xiang, Yan Xi Shan, and Li Zong Ren. This was followed by his participation in a second similarly short-lived opposition Guomindang regime in Guangzhou in 1931. Although he had no influence in the Guomindang capital of Nanjing, Wang had the support of liberal Chinese publishers in Shanghai and Tianjin, such as Tang Leang Li's China United Press, who continued to publicize his case for party leadership in a series of publications. In 1931 alone, the China United Press issued *Wang Ching Wei: A Political Biography*, and Wang's *The Chinese National Revolution*.

The Japanese invasion of Manchuria on 18 September 1931 finally prompted a drive for unification of the various party factions. Wang returned to leadership positions for the first time since 1926 and on 28 January 1932, he was appointed President of the Executive Yuan, concurrent with his appoinment as Minister of Foreign Affairs. His six years spent in the political wilderness seemed to be over, but he must have felt frustrated that his archrival Chiang Kai Shek (Jiang Jieshi) held all the real power. In theory, the regime was led by a dual leadership with Wang in charge of politics and Chiang (Jiang) the military. In reality, Wang was armed with an empty gun. Nonetheless, the theory of dual leadership was maintained with the 1935 publication by the China United Press of *China's Leaders and Their Policies*, coauthored by Chiang (Jiang) and Wang, with the latter's essay "Four Revolutions and Their Lessons" taking up the first half of the book. Wang's political rehabilitation ended abruptly on 1 November 1935 when he was the victim of an attempted assassination. After this incident, he resigned all his posts and fled to Shanghai.

The outbreak of war with Japan in July 1937 and the loss of the Guomindang capital of Nanjing to the Japanese in December once again prompted calls for national unity among China's various political factions. As a result, Wang was appointed President of the National Political Council by the Guomindang Central Executive Committee meeting, at the temporary capital of Wuhan on 16 June 1938.

Wang initially retreated to Chongqing with the rest of the Guomindang regime after the fall of Wuhan on 18 December 1938. Suddenly, he flew from Chongqing to Hanoi, where he issued a public statement calling for acceptance of Japanese peace terms. On 1 June 1939, he arrived in Tokyo to negotiate an agreement, which was finally signed on 30 December 1939. On 30 March 1940, Wang was inaugurated as head of the Japanese puppet regime in Nanjing. This finally gave him the leadership position he thought had rightfully been his since 1925.

He probably realized that as long as Chiang Kai Shek (Jiang Jieshi) lived, joining the Japanese offered him his only chance to ever occupy the Presidential Palace (Zongtongfu) in Nanjing. He would have undoubtedly been tried and executed as a traitor if he had survived the war, but he died on 10 November 1944.

The Guomindang Interlude: 1945–1949

The defeat of Japan on 16 August 1945 was followed by a brief three-and-a-half-year interlude, dominated by the Chinese Civil War of 1946–1949, in which the Guomindang resumed administration of Nanjing. The Japanese military command for China, represented by General Okamura, formally surrendered to the Chinese commander-in-chief, He Ying Qin, in Nanjing on 9 September 1945 at a ceremony held on Huangpu Lu. Eight months later, a formal ceremony was held on 5 May 1946, marking the move of the national capital from Chongqing back to Nanjing. All the government ministries resumed operations in their former headquarters, except for the Executive Yuan, which moved into the Ministry of Railways building. Politically, the Nanjing regime seemed on the surface to be modernizing: the 20 November 1946 convening of a National Assembly; the ratification by that assembly of a new Constitution on 25 December 1946; the November 1947 election of a new National Assembly; and that assembly's April 1948 election of Chiang Kai Shek (Jiang Jieshi) as President and Li Zong Ren as Vice-President.

However, economic and military disasters fueled growing popular unrest that manifested itself in university student protests, anti-inflation demonstrations, and public rallies in favor of peace negotiations with the Communists. The Huaihai campaign, that lasted from 6 November 1948 to 10 January 1949, proved to be the turning point in the civil war. The Communist commander Chen Yi defeated a Guomindang army of 500,000 men and captured the strategic railroad hub of Xuzhou in northern Jiangsu province. This defeat forced the resignation of Chiang Kai Shek (Jiang Jieshi) as President on 20 January 1949 in favor of Vice-President **Li Zong Ren** (1891–1969).

The final month of Guomindang rule in Nanjing began with a demonstration by thousands of people on 1 April 1949 in support of the peace talks between the Guomindang regime and the Communists in Beijing that were scheduled to begin that day. The latter rejected the final peace terms dictated by the Communists on 20 April. The next day, Red Army military units, led by commander Chen Yi, crossed the Yangzi River from their beachhead at Yangzhou. The Guomindang's acting President, Li Zongren, stubbornly remained in Nanjing up to the very day it was captured, before the easten China regional

PERSONALITIES

Before being elected as Vice-President in April 1948, Li Zong Ren had been one of the Guomindang's most talented military commanders. He played a crucial role in the 1926–1927 Northern Expedition (Bei Fa), and single-handedly saving Nanjing from a nearly successful counter-offensive by the warlord Sun Chuan Fang later in 1927. Later he scored the Guomindang's only major military victory of the Sino-Japanese War (1937–1945) when his troops wiped out an entire Japanese Imperial Guard division at Tai Er Zhuang in Shandong province on 7 April 1938. In his proven ability as a military strategist and a man genuinely popular with citizens under Guomindang rule as someone who cared about the public welfare, he was undoubtedly the right man for the job of trying to salvage the remains of the Guomindang regime.

Even after the disaster of Huaihai, the Guomindang still controlled all of China south of the Yangzi River, so that it would not have been impossible for a man of Li's ability to successfully follow the example of the Southern Song Dynasty, which held off the Mongols in northern China for 152 years. Unfortunately, Li was defeated not by the external enemy of the Red Army but from with the regime itself, by the continued loyalty of much of the officer corps to Chiang Kai Shek (Jiang Jieshi), especially the Huangpu Academy Classmates (Huangpu Tongxue Hui). Chiang (Jiang) continued to issue military commands to the field armies even after his sham retirement from politics. The way the Guomindang armies simply surrendered the Yangzi barrier without a fight seems to support Li's theory that Chiang (Jiang) had already planned to abandon the mainland and retreat to Taiwan by January 1949. Furthermore, it is now known that the Central Bank of China's entire gold reserve had already been secretly shipped to Taiwan by 20 February 1949, leaving Li with no funds to pay the army or the government civil servants.

commander Tang En Po forcibly escorted him to the airport, where he boarded one of the last airplanes out of the city on April 23, headed to his home town of Guilin in Guangxi province. The People's Liberation Army (Renming Jiefang Jun) successfully captured Nanjing on the night of 23–24 April 1949, and the city's residents woke up to a new regime the next morning.

Urban Development

After the Communist takeover, Nanjing became a living museum for the next 50 years as the architecture along large sections of Nanjing's main street had changed little since the Japanese occupation of 1937. In 2001, a new building boom started and in May of that year, wrecking crews began razing large parts of these areas for the first time. By the summer of 2002, most of Zhongshan Road bore little resemblance to its former self, with large areas turned into vacant lots and construction sites. A few notable structures still stand, but they are now isolated relics rather than part of a continuous period landscape.

One short two-block section of Taiping Nan Lu, stretching from Baixia Lu to Xiaohuowa Xiang has so far managed to preserve its Min Guo appearance. Historic structures include an old office building with a clock tower, a Christian church built in 1923, a Qing Dynasty Muslim mosque (Nanjing Qing Zhen Si), and many other inter-war era buildings and houses.

Another neighborhood of winding narrow alleyways, with rows of ancient Qing Dynasty two-story brick-and-wood houses, had been preserved as late as the year 2000. This was in the area lying between Hong Wu Lu to the west, Zhongshan Dong Lu to the south, Changjiang Lu to the north, and Hanfu Jie to the east. However, by December 2001, all of this neighborhood had been razed to the ground. The entire area is now an open wasteland, with the exception of one new shopping center that has already been built. The Former Presidential Palace (Tushuo Zongtongfu) now can be clearly seen from Zhongshan Dong Lu, across an open field. Deng Fu Xiang, running between Changjiang Lu and Zhongshan Dong Lu, was the last of the old Qing residential alleyways left intact, with vendors selling homemade snacks on the street; but in 2003, it too was levelled to the ground by wrecking crews.

The whole northern half of Xuan Wu Hu lake was drained of water in December 2001, and the inflow canal at He Ping Men was dammed shut, leaving open mud flats and construction cranes forming a line across the center of the lake. This was part of a project to build an east-west underground traffic tunnel under the lake so that vehicles can drive directly from Long Pan Lu, near the Railway Station, to the Zhongyang Lu in the city center without having to circle around the lakeshore as before. Since the project was completed in December 2002, six lanes of traffic have begun passing through a 2,560-m-long (1.6-mile-long) tunnel under the lake.

On 12 December 2000, construction began on Nanjing's first subway system. The first metro line is scheduled to be completed in 2005 and will run a distance of 17 km (10.6 miles) from north to south, connecting Mai Gao Qiao with Xiao Hang, traveling along the Zhongyang Lu-Zhongshan Lu axis, directly under Xin Jie Kou traffic circle and then down Taiping Nan Lu. A feasibility study, which began in September 2001, is being done for a second 27 km (16.8 mile) metro line running from east to west.

In 1997, construction of a second bridge spanning the Yangzi River began. On its completion on 26 March 2001, the six-lane Changjiang Er Qiao was the largest bridge in China and the third largest in the world. The entire structure measures 21.2 km (13.2 miles) in length and is actually formed by two bridges that meet on Ba Gua Island in the middle of the river. The bridge 11 km (6.8 miles) downstream from the site of the first Nanjing Yangzi River Bridge completed in 1968.

By November 2003, Nanjing had changed so much since the current wave of urban development started in 2001 that even local residents who live there now seem lost by the absence of previous landmarks. A huge swath of the city's eastern neighborhoods along Changjiang Lu, from Meiyuan Xincun to Zhongshan Lu, has simply disappeared, as have nearly all the Min Guo buildings along Zhongshan Dong Lu, and large sections of Zhongyang Lu. Billboards along the streets hide the entire city blocks of devastated waste land behind them. The new urban landscape seems bleak, denuded of all the small shops and quaint houses that once stood there. Only the rows of graceful old Wutong trees planted in 1929 still remain, with their natural canopies arching over the avenues, as a reminder of the pleasant urban environment the city once had.

However, a second glance shows that key historic monuments are still there, although they are now isolated without the context of their former natural surroundings. In 2003, the **Nanjing Urban Planning Institute** designated 134 historic late Qing Dynasty and Republic of China (Min Guo) buildings as protected units. Old historic sites that had been destroyed are being rebuilt, including the imperial palace gates of Dong Hua Men and Xi Hua Men, as well as Buddhist temples such as Pi Lu Si. Other long forgotten historic relics are being rediscovered, such as the home of prominent Min Guo architect Yang Ting Bao (1901–1982). The two historical residential areas of Mei Yuan Xin Cun and Yi He Lu have been marked for preservation. Mei Yuan Xin Cun included not only the more well-known home of Zhou En Lai, but also houses once belonging to the Guomindang generals, Bai Chong Xi (1893–1966) and Chiang Kai Shek (Jiang Jieshi). The Yi He Hu neigborhood west of Shanxi Lu Square includes the former homes of U.S. General George C. Marshall (1880–1959) and Wang Jingwei (1883–1944), as well as other houses that once served as foreign consulates and embassies, and residences of leaders of the Guomindang regime.

New public signs have also sprung up, calling attention to the historic significance of buildings that were occupied as war trophies by the Communist Party and Chinese military. The signs are so new that even local residents can frequently be seen stopping to read them in fascination. The block of Changjiang Lu, west of Taiping Bei Lu, still retains some of its old character. Some of its buildings include the Hanfu Hotel (Hanfu Fandian), People's Assembly Hall (Guomin Da Hui Tang), and the Jiangsu Provincial Art Museum (Jiangsu Sheng Meishu Guan), built in 1936 as the National Art Gallery (Guoli Meishu Chen Lie Guan) but demoted to provincial status in 1949. This new realization of the city's architectural heritage was displayed in 2004 when Nanjing hosted UNESCO's **World Historical and Cultural Cities Expo** from 30 April–5 May. This is an event attended by the mayors of other historic cities such as Vienna in Austria, Florence in Italy, St. Petersburg in Russia, Barcelona in Spain, and Kyoto in Japan.

Economic development has resulted in a growing disparity between the rich and poor residents. The quaint old wood timber Qing Dynasty houses between Changjiang Lu and Zhongshan Dong Lu have been razed to make way for new villas and highrise apartments. The question is: where have the neighborhood's former low income residents gone and where will they work now that their small streetside shops have been destroyed?

Incidents such as the 1 April 2000 murder of a German expat family of four living in the Royal Garden compound at Taiping Men are hard to forget when the conditions that caused it seem to be getting worse. Even as recently as November 2003, visitors to the city are in danger of being physically grabbed and mauled by poor peasants desperately seeking money.

The wealthy hide in the secure surroundings of gated communities protected by guards, such as Royal Place on Meiyuan Lu. If they can afford the monthly rent of US$8,000, the truly rich choose to live far outside the city center at Top Regent Park. Xin Jie Kou has become a copy of Shanghai's Xujiahui shopping district, complete with blindingly bright lights and Starbucks coffee shops charging 25 Rmb per cup.

All the hotels in the city have also jumped on the bandwagon, and their prices have doubled since 2002. Formerly inexpensive places such as the Tianjing Dajiudian, Xihuamen Hotel, and Hanfu Fandian have all raised their standard rates to 300 Rmb per day. No low budget accommodations seem left in a city that was once a low cost destination.

The social scene has also seen many changes. Traffic jams clog the streets, even though that Changjiang Lu has been widened from two lanes to eight and twin tunnels exist beneath Xuan Wu Hu, providing a direct link from Zhongyang Lu to Longpan Lu.

There has also been a disturbing increase in the number of "all-night hair salons," where young girls wait for customers. Expensive imported cars have been seen pulling up in the dead of night to pick them up and drop them off.

The city's attempts to balance economic development with historic preservation is illustrated by the masthead of the local newspaper, Nanjing Daily (Nanjing Ribao). It pictures modern highrise office buildings on the left side and historic sights such as Zhongshan Men on the right.

Nanjing's total population was most recently estimated at 5.32 million, but only 2.76 million of this number live in the downtown urban center. Much like other super-sized cities in China, the Nanjing municipality covers a total area of 6,516 sq km (2,515.8 sq miles), but only 976 sq km (376.8 sq miles) of this is urban area. In addition to ten fairly urbanized districts, the municipality includes five rural counties.

Nanjing Sights
Ming Dynasty City Wall (Ming Cheng Qiang)
In the Hong Wu reign of Zhu Yuanzhang, the Taizu Emperor, Ming Dynasty Nanjing had four layers of walls protecting four separate sections of the city.

The smallest of the four sections was the **Emperor's Palace** (Ming Gu Gong), the remains of which now form a city park in the southeast corner of the city near the present day Zhongshan Men on Zhongshan Dong Lu. The Ming Gu Gong had a square shape with four gates leading in each direction. The palace was built over an eleven-year period, from 1366 and 1377, making it the oldest part of Zhu's reconstruction of the city. Of the original relics, only the Wuchao Men and five stone bridges leading to it survive today. However, in 2003, a new replica of the palace's east gate, originally called Dong An Men but now called Dong Hua Men, was rebuilt east of Ming Gu Gong Park, on the south side of Zhongshan Dong Lu. First time visitors to Nanjing might be fooled by the gate's apparent authenticity, but it is in fact a clever forgery.

Surrounding the Emperors' Palace wall was the slightly larger walled area of the **Imperial City** (Huang Cheng). In the east and south, this area shared the city wall with the Emperor's Palace wall, with Chao Yang Men acting as its eastern gate, and Tong Ji Men and Zheng Yang Men (Guang Hua Men) as its two southern gates.

The Imperial Way (Yu Dao) stretched from Wu Chao Men in the north to Zheng Yang Men (Guang Hua Men) in the south, and is still commemorated by the present day street name Yu Dao Jie. Tong Ji Men, facing the Qinhuai River, had a series of four gates on an axis. These gates passing through three courtyards, built for defense, enclosed by walls known as barbicans (*weng cheng*). Outside the Tong Ji Men was the famous Nine Dragon Bridge (Jiu Long Qiao) across the Qinhuai River.

The Imperial City had its own separate wall to the north and west. The western wall had three gates, the most important of which was the Xi Hua Men. The northern gate was called Bei An Men, and is still commemmorated by the present day street name Bei An Lu. When the Ming capital was moved from Nanjing to Beijing in 1421, during the Yongle reign, the new Forbidden City in Beijing was modeled after the Imperial City and Emperor's Palace in Nanjing. During the Qing Dynasty, the Imperial City was sometimes known as the Tartar City or Manch Quarter.

Today, none of the original wall of Nanjing's Imperial City remains except for the stretch of city wall on both sides of Zhongshan Men. After being renamed Guang Hua Men in 1931, Zheng Yang Men was the main entrance point used by the invading Japanese army in December 1937. As such, it was severely damaged. A 1939 photo shows it was still standing, albeit with the exterior layer of brick blown off around the single arched portal. In 1954, the entire section of city wall from Tong Ji Men to Guang Hua Men was torn down.

In 2003, a new replica of one of the imperial city's three western gates, the Xi Hua Men, was rebuilt from scratch at the intersection of Zhongshan Dong Lu and Longpan Lu.

The **Outer City Wall** (Wai Cheng Qiang) once extended over 60 km (37.3 miles) and had 18 city gates. It was not completed until 1390, after work on the main city wall was finished. As less attention was paid to the quality of this wall, it deteriorated and disappeared fairly rapidly. In the early Min Guo period, the Guanyin Men near Yanzi Ji was the only outer city wall gate still standing. Nothing of this wall or its gates has survived to the present day.

The main **City Wall** (Cheng Qiang), which we could call the Inner City Wall (Nei Cheng Qiang), had 13 city gates and a circumference of 33.7 km (21 miles). The most impressive city gates were Jubao Men, Tong Ji Men, and Sanshan Men (Shui Xi Men), each of which had three defense barbicans (*weng cheng*) and a series of four arched portals on a central axis. Much of this wall has survived or has recently been restored.

Nanjing's 14th century Ming Dynasty city wall was built over 600 years ago. It took 200,000 workers 20 years to complete, starting in 1366 and finishing in 1386. Each brick was stamped with information regarding who made the brick, where it was made, and when it was made, in order to control the quality of the work. The Ming Dynasty capital's defenses included all the walls and moats constructed in previous dynasties. A stretch of wall, about 1.3 km (0.8 miles) long, of the **Stone City** (Shi Tou Cheng) built by Sun Quan of the Wu Kingdom was integrated into the Ming city wall. The most impressive section of the Stone City is known as the **Ghost Face** (Gui Lian). In February 2004, a new Stone City Park (Shi Tou Cheng Gongyuan) was completed, providing better access to this oldest section of the city wall.

Originally, the main city wall had 13 gates, and 200 fortresses. Its length stretched a distance of 33.7 km (21 miles) and enclosed an area of 41.3 sq km (16 sq miles). Its height ranged from 14 to 26 m (46 to 85 ft), its width 10 to 20 m (32.8 to 65.6 ft) at the base, and 7 to 14 m (23 to 46 ft) at the top.

The 13 original Ming Dynasty city gates were Taiping Men, Chao Yang Men (Zhongshan Men), Zheng Yang Men (Guang Hua Men), Tong Ji Men, Jubao Men (Zhonghua Men), San Shan Men (Shui Xi Men), Han Xi Men (Han Zhong Men), Qing Liang Men, Ding Huai Men, Yi Feng Men, Zhong Fu Men, Jin Chuan Men, and Shen Ce Men (He Ping Men). In addition there was an East Water Gate (Dong Shui Men), through which flowed a branch of the Qinhuai River, exiting out through the West Water Gate (Shui Xi Men).

Originally, some very long sections of the Ming city wall had no entry or exit points. For example, there were no gates along the shores of Xuan Wu Hu, stretching from Taiping Men to Shen Ce Men (He Ping Men). Zhong Hua Men was the only gate at the South end of the city, and there was only one gate on the city's east side between Taiping Men and Zheng Yang Men (Guang Hua Men). In 1910, Kiyoshi Uchiyama of the Japanese Consulate published a guidebook to Nanjing in which he stated that nine of the original 13 Ming city gates were still in use, although he did not clarify whether the other four had been torn down or were simply kept closed. After the 1911 Revolution, the Republican government added a number of additional gates to improve transportation in and out of the city. Eventually, there were a total of 24 gates.

POINT OF INTEREST

In 1927, the wall and its gates were still so impregnable that the resident foreign community became trapped inside the city when the gates were closed during the Guomindang army's attack on the city. In order to escape, they had to climb down the western city wall from their residential compound on Ding Shan overlooking the Hai Ling Men using ropes made out of sheets tied together.

Alice Tisdale Hobart published her account of this incident in her book, *Within the Walls of Nanking*, in which she wrote this description of the city wall as it looked in 1927:

> "...the wall descended a sheer perpendicular seventy feet, to the plain below. Everywhere we looked we could see this unscalable wall of masonry, completely separating us from the plain below. A great undulating precipice, never ending it flowed on around the city, hemming us in ... everywhere I looked I saw great reaches of the city wall. On all sides it surrounded me. From every window I saw this high wall rising out of the plain below, skirting the foot of the bluff, outlining the indentations in the hills, a sheer cliff down which no human being could climb. A great undulating precipice never ending, flowing on, as far as I could see, encircling the city. Once its huge gates were closed, barred against the invader, we should be shut in to whatever terrible things took place in the city, caught like rats in a trap."

In 1928, after making Nanjing their national capital, the newly installed Guomindang central government began renaming almost all the city gates. Several of these also had to be enlarged in order to accommodate the 1929 funeral procession of Sun Yat Sen (Sun Zhongshan). In 1930, there was still enough city wall standing for the Guomindang government to draft a plan to turn it into a ring road around the city, atop which automobiles would drive. T.Z. Tyau noted in his 1930 book, *Two Years of Nationalist China*, that the plan stated, "An elevated ring boulevard is suggested as eminently practical on top of the city wall, to afford a means of bypassing the central business districts and also to serve as a pleasure drive."

According to contemporary accounts published in the 1930s, it seems that nearly all the Ming Dynasty city walls and gates still stood at the time of the Japanese invasion in December 1937. Although sections of the wall were severely damaged, photos show that even Guang Hua Men, the main entrance point for the invading army, was still standing in 1939, albeit not in a pristine condition. After the overthrow of the Guomindang regime in 1949, some city gates and about one third of the city wall were torn down in 1954, leaving only 21.4 km (13.3 miles) of the original wall and four Ming city gates still standing. Compared with Beijing, where the entire city wall was torn down after 1949, Nanjing's city wall survived fairly well. In fact, original sections of the Ming wall are still so strong today that modern day buildings have been constructed on top of them. In some places, you can even see people actually living inside chambers in the wall.

Since 1981, the Nanjing city government has been taking steps to restore and reconstruct the city's ancient monuments. In 1994, a long section of the wall, stretching 1.7 km (1.1 miles) along the shores of Xuan Wu Hu from Jie Fang Men to Taiping Men, was reconstructed. From 2000 to 2001, the city rebuilt the northwestern corner of the wall around the base of Lion Peak (Shizi Shan), near Jing Hai Si. The western section along the **Stone City Park** (Shi Tou Cheng Gongyuan) was completed in February 2004. If you look closely, you can see that the color of the bricks changes at a certain level of the wall. This is because the bottom part is original while the top ramparts are new restorations. Unfortunately, parts of this restored wall around Shizi Shan collapsed during flooding in the rainy season of July 2003. Official estimates now state that 23.43 km (14.6 miles) of the Ming city wall is standing, an increase of over 2 km since 1979. In January 2004, in conjunction with the restoration and reconstruction of the city wall's western, southern, and eastern sections, a pedestrian promenade and park are being constructed along the river, under the auspices of the Qinhuai River Project.

Many areas of the city are still known by, and labeled on maps according to, the names of the Ming city gates which once stood there, even though the gate is long gone. For example, Taiping Men and Zhong Yang Men are still commonly used by locals as the name for the neighborhoods where these gates once stood. Even locally printed maps label neighborhoods according to the gate that once stood in that area. This has led to much confusion among Western authors (most of whom have never visited Nanjing in person) about which gates are still standing and which are not, and many English language publications provide incorrect information in this regard. Other books have made the mistake of assuming that almost all the original Ming city gates have been destroyed.

The following is an accurate and up-to-date report of the facts based on in-depth research of available records, extensive explorations of the city and in many cases, actually covering the entire course of the city wall on foot.

Ming Dynasty City Gates

Six genuine historical relics of the Ming city defenses still exist. One is an original Ming Dynasty water gate, another is a Ming Dynasty palace gate and the remaining four are part of the 13 original Ming Dynasty city gates. Their current names are provided first, with previous names in parenthesis.

Zhong Hua Men city gate, also known as the South Gate (Nan Men).

Zhong Hua Men city gate.

Zhong Hua Men (Ju Bao Men)

This impregnable fortress is an original Ming Dynasty city gate built during the period 1366–1386 when the rest of the wall was also constructed. Facing the Qinhuai River and the Yuhua Tai beyond, this was the south gate of the city. It has three defense courtyards or barbicans enclosed by separate walls, and four successive arched portals on a central axis. The city wall here was 15 m (49.2 ft) high and 15 m (49.2 ft) wide. More than just a gate, it served as a fortress which housed 3,000 soldiers who could hide inside any of its 27 caves. It has a series of four gates (Tou Dao Men, Er Dao Men, San Dao Men and Si Dao Men) which connect three courtyards known as "jar towns" or Weng Cheng. Facing the outside of the city, the

Zhong Hua Men city gate.

Looking up the flights of steps leading up to the summit of Zhong Hua Men city gate.

Looking down the flights of steps leading up to the summit of Zhong Hua Men city gate.

outermost gate (Tou Dao Men) is topped with an enormous rectangular tower. This three-story tower is 24.5 m (80.4 ft) high and has two steep flights of steps ascending to the top from either side. The whole fortress is 128 m (420 ft) long, 119 m (390.4 ft) wide, and covers an area of 15,000 sq m (161,459 sq ft). It was originally built in the same place as the Southern Tang (Nan Tang) Dynasty's Nan Men (South Gate) and continued to be called such by local residents. In 1931, two sections of city wall, on the east and west sides of Ju Bao Men, were removed to make way for the construction of Zhong Hua Lu, leaving the gate standing in the middle of a traffic circle. In the same year, Ju Bao Men (Treasure Gate) was renamed Zhong Hua Men (Central Flower Gate). A separate admission ticket must be purchased to visit this site.

A surviving piece of the original city wall standing beside the Zhong Hua Men city gate, with jagged broken ends showing where a hole for a road was punched through the wall in 1931.

Qing Liang Men

Built in 1368, this is an original single portal 14th century Ming Dynasty city gate that faces the Qinhuai River. It stands near the intersection of Huju Lu and Guangzhou Lu, at the south end of the Stone City Park (Shi Tou Cheng Gongyuan). You can now enter the park from here and walk along the Qinhuai River all the way to the recently renovated Ghost Face (Gui Lian) section of the city wall to the northwest. Qing Liang Men is named after the nearby Qing Liang Shan.

A section of the original Nanjing city wall standing beside the Zhong Hua Men city gate, casting its reflection in the water of the Qinhuai He city moat in the front. Houses along the city wall and city moat have since been demolished to make way for a newQinhuai He green belt encircling the city.

He Ping Men (Shen Ce Men)

Shen Ce Men is another original 14th century Ming Dynasty city gate that was renamed He Ping Men in 1931. Located on top of a small promontory hill overlooking the northwest corner of Xuan Wu Hu and encircled on three sides by a wide bulging bend in the city wall, the gate had a single-walled barbican enclosure extending outside of it. It is near the former site of Zhong Yang Men, close to the new train station on Long Pan Lu, and can be reached on foot from either Long Pan Lu or Zhong Yang Lu. The Long Pan Lu entrance crosses an old railroad bridge with visible wooden cross beams and steel rails. The tracks appear to lead directly to a steel gate, in the outer protective wall just in front of Shen Ce Men, and this make it seem as though the tracks may have once traveled through the city gate.

Unfortunately, this site has been closed to public visitors for decades because it is inside a military controlled area. However, with the construction of a new city park in between this section of the city wall and the canal that flows in Xuan Wu Hu, the city government began promoting the site in the past few years. Driving by on Long Pan Lu, the most obvious landmark is an original two-story wooden watchtower, with upturned roof eaves, that stands on top of the city wall. This tower may mark the inner gate, which cannot be seen, but the partly visible outer gate of the barbican stands hidden in the trees to the east. Visitors can get glimpses of Shen Ce Men by walking around the newly-built park outside of this section of wall and peering through the trees. In the winter, when foliage is off the trees, it is possible to see a single-portal arched-gate in the wall of the square barbican that descends down the hillside from the main city wall up above. Flights of steps can be seen ascending the side walls of the barbican. In February 2004, the area immediately around Shen Ce Men had been turned into a construction site, with foliage cleared away, and the earth around it ploughed up. By June 2004, the modern exterior wall blocking the view of Shen Ce Men had been torn down, allowing public access to the city gate for the first time in decade. Renovation work on the gate and its barbican was almost complete.

Zhong Shan Men (Chao Yang Men)

This three-portal gate connected to a long section of the city wall in the eastern end of the city and sits astride Zhongshan Dong Lu. The original Ming Dynasty Chao Yang Men was a single-portal gate, but it was enlarged to three portals in 1928 to facilitate the 1929 funeral procession for Sun Yat Sen (Sun Zhongshan) through the city and onward to Zijin Shan. At the time of its enlargement, it was renamed Zhongshan Men in honor of Sun. It suffered severe damage during the December 1937 Japanese attack. After the city was captured, the Japanese held a victory parade through Zhongshan Men, much as the Germans later did with the Arche de Triumphe in Paris. Photos from 1939 show the Zhongshan Men still standing, with all three of its arched portals intact. However, two of them have had the exterior brick wall blown off, and only one was completely unscathed.

Zhongshan Men city gate, at the east end of Zhongshan Dong Lu, viewed from inside the city wall.

A side view of Zhongshan Men city gate from outside the city wall.

Facing the east, this gate provides the main access to Ming Ling Lu — the road to the Ming Tombs — which branches off to the left immediately after passing through the gate on the way out of the city. On the city side of the wall, right next to the gate, are the Nanjing Museum and the Hilton Hotel.

A flight of stone steps leads up to the top of the gate. On a clear day, there is an excellent view of Zijin Shan in one direction and the long expanse of tree-lined Zhongshan Dong Lu in the other.

On top of the wall, to the right, is a small coffee and tea shop curiously decorated with Islamic artwork. Interestingly, seat cushions in the shop show pictures of the Kaaba in Mecca. Facing west, to the right, is what looks like a lake but it is actually remnants of the old city moat, Yue Ya Hu Chen He. Turning to the left, crossing the gate and following the wall will lead visitors to a hole in a newer brick wall that was erected to block access. Pass through this hole and follow a section of wall which has not been restored and is covered with vines, trees, and bushes. This section of the wall parallels Ming Ling Lu below and runs until it collapses into Qian Hu. The sight of this immense gap in the wall from the shores of Qian Hu is truly impressive. After this gap, the wall picks up again and continues past Pipa Hu, around a hill and down to the former site of Taiping Men.

Islamic design on pillows at a tea house atop Zhongshan Men city gate shows the Kaaba in Mecca.

A massive hole in the Nanjing city wall beside the small lake Qian Hu on the way to the Ming Tombs.

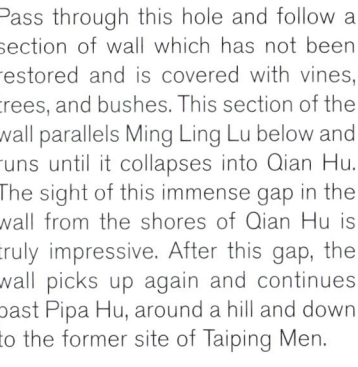

The small lake Qian Hu, with Zijin Shan in the background, on the way to the Ming Tombs.

Wu Chao Men (Meridian Gate)

This massive fortress-like gate sits on the grounds of the old Ming Palace, the Ming Gu Gong, near the interstection of Ming Gu Gong Lu and Zhongshan Bei Lu. Technically speaking, this gate was not part of the city wall, but a part of the separate Ming emperor's palace. For a full description see the section on the former Ming Palace (Ming Gu Gong).

Dong Shui Guan (East Water Gate)

An original Ming Dynasty water gate, its purpose was to let water flow in and out of the city, passing through the city wall, without compromising the city's defenses. In this sense, it is reminiscent of the Pan Men in Suzhou. The Dong Shui Dam (Dong Shui Guan) was where the Qinhuai River entered the city from the east. Made of stone blocks, it was 16 m (52.5 ft) high with 33 archways and two flood gates. Historic photos show it still intact as late as 1932. In 2000–2001, it was rebuilt with a park around it.

Qing Dynasty City Gates

Two new city gates were built during the Qing Dynasty and of these, only one still survives.

Xuan Wu Men city gate built in 1910 provides the main access to the lake of Xuan Wu Hu.

Xuan Wu Men (Feng Run Men)

Construction of this gate began in 1909. It was completed in 1910, just before the 1911 Revolution. The gate was built as an access point to the five islands and lakeshores of Xuan Wu Hu, which has recently been turned into a public park. Formerly, the area had been a private retreat for the Emperor and imperial family. In fact, public access to the lake had been almost physically impossible due to the absence of any city gates in the long section of wall running along the lakeshore from He Ping

Men to Taiping Men. It was originally named for the city governor who completed its construction, but the name was changed to Xuan Wu Men in 1931 when two more arched portals were added. The distinct outline of this gate, with its twin towers and three portals, can be seen from the islands in the lake. It can be approached on foot from the causeway linking it with Huan Zhou Island, or by car via a short road that branches off from Zhongyang Lu, near the Xuan Wu Hotel.

Xuan Wu Men city gate.

Republican Era City Gates

Five new city gates were built during the 1911–1949 Republic of China (Min Guo) period. Of these, three are still standing. Another city gate was built shortly after the founding of the People's Republic of China and this also exists today.

Han Zhong Men city gate is surrounded by this fortress wall.

Han Zhong Men (Han Xi Men)

Han Zhong Men was built in 1931, north of the Han Xi Men, an original 14th century Ming Dynasty city gate built in 1366. It now sits disconnected from the city wall, in a park at the intersection of Huju Nan Lu, Huju Lu, and Hanzhong Lu. The park itself was built in 1996, and is surrounded on three sides by a city wall, which once formed a barbican (*weng cheng*) similar to that at Zhonghua Men. The gate itself has one portal, which forms a long tunnel through the base of a high, square fortress. The fortress can be ascended by a flight of steps on one side. From the top, you can see the Qinhuai River and Mochou Hu Park. Tickets are not required for admission. The site is quite near the Sheraton Hotel on Hanzhong Lu.

Han Zhong Men city gate stands in the middle of a public park on Han Zhong Lu.

Traffic still passes through the Yi Jiang Men city gate on Zhongshan Bei Lu.

Yi Jiang Men city gate.

Wooden pavili[on] atop the Yi Jia[ng] Men city gate now houses a memorial to th[e] Communists' 1949 capture of Nanjing.

Yi Jiang Men (Hai Ling Men)

This three-portal gate sits astride Zhongshan Bei Lu, facing west of the Yangzi River. When it was built during the republican era in 1915, its original name was Hai Ling Men. This was changed to Yi Jiang Men in 1928, when the gate had to be widened to allowed Sun Yat Sen's (Sun Zhongsan's) 1929 funeral procession to pass through. Today, the gate is still connected to the city wall on both sides, and has three portals, through which modern-day traffic travels. Climb the steps to the right and purchase a ticket for 3 Rmb, then walk across to the top of the gate. A large wooden-pillared building sits on top. The inside of the pavilion contains a photo exhibition of communist party propaganda celebrating their 1949 victory.

Phone: 5880-6337

Walk around the building for incredible views of winding wooded bends in the former city moat below. Face west. To the left, is Lion Peak (Shizi Shan) and the enormous new Yue Jiang Lou pavilion which has been built on top of it. To the right are two small hills forming a series of bluffs overlooking the moat, the second of which is Ding Shan. On top of this hill is a hotel bearing the same name and three houses dating from the early 1900s. These houses were formerly occupied by a community of treaty port foreigners who fled during the Guomindang occupation of the city in 1927.

Back on Zhongshan Bei Lu, a narrow alley branches off from the left side of the road and heads up to a hilltop pagoda from which you can look down on Yi Jiang Men and across at Lion Peak (Shizi Shan). Unfortunately, the city wall cannot be followed any further in this direction due to modern day buildings blocking the way.

Return to Zhongshan Bei Lu and pass through the gate. Immediately to the right, on the other side of the gate, sits Xiu Qu Park. This is a fairly new park, having only been built in 1952, which has a lake and offers some views of the city wall section that connects with Yi Jiang Men. Tickets are to be purchased at the gate.

Across the road from Xiu Qu Park is a narrow lane (Xiao Tao Yuan Xi Jie) that branches off Zhongshan Bei Lu. This lane runs along a narrow strip of land in between the city wall and the former city moat. It is possible to follow this lane for a while to catch sights of the city wall up above, but eventually the lane stops at a dead end.

Xin Ming Men

This gate was built in 1931. However, its concrete archway is unimpressive and not really worth visiting.

Jie Fang Men

Constructed in 1952, this is the newest of the city gates and one of the two gateways allowing access to Xuan Wu Hu Park from the city. It sits astride Jiming Si Lu, which runs from He Ping Lu, which in turn connects with Beijing Dong Lu via Shi Zeng Fu Lu. Attached to the wall from the city side, sitting on top of the hill, is Jiming Si. On the other side is an area, enclosed by sections of the wall on two sides, known as Tai City (Tai Cheng). **Tai Cheng** was the site of the imperial palaces of the emperors who ruled Nanjing during the Eastern Jin (317–420 AD), Liu Song (420–479 AD), Qi (479–502 AD), Liang (502–557 AD), and Chen (557–589 AD) dynasties, although nothing remains of them now.

Jie Fang Men city gate, built in 1952, provides additional access to Xuan Wu Hu Park outside the city wall, as well as the Tai Cheng area and the City Wall Museum.

Passing through Jie Fang Men, immediately to the right is a second smaller gate in a second wall which provides pedestrian access to Xuan Wu Hu Park. Visitors who wish to take a walk around the lakeshore or to cross one of the three causeways that connect with the five islands in the middle of the lake will have to purchase a ticket for 15 Rmb.

The Tai Cheng city wall with the pinnacle of Jiming Si Buddhist Temple's pagoda visible behind it.

Sights Within the City
City Wall Museum (Cheng Qiang Bowuguan)

This museum is located at the top of Jie Fang Men in Tai Cheng. It has exhibits of old photos of long-gone city gates plus a scale model of the entire Ming walled city. An elderly couple actually lives inside this section of wall and will share some history of the place if they are so inclined. Otherwise, all visitors will be treated as trespassers on private property.

To get to the museum, buy a ticket at the bottom then climb a flight of stairs and a steeply inclined section of the wall to the top of the gate. From the museum, visitors can climb to the top of the wall and follow it all the way to Jiuhua Shan and the former site of Taiping Men. Excellent views of Jiming Si and Xuan Wu Hu can be seen from the top of this section of wall.

Phone: 8360-8359
Ticket: 8 Rmb

The double wall enclosure known as Tai Cheng, entered via the Jie Fang Men city gate, with the City Wall Museum approached via the ramp on the right to the small gate and pavilion at the top of the wall.

Looking down from the City Wall Museum at the Tai Cheng city wall and Xuan Wu Hu lake below.

One of the ivy-covered portals of Wu Chao Men, the fortress gate of the former Imperial Forbidden City, now standing in Ming Gu Gong Park.

Ruins of the Ming Palace (Ming Gu Gong)

Located at Zhongshan Dong Lu and Minggugong Lu, this is where the first Ming Emperor, Zhu Yuanzhang, built his imperial palace, a project that spanned an eleven-year period from 1366 to 1377. When Zhu Di, the future Emperor Yong Le, captured the city from Emperor Jian Wen in 1402, the original palace was completely burnt down. Although the palace was rebuilt, all the buildings were again destroyed between 1853–1864 during the ten-year occupation of the city by the Taiping rebels.

The Wu Chao Men (Meridian Gate) is now the main surviving historic relic located on this site. As you enter from Zhongsan Dong Lu, trees and thick foliage block your view of the gate, making the area look like an unassuming park. However, continue walking south until you reach a series of five parallel stone bridges, which lead to the five gates of this immense Ming Dynasty fortress.

Stone pedestals mark the site of former wooden building columns on the summit of Wu Chao Men.

Top, center and bottom: Scattered stone relics from the former imperial palace still litter the grounds of Ming Gu Gong Park.

A tea house in a traditional style building across the street from Ming Gu Gong Park.

The former north-south imperial way is now a tree-lined avenue converging on Ming Gu Gong Park, where the imperial palace once stood.

Scattered stone relics from the former imperial palace still litter the grounds of Ming Gu Gong Park.

In 1984, the parapet atop the gate was reconstructed. In addition, two flights of brick steps were built, leading up both sides of the rectangular fortress, allowing people to ascend to its flat top for a view of Zijin Shan. The top of the gate is still embedded with long rows of stone pedestals that once supported the wooded columns of now long-gone watchtowers and pavilions. While ascending or descending the steps, notice how each brick is stamped with information about who made it, when, and where. In 2001, a KTV karaoke bar was installed inside one of the gate's five portals, somewhat reminiscent of the Cambodian generals' desecration of Angkor Wat.

The plaza along Zhongshan Dong Lu was established during a May 1997 reconstruction of the park grounds and is a good place to see local people practicing their wushu and ballroom dance steps in the early morning and evening.

Ticket: 1 Rmb

Stone City Park (Shi Tou Cheng Gongyuan)

This beautiful 5-hectare (12.4-acre) park along the western city wall and Qinhuai River was newly completed in February 2004. You can now enter the park at its northwestern end from Shi Tou Chen Lu and walk along the Qinhuai River all the way to the recently renovated Qing Liang Men city gate. It is also possible to walk along the top of this whole section of renovated city wall, all the way from the National Defense Park (Guo Fang Yuan) on a hilltop above the Stone City, to Qing Liang Men at the southeast end of Stone City Park.

The most impressive part of this section of the city wall is the **Ghost Face** (Gui Lian) which can also be seen reflected in the surface of the newly created lake below. This is a section of the original Wu Kingdom city wall that bulges out in bizarre and grotesque shapes that some say resembles the face of a ghost. A model of a watchtower has been reconstructed above this section of the wall.

Sun Quan was the founding ruler of the Wu Kingdom (220–280 AD), one of the three rival states in the Yangzi River valley during the Three Kingdoms (San Guo) period. He supposedly built this section of the wall after he chose Nanjing as his capital city in 229AD. The Wu Kingdom's defeat and surrender of the Stone City to the Western Jin in 280AD later inspired **Liu Yu Xi** (772–842 AD) to write his previously cited poem about the fall of the Wu Kingdom.

Over the past year or two, the city's Qinhuai River Project has transformed the whole area. In 2000, the area was crammed with shantytown houses and factories, with coal-belching smokestacks, were built right up against the city wall. The Ghost Face (Gui Lian) was then entirely hidden from view and Shi Tou Cheng Lu ran along the river where the green park now lies. Today, the road ends at the northwestern corner of the park, green grass and flowering trees grow where the shacks and factories once stood.

The Ghost Face City (Gui Lian Cheng), reputedly the oldest section of Nanjing's city wall, before its recent restoration when the site was obscured by shanty towns and coal-burning factories.

National Defense Park (Guo Fang Yuan)

Until recently, this rather uninteresting park used to be advertised as containing the famous Stone City (Shi Tou Cheng). The best view of city is from the newly completed Stone City Park below. You can now walk along the top of the newly renovated city wall from here to Qing Liang Men, or take a stroll on **Autumn Hill** (Qiu Shan). The Guo Fang Yuan covers 5.7 hectares (14.1 acres), while the adjoining Autumn Hill covers 3 hectares (7.4 acres).

Address: 87 Huju Lu
Phone: 8652-7490

Inside the original main hall of the Nanjing Museum built in 1936.

A British ship's anchor reputedly from Zhenjiang on display outside the Nanjing Museum.

Above and left:
The Nanjing Museum has a large collection of iron British cannons bearing English inscriptions.

History Museums
Nanjing Museum (Nanjing Bowuguan)

Not to be confused with the newer Nanjing City Museum at Chao Tian Gong, this is a provincial level institution for relics from all over Jiangsu province. Founded by Cai Yuan Pei (1868–1940) as the National Central Museum (Zhongyang Bowuyuan) in 1933, the museum was designed in the style of a traditional Chinese temple and completed in 1936. The new western hall was added in 1999, and in 2003, the museum celebrated its 70th anniversary.

With Zhongshan Men on one side and the Hilton Hotel on the other, this cavernous Min Guo building has many interconnected halls separated by six internal courtyards. However, it was completely empty of historic relics on the author's last visit, the space instead being devoted to a modern painting exhibition. Nonetheless, the interior has not been changed since 1936 and the air reeks of the Min Guo era. A small theater with a stage is still intact on the first floor. In a corner of the main entrance hall stands a small bookshop with probably the best selection of publications on the history of Nanjing in the city itself. This is the only place the author has seen the invaluable but now out-of-print 1998 work, *Old Fashions of Nanjing*, by Qu Wu.

Most of the genuine relics seem to be left outside, on the museum's sprawling campus grounds and exposed to the weather. A stone sculpture garden to the east of the main entrance gate includes a stone Bixie statue from the sacred way of Liang Zhao Ming (Xiao Tong), discovered at Tai Ziao village near Yanzi Ji in 1984. North of this is a large collection of bronze cannons, including two enormous mounted ones, and a dozen smaller ones scattered on the ground. From the inscriptions on the barrels, some of these are obviously Chinese made. At least half were apparently British made, based on the engraved symbol of a royal crown and the English inscriptions "B.P. & Co." To the west of the main entrance gate is a large iron ship's anchor. The sign next to it claims it is a British anchor taken from the waterfront of Zhenjiang, a former treaty port down the Yangzi River. The sign doesn't give the name of the ship, and it's tempting to think it may have been the Amethyst. Unfortunately the rusted name engraved on the anchor's shaft is now illegible, but it seems to begin with letters "Po" and end with "cus," the rest in between being a mystery.

Address: 321 Zhongshan Dong Lu
Phone: 8480-0701, 8480-6498,
8482-2631, 8480-2119
Fax: 8480-2061
Tickets: 20 Rmb

Imperial Examination Museum (Jiangnan Gong Yuan)

This museum, located on the east side of the **Confucius Temple** (Fuzi Miao) at the south end of the city near the Qinhuai River, marks the site where the provincial level exams (*juzi*) of the imperial civil service examination system (*keju*) were held once every three years. The Nanjing imperial examinations were moved to this site in 1457, during the Ming Dynasty, and were held here until the imperial examinations were finally abolished by the Qing Dynasty in 1905.

There were three levels of examinations and corresponding degrees: county (Xiucai or Shengyuan), provincial (Juren), and national (Jinshi). The main test question involved writing what was known as an eight-legged essay (*bagu wen*). Successfully passing these tests usually guaranteed a job in the government bureaucracy. However, it has been estimated that only 1 percent of all candidates passed the exams.

Examination candidates spent a full week living in the cramped isolation of small examination cubicles, where they wrote a series of three eight-legged essays (*bagu wen*). Candidates sitting for the provincial level exams travelled from far and wide in huge numbers, creating an ever growing need to expand the examination halls. In 1534, during the Jiajing reign, there were only 3,700 examination rooms. This was gradually increased to 17,000 in the second year of the Yong Zheng reign, and 18,900 after a restoration by Zeng Guofan in 1871. By the time it was closed in 1905, there was enough space for 20,644 candidates. In 1922, the land where the cubicles stood was sold and they were all torn down. Nowadays, only 20 replica cubicles have been built since the restoration of the Fuzi Miao area in 1984.

The Nanjing City Government was housed here when Nanjing was the Guomindang national capital from 1927–1937. Later the Legislative and Executive Yuans of the collaborationist Wang Jingwei regime were housed in the Ming Yuan.

The main existing historic structure is the square, three-story, yellow-walled **Ming Yuan Tower** (Ming Yuan Lou), built in 1600 during the Wan Li reign. The exterior has been modified in a way that makes it look new, but closer inspection reveals it to be a genuine relic dating from at least 1871 when an restoration was done by Zeng Guofan. Inside the Ming Yuan Lou are two inscribed stone stele and a scale model of the original complex of examination halls. Although wooden steps lead up to the second and third floors, visitors are not permitted to ascend the tower. The interior of the Ming Yuan Lou appears to be authentic, with wooden tripod roof brackets, as well as wooden ceiling beams and pillars.

To the east and west of the Ming Yuan Lou are two stele corridors containing stone tablets inscribed with records of the site's history. One impressive looking tablet records the visit to site by the Qing Dynasty emperor Kang Xi in 1699. Behind the Ming Yuan Lou, to the east and west, is a courtyard with mock exam cubicles. On the north side of the courtyard are three genuine halls, all connected to each other, known as the Personality Hall, the Imperial Examination System Hall, and the No. 1 Scholar Hall. Inside is an interesting collection of exhibits.

Inside the courtyard of a nearby hospital (*yiyuan*) is the remains of the single-arch stone **Flying Rainbow Bridge** (Fei Caihong Qiao). Although it once crossed a rectangular pool of water, this has long since been filled in with dirt, making the bridge more of a sidewalk. Nonetheless, the stone railings and flagstone surface are still clearly visible.

An excellent portrait of the old imperial examination system can be found in the 18th century Qing Dynasty novel *The Scholars* (*Ju Lin Wai Shi*) written in Nanjing by Wu Jing Zhi (1701–1754), an examination candidate who fared poorly. For a more recent study, which uses the Nanjing Jiangnan Gongyuan as an example, see Ichisada Miyazaki's aptly titled 1981 work, *China's Examination Hell*.

Finding either the Ming Yuan Lou or Fei Caihong Qiao can be challenging. Both sit in the middle of a maze of long, winding pedestrian lanes (*bu xing jie*), which makes it difficult to approach the sites directly by car. In addition, the sites cannot be seen from any distance until you have already arrived. A vehicle can be taken to the intersection of Ping Jiang Fu Lu and the Gongyuan Lu walking street (*bu xing jie*). From here, walk west along the Gongyuan Lu walking street (*bu xing jie*) until you see a large three-portal wooden memorial gate (*pai lou*) on your right. This marks the southern entrance to the Jinling Lu walking street (*bu xing jie*). From here, walk north along the Jinling Lu walking street (*bu xing jie*) until you reach its northern end. The Ming Yuan Lou should be standing right in front of you.

Alternatively, take a vehicle to the intersection of Taiping Nan Lu and Jiankang Lu. On the south side of Jiankang Lu is a large memorial gate (*pai lou*) marking the northern entrance to the Gongyuan Xi Jie walking street (*bu xing jie*). Walk south along the zigzagging Gongyuan Xi Jie walking street (*bu xing jie*) until you reach the Gongyuan Lu walking street (*bu xing jie*). Turn left onto the Gongyuan Lu walking street (*bu xing jie*) and walk east until you see the large three-portal wooden memorial gate (*pai lou*) on your left marking the southern entrance to the Jinling Lu walking street (*bu xing jie*). Turn left onto the Jinling Lu walking street (*bu xing jie*) and walk north until you reach the Ming Yuan Lou at its northern end.

Address: Fuzi Miao district, No. 1 Jinling Lu
Phone: 8662-6556

Urban Development Exhibition Hall
For a better view of Nanjing's future, visit the Urban Development Exhibition Hall.

Address: 35 Hua Qiao Lu, Chun Feng Da Lou
Phone: 8472-2068

Zheng He Museum (Zheng He Bowuguan)
This museum is dedicated to Admiral Zheng He whose tomb is located outside the city, to the South, on Niu Shou Shan. Oddly enough, the Zheng He Museum must be entered by leaving the Zheng He Park and going around the corner to Chang Bai Jie street. The museum is a walled complex of Ming style buildings with a courtyard featuring a statue of Zheng He. Unfortunately, the exhibition hall has inexplicably been turned into a computer showroom.

Phone: 8664-6080

The Taiping Museum (Taiping Bowuguan)
Most of the Taiping exhibits and relics have now been moved to extensive new exhibits at the Tushuo Zongtongfu at 292 Changjiang Lu. This includes the imperial jade seal and imperial robes of the Taiping's Heavenly King (Tian Wang), Hong Xiu Quan, as well as military weapons.

Address: 128 Zhan Yuan Lu
Phone: 5220-1849
Tickets: 10 Rmb

Nanjing Municipal Museum
This is located inside the Chao Tian Gong.

Address: Wang Fu Da Jie
Phone: 8446-5317
Tickets: 30 Rmb

House where Zhou En Lai lived in from 1946–47 at the Plum Blossom New Village (Mei Yuan Xin Cun).

Former Residences of Famous Celebrities
Plum Blossom New Village (Mei Yuan Xin Cun)
A Communist Party (Gong Chan Dang) delegation including Zhou En Lai and Dong Bi Wu lived in a collection of three houses here from May 1946 to March 1947 during negotiations with the Guomindang. Zhou's simple house is actually No. 30 of the

village and is located right on the side street of Da Bei Xiang, but the modern entrance gate is a block away on Mei Yuan Lu. The modern exhibition hall just inside the front gate on Mei Yuan Lu was added in 1990.

Address: 81 Meiyuan Lu
Phone: 8454-2362

Club House of Chiang Kai Shek (Jiang Jieshi Guan Gong)

This house where Chiang Kai Shek (Jiang Jieshi) once entertained close personal friends after hours is now a military officers' dining hall (Can Yin Bu) of the Nanjing military district (Jun Qu Kong Jun Zhen Bu). Despite the military nature of this facility, dining hall staff were polite enough to entertain the author with a quick look inside, as well as answer some questions. However, their attitude to future visitors is hard to judge.

Address: 6 Yong Yuan Lu
Phone: 8454-2585

PERSONALITIES

Bai Chong Xi was known as the Guomindang's most ruthless general because of his slaughter of the Communists in Shanghai in April 1927. However, he is also considered the most courageous because he refused to surrender to the Communists in 1949 and was the last Guomindang commander still in the field on mainland China in 1950, long after his comrades had fled to Taiwan.

Residence of Bai Chong Xi (Bai Chong Xi Gu Ju)

The Nanjing residence of Bai Chong Xi (1893–1966) was located somewhere on the north side of the short back street of Yong Yuan Lu, running between Da Bei Xiang and the Zhu Qiao. Unfortunately, the author has not yet been able to determine exactly which house it was. Both No. 31 and No. 29, across the street from Jiang Jieshi's Guan Gong, seem like possible candidates based on their age, architectural style, and location. Possibly the city will place a marker at this site some time in the near future, as they have recently done with a number of other forgotten relics.

Address: Yong Yuan Lu

Residence of Yang Ting Bao (Yang Ting Bao Gu Ju)

Yang's simple house stands appropriately across the street from Southeast University where he worked as a professor of architecture. He continued to live in this house from 1946 until his death in 1982. Despite having been closely associated with the Guomindang regime, Yang chose to remain in Nanjing after its capture by the Communists in April 1949, although there is no record of any further architectural achievements during the last 30 years of his life. At the time of his death, he was President of the Architectural Society of China. In 1997, a collection of his written essays on architecture was published in Beijing under the title, *Yang Ting Bao Jianzhu Lun Shu Yu Zuo Pin Xuan Ji*.

Address: East side of Cheng Xian Jie, near its intersection with Si Pai Lou

PERSONALITIES

Yang Ting Bao (1901–1982) was one of the most prolific Chinese architects in Nanjing during the first decade of Guomindang rule (1927–1937). He was friends with the American architect Henry K. Murphy and seems to have shared a similar taste for the Chinese renaissance style of architecture that combined the traditional and modern forms. After returning from the United States, where he attended the University of Pennsylvania, he designed three of the most impressive government compounds along Zhongshan Dong Lu. His first government project came in 1929 when he designed the complex of three buildings once collectively known as the Lizhi Association of Huangpu Classmates Society at 307 Zhongshan Dong Lu, which now stands on the grounds of the modern day Zhongshan Hotel. His next major project was in 1931 when he designed the domed Auditorium (Da Li Tang) of National Central University. In 1934, he designed the Guomindang Historical Relics Exhibition Building and offices of the Guomindang Party History Compilation Committee at 309 Zhongshan Dong Lu, which now serves as China's Second National History Archives (Zhongguo Di Er Lishi Dang An Guan). In the same year he also designed the Guomindang Central Supervisory Committee at 311 Zhongshan Dong Lu, now the Military Archives (Jun Shi Dang An Guan).

Presidential Palace (Tushuo Zongtongfu)

Behind the enormous three-portal entrance gate of the Presidential Palace, with its Greco-Roman columns and center guard tower, is a 5-hectare (12.4-acre) site which began as the 14th century palace of a Ming prince. The oldest surviving part of the site is the beautifully landscaped Ming Dynasty Xu Yuan west garden, with its many lakeside pavilions and famous stone boat, where a succession of rulers have held their private meetings throughout the centuries. During the Qing Dynasty it was converted to the offices and residence of the Liangjiang Viceroy, an official who governed the three provinces of Jiangsu, Anhui, and Jiangxi.

The West Flower Hall (Xi Hua Dian) inside the Tushuo Zongtong Fu complex.

After the Taiping rebels captured Nanjing in March 1853, the Taiping Heavenly King (Tian Wang), Hong Xiu Quan, had his throne room and residence here. Recently, this has been restored to look as it did from 1853 until the Qing reconquest of July 1864, when the original building was burned down. Near the restored throne room is another pavilion with an extensive exhibit of genuine artifacts from the Taiping rebellion.

Once the Taiping rebellion had been quelled, the site again became the offices and residence of the Qing Dynasty Viceroy for the three Liangjiang provinces. In 1910, the **West Flower Hall** (Xi Hua Dian) was built to the west of the Xu Yuan garden to serve as the official residence of the Liangjiang Viceroy.

After the Revolution of 1911 overthrew the Qing Dynasty, Sun Yat Sen (Sun Zhongshan) was inaugurated as provisional president of the new republic in the West Flower Hall (Xi Hua Dian) on 1 January 1912. From January to April of the same year, this hall served as the offices of his provisional government, while his personal residence was located in another small, two-story wooden house near the northeast corner of Xu Yuan garden.

Entrance gate leading into the separate walled enclosure of the West Flower Hall (Xi Hua Dian), inside the larger Tushuo Zongtong Fu complex.

When the Guomindang captured Nanjing in March 1927, they made it their capital city and chose this location for the offices of their central government and its leader Chiang Kai Shek (Jiang Jieshi). In 1929, the large main entrance gate was constructed and the whole site was renamed the **Guomin Zhen Fu**. The street out in front, now known as Changjiang Lu, was then named **Guo Fu Lu** (National Government Road). In 1934, the **Zi Chao Building** was constructed on the site to serve as the Guomindang's central government headquarters.

The West Flower Hall (Xi Hua Dian) inside the Tushuo Zongtong Fu complex.

During World War II, the same site was used by the collaborationist puppet regime of Wang Jingwei, the former Guomindang leader who defected to the Japanese in 1940. After the war was over in 1946, it once again became the Guomindang central government headquarters, and in 1948, the whole site was again renamed the **Zongtongfu** (Presidential Palace). It kept this name until Nanjing was captured by the Communists on 23 April 1949.

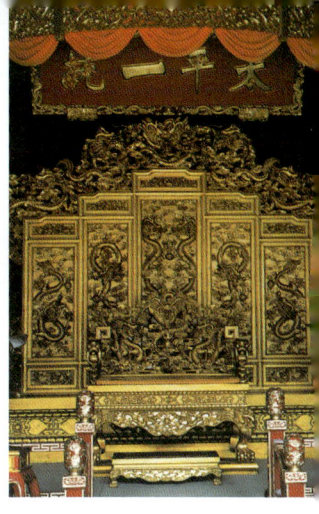

Above left: The Stone Boat (Shi Chuan) in the Xu Yuan garden where Taiping leaders once met.
Above right: The restored throne room of the Taiping Heavenly King (Tian Wang) Hong Xiu Quan.

Above left: A moon gate leading from a side courtyard into the central garden of the Xu Yuan.
Above right: The lake in the Xu Yuan.

Below left: A traditional two-story lake-side pavilion in the Xu Yuan.
Below right: A bronze statue of the Taiping Heavenly King (Tian Wang) Hong Xiu Quan outside his throne room.

Traditional Chinese furniture, made from twisted tree roots, in the pavilions of the Xu Yuan.

After the 1949 Revolution, the Zongtongfu became the headquarters of the Jiangsu Provincial Communist Party. During this time, it was strictly off limits to outside visitors until the site was finally opened to the public as a museum in February 2000. In that year, it regained its former pre-revolutionary name, in a slightly modified form, as the Tushuo Zongtongfu (Former Presidential Palace).

Today, you can see the restored offices of Chiang Kai Shek (Jiang Jieshi), his personal air raid shelter used between August and December 1937 during the first few months of the war with Japan, and the auditorium where he was inaugurated president on 20 May 1948. There are also several rooms exhibiting historic photos from the Guomindang era, including many of Chiang (Jiang) and one very eerie group photo of the entire Guomindang government taken in May 1948, just one year before the city fell to the Communists.

Many changes happened to the site in 2003. The former presidential compound covers an entire city block between Changjiang Lu, Hanfu Hou Jie, Cheng Xian Jie, and Taiping Bei Lu. However, only a small part of this compound was initially opened to the public in the year 2000. In 2003, a rear gateway to the compound dating from 1934 was rebuilt, providing public

The entrance to the private underground air raid shelter of Chiang Kai Shek (Jiang Jieshi).

Newly rebuilt entrance gate to the former site of Guomindang Executive Yuan (Xing Zheng Yuan).

access to the former Education Ministry and **Executive Yuan** (Xing Zheng Yuan) buildings. The old neighborhoods along Taiping Bei Lu and Hanfu Hou Jie were razed to the ground in 2003. In their place, replicas of Min Guo era mansions, villas, and houses are being built. The original screen wall outside the main gate on the south side of Changjiang Lu was also torn down in 2003.

Address: 292 Changjiang Lu
Phone: 8440-3763, 8457-8717
Tickets: 30 Rmb

The Jiangsu Provincial Assembly (Jiangsu Zi Yi Ju)

In the late Qing Dynasty, a special building was constructed for meetings of the **Jiangsu Provincial Assembly** (Jiangsu Zi Yi Ju). It is an impressive two-story, rectangular hall with a clock tower in the center and domed cupolas at either end, built in French Baroque-style. It is probably the most impressive example of Western architecture in Nanjing.

In 1911, this building played an important role in the Xin Hai Revolution that established the Republic of China (Min Guo). An assembly of 44 delegates, representing 17 provinces of China, convened, for the first time, at Nanjing's Jiangsu Provincial Assembly (Jiangsu Zi Yi Ju) on 14 December 1911. On 29 December 1911, this assembly elected Sun Yat Sen (Sun Zhongshan) as the first President of the newly declared Republic of China. Sun arrived in Nanjing for his inauguration here on 1 January 1912.

After Chiang Kai Shek (Jiang Jieshi) established his new central government in Nanjing in 1929, the **Guomindang Central Party Headquarters** was housed in this same building. It is here that the Guomindang Central Committee held its regular meetings.

This building still stands on the north side of Hunan Lu at its intersection with Yunnan Lu, in an area once known as Ding Jia Qiao, a few blocks west of Zhongyang Lu. Unfortunately, it is regarded by the current Communist regime as a major war trophy demonstrating their 1949 victory over the Guomindang. As such, it is kept strictly off limits to public visitors and guarded by armed soldiers who stand rigidly at attention at the walled compound's entrance gate. A small bilingual sign on the compound wall states clearly that even taking photographs from the public sidewalk is not permitted. Two vertical sign boards on either side of the gate tell us that it is now the Nanjing Headquarters (Nanjing Jing Bei Si Ling Bu) of the Jiangsu Provincial Military District (Jiangsu Sheng Jun Qu).

Historic Universities
The University of Nanking (Jinling Daxue)
Across the street from the Drum Tower (Gu Lou) traffic circle, on Beijing Xi Lu, still stand some of the original buildings which

comprised the University of Nanking (Jinling Daxue). The campus actually covers a huge area stretching from Guangzhou Lu in the south to Beijing Xi Lu in the north, and is divided in half by Hankou Lu running from east to west. This school was formed in 1910 through the merger of three colleges established earlier by Christian missionaries, including the Methodist Nanking University founded in 1888 by John C. Ferguson. In 1911, the school was granted a charter by the State University of New York (SUNY). By 1914, the campus covered 28.3 hectares (70 acres) of land, and included three dormitories, three lecture halls, a science hall, a chapel, a YMCA, a hospital, and 13 faculty houses. In 1915, a school of agriculture and forestry was opened under Professor Joseph Bailie.

POINT OF INTEREST

Much like Ginling College, the University of Nanking seems to have had a fairly close relationship with the Guomindang central government. The annual commencement ceremonies featured three minutes of silent prayer before a portrait of Sun Yat Sen (Sun Zhongshan), founder of the Guomindang party. The 1934 commencement was attended by Sun Fo, the founder's son, and the then President of the Legislative Yuan. In 1936, President Chiang Kai Shek (Jiang Jieshi) visited the campus, joined by the heads of the Examination Yuan (Kaoshi Yuan) and the Guomindang party students' organization. In fact, the Guomindang's long-serving military chief of staff, General He Ying Qin, lived in a house on the university's campus. Although the original one was destroyed during the Japanese occupation of the city, he rebuilt it after the war and it is still there now, serving as the university's Foreign Affairs Office.

By 1925, the school had an enrollment of 293 students, with 27 full-time foreign faculty and a library collection of 67,000 volumes which was by far the largest of any of the dozen missionary universities in China. By 1935, the urban campus had grown to 44.5 hectares (110 acres), and a 48.6-hectare (120-acre) Agricultural Experimentation Station, known colloquially as "Bailie's Farm," had been established outside the city at the northwestern foot of Zijin Shan. There were two chapels, the first one was Sage Memorial Chapel, later supplemented with the Paul D. Twinem Memorial Chapel. The architecture was in the neo-classical Chinese renaissance style also used for the buildings of nearby Ginling College. By March 1935, the library had a collection of 194,253 books, including 23,812 volumes in Western languages.

PERSONALITIES

John Leighton Stuart began his term of service as president of the University of Nanking in 1916. Two years later, in 1918, he was appointed president of Peking-Yenching University in Beijing. He held this post until 1946 when he became U.S. Ambassador to China, a position he held until 1949.

From 1916–1918, John Leighton Stuart was president of the University of Nanking, after which he was replaced by Arthur J. Bowen. John E. Williams, who had been appointed the school's very first vice-president at the time of its founding in 1910 continued to serve in this role until March 1927, when he was executed by Chinese soldiers during the Guomindang's occupation of the city. The events of 1927, coming after several years of public pressure known as the "Educational Rights Recovery Movement," finally forced the appointment of the university's first Chinese president, Y.G. Chen (Chen Yu Guan), who formally replaced Arthur J. Bowen in May 1928.

One of the original halls of the former University of Nanking standing on the main quad.

In November 1937, the faculty and students retreated to Chengdu, just prior to the Japanese attack on Nanjing. During the first few months of the city's occupation by the Japanese, the university campus served as neutral territory for refugees, in much the same way as Ginling College did. At that time, it is said that the university's hospital was the only one functioning in the entire city.

The faculty returned to the Nanjing campus in May 1946. During the war, the collaborationist regime of Wang Jingwei used the main quadrangle buildings for their own Central University, while the Japanese military occupied the faculty houses. The chapel was used as a warehouse. Sadly, the original library collection of 440,000 volumes was looted.

Although it had previously had a close relationship with the Guomindang government, the student body became affected by rising dissatisfaction with the regime in the immediate postwar years. In 1947, University of Nanking students went on strike, in sympathy wih those who were striking at the government-run National Central University (Guoli Zhongyang Daxue).

After the April 1949 Communist capture of Nanjing, the university maintained its Christian atmosphere and missionary management for some time. The 1949 commencement was held with a church choir in attendance. On 24 December 1949, a Christmas party was held, complete with a nativity scene and religious play performed by students. The very last commencement ceremony held under the management of missionaries was on 3 July 1950. The administration of the school was taken over by government authorities in early 1951, when foreign missionary organizations were prohibited from operating in China, and all remaining foreign faculty left at that time. The name of the school was changed to Nanjing University (Nanjing Daxue), under which it continues to function today.

Although nearly all the original buildings have survived, it is unfortunate that Nanjing University follows the example of Nanjing Normal University (Nanjing Shifan Daxue) in denying its Western missionary heritage. Instead, it insists on promoting the lie that its origins can be traced to the Sanjiang Normal College founded by Zhang Zhi Dong in 1902. The university's official history makes absolutely no mention of the missionaries' founding, constructing, and managing the school from 1911 to 1951. The school's coat of arms, prominently displayed everywhere, carries the date 1902. All evidence that would testify to the unversity's true origins has been carefully cleansed from the buildings and campus.

Today, most of the surviving historic buildings are found in the half of campus north of Hankou Lu, although there are three historic buildings in the southern half as well. Historic houses where the foreign faculty members formerly lived can be found on both sides of tree-lined Hankou Lu.

Heading north from Hankou Lu and walking up Zhong Da Lu will lead you past a two-story Spanish Colonial house on the left side of the road. This is by far the nicest of the historic houses on campus, so it is likely to have belonged to either the university president or General He Ying Qin, who is known to have lived somewhere on university grounds.

On the east side of Zhong Da Lu is a small, one-story, red brick hall with upturned roof eaves that was once the **Twinem Memorial Chapel**. The chapel was named after Paul D. Twinem, a former faculty member at the university. Outside is an iron bell, hanging from a wooden frame, that is inscribed with the words "Weneely N.V.," possibly providing a clue to where it was made.

North of the chapel, pathways lead to the main quadrangle of historic buildings and a smaller one on its west side. At the north end of the main quadrangle is the two-story former **Severance Hall** with its five-story tower. This hall originally served as

Severance Hall of the former University of Nanking still stands at the north end of the main quad.

the combined administration-library building. A foundation stone in the southwest corner still bears the date "1919." Inside the first floor lobby, the original chandelier still hangs from a coffered ceiling, colorfully painted with a phoenix pattern. The stairwells on either side bear a total of four sets of stone Chinese inscriptions, embedded in the walls that have been covered up with thick white paint to make them illegible.

The two-story hall on the western side of the main quadrangle was formerly the **Joseph Bailie Agricultural Hall** and has a foundation stone in its southeast corner bearing the date "1925." The two-story hall on the eastern side of the main quadrangle has no visible cornerstone, but was formerly the **Swasey Science Hall**. Inside its entrance lobby, a curious relic has survived in the form of a round, bronze, Western astrological calendar embedded in the floor.

West of this main quad is a second smaller one surrounded by a collection of historic halls that were the university's original dormitories. The larger of the university's two chapels, the two-story brick **Sage Memorial Chapel** built about 1920, once stood in the center of this smaller quadrangle, but now seems to have disappeared.

The university's History Department has an Exhibition Hall for Cultural Relics. Call ahead, at phone: 8359-3512, for an appointment.

Address: Gu Lou, Beijing Xi Lu

Ginling College (Jinling Nuzi Daxue)

A Christian school for young Chinese women, Ginling College (Jinling Nuzi Daxue) was established by American missionaries in 1913 when Matilda Thurston (Mrs. Lawrence Thurston) was chosen as its first president. Its first classes started informally in 1915 in a few rented houses, but in 1916, the founders began purchasing parcels of land. By 1918, a 10.9-hectare (27-acre) site was ready in **Peach Valley** (Tao Gu), between Qing Liang Shan and Wu Tai Shan, southwest of the University of Nanking (Jinling Daxue), along present-day Ning Hai Lu.

An American Building Committee for Ginling College was established in New York to raise funds for construction. Henry K. Murphy was the architect for Ginleng College, and his idea —

POINT OF INTEREST

In 1918, American architect Henry K. Murphy was chosen to design Ginling College. At that time, the firm of Murphy and Dana was based in New York, but they had just opened an office in Shanghai. Murphy had already designed the Yale-in-China (Yali) campus in Changsha in 1914. In 1918, he was also involved in designing plans for Qinghua University in Beijing and Fudan University in Shanghai. Later he designed Peking-Yenching University in Beijing, which still stands today.

This pre-revolutionary monument on the campus of Ginling College remains a mystery till today.

unique at the time — was to combine traditional Chinese style with modern Western construction methods. He was one of the founders of what became known as the neo-classical Chinese renaissance in architecture, a style that later became a trademark of the Guomindang era. Murphy's plan for Ginling called for administrative and residential buildings to be constructed around several quadrangles. The buildings were to include a Chapel, Library, Science Building, Recitation Building, Faculty House, and two dormitories. Construction of the first six buildings lasted from 1921 to 1923.

The new campus formally opened in October 1923, with ceremonies attended by provincial government officials and foreign journalists. One observer commented that it was "the first time that foreigners had ever successfully adapted Chinese architecture to modern requirements." Other observers compared the campus buildings to Chinese palaces or temples. By 1925, the college had an enrollment of 133 students, with 17 full-time foreign faculty and a library housing a collection of 10,000 volumes of books. In April 1934, the library collection contained 21,803 volumes, including 10,038 in Western languages.

As it was with the University of Nanking, the 1924–1927 "Educational Rights Recovery Movement" finally forced the appointment of the university's first Chinese president, Wu Yi Fang. He replaced Matilda Thurston (Mrs. Lawrence Thurston) in May 1928, and continued to serve in this post for the next 23 years, until the school was closed down by the new Communist government in 1951.

Ginling College seems to have had a very close relationship with the national government authorities, as many high level representatives paid visits to the campus in the decade when Nanjing served as the Guomindang's capital city. The 1934 commencement ceremony was attended by President Chiang Kai Shek (Jiang Jieshi) and his wife Song Meiling. The latter then donated a dormitory to the campus, and continued to visit the school after its exodus to Chengdu. Both Hu Shih and Finance Minister, H.H. Kung, attended the November 1934 dedication and formal opening of two new campus buildings, the Library-Administration Building and the Chapel-Music Hall. Sun Fo, the son of Sun Yat Sen (Sun Zhongshan), visited the school in 1936.

By 1937, the campus had grown to 16.2 hectares (40 acres) in size. Just prior to the Japanese attack on the city, most of the school's students and faculty retreated to Chengdu, in Sichuan province. Here, they set up an alternate campus, in exile, for the next eight years. From December 1937 to May 1938, the campus at Nanjing served as a safe haven for an estimated 10,000 civilian Chinese refugees who sought to escape from the Japanese army which was ravaging the rest of the city. Some faculty members who had chosen to stay behind directed the relief efforts. As an American-run institution, its campus was treated as neutral territory until after the Japanese attack on Pearl Harbor in December 1941. In June 1942, the campus was finally occupied by Japanese troops who used it as living quarters until the end of the war in August 1945.

In February 1946, the faculty returned to the Nanjing campus. They found severe war damage from the Japanese occupation, including empty laboratories, looted libraries, missing furniture, newly dug trenches and constructed walls, warehouses, and horse stables. Watchtowers had been built on top of many of the buildings.

After Ginling's resumption on its old campus, it regained its previous prominence with the national government. Four Ginling graduates were elected to the April 1948 National Assembly, after which the newly elected Vice-President, Li Zong Ren, paid a visit to the campus to give a speech on 3 May 1948.

After the Communist occupation of Nanjing, Ginling College still managed to hold its commencement ceremony on 27 June 1949. The school continued to function until early 1951 when all overseas sources of funding for missionary-run institutions were cut off by the Communist government, which then began to take over their administration. Ginling was initially merged with Nanjing University (Nanjing Daxue), but in 1952, it become an independent university with the name of Nanjing Teachers College (Nanjing Shifan Xueyuan). In 1984, this was changed to Nanjing Normal University (Nanjing

One of the main halls of the former Ginling College stands on the main square.

Shifan Daxue), the name it goes by today. It is now a co-educational institution for both boys and girls.

The former site of Ginling College is now known as the Sui Yuan Campus of Nanjing Normal University. The original monumental red entrance gate (*pai lou*) is still there, facing Ning Hai Lu. Passing through the gate and walking up the tree-lined main avenue of the campus, you will reach a square green lawn surrounded on all four sides by the original halls of Ginling College. Amazingly, they are intact and in pristine condition, complete with yellow walls, red columns, blue trim around the doors and windows, green and red tripod roof brackets, upturned roof eaves, and sloping tiled roofs. There are a total of 17 historic buildings from the Ginling College still standing here, and still in use by the modern day university. Many of the building interiors are unchanged, although some have been renovated.

Although the Ginling campus has been well preserved, the sad part is the near total denial of its American missionary origins. There are no monuments to its founder, Matilda Thurston (Mrs. Lawrence Thurston), nor to Henry K. Murphy, the American architect who designed the college. The only admission of Ginling's previous existence at this site is a memorial plaque on the outside of the Hua Xia Library Building. It notes that the former office of Wu Yi Fang, president of Ginling from 1928 to 1951, was once in this building. The official history, displayed on public signs at the campus as well as on the university's web site, falsely claims the university's origins as having started with Zhang Zhi Dong's founding of Sanjiang Normal College in 1902. It neglects any mention of Thurston, Murphy, Ginling's true founding in 1913, nor the grand opening of the campus in 1923. This anti-American attitude seems to pervade even the School of Foreign Languages which pointedly lacks an American Studies Center, even though it has centers for Canadian, Australian, and French studies.

The present day foreign language school on the site of the former Ginling College.

Despite the denial of its American missionary origins, the modern day university is probably more open to international exchange than most Chinese universities. The School of Foreign Languages in Building No. 500 does have an active English language learning program that recruits foreign teachers to prepare Chinese students for such English tests as BEC. Furthermore, the International College for Chinese Studies (ICCS) in Building No. 200 was, in the 1980s, one of the first two Chinese language training centers for foreigners in China, authorized by the Ministry of Education. Currently, the ICCS is one of only eight such public training centers.

University Address: 122 Ning Hai Lu
University web site: http://www.njnu.edu.cn

School of Foreign Languages

Address: Building No. 500
Phone: 8320-1260,
8373-2062, 8324-7123

International College for Chinese Studies (ICCS)

Address: Building No. 200
Phone: 8359-8374
Fax: 8371-7160
Web site: http://www.lxnjnu.com
E-mail: iso@njnu.edu.cn

> **POINT OF INTEREST**
>
> The "Nanking Incident" of 24 March 1927 refers to the incident in which marauding Guomindang troops massacred the city's foreign residents and looted the property belonging to resident foreign community.

Nanjing Theological Seminary (Jinling Xie He Sheng Xueyuan)

Located west of Xin Jie Kou, the remnant of this former missionary seminary's campus is now hidden on a narrow back alleyway, half a block north of Hanzhong Lu. In 1904, it was founded by American missionaries as a Presbyterian Seminary. However, in 1911, it became a non-denominational Union Seminary which merged the efforts of American missionaries belonging to the Presbyterian, Methodist, and Baptist churches. Its most famous faculty member was John Leighton Stuart.

As a result of the "Nanking Incident", the Seminary closed down for two years. During this interval, the Seminary's property was taken over by the Guomindang national government's Supreme Court (Zui Gao Fa Yuan), which continued to occupy it until their new quarters were completed on Zhongshan Bei Lu in 1933. In the meantime, the Seminary's original campus was cut in half by the newly constructed Hanzhong Lu, which was built in 1931. After finally recovering their property in September 1933, the Seminary continued to function until the Japanese invasion of 1937.

On 20 November 1937, the Guomindang government announced that it would be moving to Chongqing. Two days later, the Seminary closed down. The Japanese capture of Nanjing on the night of 12 December 1937 left the Seminary's campus largely intact. Later it would serve as barracks for the Japanese soldiers. The Seminary was finally able to reopen again in February 1946, after having operated in exile in Chengdu for nine years during the Sino-Japanese War.

The Seminary managed to keep functioning normally after the 1949 revolution until as late as the fall of 1950, when the faculty still included half a dozen foreign missionaries. However, new regulations governing religious organizations were issued in January 1951, which prohibited any financial support from foreign countries, thus cutting the Seminary off from its overseas missionary founders. A national conference of Protestant church leaders held in Beijing in April 1951 resulted in the expulsion of the final remaining foreign missionaries from China. Soon after this, the name of the school was changed to Jinling Union Theological Seminary (Jinling Xie He Sheng Xue). Under this new name, and with an all-Chinese leadership, it continued to enroll students.

However, in 1966 it was closed down at the start of the Cultural Revolution, and did not reopen until 15 years later, in February 1981, when it began to enroll students again. The seminary still functions today, under the name **Nanjing Union Theological Seminary** (Jinling Xie He Sheng Xue). In recent years has issued its own periodical, "The Nanjing Theological Review" ("Jinling Sheng Xue Zhi"), which often includes photos of the campus and its historic buildings.

A tour of the site in November 2003 revealed a campus of green lawns behind a red brick wall surrounded by urban construction. The institution is apparently now co-educational, as men and women could be seen walking around the campus together. A walkway leading from the main gate heads straight to the main historic structure, a two-story red brick building with a three-arched arcade in front supported by four white pillars. A red brick chapel extends out of the back of this hall's ground floor and into the rear garden. The interior of this main hall

The Nanjing Union Theological Seminary (Jinling Xie He Sheng Xue) built in 1904.

seemed largely unchanged. Of the other two three-story historic houses on the campus, one was in the midst of a major restoration that had completely gutted its interior. A new library building on the east side of the main hall contained a fairly large number of books — all related to Christianity — including some old hardcover English ones that looked as if they might have been survivors of an earlier pre-revolutionary collection.

Address: 17 Da Jian Yin Xiang
Phone: 8470-4108
Fax: 8472-7204

The original library building of South East University in Nanjing, completed in 1933.

Southeast University (Dong Nan Daxue)

Sanjiang Normal College (Sanjiang Shifan Xuetang), the ancestor of Southeast University, was established in 1902 by Zhang Zhi Dong, then Governor-General of the Liangjiang provinces. It was renamed Liangjiang Normal College (Liangjiang Shifan Xuetang) in 1905, and evolved into Southeast University (Dong Nan Daxue) between 1921 and 1923. After briefly being known as the Fourth Zhongshan University for just one year, in 1928, the name was changed again to National Central University (Guoli Zhongyang Daxue). As the main public university of the Guomindang regime, this was the scene of countless student protests and demonstrations against the government during the 1930s and 1940s. After the 1949 revolution, the name was changed again in 1952 to the Nanjing Institute of Technology (Nanjing Gong Xueyuan). However, in May 1988, the name was changed back to its pre-1928 name of Southeast University (Dong Nan Daxue).

A plaque on a corner stone of the library building of South East University.

The university's enormous green campus campus is still dominated by historic relics of the Min Guo era. Located in an area known as Si Pai Lou (Four Memorial Gates), the campus is bounded on the east by Cheng Xian Jie, on the north by Beijing Dong Lu, and to the west by Jin Xiang He Lu, a street named after a stream that once flowed past the campus there. The monumental gateway to the campus, with its four

The original entrance gate to the campus of South East University facing Si Pai Lou road.

square pillars, still stands on its southern boundary facing Si Pai Lou road. The top of this gate has borne all the many name changes experienced by the university over the years, just as its flagpole has borne witness to the rise and fall of many political regimes.

Straight ahead from this main gate, down the central tree-lined campus avenue, is National Central University's impressive **Auditorium** (Da Li Tang) with its octagonal dome. The Da Li Tang was completed on 10 October 1931 and was last repaired in 1994. It was designed by architect Yang Ting Bao, a professor at the university whose house still stands across the street from the campus on Cheng Xian Jie. The original weather-beaten foundation stone can still be found in the southeast corner of the building. Inside, an octagonal hallway leads in two directions from the front lobby to various entrances into the theater. Inside the theater itself, a stage stands at the north end, double rows of balconies look down upon the stage from the three other directions, and a glass skylight at the very top of the octagonal dome overhead lets in natural sunlight.

Guomindang Party Congresses were held in this hall, starting with the May 1931 Fourth Party Congress that adopted the 1931 Constitution. During the Sino-Japanese war, this auditorium was converted into a Japanese military hospital, and a giant red cross was painted over the outside of its dome to prevent it from being bombed.

To the west of the central avenue, before reaching the Auditorium (Da Li Tang), is the original **Library** (Tushuguan) building of Southeast University, built between 1922 and 1923, and expanded again in 1933. Its exterior is dominated by four large Roman columns, while its interior has the musty air of a historic building that has yet to be renovated. A Chinese language exhibit on the university's history is displayed inside on the ground floor.

Several other Min Guo halls frame the main quadrangle of the campus, but none as impressive as the Library or Auditorium

(Da Li Tang). An odd ommission is the absence of any statue or memorial devoted to the school's founder Zhang Zhi Dong.

Address: No. 2 Si Pai Lou
Tel: 379-2412
Fax: 361-5736

Johns Hopkins Center

During the 1980s, this Nanjing campus of Johns Hopkins University in the United States was where some of the very first American graduate students came to study in China after the country's reopening to the West in 1979.

Address: 162 Shanghai Lu

Colonial Relics
Former British Consulate (Xiao Bai Lou)

The former British Consulate, now known as the **Little White House** (Xiao Bai Lou), is today a luxurious banquet facility with 15 dining rooms. Since 1954, it has been owned by the Shuang Men Lou Hotel. Built in 1919, this was the British Consulate where the British consul was assassinated by Guomindang troops during their occupation of the city in March 1927. It was his murder which sparked the flight over the city wall by the foreign residents on Ding Shan. The building is now kept in an immaculate and pristine condition with one of the cleanest and most luxurious interiors in China. Staff are happy to allow visitors to look around inside, and can even provide an English language brochure describing some of the buildings' history.

Address: 185 Huju Bei Lu

The former British Consulate in Nanjing, now a restaurant known as the Xiao Bai Lou.

Ding Shan

Now the site of the enormous Shangri-La Ding Shan Hotel complex, this hill overlooking the low river bottom land towards the Yangzi was once the site of a community of foreigners during treaty port days.

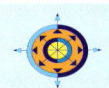

POINT OF INTEREST

Ding Shan was the place where a large group of Nanjing's foreign residents took shelter from the invading Guomindang troops who occupied and ransacked the city in March 1927. As the troops began summarily executing whatever foreigners they could find, including the British consul, the Ding Shan group decided to escape. Foreign warships were waiting for them on the Yangzi, but the trouble was how to get there. The city wall was still impregnable at this time and all the gates had been closed. In order to get out of the city, they had to climb down the city wall, using ropes made out of bed sheets tied together. After the descent, there was still a long run across the bottom land of Xia Guan to the safety of ships waiting in the Yangzi River.

Three of these obviously Western houses can be still be seen here today. Two of them are now guesthouse villas belonging to the Ding Shan Hotel — the ones with a big number 1 and 4 on them — while the third is part of the Nanjing International School. Their current owners do not seem to have any knowledge of the buildings' history. Look for the Ding Shan Health Center with its enormous neon sign and you'll find all three houses.

Ding Shan can be reached by several narrow side lanes. The easiest is probably to approach by taking Cha Haer Lu from Huju Bei Lu. Another alternative is to take Dai Jia Xiang, off Huju Bei Lu, then turn right onto Gui Yun Tang Shi Wu Xiang, and then left onto Zhenjiang Lu.

Parks in the City Center
Xuan Wu Hu Park (Xuan Wu Hu Gongyuan)

Known as Xuan Wu Lake (Xuan Wu Hu) since 446AD, it was originally a naval training ground and a private retreat for the imperial royal family. It was opened as a public park in 1910, the year before the 1911 Revolution, and underwent major renovations in 1928.

A foot bridge connecting the two islands of Ling Zhou and Huan Zhou in Xuan Wu Hu lake.

The 472-hectare (1,166.3-acre) park consists of a lake shore path around the entire circumference of Xuan Wu Hu, plus five islands in the center of the lake which are connected to the shore by three narrow causeways. The five islands are now named Ling Zhou, Huan Zhou, Ying Zhou, Liang Zhou and Cui Zhou. Except for Cui Zhou, these are the same names they have had since at least 1937, although at one time they were also named after the Earth's five continents (*wu zhou*), causing the park to sometimes be called Wu Zhou Gongyuan.

During the Min Guo era, it was also known as Rear Lake (Hou Hu). Historic maps and photos show that as late as 1937, the causeway linking the islands to the lake shore ran from near the Taiping Men city gate to the island of Cui Zhou, then known as Cai Zhou. Nowadays, the two main causeways run from Jiefang Men to Ling Zhou, and from Xuan Wu Men to Huan Zhou, with a third connecting Cui Zhou to Long Pan Lu. When these changes were made to the network of causeways is unclear, but it was certainly after 1937, and thus must have occurred sometime after the end of the Japanese occupation in 1945.

Dragon head ornaments protrude from a wall on an island in Xuan Wu Hu lake.

The Friendship Hall built in 1941 on Liang Zhou island in Xuan Wu Hu lake.

Ling Zhou

The main sight here is an aviary, for which there is a separate entrance fee of 15 Rmb. The island can be reached by a bridge from Huan Zhou or a long narrow causeway connecting it to the Jie Fang Men area. Pictures from the 1930s show that Ling Zhou was then not connected by bridges to either Huan Zhou or the lake shore, as it is today. It's not clear exactly when the Ling Zhou causeway was constructed.

Ying Zhou

This small island sits entirely inside the enveloping island of Huan Zhou, separated only by a lotus-filled moat.

The Tibetan Buddhist temple Nuona Si and its pagoda Nuona Ta built in 1937 on Huan Zhou island in Xuan Wu Hu lake.

Huan Zhou

A man-made waterfall is the first sight one sees when approaching from the Xuan Wu Men causeway. When crossing the footbridge from Ling Zhou, you can see from a distance the **Nuona Si** or Tibetan Buddhist Temple with its tall white pagoda (Nuona Ta). Both buildings were constructed in 1937, but the statues inside the temple are from a 1993 restoration. Tibetan prayer flags are draped across the outside, and tape recordings of relentless chanting of the phrase "om padi om" are played by an attendant. However, there are no resident monks and no real religious worship seems to go on here. The temple and pagoda were built in dedication to the Tibetan monk **Nuona** who died in China in 1937. Another temple and pagoda (also called Nuona Si and Nuona Ta respectively), built in a more authentic Tibetan style, marks his grave on top of Mount Lushan in Jiangxi province.

Liang Zhou

Out of the five islands, Liang Zhou features the most genuine historic artifacts in the form of four Qing Dynasty buildings and a fifth dating from the Japanese occupation. A Ming Dynasty **Temple to the Lake God** (Hu Shen Miao) located here was rebuilt in 1872 by Zeng Guofan, then the resident Viceroy of the Liangjiang provinces, and has been undergoing extensive renovation since 2000. In 1937, the Lake God Temple was called Hu Cheng Miao, and was accompanied by a Guanyin Pavilion and two other memorial halls. Another historic building still standing on the island is the two-story **Sightseeing Pavilion** (Lan Sheng Lou), built in 1909 by the Qing prince Xu Shao Zhen as a writers' retreat. Two other Qing dynasty buildings are the **Wen Ji Pavilion** (Wen Ji Ting) and the **Xuan Wu Hall** (Xuan Wu Dian). A fifth, more modern building, is an odd 1941 strucure, which is dubbed the **Friendship Hall**.

Cui Zhou

This island is connected to the Long Pan Lu causeway. Its main feature is some recently constructed gardens. It is currently suffering blight from the draining of this half of the lake for the construction of the new cross-lake traffic tunnel.

A fleet of Dragon Boats lie patiently waiting for the annual race held during Du Wan Wu Jie festival.

Xuan Wu Hu park can be reached in basically three ways. The first is through Xuan Wu Men gate, which is reached by turning off Zhongyang Lu. The second way is via Jie Fang Men gate, which sits astride Ji Min Si Lu. The third approach is from the East side where a causeway connects to the shore beside Long Pan Lu, across the street from the train station. The price of admission to the park is 15 Rmb.

North Pole Tower (Bei Ji Ge)

Beside the peak of Jiming Si is a second hill, known as Bei Ji Ge, which has excellent views of Jiming Si and Xuan Wu Hu. This was formerly the site of a Taoist Temple and an earlier Ming dynasty astronomical observatory. In 1928, it was chosen by the Guomindang as the location for several institutes of the newly established **Academia Sinica** headed by Cai Yuan Pei. The Institute of Meteorology was establishd on the summit in 1928 as a weather observatory. With a curious mixture of traditional Chinese and early 20th century Western architecture, these buildings can still be seen today. In the autumn of 1934, the Institutes of Historical Studies, Linguistics, Archaelogy, and Anthropology were also moved here and set up inside a special new building. In the same year, a new building was erected here for the Institute of Geology. The Guomindang's long-serving Finance Minister T.V. Soong (Soong Zi Wen) also reportedly lived in a house on this hill, although the exact location is now unclear.

Weather Observatory built in 1928 atop the North Pole Tower (Bei Ji Ge) hill.

The rooftop of a traditional pavilion at the Black Dragon Pool Park (Wu Long Tan Gongyuan).

A long winding road makes a very steep climb to the top. Although the road to the top travels through a public park, the very top of the peak, where the tower stands within a walled compound, generally is not open to visitors. However, friendly staff will occasionally allow escorted visits.

The tower is located on Ji Long Shan overlooking the Xuan Wu Hu lake. The road to Ji Long Shan branches off He Ping Lu, near its intersection with Bei Jing Dong Lu. No ticket is required.

Black Dragon Pool (Wu Long Tan Gongyuan)

Formerly known as Ma Long Tan, this is a pleasant park, with green willow trees lining both sides of a long oval pool, footbridges, islands, traditional pavilions, and an uncrowded, peaceful, relaxing environment. Five fake dragons grace the center of the lake, in honor of the park's tradition as the site where dragons appeared once each year. The park stretches from Guangzhou Lu to Huju Lu and has entrance gates at both roads.

Address: 217 Guangzhou Lu
Phone: 8371-9394
Ticket: 4 Rmb

Qing Liang Shan

This was originally an imperial summer retreat used by vacationing emperors from as far back as the Song Dynasty (960–1279). During the Song Dynasty, there was a Buddhist Temple here called Guang Hui Si. The locale's unusual topography consists of two small hills with a valley in between. As a result, it has traditionally been considered a good place to cool off during Nanjing's infamously hot summers.

The Ming Dynasty city gate nearby was named after this hill. As late as 1937, there was still an active Buddhist temple located there, the **Qing Liang Si**. The temple had three halls and a building supposedly dating from the Ming Dynasty known as the Sweeping Leaves Tower (Sao Ye Lou). Within the temple compound was the Nan Tang Jing, a well supposedly dating from the reign of Emperor Li Jing (943–961 AD) of the Southern Tang (Nan Tang) Dynasty

Today, several traditional pavilions grace the tops of the hills. However, there is no functioning temple nor are there any Buddhist monks. The Nan Tang Jing was still there as recently as 1980. On a hot summer's day, one can still enjoy the natural cool air that seems to inhabit this place. Unfortunately, the summit of the main central peak now has a foul shanty town slum, as does the base of the hill just outside the park. The main entrance gate is at the intersection of Huju Lu and Guangzhou Lu.

Mo Chou Lake (Mo Chou Hu)
This park sits outside the city wall, in between Han Zhong Lu and Shui Xi Men Lu, with gates entering from both roads. It contains a fairly large lake with an island in the center. Several traditional Ming-Qing style pavilions grace the park, including a small one on the island which is reachable only by boat. Boats can be rented at the park.

According to a famous story, the Ming general, Xu Da, received the park as a gift from the first Ming Emperor, Zhu Yuanzhang, when the former beat the latter in a famous chess (*weiqi*) game. One of the buildings is known as the **Winning at Chess Pavilion** (Sheng Qi Lou). Xu Da is buried in his own tomb on the Northern slope of Zijin Shan, beside Ban Cang Lu.

Next to the Sheng Qi Lou is a walled garden containing a white statue of the mythical heroine Mo Chou, whom the park is named after.

These two sites are most easily reached from the Shui Xi Men Lu entrance. The park stays open after dark, but the pavilions close at dusk.

Tickets: 8 Rmb

Zheng He Park (Zheng He Gongyuan)
Devoted to the famous Chinese Muslim Ming Dynasty admiral, Zheng He (371–1435) whose ships sailed the seven seas during the early 15th century. Zheng He Park was established in 1985 and sits on Xiao Huo Wa Xiang street, half a block from its intersection with Taiping Nan Lu.

Tickets: 1 Rmb

White Egret Isle (Bai Lu Zhou Gongyuan)
Situated near Fuzi Miao, this new Buddhist temple was completed in 2003 and has a resident monk population.

Address: Chang Bai Jie
Tickets: 5 Rmb

PERSONALITIES

In 629AD, the Buddhist monk Xuan Zang (596–664 AD) left China against the explicit orders of the Tang Emperor Tai Zong (626–649 AD). Sixteen years later, in 645AD, Xuan Zang returned, bringing with him some 657 Buddhist texts, which were later translated from Sanskrit into Chinese. He later wrote about his travels in the book, *Record of the Western Regions*, published in 646AD. However, the best known version of his story is the one contained in one of Chinese literature's four greatest novels, *The Journey to the West* (Xi You Ji), a Ming Dynasty work written by Wu Cheng En (1500–1582) during the Jiajing reign.

Right: Distant view of the pagoda on top of Xiao Jiu Hua Shan from the foot of the hill.
Far right: A close up view of the pagoda on top of Xiao Jiu Hua Shan.

The Peace Pagoda (He Ping Ta), built in 1941.

Small Nine Flower Hill (Xiao Jiuhua Shan)

Not to be confused with the much larger Buddhist mountain of the same name in Anhui Province, this is a hill on the shores of Xuan Wu Hu. On this site sits a Buddhist pagoda dedicated to the famous monk, Xuan Zang. This tower competes with Ling Gu Si as the supposed site of Xuan Zang's skull. The Japanese claimed that they discovered his skull buried on top of this hill in 1943 and built this tower in commemoration the following year, placing the skull inside a concrete block. Ling Gu Si claims to have the real skull. The latter seems to be winning the battle as it is a popular, functioning temple frequented by visitors, while Jiuhua Shan seems forlorn and abandoned. Either way, how the skull of someone who lived in Xian would have made it to Nanjing is something of a mystery.

Nonetheless, despite its questionable origins, Jiuhua Shan Ta has a beautiful view of Xuan Wu Hu, Zijin Shan, and the whole city in all four directions. The tower itself is five storys high with a square shape and is modeled on one at Xing Jiao Si in Xian. On the side of the tower's base is a map of Xuan Zang's world travels inscribed in stone.

This pagoda, along with Jiming Si and the North Pole Tower (Bei Ji Ge), can be seen from long distances throughout the city and together the three of them help shape the city skyline when viewed from the East. Jiuhua Shan can be reached from a long narrow lane which turns off from Beijing Dong Lu at the **Academica Sinica** campus and ends at the bottom of a long flight of steps. Buy a ticket at the bottom of the steps for 5 Rmb. Alternatively, approach from the direction of Taiping Men and then climb the hill by another trail.

The area below Jiuhua Shan also offers access to the top of the city wall. This can be followed on foot all the way to the city wall museum and Jie Fang Men. Descend the hill using one of the trails headed towards the lakeshore and you will find the wall entrance marked by a small ticket booth, wherr you can buy a ticket for 8 Rmb.

Peace Pagoda (He Ping Ta)

Another Buddhist pagoda built by the Japanese occupiers in 1941. It is made out of grey stone and sits in the middle of He Ping Park, between Bei Jing Dong Lu and He Ping Lu. On the inside, a spiral metal staircase ascends to the fourth floor. Some peeling Buddhist paintings adorn the inner walls. No ticket is required.

The entrance gate to Drum Tower Park (Gu Lou Gongyuan).

Drum Tower (Gu Lou)

This large rectangular brick tower is 40 m (131.2 ft) high which sits on a small hill in the middle of a round park in the center of a traffic circle on Bei Jing Xi Lu. The tower was first built during the Ming Dynasty in 1382. The Gu Lou originally had three arched gateways which passed through the center of its base. In 1894, a paved road was built across the city, from Yi Feng Men in the west to Tong Ji Men in the east, passing through the Gu Lou on the way. This modern road replaced a stone paved trail that had passed through the Gu Lou before. In 1923, the area around the Gu Lou was converted into a green-traffic circle park, the road no longer passing through its three arched portals. Nonetheless, photos from 1930 show that these portals were still open at that times. These days, the three gates are no longer visible, having been walled up and converted into interior rooms used for shops selling trinkets.

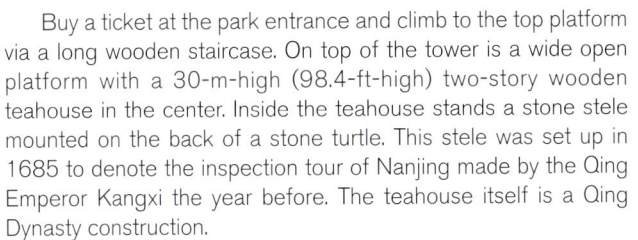

The bronze bell that now hangs atop the Drum Tower (Gu Lou).

Buy a ticket at the park entrance and climb to the top platform via a long wooden staircase. On top of the tower is a wide open platform with a 30-m-high (98.4-ft-high) two-story wooden teahouse in the center. Inside the teahouse stands a stone stele mounted on the back of a stone turtle. This stele was set up in 1685 to denote the inspection tour of Nanjing made by the Qing Emperor Kangxi the year before. The teahouse itself is a Qing Dynasty construction.

Outside the teahouse sits a large bronze bell hanging from a wooden frame. For a small fee you can ring the bell by pulling back a long wooden log and pushing it into the side of the bell. Listen to its loud echo ring out across the city. This used to be the signal for the opening and closing of the city gates in the mornings and evenings, as well as in times of danger. Although it is called the Drum Tower, there do not seem to be any drums kept there anymore.

From the flat platform on the top of the tower, you can enjoy one of the best views in the city. To the east is Zijin Shan, Jiming Si, and Bei Ji Ge. To the right are the old historic buildings of Nanjing University across the street.

Address: Gu Lou, Beijing Xi Lu

White Horse Park (Bai Ma Gongyuan)

This is a park that has been recently constructed at the western foot of Zijin Shan.

Temples in the City Center
Quiet Sea Temple (Jing Hai Si)

This temple was originally built by Ming Emperor Yong Le in honor of Admiral Zheng He, whose ships sailed farther around the world than any other of his day. It was intentionally located outside the city wall, in the Xiaguan district near the Yangzi River because its main purpose was to bless the ships of Zheng He before they left on their voyages across the oceans, and to give thanks for their safe return afterwards. The temple was dedicated to the goddess Tian Fei who was thought to protect sailors at sea. In fact, the name "Jing Hai" means "quiet sea," conveying the wish that Zheng He's fleet would have a safe journey.

Ironically, 400 years later, this was also the location of the Sino-British negotiations which resulted in the 29 August 1842 Treaty of Nanking, ending the First Opium War of 1840–1842, although the treaty was actually signed on board the HMS Cornwallis as it sat anchored in the Yangzi River. It was this treaty which ceded Hong Kong to Britian and opened up the first five coastal treaty ports to foreigners. Quite a reversal of fortune in a fairly short time.

The original Jing Hai Si was burned down by the Japanese in December 1937, shortly after their capture of the city; but it was rebuilt again in 1987. In 1990, a museum devoted to the Treaty of Nanking was opened here. In June 1997, celebrations were held here in honor of the return of Hong Kong to China. A courtyard off to the side contains the large bronze Awakening Bell, placed there for the 1997 ceremony. There are now three Ming-style exhibition halls. Unfortunately none of them carry English captions.

The Quiet Sea Temple sits at the foot of Lion Peak (Shizi Shan), immediately outside the old city wall and city moat, both of which were rebuilt during 2000–2001. You can approach from Re He Lu, where a gate marks the lane leading to the temple gate at the far end. Now, you can also approach on foot by descending the pathway down Lion Peak from the newly built Yue Jiang Lou.

Address: 116 Re He Lu
Phone: 5880-2973
Admission: Included in the 30 Rmb ticket
for Lion Peak (Shizi Shan)

POINT OF INTEREST

At the Quiet Sea Temple (Jing Hai Si) is a copy of the original 6-m-high (19.7-ft-high), 27-ton Ming Dynasty stele, sitting on top of a turtle, on which Emperor Yong Le had inscribed his dedication to the goddess Tian Fei in 1416.

A 1933 guidebook to Nanjing published a rough translation of this lengthy inscription consisting of 699 characters. The text provides an incomparable understanding of the significance the goddess Tian Fei had to the early Ming:

"Stele of the Temple of the Goddess Tien Fei (Tian Fei),
the magnanimous and universally beneficient.

Successor of Hung Wu (Hong Wu),
I initiate him by sending abroad my civilizing embassies.
The first of these was overtaken by a great tempest and
saved by the appearance of Tien Fei (Tian Fei).

To her I dedicate a temple outside the walls,
on the River of the Dragon (Long Jiang).
The goddess has shown to embassies coming from
foreign lands her favor by innumerable miracles.

To her I inscribe a tablet with these verses:

> The beautiful soul of the divine daughter of Mei Chou walks by morning in the blue garden and by night in the isle of Peng Lei and Ying Chou (Ying Zhou). She raises the trembling, she succors the weak and comforts them. When appealed to she replies immediately, and prayed to, she harkens. The Heavenly Father confides to her care the seas; she orders and the evil spirits are dissipated. Wind, rain, thunder, lightning, all are beneath her sway and hers the power, according to her desire, to loose them or to withhold them. Great tides and waves become calm and motionless; travelers cross the seas in tranquility as though walking on a plain. All the foreign peoples, children of the same father, with tattooed skin and multicolored garments, all come to visit me, after passing through more than ten thousand kingdoms. Our goddess protects them, her great and universal power extends over them. She leads them, she helps them; is it not evident?
> Behold Goddess your temple so majestic, so high and wide, built to reward you for your merits. Pure and fragrant sacrifices are offered to you.
> When the goddess arrives, from her ears hang beautiful sonorous pendants; in her carriage preceded by the clouds which serve as banners, before her the mists. In an instant she mounts into the skies, whence looking down upon the Earth, she blesses her people, who live happily in peace bestowed by the goddess. The waves of the oceans are calm, the universe lives in prosperity. May her great and miraculous beneficience resound everywhere even unto tens of thousands of years.

>> Sixth day of the fourth moon
>> of the fourteenth year of
>> Yung Lo [Yong Le]."

Rooster Crow Temple (Jiming Si)

Previous Buddhist temples of various names have existed on this site as early as the Eastern Jin and Liang Dynasties. Rooster Crow Temple (Jiming Si) was established here in 1387 by the first Ming Emperor Zhu Yuanzhang. It was later reconstructed in the Qing Dynasty during the Guang Xu reign (1875–1908). During the Cultural Revolution (1966–1976), the temple was completely burned down by a great fire in 1973. The main temple buildings were rebuilt in 1981, after which new bronze statues of Buddha and Guanyin were contributed by Thailand. It was only eight years later that the landmark seven-story **Yao Shi Ta** pagoda was reconstructed in 1989. The pagoda is named after the Yao Shi Fo Buddha. Since then, this Buddhist temple has once again become a functioning nunnery. Its tall seven-story tower, perched on top of a sharp peak, offers views of Xuan Wu Hu and Zijin Shan. This tower can be seen from many parts of the city and is a symbol of Nanjing. However, you must climb many flights of steep steps, up the hillside, and purchase a second ticket to access to the tower itself.

Another sight at Jiming Si is the **Ci Hang Qiao**, a footbridge which connects the temple with the Tai Cheng city wall, but this is normally kept closed. Inside the temple grounds, on the lower eastern slope of the hill, is the **Rouge Well** (Yanzhi Jing), where Chen Hou Zhu, the last emperor of the Chen dynasty (557–589 AD), supposedly hid with his two favorite concubines to escape the Sui conquest of the city in 589 AD.

Seen from the base of the hill, this is the Yao Shi Ta pagoda of Jiming Si that was rebuilt in 1989.

A closer view of the Yao Shi Ta pagoda of Jiming Si from a lower terrace down below.

The main entrance gate to the Chao Tian Gong.

The temple entrance is on Jiming Si Lu, just before the Jie Fang Men and Tai Cheng. It can be reached by turning off Bei Jing Dong Lu onto Shi Zeng Fu Lu, which crosses He Ping Lu and becomes Jiming Si Lu.

Address: 1 Jiming Si Lu
Phone: 8360-0842

Confucius Temple (Fuzi Miao)

This has been the site of a Confucius temple ever since the year 1034 in the Ren Zong reign (1022–1063) of the Northern Song Dynasty (960–1126). However, in the Qing Dynasty, the previous temple buildings were destroyed when the Taiping rebels occupied the city from 1853–1864. The temple was rebuilt by the resident Viceroy of Liangjiang, **Zeng Guofan**, in 1869. This restored temple survived until it was completely burned down by the Japanese during their 1937–1945 occupation of the city. The current temple and surrounding shopping district were constructed in faux Ming-Qing style beginning in 1984. The three-story **Wen Xing Ge** pavilion, standing in a bend of the

A stretch of the Qin Huai He city moat near Fuzi Miao.

The center of the Fuzi Miao area, bisected by the Qin Huai He city moat, with the three-story Wen Xing Ge pavilion on the left.

Qinhuai River across the plaza from the Fuzi Miao, is where the scholar with the highest examination score would be honored by making a public appearance from the top floor. It is not clear whether this is the original pavilion dating from 1869 or a 1984 reproduction, but its presence gives the area a look exactly identical with photos taken in the 1930s. The area now has the same fake Disneyland quality as the Fang Bang Zhong Lu area of Shanghai. For a look at a real Confucius Temple, a visit to Chaotian Gong is a much more rewarding experience.

Although the name Fuzi Miao means Confucius Temple, it is usually used to describe the entire shopping district surrounding the temple. During the Qing Dynasty, the section of the Qinhuai River which runs past the temple was the place where pleasure boats carried important officials and merchants who were holding secret meetings or having rendezvous with high class prostitutes. The age-old tradition of the Qinhuai River serving as a pleasure ground full of sing-song girls started as far back as the Ming Dynasty and continued right up to the Japanese occupation of December 1937. The pleasure boats of the Qinhuai River have been well described by the Qing Dynasty author Wu Wo-yao in his book, *Vignettes from the Late Chi'ing: Bizarre Happenings Eyewitnessed Over Two Decades.*

A stone foot bridge over the Qin Huai He city moat in the Fuzi Miao area.

Phone: 8662-8639

Chaotian Palace (Chaotian Gong)

Located in a large rectangular space between Mochou Lu, Jian Ye Lu, and Wang Fu Lu, this was formerly the site of a Ming palace built by Emperor Zhu Yuanzhang in 1384. The only authentic structures left are those of a Confucius Temple, which itself is a Qing Dynasty restoration dating from the reign of Emperor Tongzhi (1862–1874). Many new Ming-style buildings are currently being thrown up in the area surrounding the Qing-era palace. Nonetheless, the Chaotian Gong Confucius Temple is still quite impressive, much more so than the other Confucius Temple at Fuzi Miao, which was only constructed in 1984.

The Chaotian Gong Confucius Temple covers a large site, consisting of four courtyards and three main buildings, all within a walled compound. Several of the buildings now house historical exhibits of the Nanjing Municipal Museum. The first two courtyards, where entry is free, contain lively outdoor market bazaars where peddlers sell antiques, arts and crafts, and old books. The first courtyard contains the Crescent Pool, while the second contains a statue of Confucius and is entered by passing through the Lin Xin Men.

Buy a ticket at Da Cheng Men and walk through the third courtyard to Da Cheng Gong palace, which is a two-story building now devoted to exhibits of historical relics from the Six Dynasties period of Nanjing's history. From Da Cheng Gong palace, you can walk into the fourth courtyard and on into the Chong Sheng Gong palace, which currently exhibits a ghoulish mummified corpse. Facing Chong Sheng Gong palace, to the left of the fourth courtyard, is a new building housing one floor of relics from the Ming Dynasty era of Nanjing's history. Two English language brochures are available for 10 Rmb each. Costume performances of Ming court ceremonies are occasionally held in the third courtyard.

Phone: 8446-5317
Tickets: 15 Rmb

Top: A small pavilion on the grounds of the Chao Tian Gong.
Above: A recently rebuilt pavilion on the grounds of the Chao Tian Gong.

An ancient golden belt on display in the Chao Tian Gong museum.

Nanjing Mosque (Nanjing Qingzhen Si)

Located at the intersection of Taiping Nan Lu and Xiao Huo Wa Xiang, this mosque is near the park and museum named for the famous Admiral Zheng He, who was also a Muslim. Nanjing Mosque is fully functioning and services are held every Friday. The building is inside a series of Qing Dynasty buildings with several courtyards, all surrounded by a wall. Enter through a gate from Taiping Nan Lu. There is no price of admission and the gatekeeper is happy to show visitors around.

Address: Taiping Nan Lu and Xiao Huo Wa Xiang
Phone: 5220-0115

Entrance gate to the Nanjing mosque (Qingzhen Si).

Churches

Nanjing Catholic Church (Nanjing Tian Zhu Jiao Tang)

Address: 112 Shi Gu Lu
Phone: 8470-4129

Nanjing Protestant Church (Nanjing Jiao Tang)

Address: 388 Mo Chou Lu
Phone: 8446-9257

St. Paul's Church

Address: 396 Taiping Nan Lu
Phone: 8664-7225

Military Controlled Areas

Unlike Shanghai, where the municipal police seem to be in charge and you rarely see soldiers on the streets, Nanjing is much more under the control of the military. Green army jeeps are frequently seen driving up and down the city streets while green uniformed army soldiers can be found walking on every street and sitting in every restaurant. This close contact with the soldiers does require some added tact, caution, and politeness. It is possible that one of them may cover your camera lense with their hand and ask you not to take a picture of something he thinks is unflattering or confidential.

Most of all, you need to be aware that numerous buildings, compounds, and even whole neighborhoods in the city, are restricted to Chinese military personnel and communist party officials only. As such, it is forbidden for foreigners to enter. This can be frustrating, as the army seems to have intentionally taken over many of the most impressive historic pre-1949 buildings lining the main streets of Zhongshan Dong Lu, Zhongshan Bei

Lu, Zhongyang Lu, and Beijing Dong Lu. Walking down the street, you can often just catch a glimpse of some fascinating traditional Chinese style buildings hidden behind a high wall and large ornamental gateway. However, at the gate will be some green uniformed soldiers and sometimes an English language sign stating "Military Controlled Area." Don't try to go inside the gate. You will get into trouble. Here are some specific examples of off-limits areas:

List of Military Controlled Areas
Nanjing Municipal Government
This is located in a large walled compound just below the Rooster Crows Buddhist Temple (Jiming Si) and beside Beijing Dong Lu, across the street from He Ping Park. The area is like an enormous campus, full of lush, green gardens and huge 1930s-era Chinese-style buildings, all inside a high yellow wall with several colorful ornamental gates. The existing buildings, built between 1930 and 1934, served as the **Examination Yuan** (Kaoshi Yuan) when Nanjing was the Guomindang national capital. Prior to that it was the site of the Qing Dynasty **War God Temple** (Guandi Miao) built by Zeng Guofan. It is a tempting sight to explore, but uniformed soldiers at the gates will tell you not to come in.

Address: 43 He Ping Lu

Second National History Archives
(Zhongguo Di Er Lishi Dang An Guan)
Before 1949, this was the Guomindang Historical Relics Exhibition Building and offices of the Guomindang Party History Compilation Committee. Now this is China's second most important national archives facility, with the first located in Beijing. Important historical documents dating back to the Ming Dynasty are kept here. Soldiers armed with rifles at the gates seem to be rather paranoid about anyone lingering outside the fence to admire the building's beautiful architecture and may be a trigger-happy. You can try calling ahead for an appointment.

Address: 309 Zhongshan Dong Lu
Phone: 8480-9328

Entrance gate to the China Second National History Archives (Zhongguo Di Er Lishi Dang An Guan).

Military History Archives (Jun Shi Dang An Guan)

This is a block east of the Second History Archives and the former Ming Palace (Ming Gu Gong), on the north side of Zhongshan Dong Lu. It is clearly labeled as a Military Controlled Area and protected by armed soldiers.

Address: 311 Zhongshan Dong Lu

Side view of the original main hall of China Second National History Archives (Zhongguo Di Er Lishi Dang An Guan).

He Ping Men (Shen Ce Men)

One of the four surviving original Ming Dynasty city gates still stands off Zhongyang Lu. However, it is now inside a military compound.

The Former Presidential Palace (Tushuo Zongtongfu)

The main gate is now open to visitors. Unfortunately, west of this gate is a military base occupying part of the Presidential Palace (Tushuo Zongtongfu) compound.

Address: 288 Changjiang Lu

The Former Foreign Ministry

Located at the intersection of Zhongshan Bei Lu and Yunnan Lu, with the back side facing Hubei Lu.

The Former Railway Ministry

Address: 252 Zhongshan Bei Lu

The Former Communications Ministry

Address: 303-305 Zhongshan Bei Lu

Entrance gate to the PLA Military Archives (Junshi Dang An Guan).

The Former Jiangsu Provincial Assembly (Jiangsu Zi Yi Ju).

Address: Intersection of Hunan Lu and Yunnan Lu

Sights on Zijin Shan (Purple Gold Mountain)
Ming Tombs (Ming Xiao Ling)

The tomb of the first Ming Dynasty Emperor Zhu Yuanzhang took 100,000 workers 32 years to complete, starting in 1381 and finishing in 1413. It is located on the southern slope of Zijin Shan. The wall surrounding the tomb itself is 22.5 km (14 miles) long. The approach to the tomb formed a long winding "S" shape, rather than the straight lines often found at previous tombs. Modern day visitors often miss much of the original **Sacred Way**

(Shen Dao) leading to the tomb because Ming Ling Lu has been built directly to the gate of the tomb itself.

In fact, the original Sacred Way started far from the tomb, near the town of Weigang which now sits on the Nanjing-Shanghai highway. At Weigang, you can still find the **Xia Ma Men**, a stone gate which is engraved with the instructions, "Get down from your horses." This was the place where all horseback riders were supposed to dismount, in respect to the emperor, and walk the remainder of the way to the tomb. In 2003, Xia Ma Men was restored at a cost of 3 million Rmb (USD360,000).

A long distance separates Xia Ma Men from the next site on the Sacred Way, the **Grand Gold Gate** (Da Jing Men), which sits on Zhongshan Ling Lu. Across the road from Da Jing Men is the **Square City** (Si Fang Cheng). This is a square, roofless pavilion, with arched gateways in each of its four walls. In the middle stands a stele mounted on the back of a turtle. On one side of the stele is an inscription, carved by the sailors of the U.S. naval

Stone animal statues line the Sacred Way (Shen Dao) leading to the Ming Tombs (Ming Xiao Ling.)

Map labels

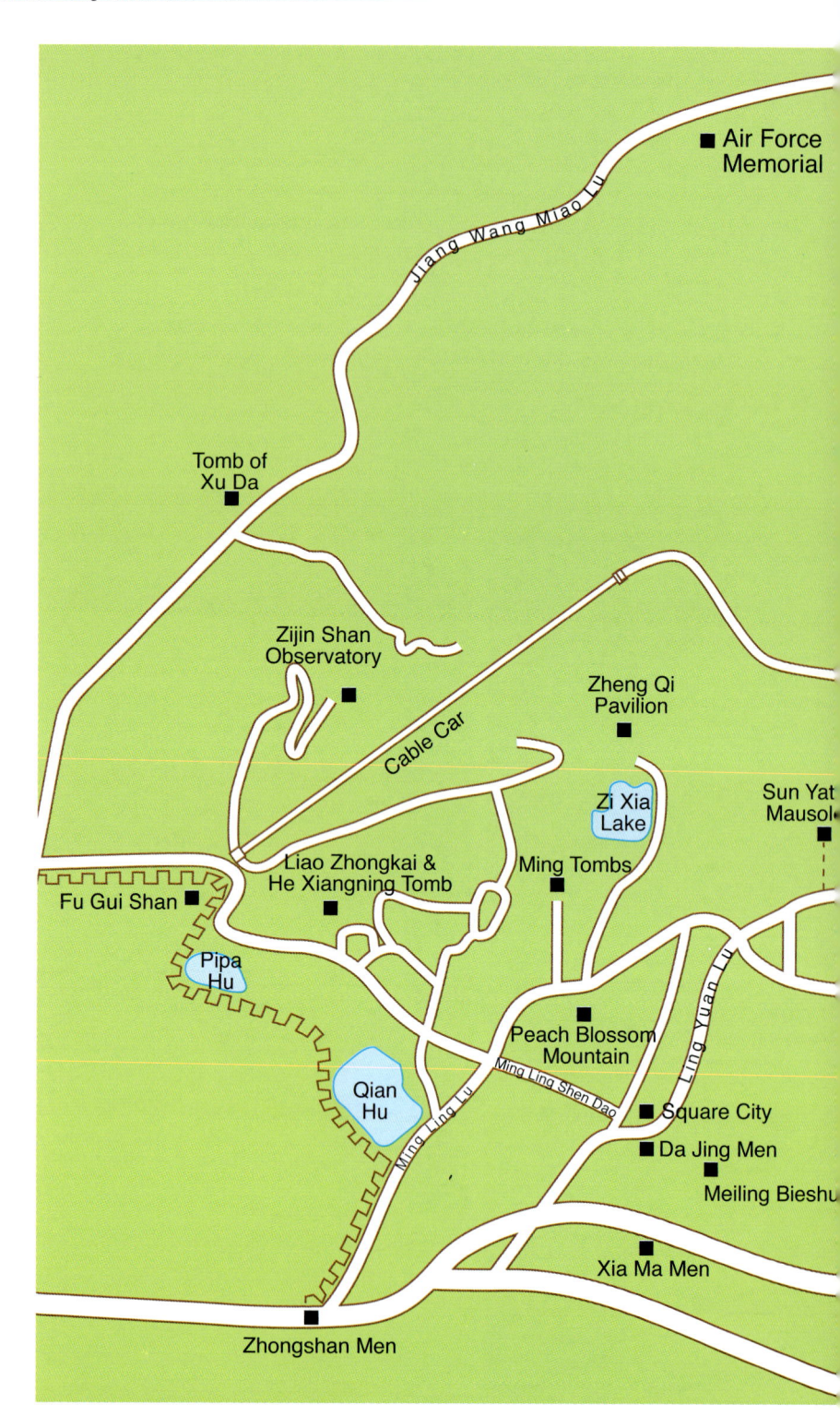

- Air Force Memorial
- Jiang Wang Miao Lu
- Tomb of Xu Da
- Zijin Shan Observatory
- Cable Car
- Zheng Qi Pavilion
- Zi Xia Lake
- Sun Yat Mausol[eum]
- Fu Gui Shan
- Liao Zhongkai & He Xiangning Tomb
- Ming Tombs
- Pipa Hu
- Ling Yuan Lu
- Peach Blossom Mountain
- Qian Hu
- Ming Ling Lu
- Ming Ling Shen Dao
- Square City
- Da Jing Men
- Meiling Bieshu
- Xia Ma Men
- Zhongshan Men

Jiangsu Province: Nanjing 125

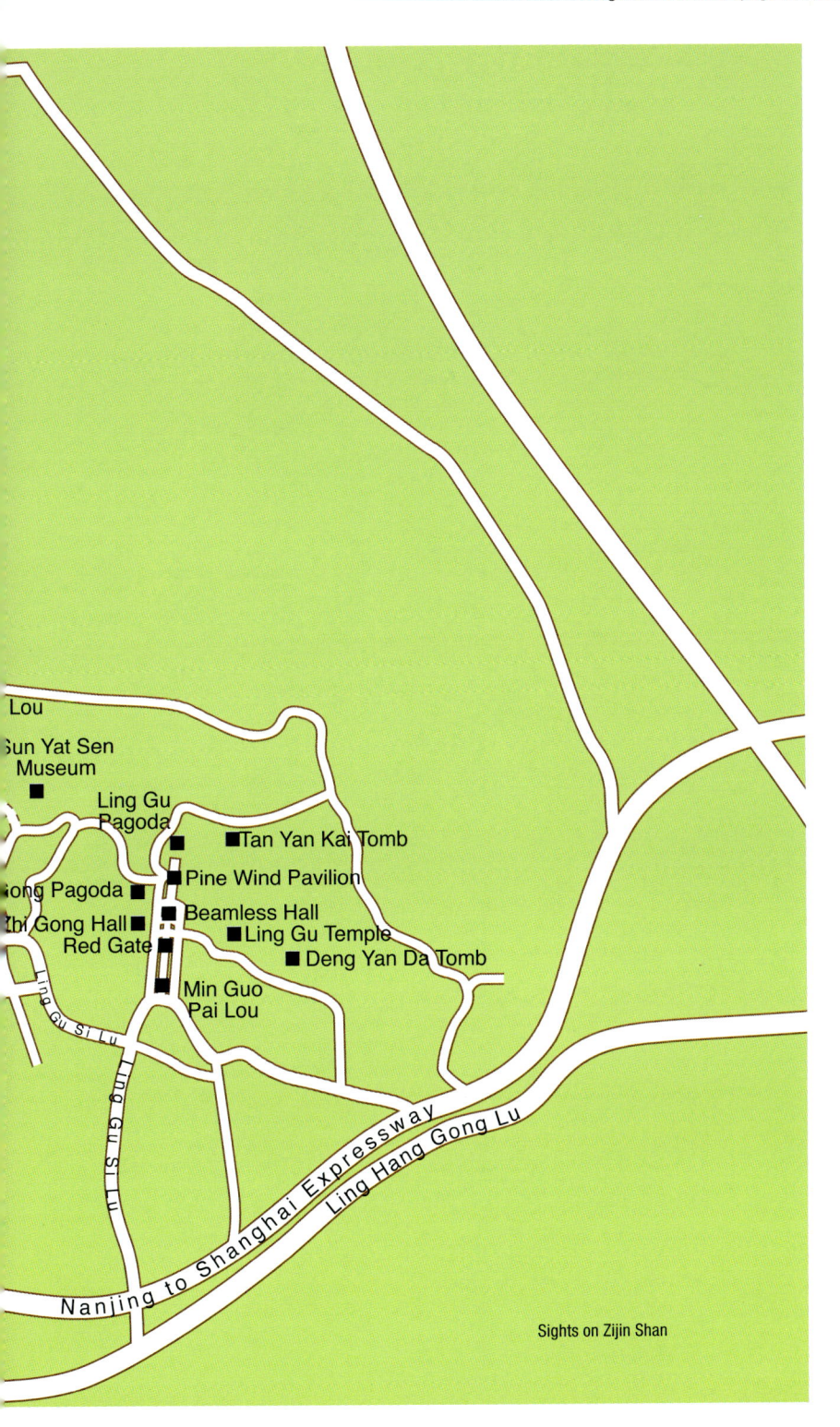

Lou
Sun Yat Sen Museum
Ling Gu Pagoda
Tan Yan Kai Tomb
Pine Wind Pavilion
Gong Pagoda
Beamless Hall
Zhi Gong Hall
Ling Gu Temple
Red Gate
Deng Yan Da Tomb
Min Guo Pai Lou

Ling Gu Si Lu
Ling Gu Si Lu

Nanjing to Shanghai Expressway
Ling Hang Gong Lu

Sights on Zijin Shan

POINT OF INTEREST

One of the most fascinating events in the history of the Ming Tombs happened on 15 February 1912, three days after the abdication of the Manchus. The provisional President of the new Republic of China, Sun Yat Sen (Sun Zhongshan) took the leading role in a ceremony of sacrifice, kowtow, and prayer before the ancestral tablet of Zhu Yuanzhang (Hong Wu), thus paying homage to one who had driven out alien rulers and founded a Chinese dynasty. The following are excerpts from President Sun's speech given on that day:

"Of old, the Song dynasty became effete, and the Liao Tartars and Yuan Dynasty Mongols seized the occasion to throw this domain of China into confusion … It was then that Your Majesty, our founder, arose in your wrath from obscurity and destroyed those monsters of iniquity, so that the ancient glory was won again … Often in history has our noble Chinese race been enslaved by petty frontier barbarians from the North. Never have such glorious triumphs been won over them as Your Majesty achieved.

"But your descendants were degenerate and failed to carry on your glorious heritage; they entrusted the reigns of government to bad men, and pursued a short-sighted policy. In this way they encouraged the ambitions of the Eastern Tartar savages, and fostered the growth of their power. They were thus able to take advantage of the presence of rebels to invade and possess themselves of your sacred capital.

"From a bad eminence of glory basely won, they lorded it over this most holy soil, and our beloved China's rivers and hills were defiled by their corrupt touch … As time went on, the law became ever harsher … The Manchu despotism became so thorough and so embracing that they were enabled to prolong their dynasty's existence by cunning wiles.

"Even so, rebellions occurred … Although these worthy causes were destined to ultimate defeat, the gradual trend of the national will became manifest. At last our era dawned, the son of freedom had risen, and a sense of the rights of the race animated men's minds … Then did patriots arise like a whirlwind or like a cloud which is suddenly manifested in the firmament … An earthquake shook the barbarian court of Peking, and it was smitten with paralysis.

"Today it has at last restored the Government to the Chinese people, and the five races of China may dwell together in peace and mutual trust. Let us joyfully give thanks.

"How could we have attained this measure of victory had not Your Majesty's soul in heaven bestowed upon us your protecting influence? … I have heard that in the past many would-be-deliverers of their country have ascended this lofty mound wherein is your sepulcher. It has served them as a holy inspiration. As they looked down upon the surrounding rivers and upwards to the hills, under an alien sway, they wept in bitterness of their hearts, but today their sorrow is turned into joy. The spiritual influences of your grave at Nanking have become once more into their own. The dragon crouches in majesty as of old, and the tiger surveys his domain and his ancient capital. Everywhere a beautiful repose doth reign. Your legions line the approaches to the sepulcher; a noble host stands expectant. Your people have come here today to inform Your Majesty of the final victory."

ship Palos which was part of the Yangzi Patrol, denoting the name of their vessel and the date "December 1904". Up to this point, no tickets are required.

A few steps away from Si Fang Cheng is **Shi Xiang Lu**, the section of the Sacred Way which contains twelve pairs of stone statues of six different species of animals, both real and mythical. A separate ticket is required to enter the stone animals walkway. This is a pedestrian walkway which passes through a beautiful garden which vehicles cannot enter.

The next section of the Sacred Way sits in the middle of a traffic strip dividing the two lanes of Weng Zhong Lu. This section is free and begins with two large round stone pillars known as **Hua Biao**. Following this are stone statues of four civil officials and four generals. The statues are much larger than life-sized, and contain an amazing amount of detail, right down to their hairstyles and clothing.

Continuing on up Weng Zhong Lu, you reach the main gate, **Ling Xing Men**. Here, three parallel stone-arched bridges known as the **Jing Shui Qiao** cross over a small stream. Another ticket purchase is needed to enter this walled area of the mausoleum. Follow the straight brick-paved avenue lined with cedar trees on both sides and you will eventually reach the first **Outer Wall** and its five gates known as the **Weng Wu Men**.

Pass through the Weng Wu Men to reach the **Stele Pavilion** (Bei Dian) containing five stone stele, including one engraved by Qing Emperor Kang Xi in 1699. A plaque, posted by the Qing government in 1909 on the outside of the building, commands the preservation of the tomb. These commands are in six foreign languages (Japanese, German, Italian, English, French, and Russian).

Next comes the **Sacrificial Hall** (Xiao Ling Dian). The original was constructed in 1383, but was destroyed during the Taiping Rebellion of 1851–1861. This Qing reconstruction was built in 1873, and is a much smaller one than the original. It sits on top of a raised rectangular flat platform with several tiers. The stone base of this platform and its tiers are decorated with the remains of

This page, top: Stone turtle stele stands inside the walled enclosure of the Square City (Si Fang Cheng) on the Sacred Way (Shen Dao) leading to the Ming Tombs (Ming Xiao Ling.)
This page, center: Graffiti left behind by sailors from an American gunboat in 1904 is still clearly legible on the Stone turtle stele inside the Square City (Si Fang Cheng).
This page, bottom: One of two stone soldiers guarding the approach to the Ming Tombs along the Sacred Way.

protruding stone animal heads resembling alligators. In fact they represent a legendary animal, the Lishou, which was a particular Ming symbol. The piles of loose broken stones in this area attest to the decay of the site's previous grandeur.

Continuing on up the long tree-lined avenue, you reach the **Inner Wall**, which is painted red and has a single gate. Passing through this **Inner Red Gate**, the avenue continues until you cross a large stone arched bridge known as the **Da Shi Qiao** and reach the giant rectangular **Ming Tower** (Ming Lou). A tunnel cuts through the center of the building at an inclined angle and emerges on back side, from where two flights of steps ascend to the top of the tower. Four walls are all that remain of the building that once stood there. From the top, you have a view of the whole approach.

Behind the Ming tower sits the **Treasure Mound** (Bao Cheng). Inside this large man-made circular mound are the unexcavated tombs of the first Ming Emperor, and his wife, Empress Ma, his eldest son who died before he could inherit the throne, and countless concubines. Passing through a gate in a chainlink fence behind the Ming Tower, you can follow a steep dirt trail that ascends to the top of the treasure mound. From the summit, you can see that it is really the size of a small mountain, descending sharply on all sides. At the foot of the mound, just visible through thick trees, is yet another ancient brick wall which encircles it and connects to the separate red brick Inner Wall.

To reach the Ming Tombs, take either Ming Ling Lu and Weng Zhong Lu from Zhongshan Men to the main gate of the mausoluem, or take Zhongshan Ling Yuan Lu from Ling Hang Gong Lu, near Weigang village, to see the whole Sacred Way from its starting point.

The Inner Red Gate on the foot path to the Ming Tombs.

Horizontal stone alligator statues protrude by the hundreds from the stone foundations of the Sacrificial Hall (Xiao Ling Dian) of the Ming Tombs.

The Jing Shui Qiao bridges now mark the beginning of the walk to the Ming Tombs, with the Weng Wu Men gate visible in the distance.

Lush public gardens on Zijin Shan at the foot of Plum Blossom Hill (Mei Hua Shan).

The Ming Tower (Ming Lou) at the foot of the Ming Tombs' Treasure Mound (Bao Cheng).

Like Zhongshan Ling, Ming Xiao Ling is wide open, uncrowded, unguarded, and open even at night. However, one difference between the two is that Ming Xiao Ling is not lighted at night so it is advisable to bring a flashlight. After dark, the place has an air of romance and mystery.

Disreputable tour guides often tell foreign tourists that there is nothing worth seeing at the Ming Tombs, only because there are no souvenir shops there for them to earn sales commissions from. Don't believe them. In July 2003, UNESCO added Ming Xiao Ling to its list of World Heritage sites, along with the Ming Tombs outside Beijing.

Address: Weng Zhong Lu
Tickets: 10 Rmb

Peach Blossom Hill (Tao Hua Shan)

This was supposedly the site of the Wu King Sun Quan's tomb, and the reason for the circuitous roundabout route taken by the Sacred Way to Ming Xiao Ling. The summit has a view of Zhongshan Ling's main hall with its blue-tiled roof. Wang Jingwei, the Japanese collaborator and former heir apparent to Sun Yat Sen (Sun Zhongshan), had his tomb placed at the summit of Peach Blossom Hill during the Japanese occupation. However, his tomb was "blown up" by the returning Guomindang in January 1946. It was replaced with the existing pavilion built by Sun Ke in 1947, as he was then the administrator of Zhongshan Ling park. Entrance is included in admission to Ming Xiao Ling.

A view of Zhongshan Men city gate from inside the city wall.

Zi Xia Lake (Zi Xia Hu)

A beautiful lake located between Ming Xiao Ling and Zhongshan Ling at the end of long forested stone paved road. Take a walk around the lakeshore and watch people swimming and fishing. On a sunny day, the place has a summer camp feel to it. You must buy a 10 Rmb ticket at the gate on Weng Zhong Lu, but the same 10 Rmb Ming Xiao Ling ticket will get you in here as well.

Zheng Qi Pavilion (Zheng Qi Ting)

This is the site Chiang Kai Shek (Jiang Jieshi) chose for his tomb in November 1946, but was never able to enjoy due to his flight to Taiwan three years later. The size of the man's ego is

Left: The crystal clear waters of Zi Xia Hu on Zijin Shan.
Right: A stone foot bridge crosses a small tributary stream flowing into Zi Xia Hu on Zijin Shan.

Left: A rustic log cabin stands beside the shores of Zi Xia Hu on Zijin Shan.
Right: A flowing mountain stream near Zi Xia Hu on Zijin Shan.

evident in the fact that he expected to be buried between the first Ming emperor and the founding father of modern China. The Pavilion is inscribed both by Chiang and Sun Ke, and a single Guomindang symbol adorns the center of the ceiling. Although it has been allowed to stand, the monument is not well maintained. The blue-tiled roof has been vandalized, with broken shards littering the ground, the paint is peeling, and plants grow on the roof. The pavilion sits at the end of a long, steep foot trail which climbs up from the back side of Zi Xia Hu.

Sun Yat Sen Mausoleum (Sun Zhongshan Ling)

Although Sun Yat Sen (Sun Zhongshan) died in Beijing in 1925 and his body was temporarily laid to rest in the White Cloud Temple there, his wish had always been to be buried on Zijin Shan in Nanjing.

A visit to the tomb today begins by ascending a short flight of steps to the bright white granite archway with three gates. Over the center gate is inscribed the two characters for **Universal Love**. Pass through this gate and walk up a 480-m-long (1,574.8-ft-long) tree-lined avenue and ascend two flights of steps before reaching the first terrace with its granite **Mausoleum Gate** (Ling Men), which has three arched doorways. Inscribed over the center door are the four characters variously translated as "All for the nation," "Serving the public under heaven," or "The world belongs to the public."

The inside ceiling of the Zheng Qi Ting pavilion is still painted with the Guomindang symbol.

The Zheng Qi Ting pavilion near Zi Xia Hu marks the spot chosen by Chiang Kai Shek (Jiang Jieshi) for his mausoleum.

After passing through the Masoleum Gate, ascend two more flights of steps and reach the second terrace with its **Tablet Pavilion** (Bei Ting), inside which is a stone stele engraved with the words, "the Guomindang party buries its prime minister Sun Yat Sen (Sun Zhongshan) here on 1 June 1929."

From the Tablet Pavilion, ascend eight more flights of steep steps to the third terrace and its **Ceremonial Hall** (Ji Tang), behind which is the tomb chamber itself. Above the three arched doorways of the Ceremonial Hall is engraved the characters for the Three People's Principles (San Ming Zhu Yi) of Nationalism

The Tablet Pavilion (Bei Ting) on the steps leading up to the Sun Yat Sen Mausoleum (Zhongshan Ling).

(*minzu*), Democracy (*minzhu*) and People's Livelihood (*minsheng*), which were the core of Sun's ideology.

Ascend the final short flight of steps leading into the Cermemonial Hall and you will see a white marble statue of a seated Sun Yat Sen (Sun Zhongshan). At the base of the statue

POINT OF INTEREST

The site for Sun Yat Sen's (Sun Zhongshan's) tomb was selected by his wife, Song Qingling, on 21 April 1925. The design chosen for the tomb was drafted by Lu Yan Zhi (1894–1929), an American-trained architect who graduated from Cornell University in 1918 and was a former assistant to the American architect Henry K. Murphy. Construction of Sun's tomb started on 15 January 1926 and most of it had been completed by the spring of 1929. However, some finishing touches continued to be made until January 1932, including the white marble seated statue of Sun now seen in the Ceremonial Hall.

Unable to wait for the tomb's final completion, on 28 May 1929, the Guomindang had Sun's body shipped to Nanjing on a special ceremonial train from Beijing. Arriving at Pukou railway station on the North bank of the Yangzi River, the body was then sent across the river to Xiaguan on board the Chinese warship Wei Sheng. From Xiaguan, it then travelled through the city along the newly constructed system of roads and city gates named after him. The body started on Zhongshan Bei Lu and travelled to Gu Lou, then to Xin Jie Kou along Zhongshan Lu. From there it passed through Zhongshan Men along Zhongshan Dong Lu, and then up the southern slopes of Zijin Shan where the nearly completed tomb awaited.

The funeral service held on 1 June 1929 was an official state ceremony attended by diplomatic representatives of all the major foreign powers and all the Guomindang party and government officials. Song Qingling returned from her self-imposed exile overseas and joined the funeral procession, accompanied by Chiang Kai Shek (Jiang Jieshi), despite her intense opposition to his leadership of the Guomindang party. Journalists, newsreel cameramen, and photographers from around the world recorded the event for posterity, flashing news reports of the procession to a global audience. This funeral ceremony served as a major opportunity for the Nanjing regime to establish its legitimacy as the central government of China. Having started its reign just two years earlier by outraging Western governments with the massacres of foreigners in Nanjing in March 1927, and then alienating many Chinese with the massacre of workers in Shanghai in April 1927, the positive publicity generated by this event was worth any price.

POINT OF INTEREST

In fact, Sun's tomb continued to play a role of great political significance for all succeeding Chinese regimes. Chiang (Jiang) is said to have paid a tearful farewell to the tomb just before he evacuated the government from Nanjing to Wuhan in December 1937. Even during the Japanese occupation, the tomb was well cared for because the puppet collaborationist regime of Wang Jingwei also sought to use its legitimacy for their own rule. After the Guomindang central government returned to Nanjing at the end of the 1937–1945 Sino-Japanese War, a massive ceremonial procession was held at Zhongshan Ling on 5 May 1946, attended by the entire civil and military leadership of the Guomindang regime. When Chiang (Jiang) left Nanjing for the last time, just before it fell to the Communists in May 1949, he apparently paid one final solemn visit to Sun's tomb on his way.

After the 1949 Revolution, Sun's tomb continued to be shown to visiting delegations of foreign diplomats by Communist Party officials, as can be seen from the photo exhibits at the nearby Sun Zhongshan Museum in the Cang Jing Lou. Since the death of Mao Zedong in 1976, Sun has largely replaced him in the current regime's ideology as the officially recognized founding father of modern China, and as such his tomb has experienced a huge resurgence in popularity with Chinese visitors.

---

is chiseled "P. Landowski, Paris, 1931," denoting who, where, and when the statue was made. This statue, which now dominates the hall, had not actually been completed in time for the 1 June 1929 funeral, and was added later. On the east and west walls of the hall is engraved the complete text of Sun's book, *Outline of National Reconstruction* (*Jian Guo Da Gong*). If you look up at the ceiling over this statue, you will see a giant blue and white Guomindang flag painted on the ceiling, still in immaculate condition.

At the back of the room is a small doorway which leads into the **Tomb Chamber** (Mushi Liceng). Between 1929 and 1949, this chamber was only open to the public once a week on Sundays. Now, it can be entered at any time. This is a circular room with a dome over the top. In the center of the room lies a white marble

The Universal Love gate marking the start of the long climb up to the Sun Yat Sen Mausoleum (Zhongshan Ling).

statue of Sun Yat Sen (Sun Zhongshan) in a reclining position. Below this lies his coffin. Look up again and see another immaculate blue and white Guomindang flag painted on the ceiling of the dome overhead. The Mausoleum Gate, Tablet Pavilion, and Ceremonial Hall are all decorated with the Guomindang party colors and feature bright blue roofs with white walls.

Exit the Ceremonial Hall. Walk to your right, around the outside of the building, and you can visit the back of the domed Tomb Chamber which is known as the **Tomb Fort** (Mushi Waiceng). Here, there is usually an outdoor display of photographs showing the construction process and design of the tomb.

The full distance from the Gate of Universal Love to the Ceremonial Hall is 700 m (2,296.6 ft). There are a total of 14 flights of 392 stone steps. The perimeter of the entire site was originally meant to take the shape of a giant bell, symbolic of Sun himself as the human alarm bell, and his own *nom d' guerre* of "Zhongshan" meaning "Bell Mountain." Unfortunately, the growth of fir trees that have been planted since then obscures this.

The view from the top is spectacular in the daytime. However, a visit at night is worthwhile because of the floodlights which shine on the mausoluem. Also, after dark the crowds are gone and admission is free. Daytime visits require a 20 Rmb ticket.

The effigy of Sun Yat Sen (Sun Zhongshan) lies in state over the coffin bearing his actual remains inside the Tomb Chamber (Mu Shi Li Ceng).

Sun Yat Sen Museum (Sun Zhongshan Ji Nian Guan)

Located inside the Buddhist Scripture Hall (Cang Jing Lou) is an important museum devoted to Sun Yat Sen (Sun Zhongshan). The building was first constructed from 1935–1936, and completely renovated in 1982. It sits in between Zhongshan Ling and Ling Gu Si on a separate narrow mountain road which forms a loop off Ling Gu Si Lu. The museum has a photo exhibition depicting the construction of Zhongshan Ling, as well as famous visitors to the mausoleum over the years. A film of Sun's elaborate 1929 funeral ceremony is shown continuously. There is an excellent book shop which sells a VCD of the film.

Phone: 8443-2799
Tickets 5 Rmb

Sun Ke Lou

The home of Sun Ke — the son of Sun Yat Sen (Sun Zhongshan) — this is sometimes known as the Yi Zhen or Ying Qiao Pavilion. This is now a ruin of broken stone walls. It sits right next to the Yong Mu Lou, outside of its enclosing wall.

Yong Mu Lou

This is the house where Sun Ke and Song Chingling stayed during their 1929 period of mourning, immediately after Sun Yat Sen's (Sun Zhongshan's) funeral. Sun Ke Lou and Yong Mu Lou can both be reached by a stone paved road from Ling Gu Ta. It can also be approached by a steep stone-paved trail that ascends the hillside, starting from the road to Zhongshan Bowuguan, across the road from a small restaurant. The trail is not marked by any sign. An old couple now live at Yong Mu Lou, and they sell drinks and snacks to passers-by. This is the only such place to find refreshment this high up on the mountain.

The Sun Yat Sen Memorial Hall (Sun Zhongshan Ji Nian Guan) also known as the Buddhist Scripture Hall (Cang Jing Lou) because of its original intended purpose.

Spirit Valley Park (Ling Gu Gongyuan)

The admission ticket to this park will grant entry to an array of historic sites. The memorial archway (*pai fang*) at the entrance to the park is remarkable for its five blue-and-white Guomindang symbols, mounted over the top of each of its five gates.

Beamless Hall (Wu Liang Dian)

When the Danish architect Johannes Prip-Moller first visited Nanjing's Spirit Valley (Ling Gu) in August 1929, the Beamless Hall (Wu Liang Dian) was a roofless ruin with grass growing inside its still erect brick walls. At that time, the ruins stood along the central axis of an earlier incarnation of the Ling Gu Buddhist Temple (Ling Gu Si). This row of temple halls started with a Heng Ha Dian, followed by a Tian Wang Dian, and then a Da Xiong Bao Dian, before reaching the Wu Liang Dian. Behind the Wu Liang Dian lay "the remains of what was formerly a pagoda erected over the Buddhist saint Chih Kung of Liang Dynasty…" The entire temple was in a dilapidated state, having never fully recovered from damage inflicted during the Taiping Rebellion. Before the Rebellion, it was estimated that 1,000 monks had lived there, but in 1929, their numbers had been reduced to "half a score." A map from the temple history (Ling Gu Si Zhi) published by Prip-Moller in 1937 shows that it also once had a Pi Lu Dian and Guan Yin Dian on its central axis, behind the Wu Liang Dian, but neither of these were still standing when he visited in 1929.

The Beamless Hall structure was remarkable for having been built with no nails and no wooden beams. The ceiling was originally made of bricks, forming a rounded vault over the walls. More than a million bricks went into building the original structure. It was 50.3 m (165 ft) long, 33.5 m (110 ft) wide, and the central vaulted ceiling of large bricks was 15.8 m (52 ft) high.

In 1398, a visitor recorded the following description of the hall, "The Wu Liang Dian is entirely made of brick, no wood is employed. It consists of three big vaults, no wood employed for making beams … The way in which this hall is built is mostly from the time of Liang Wu Di (502–549 AD), although a thorough repair was made in this dynasty (Ming)…" Although the hall's exact date of construction remains an unsolved mystery, this visitor's record tells us that it was already standing in the Soul Valley when the Ling Gu Buddhist Temple (Ling Gu Si) was moved there from the present site of the Ming Tombs (Ming Xiao Ling) in 1381.

The Beamless Hall (Wu Liang Dian) of Spirit Valley Park (Ling Gu Gongyuan).

According to the Ling Gu Temple history (Ling Gu Si Zhi), part of the central vault had first collapsed back in 1832. It was repaired, but in such a way that the two side vaults would collapse later, followed by the final collapse of the central vault. Photos in Kiyoshi Uchiyama's 1910 guide to Nanjing show that the roof over the Beamless Hall had already entirely caved in by then, 19 years before Prip-Moller's 1929 visit.

By 1932, the Wu Liang Dian site had undergone considerable change, under the direction of the American architect Henry K. Murphy, as part of the Guomindang's Memorial Cemetery for Heroes of the Revolution. All other temple buildings along the central axis had been demolished. The Ling Gu Buddhist Temple (Ling Gu Si) had been moved several yards to the east, to the former site of the Dragon King Temple (Long Wang Miao), where it still stands today. To the south of the Wu Liang Dian, a memorial archway (*pai fang*) had been erected with five blue and white Guomindang symbols mounted over the top of each of its five gates. Immediately behind the north side of the Wu Liang Dian, Murphy had built the **Pine Wind Pavilion** (Song Feng Dian) and the Ling Gu Pagoda (Ling Gu Ta).

The entrance gate to Spirit Valley Park (Ling Gu Gongyuan).

The Beamless Hall (Wu Liang Dian) itself had been restored and turned into a memorial to the Guomindang military officers and soldiers who perished as members of the **National Revolutionary Army** (Guomin Geming Jun) in the **Northern Expedition** (Bei Fa) of 1926–1927. The names and ranks of all 33,224 martyrs are still listed on a stone tablet inside. Today it contains an exhibit of mannequins acting out scenes from China's revolutions.

Ling Gu Pagoda (Ling Gu Ta)

Although it looks like a typical Buddhist tower, this nine-story, 60-m (196.9-ft), octagonal structure was constructed between 1930 and 1932 as a memorial to the Guomindang officers and soldiers of the **National Revolutionary Army** (Guomin Geming Jun) who perished in the 1926-1927 **Northern Expedition** (Bei Fa). The walls inside the pagoda are inscribed with the text of two speeches given by Sun Yat Sen (Sun Zhongshan) at the Whampoa Military Academy in Guangzhou. A circular staircase inside allows you to climb all the way up to the top.

The pagoda and surrounding memorial area was designed in 1929 by the American architrect Henry K. Murphy. He consciously chose to model the Ling Gu Pagoda after the Porcelain Pagoda (Bao En Ta) that once stood outside Nanjing's southern gate but was destroyed by the Taipings.

The rows of 1,000 white tombstones which previously marked the graves of Guomindang soldiers on the round lawn outside the pagoda have been removed since 1949. This cemetey was completed in 1932 and included some of those who died in the defense of Shanghai against the Japanese invasion of that year.

A stone turtle missing its stele.

Ling Gu Buddhist Temple (Ling Gu Si)

This is a functioning Buddhist temple with a resident population of monks. The original temple was built in the 6th century at the site where the Ming Tombs (Ming Xiao Ling) now stands. When the tomb of the first Ming Emperor Zhu Yuanzhang (Hong Wu) was constructed in 1381, the temple was moved to the present site of the Beamless Hall (Wu Liang Dian). The temple buildings were severely damaged during the Taiping Rebellion and rebuilt by Zeng Guofan in 1867. In 1932, the entire Ling Gu Buddhist Temple was moved a few yards east to the former site of the Dragon King Temple (Long Wang Miao), where it now stands today, in order to make room for a new Guomindang military cemetery and memorial.

A stone turtle with its stele still intact on its back.

The Spirit Valley Pagoda (Ling Gu Ta) built in 1929

The Temple has a special hall devoted to the famous travelling Buddhist monk **Xuan Zang** (596–664 AD) from the Tang Dynasty. This hall, devoted to him, holds what is purported to be a piece of his skull, which is kept on public display in a clear wine glass sitting inside a small model pagoda. In addition to the ticket for the Ling Gu Park area, a separate ticket must be purchased to enter the temple.

Bao Gong Pagoda (Bao Gong Ta)

Both the Bao Gong Pagoda (Bao Gong Ta) and the Zhi Gong Hall (Zhi Gong Dian) are dedicated to the memory of the Liang Dynasty (502–557 AD) Buddhist monk **Bao Zhi Gong** (436–514 AD), who was a trusted advisor to Emperor Liang Wu Di (502–549 AD). Bao Zhi Gong was originally buried on the site of the Ming Tombs (Ming Xiao Ling), but his grave was moved to the Spirit Valley (Ling Gu) in 1379, when the tomb of the first Ming Emperor Hong Wu was being built.

The entrance to the modern day Spirit Valley Buddhist Temple (Ling Gu Si).

The Bao Gong Pagoda (Bao Gong Ta) has been destroyed and rebuilt three different times. Johannes Prip-Moller was able to identify the site in August 1929 as being directly behind the present Beamless Hall (Wu Liang Dian). However, it is now said that the location of the previous grave site has been lost to memory and is now not known. From Prip-Moller's description, it must have been about where the Ling Gu Pagoda (Ling Gu Ta) now stands.

The current Bao Gong Pagoda (Bao Gong Ta) is a new construction dating from 1981. It no longer marks the actual grave site, and stands in a forested area a few yards west of the Beamless Hall (Wu Liang Dian). The present Bao Gong Pagoda (Bao Gong Ta) does not resemble a normal Chinese pagoda, but is more of a low, rounded, mound resembling a

Tibetan stupa. Interestingly, Prip-Moller's 1937 map of the site, copied from the Ling Gu Temple history (Ling Gu Si Zhi), shows that Bao Gong Pagoda (Bao Gong Ta) was previously a five-story pagoda.

The Three Treasures Tablet (San Bao Bei)

Before the reconstruction of the Ling Gu site in 1932, a stone tablet in honor of Bai Zhi Gong was erected in 1757, by order of the Qing Dynasty emperor, Qian Long. This, in itself, was a reproduction of a much more ancient tablet that no longer existed. This tablet was considered a special treasure for three reasons. It had a portrait of Bao Zhi Gong by the painter Wu Dao Zi, a poem about Bao by the poet Li Bai (Li Tai Po) (701–762 AD), and an inscription which was written by the calligrapher Yan Zhen Qing. All three lived during the Tang Dynasty (618–907 AD) and were then considered the most skillful craftsmen of their various trades. Unfortunately, this precious stone tablet was broken into fragments during the construction of Ling Gu Pagoda (Ling Gu Ta) and the Guomindang military cemetery. A modern copy of the tablet is now inset in the base of the Bao Zhi Ta stupa. Sadly, it is so black from the making of paper rubbings that it is almost impossible to see any of the artwork or inscriptions.

Zhi Gong Hall (Zhi Gong Dian)

A few yards south of the stupa stands the **Zhi Gong Hall** (Zhi Gong Dian), which was first built in 1934 and renovated in 1941. This hall contains two stone tablets. The first is dated 1382 and records the moving of Bao Zhi's grave from the present site of the Ming Tombs (Ming Xiao Ling) to the Spirit Valley (Ling Gu). The second is a more modern tablet that records the renovation of this hall in 1941. Visitors will need to purchase a ticket for Ling Gu Park in order to access this hall.

Guilin Stone House (Guilin Shi Lou)

This was the home of Lin Sen, built completely out of stone in 1932, at a time when Lin had reached the peak of his political career. It sits on top of a high promontory on the southern slope of Zijin Shan, west of Spirit Valley Park (Ling Gu Gongyuan), and east of the Buddhist Scripture Pavilion (Cang Jing Lou). An incredibly steep, narrow stone-paved road approaches it from either of these two directions. Approaching from both sides at impossibly steep angles, the road reaches an apex at a small plateau where cars can park. From this small plateau, 170 stone steps lead up the hillside to the house. Even more impregnable than Chiang's (Jiang's) home, this site descends downward sharply in three directions and upward sharply in the fourth.

The house was destroyed by the Japanese during their 1937–1945 occupation of Nanjing, and the walls are scarred black from the fire. The remains include the foundation, some ruined walls, and a staircase that now ascends into the air. There are also some Ming-style stone statues Lin had used to decorate his house. (Copies of some of these statues can also be seen at the Ming Tombs.) In 2000, plans were announced for the reconstruction of the house, but as of May 2001, no work had yet been done. Purchase a ticket to Ling Gu Park in order to enter this area.

The fire-scarred ruins of Lin Sen's former home, the Guilin Stone House (Gui Lin Shi Lou).

Tomb of Deng Yan Da (Deng Yan Da Mu)

Although Deng died in 1931, this monument was not constructed until 1957, after the Communists had come to power and his erstwhile nemesis Chiang (Jiang) had fled to Taiwan. The tomb is located inside Ling Gu Park and entry is included in the ticket.

Tomb of Tan Yan Kai (Tan Yan Kai Mu)

Tan Yan Kai's tomb was built on the southern slope of Zijin Shan between 1931 and 1933, using some of the original materials from the ruined Summer Palace (Yuan Ming Yuan) in Beijing. It is located inside Ling Gu Park at the end of a very long trail that ascends the forested hillside and passes through several

---

PERSONALITIES

Lin Sen (b.1864) was one of the top Guomindang party leaders during the decade when Nanjing served as the national capital from 1927 to 1937. Lin was a member of the Chinese parliament from 1912 to 1923, and in 1924 joined the Central Executive Committee of the Guomindang. When the left wing and moderate center of the Guomindang split with Chiang Kai Shek (Jiang Jieshi) in 1927, Lin Sen was initially one of the few civilian intellectual leaders who first supported the new national government in Nanjing. The paucity of civilian intellectuals supporting the new regime gave Lin Sen the opportunity to fill some very high positions in the Nanjing national government. In 1928, he joined the State Council and also became Vice-President of the Legislative Yuan, one step below President Hu Han Min, the top civilian leader in the new regime. When Hu resigned the Presidency of the Legislative Yuan in March 1931 as an act of protest against the dictatorship of Chiang Kai Shek (Jiang Jieshi), Lin Sen gladly took his place. The next year, Lin Sen was given the newly created title of President of the National Government. This was a largely honorific title since Chiang (Jiang) held all the real power, but it was one which he would continue to hold until after the regime had retreated to Chongqing.

The stone gate (pai lou) marking the start of the long trail uphill to the Tomb of Tan Yan Kai.

monumental memorial archways (*pai lou*) before reaching a very quiet, isolated spot. It makes for a nice walk and a good place for a picnic, even if the significance of the memorial escapes you. Entry to this site is included in the Ling Gu Park ticket.

PERSONALITIES

Deng Yan Da (1888–1931) was an early follower of Sun Yat Sen (Sun Zhongshan) and one of his close aides during Sun's various Guangzhou regimes. Deng had been an instructor at the Guomindang's Whampoa Military Academy established in Guangzhou in 1924. He also served as head of the National Revolutionary Army's (Guomin Geming Jun) political department during the 1926–1927 Northern Expedition (Bei Fa). However, Deng split with the commander-in-chief Chiang Kai Shek (Jiang Jieshi) in 1927 and joined the ephemeral left Guomindang regime in Wuhan. After the demise of the Wuhan regime in September 1927, Deng went into exile in the Soviet Union and Germany, returning to China in 1930. By 1931, Deng had become the leader of an opposition political group opposed to Chiang's (Jiang's) Nanjing regime. This group is sometimes referred to as the Third Party because it stood in between both the Guomindang on the right and the Communists on the left. After being arrested in Shanghai on 13 August 1931, Deng was secretly executed for treason in Nanjing on either 29 November or 16 December 1931, according to various accounts.

PERSONALITIES

Tan Yan Kai (1876–1930) was a Guomindang official with an illustrious career cut short by an early death. His political career began when he served as Military Governor of Hunan after the 1911 Revolution (Xin Hai Geming). He supported the Second Revolution in 1913, declaring independence from Beijing on 25 July, but retracted it on 13 August when the movement was clearly failing. He managed to remain Governor of Hunan until 1920, when he declared provincial autonomy from the central government in Beijing on 22 July. On 2 March 1923, he was appointed the Minister of the Interior of Sun Yat Sen's (Sun Zhongshan's) Guangzhou regime. Shortly thereafter, on 16 July, he was reappointed Governor of Hunan. On 16 January 1926, he was elected to the Guomindang Central Executive Committee by the Guomindang Second National Congress. On 10 October 1928, he was appointed President of the central government's Executive Yuan in Nanjing. On 27 March 1929, the Guomindang Third National Congress again elected him a member of the Guomindang Central Executive Committee. He died on 22 September 1930 in Nanjing.

Song Meiling Villa (Meiling Bieshu)

This is the former home of Chiang Kai Shek (Jiang Jieshi) and his third wife Song Meiling. It was built on the southern slope of Zijin Shan in 1931 and served as the official presidential residence (Xiao Hong Shan) until 1949. It was off limits to the public for decades, but since 2002, it has been open to visitors. The three-story house is decorated with period furnishings meant to show how it looked when Chiang (Jiang) lived there, including his bedroom, office, living room, and even toilet. Photos of its famous former residents grace the walls, and Chiang's (Jiang's) original car, a black Buick, is parked outside the house. A map room even displays the military situation in 1949. The whole site forms a teardrop shape, with a single long access road approaching from the west and then forming a loop around the

The abandoned Sacrificial Hall of Tan Yan Kai Mu on the trail to the tomb.

Meiling Villa, the former home of Chiang Kai Shek (Jiang Jieshi) and Song Meiling.

Below: The former car of Chiang Kai Shek (Jiang Jieshi) parked in front of Meiling Villa.
Bottom, left: The home office of Chiang Kai Shek (Jiang Jieshi) inside Meiling Villa.
Bottom, right: Another room inside Meiling Villa.

house. The hillside descends downward sharply from the loop road in three directions, allowing access from only one side, making it an eminently defensible location.

Address: No. 9 Zhongshan Ling Yuan Lu
Phone: 8443-1491

Tomb of Liao Zhong Kai and He Xiang Ning

Liao Zhong Kai (1877–1925) was a leading Guomindang official who was assassinated in Guangzhou in 1925. He was a close associate of Sun Yat Sen (Sun Zhongshan) and went into exile with him in Japan after the failure of the Second Revolution in 1913. Liao and his wife, He Xiang Ning (1879–1972), had been one of the few to attend the wedding of Sun Yat Sen (Sun Zhongshan) and Song Qingling in Tokyo in 1915.

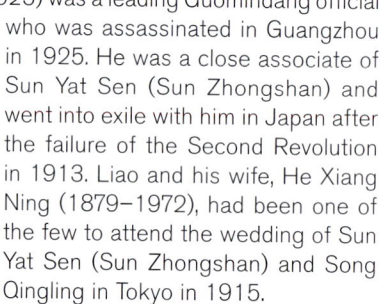

On 7 May 1923, Liao was appointed Governor of Guangdong by Sun's Guangzhou regime. He was the first political director of the Guomindang's Whampoa Military

Academy established in Guangzhou in 1924. On 1 July 1925, he was appointed the Guomindang's Minister of Finance. Sadly, he was assassinated in Guangzhou on 20 August in that same year. This tomb was built for him in 1935.

Liao's wife, was a close friend of Sun's wife, Song Qingling. He Xiang Ning served as Chair of the Guomindang Revolutionary Committee, a Communist puppet organization on the mainland, until her death in Beijing in 1972.

Zijin Shan Cable Car (Zijin Shan Suo Dao)
The cable car takes passengers up to Shan Ding Gongyuan on the highest central peak of Zijin Shan's three peaks. The top of this peak can also be reached via a stone-paved road that begins from behind Ling Gu Ta. The road ascends the ridge, traverses the third peak and then ascends the second peak. This is a very long walk so you can choose to go on foot or hire a taxi driver to take you there.

Zijin Shan Observatory (Zijin Shan Tian Wen Tai)
Built by the Guomindang between 1929 and 1932, this observatory sits on the first and lowest peak of Zijin Shan's three peaks. It can be reached by a road, built in 1930, that branches off from the bottom cable car station. You can opt for a long walk or a hired taxi ride.

The silver domes of the Zijin Shan Observatory (Tian Wen Tai) that were completed in 1932.

Some maps show the Observatory peak and Cable Car peak as being connected by a road. However, this is a dirt road that is usually blocked by closed gates, guarding the more modern observatory facilities still in use. Nonetheless, a narrow foot trail does skirt around the edge of this facility, making it possible to hike from here to a crossroads where three dirt roads lead in different directions. The one to the right is a dead end which

Left: The original stone entrance gate to the Zijin Shan Observatory (Tian Wen Tai) built in 1929. *Right*: Ming Dynasty bronze astronomical instruments on display outside the Zijin Shan Observatory.

leads down to a closed gate and brick wall guarding the boundary of Ming Xiao Ling. The road to the left descends to the site of Xu Da's Tomb (Xu Da Mu). The upper road to the right leads up to another crossroad. At this second junction, the left road heads up to the summit of Zijin Shan. The paved road to the right continues for a long distance along the ridge, past a trail which turns off to Sun Ke Lou, until eventually it descends to Ling Gu Ta and the Ling Gu Gongyuan area.

Sights to the South of the City
The Porcelain Pagoda (Bao En Ta)

Commissioned by the Ming Emperor Yong Le and built under the direct supervision of Admiral Zheng He, the famous Porcelain Pagoda is a memorial to Yong Le's mother, the Empress Ma. Once the most impressive landmark of Nanjing, it sadly no longer exists. Construction began in the tenth year of the Yong Le reign on 15 June 1412 and was not completed until 19 years later. At an estimated height of over 100 m (328.1 ft), its exterior was covered with white glazed tiles, its roof eaves with green tiles, and over 100 porcelain bells hung from the octagonal corners.

The first European visitor to see the pagoda was the Portuguese missionary Alvare de Samedo. He lived in Nanjing for three years, starting in 1613, and later published his memoirs. The next Westerner to see it was the French missionary Louis le Comte who described a visit he made to Nanjing in 1687. Finally, in 1768, the French missionary Francois Bourgeois not only visited the pagoda, but took the most detailed measurements of it ever made. According to the data collected by Bourgeois, the nine-story octagonal pagoda had a circumference of 78 m (256 ft), 3.7-m-thick (12-ft-thick) walls at the base, a total height of over 61 m (200 ft), and 198 steps from the bottom to the top floor. Above the top floor was a 9.1-m (30-ft) high pole decorated with iron rings, at the very pinnacle of which was a golden ball. The pole had eight iron chains tying it to the roof, and hanging from these chains were 72 copper bells. On the ninth floor were 128 lanterns, and on the first floor 12 enormous porcelain oil lamps, each one weighing more than 36.3 kg (80 lbs). There were also more than 400 porcelain statues of Buddhist saints known as Arhats (*Luohan*).

In August 1842, at the end of the First Opium War, the British fleet were anchored off Nanjing. Several group of British officers visited the pagoda and climbed to its top, after which they wrote many descriptions of the structure.

Captain Arthur Cunnynghame visited the pagoda twice, climbing to its top each time, and taking detailed measurements. He described the ninth floor as being 61 m (200 ft) high, with a stone balcony around its outside. Not counting the balcony, the circumference of the pagoda's walls at the top floor was 14 m (46 ft), but 25.6 m (84 ft) around the outside edge of the balcony. However, it tapered from the bottom to the top, with the walls at the base being 3.2 m (10.5 ft) thick. Including what he described as the "golden pear-shaped ball at its summit," the nine-story pagoda was, by his estimate, 82.3 m (270 ft) high. In addition to the eight iron chains connecting the golden ball with the eight corners of the roof, Cunnynghame described an additional 152 chains hanging down from the roof pole, and 140 oil lamps set in niches of the exterior walls. Each of the nine floors had an exterior balcony and roof eaves.

Cunnynghame noted that the many-colored porcelain tiles still had an almost new appearance, but claimed each one was stamped with an image of Tian Hou (Mazu), the goddess of the sea who protects sailors and fishermen. This was an observation not reported elsewhere. The interior walls were reportedly scribbled with the graffiti of signatures left by the many previous Chinese visitors, an observation later made about the pagoda in Anqing as well. At the base of the pagoda, the Bao En Buddhist Temple was described as a "superb temple," still functioning and staffed with resident monks who sold woodcut prints of the pagoda along with descriptions of its history.

Many 19th century European visitors made engravings, sketches and paintings of the pagoda, but before it could ever be photographed, the structure was destroyed by the Taiping rebels in 1856. As late as 1928, there was still a **Bao En Temple**, although the pagoda itself was long gone. The only remains of the tower at its original location was the bronze cap that once topped the pagoda. A few of the porcelain tiles made it to the Metropolitan Museum in New York. Photos taken of the bronze cap in 1933 show it looking like an enormous bowl, sitting upside down, balanced atop a specially made pedestal. Sometime during the 1937–1945 Japanese occupation of the city, the bronze cap disappeared and its fate is now unknown, although it was presumably destroyed. The spot where it once stood is on the slopes of the Rainflower Terrace (Yuhua Tai) just outside the South Gate or Zhonghua Men.

In April 2003, Nanjing city officials suddenly announced plans to spend an estimated USD53 million to reconstruct an 80-m-high (262.5-ft-high) version of the pagoda over a period of three to four years. A 9.4 hectare (23.2 acre) piece of land has been set aside for the project.

Rainflower Terrace (Yuhua Tai)

This site has played a strategic role in Nanjing's history. As high ground just south of the Zhong Hua Men city gate, it was the focus of military battles during the Taiping's occupation of Nanjing and in the 1911 Revolution (Xin Hai Geming). It had been the site of military fortifications, temples, and tombs of important persons since at least the Ming Dynasty. In recent years, nearly all of the hilltop has been taken up by a gigantic monument dedicated to the Communist martyrs of 1927 and 1949 and this stretches all the way from the south to the north end of the park's central axis.

Off the central axis, a few small non-Communist monuments from earlier times have survived. These include one memorial to the 1911 Revolution (Xin Hai Geming), a stone stele inscribed by the Qing Dynasty emperor **Qian Long** (Qian Long Yu Bei Ting), and the tomb of **Fang Xiao Ru**, a Ming Dynasty official executed for refusing to sanction the overthrow of the second Ming emperor, Jian Wen (1399–1402) by Zhu Di, the rival Prince of Yan who became known as the Yong Le emperor (1403–1425).

Several other modern buildings, constructed in traditional style, have recently been built here. These include the five-story Yuhua Pavilion (Yuhua Ge), the Yuhua Stone Museum (Yuhua Shi Bowuguan), the Two Springs Tea House (Er Quan Cha Sha), the The Two Loyalists Ancestral Temple (Er Zhong Ci), and the Plum Flower Garden (Mei Gang).

Rainflower Terrace (Yuhua Tai) is also famous as the supposed place of origin of the colorful rainflower pebbles (Yuhua Shi) sold by street vendors all over the city, but especially found for sale outside the park's north gate on Yuhua Dong Lu.

The whole park is shaped like an upside down Liberty Bell, with its apex pointed north. The park is surrounded by a triangle of roads. To the east and north is Yuhua Dong Lu, to the south is Yuhua Dong Lu, and on the west side runs Gong Qing Tuan Lu.

Phone: 5243-0132, 5242-1628
Web site: http://www.travel-yuhuatai.com
Tickets: 25 Rmb

Sights on Niu Shou Shan
Up until as late as 1981, this mountain had always been referred to in all English publications as Niu Tou Shan (Ox Head Hill). However, since current maps of Nanjing and local residents now refer to the same hill as Niu Shou Shan, this is the name we shall adopt here.

The Tomb of Zheng He (Zheng He Mu)
This is the tomb of the famous Chinese Muslim Ming Dynasty Admiral Zheng He (1371–1435). His body was actually buried at sea on his last voyage, but this is still an impressive monument to an amazing man.

Take Zhongshan Nan Lu to Yuhua Xi Lu, travelling out of the city heading south. When Yuhua Xi Lu forks into two directions, take the left fork onto Ning Dan Lu. Follow this all the way out to Niu Shou Shan which will eventually appear on your right after a long drive through farmland and rolling hills.

Yue Fei's 12th Century Fortifications
The remnants of Yue Fei's Nanjing fortifications stretch from Hanfu Shan to Niu Shou Shan, south of the city. To reach this area drive south out of the city, taking first Zhongshan Nan Lu, then Yuhua Xi Lu, and finally Ning Dan Lu until you reach Niu Shou Shan.

> **PERSONALITIES**
>
> Yue Fei (1103–1141) was a famous Southern Song Dynasty (Nan Song) general. He wanted to recapture the north after the Song had been driven south to their new capital in Hangzhou. In 1129, Yue Fei recaptured the Nanjing area and was able to hold a frontline along the Yangzi. In 1136, he advanced to the Yellow River and from 1139–1140, was raiding Henan Province and approaching the old Song capital at Kaifeng. However, at that point he was ordered to withdraw from North China by the Song Emperor Qin Gui who preferred reaching a diplomatic solution with the Jin invaders. Yue Fei was recalled to the capital at Hangzhou and imprisoned, dying a mysterious death in 1141. A popular temple is devoted to him in Hangzhou on West Lake.

Yu Qi Buddhist Temple (Yu Qi Si) and Lan Yong Cave (Lan Yong Dong)
Yu Qi Si was a Buddhist temple erected on the southern slope of Niu Shou Shan in the Tang Dynasty. The nearby cave is known for a "Fo" character drawn in the cave's stone floor by the former resident hermit Lan Yong.

When Prip-Moller visited the cave in the 1930s, there were no hermits living there. The "Fo" character was still visible on the

> **PERSONALITIES**
>
> Lan Yong was supposedly an acquaintance of the Fourth Patriarch of the Chan sect (Chan Zong) of Chinese Buddhism. The Patriarch was said to have visited him in his cave during the Zheng Guan reign (626–649) of Li Shi Min, the Tai Zong Emperor of the Tang Dynasty.

floor of the cave and monks were apparently still living in the nearby Yu Qi Buddhist Temple (Yu Qi Si). A small structure had been built over the entrance to the cave. Barry Till explored this same area in 1980 and mention "a small niche in a cliff with several small Buddhist statues." This sounds enticingly lilke Lan Yong Dong, but Till does not make the connection.

Hong Jue Pagoda (Hong Jue Ta)

This octagonal, 45-m-high (147.6-ft-high), seven-story pagoda was, by some accounts, originally built in 774AD, during the Dai Zong reign (762–779) of Emperor Li Yu of the Tang Dynasty. However, Xing Ge in her 2003 work, *Fo Bao*, argues that although the temple, Hong Jue Si, was founded in the 6th century, the existing pagoda was built in 1433 in honor of Zheng He.

During the Qian Long reign of the Qing Dynasty, the pagoda caught fire, burning off all of the wooden exterior balconies and roof eaves. For centuries, the brick core of the pagoda continued to stand as a weathered and majestic ruin.

In July 1956, some children accidentally discovered an underground treasure chamber hidden beneath the pagoda. Inside was a 32.7-cm-high (12.9-inch-high) gilded copper Tibetan stupa (Lama Ta), an 8.9-cm-long (3.5-inch-long) gilded copper reclining Buddha (Shi Jia Nie Pan Fo Xiang), and a set of four blue and white porcelain jars. The items are now part of the Nanjing Museum collection.

Later, from 1995 to 1997, the Hong Jue Ta underwent two years of restoration, which left it with its current appearance.

Sights on Zu Tang Shan
Two Southern Tang Dynasty Tombs (Nan Tang Er Ling)

On the southern slope of **Zu Tang Shan** are the tombs of two Southern Tang Dynasty (Nan Tang) emperors, Li Bian or Li Sheng (937–943), and Li Jing (943–961). The two underground tombs are open, well-lit on the inside, and can be entered on foot without any escort or guide. Crowds are not a problem, because the place is nearly deserted as it is well off the beaten tourist track.

Located to the right of Li Jing's tomb is the one belonging to Li Sheng and his is the more impressive of the two. Inside, you will find three main rooms with domed ceilings, marble columns, detailed bas relief rock carvings of warrior guardians armed with swords, and other decorations such as dragons as well as stone tripod roof brackets just like those used on traditional wooden Chinese buildings today. Lay down on the emperor's stone slab burial bed to see how it must have felt. Notice the ten side chambers where his wives and retainers were buried with him while they were still alive.

Just inside the entrance gate, off to the left, is a small museum displaying some of the 640 artifacts discovered in the tombs when they were first opened in 1950. Unfortunately, there are no English language materials available.

Step behind the museum and look over the wall encircling the grounds. Here, there are three stone statues standing in a farmer's field overgrown with vines. There are two soldiers facing each other and one scholar. This is the remains of the Sacred Way leading to the tombs. You can reach it by exiting the site and following a dirt road from the parking lot, through a small village, then descending a dirt path down to the fields.

To reach Nan Tang Er Ling, follow the same directions as for Zheng He Ling, but continue on a bit farther, going past Niu Shou Shan onto Zu Tang Shan.

The main entrance gate to the grounds of Nan Tang Er Ling in Nanjing, where two former emperors of the Southern Tang Dynasty were buried in ornate underground chambers.

Pass through a road toll gate, where you have to pay 10 Rmb, and watch for a sign on your right that says *"Nan Jin Zu Tang Shan Ling Yuan."* Turn right onto a two-lane road. Then turn right again at the next sign onto a one-lane dirt road which takes you to the dirt parking lot. Tickets are only 8 Rmb, but you'll probably have to pay a taxi driver at least 100 Rmb to take you there.

Beamless Hall (Wu Liang Dian)
In his 1935 study of the famous Beamless Hall (Wu Liang Dian) at Spirit Valley (Ling Gu Gongyuan) on Zijin Shan, Johannes Prip-Moller mentions the existence of another similar brick beamless hall. This one has only two barrel vaults, apparently dating from the Ming Dynasty, and is standing somewhere on Zu Tang Shan. Unfortunately he did not provide a more specific location.

Cave of the Fourth Patriarch (Si Zu Dong)
This cave is located on the northern slopes of Zu Tang Shan. It was supposedly visited by the Fourth Patriarch (Si Zu) of the Chan sect (Chan Zong) of Chinese Buddhism. His visit was believed to have taken place during the Zheng Guan reign (626–649) of Li Shi Min, the Tai Zong Emperor of the Tang Dynasty. When Prip-Moller visited it in the 1930s, it still contained a stone altar with an ornamental design implying it dated from the Tang Dynasty.

Sights along the Yangzi River
Lion Peak (Shizi Shan)
Located in the northwest corner of the city, this site marks a turning point in the city wall and city moat which envelope it on two sides. The entrance to the park can be reached from Jian Ning Lu, near its intersection with Da Qiao Lu. The impressive **River Viewing Tower** (Yue Jiang Lou) was rebuilt in 2001 to replace

a previous structure of the same name that stood here in 1937 but was later destroyed. An even earlier pavilion seems to have been built on this same spot by the first Ming emperor, Zhu Yuanzhang, in 1374.

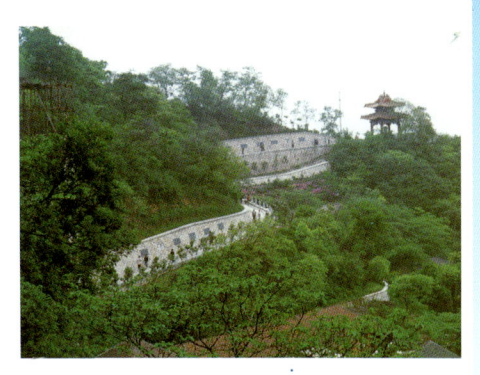

The top of Lion Peak (Shizi Shan) affords an incredible view of a long stretch of the Yangzi River and the Da Qiao bridge crossing over it. Perched on top of the narrow knife-edge peak, that drops off sharply on all sides, the stone block foundation of the building takes up literally every inch of space here. The building itself is a multi-story Ming-style wooden structure decorated in bright colors of blue, yellow, and red. In some ways, it resembles Himeji Castle in Japan. It is like no other traditional building in China, something of a Ming-style wooden skyscraper.

The winding foot trail heading up the eastern slope of Lion Peak (Shizi Shan) in Nanjing.

A stone archway atop Lion Peak (Shizi Shan) frames Ding Shan and Yi Jiang Men in the distance. You can watch the sun set over the pavilion. At night, the entire Yue Jiang Lou is lit up with bright lights that illuminate its colors. There are three pedestrian approaches to Yue Jiang Lou. One is a long frightening ascent up stone steps, climbing a knife blade ridge, while the other is a stone-paved road that follows a more gradual incline up a slightly wider ridge. A third approach is via a newly-built trail of stone steps which connects Lion Peak (Shizi Shan) and Jing Hai Si. The latter is reached by going into a tunnel that passes through the city wall and then by crossing a footbridge over the city moat.

The city wall and moat have been rebuilt all around the base of Lion Peak (Shizi Shan) and there are now pedestrian promenades which follow the course of both the wall and moat. Another small Buddhist temple, **Dizang Si**, has been built on the western slope of Lion Peak (Shizi Shan), along the trail to Jing Hai Si. A giant bronze statue of the Ming Dynasty Admiral Zheng He stands at the main entrance to the park at the eastern foot of the hill.

Address: 202 Jian Ning Lu
Phone: 5881-5369
Admission: 30 Rmb,
including entrance to Jing Hai Si

Yangzi Water Front and Former Bund
With the exception of the Pu Kou and Da Chang industrial suburbs across the river on the north bank, most of Nanjing has always been on the south bank of the Yangzi River, approximately

400 km (248.5 miles) upstream from the river's mouth. The Yangzi River waterfront and former bund area lie in the Xia Guan district of the city, a flat river bottom area outside the northwestern city wall.

From Re He Lu, turn down Long Jiang Lu until you reach Jian Bian Lu. Turn left and follow Jian Bian Lu for several blocks. This is the old Yangzi River waterfront. Almost all the shipping industry is now located across the river on the Pu Kou side, which you can see is wall to wall with loading cranes and container facilities. Jian Bian Lu has an old waterfront breakwater with a raised pedestrian promenade that allows you to see over the top and look at the river. Rusted, broken, iron lampposts mark the pathway.

After several blocks, turn left onto Da Ma Lu and see three impressive pre-1937 European-style buildings which somehow have survived the wars, revolutions, and economic development of the city since then. This was the old pre-war business and finance center. The buildings here look much like those on the Bund (Waitan) in Shanghai. One has a large dome over the top, and Greco-Roman columns, making it resemble the Hong Kong and Shanghai Bank building. The buildings now seem abandoned and the street itself is dusty and deserted, devoid of all activity.

Continue down Jian Bian Lu along the waterfront. At its intersection with Zhongshan Bei Lu is Zhongshan Wharf. This is the arrival and departure point for passenger ships traveling the Yangzi River.

The Nanjing Yangzi River Bridge (Nanjing Changjiang Da Qiao)

Opened in December 1968, the Nanjing Yangzi River Bridge (Nanjing Changjiang Da Qiao) was only the second bridge ever to cross the Yangzi River. The first one, connecting Hanyang with Wuchang in Wuhan, was completed in 1957. This 1.6-km (1-mile) double-decker bridge for cars and trains was one of the longest in China when it was completed. The bridge was completely designed and built by the Chinese themselves after the Russians withdrew support and took away the design plans in 1960.

The lower rail section of the two-tier bridge was opened on 1 October 1968, and the upper road section more than two months later on 29 December. Both ends of the bridge feature statues of socialist labor heroes. Although a second even longer Yangzi River bridge (Changjiang Er Qiao) was completed in Nanjing in March 2001, the original bridge continues to be jammed with the bulk of the cross-river traffic. This is because its location is more central and it is free to use. The new bridge is located far in the northeastern suburbs and requires a steep toll to be paid.

Swallows Crag (Yanzi Ji)

This peak is formed by a completely freestanding rock outcropping with a hollowed-out cove facing the water. The cove cannot be entered from either side except by climbing through caves and narrow openings in the natural rock walls which enclose it on all three sides.

The ridge line trail along a knife-like extension from the peak of Yanzi Ji.

The hillside is decorated with bright, colorful flowers, and the whole site is arranged in the style of a traditional Chinese garden, dotted with small pavilions offering views of the Yangzi River. One small pavilion, surrounded by the river, sits at the foot of a cliff face with carved Chinese characters in many places. A small cave tunnels underneath, through the rocks to the concave, half oval beach enclosed by the cliff face on three sides and water on the fourth.

The Wang Jiang Bei Ting pavilion atop the summit of Yanzi Ji in Nanjing.

The other main pavilion, **Wang Jiang Bei Ting**, sits on top of a small peak. It is swarming with butterflies and offers a 360-degree view of the Yangzi River. A steep flight of steps ascends the peak. To the left is the forested **Mu Fu Shan**, dotted with tombs and graves, but blighted by some industrial plants along the water's edge. To the right is Nanjing's recently built second bridge over the Yangzi River, the **Changjiang Er Qiao**. Inside the peak-top pavilion stands a stone stele decorated with dragons. Called the "Imperial Stone Tablet," the inscription on it was supposedly carved by the Qing Dynasty Emperor Qian Long himself during his visit here in 1751. Indeed, it does seem to be a genuine historical artifact.

At the foot of Yanzi Ji stands a small stone pavilion, the Da Tu Sha Ji Lia Bei Ting, dedicated to the memory of those who perished during the December 1937 Nanjing Massacre.

A third pavilion, the **Massacre Memorial Stele Pavilion (Da Tu Sha Ji Lia Bei Ting)**, is found at the right foot of the peak. It contains a more recent, although not new, granite stele decorated with fresh cut flowers — a memorial to someone still remembered. A wooden English language sign pointing the way there calls it the "Memorial to the Massacre," apparently a reference to the events of November 1937. The main modern-day memorial to this event is a much larger monument located at the opposite end of the city in Xiaguan. It is not clear if this smaller one pre-dated the other, when it was built exactly, or why it was located here.

Getting There

Swallow's Crag (Yanzi Ji) is fairly far north of the Nanjing city center. To reach it you have two choices. You can take Zhonyang Bei Lu to its intersection with He Yan Lu and follow it all the way to Swallow's Crag (Yanzi Ji). Alternatively, you can take Long Pan Lu to the Xinzhuang Overpass and turn right onto Hong Shan Lu, following it until it merges with He Yan Lu. Follow He Yan Lu north all the way to Yanzi Ji.

You can also take a taxi from the Xin Jie Kou area out to Swallow's Crag (Yanzi Ji), going via Long Pan Lu, Hongshan Lu, and He Yan Lu. The ride will cost 36 Rmb. Be advised that the last road is a narrow, bumpy one-lane paved road choked with traffic.

Mu Fu Shan Cave Temples

The much more fascinating cave temples are not located on Swallow's Crag (Yanzi Ji) itself, but are carved into the slopes of nearby **Mu Fu Shan** facing the Yangzi River. They can be reached by following Xia Yan Lu. There are a total of 12 sacred caves spread out over this lengthy mountainous area along the river's edge. The caves are grouped together into three separate walled temple complexes known respectively as **Guanyin Dong**, **Tou Tai Dong**, and **Three-Terrace Cave** (San Tai Dong). These Buddhist temple complexes feature shrines located inside caves, their entrances covered with temple halls and pavilions built on terraces (*tai*) that are halfway up the mountainside, against the rock cliff face. Networks of natural tunnels through the rock connect some of the caves. The original Buddhist statues seem to have been smashed by the Red Guards, but new ones have, in recent years, replaced the originals. Today, no resident Buddhist monks can be seen living at any of these sites. However, some devout lay worshippers have been seen praying and the remains of burnt incense and red candles are visible inside the caves.

Guanyin Dong

About 200 m (656.2 ft) west, down Xia Yan Lu, from the village of Yanzi Ji is Guanyin Dong, the first of the Buddhist cave temples. The **Guanyin Hall** (Guanyin Ge) was built during the reign of the first Ming Dynasty Emperor Zhu Yuanzhang (Hong Wu). During the Zheng De reign of the Ming Dynasty, **Hong Ji Temple** (Hong Ji Si) was built beside the Guanyin Ge. The temple's name was changed to **Yong Ji Temple** (Yong Ji Si) during the reign of Qing Dynasty Emperor Qian Long.

Yong Ji Temple's single hall still sits on a terrace halfway up the hillside overlooking a lake down below. It appears today much as it did in a 1931 photo. The outside of Yong Ji Temple is decorated with authentic wood carvings along the roof beams. Inside, it contains statues of 18 gilded Arhats (*Shi Ba Luohan*), nine on each side. Although the presence of the *Luohan* is not unusual, their renderings here are very unusual, as they are much more expressive than the typical generic ones. Four Heavenly Kings sit inside glass cases at the back of the hall. In the center is a seated Sakyamuni Buddha flanked by two standing disciples, one very young man on the left and a very old man on the right. Hidden behind a partition is a rear exit leading to a small outdoor are, completely enclosed between the temple's back wall and the hillside. Here, there are three Buddhist shrines inside recesses in the natural rock, but no actual caves. There are no resident Buddhist monks living here, but one woman lay believer was observed diligently chanting devotions.

The hillside pavilions of Yong Ji Si and the Guanyin Ge at Guanyin Dong.

Beside the Yong Ji Temple hall is the smaller **Guanyin Hall** (Guanyin Ge). It contains three statues, including the bodhisattvas Dizang and Guanyin, and a second unidentifiable woman. Carved on the rock face of the hillside, behind the Guanyin Ge, used to be an image of Guanyin painted by Wu Dao Zi of the Tang Dynasty. However, this no longer seems to be there.

A trail along the lake below the two halls and a second path leading from the Guanyin Ge provided access to the Guanyin Dong, a large cave halfway up the hillside. Although the mouth of the cave can still be seen from down below, both trails leading to the cave were closed in October 2003 for some reason.

The lower cave mouth of Tou Tai Dong.

Tou Tai Dong

The second cave temple is 850 m (2 788.7 ft) farther west of Guanyin Dong, down Xia Yan Lu. Although the temple halls on the mid-mountain terrace were closed on the author's last visit, the cave itself was open. The upper mouth of Tou Tai Dong starts from this terrace beside the temple halls. From here, it tunnels downwards at a sharp angle to a second, much wider cave mouth below. New cement steps and metal handrails make the descent through this natural tunnel much easier. The main lower cavern is a wide open space with many recesses in the walls, burnt black from incense but missing their original shrine images. The floor is paved with old bricks. In October 2003, the cave housed three new statues that it had not had a year earlier. One was a new Maitreya Buddha (Mi Le Fo), but the other two were a

The hillside temple halls at Tou Tai Dong.

The cave mouth of Tou Tai Dong with statues visible inside.

mysterious man and woman, the man looking like a traditional Chinese military general. The wide mouth of the lower cave has at some time been made smaller by a man-made rockery.

Immediately outside the lower cave mouth is the **Arhat Hall** (Luohan Dian). Inside it contains 16 statues of the Sakyamuni Buddha's original disciples, unlike most Chinese Buddhist temples which display 18 Arhats (*Luohan*).

On the west side of the lower cave mouth are two important genuine historic relics. These are in the form of stone inscriptions. A short flight of steps leads up to an enormous and elaborate inscription, in the natural rock hillside, of the Chinese character "Shou" which stands for longevity. This character was supposedly written during the Hong Wu reign (1368–1398) by the first Ming emperor Zhu Yuanzhang himself. It is said that Zhu and his wife Empress Ma used to visit these caves by boat. Beside this is a faded, stained, and moss-covered stone tablet of uncertain age with a lengthy inscription.

From the Luohan Dian, a foot trail continues west to a natural rock archway and a long flight of steps that winds halfway up the mountainside to the mouth of another cave. According to a stone inscription beside its entrance, this cave is now known as **Immortal's Cavern** (Xian Ren Dong). It may have once been called Eight Immortals' Cave (Ba Xian Dong), the place where the Taoist Eight Immortals (Ba Xian) supposedly used to meet.

The large rock inscription of a single character meaning "longevity" (*shou*), supposedly written by the first Ming Dynasty emperor, Zhu Yuanzhang, outside the lower cave mouth of Tou Tai Dong.

Trail up a rock cliff at San Tai Dong.

Three-Terrace Cave (San Tai Dong)

Also on Xia Yan Lu, 450 m (1476.38 ft) further west of Tou Tai Dong, is the Three-Terrace Cave (San Tai Dong). As the name implies, this is a network of various connected caves on three different levels of the mountainside. Walking along a lakeshore, you reach the lowest of the four caves, which has a wide mouth and a pool of water inside known as the **Goddess of Mercy Spring** (Guanyin Quan). A new stone railing runs along the edge of the pool at the cave's mouth. A stone footbridge crosses the center of the pool to the back wall of the cave where several old and new inscriptions can be found. The most famous inscription is a faded one of the three characters for "San Tai Dong." This same inscription appears in photos of the site taken in 1931. Outside the first cave mouth is an octagonal old stone well, a small open-air pavilion known as the **Guan Quan Pavilion** (Guan Quan Ting), and a new stone tablet featuring a copy of a portrait of Guanyin originally made by the painter Wu Dao Zi in the Tang Dynasty.

Inscription reading "Gu San Tai Dong," or "Ancient Three Terrace Cave."

Branching off from the right side of the San Tai Dong is a second long and narrow cave known as **Tong Tian Dong**. This natural passageway ascends through natural stone to a pavilion on the second terrace, halfway up the mountainside. Inside the Tong Tian Dong, there are many genuine relics in the form of faded inscriptions chiseled into its natural stone walls. One of them mysteriously points the way to the Dragon King Temple (Long

Wang Dian), a building that no longer seems to exist. At one point natural sunlight streams into the cave through holes in its roof but in other sections, it is as dark as night, making a flashlight necessary. The original stone steps, worn smooth from centuries of pilgrims' feet, lead visitors through several twists and turns upward before they emerge through the foundation floor of the second terrace pavilion.

This second terrace pavilion is apparently known as the **Jade Emperor's Pavilion** (Yu Huang Ting). This enclosed square pavilion protects the mouth of a third natural cave in the hillside. Inside the second terrace cave is an impressive shrine with a collection of statues. Two small stone statues of standing disciples flank a third, much larger, white stone statue of a seated man. The man is barefoot, wears long robes from under which a turtle emerges, has a long pointy beard and moustache, and is seated in a chair with a red cloth draped over his head. According to a sign at his feet, he is supposed to be Zhen Wu Da Di. In the left corner of the cave is an altar, formed by a simple wooden office desk. Behind the altar, standing against the back wall, is a glass case containing images of a man and woman dressed in orange robes, similar to another pair just outside the cave's entrance. On the right side of the cave a new stone tablet commemmorates those donors who contributed to its reconstruction in 1999.

The Min Guo gatehouse bearing the "Gu San Tai Dong," inscription and housing a small shrine to the God of Fortune Cai Shen inside.

From the Jade Emperor's Pavilion (Yu Huang Ting), a flight of old, worn, stone steps lead up to the third terrace where a three-story orange pagoda and the mouth of a fourth cave can

PERSONALITIES

China's Chan (Zen) sect reveres Bodhi Dharma (Pu Ti Da Mo) as their First Patriarch. He is said to have arrived in China sometime between 520 and 526 AD, during the reign of Liang Wu Di (502–549 AD). When Bodhi Dharma arrived in the Liang Dynasty's capital city of Nanjing, Emperor Wu Di invited him to the palace for a meeting. However, Bodhi Dharma was, for some reason, dissatisfied with the conversation he had with the emperor, and decided to leave the city by crossing the Yangzi River. Tradition says he floated over the river on a reed. From Nanjing, he made his way to the city of Luoyang. He was, in the past, often portrayed as carrying one shoe because of another legend, one which says that only one shoe was found in his grave when it was later reopened. Images of him typically illustrate his distinctively non-Chinese face, a heavy black beard and extremely long eyebrows growing down to his feet.

be found. This last cave winds upwards, like a tunnel, through the mountain to an exit out on a wooden platform covered by an open-air pavilion known as the **Wang Jiang Ting**. Fom here you can get spectacular views of the Yangzi River.

West of the Three-Terrace Cave (San Tai Dong) is a red brick one-story Min Guo gate house inscribed with the sign "Ancient San Tai Dong" ("Gu San Tai Dong"). Inside one of the two rooms in the gate house is a small shrine devoted to the **God of Wealth** (Cai Shen). Past this gate house is a garden, another Min Guo structure now apparently used as a residence, and a flight of steps providing an alternate way of reaching the Guan Quan Pavilion (Guan Quan Ting).

In the 1920s, visitors to the Three-Terrace Cave (San Tai Dong) reported that the caves then had an active shrine. This shrine was devoted to the Indian Buddhist monk **Bodhi Dharma** (Pu Ti Da Mo), and was attended to by resident Buddhist monks. Nowadays the previous shrines and the monks are all gone. Although new shrines have been erected since 1999, none of them seem devoted to Bodhi Dharma. According to one source, there may be another cave known as **Da Mo Dong**, located somewhere west of Three-Terrace Cave (San Tai Dong). This does not appear on the local maps nor has the author been able to find it.

Getting There

Visiting this area can be dangerous. The first cave temple can be reached in a few minutes by walking down the dusty one-lane road that follows the narrow strip of flat land between the foot of Mu Fu Shan and the Yangzi River's edge. However, walking all the way from Swallow's Crag (Yanzi Ji) to Three-Terrace Cave (San Tai Dong) and back can be an

Top: A modern replica of Wu Dao Zi's portrait of Guanyin on a new stone tablet at Guanyin Quan.
Above: The hillside pavilion of Yu Huang Ting at San Tai Dong.

exhausting experience once you figure in all the hillside climbing and cave exploring. Alternatively, you could choose to hire a local pedicab or motor tricycle driver. Beware of their criminal expectations of exorbitant financial rewards for a few minutes work. This is an isolated area, cut off for a long distance from the rest of the city by Mu Fu Shan, and the local inhabitants are poor peasants. The combination of their poverty, isolation, and yet close proximity to the city seems to motivate them to extortionist strong arm tactics when it comes to visitors. However, you will not find any taxis traveling this road, and all public buses stop at the end of the line in Swallow's Crag (Yanzi Ji) village.

Phone: 8531-1337

Sights Northeast of the City
Tomb of Xu Da (Xu Da Mu)
This is the tomb of Xu Da, the commander-in-chief under the first Ming emperor. It has a Sacred Way (*shen dao*) of stone animal statues similar to that at the Ming Tombs, as well as one stone stele tablet balanced on the back of a turtle. Entering the gate of the walled compound, the Sacred Way proceeds between two stone columns, then two stone horses, followed by two stone rams, two stone lions, two stone soldiers, and finally two stone civil officials, before ascending four flights of steps up to the unexcavated round burial mound. A modern-day exhibit hall stands empty beside the gate. The tomb sits on the north side of Bang Cang Lu, at the foot of the north slope of Zijin Shan. To reach it, take Long Pan Lu until you reach its intersection with Bang Cang Lu, just past the former site of Taiping Men. Turn off onto Bang Cang Lu and follow it for several kilometers until you reach the site.

Air Force Memorial (Hang Kong Lie Shi Gong Mu)
Originally built by the Guomindang in 1932, this was badly damaged during the Japanese occupation. It was restored and expanded in 1994. It now includes the names of all the pilots, both Chinese and foreign volunteers, who died in all the air battles with Japan from 1932 to 1945.

A battle-scarred four-pillar gate marking the entrance actually seems to still be scorched by the flames of war. Long flights of steps lead up to the hillside, to the highest terrace where the new name tablets and a heroic statue have been erected. The names seem equally divided between Americans, Russians, and Chinese. This would probably be a good site to visit for anyone researching the history of the volunteer American pilots known as the Flying Tigers, or the genealogy of one of its members. What's most remarkable about this memorial is not so much the respect it shows to Americans, but how it highlights that the Chinese Communist Party (Gong Chan Dang) had no air force or pilots of their own. All the Chinese pilots remembered here flew for their rivals, the Guomindang; in some cases in civil war battles against the Communists rather than against the Japanese. A similar Guomindang military cemetery at Ling Gu Gongyuan, on the south slope of Zijin Shan, had all of its tombstones removed decades ago. Mistreatment of some of the original tombstones at the Air Force Memorial is also evident, as they can be found overgrown with weeds or pushed off to the side. Likewise, the original memorial halls remain ghostly empty of any artifacts, and no attempt has been made to establish any kind of educational exhibits or bookshop.

The memorial sits just off Jiang Wang Miao Lu, on the North slope of Zijin Shan. To reach it, turn off Long Pan Lu onto Bang Cang Lu and follow it past Xu Da Mu. Continue following the same road around the base of the mountain until its name changes to Jiang Wang Miao Lu. Eventually you will see the memorial off to your right.

Liang Dynasty Tombs

Although the more important tombs of the Liang Dynasty (502–557) emperors and princes are found in the Danyang and Jurong counties of Zhenjiang municipality, several of the lesser Liang princes were buried in Nanjing. Ancient stone statues of mythical winged Bixie animals and one stone column can be found marking the site of several Liang tombs. The tombs are near the village of Gan Jia Xiang, just off the newly built highway of Xi Xia Da Dao, on the way out to Xi Xia Zhen and Qi Xia Shan.

Just before reaching the turn off to Gan Jia Xiang, on the south side of the highway in the middle of the farmers' fields, is the tomb of **Liang Xiao Jing** (d. 528). This is marked by one large stone statue of a roaring, winged Bixie, and one tall stone column with a smaller Bixie balanced on top of a round disc on its summit. The tall stone fluted pillar is 6.5 m (21.3 ft) high and bears a remarkable resemblance to Greco-Roman Corinthian columns. At the base of the pillar are two dragons playing with a pearl, and just below the disc is a rectangular tablet with a faded inscription. Both relics can be seen from the highway, but a paved access road now runs in between them to the gate of a factory. A new stone tablet has been erected where the access road leaves the main highway.

A short distance further east on Xi Xia Da Dao, an unmarked paved road veers off to the left and heads northeast to the village of Gan Jia Xiang. Along the way, it passes three more stone statues of winged Bixie

An ancient stone bixie statue marking a Liang Dynasty tomb near Gan Jia Xiang village.

standing at two sites on the left (west) side of the road, in the middle of the farmers' fields. A dirt road leads into the fields to the two sites.

The first Bixie on the left has a broken head, with two much smaller Bixie hidden beneath its belly. Behind this Bixie is a two-story, red brick Min Guo tower. Inside this tower is an enormous stone stele tablet balanced on the back of a turtle. It is 5.6 m (18.4 ft) high, and weighs 10.2 tonnes (10 tons). Its lengthy inscription of 2,840 characters describes this site as the tomb of **Liang Xiao Dan** (d. 522), the brother of Emperor Liang Wu Di (502–549 AD). A white marble corner stone in the tower's wall bears a newer and more readable inscription.

The two other stone Bixie to the northeast stand within the fenced area of a farm, and you must ask the resident peasants to open the gate. These two Bixie are much better preserved, and face each other as if they once marked a sacred way (*shen dao*) to a tomb. According to Barry Till, this was the tomb of **Liang Xiao Hui** (d. 526), another brother of Emperor Liang Wu Di (502–549 AD).

A Qing Dynasty brick tower housing an ancient inscribed stone tablet marking the tomb of Liang Xiao Dan.

Qi Xia Buddhist Temple (Qi Xia Si)

Located 22 km (13.7 miles) northeast of Nanjing is this large, functioning Buddhist temple, nestled in a low valley at the foot of Qi Xia Shan. The main east-west street of Xi Xia town ends at large new monumental gate (*pai lou*) to the mountain of Qi Xia Shan. Once inside the gate, a new motor vehicle road heads up the forested mountain to your left. However, if you take this new road to the summit, as all the tour buses seem to do, you will miss all the genuine historic sights which are located off the beaten track. Walking from the *pai lou* to your right takes you to a new Heng Ha Dian, which acts as a ticket booth for admission into the grounds of Qi Xia Temple. From here the original cobblestone footpath to the temple winds through a valley and around the shore of the **Rainbow Reflection Pool** (Cai Hong Ming Jing Chi). This lake was supposedly built when the Qian Long emperor first visited.

From the east shore of the Rainbow Pool, the actual complex of temple halls begins. However, most of these are of very recent construction and seem to be completely brand new structures rather than restorations. In November 2003, there was a massive reconstruction project under way. The Bell Tower (Zhong Lou) and Drum Tower (Gu Lou), both new and made of cement, were being built on opposite

Signs pointing the way at the intersection of several foot trails on Qi Xia Shan.

sides of a half-circle Animal Releasing Pool (Fang Sheng Chi). Past this pool, the first building is a new orange-walled Heavenly Kings Hall (Tian Wang Dian) housing statues of the Four Heavenly Kings and the Maitreya Buddha (Mi Le Fo). On the terrace outside the front entrance are two new bronze elephants.

Exiting the east side of the Heavenly Kings Hall (Tian Wang Dian) leads you into an enclosed courtyard, with side halls to the north and south. Straight ahead to the east, on a raised platform, is the Precious Hall of the Great Hero (Da Xiong Bao Dian). It also seems to be brand new, although it features a second story sidewall glass skylights like those found at Jiuhua Shan.

It's only behind the new Da Xiong Bao Dian that the historic structures are found. Sealed off from the new structures by a high wall and a large closed wooden gate, is a completely separate courtyard compound of red brick and stone-walled structures dating from the temple's last reconstruction in the Min Guo era. Since the central gate in the wall is kept closed, the way into this rear compound is through a side entrance to

The ancient stone pagoda She Li Ta beside the Buddhist temple of Qi Xia Si.

POINT OF INTEREST

The original Qi Xia Temple was built in in the year 489AD, during the 7th year of the Yong Ming reign (483–493 AD) of Xiao Ze during the Qi Dynasty (479–501 AD), when Ming Seng Shao donated the land he lived on to the monk, Zhi Du Chan Shi. In the year 676AD, during the Gao Zong reign (649–683 AD) of the Tang Dynasty, Emperor Li Zhi erected a memorial stele in honor of the Qi Dynasty monk Ming Seng Shao, who was the temple's founding ancestor. During the Taiping Rebellion, the temple buildings were completely destroyed, but this stele has survived to the present day. Some buildings were rebuilt from 1908 onwards. During the Guang Xu reign of the late Qing Dynasty, a major reconstruction project started at Qi Xia Temple in 1920 and continued for the next 20 years. During this time, an entirely new complex of brick and stone wall halls were completed.

Like other temples, Qi Xia Temple received no government subsidies during the Min Guo era (1911–1949). After Lin Sen became the President of the Guomindang government in 1931, he extended his personal protection to the temple and its surrounding lands, and often visited the temple. It is said that even Chiang Kai Shek (Jiang Jieshi) had a private apartment reserved for himself there. In 1933, visitors found the temple protected by Guomindang troops.

In the 1940s, Qi Xia Temple had 110 resident monks, but by 1955, this number had dropped sharply to only 22 resident monks, just one-fifth of its previous total before the 1949 revolution. By 1962, the numbers had recovered slightly to 40 monks, still about two-thirds less than before the 1949 revolution. With the start of the Cultural Revolution in 1966, all the remaining monks were forced to move out. According to Barry Till, the temple buildings were occupied by Chinese military units from 1966 to 1979, after which resident monks began to return. The current population in November 2003 seemed, by the author's estimate, to be somewhere between 40 and 50.

your right, behind the southeast corner of the Da Xiong Bao Dian. The side halls of this rear compound now seem to be the monks residential quarters. The main hall at the far eastern end of the compound may have once been the Da Xiong Bao Dian, but is now used as a classroom with rows of approximately 50 desks and chairs laid out facing a black board, looking much like a grade school. There are no Buddha images in this hall at all. The only Buddhist decoration is one large hanging scroll painting displayed behind the blackboard depicting a man who may be Bodhia Dharma (Pu Di Da Mo). To the north of this hall is a large vegetable garden, indicating that the monks still follow a vegetarian diet and grow their own food. In the middle of the garden is a tomb stone.

Outside the walls of both the new and the old temple compounds, hidden behind the southeast corner, stands the massive **She Li Ta**. This is an 18-m-high (59-ft-high) octagonal stone pagoda originally built in the year 601 AD, during the Ren Shou reign of the Sui Dynasty Emperor Wen Di (581–604 AD). It was later destroyed during the Hui Chang reign of the Tang Dynasty, and rebuilt during the Southern Tang (Nan Tang) Dynasty (937–975 AD). A photo taken in 1930 shows the pinnacle having been broken off. Later, it was reconstructed back to its present condition of five levels, balanced on the foundation of a large stone pedestal with a tall stone pinnacle at the top. The pagoda is solid stone with no entrance, no windows, and apparently no hollow space inside, so it cannot be ascended. Stone roof eaves project out from five of the six levels, although in some places pieces of these stone eaves have been broken off. On the second level, which is a wider band than any of the others, stone-carved images of fierce looking warrior gods decorate four of the pagoda's eight sides. Although other stone pagodas exist in Jiangnan — such as the Tang Tuo Luo Ni in Songjiang — this is the thickest and tallest one the author has ever seen.

Immediately behind the She Li Ta stone pagoda is the **Thousand Buddha Cliff** (Qian Fo Yan), decorated with hundreds of niches and grottoes containing stone sculptures of Buddhist deities. Although additions continued to be made as late as the Qing Dynasty, most of these rock carvings date as far back as 484 AD, the 2nd year of the Yong Ming reign (483–493 AD) of Xiao Ze of the Qi Dynasty (479–501 AD), and continued through the end of the reign of Liang Wu Di (502–549 AD). There are a total of 295 grottoes (*Fo kan*) and 515

The temple hall of Qi Xia Si.

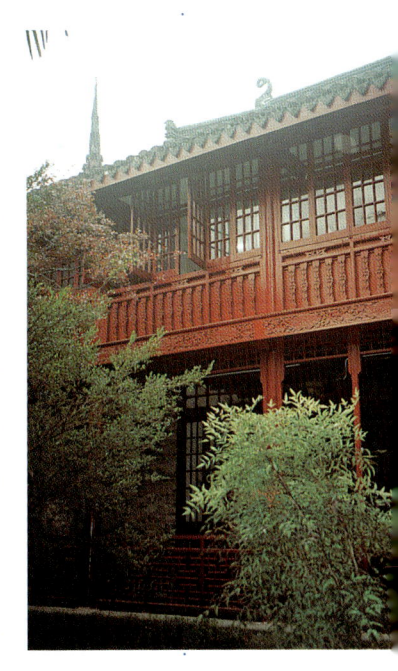

The ancient Buddhist grottoes at Sha Mao Feng on Qi Xia Shan.

One of the many Buddhist grottoes at Qian Fo Yan at the foot of Qi Xia Shan.

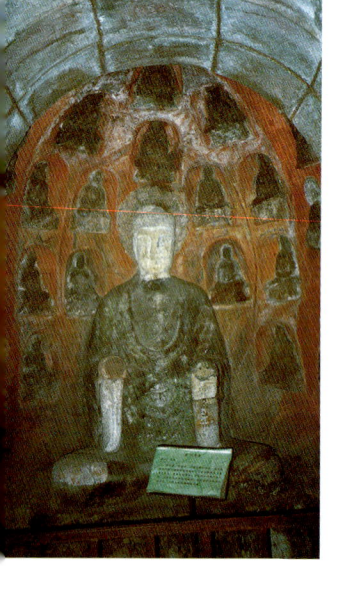

Buddhist rock sculptures (*Fo xiang*), including both those at the Qian Fo Yan and a second collection of grottoes higher up the mountain known as **Sha Mao Feng**. Many of the Buddhist sculptures were damaged during the Taiping Rebellion and later repaired by Abbot Ruo Shen with cement over a two-and-a-half year period from 1923 to 1925. Despite the effects of the Taiping damage and later repairs, these Buddhist rock carvings are easily comparable in quality to those at Fei Lai Feng in Hangzhou.

Built right into the cliff face is the massive, fortress-like, stone block **Amitabha Hall** (O-Mi-Tuo-Fo Dian), sometimes also known as the **Three Saints Hall** (San Sheng Dian), or **Big Buddha Pavilion** (Da Fo Ge). This hall has a high peaked roof, shaped like the tiled roof, with wooden upturned eaves found on traditional wooden Chinese halls. However, this one is made entirely from cut stone blocks, as are all three of its exterior walls. The appearance of the structure is very much like a Ming Dynasty fortress or city gate.

In the center of the hall is a single enormous, arched, stone gate, inside which stands a 10.7-m-high (35.1-ft-high) stone statue of a seated Amitabha Buddha (O-Mi-Tuo-Fo) flanked by two 10-m-high (32.8-ft-high) stone standing statues of the bodhisattvas Guanyin and Da Shi Zhi. On either side of this central archway are arcades of smaller arched niches filled with stone Buddha statues. Many of the niches and statues are numbered according to some kind of cataloguing system, and some niches feature explanatory signs in Chinese. Although the exact age of the Amitabha Hall seems unkown, photos taken in 1930 show it looking remarkably the same as it does today. Barry Till referred to this structure as the Three Saints Hall (San Sheng Dian) in his 1982 work, but Wang Neng Wei's 1998 work, *Nanjing Jiu Ying*, refers to it as the Amitabha Hall. According to Chen Ping's 1998 *Nanjing De Wen Wu*, this hall was originally built by the monk Zhi Du Chan Shi shortly after the temple's founding in 489AD; but it's hard to believe the existing hall is exactly the same one, despite its impressively aged appearance. Chen also calls the Amitabha statue the Wu Liang Shou Fo, and calculates its height in Chinese measurements as three *zhang*, 2 *chi*, and 5 *cun*.

From behind the Amitabha Hall, a stone-paved trail heads up into the thickly forested hills of Qi Xia Shan. At a crossroads in the trail, the route to the left heads to the Buddhist grottoes of Sha Mao Feng. The route to the right goes to the former site of **Qi Xia Palace**, Emperor Qian Long's temporary imperial palace built in 1757 during the 22nd year of his reign. This was where Emperor Qian Long stayed during his five visits to Qi Xia Si, on his journeys to the south from the capital in Beijing. The palace was completely destroyed during the Taiping Heavenly Kingdom (Taiping Tian Guo), and all that remains now are scattered stone wall ruins. Past the ruins of the palace, the trail continues upwards through thick forest, past many isolated sites of stone inscriptions on natural rock formations and stone wall ruins. However, there are no further sites even comparable with the grottoes at Sha Mao Feng, so if your time is limited you should definitely focus your energy in this direction.

The Buddhist rock sculptures and grottoes at **Sha Mao Feng** are even more impressive than those at Qian Fo Yan. They are also less visited due to the need to hike halfway up the mountain to reach them. Ascending a gradual incline through the forest to a ridge line, you emerge from the trees, at a pass, to find your eyes dazzled by a feast of Buddhist sculptures on all sides. Straight ahead, the trail passes through a natural cleft in the rock ridge, with rock carvings towering over both sides of the trail. On the left is a natural rock pinnacle riddled with grottoes from top to bottom. On the right is a rock ridge full of grottoes and rows of niches housing stone statues. Many of the caves have decorated stone block archways. At least one old Buddhist hermit was still seen living inside one of these grottoes in November 2003. Further to the right, a steep side path climbs up along the edge of the rock ridge. This is the route to take for those ascending views of even more grottoes built ever upward towards the summit.

The classroom for Buddhist monks inside an old temple hall at Qi Xia Si.

Unfortunately, no local maps, brochures, visitors' guides, or any kind of publications on this fascinating sight seem to be available for sale anywhere at or near the temple. Even picture postcards seem unavailable. Furthermore, the rather expensive admission tickets come without the standard thumbnail history of the site usually found printed on the back side, the space instead being devoted to unrelated commercial advertising. Another confusing mystery for visitors is why the area's name has in recent years been changed to "Xi Xia." Throughout its history it has always been known as "Qi Xia," as it was still called in two seminal local histories published in 1998, Wang Neng Wei's, *Nanjing Jiu Ying*, and Ye Zhao Yan's, *Lao Nanjing: Jiu Ying Qinhuai*.

The easiest way to get there is to take a taxi along the newly built highway Xi Xia Da Dao, past the village of Gan Jia Xiang, to the town of Xi Xia (Xi Xia Zhen). Taking a taxi will allow you the freedom to ask the driver to stop at the Liang Dynasty tombs in Gan Jia Xiang on your way. This convenience should be worth the added cost one way. However, when you're ready to return to the city center, cheap and plentiful public buses can easily be boarded at the main intersection of Xi Xia town, one block outside the Qi Xia Shan mountain gate. The fare back to the Nanjing Railway Station should only be 2.5 Rmb.

Address: Xi Xia Zhen
Phone: 8576-1831, 8576-6780
Tickets: 25 Rmb

Nanjing Practical Information

Nanjing Area Code: (025)

Shopping
Most shopping is centered in the Xin Jie Kou area, named after a giant traffic circle where Zhongshan Dong Lu, Zhongshan Lu, Zhongshan Nan Lu, and Hanzhong Lu all converge on a giant statue of Sun Yat Sen (Sun Zhongshan). This is also where most of the five-star hotels and restaurants are located. For daily necessities, there are many branches of the CVS/Suguo drugstore chain spread about the city, most of which stay open 24 hours.

Orient Department Store
Address: 2 Zhongshan Nan Lu
Phone: 8478-4000

Xin Jie Kou Department Store
Address: 3 Zhongshan Nan Lu
Phone: 8471-5188

Shang Mao Department Store
Address: 49 Zhongshan Nan Lu
Phone: 8689-3000

Central (Zhongyang) Department Store
Address: 79 Zhongshan Nan Lu
Phone: 8471-8288

Jinling Shopping Center
Connected to the Jinling Hotel, this was recently expanded to include a new wing stretching down Zhongshan Lu. High-priced brand name shops including Bally, YSL, and Lacoste.

Address: 2 Hanzhong Lu
Phone: 8470-3360

Jinying International Shopping Center
Address: 89 Hanzhong Lu
Phone: 8470-8899

Pacific Department Store
Address: 86 Zhongshan Bei Lu
Phone: 8324-4728

Shanxi Lu Department Store
Address: 107 Zhongshan Bei Lu
Phone: 8323-8072

Carrefour Hypermarket
Address: 7 Da Qiao Nan Lu
Phone: 5877-1118

Taiping Department Store
Address: 279 Taiping Nan Lu

Jinling Flower Market
Address: 262 Yuhua Xi Lu

Restaurants (Can Ting)
Surprisingly enough for a city located deep in the interior of eastern China, Nanjing's restaurants offer a wide range of cuisines from around the world, including Italian, Korean, Thai, Indian, and Brazilian.

Most of China's regional cuisines are also represented. The range of culinary choices took a great leap forward in 2002 with the opening of the new Hunan Lu food street. For Western fast food, many branches of McDonalds and Kentucky Fried Chicken have been opened up in all parts of the city.

Hilton Hotel Paris Café
All you can eat buffet for 118 Rmb.
Address: 319 Zhongshan Dong Lu.

Aloha
All you can eat buffet 48 Rmb.
Address: 50 Hong Wu Lu.
Phone: 8471-7809.

Henry's Home (Hengli Zhijia)
This is probably the best Western style restaurant in the city. English language menu offers a wide assortment of Italian pasta and salads. Located in the Xin Jie Kou area, near the intersection of Guan Jia Qiao Lu and Hua Qiao Lu, next to the City Garden Coffee Shop.

Address: 33 Hua Qiao Lu
Phone: 8470-1292, 8471-7819

Venice Pizza
On the corner of Hua Qiao Lu and Zhongshan Bei Lu.

Golden Palm
At the intersection of Hua Qiao Lu and Guan Jia Qiao.

Topone Tepanyaki
Located on Gua Qiao Lu, next to the House Disco and across the street from the Jinling Hotel.

Swede and Kraut (Yun Zhong Canting)
Located in between Hankou Xi Lu and Shanghai Lu. Owned and operated by a Swedish-German couple, this was one of the first Western restaurants to open in the city.

Address: 14 Nan Xiu Cun
Phone: 8663-8798

Carioca (Li Yue Ren Ladin Canting)
Brazilian barbecue restaurant with two branches in the city. One is located inside the Sheraton Hotel, while the other is beside the former Soldiers' Club.

Address: 103 Zhongshan Bei Lu
Phone: 8323-2163

10,000 Buddhas Vegetarian Restaurant (Qian Fo Canting)
Located inside the grounds of the newly rebuilt Pi Lu Buddhist Temple (Pi Lu Si), just east of Mei Yuan Xincun, and before the Royal Place gate. The temple seems to have no exact street number yet.

Address: Mei Yuan Lu
Phone: 8451-8531

Golden Harvest Thai Café (Jin He Tai Da Canting)
Thai cuisine prepared by Thai chefs imported from Thailand.

Address: 2 Lion Bridge (Shizi Qiao), Hunan Lu Food Street
Phone: 8324-1823, 8324-5887.

Tudali Korean Barbecue (Tudali Han Guo Shao Kao)
Located near the intersection of Taiping Bei Lu and Zhongshan Dong Lu. Barbecued shish kebabs are the specialty.

Address: 118 Cheng Xian Jie
Phone: 8335-0910

Punjabi (Ben Jie Bi Canting)
Indian restaurant.

Address: 2 Lion Bridge (Shizi Qiao),, Hunan Lu Food Street
Phone: 8324-5421

La Zi Cun
Sichuan restaurant serving spicy Chinese dishes.

Address: 173 Sheng Zhou Lu
Phone: 5224-2389

Sichuan Jiu Jia
Sichuan Restaurant.

Address: 171 Taiping Nan Lu
Phone: 8664-5141 x 3030

Fuzi Miao Ding Shan Meishi Cheng
Offers a wide selection of traditional Nanjing delicacies.

Address: 5 Zhan Yuan Lu
Phone: 5220-7218

Ma Xiang Xing Muslim Restaurant
Founded in 1840 by the Muslim family of Ma Si Fa. The restaurant became famous in 1927 after the Guomindang official Tan Yan Kai enjoyed a meal there.

Address: 5 Zhongshan Bei Lu, just west of Gu Lou.

Coffee Shops (Kafei Guan)
Starbucks arrived in Nanjing in November 2003 and opened their first shop at Xin Jie Kou on Zhongshan Nan Lu. There is

also a growing assortment of homegrown coffee shops spreading throughout the city.

City Garden Coffee Shops (Cheng Shi Hua Yuan)
Several branches.

Address: 2 Bai Xia Lu (near Zhongshan Nan Lu)
Phone: 8441-1639

Address: 87 Guan Jia Qiao (near Hua Qiao Lu)
Phone: 8471-3515

Hedera Helix (Chang Chun Teng)
Several branches.

Address: 100 Shanghai Lu
Phone: 8323-2531

Address: 87 Shanghai Lu
Phone: 8663-6665

Address: Hua Qiao Lu (across the street from Henry's).

Nightlife

World Trade Center German Brahaus
In the basement of this building which is connected to the Jinling Hotel. Enter from Guan Jia Qiao. Has a live band.

The Black Cat
Address: 1 Ci Bei She Lu
Phone: 8472-8973

77 Music Studio
Serves pizza. Sometimes has live music.

Address: 129 Han Zhong Lu
Phone: 8470-2006

House Disco
Address: Guan Jia Qiao, across the street from the Jinling Hotel

Orgies Bar
Located next to the Hongqiao Hotel. Heavy metal bar whose interior is decorated with posters of Western rock bands like Guns N' Roses.

Address: 202 Zhongshan Bei Lu
Phone: 8343-3338, 8341-9991

Top One
Address: 187 Zhongshan Nan Lu
Phone: 8450-0423

The Answer Bar
Address: 13 Jin Yin Jie
Phone: 8323-2486

Theaters
Jiang Nan Theater
Address: 5 Yan Ling Jie
Phone: 8441-9786

Zijin Grand Theater
Address: 20 Xiao Huo Wa Jie
Phone: 8452-2015

People's Theater
Address: 25 Yang Gong Jing Lu
Phone: 8664-4605

Nanjing Culture and Arts Center
Address: 101 Chang Jiang Lu
Phone: 8470-6390

Nanjing Hotels

Five Star Hotels
Hilton International Hotel ***
Address: 319 Zhongshan Dong Lu
Phone: 8480-8888
Fax: 8480-9999

Sheraton Nanjing Kingsley ***
Address: 169 Hanzhong Lu
Phone: 8666-8888
Fax: 8666-9999

Jinling Hotel ***
Address: 2 Hanzhong Lu
Phone: 8471-1888
Fax: 8471-1666

Golden Eagle Crowne Plaza Hotel ***
Address: 89 Hanzhong Lu
Phone: 8471-8888
Fax: 8471-9999

Mandarin Garden ***
Address: 9 Zhuang Yuan Jing Lu
Phone: 5220-2555
Fax: 5220-1876

International Conference Hotel *****
Address: 2 Sifancheng, Zhongshan Ling Lu (Zijin Shan)
Phone: 8443-0888

Nanjing Dong Jiao Guest House
Officially unrated, mainly because it was formerly the secluded mountain retreat of China's national political leaders. Now open to the public. Expect five-star quality service.
Address: 5 Zhongshan Ling (Zijin Shan).
Phone: 8664-5181
Fax: 8440-1434

Xuan Wu Hotel ****
Address: 193 Zhongyang Lu
Phone: 8335-8888

Four Star Hotels
Grand Central Hotel ****
Address: 75 Zhongshan Lu
Phone: 8473-3666
Fax: 8473-3999

Yihua Ramada Plaza ****
Address: 45 Zhongshan Bei Lu
Phone: 8330-8888
Fax: 8330-9999

Ding Shan Shangri-La ****
Address: 90 Cha Ha Er Lu
Phone: 5880-2888
Fax: 5882-1729

Phoenix Palace Hotel ****
Address: 47 Hunan Lu
Phone: 8330-3388
Fax: 8663-0510
Web site: http://www.pphotel.com.cn

Three Star Hotels
Paradise Hotel (Tian Jin Da Jiudian) ***
Address: 238 Zhongshan Nan Lu (near Xinjie Kou)
Phone: 8420-9888, 420-9818
Fax: 420-9140

Hong Qiao Hotel ***
Address: 202 Zhongshan Bei Lu
Phone: 8340-0888

Shuang Men Lou Hotel ***
85 Huju Bei Lu
Phone: 5880-5961

Hanfu Hotel ***
Address: 264 Changjiang Lu
Phone: 8440-0400, 440-0415
Fax: 8440-0184

Yishi Hotel (Jiangsu Yishi Yuan Jiudian)
Address: 81 Zhongshan Bei Lu
Phone: 8332-6826
Fax: 8663-3110
E-mail: yshotel@public1.ptt.js.cn

Unrated Hotels
Zhongshan Hotel
Address: 307 Zhongshan Dong Lu
Phone: 8481-8888

Jiangsu Hotel
Address: 278 Taiping Nan Lu
Phone: 8664-6101

Transportation

Air Travel
Lukou International Airport (Lukou Feiji Chang) opened in 1997. It is located 35.8 km (22.2 miles) south of the city, or about one hour's drive.

Airport Information
Domestic Flights: 5248-0488
International Flights: 5248-0480

**Airport Ticket Booking Office
(Feiji Chang Shou Piao Chu)**
Phone: 248-0482, 5248-0710.

Unified Ticket Booking Office
Sells tickets for all domestic and foreign airlines serving Nanjing.
Address: 180 Hanzhong Lu
Domestic Flights Phone: 8660-2902, 8660-5015
Domestic Flights Fax: 8660-0250
International Flights Phone: 8660-2912

CAAC (Civil Aviation Adminstration of China)
Address: 52 Rui Jin Lu
Phone: 8664-9275

Train Stations (Huoche Zhan)
The main station is the East station on Long Pan Lu. A new train station has been under construction here, from 2002 to 2004, and unfortunately has caused considerable chaos in buying tickets and boarding trains. There are four train stations in Nanjing: North, South, East and West. Although it should be obvious, taxi drivers do sometimes take you to the wrong one. Nanjing is 310 km (192.6 miles) from Shanghai by rail.

Phone: 8582-2222, 99-820

Ships (Chuan)
Yangzi River ferries arrive and depart from Zhongshan Wharf, located in the Xia Guan district at the intersection of Jian Bian Lu and Zhongshan Bei Lu. Nanjing is 72.4 km (45 miles) up the Yangzi River from Zhenjiang, and 365 km (228 miles) from the East China Sea.

Address: 21 Jiang Bian Lu, Xia Guan.
Phone: 5880-2803, 5880-5501

Taxis (Chuzu Qi Che)
The basic cab fare is 7 Rmb for the first 3 km (1.9 miles). Take note that taxis in Nanjing will not stop and pick up passengers except at designated taxi stations, which act like bus stops.

Buses (Gong Gong Qi Che)
Most buses seem to converge on the Xin Jie Kou traffic circle, including the famous No. 9 which takes passengers all the way up Zijin Shan to Zhongshan Ling.

Subway (Di Tie)
On 12 December 2000, construction began on Nanjing's first subway system. However, the first metro line is not scheduled to be completed until 2005.

Travel Agencies (Luxing She)

CITS (China International Travel Service)
Address: 202-1 Zhongshan Bei Lu
Phone: 342-8999
Fax: 8342-8954

CTS (China Travel Service)
Address: 313 Zhongshan Bei Lu
Phone: 8343-1502

CYTS (China Youth Travel Service)
Address: 160 Hanzhong Lu
Phone: 8652-3344
Fax: 8652-3344
E-mail: cyts@public.ptt.js.cn

Nanjing Tourism Bureau
Address: 4 Nan Dong Gua Shi
Phone: 8360-8901

Qi Xia Shan District Tourism Bureau
Address: 234 Shao Shan Lu
Phone: 8562-4425

Antiques, Arts & Crafts

Fuzi Miao
Chao Tian Gong

Book Stores (Shu Dian)

Jiangsu Foreign Languages Bookstore
Address: 165 Zhong Yang Lu at corner of Hunan Lu
Phone: 8663-3094

Nanjing Xinhua Bookstore
Address: 130 Zhongshan Dong Lu, near Hong Wu Lu
Phone: 8450-0613, 8452-3713

Address: 58 Zhongshan Dong Lu
Phone: 8472-0344

Hunan Lu Xinhua Bookstore
Address: 47 Hunan Lu
Phone: 8330-0360

Nanjing Museum Bookstore
Address: 321 Zhongshan Dong Lu

Nanjing Gu Ji Shu Dian
Address: Taiping Nan Lu and Yang Gong Jin Lu.

Nanjing Book Mall
Address: Nanjing International Trade Center, 18 Zhongshan Dong Lu, near Xin Jie Kou.
Phone: 8479-1688
Web site: http://www.njbooks.com.cn

English Periodicals

Compared to Shanghai, Nanjing has been quite slow in developing any kind of local English language magazines. A brief attempt by *City Weekend* to expand their range of local editions to Nanjing was apparently shut down by the local authorities, while other local entrepreneurs met similar resistance from the powers that be, whose permission was needed to get the proper license. Finally, in 2002, a publication called *Map Magazine* began publishing on a bimonthly basis, with the support of the Jiangsu Tourism Bureau and, as of June 2004, has put out 28 issues.

Executive Publisher: Brett Sutcliffe
Address: 188 Hong Wu Bei Lu, 11th floor, Suite B, Nanjing
Phone: 8472-7680, 8471-9507, 8472-2466
Fax: 8470-5171
Web site: http://www.mapmagazine.com.cn
E-mail: editor@mapmagazine.com.cn

Life Nanjing

Like *That's Shanghai*, this is a slick, glossy magazine, mainly full of colorful advertising and lurid 'lifestyle' essays about hip, swinging Chinese yuppies. Nonethelss, its classified listings contain some useful local addresses and phone numbers.

Phone: 8452-0072
Web site: http://www.njlife.xici.net
E-mail: LifeNanjing@163.com

Anhui Province

Ma An Shan

The modern city of Ma An Shan was founded completely from scratch in October 1956 as an early Communist experiment in planned urban development. It covers 1,706 sq km (658.7 sq miles), is divided into four districts and one county, and has a total population of 1.18 million people.

Ma An Shan has a largely deserved reputation as a polluted industrial armpit that extends like a rust belt from the western outskirts of Nanjing to the eastern border of Wuhu, along the south bank of the Yangzi River. Because of its bad reputation, it has never even come close to being considered a travel destination, and most guide books either ignore it or even advise against visiting it.

Nonetheless, an exploration of the large area falling within the borders of the Ma An Shan Municipality (Ma An Shan Shi) reveals the surprising discovery of some genuine historic relics. Before 1949, Ma An Shan Municipality was known as the Prefecture of Taiping (Taiping Fu). In the Tang Dynasty, it was the haunt and final resting place of the poet Li Bai (Li Tai Po) (701–762 AD), who has left behind many sights and relics associated with his life. Over the centuries, many pagodas and temples, as well as tombs of princes and cultural celebrities, were erected here. A surprising number of these have survived. Most of these interesting sights lie in the western border area of the present municipality, in Dangtu County (Dangtu Xian), named after a tributary of the Yangzi River, the Dangtu Xi.

Cai Shi Ji National Park

About 7 km (4.3 miles) upriver, to the west of downtown Ma An Shan, in between the city center and the eastern border of Dangtu County (Dangtu Xian), stands a natural rock outcropping known as the **Cai Shi Ji**. This is perched on the south bank of the Yangzi River, at the base of 131-m-high (429.8-ft-high) Green Snail Mountain (Cui Luo Shan). This is one of the three most famous rock formations of this kind along the Yangzi, the other two being the Cheng Ling Ji in Yueyang, and Yanzi Ji in Nanjing. It was here that the Tang poet **Li Bai** (Li Tai Po) (701–762 AD) supposedly wrote many of his poems. According to legend, Li

Bai drowned in the Yangzi River near this rock when he fell out of his boat while trying to catch the reflection of the moon in the water's surface.

In Li Bai's time, Cai Shi Ji was known as Cow Island Rock (Niu Zhou Ji) and it is by this name that he refers to it in several of his poems. Later the name was changed to Colorful Stone Rock (Cai Shi Ji). Today, the main sights include the Li Bai Memorial Hall (Li Bai Ji Nian Guan), Tai Bai Tower (Tai Bai Lou), Guang Ji Buddhist Temple (Guang Ji Si), Li Bai's Garment Tomb (Li Bai Yi Guan Zhong), San Tai Pavilion (San Tai Ge), Capturing the Moon Terrace (Zhuo Yue Tai) or Lian Bi Tai, the newly built Ancient Plank Road (Gu Jian Dao), pleasure boats, as well as sandy beaches at low tide. There are five natural caves, the largest of which is the Three Officials Cave (San Guan Dong), covered by the Miao Yuan Pavilion. The Golden Cow Cave (Jin Niu Dong) gave the area its original name. Since 1989, the International Poet Chanting Festival has been held here every year on 9 September.

Turn off from National Highway 205 (Ning Wu Gong Lu) onto Tang Xian Lu to Cai Shi Town. A footbridge crosses the **Cuo Xi He** canal that encircles Cui Luo Shan and leads you to the park's main gate (Da Men) where you pay a 40 Rmb admission charge. Frome here, at the foot of Cui Luo Shan, the enormous five-story San Tai Pavilion on the summit is already visible, as is the cable car that can take you there if you choose not to climb up. It's much larger than Swallow's Crag (Yanzi Ji), and more the size of Shi Zhong Shan or She Shan. It also goes by the name of Cai Shi Ji National Park or Cai Shi Ji Scenic Area.

Entering the park, you are immediately surrounded by thick bamboo forests, lakes, chirping birds with long brightly colored tail feathers, and networks of winding trails ascending the mountain.

Walking around the northwestern base of the hill, you pass through the Bamboo Forest (Wan Zhu Wu) and then come to the first two main sights – the Li Bai Memorial Hall and Tai Bai Tower, side by side at the end of the road – followed shortly by the lower cable car (*suo dao*) station and Guang Ji Temple.

The **Tai Bai Tower** (Tai Bai Lou) is a three-story traditional wooden structure that looks like a Confucian temple, with double rows of upturned roof eaves covered by glazed tiles. This hall was supposedly built in 1877, during the Qing Dynasty, by Peng Yu Lin, one of Zeng Guofan's key lieutenants during the Taiping Rebellion. Interestingly, Tai Bai Tower has been erected on the same site as an earlier memorial hall devoted to Li Bai known as the **Banished Immortal Tower** (Zhe Xian Lou). This was built in the Yuan He period (806–820 AD) of the Xian Zong reign (805–820 AD) during the Tang Dynasty. The present walled compound actually consists of three main courtyards and three buildings on a central axis, with two smaller side courtyards. Inside the first courtyard, some inscribed tablets are cemented into the wall. There is a second courtyard and hall behind the first. Inside the second hall is a wooden carved statue of a standing Li Bai and some exhibits in glass cases. Climbing up to the second floor of the first hall, you find another carved wooden statue of Li Bai in a seated position. Behind the second hall is a third courtyard at the rear in which stands a modern building known as **Li Bai's Drunken Moon Tea House** (Tai Bai Zui Yue Zhai Cha Lou). From this third courtyard, a portal in the wall leads into the rear garden behind the neighboring Li Bai Memorial Hall (Li Bai Ji Nian Guan).

Li Bai Memorial Hall (Li Bai Ji Nian Guan) has a large stone entrance gate similar to that of the Loyalties Temple at Shi Zhong Shan. Passing through a courtyard leads you into the main hall lined with shelves of Li Bai's written works. Behind this is a beautiful garden bisected by moss-covered brick paved paths. Although it was only built in November 1987, the garden somehow manages to appear older than its Qing Dynasty neighbor. All together the complex includes seven halls and pavilions. Several derelict wooden structures in the rear garden seem to be older relics, with intricate woodwork carvings, weathered exteriors, and peeling paint. As is usually the case, some authentic broken stone tablets with decorative artwork lie on the ground in the back corner of the garden next to a trash heap.

Guang Ji Buddhist Temple (Guang Ji Si) was under reconstruction in January 2004, and consisted of only one small hall with no resident monks. However, stone pillar pedestals scattered about on the ground and a series of flights of stone steps showed that an earlier temple probably once occupied a larger area here, covering three hillside terraces. The original Guang Ji Si was supposedly built here in 239AD during the Three Kingdoms (San Guo) and was reportedly still flourishing during the reign of Zhu Yuanzhang (1368–1398) in the Ming Dynasty. Exactly what its relationship is with the temple of the same name in nearby Wuhu is unclear. Just below Guang Ji Si is the site of the **Dark Red Well** (Chi Wu Jing), which is supposedly over 1,700 years old.

For an additional 20 Rmb, you can take a round trip ride on the cable car (*suo dao*) to the summit. However, the more interesting sights lie at the water's edge and along the fairly easy hillside trail to the top of the peak. Walking along the water's edge, just below Guang Ji Si, takes you to a natural rock outcropping, that extends out into the water, which has fantastic views of the Yangzi River and the ships traveling on it in both directions. This rock is known as the footprint of Ming General Chang Yuchun, or simply the **Giant Footprint** (**Da Jiao Yin**). Waves crash against the rocks, small wooden boats row around the promontory, and half a dozen house boats are anchored nearby with families living on board them. One is tempted to believe that this is the very spot where Li Bai once sat drinking wine, gazing at the river, and writing poetry. Nonetheless, modern-day residents reserve that fame for the more inaccessible area around the Seizing the Moon Terrace. Just behind this promontory is a rock cliff face with flights of stone steps etched into it. However, a climb up the nearby hillside makes for a much easier route to rejoin the trail to the summit.

The trail to the summit of Cui Luo Shan gradually climbs a ridge line and passes by three small pavilions known as the **Ran Xi Pavilion** (Ran Xi Ting), **Emei Pavilion** (Emei Ting), and **Huai Xie Pavilion** (Huai Xie Ting), located at various spots. The Huai Xie Pavilion is dedicated to General Xie Shang of the Eastern Jin Dynasty, who appears in Li Bai's most famous poem about Cai Shi Ji. Part of the path between the Emei and Huai Xie Pavilions is lined on both sides with six pairs of stone animal sculptures similar to a sacred way (*shen dao*) leading to the tomb of an emperor, prince, or other important person. In fact, shortly past the Huai Xie Pavilion, dedicated to General Xie Shang of the Eastern Jin Dynasty, you reach the site of **Li Bai's Garment Tomb** (Li Bai Yi Guan Zhong). The tomb is a mound of earth, surrounded by a round stone block wall, seated on a raised stone terrace with an inscribed tablet erected in front of it. Although Li Bai's real tomb lies in the nearby Cai Shi Ji at the foot of Qing Shan, this tomb supposedly contains his personal effects. Unlike the stone animal sculptures of the *shen dao*, which appear as if they could be real historic relics, this tomb's current construction is obviously brand new.

Past the tomb, the trail ascends uneventfully to the enormous **San Tai Ge** pavilion on Cui Luo Shan's summit. Although the name San Tai Ge means Three Terrace Pavilion, the current four-sided tower actually has five floors, each one featuring projecting upturned roof eaves covered with glazed tiles. The entire structure is 30 m (98.4 ft) high, and from the top you can supposedly see as far as Tian Men Shan and Jiuhua Shan, as well as the nearby Yangzi River. The present structure was not mentioned in a 1989 local guide book and seems to have been built in the late 1990s. However, it is modeled on an earlier pavilion of the same name, built here during the Chong Zhen reign (1628–1644) of the Ming Dynasty.

From the summit and ridge line, several steep trails lead downward to the San Guan Dong, Heng Jiang Guang, Xi Da Wa, Capturing the Moon Terrace (Zhuo Yue Tai), and so-called **Ancient Plank Road** (Gu Jian Dao) at the eastern foot of the mountain. Despite its name, the Ancient Plank Road is, in fact, a brand new construction, which has been impressively built into the cliffside over the Yangzi River and even has tunnels running through several long sections of man-made caves in the natural rock. An easier alternative for reaching this relatively inaccessible eastern foot of the mountain is to travel from Cai Shi Town to where a road ends at the site of the local cross-river ferry landing (*matou*), where you'll also see anchored a large ship used as a floating restaurant. From here, it is possible — in the low tide winter months — to take a romantic walk along the sandy beach beside the Yangzi until you pick up the cliffside Plank Road that will take you directly to the Capturing the Moon

Terrace. Best of all, this route provides you with free access to the whole national park without paying the rather exorbitant 40 Rmb admission charge.

Address: Tang Xian Lu, Cai Shi Town
Phone: (0555) 210-1058
Admission: 40 Rmb

POINT OF INTEREST

Two variant translations exist of Li Bai's most famous poem about Cai Shi Ji, each with quite different titles, and both of which are hard for the untrained eye to identify with this place since they use the site's earlier name of Cow Island Rock (Niu Zhou Ji). In *The Jade Mountain* (1929), Witter Bynner calles it "... A Night Mooring Under Mount Niu Chu (Niu Zhou Ji)." Here, the poet is made to say:

"This night to the west of the river brim
There is not one cloud in the whole blue sky
As I watch from my deck the autumn moon,
Vainly remembering old General Hsieh* ...
I have poems; I can read;
He heard others, but not mine.
... tomorrow I shall hoist my sail,
with fallen maple leaves behind me."

* General Xie Shang of the Eastern Jin Dynasty

However, Minford and Lau (1996) entitle their version, "Night Mooring at Cow's Creek..." Here, an attempt is made to present the intended rhythm of Li Bai's prose:

"At Cow's Creek
on Western River*,
the night
sky still blue.
not a rag of cloud.
I go on deck
To look at the bright moon,
Thinking of
The great General Xie** of old.
I also
can make poetry,
but that man's like
will not be found again.
In the morning
We make sail and go.
The maple leaves
Fall as they will."

* Cuo Xi He
** General Xie Shang of the Eastern Jin Dynasty

Huang Shan Bao Ta

Driving westward out of the industrial center of Ma An Shan on the Ning Ma Expressway, about 30 km (18.6 miles) from the city center, you suddenly pass the Huang Shan Bao Ta, a large stone pagoda perched on the very summit of a 54-m-high (177.2-ft-high) forested hilltop to your left, on the south side of the road. From a distance, only the top three levels can be seen emerging above the natural thick canopy of the tree line, but there are two more stories hidden from view. It has no balconies, no roof eaves, and no metal spiral on top, appearing like a cylindrical stone pillar.

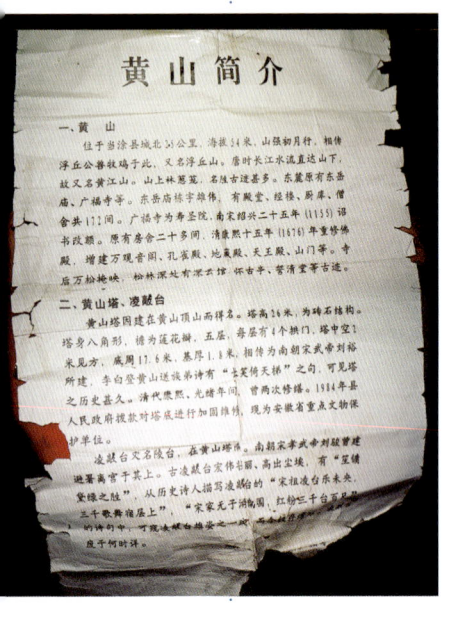

There is no visible way to approach the summit from the front of the hill facing the highway. A path exists up the back side, if one has time to circle around the hill to find the way up. Turning off the main highway and driving one block until you reach a traffic circle marking the location of the small township of Huang Shan Zhen, you turn left onto a dirt road and drive until you reach a small roadside shop on your right. Park here and follow a foot trail that begins on the left side of the road. A climb to the top on foot takes about half an hour.

After crossing the railroad tracks and walking through some fields, you come to a small newly rebuilt Buddhist temple at the foot of the hill. **Huang Shan Guang Fu Si** has three small halls and it appears that at least one Buddhist nun is a resident there. The nun possesses a single long torn paper scroll describing the temple's history. According to the scroll, this hill was known as Huang Jiang Shan in the Tang Dynasty, because the Yangzi River then flowed much closer to its northern base. Guang Fu Si was first built on this spot in 1155, during the Northern Song (Bei Song) Dynasty. In 1676, during the early Qing Dynasty, the temple was greatly expanded with the building of many new halls. The current halls were built in 1984.

From the temple you hike up the ridge, past a new hall under construction, and many tomb mounds with inscribed tablets. This is an indication that this place has been considered sacred for some time. In fact, the southern slopes of the hill are known as the Tomb Terrace (Ling Chao Tai or Ming Ling Tai).

At the summit is the five-story, 26-m-high (85.3-ft-high), octagonal Huang Shan Ta. The walls are made of brick and stone, over which white plaster was once spread. Broken wooden

The single torn paper scroll recording the full history of Guang Fu Si Buddhist Temple on Huangshan in Ma An Shan.

Huangshan Guang Fu Si Buddhist Temple.

beams stick out at each level to show where roof eaves and verandas probably once existed. Every other side of the pagoda has an open window, including four on the ground floor, but there seems to be no doorway. Looking through the open ground floor windows, one can see that the pagoda is hollow inside, with no stairs or upper interior floors. Unfortunately, there are no original inscriptions left on the pagoda's exterior, and the one modern tablet standing beside it has had its inscription completely rubbed off. In style, it appears to be similar to those from the Northern Song (Bei Song) Dynasty. However, according to the scroll possessed by the Buddhist nun at the temple below, the pagoda was first built during the Southern Dynasties (Nan Chao) period, in the Liu Song Dynasty (420–479 AD) reign of Emperor Wu Di (420–422 AD). During the Qing Dynasty (1644–1911), it was repaired in the reigns of both Kang Xi and Guang Xu. In 1984, it was repaired by the Dangtu county government.

Incredible views can be had from the summit of the entire Wuhu and Ma An Shan areas. The pagoda stares out at the Yangzi River, and can be seen from the confluence of the Dangtu Xi and the Yangzi.

Address: Huang Shan Zhen, Dangtu Xian

Huangshan Precious Pagoda (Bao Ta).

Li Bai Tomb (Li Bai Wen Hua Yuan)

Ma An Shan's biggest claim to fame is as the site where the 8th century poet **Li Bai** (Li Tai Po) (701–762 AD) supposedly drowned in the Yangzi River near the Cai Shi Ji in 762 AD. As the romantic tale goes, after a drinking party on board a boat, he fell into the river while trying to embrace the reflection of the moon in the water's surface. Another legend says he was carried away on the back of a Yangzi River dolphin to the land of the immortals. However, Li Bai's two biographers, Shigeyoshi Obata and Arthur Waley, both disregard these legends. Waley states that Li Bai died in the home of Li Yang Ping s(693–772 AD), the Prefect of Dangtu; a statement which at least supports the historical authenticity of the location of his present tomb here.

Today, Li Bai is commemmorated in Ma An Shan by a reconstructed tomb and new memorial temple set in a beautiful garden known as the **Li Bai Wen Hua Yuan**. This garden is located west of the Dangtu Xi, in Dangtu County, near Ma An Shan's border with Wuhu. From the Ning Ma Expressway, you need to turn off onto a side road heading south towards the industrial center of Da Long Qiao. After driving 3 km (1.9 miles) through an industrially unsavory area, you will reach the site of the garden which is set in beautiful surroundings at the foot of a range of wooded hills. Oddly enough, it is nowhere within sight of the Yangzi River where Li Bai supposedly drowned.

PERSONALITIES

Li Bai's career fascinates us not only because of the quality of his poems, but because of his strikingly unorthodox lifestyle. Unlike all his contemporary poets of the Tang Dynasty, Li Bai was the only one to never even attempt to take the imperial civil service examinations. Because of his lack of a scholarly degree, he never once held a single government post as an official, with the exception of a brief stint as a court poet attached to the Hanlin Academy in Changan (Xian). For all other Tang poets, writing poetry was a hobby conducted in retirement from the civil service or during brief periods of political banishment from the capital. For Li Bai, poetry-writing was his sole vocation and means of employment. At that time, commercial publishing was in its infancy so this was not really an economically viable career choice and explains the absence of others following his example. As a result, Li Bai always relied on the kindness of strangers. He would introduce himself to people who happened to share his quite common surname as supposedly being one of their distant relatives. When invited as a guest for dinner, he would often end up staying with his host for as long as a year. Many of his poems are written in gratitude or fond farewell to these sometimes unwitting patrons. He was truly a bohemian vagabond before the terms were coined. Dabbling superficially in Taoist studies, he liked to be called by his nickname, "The Banished Immortal." Traveling extensively throughout the Yangzi River region, he lived for brief periods at Yangzhou, Nanjing, Susong, Jiujiang, Mount Lushan, Wuhan, and Yueyang, leaving us his impressions of these places in his poetry.

The garden covers 60,000 sq m (645,835 sq ft) and includes the **Tai Bai Tablet Corridor** (Tai Bai Bei Lin), **Tai Bai Ancestral Temple** (Tai Bai Ci), and **Li Bai's Tomb** (Li Bai Mu). A memorial gateway (*pai lou*) marks the entrance. This is followed by a long pathway, lined on both sides with scenes from Li Bai's life, which leads you to a lake around whose shores are scattered the various halls. The Tablet Corridor displays modern reproductions of one hundred of Li Bai's most essential poems. The Tai Bai Ancestral Temple consists of two modern reproductions of traditional halls, on a south-north axis, separated by a courtyard and surrounded by a wall. A weathered stone tablet bearing an inscription stands in front of the first hall's southern entrance. The official record of the site dates this tablet to the year 1241, in the Li Zong reign of the Southern Song (Nan Song) Dynasty.

Passing through the second hall of the temple and exiting from its northern side, you come to another walled enclosure in the middle of which is Li Bai's Tomb. The tomb consists of a round earthen mound surrounded at the base by a round stone wall, with a stone tablet in front. Although it has obviously been repaired, at least part of the tomb's stone tablet appears to be a genuine relic. According to the official story, the tablet dates from the Qing Dynasty. It is inscribed with one vertical line of eight characters that read, *Tang Ming Xian Li Bai Mu Zhi Mu*, meaning, "The Tomb of Li Bai: a famous person of the Tang Dynasty."

The overall new appearance of the site tempts one to view this simply as an attempt by Ma An Shan to cash in on its most famous former resident. However, the official record of the site states that a Li Bai Tomb was built on this spot in 817 AD, during the 12th year of the Xian Zong reign (805–820 AD) of the Tang Dynasty. Arthur Waley's 1950 biography of Li Bai, *The Poetry and Career of Li Po*, testifies that he did, in fact, die here in Dangtu, but it says nothing about his tomb. Shigeyoshi Obata's 1922 biography of Li Bai, *The Works of Li Po*, explains the mystery of the long gap between the poet's death

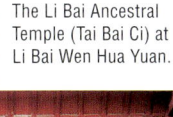

The new Da Men of Li Bai Wen Hua Yuan, the site of Li Bai's Tomb in Ma An Shan.

The Li Bai Ancestral Temple (Tai Bai Ci) at Li Bai Wen Hua Yuan.

Left and right: Li Bai Wen Hua Yuan

and his burial at the site of his present tomb. According to Obata, Li Bai had expressed a wish to be buried on Qing Shan, but instead was buried without ceremony at the eastern foot of another hill in the area known as Long Shan. When Bai Ju Yi (772–846 AD) visited the grave sometime in the second decade of the 9th century, he was surprised to find it in a neglected state of overgrown decay. Public embarrassment at the tomb's condition coincided with the rediscovery that it was not even located where Li Bai had wanted it to be. Shortly thereafter, the grave was moved to a newly constructed tomb at its present location on the north side of Qing Shan, where Obata says "two new monuments" had been erected by January 818AD. This story is confirmed in the biography of Li Bai by Song Zhi, published in 1060 in the dynastic history, *The New Book of Tang* (*Xin Tang Shu*). Since then, the present tomb has been repaired 12 different times. In 1954, the Anhui government designated the tomb as a provincial level protected cultural unit.

Address: Li Bai Wen Hua Yuan, Dangtu Xian
Phone: (0555) 671-1309, 668-3504
E-Mail : libai_817@163.com
Web site: http://www.libaidt.com

Li Bai Wen Hua Yuan.

Green Hill (Qing Shan)

The 372 m (1,220.5 ft) forested hill just behind Li Bai's Tomb is called Qing Shan. Li Bai is said to have often visited the hill during his lifetime, so it is sometimes called Li Jia Shan. Historic sites on the hill include some **Imperial Tombs of the Eastern Jin Dynasty** (317–419 AD), which had its capital in Nanjing, and the **Palace and Pool of Xie Tiao** (Xie Gong Chi). Xie Tiao was a poet of the Qi Dynasty (479–501 AD), which also had its capital in Nanjing. There are two Buddhist temples on the hill: **Stone Buddha Nunnery** (Shi Fo An) and **Cloud and Mist Zen Buddhist Temple** (Yun Wu Chan Si).

Li Bai's Tomb (Li Bai Mu).

The Jin Zhu Bao Ta stands at the confluence of the Dangtu Xi and the Yangzi River.

Jin Zhu Ta (Bao Ta)

Farther west on the Ning Ma Expressway, you cross a bridge over the Dangtu River (Dangtu Xi), a tributary that flows into the Yangzi from the south. As you cross the bridge, turn your head to the right and you will see a very tall stone pagoda in the distance, near the shores of the Yangzi River. This pagoda can be reached by turning right off the main highway onto a dirt road that follows the western bank of the Dangtu Xi. Along the way, you will pass fleets of river barges tied up to the shore. As you get closer to the pagoda, its massive size and impressive image become clearer and clearer. Arrival at the site shows that the pagoda stands precisely at the confluence of the Yangzi and the Dangtu Xi, an auspicious location to say the least. All ships sailing up or down the Yangzi River should be able to get a clear view of this impressive tower.

Stone tablets at the foot of the Jin Zhu Bao Ta.

The pagoda is a seven-story, octagonal structure made of brick and stone. It has no wooden parts, and even the roof eaves and the brackets that support them on each floor are made entirely of stone. Grass and plants growing out of the pagoda's summit and its six levels of eaves illustrate its natural, unrestored condition. It is a miracle to find a pagoda in China that has neither fallen to ruins nor has been so heavily restored as to appear brand new and lose the mystique given it by its true age. There are open windows on each of the six upper levels, and on the ground floor, a metal gate in the entrance can actually be opened to allow visitors to climb up the winding flights of stone steps all the way to the top.

The Jin Zhu Bao Ta.

A shrine at the foot of the Jin Zhu Bao Ta.

Although there are no original inscriptions remaining on the tower itself, several broken stone tablets and a few faded modern-day signs scattered around the base tell the pagoda's story. One faded tablet bears the three characters for "Jin Zhu Ta." Two male octagenarians living in shacks at the base of the tower welcome visitors warmly with the "O-Mi-Tuo-Fo" greeting and hands pressed together. They seem to be old Buddist monks (*Lao Hou Shang*) who have voluntarily assigned themselves the task of caring for the tower. According to these oral sources, the pagoda was built in 1589 during the Wan Li reign of the Ming Dynasty. They also call it the Jin Zhu Ta or Bao Ta, the latter being the standard name given to all pagodas that form part of a Buddhist temple. However, there is no sign of even the remains of any temple buildings nearby. There is a make-shift shrine with the figures of two people, a man and woman, inside. A few shards of a broken porcelain Guanyin are set in a recess in the pagoda's ground floor exterior. Active Buddhist and popular worship of an informal sort is obviously still carried out here by the local people.

Address: Dangtu Xi, Dangtu Xian

Anhui Province
Wuhu

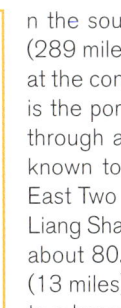

On the south bank of the Yangzi river, about 449 km (289 miles) upstream from the river's mouth, situated at the confluence of the Yangzi and the Qing Yi River, is the port of Wuhu in Anhui Province. After passing through a narrow gap between two hills, historically known to Europeans as "the Pillars," but called the East Two Mountains and West Two Mountains (Dong Liang Shan and Xi Liang Shan) by the Chinese, located about 80.5 km (50 miles) above Nanjing and 21 km (13 miles) below Wuhu, the Yangzi River here widens to a breadth of about 8 km (5 miles).

The city of Wuhu has a history of over 2,000 years. During the Spring and Autumn (Chun Qiu) Period (770–476 BC) of the Later Zhou Dynasty, it was known as Jiu Zi Yi. However, during the Eastern Han Dynasty (25–20 AD), the place name was first changed to Wuhu (Five Lakes) when it was designated as a county (*xian*) in 109 AD. In 719 AD, during the Kai Yuan era (713–741 AD) of the Xuan Zong reign (712–756 AD) of the Tang Dynasty, the Korean prince Kim Gio Gak (Jing Qiao Jue) supposedly stopped here on his way to nearby Jiuhua Shan, where he was later recognized as the reincarnation of the bodhisattva Dizang after his death in 794 AD. Kim's visit seems to have sparked the founding of the city's still functioning Buddhist temple, Guang Ji Si, later in the 12th century.

During the Taiping Rebellion, Wuhu was occupied by the Taipings for about six years, from 1854 to 1860. Wuhu first fell to the Taipings on 4 March 1854 after they sailed downriver from Anqing. After this, it became an important point in the western defense of the Taiping capital in Nanjing. When Lord Elgin commanded a flotilla of British ships that sailed up the Yangzi River in November and December 1858, he reported that the Taipings still controlled Wuhu. The Taiping's Zhong Wang, Li Xiu Cheng, was able to briefly recapture Wuhu in November 1860.

Wuhu was still in the hands of the Taipings when Captain Blakiston stopped there in March 1861, on his way up the Yangzi River as part of Admiral Sir James Hope's naval expedition. Blakiston reported that at that time, the suburbs of the town started at the confluence of the Yangzi and the Qing Yi River (Qing Yi He), a tributary flowing into the larger river from the south, at a spot marked by the Zhong Jiang Ta pagoda, which still stands today. However, the walled town of Wuhu was actually located at least 1.6 km (1 mile) away from the Yangzi, up the Qing Yi He. This was apparently still the location of the walled town as late as 1895 when Villard published his map of the Yangzi, although the city center moved towards the shore of the larger river later. His map shows four gates facing the Qing Yi He, two to the south, one to the east, and one gate facing north towards the Yangzi. The entire walled town was south of the line of Wuhu's dozen hills.

Wuhu was opened as a treaty port in April 1877, in accordance with the 13 September 1876 Chefoo (Yantai) Convention signed with Britain. It was the only treaty port in Anhui Province, since the provincial capital of Anqing located upriver was never opened to foreign trade. In 1884, the British firm of Butterfield & Swire opened an office here for their steamship line, the China Navigation Co. By the 1890s, it was an important port of call for river steamers, and had a British Consulate, a Customs House, and a Roman Catholic Jesuit mission. This influx of foreign immigrants was not entirely welcome by the local population, and on 13 May 1891, a mob attacked and destroyed the Catholic mission in Wuhu. A new **Roman Catholic Cathedral**, which still stands today, was completed in 1895 on a knoll facing the Yangzi River where ships sailing by could easily see it. In 1899, Episcopalian missionaries began constructing a residential community and educational compound known as the **St. James Episcopal School** on top of **Lion Hill** (Shizi Shan). The St. James School continues to be a functioning educational institution today, albeit under new management.

By the time Gretchen Mae Fitkin visited Wuhu in 1921, most of the foreign residents and institutions were perched on the city's seven hilltops. Residences for the foreign staff of the Standard Oil Co. of New York (Socony) and the Asiatic Petroleum Co. (APC) were atop **Da Guan Shan**. Replacing an earlier version of the facility they had established in the same spot in 1913, American Methodist missionionaries in 1926 completed the new **Wuhu General Hospital** at the top of **Yi Ji Shan**, the hill nearest the Yangzi River. A modern day hospital, Yi Ji Shan Yiyuan, still stands on this hill, with the Methodists' 1926 building continuing to serve as the facility's core.

When the city was captured by the Guomindang army in March 1927 during their Northern Expedition (Bei Fa) from Guangzhou, the resulting outbreak of antiforeign riots forced the foreign community to be evacuated downriver to the safety of Shanghai by British and American warships patrolling the Yangzi. By 1931, the only foreign consul resident at Wuhu was Japanese, and those foreign residents who remained lived several miles inland on a series of low foothills, including Lion Hill (Shizi Shan). The town had a population of 136,000 inhabitants in 1931. However, when Commander F.H.E. Skyrme published his guide to the Yangzi in 1937, he reported that Wuhu was still the home of several "foreign missions and hospitals." During the first decade of Guomindang rule, urban development came to Wuhu with the destruction of the city walls in 1936, as well as the construction of road and rail links with Nanjing.

The final blow to this city of the Min Guo era came on 10 December 1937 when Wuhu fell to the Japanese, three days before Nanjing. After the Japanese defeat in August 1945, Wuhu did not really return to its prewar normalcy. For one whole week in 1947, from 2nd to 9th May, the city experienced rice riots in response to hyperinflation and food shortages. Not until the 1990s did Wuhu achieve its current level of prosperity and stability.

Wuhu Today

The Wuhu municipality (Wuhu Shi) covers a total area of 3,317 sq km (1,280.7 sq miles), with a population of 2.2 million people. However, the urban center occupies just 230 sq km (88.8 sq miles), and is inhabited by only 659,000 urban residents.

Wuhu is Anhui Province's most important Yangzi River port. Since it was opened to visits by foreign ships in April 1992, the city has had an increasing amount of economic investment. An Economic and Technology Development Zone was set up here in April 1993, and there is now also a special Export Processing Zone. Both developments are in the eastern suburbs, outside of town.

For travelers, it is one of the jumping-off points for trips to the Buddhist temples on **Nine Flower Mountain** (Jiuhua Shan), one of the Four Sacred Buddhist Mountains in China, and to the **Yellow Mountain** (Huang Shan), both located south of the Yangzi in southern Anhui Province.

Wuhu is a fairly important transportation hub where four rail lines and a cross-river highway converge. From here, the main East-West rail line from Nanjing divides in two directions. One line heads north to Hefei, the capital of Anhui province, while another goes south to Tunxi, which has the nearest train station to Yellow Mountain (Huang Shan). A fourth spur line continues westward upriver a short distance to the next Yangzi river town of Tongling, where it ends. The completion of a new highway and railway bridge (Changjiang Da Qiao) across the Yangzi River at Wuhu on 30 September 2000 has, for the first time, provided direct rail and road access to Anhui's provincial capital of Hefei.

For a small inland city relatively unknown to foreigners, Wuhu is an incredibly prosperous place today. Department stores and clothing shops along the Zhongshan Road pedestrian mall sell the latest fashions, while night spots such as the Celebrity Club put on impressive Las Vegas-style shows complete with musicians and performers imported from such big cities as Guangzhou. It is also an extremely livable city, full of parks, lakes, and green hills. This is in stark contrast with the extremely bleak, inhospitable, and undeveloped city of Hefei.

Map of Wuhu

Wuhu Sights
Middle River Pagoda (Zhong Jiang Ta)

The five-story Zhong Jiang Pagoda (Zhong Jiang Ta) stands right at the confluence of the Yangzi River and the Qing Yi River (Qing Yi He), a tributary flowing into the larger river from the south. The pagoda has an octagonal shape, with walls made entirely of red brick, and four sets of wooden roof eaves with tripod brackets supporting them. There are no original inscriptions or Buddha images on the tower's exterior. Furthermore, there seems to be no entrance at all, with even the windows on the first and second floors having been sealed up. There are some windows open on the 3rd and 5th floors, and a metal spiral on the top of the roof. However, there are two modern day plaques on the base of the pagoda, with the dates of the construction (1618), reconstruction (1669), and its height of 43 m (141.1 ft). Views of the tower, and access to it, are somewhat obscured in all directions by surrounding shops and residences. Strangely, it is not the centerpiece of a public park as one might expect of the city's key historic sight. You can approach the base of the pagoda from a flight of steps to the left of it, which lead up to a terrace. The Zhong Jiang Ta stands on Yan He Lu, at its intersection with Ji He Nan Lu, on the eastern bank of the Qing Yi He.

Top: A commemorative plaque on the Middle River Pagoda (Zhong Jiang Ta) in Wuhu.
Above: The Middle River Pagoda (Zhong Jiang Ta) in Wuhu.

Roman Catholic Cathedral (Wuhu Tian Zhu Jiao Tang)

This 108-year-old cathedral was completed by French Jesuits in June 1895 and has twin four-story bell towers which were added only in 1931. It was last repaired in 1993, over a period

The Roman Catholic Cathedral (Tian Zhu Jiao Tang) in Wuhu.

of three months from September to December. Each tower is topped by a dome adorned with crosses, but only the right dome has a round clock-face embedded in it. A round rose window on the front of the cathedral's main hall still has the Jesuit logo of "JHS" in the center. A new giant white statue of Jesus stands over the center peak of the central hall's roof. The three-story building is of stone block construction, but the twin towers' fourth floor is made of red brick. There are three arched double wooden entrances on the front of the main hall, but access to the inside is actually through a smaller side door. The interior of the church is covered with peeling yellow paint, but has a total of 11 altars, three in the front with four along each side. The ceiling consists of ten vaulted domes, similar to the style of the catholic cathedrals in Shanghai on She Shan and at Xujiahui. There is a memorial inside, dedicated to a former bishop who died in 1990 and which lists important events in his life from 1915, 1927, 1935, and 1942. Today, the church has a relatively young resident priest and a congregation of active worshippers. It stands a few blocks east of the Zhong Jiang Ta, which can be seen at the end of tree-lined Ji He Nan Lu, and across the street from a large open plaza that occupies the city block between the church and the Yangzi River. The cathedral was built on a knoll facing the Yangzi River, which can be seen from the church's front terrace. Ships sailing up and down the river could see the cathedral and its towers, making for an impressive sight.

Address: 28 Ji He Nan Lu
Phone: 383-5418

Guang Ji Buddhist Temple (Guang Ji Si)

At the southern foot of Zhe Shan is a Buddhist temple with a history dating back to the Tang Dynasty. In 719AD, during the Kai Yuan era (713–741 AD) of the Xuan Zong reign (712–756 AD) of the Tang Dynasty, the Korean prince **Jing Qiao Jue** (Kim Gio Gak, also known as Kim Kiao Kak) stopped here on his way to Jiuhua Shan, where he was later recognized as the reincarnation of the bodhisattva Dizang after his death in 794AD. As a result, this temple was sometimes called Xiao Jiuhua (still the name of a nearby lane) or Jiuhua Gong. The temple still possesses a gold signet which dates from the reign of the Tang emperor Su Zong (756–762 AD). However, the temple itself was built between the years 894 to 897 AD, a hundred years after Jing Qiao Jue's death, during the reign of the last Tang Emperor, Zhao Zong (888–904 AD). Its stone pagoda (Zhe Ta) was added in the year 1065, during the Northern Song (Bei Song) Dynasty. The most recent version of the temple's Da Xiong Bao Dian was built in 1783. In 1983, Guang Ji Si was named a "national key temple" by the central government's State Council. Since 2000, the temple has been undergoing a massive reconstruction that was still underway in July 2003. Nowadays, the temple complex consists of six main halls built into the hillside, with 20 resident monks living there. An annual temple fair is held every 30 July.

The new entrance hall of Guang Ji Si Buddhist Temple in Wuhu.

A commemmortive plaque on the wall of Guang Ji Si Buddhist Temple in Wuhu.

statue of one of the Four Heavenly Kings (Tian Wang) at Guang Ji Si Buddhist Temple.

The temple can be approached across a large new plaza from Jiuhua Zhong Lu. For a more picturesque route, travel along the narrow market street of Xiao Jiuhua Jie from Beijing Dong Lu. The first hall is a colorful new building which serves simply as a souvenir shop and ticket booth. Exiting the first hall, you see is an open field, with the rest of the complex still hidden from view down at the end of a pathway. Along the path is a sign with a map and a brief history of the complex.

Reaching the front of the main complex, you find a screen wall, an open area containing three incense burners, and the entrance gate hall or **Shan Men Dian**. The Shan Men Dian is flanked on the left by a two-story **Drum Tower** (Gu Lou) and on the right by a two-story **Bell Tower** (Zhong Lou). At this stage, only the top three storys of the five-story brick pagoda (Zhai Ta) are visible up on the hillside behind the temple's halls, with the two lower floors hidden from view.

The **Shan Men Dian** contains two large statues of the fierce-looking temple guardians **Heng** and **Ha** on either side. In the center is a glass case containing a statue of the Maitreya Buddha (Mi Le Fo) facing south, and behind him Putuo Pusa facing the northern exit.

The second hall on the central axis is the **Yao Shi Fo Dian**. This diety's origins are somewhat mysterious and cannot be traced precisely to any Sanskrit names of the original Buddhist deities in India. His special role in China is to serve as a heavenly Buddha who is capable of healing all diseases without the aid of any medicine. This hall contains a seated Yao Shi Fo Buddha in the center, with two standing disciples on either side of him. Behind the central partition of the Yao Shi Fo Dian is a reclining gilded Buddha facing the northern exit.

Twenty-four colorful standing figures line both sides of the Yao Shi Fo Hall, with 12 on each side. Some of them have long flowing black beards and are dressed like Confucian scholars, while others are women. These seem to be the same **24 Devas** (Zhu Tian) who were described by Reichelt as frequently appearing in Chinese Buddhist temples during the Min Guo era. According to him, they included such non-Buddhist figures from Chinese tradition as Confucius (Kong Fuzi), the War God (Guandi), the God of Literature (Wen Chang), and the Kitchen God; Hindu gods such as Brahma, Indra, and Yama (Yen Lo); as well as Buddhist deities such as the Four Heavenly Kings (Si Tian Wang) and the bodhisattva Wei Tuo. Nowadays, it is extremely rare to see this group of Devas with its many non-Buddhist gods, kings, and judges in Chinese Buddhist temples. The only other example in the area covered by this book is at the Ying Jiang Si temple in Anqing, which for some reason only has 20 figures.

Another one of the Four Heavenly Kings (Tian Wang) at Guang Ji Si Buddhist Temple.

Statues of four of the 24 Devas (Zhu Tian) at Guang Ji Si Buddhist Temple in Wuhu.

The third building on the central axis is the **Precious Hall of the Great Hero** (Da Xiong Bao Dian). This hall contains three gilded Buddhas in the center, with Sakyamuni Buddha (Shijiamouni Pusa) in the middle. Nine gilded Arhats (*Luohan*) stand along each side of the hall, giving a total of 18.

The fourth hall, the **Dizang Dian**, is dedicated to the bodhisattva Dizang (Kshitigarbha) who can rescue departed souls from Hell. This hall sits on a terrace high above the first three and can only be reached by climbing a flight of 88 stone steps. There are three separate stairways, two new ones on either end and an older one in the center. The older stone stairway is lined on both sides with iron chains weighted down with padlocks. On Yellow

Mountain (Huang Shan), this is a custom practiced by young lovers as an act of devotion to each other, but it is not clear what the meaning is here.

To the left of the Dizang Dian is a two-story, red brick building with arched verandas from the Min Guo era. A modern plaque on it has the dates 1045–1105, 1094, and 1918.

Immediately behind the Dizang Dian, and actually touching its rear wall, is the five-story **Zhe Ta**, a brick pagoda built in 1065 during the Northern Song (Bei Song) Dynasty reign of emperor Ying Zong. A line of small decorative stone Buddha images once lined the exterior of each floor, but those on the ground floor have been chiseled off. Three steps lead up to an arched entrance with a locked wooden gate. The brick pagoda has no wooden parts, with even its roof eaves and supporting brackets being made of stone. The decorative Buddha images on the second floor seem to have survived better if you climb up onto the terrace behind the tower to take a look at the upper floors. This pagoda cannot be seen from the Yangzi River, as it stands on the southern slope of Zhe Shan, and not on the hill's summit.

Address: Jiuhua Zhong Lu, near the intersection with Beijing Dong Lu
Phone: 383-5195, 382-3683
Mobile phone: 13955309118

The original Entrance Hall (Shan Men) of Guang Ji Si Buddhist Temple in Wuhu.

The new stone First Gate of Heaven (Yi Tian Men) of Guang Ji Si Buddhist Temple facing Jiuhua Zhong Lu.

Zhe Shan Park
(Zhe Shan Gongyuan)

This park covers a large area of 540 mu in the center of the city, including two forested mountain peaks with a green valley in between them. The higher peak, Da Zhe Shan, is 85 m (278.9 ft) high.

Zhe Shan was supposedly the sight of several historic events, most notably the surrender of the Hong Guang emperor — the last Ming Dynasty ruler to govern central China — to the invading Manchus. After the fall of the Ming capital in Beijing in April 1644, remnants of the old regime established the Southern Ming Dynasty in Nanjing, placing the Prince of Fu, Zhu You Song, on the throne as the Dong Guang emperor on 19 June 1644. After the Manchus captured Nanjing on 1 June 1645, the Hong Guang emperor fled westward to Wuhu, where he was captured about ten days later.

Other famous leaders who visited Zhe Shan in the past include Qing Dynasty Emperor Qian Long and Mao Zedong, who came here in 1969. Sadly, there aren't really any genuine historic relics here nowadays. Nonetheless, a stroll through the park makes for a pleasant hike.

The old stone entrance gate to Da Zhe Shan inside Zhe Shan Park.

A stone memorial monument on the summit of Da Zhe Shan inside Zhe Shan Park.

After a steep ascent up long flights of steps, the north peak (Xiao Zhe Shan) offers spectacular views of the Yangzi River and the surrounding city. Currently, its summit is occupied by a radar station (Wuhu Dian Shi Tai), which is closed to visitors. From a distance, it appears deceptively like a temple in its architectural style. On a terrace below the summit of the north peak is a tomb of an army general named Dai An Lan (Dai An Lan Jiangjun Mu).

The south peak (Da Zhe Shan) has two modern reproductions of traditional Chinese style buildings, including a three-story pagoda (Yi Lan Ting) and the two-story Heavenly Comfort Pavilion (Shu Tian Ge). Built in 1990, this pavilion covers 477 sq m (5,134.4 sq ft) and is supported by 20 round wooden columns.

From the south peak you can descend down to the Sun Zhongshan Memorial Hall (Zhongshan Tang), the Green and Bright Garden (Chi Ming Yuan), and the Tie Shan Hotel.

Anhui Province: Wuhu 203

The Wu Dian Shi Tai on the summit of Xiao Zhe Shan inside Zhe Shan Park.

Below, left: The Yi Lan Ting pavilion on the summit of Da Zhe Shan inside Zhe Shan Park.
Below, right: The Shu Tian Ge pavilion on the summit of Da Zhe Shan inside Zhe Shan Park.

Located in the valley in between is a statue of Mao Zedong overlooking a lake. The statue is dated 3 March 1969, apparently commemorating a visit by Mao to Wuhu.

Address: East Gate (Dong Men)
at 345 Jiuhua Zhong Lu
Phone: 383-3361

Gracefully arched stone footbridge dividing Da Jing Hu from Xiao Jing Hu in Wuhu.

Mirror Lake (Jing Hu)

Jing Hu lies in the middle of downtown Wuhu and is much more the center of urban social life today than is the Yangzi River waterfront. The shore is surrounded by a beautiful green park, where families, couples, and friends can be seen strolling in the evening. Free music wafts through the air, and many restaurants line Jing Hu Lu, the road that runs beside the lakeshore park. The lake is actually divided up into two parts, **Small Mirror Lake** (Xiao Jing Hu) and **Big Mirror Lake** (Da Jing Hu). The two lakes are divided by a pedestrian causeway, in the center of which is a new but graceful sloping arched stone footbridge, beneath which flows the channel connecting the lakes. Together, the two lakes cover 230 *mu* of water, and have 54 *mu* of parkland along their shores. Xiao Jing Hu has one large island, which is occupied by the City Garden Restaurant and can reached by a bridge. Da Jing Hu has three islands. One of these islands can be reached only by boat, a second is connected by a bridge and is occupied by a bar with an outdoor beer garden set amidst green trees, while the third, with some houses on it, has a bridge with a locked iron gate. Docked on the shore in between Da Jing Hu's two main islands is a floating bar inside a traditional wooden boat.

Small Mirror Lake (Xiao Jing Hu) in Wuhu.

A small island in Big Mirror Lake (Da Jing Hu) in Wuhu.

A floating tea house on board a wooden boat on Big Mirror Lake (Da Jing Hu) in Wuhu.

The new and luxurious Garden Hotel on the shore of Big Mirror Lake (Da Jing Hu) in Wuhu.

Zhongshan Road Pedestrian Mall (Zhongshan Lu Shang Ye Bu Xing Jie)

Zhongshan Road, located a block away from the shores of Da Jing Hu, has been turned into a pedestrian mall just like that of Nanjing Dong Lu in Shanghai. It is along this street that you will find many Western-style restaurants such as Kentucky Fried Chicken, McDonalds, and Ristorante Italiano. Nearby, on Jing Hu Lu, is the plush new Garden Hotel with its restaurants, coffee shop, and book store. In the evenings, Zhongshan Road plays host to many free performances of dancers and musicians, on stages set up in the street. Walking along the shores of nearby Da Jing Hu, you can hear the strains of Joan Jett blasting from the outdoor stages. It is also on Zhongshan Road that you will find branches of most major Chinese banks with ATM machines. The Wuhu Conference and Exhibition Center is located on this road as well.

The Old City (Shi Men Kou)

The Wuhu old town is about two blocks west of Jing Hu and starts near the Jing Hu Police Station on Zhong Er Jie. It is bounded by Zhong Er Jie to the east, Tian He Lu to the west,

Wuhu's old city district of Stone Gate Mouth (Shi Men Kou).

Hua Jin Bei Lu to the north, and Jiuhua Zhong Lu to the south. Within this area, you will find many narrow pedestrian lanes lined with Shikumen-style houses, dating from the late Qing Dynasty and Min Guo periods. There are also a few stone wells and the occasional old Western-style house. The area is generally known as Stone Gate Mouth (Shi Men Kou), and probably once stood within or around the now long gone city walls. Some of the more interesting lanes bisecting it include You Fang Xiang, He Ping Xiang, Tang Zi Xiang, Yong Ping Li, Chun Liang Li, and Shang Cai Shi Xiang. All of these are much too small to appear on any city map. You can spend an interesting morning or afternoon walking along these narrow lanes.

On the east side of Zhong Er Jie, in between Zhongshan Lu and Liu Chun Lu, stands one of the most impressive surviving Min Guo buildings in the city. It is a white, stone block structure built in a monumental style, with four large Greco-Roman columns standing out in front. At the foot of the building's right corner are two small original Chinese inscriptions embedded in the corner stones. This is now a branch of the ICBC Bank (Zhongguo Gongshang Yinhang).

Left and right: Wuhu's old city district of Stone Gate Mouth (Shi Men Kou).

Wuhu Mosque (Wuhu Qing Zhen Si)

The most impressive historic sight of the old city is the **Wuhu Mosque** (Wuhu Qing Zhen Si). The high blank windowless back walls of this mosque are visible from Zhong Er Jie, but no clue as to its contents appear until you turn up the narrow lane of Shang Cai Shi Jie. Even the front of the mosque's exterior seems unassuming, except for some faded Arabic inscriptions. Signboards framing the entrance announce that this is the headquarters of the Wuhu Islamic Committee (Wuhu Shi Yi Si Lan Jiao Xue Hui).

The modern street entrance to Wuhu's Mosque (Qing Zhen Si).

Entering the front door and passing through the first building leads one into a courtyard sandwiched between two traditional Qing Dynasty red-painted, wooden pillar halls with intricate wood carvings. The building to the left is the prayer hall. Local Muslims take off their shoes at the entrance before going inside to kneel on prayer carpets on the floor. These are by far the most impressive authentic Qing Dynasty buildings in the city, the ones at Guan Ji Si being new restorations and the Tian Zhu Jiao Tang, a Western style structure. There are three resident Muslims living in the mosque. According to them, Wuhu has a very large Muslim population. Visitors are welcome, and it helps if they know a few words of Arabic, such as the traditional greeting of "Asalaamu 'alaikum."

Address: 1406 Shang Cai Shi Jie
Phone: 383-4182

Inside the remarkably well-preserved wooden Qing Dynasty prayer hall of Wuhu's Mosque (Qing Zhen Si).

Customs House (Hai Guan)

Just beside the modern-day Yangzi ferry terminal, hidden from side view by billboard signs, stands the old Customs House, a genuine historic relic left over from treaty port days. Although in a ramshackle state, it still presents a striking image with its four-story clock tower, decorated with four round iron clock faces on each side, their roman numerals frozen in time. Rows of residential shacks have been tacked on to the front and sides of its ground floor, and a large number of families apparently live inside, the interior of which has been divided up into rabbit hutches. The current residents do not welcome visitors to look around inside. No original inscriptions seem to have survived.

A walk along this section of Bin Jiang Lu reveals the curiously derelict state of Wuhu's Yangzi waterfront. A high wall blocks any view of the river just on the other side. Except for the Disco KTV bar inside the ferry terminal, there are no restaurants, shops, cafes, or bars along the water. Unlike other river towns such as Yichang, Jiujiang, and Anqing, Wuhu has not built a pedestrian promenade along its flood wall, nor even tried to develop its Waitan into a scenic sightseeing area. All the focus has been on developing the Jing Hu area in the center of town, which is now where everyone goes for an outdoor stroll on a warm day or cool evening.

Address: 40 Bin Jiang Bei Lu

Lion Hill (Shizi Shan)

This forested hill was once the site of an Episcopolian foreign missionary community before 1949. Between 1899 and 1937, the missionaries constructed a large three-building compound here for the **St. James Episcopal School**, as well as a whole community of residential houses. Much of this former missionary community is still intact, with their buildings continuing to serve the useful purposes of educating youth and housing people.

Since 1958, the St. James School has been known as the **No. 11 Middle School** (Shi Yi Zhong Xue), and its former campus now also serves a branch of the **Anhui Normal University School of Foreign Languages** (Anhui Shi Dafushu Waiguo Yu Xuexiao). Approaching from the gate on Ji He Bei Lu, walk uphill along a road through a forested hill to a second gate that is sometimes closed, but can be opened by a friendly gatekeeper inside. Entering the second gate, continue uphill past the small old open-air Good Rain Pavilion (Hao Yu Ting) on the right until you reach the northern summit where the former St. James Episcopal School still stands, fully erect.

The main hall is a three-story, red brick structure with arched arcade verandas. A six-story red brick tower is connected

A modern tablet recording the history of Wuhu's Lion Hill (Shizi Shan).

to the main hall. Inside, the interior seems unchanged from its missionary days, the stairways' wooden steps sagging from the imprint of over a hundred years worth of students' feet. The hall was built in 1910, and is known in Chinese as the Sheng Ya Ge Xue Tang.

A second two-story brick hall is known as the Yi De Lou in honor of the school's American founder, now known only by the Chinese name of Lu Yi De. The same building is sometimes also called the Reading Place (Du Shu Chu) of Wang Jia Xiang, a famous Chinese scientist who studied here from 1924 to 1925. A third hall was added in 1936, and as such it is commonly referred to as the 1936 Hall (Yi Jiu San Liu Tang). It is sometimes also known as the Jing Fang Hall (Jing Fang Tang), because Li Jing Fang, the son of Li Hong Zhang, donated the money for its construction in 1936. All together the three original school buildings form a horse-shoe pattern.

Cross the large modern playground area to the southern end of the summit to find the Episcopalian community's original two- and three-story red brick residential houses still standing. One of them now bears the sign, "Apartment House for Foreign

The former St. James Episcopal School still stands on Wuhu's Lion Hill (Shizi Shan).

Teachers," a fitting use for a building originally constructed as the home of foreign missionaries. From here, a second road descends the southern end of the mountain to Zhongshan Bei Lu. Just before the gate exiting out onto this street is a narrow side lane which leads along the inside of the compound wall to a number of other Min Guo era red brick houses. These are in a more dilapidated condition than those on the summit.

Also on Shizi Shan is the **Wang Jia Xiang Memorial Garden** (Wang Jia Xing Jinian Yuan), which is housed inside a number of Min Guo era red brick houses formerly belonging to the Episcopalians.

Address: No. 11 Zhong Xue, enter from either Ji He Bei Lu or Zhongshan Bei Lu

Above: Caption D28

The colorful entrance Gate (Da Men) to Yi Ji Shan in Wuhu.

Yi Ji Shan

The summit of Yi Ji Shan is the best spot in Wuhu for observing the Yangzi River. This is also the location of one of the city's few remaining historic structures from the Min Guo period.

After passing through a series of gates, including a new but colorful *pai lou*, the main road through the hospital's green campus ascends to the top of Yi Ji Shan's flat summit. It is here that you find the original **Wuhu General Hospital** built by American Christian missionaries in 1926. It is not only still standing, but continues to serve the sick and injured of China today. The horse-shoe-shaped, red brick, three-story structure is built in American

The covered open-air corridor along Yangzi River waterfront at Yi Ji Shan offers by far the best view of the river in Wuhu.

Traditional twin pavilions on the Yangzi River waterfront at Yi Ji Shan in Wuhu.

Colonial style with four white columns marking the former main entrance at the top of a short flight of steps. The original lamp posts still stand on either side of the landing. Beside the original building is a new wing connected to the old one.

In the center of a green lawn, in front of the original building is a white standing statue of an obviously Western man with a moustache, bald head, and clothes resembling those worn by a Christian priest. The statue is mounted on a new pedestal with a plaque containing a Chinese language inscription. Unfortunately,

One of several old Western style houses at Yi Ji Shan in Wuhu.

this is not a monument to the hospital's American founder, but a commemoration to the Communist traveler Norman Bethune (Bai Qiu En). The statue was erected in July 1994.

A trail of steps leads down from the bluff promontory overlooking the river to the water's edge. The steps pass two old Western-style houses that were renovated in October 2002 to give them a new appearance. However their architectural style, including double rows of verandas, date them from the Min Guo era. Just past the houses is a beautiful landscaped garden. At the bottom of the steps is a long, open-air, covered pedestrian corridor running along the Yangzi River just above the water's edge. From the corridor, built in 2001, one can get a great view of the river and the Wuhu waterfront. At the east end of the corridor is a colorful three-story octagonal traditional style pavilion with an ascending circular staircase within.

stone marker commemorating the restoration the Western houses at Yi Ji Shan in 2002.

The original building of the Wuhu General Hospital built during the Min Guo era by American missionaries. A statue of the Communist fellow traveler Norman Bethune (Bai Qiu En) erected in 1994 now stands in front of the building.

Lush gardens on Yi Ji Shan, located on a terrace halfway between the hilltop and the Yangzi.

Ting Tang Park (Ting Tang Gongyuan)

Built in the northern suburbs of Wuhu in 1984, this park covers 1,000 *mu*, half of which is covered by water. Several different lakes are connected by causeways and footbridges. The main lake has two islands, one of which is connected to the shore by a footbridge, and the other which can only be reached by boat.

This page: Sights of the Ting Tang Park (Ting Tang Gongyuan) in Wuhu.

Curious-looking house boats float on the surface of the main lake. This is a swimming lake, and you will see large groups of swimmers in the water and walking around the park in their swimsuits. Army troops also occasionally perform aquatic military exercises here.

Address: Jiuhua Zhong Lu

Ting Tang Park (Ting Tang Gongyuan) in Wuhu.

Wuhu Practical Information

Wuhu Area Code: (0553)

Wuhu Hotels
Garden Hotel***
This is the most luxurious and most expensive hotel in the city, and is located on the shores of Big Mirror Lake (Da Jing Hu), just one block away from the Zhongshan Road pedestrian mall. Its classical dome with four round clock faces can be seen from far away. A bookstore inside the hotel sells maps of the city, and its ground floor coffee shop has views of the lake.

Address: 12 Jing Hu Lu
Phone: 382-2666, 382-2688, 381-8688
Fax: 382-2988

The Seaman Hotel (Hai Yuan Lou Binguan)**
This hotel's unfortunate name conjures up images of a cheap flophouse for sailors when, in fact, it is in close competition with the Garden Hotel as one of the best places to stay in the city. Located right beside the Yangzi River waterfront, one block from the Catholic Cathedral (Tian Zhu Jiao Tang), and two blocks from the Zhong Jiang Ta, it is close to a few of the key historic sights. In addition to a clean restaurant in a separate building next door, some of its unique features include a public sauna and bathing pools, a foot massage facility, an Internet computer bar, and a video hall. A travel agency office is also conveniently located inside the hotel if you need assistance with your travel plans. Seventh floor guest rooms on the north side are the only ones in Wuhu with views facing the Yangzi River.

Address: 18 Jiang An Lu,
two blocks down a lane off of Ji He Nan Lu,
where a gate marks the way
Phone: 380-6088, 380-6000, 385-2624
Fax: 380-6499, 380-6421
Prices: 180–220 Rmb

The Alton Hotel
This hotel has two buildings. The newer wing facing Beijing Dong Lu has small rooms with new interiors and goes for 188 Rmb. However, this building has no elevators which may mean walking up and down four flights of stairs. The older building facing Jiuhua Zhong Lu has larger rooms with balconies that show a bit wear and tear. These rooms go for 148 Rmb, and the building does have an elevator. Although the location is central and the prices reasonable, foreigners should beware — the hotel has a strange

habit of letting foreigners check in, taking their money, and then calling the police to come and have a nice long chat with you about exactly who you are and why you're in town.

Address: 10 Beijing Dong Lu
Phone: 383-5198,
E-mail: Altonm@mail.ahwhptt.net.cn
Web site: http://www.altonhotel.com

East Garden Hotel (Dong Yuan Binguan)
Although the hotel is a bit seedy now, it has definitely seen better days. However, the location is ideal if you are catching an early morning train or bus out of town. Located right next door to the city's long-distance bus station (*gong gong qiche zhan*) and across a large open plaza from the train station (*huoche zhan*). Equally low prices can be found at nicer hotels in the city center, but staff at the Dong Yuan seem a bit friendlier towards foreigners than the other hotels, maybe because they need the business too badly to hassle you with a lot of inquisitive questions. If you like a no-questions-asked policy, this is the place for you. Half of the seventh floor has been somewhat redecorated, but be warned that rooms facing the railway station are exposed to high-powered train whistles throughout the night.

Phone: 382-9041
Prices: 120-150 Rmb

Tai Xing Long Hotel
Traditional Chinese style buildings centered around a beautiful landscaped garden at the foot of Zhe Shan. It was closed for remodeling in July 2003, but should be a wonderful place to stay in when it reopens.

Address: Jiuhua Zhong Lu,
beside the Guang Ji Temple gate
Phone: 382-9768, 381-7182

Iron Mountain Hotel (Tie Shan Binguan)
Located at the western foot of Zhe Shan.

Address: 3 Gen Xin Lu
Phone: 383-5981, 371-8888
Fax: 383-0240
Prices: 150-200 Rmb

Wuhu Restaurants
City Garden Restaurant
This is located on a beautiful forested island in Small Mirror Lake (Xiao Jing Hu). The bridge to the island can be reached from Huangshan Zhong Lu.

Phone: 381-8888

Italian Pizza House

Located just across the street from the shore of Big Mirror Lake (Da Jing Hu).

Address: 1 Jing Hu Lu
Phone: 387-7778

Ristorante Italiano

Located on the Zhongshan Road pedestrian mall, one block from Big Mirror Lake (Da Jing Hu).

Kentucky Fried Chicken (KFC)

Located on the corner of Guo Huo Lu and the Zhongshan Road pedestrian mall.

McDonald's

Located inside the first floor of the Wuhu Shang Zhi Du Building on the Zhongshan Road pedestrian mall.

Nightlife

The Celebrity Club

A disused bowling alley on the ground floor disguises the windowless upstairs night club. Visitors will be treated to Las Vegas-style stage performances by busty showgirls in exotic and risque costumes, backed by an extremely professional hard rock band imported from Guangzhou. The bar serves imported beer, such as Corona. Private rooms are available with the hostess of your choice from a limitless selection of young female companions. A veritable pleasure dome where fantasies come true for those who can afford it.

The Hard Rock Bar (Ha De Nuo Ke Qing Diao)

On Beijing Dong Lu, across from the Jing Hu Xiao Xue, upstairs on the second floor.

Jin Bi Hui Huang

Opposite Small Mirror Lake (Xiao Jing Hu).

Da Jing Hu Island Beer Garden and Bar

Address: Jing Hu Lu
Phone: 383-8370

Bookstores
Wuhu Library (Wuhu Shi Tushuguan)
Has an Internet computer bar on the first floor.

Address: Jing Hu Lu,
across the street from Big Mirror Lake (Da Jing Hu)

Wuhu Transportation
Wuhu's train station (*huoche zhan*) is at the east end of town, facing the long-distance bus station (*gong gong qiche zhan*) and the Dong Yuan Binguan across a large open plaza (*zhan guangchang*).

Yangzi ferry terminal (*matou*)
This is located at the north end of Beijing Xi Lu, at its intersection with Bin Jiang Lu. It doubles as a large Disco KTV bar at night, with an enormous neon sign advertising the night club. Wuhu is 449 km (281 miles) upriver from the mouth of the Yangzi.

Tongling
The next upstream Yangzi River port of Tongling is 83 km (51.6 miles) from Wuhu by road. A spur railway line continues from Wuhu to the town of Tongling where it ends. This is currently the farthest up the Yangzi River valley you can travel by train from Shanghai via Nanjing. However, a construction project is currently underway to connect Tongling with the town of Jiujiang in Jiangxi Province, as part of the great Shanghai to Chongqing railroad project.

Tongling is another one of Anhui Province's top five river ports. It is an industrial city and is home to China's largest cement plant, as well as being the largest producer of copper in Eastern China. It has been an important center of copper production for over 3,000 years.

The main tourist sight in Tongling is the nature reserve established for the endangered species of Yangzi River dolphin. These dolphins were once a common sight in the whole stretch of river between Chongqing and Shanghai. These days, their numbers have dwindled down to the point of extinction.

Jiuhua Shan
By road, Jiuhua Shan is 168 km (104.4 miles) from Wuhu. The important crossroads of Qing Yang town, on the way to Jiuhua Shan is 120 km (74.6 miles) from Wuhu by road.

Qing Yang

This town is is 32 km (19.9 miles) away from Jiuhua Shan, 41 km (25.5 miles) from Chi Zhou city (en route to Anqing), and 120 km (74.6 miles) from Wuhu, which has the nearest train station and provides a route to either Hefei, which has the nearest airport, or Shanghai.

Sights include a **Roman Catholic Cathedral** (Tian Zhu Tang) with twin bell towers that must be among the largest ever built in China. Locals will tell you it no longer exists (*xianzai meiyou*), but what they really mean is that it is closed now. Despite being closed, visitors are still able to appreciate the incredible views of its exterior from outside the locked gates on the narrow lane, He Jia Nan Xiang. Hotels include the Jiuzi Shan (closed for repairs), Hua Lin, Xi Feng, and Qing Yang Guest House.

Qing Yang is the most important transportation crossroads in this area. It has a large bus station with long distance buses traveling in three directions: east to Shanghai via Wuhu, south to Jiuhua Shan and northwest to Anqing via Chi Zhou city. However, the bus station closes for the day at 5:00PM, and the last daily departures seem to be around 4:00PM. Since there is no airport or train station, the bus is your only option for getting out of town.

Above: Caption D40

Anhui Province
Jiuhua Shan

Located in the south of Anhui Province, Jiuhua Shan stands on the south bank of the Yangzi River with Huang Shan and Tai Ping Lake as its background, within the borders with the former Chi Zhou Fu prefecture (now Chi Zhou Shi municipality). The Jiuhua Shan Scenic Area covers 120 sq km (46.3 sq miles).

Jiuhua Shan covers more than 100 sq km (38.6 sq miles) in the southwest corner of Qing Yang County, Chi Zhou Municipality, Anhui Province. Qing Yang Zhen is the closest town to the mountain and can be reached by road from Tongling, the nearest town on the Yangzi River, and Wuhu, a bit farther downriver. Although it is said to have 99 peaks, nine of these have always stood out as the main ones. The **Ten Kings Peak** (Shi Wang Feng) is the highest at 1,342 m (4,402.9 ft).

Natural attractions include the Tao Yan Waterfall (Tao Yan Pubu), the Shu Tan pool, the East Cliff (Dong Ya), the Lotus Peak (Lianhua Feng), the Heavenly Pillar, and the Heavenly Terrace (Tian Tai). There are also the five streams at the mountain's base — the Ming Yuan Garden's bamboo forest and the Phoenix Pine (Feng Huang Song) — reputed to have been planted more than 1,400 years ago during the Southern Dynasties.

Mount Jiuhua was originally known as Jiuzi Shan (Nine Peak Mountain) because it consists of nine main peaks that soar into the clouds. However, the name was changed in the Tian Bao era (742–756 AD) during the Xuan Zong reign (712–756 AD) of the Tang Dynasty, after the poet Li Bai (Li Tai Po) (701–762 AD) wrote a poem about it which included the lines, "Sailing down the Jiujiang River the other day, I saw the Jiuhua Peaks in the distance, looking like a heavenly river hanging in heaven, its green water embroidering nine flowers."

In addition to its natural beauty, the mountain is also famous as one of the four sacred Buddhist mountains in China. According to the local history of Chi Zhou prefecture (Chi Zhou Fu Zhi), the first Buddhist monk to begin living on the mountain was a man named **Bei Du**. He arrived from India in 401 AD, the 5th year of the Long An reign (397–408 AD) during the Eastern Jin (Dong Jin) Dynasty (317–419 AD).

In 719 AD, in the 7th year of the Kai Yuan era (713–741 AD) during the Xuan Zong reign (712–756 AD) of the Tang Dynasty, Prince **Kim Gio Gak** (Jin Qiao Jue) of the Korean Silla Kingom's royal family came to Jiuhua Shan. He spent the remaining 75 years of his life here as a Buddhist monk until his death at the age of 99 in 794 AD in the Zhen Yuan era (785–805 AD) during the De Zong reign (779–805 AD) of the Tang Dynasty. According to legend, when his tomb was reopened three years later, his body still appeared so lifelike that the local monks decided Kim was the reincarnation of the Bodhisattva Dizang (Kshitigarbha). A Dizang sutra (Dizang Jing) had been incorporated into the Chinese Tripitaka (San Zang) dating from the end of the 7th century.

The result was a "construction spree" of temple building lasting from the Song Dynasty (960–1279) through the Qing Dynasty (1644–1911). By the end of the Qing Dynasty in 1911, there were hundreds of temples on the mountain. In the Ming and Qing dynasties, there were over 300 temples with about 5,000 monks and nuns.

Despite its importance as one of the four most sacred Buddhist mountains in China, English language descriptions of Jiuhua Shan have been few and far between. **Reginald F. Johnston**, better known as the tutor to China's last emperor Pu Yi, devoted a considerable amount of space to Jiuhua Shan in his book, *Buddhist China*, published in London in 1913. In the same year, Carl F. Kupfer, president of the William Nast College in Jiujiang, published his slim volume, *Sacred Places in China*, which includes a chapter on Jiuhua Shan. After those first two volumes, there was a 24-year silence until Danish architect Johannes Prip-Moller visited and included some of Jiuhua Shan's sights in his 1937 work on Chinese Buddhist temples. Thirty years later, Holmes Welch studied the history of the temples there, without being able to actually visit them, and included his findings in his three-volume series on Chinese Buddhism published between 1967 and 1972.

According to Holmes Welch, there were 1,000 resident Buddhist monks on Jiuhua Shan in the 1930s. However, the mountain became almost entirely depopulated within a few years after the 1949 Communist revolution. By 1953, the number of resident monks had already been reduced by over 80 percent, down to just 178 people. The Jiuhua Temple Fair, traditionally held every year on the 30th day of the 7th lunar month, was banned after 1949, and only resumed in 1983.

According to officially published statistics, there are 78 historic temples on the mountain and over 6,000 Buddhist statues today. Nine of the temples are protected by the State Council. Jiuhua Shan has four Buddhist mummies, and the most temples of any one place in China, with the most monks and nuns. There are over 2,000 relics, some of which are kept on the mountain. However, unofficial estimates place the number of surviving temples at only 60, while just seven main temples seem to have been actually restored. Furthermore, although resident monks once again live there, the atmosphere of many of the temple halls is more like a Buddhist museum than living centers of active worship. Some of the 2,000 other Buddhist cultural artifacts include Wu Xia's Hua Yang sutras, sutras written in the original Sanskrit script, and Qing dynasty sutras produced by imperial command.

The most notable existing temples include the Tending Garden Temple (Qi Yuan Si), The Transformation Temple (Hua Cheng Si), the Hundred-Year-Old Palace which is also known as the Temple of Longevity (Bai Sui Gong), the Precious Hall of the Holy Body (Rou Shen Bao Dian), the Temple of the Heavenly Terrace (Tian Tai Si), the Ming Yuan Nunnery (Ming Yuan An), and the Gan Lu Temple (Gan Lu Si).

Temples Below the Second Gate

When Reginald F. Johnston and Carl F. Kupfer separately visited Jiuhua Shan in 1913, the approach to Jiuhua Village from the flat plains down below was via a foot trail that passed through a series of four heavenly gates (Si Tian Men), and stopped at three Buddhist temples – the Two Saints Hall (Er Sheng Dian), Sweet Dew Temple (Gan Lu Si), and Dragon Pool Buddhist Nunnery (Long Chi An), named after the nearby Dragon Pool Waterfall (Long Chi Pubu) – before reaching the hard-earned reward of the temple valley around the village itself. Although these sights are still there, their location far down the mountain from the Jiuhua Village gate where the buses stop, tickets are checked, and the string of hotels begins, means that few people now visit them, especially with the Everest-like determination of most people to get to the very top of the mountain at Da Tian Tai. In much the same way as Ming Xiao Ling in Nanjing, the pushing of a modern road all the way up to the doorsteps of the main sights has destroyed the original spiritual experience of slowly approaching along a Sacred Way that gradually built to a climax. Nonetheless, purists can still follow a stone step trail that begins on the plains below and cuts straight up through the switchback corners of the modern highway to Jiuhua Village. The First Gate of Heaven (Yi Tian Men) stands below Gan Lu Si, the Second Gate of Heaven (Er Tian Men) is below Long Chi An, and the Third Gate of Heaven (San Tian Men) is reached just before dropping down into the valley of Jiuhua town below.

Jiuhua Village (Jiuhua Jie Qu)

In 1913, Carl F. Kupfer described Jiuhua Village as "a restful valley nestled in the top of the mountain." Today, unfortunately, it is a much more urbanized and less restful place, particularly depending on the time of year you visit. Deafening choruses of car horns seem to blare incessantly, and traffic jams of speeding motor vehicles make the main street almost unsafe for pedestrians.

Buses from Qing Yang town stop at a parking lot outside the First Gate (Di Yi Da Men) of Jiuhua Shan, located on the flat plain of a broad valley floor. Here you must dismount, buy a 90 Rmb admission ticket, and walk across the border. Immediately inside the gate is the first of three local bus stations on Jiuhua Shan between which shuttle buses run up and down the mountain.

The first shuttle bus stage takes you up the mountain via winding switchbacks and hairpin corners, past the Buddhist temples of Gan Lu Si and Long Chi An, until you reach the Second Gate (Di Er Da Men). Here you must dismount again, show your admission ticket, and walk across the border into Jiuhua Village, located in a small mountain valley. Although the main street through town is lined with hotels such as the Long Quan, most of their rooms suffer from direct exposure to the constant horn honking of endless traffic jams on the road. Many others, such as the Fu Gu Yuan, appear to be quite derelict or semi-

A five-arched road bridge crosses over a lotus pool in Jiuhua Village.

abandoned. The two best hotels on the mountain, the Ju Long and Fo Jiao, are conveniently situated directly inside the Second Gate, both of them on the right side of the road. If you choose to stay somewhere further up the mountain, you will need to transfer to a second shuttle bus that travels the route from the Second Gate (Di Er Da Men) to Zhong Ming Yuan.

Many of the major temples are on the main road, Jiuhua Jie, or along a ridge up above the village. The route to Da Tian Tai still seems challenging, though a cable car now goes to Bai Jin Tai from Zhong Ming Yuan where the road ends.

Ju Long Binguan is across the street from Qi Yuan Si, immediately inside Di Er Da Men. It seems to be the most pleasant hotel but it is also the most expensive at 400 Rmb per day. Although it claims to be a three-star hotel, it serves unpalatable food in a single dining hall-style restaurant, has poor customer service and an ill-stocked bookshop with no English guides or maps to the mountain. The architectural style of the building is a series of horizontal terraces connected by flights of steps and open-air covered corridors, rather than a vertical tower.

Right next door to the Ju Long is the Fo Jiao Binguan, a newer facility built around a central courtyard designed to look like a Buddhist Temple. Prices here are only 200 Rmb.

The climate here tends to be cold and shrouded in wet fog, making warm clothes and an umbrella necessary equipment, even in summer. Thanks partly to the surrounding high mountain peaks, it gets pitch black outside once the sun sets at 6:00PM. One of your first purchases should be a flashlight, which you should carry with you at all times in case you accidentally get stuck far from your hotel after dark.

Jiuhua Village (Jiuhua Jie Qu) nestled in a high mountain valley filled with thick fog.

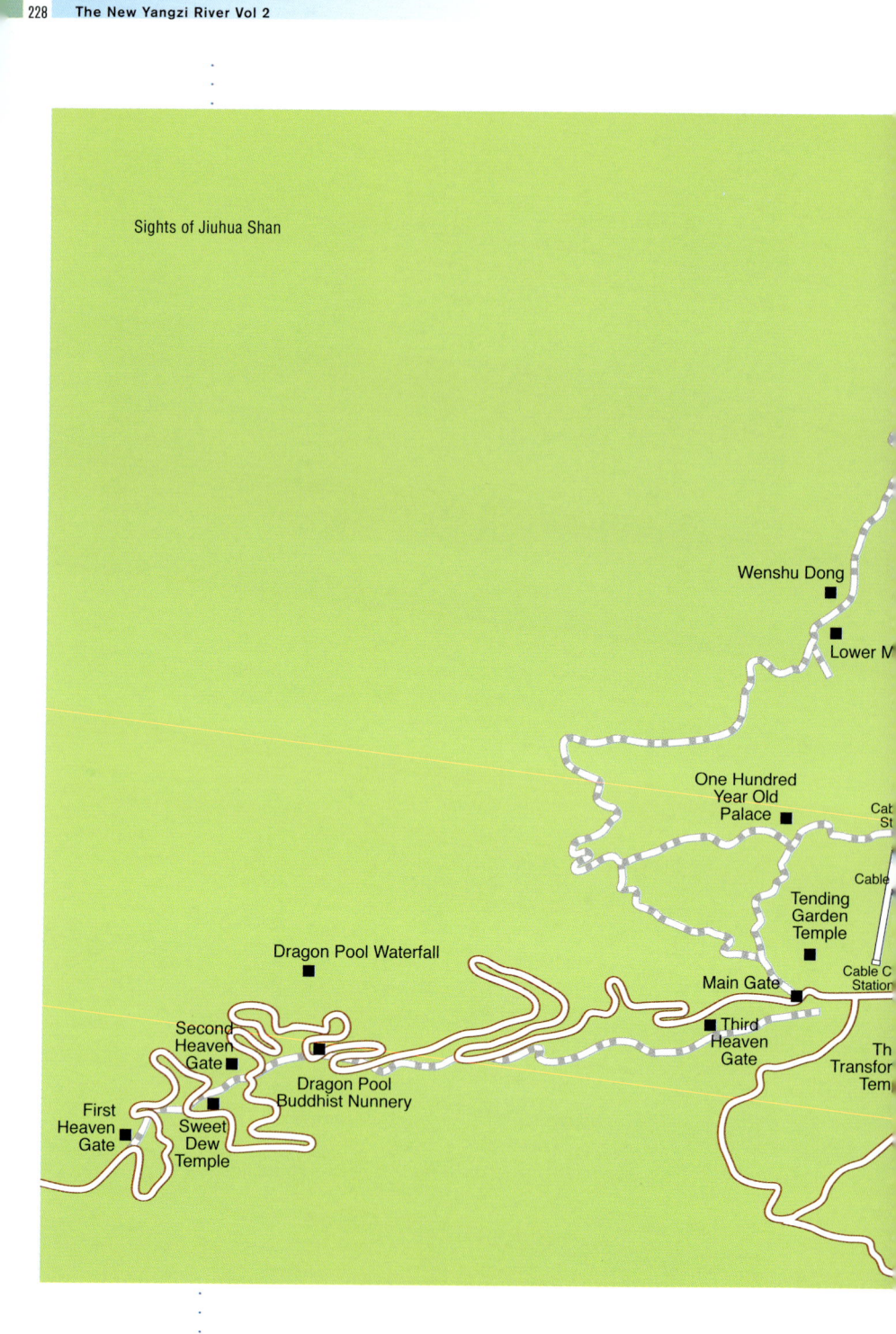

Sights of Jiuhua Shan

- Wenshu Dong
- Lower M[...]
- One Hundred Year Old Palace
- Cab[le] St[ation]
- Cable
- Tending Garden Temple
- Cable C[ar] Station
- Dragon Pool Waterfall
- Main Gate
- Second Heaven Gate
- Third Heaven Gate
- Th[...] Transfor[mation] Tem[ple]
- First Heaven Gate
- Dragon Pool Buddhist Nunnery
- Sweet Dew Temple

Anhui Province: Jiuhua Shan

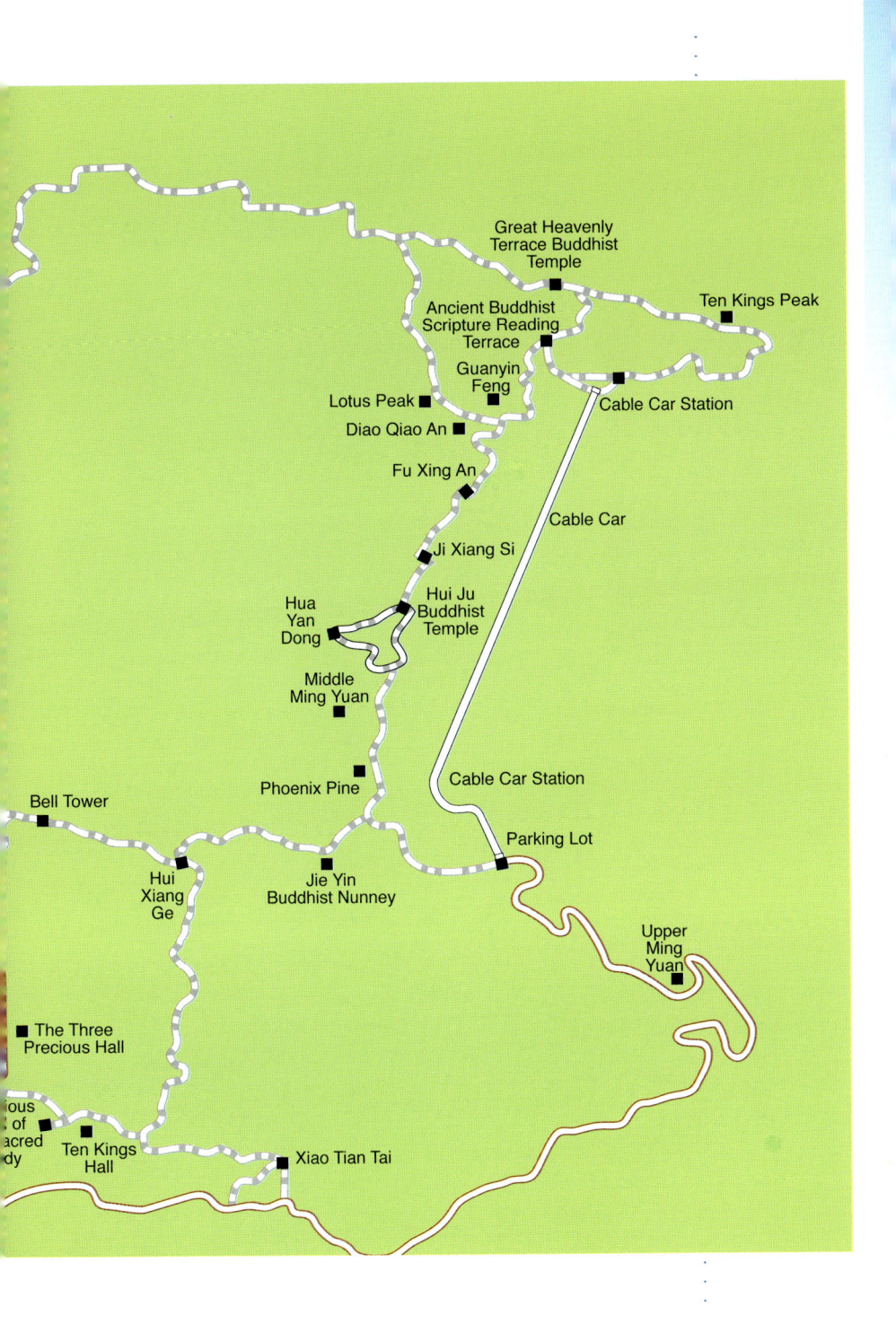

- Great Heavenly Terrace Buddhist Temple
- Ten Kings Peak
- Ancient Buddhist Scripture Reading Terrace
- Guanyin Feng
- Lotus Peak
- Cable Car Station
- Diao Qiao An
- Fu Xing An
- Cable Car
- Ji Xiang Si
- Hua Yan Dong
- Hui Ju Buddhist Temple
- Middle Ming Yuan
- Phoenix Pine
- Cable Car Station
- Parking Lot
- Bell Tower
- Hui Xiang Ge
- Jie Yin Buddhist Nunney
- Upper Ming Yuan
- The Three Precious Hall
- Ten Kings Hall
- Xiao Tian Tai

Temples in Jiuhua Village (Jiuhua Jie Qu)
Tending Garden Temple (Qi Yuan Si)

This is one of the nine temples on Jiuhua Shan that is protected by the State Council, and among the four largest temples on the mountain. Although it was first built in the 16th century during the Jiajing reign (1522–1566) of the Ming Dynasty, the oldest existing buildings today date from the Tongzhi reign (1862–1874) of the Qing Dynasty. Other buildings were added during the Xuan Zong reign (1909–1911), and in the early Min Guo period (1912–1949).

The first hall is a Heng Ha Dian with a three-story pavilion over the entrance. Statues of the two martial protectors Heng and Ha stand inside. After a small courtyard, the next building is the Heavenly Kings Hall (Tian Wang Dian). Inside are statues of the Four Heavenly Kings (Si Tian Wang).

A flight of stone steps leads up to a raised terrace where you find the third main hall, the Precious Hall of the Great Hero (Da Xiong Bao Dian) with its red-painted walls. In the center of the hall are three enormous gilded Buddha statues (San Fo) seated on lotus flowers. Each one is 6.7 m (22 ft) high, and together they are reputed to be the largest on Jiuhua Shan. While the faces and bodies of the three Buddhas are identical, the hand gestures are different. On the left is Amitabha (O-Mi-Tuo-Fo), in the middle Sakyamuni (Shijiamouni), and on the right is Yao Shi Fo, who is known as "the medecine Buddha." In front of the three Buddhas are seven rows of prayer cushions. Overhead is a three-story high raised ceiling, with glass skylights in the upper side walls. Although the statues are new, the hall itself seems to be quite an authentic historic relic, with an all-wood beam construction. There are nine gilded Arhats (*Luohan*) on each side, giving a total of 18 (Shi Ba Luohan). One of these is the Bodhi Dharma (Pu Ti Da Mo) with long eyebrows. On the back side of the San Fo partition is a giant Guanyin standing on the head of a sea serpent amidst ocean waves, with a massive mountain landscape behind her containing hundreds of figurines. This Guanyin statue is also supposedly the largest one on Jiuhua Shan. Unfortunately, rules against taking pictures are strictly enforced here.

A wooden temple hall at Qi Yuan Si on Jiuhua Shan.

The Heng Ha Dian of Qi Yuan Si on Jiuhua Shan.

A hillside terrace of Qi Yuan Si facing the rear of the Da Xiong Bao Dian.

From the Da Xiong Bao Dian, flights of stone steps lead up to more hillside terraces containing many other courtyards and halls belonging to the same temple. This includes an old wooden structure that was being restored in October 2003 and another structure containing paper effigies of ships and other objects ready to be set afire and ceremonially burned.

There are many signs of active devout worship by an extremely large resident monk community. Despite being located near the main street and entrance gate of the village, the atmosphere inside the temple's walled compound was one of spiritual tranquility. At about 10:30AM, a group of 150–200 Buddhist monks paraded into the Da Xiong Bao Dian to perform a chanting ceremony. Later the same day, hundreds of monks were seen seated along rows of tables in the dining hall eating lunch in strictly enforced silence. Qi Yuan Si seems to have the single largest monastic population of any of the temples on the mountain. The monks here say that they follow the practices of both the Pure Land (Jing Tu) and Chan (Zen), a sign that the two formerly separate sects (*zong*) have been completely merged.

Other halls include a Pure Land Hall (Jing Tu Tang), Ancestor Hall (Zu Shi Tang), Buddhist Law Hall (Fa Tang), Meditation Hall (Chan Tang), and Buddhist Scripture Library (Cang Jing Lou).

In his 1913 account, Reginald F. Johnston described the temple as possessing the gilded mummy of a Buddhist monk named Long Shan. However, a tour of the site in October 2003 revealed no sign of it, resident monks knew nothing about it, and no mention of it is made in current Chinese guide books.

Qi Yuan Si is located near Jiuhua Village (Jiuhua Cun) at the entrance gate to the mountain, and is thus usually the first temple that visitors see.

Ticket: 2 Rmb

The Transformation Temple (Hua Cheng Si)

In his 1913 account, Reginald F. Johnston described Hua Cheng Si as the oldest temple on the mountain, dating back to the 8th century. According to legend, this is the same location where the Indian monk **Bei Du** built his house in 401 AD during the Eastern Jin Dynasty. In 757 AD, the second year of the Zhi De era (756–758 AD) of the Su Zong reign (756–762 AD) during the Tang Dynasty, Zhu Ge Jie of nearby Qing Yang Town built this temple as a residence for the Korean prince Kim Gio Gak (Jin Qiao Jue). In 781 AD, the second year of the Jian Zhong era (780–783 AD) during the De Zong reign (779–805 AD) of the Tang Dynasty, Kim's former residence was rededicated to Dizang, and renamed the Hua Cheng Temple (Hua Cheng Si). At the time of Johnston's visit in 1913, the temple's Buddhist Scripture Pavilion (Cang Jing Lou) had a copy of the Buddhist Tripitaka (San Zang) printed during the Wan Li reign of the Ming Dynasty, as well as scrolls from the Kang Xi and Qian Long reigns of the Qing Dynasty. The Cang Jing Lou itself was reportedly built during the Xuan De reign (1426–1435) of the Ming Dynasty. The three other temple halls were last restored in 1889, during the Guang Xu reign (1875–1908) of the Qing Dynasty.

An iron incense burner in the courtyard of Hua Cheng Si on Jiuhua Shan.

The Heavenly Kings Hall (Tian Wang Dian) of Hua Cheng Si with the Animal Releasing Pool (Fang Sheng Chi) full of dead turtles at foot of the steps.

Sadly, neither the Cang Jing Lou described by Johnston nor its treasured library seem to have survived to the present day. The temple itself has been turned into a lifeless Buddhist history museum (Jiuhua Shan Lishi Wenwuguan), which claims to have such authentic relics as Ming Dynasty editions of both the *Dizang Jing* and Wu Xia's *Xie Jing*, as well as the *Bei Ye Jing*, but these were nowhere in sight.

Hua Cheng Si stands at the far end of a large public square in the center of Jiuhua Village. The square is surrounded by tacky shops on all four sides. In the middle of the square is a stone block platform that looks like a genuine historic relic. In front of the stone steps leading up to the temple is semi-circular Animal Releasing Pool (Fang Sheng Chi). Strangely, it was full of dead turtles and vendors all around were selling more captive turtles to be 'released' into the lifeless pool.

Heng and Ha guardians stand in outside alcoves at either end of the entrance hall. Inside the first hall are new statues of the Four Heavenly Kings (Si Tian Wang), two at either end, but these are partially obscured by the gift shops. One hall is devoted to the Literature and History of Buddhism.

Past the Heavenly Kings Hall (Tian Wang Dian) and the exhibition hall is a courtyard. After this is the Precious Hall of the Great Hero (Da Xiong Bao Dian). Inside the inner courtyard, the low one-story structures seem older, with weather-beaten wooden pillars and wooden exteriors decorated wth ornately carved roof beams. Dating the building's exact age is difficult. It may be a mixture of new reconstruction and original restoration.

In the Da Xiong Bao Dian, there are three Buddha statues (San Fo), with incense and candles burning. There is an attending monk, but he seems to know little about Buddhism. The stone floor and walls of the hall are clearly Min Guo or late Qing, but the roof overhead is brand new.

· The newly built Scripture Pavilion (Cang Jing Lou) of Hua Cheng Si on Jiuhua Shan.

· One of the four statues of the Heavenly Kings (Tian Wang) at Hua Cheng Si.

At the back of the Da Xiong Bao Dian, original stone steps lead up to a slightly raised terrace where a fourth and final hall was still under construction in October 2003. Unlike the Da Xiong Bao Dian, the foundation, floor, and pillar pedestals are clearly brand new. An attendant monk says this is the Cang Jing Lou. Official written accounts claim that the exhibtion hall is the original Cang Jing Lou, but this would not fit with the normal floor plan of Chinese Buddhist temples.

Official statements continue to claim that the Cang Jing Lou contains a collection of more than 1,300 Buddhist cultural artifacts, including an edict issued by Emperor Wan Li (1573–1620) of the Ming Dynasty, and 6,777 volumes of Buddhist scriptures. However no evidence to support these claims was visible on the author's last visit in October 2003. The horrible truth seems to be that the far-famed original Cang Jing Lou was at some time destroyed, along with its precious contents, most likely during the Cultural Revolution.

The rear gate of the Da Xiong Bao Dian at Hua Cheng Si on Jiuhua Shan.

The golden pagoda (Jin T. at Long An Buddhist Nunnery on Jiuhua Shan.

Long An Nunnery

This is located near the Mi Le Fo Dian, over a bridge crossing a pool with a golden seven-story pagoda covered with Buddhas. Resident nuns stay here.

The nunnery's three main halls have the same unusual style. The outside looks like a three-story square house with windows. On the inside, the main chamber opens up all the way to the roof with a skylight and an inner balcony like a church choir loft looks down upon the altar. This style is unusual elsewhere in China, but is commonly found on Jiuhua Shan. Although not mentioned by R.F. Johnston, this is clearly a genuine Min Guo or late Qing structure.

The Three Precious Halls
(Zhan Tan Chan Ling San Da Bao Dian)
This is a collection of three new Buddhist halls beside the main road (Jie Qu Gong Lu) that runs through Jiuhua Village (Jiuhua Jie Qu). The Da Bei Bao Dian was built between 1992 and 1994 and is a shrine dedicated to the bodhisattva Guanyin. It features a statue of her with 1,000 hands and 1,000 eyes. In the middle of the shrine stand statues of the first six Chinese patriarchs of the Chan (Zen) sect. There are also many marble carvings. The Da Yuan Bao Dian was completed in 1998. The Ling Shan Bao Dian was still under construction in October 2003. Plans call for two more halls to be added, along with a proposed pagoda, which already appears on maps although it does not yet exist. These three massive but gaudy new halls with concrete structures are across the street from the Long An Nunnery.

One of the new Three Precious Halls in Jiuhua Village.

Kshitigarbha Hall (Dizang Dian)
The Kshitigarbha Hall (Dizang Dian) has a massive triple arch red gateway. It is so new that the rock saws are still buzzing here. The hall houses the biggest copper statue of Kshitigarbha, as well as "the newly found" meditating mummy of Master Chi Ming, displayed as a seated golden statue.

The new Dizang Dian in Jiuhua Village.

An extremely difficult and long flight of 99 vertical stone steps leads straight up from behind the Dizang Dian to the Precious Hall of the Sacred Body (Rou Shen Bao Dian), but a much easier way exists. The hall can be easily reached from the main road passing through Jiuhua Village. In fact you can drive right up its massive entrance gate.

Temples on the Shen Guan Ridge

A moderately easy trail, consisting of flights of steps, begins from Jiuhua street beside the **Pure Land Nunnery** (Jing Tu An). It gradually winds up through a forested hillside of cedar trees shrouded in thick fog and mist to the Precious Hall of the Sacred Body (Rou Shen Bao Dian). Along the way, the trail passes a series of other temples, including the **Shang Chan Tang** and the **Ten Kings Hall** (Shi Wang Dian).

An ancient stone foot bridge over a pool inside the Ten Kings Hall (Shi Wang Dian).

Ten Kings Hall (Shi Wang Dian)

Located just below the **Precious Hall of the Sacred Body** (Rou Shen Bao Dian), on a slightly lower terrace, the **Ten Kings Hall** (Shi Wang Dian) is definitely worth a visit.

A courtyard in the center of the Shi Wang Dian has a weathered stone bridge over a stone pool, with a skylight above. This bridge seems to be a genuine historical relic, although the rest of the hall appears new. It resembles the Bridge of No Return on Ming Shan in Fengdu. In fact, many of the figurines in the hall seem to depict scene of frightening punishments in the afterlife.

From the Shi Wang Dian, there are two ways to get up to the higher terrace where the Rou Shen Bao Dian stands. As is usual in China, there is a difficult way to the top for tourists, and a much easier way used by the local inhabitants. To your left is an extremely difficult and long flight of vertical stone steps leading straight up from behind the Shi Wang Dian to the Rou Shen Bao Dian. To your right, however, is hidden a much easier climb that reaches the same destination.

POINT OF INTEREST

As the site has undoubtedly changed over the years, it seems useful to quote directly from the 1913 visit of Carl F. Kupfer in which he describes the Ten Kings Hall (Shi Wang Dian):

"At the entrance of the south door stand two black and red, ferocious looking guards. At the north door two yamen runners with ox and horse heads. In the northeast corner is a scribe who keeps the accounts of men's lives; by his side a fierce, black image, holding a banner... In the northwest corner stands a military officer holding a sword... On the east and on the west sides of this hall the Ten Divisions of Hades are represented, each presided over by one of the ten kings. They are holding court and mete out indescribably cruel punishments... these ten courts... terrible exhibitions of punishment... awful scenes of the future state."

Precious Hall of the Sacred Body (Rou Shen Bao Dian)

The route to the right emerges on a new stone plaza terrace just below the Rou Shen Bao Dian, overlooking the forested hillside below and a difficult flight of 99 stone steps that lead up to the hall's entrance from the Dizang Dian down below in the valley. The knoll is shrouded in thick fog. Two new, but closed, Bell and Drum Towers stand at either end of the terrace. The atmosphere is somewhat tacky with hot air balloons and the pervasive smell of cigarette smoke, the latter activity being forbidden at most functioning temples elsewhere in China. A Communist flag flies from a flag pole.

The exterior of Rou Shen Bao Dian is a two-level pavilion with glass window skylights on the upper side walls. It looks like an almost brand-new concrete beam structure. Inside is the Rou Shen Ta, an octagonal, seven-story, 17-m-high (55.8-ft-high), wooden pagoda that reaches all the way to the ceiling. Along the side walls, with six on each side, are statues of the 12 Devas, all bearded. The foundation of the pagoda, altar, and floor are all made of white marble.

It was in 719 AD that the Korean prince, Kim Gio Gak (Jin Qiao Jue) came to Jiuhua Shan. After 75 years of living on the mountain, Kim passed on but his body remained intact, much like a mummy, and he was recognized as the reincarnation of Kshitigarbha (Dizang). Since then Kim has been known as Jin Dizang. In 781 AD, the second year of the Jian Zhong era (780–783 AD) of the De Zong reign (779–805 AD) during the Tang Dynasty, Buddhists built the Rou Shen Ta as a shrine to Jin Dizang. It was renovated in the Ming Dynasty (1368–1644) when an enclosing hall was built around the pagoda and the shrine received its present name, the Precious Hall of the Sacred Body (Rou Shen Bao Dian).

The Precious Hall of the Sacred Body (Rou Shen Bao Dian) on Jiuhua Shan obscured by thick fog and smoke from burning incense.

A new inscription in ancient Chinese characters on the side of the Precious Hall of the Sacred Body (Rou Shen Bao Dian) on Jiuhua Shan.

According to R.F. Johnston's 1913 account, the Rou Shen Bao Dian was restored in 1867, during the Tongzhi reign (1862–1874) of the Qing Dynasty. The building was most recently "renovated" again in 1989 by Master Shen Fu, and additional temple buildings were added to the site at the same time. However, this renovation seems to have been much more of a reconstruction, as the building's exterior and interior now appear to be completely new. Accurate dating of the Rou Shen Ta inside the hall is more problematic. The temple is now protected by the State Council.

From the Ten Kings Hall, a trail heads up the hillside to a crossroad known as Cha Lu Kou. From here, you can turn right to Xiao Tian Tai or left to the Yin Ke Song and Hui Xian Ge. At Hui Xian Ge, there is another crossroad, with one trail heading up the ridge line of the East Cliff (Dong Ya) towards Bai Sui Gong, and another heading down to Jie Yin Buddhist Nunnery and the Feng Huang Song in the Zhong Ming Yuan valley.

POINT OF INTEREST

In Carl F. Kupfer's 1913 account of his visit, he described the Precious Hall of the Sacred Body (Rou Shen Bao Dian) as such:

> "Here rest the mortal remains of Dizang Wang. They buried him where once stood the little stone hut. A pagoda is erected over this spot, and around this pagoda a temple is built. In this pagoda rests the undecayed body of Dizang Wang. ... This building is square. On the east and west sides stand the Ten Rulers of Hades. In the southeast and southwest corners are two Police of Hades, one having an ox-head and the other a horse-head. In the northeast corners the civil and military judges preside. In the center of this hall stands a square altar. Upon this altar a pagoda is erected, which reaches up through the roof of the building. On the south side of this altar are five images of Dizang Wang and two servants; on the north four images of Dizang Wang and six servants; on the west two images of Dizang, one Laughing Buddha, and seven servants; on the east two images of Dizang and two servants."

One Hundred Year Old Palace (Bai Sui Gong)

The East Cliff (Dong Ya) ridge trail from Hui Xian Ge is like a knife blade dropping off sharply on both sides down into the two valleys on either side of it. An easier route up is to take the Bai Sui Gong Funicular Railway from Jiuhua Village. The ride up takes only five minutes and costs 40 Rmb for a one-way trip, or 70 Rmb for a round-trip.

The terrace at the top of the funicular provides a view of a sea of thick white clouds down in the next valley below on the other side of the ridge. To the right is the ridge trail coming from Hui Xian Ge. To the left, the trail to Bai Sui Gong leads along a moderately-leveled cliff-side trail lined with stone railings adorned with iron chains of padlocks inscribed with lovers' names. The trail passes a small temple building — now turned into tacky shops — and two small stone chortens before rounding the shore of a semi-circular **Animal Releasing Pool** (Fang Sheng Chi) and reaching the original entrance gate to Bai Sui Gong.

The entrance is up steps that tunnel through a small **Maitreya Buddha Hall** (Mi Le Fo Dian) that appears to be an original structure. Here you buy a ticket for 8 Rmb. The steps lead up to the original small terrace atop **East Cliff Peak** (Dong Ya Feng) where the three white-walled original main halls stand in a horseshoe shape set amidst natural rock formations. The hall to the right now functions as business offices, the one to the left is the monks' residential quarters, and straight ahead is the **Precious Hall of the Great Hero** (Da Xiong Bao Dian). The exteriors of these three halls look the same as in Johannes Prip-Moller's 1937 photos and sketches, implying that the buildings themselves survived the political turmoil of the 1937–1945 Japanese occupation, 1946–1949 Chinese Civil War, and 1966–1976 Cultural Revolution.

Inside the Da Xiong Bao Dian is a wood-beamed structure that clearly dates from the early Min Guo or late Qing Dynasty. The Da Xiong Bao Dian has wood-framed glass cases along both sides containing new gilded statues of the 18 Arhats (Shi Ba Luohan), nine on each side. Along the back side of the hall are gilded, seated statues of three Buddhas (San Fo), also inside wood-framed glass cases. Sakyamuni Buddha (Shijiamouni) sits in the center, framed by Pu Xian on an elephant and Wenshu on a blue animal. Seated to the left of Shijiamouni is Amitabha (O-Mi-Tuo-Fo), and seated on

Buddhist worshippers burning incense at Hundred Year Palace (Bai Sui Gong) on Jiuhua Shan.

Inside one of the inner courtyards of Hundred Year Palace (Bai Sui Gong).

the right is Yao Shi Fo. Two other portable wooden cases contain statues of Wei Tuo Pusa and a bearded Guandi holding a sword. Rock boulders emerge through the hall's floor. On the right side of the Da Xiong Bao Dian is a Dining Hall with eight rows of wooden tables. A wooden fish hangs from a beam for signaling meal times.

According to one friendly monk, there are now between 50 to 60 resident monks living at Bai Sui Gong, with some seasonal fluctuations. As such, it is considered to be one of the four largest temples on Jiuhua Shan today. Like the monks at Qi Yuan Si, they practice a combination of both Jing Tu Zong and Chan Zong. The current Abbot (Zhu Chi) of Bai Sui Gong is Shi Hui Qing. He is a member of both the Anhui Province Political Consultative Committee and Qing Yang County Political Consultative Committee.

Behind the Da Xiong Bao Dian is a second two-story wooden hall that is now connected to the first, but seems to have once been separated by a narrow courtyard. Here, seated upright inside a glass case are the gilded remains of the temple's founding ancestor (*zu*), Master Wu Xia, looking impressively realistic.

The third hall holds wooden memorial plaques for the dearly departed, while the fourth hall is a private residential area. Prip-Moller's 1937 floor plan of the temple depicts these two rooms as the Ten Thousand Buddha Hall (Wan Fo Dian) and the 18 Arhats Hall (Shi Ba Luohan Dian) respectively.

PERSONALITIES

Wu Xia (1497-1623) lived here in the 17th century. At that time, the existing temple was called Ten Thousand Year Temple (Wan Nian Si) and had been built during the Wan Li reign (1573–1620) of the Ming Dynasty. Wu Xia spent eight years writing the 81-volume Huang Yan Sutras (Da Fang Guang Fo Huang Yan Jing) using only a mixture of gold dust and his own blood for ink, before it was finally completed in 1623. Three years after his death at the age of 126, his body was found preserved as a mummy. In 1630, during the Chong Zhen reign (1628–1644) of the Ming Dynasty, the Emperor Zhu Yu Jian issued an imperial edict designating Wu Xia as a bodhisattva and giving him the posthumous honorific name, Ying Shen Pusa. The emperor also ordered that Wu Xia's mummy to be gilded and the Bai Sui Gong temple be built to house it.

Creaky wooden floor boards betray the fact that the main floor is actually a second floor above another sub-floor below, making the structures three storys high in all. The main floor is supported by wooden pillars embedded in solid rock boulders down below. All the halls are connected but also separated by narrow courtyards. The wooden exteriors facing the courtyards are covered with ornate wood carvings of figurines and other decorations.

Inscribed gilded signboard over the entrance to the Da Xiong Bao Dian of Bai Sui Gong.

Johannes Prip-Moller's 1937 floor plan of Bai Sui Gong shows a two-story structure built into the hillside. The first floor was dedicated to the more practical needs of storing and preparing food, and providing lodging, for the masses of lay pilgrims who then visited the site. Spiritual needs were attended to on the second floor where the Da Xiong Bao Dian was located. At the time of Prip-Moller's study, the Da Xiong Bao Dian featured the 24 Devas, 12 on each side, with Sakyamuni Buddha (Shijiamouni) in the center of the back wall flanked by Amitabha (O-Mi-Tuo-Fo) and other attendants. Behind a partition were statues of the bodhisattva Guanyin and Yao Shi Fo. Comparing Prip-Moller's description with the present structures, it seems little has changed except for the absence of 12 Devas. It would therefore be safe to conclude that today's existing structure is probably the same one that stood here in 1937.

On a slightly higher flat terrace beside the original Bai Sui Gong buildings is a much larger new two-story **500 Arhat Hall** (Wubai Luohan Tang) built in 1996. The design is more ostentatious, with white walls, red pillars, and a massive high-peaked red-tiled roof featuring two layers of upturned eaves. It stands in stark contrast to the simple but somehow more impressive original halls with their rectangular white walls and nearly flat roofs. The cliff behind this hall drops off into a sea of clouds filling the valley below.

Phone: 501-1293, 501-3118,
251-6480, 790-0183, 672-2500
Fax: 501-1292
Mobile phone: 13905664137

Jie Yin Buddhist Nunnery (Jie Yin An)

After a seemingly endless descent down flights of stone steps from Hui Xiang Ge, hikers finally reach a small Buddhist nunnery known as Jie Yin An. Standing beside a pleasantly gurgling

An ancient stone footbridge over a rushing mountain stream beside the Jie Yin An Buddhist nunnery.

stream in a hollow of the Zhong Ming Yuan valley, the trail actually passes through the ground floor of the nunnery via a kind of tunnel providing cover from the fall rains and winter snows. In their manic need to push on to a final destination, most hikers pass through the nunnery's tunnel without pausing long enough to even realize that a temple lies behind the closed wooden doors. Unknown to all but a few, two Buddhist nuns live a tranquil existence inside the wooden-beamed temple halls. Accessible only by walking through the temple's two chapels, their private outdoor stone terrace overhangs the rushing stream below. The two nuns are quite friendly and seem eager to chat with visitors from the outside world. Beyond tending their vegetable garden and watching the stream flow by, they do not have a lot to do. Amazingly, they do have a telephone, allowing you to call them for spiritual guidance.

Phone: 501-1681

Following the trail straight ahead, a stone footbridge that seems to be a genuine historic relic crosses the stream to the village of Phoenix Pine (Feng Huang Song) on the other side. Formed by three long stone beams, the bridge is cantilevered at either end by projecting stones balanced on stone foundation blocks at either end.

Upon crossing the bridge and reaching the other side of the stream, you find yourself at a crossroads. Here, a branch trail veers off to the right heading towards the Zhong Ming Yuan parking lot and bus station at the present end of the paved road up the mountain. The trail straight ahead leads to Phoenix Pine (Feng Huang Song), passing between a half-mile long unbroken row of more than a dozen small Buddhist temples lined up on either side. This concentration of temples, all occupied by chanting monks and nuns, is almost a sensory overload even for the most seasoned of temple visitors. In the daytime, a bewildering chorus of chanting, bell ringing, drum beating, and rhythmic tapping of wooden fish (*mu yu*) assaults the ears from all directions.

Phoenix Pine (Feng Huang Song)

After this stunning experience, you cross another footbridge over a second stream and arrive at the foot of the famous Phoenix Pine (Feng Huang Song). The well-preserved tree looks in real life just as it does in the widely distributed photographs, resembling somewhat the even more famous Welcoming Pine on Mount Huang Shan, about 100 km (62.1 miles) away. Its canopy of foliage stretches out horizontally forming a green plateau with a wingspan so wide that it is almost impossible to photograph the whole tree in one shot.

Stone dagobas marking the tombs of Buddhist monks on the trail to Bai Sui Gong.

Unfortunately, the tree now sits on the edge of a paved parking lot encircled by shops and occupied in the daytime by a frightening mob of vendors and touts hawking their wares. If you have just descended the forest trail from Hui Xiang Ge, it is like parachuting into an urban nightmare. Remarkably, the whole circus environment completely changes by 6:00PM when the sun goes down and all the shops close. However, this peaceful tranquilty comes at the price of being submerged into total darkness. Be prepared with a flashlight, an item that should always be with you while on the mountain. Keep in mind that the last bus leaves the Zhong Ming Yuan parking lot at 6:00PM, and it is an extremely long walk back to Jiuhua Village in the valley on the other side of the ridge.

One sight not to be missed in the Phoenix Pine (Feng Huang Song) area is a row of five ancient stone dagobas marking the graves of eminent Buddhist monks. Not far away, a sixth stone dagoba stands hidden in the trees. Oddly, no pathway to these monuments exists, short of crossing a field of thorny bushes, although they can be seen in the distance from the Wenshu Dong trail. Normally, they would be in sight from the Phoenix Pine (Feng Huang Song) parking lot, but are now obstructed by a large new building housing a water closet.

Ming Yuan is the name commonly used for the valley where the Phoneix Pine (Feng Huang Song) stands. However, visitors should know that this long valley is actually divided up into a Lower Ming Yuan (Xia Ming Yuan), Middle Ming Yuan (Zhong Ming Yuan), and Upper Ming Yuan (Shang Ming Yuan). From the Phoenix Pine (Feng Huang Song), a foot trail used to veer off to the left heading up to Upper Ming Yuan and the Wenshu Dong. Unfortunately, in October 2003, the trail was well into the process of being converted into a super highway extension of the paved road that currently ends at the Zhong Ming Yuan parking lot.

The Trail to Da Tian Tai

From the Feng Huang Song parking lot, the main trail to Da Tian Tai begins near a big rock covered with a large inscription. It then passes another fork trail to **Yong Xin An**, then tunnels through a covered portico of a trailside temple. Past this temple, the trail soon encounters two more stone dagobas and then passes an even larger stone boulder with a massive inscription just below the trail to your right. A spur trail leads off to the right toward the **Guardian Warrior Temple**, passing another stone dagoba on the way. Making a gradual ascent up a rocky ridge, the trail repeatedly passes straight through people's houses and small Buddhist temples via these covered corridors that seem a uniquely common architectural feature of Jiuhua Shan. These corridors or tunnels provide the hiker with frequent periodic opportunities for convenient shelter from bad weather. More stone shrines and dagobas line the path, becoming too many to number as you lose count during your ascent. A surprising number of people live up here, with each house seeming to offer an informal restaurant set up for passers-by in their front room. A few relatively well stocked shops sell bottled drinks and sundries, albeit at prices marked up to cover the back-borne transportation.

Eventually the relatively easy hike up the populated ridge line ends at a junction in the trail where the left branch descends to the **Hua Yan Dong**. The right branch begins a much steeper climb up flights of stone steps to the first major temple on the Da Tian Tai trail, Hui Ju Chan Si.

Hui Ju Buddhist Temple (Hui Ju Chan Si)

Once named Hui Qing Temple and dating from the Qing Dynasty, this temple stands in the green bamboo forest of Ming Yuan.

Since Master Wu Chan took over, several new halls have been built, including a Maitreya Buddha Hall (Mi Le Fo Dian), and Buddhist Scripture Library (Cang Jing Lou).

After leaving Hui Ju Chan Si, the next four sights encountered during the ascent upward to Da Tian Tai are in order: Ji Xiang Si, Fu Xing An, Diao Qiao An, and Guanyin Feng.

Ancient Buddhist Scripture Reading Terrace (Gu Bai Jing Tai)

This the second main temple reached on the Tian Tai trail from Zhong Ming Yuan, after first passing Hui Ju Temple. The oldest hall here was built in the late Qing Dynasty. In 1994, a 'renovation' was conducted by Master Shen Ming (Fa Shi), in which some of the older halls were torn down and a completely new Precious Hall of the Great Hero (Da Xiong Bao Dian) was built. It is a much larger and more ostentatious multi-story hall with red pillars, yellow walls, and a huge high-peaked red-tiled roof with two layers of upturned eaves. It now stands beside the remaining original low, white-wall, two-story rectangular hall with a nearly flat roof. Both the original and new halls now stand on a greatly expanded three-story high concrete terrace, built up against the rocky mountainside. According to legend, Kim Gio Gak (Jin Qiao Jue) used to chant sutras in a cave near here and left a pair of his footprints embedded in a rock outside its mouth. The footprints are now on display inside the newly built Da Xiong Bao Dian and may be viewed by visitors.

Great Heavenly Terrace Buddhist Temple (Da Tian Tai Chan Si)

Standing at the summit of Jiuhua Shan, at an elevation of 1,306 m (4,284.8 ft), this is the highest temple on the mountain. From the Heavenly Terrace Peak (Tian Tai Feng), you can see two other peaks: Dragon Head Peak (Long Tou Feng) and Dragon Ball Peak (Long Zhu Feng).

A temple was first built here in the third year of the Hong Wu reign during the Ming Dynasty. In 1913, R.F. Johnston wrote that the buildings were small but old, dating from the first year of the Ming Dynasty (1368), and had last been restored in 1890 during the Guang Xu reign of the Qing Dynasty. Along the beams of the old temple hall, visitors could find 1,000 well-carved Buddha images.

Much like at Bai Jing Tai and Bai Sui Gong, a completely new temple was recently built here. Unlike at these two sites, where old and new coexist side by side, the earlier building had to be completely destroyed in order to build the new one. This is despite being supposedly protected by the State Council. The original temple, which still stood in 1997, was a one-story, white-wall, rectangular hall with a nearly flat roof. It has since been replaced by a new much larger and elbaorate hall, complete with yellow walls, red pillars, and a red-tiled, high-peaked, with upturned eaves.

What has not changed is the spectacular view from the summit. From the terrace in front of the temple, you can enjoy watching the sun rise over such sights as Huang Shan, Tai Ping Lake, and the Yangzi River.

The trail to the summit is also still the same today: a nearly vertical flight of endless steps, in a perfectly straight line up the mountainside, to the first of four stone wall terraces, each higher than the other, but with the lower three vacant of any structures. The existence of a cable car (*sui dao*) from Zhong Ming Yuan to Bai Jing Tai makes the ascent much easier.

Tian Tai Si is sometimes called Da Tian Tai to distinguish it from the Xiao Tian Tai. Other variant names include Dizang Chan Lin and Tian Tai Zhen Ting.

The **Jiuhua Shan Buddhist Fair** (Jiuhua Miao Hui) is an annual event which usually falls on 30 July. It commemmorates the death of Korean Prince Kim Gio Gak (Jin Qiao Jue) and his reincarnation as the bodhisattva Dizang. The traditional fair was banned at the start of the Cultural Revolution in 1966, and only resumed 17 years later in 1983. It is now once again a popular event.

Phone: 501-1228
Admission: There is a 90 Rmb admission fee to enter the Jiuhua Shan Scenic Area
Cable car: The Eastern Peak Cable Car costs 48 Rmb to ascend and 20 Rmb to descend
Web site: http://www.jiuhuashan.com.cn

Jiuhua Shan Practical Information

Jiuhua Shan Area Code: (0566)

Jiuhua Shan Transportation

The nearest train station to Jiuhua Shan is in the Yangzi River town of Tongling, although most trains stop at the larger city of Wuhu. The closest airport is in the Anhui provincial capital of Hefei. Either of these options will still require you to take a long-distance bus the remainder of the way to the mountain. Few long-distance buses travel the full distance from Shanghai to Jiuhua Shan, with most stopping in Wuhu, where you will need to transfer to another local bus.

Long distance buses from Tongling (40 km; 24.9 miles) take about 2 hours, from Wuhu (100 km; 62.1 miles) 4 hours, or from Hefei (200 km; 124.2 miles) 4 hours. Nanjing is 6 hours away from Jiuhua Shan by bus, and Shanghai 10 hours. Many long-distance buses stop at the nearby town of Qing Yang (Qing Yang Zhen), from where minibuses leave for the short ride to Jiuhua Village (Jiuhua Cun) throughout the day. However, there is a long-distance bus stop at Jiuhua Village itself, beside the Qi Yuan Temple.

Maps of the mountain's trails can easily be bought in Jiuhua Village (Jiuhua Cun). There are also two cable cars on the mountain. One leaves from the back of the Qi Yuan Si and ascends to a spot about halfway between the Bai Sui Gong and the Bell Tower (Zhong Lou). The other one takes a much longer ascent to the top of Tian Tai Feng, and can be boarded east of the village, near the Phoenix Pine (Feng Huang Song).

Jiuhua Shan Hotels

Ju Long Hotel (Ju Long Da Jiudian)***

Address: Opposite the Qi Yuan Temple, Jiuhua Village
Phone: 501-1368
Price: 320–650 Rmb

Long Quan Hotel (Long Quan Fandian)

Address: Jie Qu Gong Lu, Jiuhua Village
Phone: 501-1320

Bell Tower Hotel (Zhong Lou Fandian)

Address: Jie Qu Gong Lu, Jiuhua Village
Phone: 501-1251
Price: 25–100 Rmb

Nan Yuan Guest House (Nan Yuan Lu Guan)

Address: Jie Qu Gong Lu, Jiuhua Village
Phone: 501-1122
Price: 25–100 Rmb

The Buddhism Hotel (Fo Jiao Binguan)

Address: Beside the Qi Yuan Temple, Jiuhua Village
Phone: 501-3117
Fax: 501-3118
Price: 60–140 Rmb

Anhui Province

Anqing

Anqing lies on the north bank of the Yangzi River, 592 km (370 miles) west of Shanghai. The town is almost entirely surrounded by water, with the mouth of the Wan He on its western border, the Yangzi to the south, the Xin He on its eastern border, and three lakes to the northeast. This accounts for legends that the town would float away if the anchors at Yin Jiang Temple were ever removed. Beyond the lakes and rivers marking the town's outskirts is a ring of mountains, the largest being the 914.4-m-high (3,000-ft-high) Great Dragon Mountain (Da Long Shan), 16 km (10 miles) to the north.

Anqing's History

During the Spring and Autumn (Chun Qiu) period (770–476BC), Anqing was known as the Wan Kingdom (Wan Guo) or Wan City (Wan Cheng). During the Eastern Jin (Dong Jin) Dynasty (317–419 AD), Wan Cheng adopted the new name of Yi Cheng. Today there is still an Yi Cheng Road in the city. Huailing county (*xian*), of which Anqing was the capital, first appears in historic records in the year 380AD during the Xiao Wudi reign (373–396 AD) of the Eastern Jin Dynasty. The name Huailing continued to be used for the area surrounding Anqing until 1949. The town was refounded and renamed Anqing in 1217. The Mongols captured Anqing in 1274, the last year of the Du Zong reign (1264–1274), during their final drive south. In the next year, they captured the Southern Song capital in Hangzhou, and took the child emperor Gongzong (1274–1276) hostage, effectively ending the dynasty. Anqing was one of the first towns captured by Zhu Yuanzhang in the 1350s, when his base was still the town of Chuzhou, before he crossed to the south bank of the Yangzi River in 1355, occupied Nanjing in 1356 and proclaimed himself the first emperor of the new Ming Dynasty (1368–1644). In 1646, the city changed hands again when it was captured from its Ming defenders by the invading Manchu forces moving southward from their base in northeastern China.

During the Qing Dynasty and Min Guo era, Anqing served as the capital of Anhui Province from 1760 to 1949, even though it was occupied by the Japanese from 1938 to 1945. In fact, the name "Anhui" was formed by combining the first portions of two prefectures, Anqing and Huizhou, the latter being the home of the famous Yellow Mountain (Huang Shan). As well as being the provincial capital, it was also the seat of government of the Anqing prefecture (*fu*), and the county (*xian*) of Huailing. As the headquarters for three different levels of government, the city had a large number of public buildings and state temples, including two City God Temples (Cheng Huang Miao), one for Anqing prefecture and another for Huailing county, and a Confucius Temple (Wen Miao or Kong Fuzi Miao).

Anqing was a major stronghold of the Taiping Rebels for eight and a half years, from February 1853 to September 1861. During that time, it played a key role in protecting the western approach to the capital city of Nanjing. Taiping forces led by Shi Da Kai first captured Anqing on 24 February 1853. After briefly losing the city, the Taipings recaptured Anqing on 10 June 1853. Shi Da Kai returned to Anqing on 25 September 1853 with a Taiping army of 6,000 troops.

The Qing siege of Anqing began on 15 October 1858. In November and December 1858, after the signing of the Treaty of Tientsin, Lord Elgin commanded a flotilla of British ships that sailed up the Yangzi River. He reported that the Taipings were in control of all the important towns along the river from Nanjing to Anqing. The latter was still in the hands of the Taipings when Captain Blakiston passed by there in March 1861, on his way up the Yangzi River as part of Admiral Sir James Hope's naval expedition. Blakiston reported that the walled city was under siege by surrounding Qing land forces. Two fleets of Qing ships were blockading the Yangzi River, to the east and west of the town, while the Taiping garrison itself had no ships of its own. Blakiston noted that the Taipings had heavily fortified the hilltop area, at the east end of the walled town around the Zhen Feng Ta pagoda, which still stands today.

More than two years later, when the siege yielded no results, Zeng Guofan's brother Zeng Guoquan took over command of the Qing forces on 5 May 1861. He succeeded in recapturing Anqing on 5 September 1861. The fall of this city, described by some as the Taiping's second most important city, was probably the decisive turning point in the war. After its recaputure, Zeng Guofan moved his headquarters to Anqing in preparation for the final reconquest of Nanjing. In December 1861, Zeng Guoquan set up an arsenal in Anqing to manufacture weapons for the attack on Nanjing.

Even though the walls and city gates have all since been torn down, Anqing remained a walled city until 1927. The city wall had a circumference of 4.8 km (3 miles), with four gates each pointing in the directions of the compass.

As late as 1927, Anqing still had enough functioning temples of various creeds that the city served as the focal point for an American academic's study of religion in China, John K. Shryock's *The Temples of Anking and Their Cults*. Shryock lived in Anqing for eight years, and counted a total of 125 temples there, 99 of which were still actively functioning as religious institutions.

Sadly only a few of these religious sites still stand today. Part of the reason is undoubtedly the Japanese occupation of Anqing, which began with their capture of the city on 12 June 1938. However, much of the destruction was caused by the Chinese themselves during the 1966–1976 Cultural Revolution.

Anqing Today

Anqing is one of the largest cities in Anhui Province. Although it has lost its role as the provincial capital to Hefei, Anqing city is the capital of a municipality which includes eight counties spread out over 243 km (151 miles) of the Yangzi's north bank, and far into northern Anhui. The eight counties include four along the river bank — Su Song at the far western end, Huai Ning, Wang Jiang, and Zong Yang at the far eastern end — as well as four inland counties to the north of the Hefei-Jiujiang railway: Tong Cheng, Yue Xi, Qian Shan, and Tai Hu. The current municipality is largely similar in territory to the old Anqing Prefecture prior to 1949. The total area of the municipaity is 15,200 sq km (5,869 sq miles), and its population in 1992 was 5.57 million. However, the urban area of Anqing city itself is only about 46 sq km (17.8 sq miles), still a large increase from its 1992 size of 19.5 sq km (7.5 sq miles) and its pre-1949 size of 3.5 sq km (1.4 sq miles). Today, the population of Anqing city is 585,000.

Before 1992, Anqing city had no airport or train station, and this was before China's highway system had been developed to allow the current long-distance bus service. As recently as ten years ago, Anqing could only be reached by ships traveling the Yangzi River.

A local guidebook published in 1992 admitted that the city had already changed beyond recognition, and at first glance there does not seem to be any remaining old town district at all. However, a closer look will show that some historical relics have survived.

Anqing Sights
Welcome the River Temple (Ying Jiang Si)

This is located at the east end of town near the former location of the East Gate (Dong Men) of the city wall, on a small hill beside the Yangzi River, at the intersection of Hu Xin Nan Lu and Yan Jiang Dong Lu. This large complex of buildings covers 30,000 sq m (322,917 sq ft) and features four main halls, plus the famous pagoda, and numerous minor side halls. The grounds can be entered from the east by entering a side gate from Hu Xin Nan Lu and walking up a road which ascends the hill to the central courtyard where the pagoda stands. You can also begin at the front entrance facing Yan Jiang Dong Lu and the Yangzi River to the south and ascend up several flights of steps. Since Chinese temples are typically organized along a central axis with the first hall at the southern end, it would make more of a logical progression to begin from the Yan Jiang Dong Lu entrance.

At the south entrance facing Yan Jiang Lu and the Yangzi River are two legendary four-pronged iron ships' anchors cemented into the steps. The first building is the **Four Heavenly Kings Hall** (Si Tian Wang Dian). It is an obviously new reconstruction with a concrete frame structure, completed around 1992. Inside are four

One of two iron ship's anchors embedded in the terrace in front of the Heavenly Kings Hall (Tian Wang Dian) of Ying Jiang Si at Anqing.

The Wind Mc Pagoda (Zhe Feng Ta) of th Welcome the River Temple (Ying Jiang S in Anqing.

brand new but impressive looking wooden statues of the four heavenly kings, two on each side. In the middle of the hall facing the southern entrance is a Mi Le Fo, the Maitreya Buddha of the future, inside a glass face, while behind him facing the north exit is a Pu Tuo Pusa, the martial warrior Buddha who protects temples.

Leaving the first hall, you ascend up a flight of steps to a second terrace where stands the comparatively small **Precious Hall of the Great Hero** (Da Xiong Bao Dian). This hall contains three giant gilded Buddhas in the center, with O-Mi-Tuo-Fo (Amitabha) on the far left. Because this is a Chan temple, Amitabha has less importance. Eighteen gilded Arhats (*Luohan*) stand along the side walls, nine on each side.

To the left of the Da Xiong Bao Dian is a small gate leading to a hall known as the **Wen Wu Chen Lie Shi Dian**, but the main progression through the temple leads to your right. Walking east from the second hall leads you to an intersection of pathways. To the south, the path heads to the second floor of the temple's **Vegetarian Restaurant** (Ying Jiang Lou Su Cai Guan), which offers wonderful views of the Yangzi River and is open to the public.

The small Da Xiong Bao Dian of the Welcome the River Temple (Ying Jiang Si), with the Wind Moved Pagoda (Zhen Feng Ta) rising behind it.

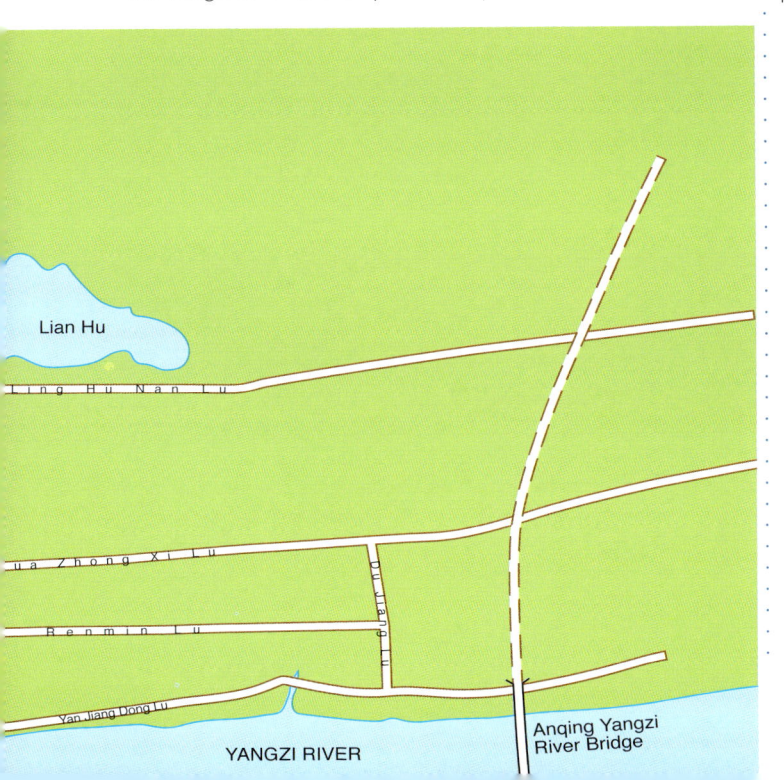

A stone statue of a warrior embedded in the walls of the Wind Moved Pagoda (Zhen Feng Ta).

A stone Buddhist statue of the Jie Yin Fo inside the Wind Moved Pagoda (Zhen Feng Ta).

The path to the north lead to the temple's main courtyard, in the center of which stands the famous **Wind Moved Pagoda** (Zhen Feng Ta). This was built in 1570 during the Wan Li reign (1573–1620) of the Ming Dynasty. Despite having been built by their predecessors, the Qing emperors took good care of the pagoda. During the Shun Zhih reign (1644–1661), a local official had the pagoda rebuilt in 1651, and in the Kang Xi reign (1661–1722), it was repaired in 1664. Although most other temple buildings were destroyed during the Taipings' eight-year occupation of the city, Shryock concluded that the original pagoda had in fact survived without needing to be rebuilt later. However, it did receive minor renovations during the Tong Zhi reign (1862–1874) and again under the early republic.

The 72.74-m-high (240-ft-high) stone pagoda is fully intact today, but has obviously been repaired and restored. Niches in the exterior walls where Buddha figurines must have once sat are now empty. The pagoda's spire has a series of six round balls of various sizes. Small bells still hang from all the corners of the pagoda's roof eaves extending from each floor. The base of the octagonal pagoda originally seems to have had eight entrances, but six of these have now been filled up with Inscribed Tablets. The only one still open is that leading to the stairwell.

For a separate 3 Rmb ticket, you can now climb 168 stone steps, all the way to the top of the pagoda, and even get to visit the once mysterious seventh floor that was previously off limits. Six of the floors feature doorways exiting out on all eight sides onto narrow stone balconies with low stone railings that encircle the pagoda. In 1911, the American visitor William Edgar Geil noted that more than one hundred poems had been inscribed on the inside walls of the pagoda by previous Chinese visitors describing their impressions.

Authentic stone carvings decorate the inside walls of the narrow winding stone stairwell. Inside the ground floor entrance, visitors first see the **Welcoming Buddha** (Jie Yin Fo) a 5-m-high (16.4-ft-high) stone statue embedded in the wall. In the center of the second floor is a soapstone statue of the **Maitreya Buddha** (Mi Le Fo). On the third floor is another Buddha statue, this one representing **Wu Fang Fo**. In total there are supposedly 1,178 stone Buddha statues inside the pagoda. The poetic graffiti reported about in 1911 is now gone. It has been whitewashed over, only to be replaced by newer, less poetic graffiti that in some cases even covers the faces of the statues.

Just north of the pagoda is the **Pi Lu Dian**, the temple's third main building with its two tiers of upturned roof eaves. Pi Lu Fo, also known as Pi Lu Zhe Na, is the Chinese name of **Vairocana**. As Vairocana represents the Buddist law or doctrine, the Pi Lu Dian would be where lectures and education on the Buddhist doctrine take place. This is the temple's largest hall, and contrary to normal practice, this one seems to function as the main hall of the temple rather than the much smaller Da Xiong Bao Dian. It has an unusual arrangement of effigies inside. A seated Pi Lu Fo Buddha sits all alone on a lotus flower wearing a crown on his head, with his hands clasped together, one finger of each hand extended and their tips touching. Two very non-Buddhist looking disciples stand on either side of him, one with a long flowing black beard. A giant drum (*gu*) sits in the front corner on the left, while a giant bronze bell (*zhong*) stands in the front corner on the right. Behind the main screen is a giant standing Guanyin facing the hall's north exit. Guanyin stands in front of an amazingly colorful landscapes wall covered with hundreds of smaller figures of people, pagodas, and pavilions.

One of four statues of the Heavenly Kings (Tian Wang) inside the Tian Wang Dian of Ying Jiang Si.

Along both sides of the Pi Lu Fo Dian are 20 statues of figures who do not appear at all like the typical portrayal of Buddhist Arhats (*Luohan*). Most have a Confucian scholar appearance, with long flowing black beards and colorful robes of blue, red, and yellow. These seem to be the same Devas (Zhu Tian) who were described by Reichelt as frequently appearing in sets of 24 statues in Chinese Buddhist temples during the Min Guo era. Nowadays, it is extremely rare to see this group of

Some of the 20 Devas (Zhu Tian) portrayed inside the Pi Lu Dian of Ying Jiang Si.

Devas with its many non-Buddhist gods, kings, and judges in Chinese Buddhist temples.

On the east side of the courtyard is the temple's **Book Store** (Shu Dian), where you can purchase informative publications on the history of Anqing as well as the temple itself.

Behind Pi Lu Dian is the fourth main building of the temple, the three-storey **Scripture Storage House** or Library (Cang Jing Lou). Inside this hall is a rather chunky looking obese reclining Buddha. The hall's main purpose is to store the many volumes of Buddhist scriptures or sutras.

Behind the Cang Jing Lou is a garden with a man-made rockery known as **Jia Shan**, and an **Animal Releasing Pool** (Fang Sheng Chi). Beside this garden are several small open-air pavilions, including the Wang Ta Ting and Ban Bian Ting.

In addition to the main halls along the north-south axis, there are several others hidden off to the sides. The Guang Si Dian and Da Shi Ge are both west of the main courtyard containing the Zhen Feng Ta. The **Da Shi Ge** is a two-story red brick hall with a series of arched arcades on both floors and a veranda on the second. Its appearance is that of a Min Guo era structure. It is somewhat isolated from the rest of the temple, having a separate entrance gate (Da Shi Ge Shan Men) from Yan Jiang Lu, and being surrounded by its own wall that cuts it off from the other halls and courtyards. Insde its walled enclosure, the Da Shi Ge has its own courtyard where you can find the small open-air Qi Xin Ting. Despite having many halls, there no longer seems to be a genuine Meditation Hall (Chan Tang). Such a hall did exist before the 1949 revolution, as witnessed and recorded by Shryock in 1927.

The temple now has an apparently large resident monk population, although the exact number is difficult to determine. Although the temple's population may have somewhat recovered, their practices are not necessarily in line with former rigid customs. When it was meal time, the monks were seen eating separately

The East Gate of Ying Jiang Si facing Hu Xin Nan Lu.

The Pi Lu Dian of Ying Jiang Si.

as individuals in widely dispersed locations around the grounds, rather than together in one dining hall under the watchful eyes of a master. In the past, monks were restricted to their temple grounds, but now they seem to wander around the city freely, taking taxis and shopping in stores. Some were even seen smoking.

Unlike most temples which tend to close fairly early around 4:00PM, this one seems to stay open to visitors late into the evening, possibly to encourage customers to eat at their restaurant. This also allows visitors to mingle with the monks who are off cuty as they wasnder about the temple grounds in their simple white tunics.

The temple's own historical records state that it was founded during the Northern Song (Bei Song) Dynasty in 974AD. The pagoda was added to the temple in 1570, during the Long Qing reign (1567–1572) of the Ming Dynasty. The original names were Ten Thousand Buddha Temple (Wan Fo Si) and Ten Thousand Buddha Pagoda (Wan Fo Ta). When the temple was repaired between 1619–1620, its name was changed to Yong Chang Si. This new name did not last long, as it was renamed again in 1650 to the present day Ying Jiang Si.

The iron gong for calling meal times at Ying Jiang Si.

Address: Hu Xin Nan Lu and Yan Jiang Dong Lu
Phone: 551-0382
Admission: 3 Rmb for the temple and another 3 Rmb for the Pagoda

Anqing Museum (Anqing Shi Bowuguan)

The architectural style of the building housing the Anqing Museum (Anqing Shi Bowuguan) immediately attracts the eyes of the visitor. Its red brick hall is obviously much older than the new Tian Wang Dian of Ying Jiang Si standing beside it. There are a number of stone inscriptions on its façade, and three arched gateways with double wooden doors pierce the front of the two-story hall. Above each of the three gateways is a white stone block with an inscription in Chinese characters. At first glance it would appear that this hall clearly once belonged to the Buddhist temple next door. Museum staff claim that the hall was built in the Ming Dynasty as part of neighboring Ying Jiang Si and served as a hall devoted to the Buddhist bodhisattvas Guanyin and Da Shi Zhi (Guanyin Da Shi Zhi Dian). However, the stone inscriptions call it the Two Martyr's Ancestral Temple (Xiong Fan Er Lieshi Zhuan Ci).

A new inscribed tablet outside the Anqing Museum.

Left and right: Rows of 19th century iron cannons inside the courtyard of the Anqing Museum.

The building certainly has a confusing array of names and purposes, as testified by the profusion of signs on the exterior. In addition to wooden signboards labeling it as the Anqing Museum (Anqing Shi Bowuguan), and the stone inscriptions commemmorating it as an Ancestral Temple (Zhuan Ci), it also has a sign dedicating it, in 1990, as a memorial to the Taiping rebels (Taiping Tianguo Wan Fu). Furthermore, a long red banner stretched across the façade adorned with red hammer and sickle symbols proclaims it as a Communist Party (Gong Chan Dang) history exhibition hall.

Although the Communist propaganda exhibits inside the hall fail to inspire, a step into the inner courtyard behind it reveals an impressive collection of genuine historical artifacts. Eight iron cannons are lined in two rows of four, and another nine cannons

The front entrance to the Anqing Museum, formerly a hall of Ying Jiang Si.

Headless ancient stone statues lined up in the courtyard of the Anqing Museum.

Inscriptions are still legible on some of the 19th century iron cannons at the museum.

lay on the ground beside the wall to your right. All are obviously genuine 19th century relics and together they comprise one of the largest collection of historic iron cannons in China. According to the attendant, the row of four cannons on the right date from the Taiping Rebellion, when Anqing was controlled by the Taipings for eight years. The row of four cannons on the left date from the "English War." Whether this refers the Opium War of 1839–1842 or the war of 1860 is not clear. In the First Opium War, the British did not sail any further upstream than Nanjing, but in 1860 the Earl of Elgin sailed as far west as Hankou. Most of the cannons have Chinese inscriptons engraved on their muzzles, illustrating the practice then of giving each gun some kind of inspirational name. A horseshoe shaped wooden second story of the hall surrounds the courtyard on three sides and provides another angle to view the relics down below.

In addition to the cannons, the courtyard holds three impressive standing stone statues of men, whose heads have been broken off, and a number of stone stele tablets seated upon the backs of turtles, a style that was common during the Ming Dynasty. Furthermore, there are wonderful views of the Zhen Feng Ta pagoda next door from here. The pagoda is so large that it is difficult to get a good view of it from within the temple itself, but the view from here provides a better perspective. You can see the people ascending to the different floors of the pagoda and walking around its exterior stone balconies. However, a wall around the courtyard separates it from the temple grounds.

Address: Yan Jiang Zhong Lu
Phone: 551-2797, 550-4935

The Old Town

Start out from the Qing Zhen Si, and walk uphill along **Nan Men Jie**. Nan Men means South Gate, and this was the southern entrance to the walled city. Notice the many shops and restaurants with flowing Arabic script on their signs.

Anqing Mosque (Anqing Qing Zhen Si)

The entrance is through an unassuming, plain-looking modern-day building facing a courtyard and gate that faces the uphill main street of Nan Men Jie, one block uphill from the Yangzi waterfront. However, the original gate and views of the main halls, that are built in traditional Chinese-style architecture, can be seen by turning right off of Nan Men Jie onto Qing Zhen Si Jie, just downhill from the new entrance. Qing Zhen Si Jie makes an L-shape around two sides of the mosque complex and provides a look at the original double wooden gate now kept closed, with two screen walls opposite it.

Passing through the new modern entrance, you descend a flight of steps to the main hall and its side halls. Although these seem to be fairly recent reconstructions, they are impressively designed in traditional Chinese style architecture. The main hall has an enormously high roof supported by row upon row of thick round wooden columns. Ornate inscriptions in Arabic script can be found on signboards inside and out. Prayer mats are spread on the floor. Inside the main gate is a sign commemmorating its construction in 1422 by Ma Zhao Tie and Ma Cui Ying. Shryock noted that Anqing had two mosques when he lived here in the 1920s, but this seems to be the only one now. Despite the mosque's undoubtedly long history, authentic historic relics seem in short supply today. One diagonal stone sculpture on the steps is barely identifiable, one stone tablet bearing an inscription has been extensively repaired with cement patches to such extent the original stone parts can barely be seen. A stone wall beside the main hall is marked by a sign.

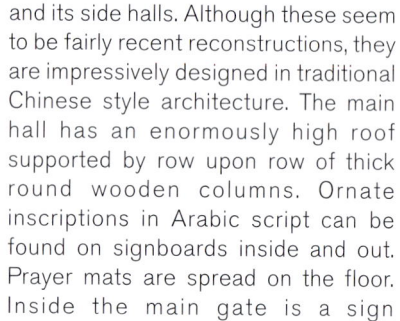

Address: 48 Nan Men Jie
Phone: 554-3543

Both pages: The Anqing Mosque (Qing Zhen Si).

Ren Jia Po Jie

At the summit of a ridge, you reach the intersection with a narrow east-west lane known as Ren Jia Po Jie. A few blocks to the east is the remains of a small red brick church, which is in sad disrepair and apparently closed. However, turning left at the intersection and heading west leads one into a fascinating area of narrow pedestrian lanes with outdoor street markets. At No. 47 is the oldest building on the block, a structure which seems to have once been a temple. The two round stone gate markers lie on the ground outside, and a plaque with Chinese characters is embedded in the wall. The structure has wooden walls and inside, part of a seal is still visible in the floor with a motife of flying bats — a lucky symbol in Chinese mythology — and a hexagram in the center. Many families now live in this rustic space.

Turn right and head downhill to the north. The next east-west cross street has at No. 62 the best preserved Min Guo building in the city. This is a three-story structure which is now used as a neighborhood Post Office. The original inscription at the top of the façade has been intentionally covered up, hiding its original name and date of construction. However, along the side alley, to the left, a plaque embedded in the wall. In Chinese, the plaque states that the building was formerly the Postal Service Headquarters for all of Anhui province (Anhui You Wu Guanli Ju Jiu Zhi) during the Min Guo era when Anqing was still the capital of Anhui.

Dao Pa Shi Jie

Turning left and heading east on this street takes you to a building built over the street and made to look like traditional Chinese architecture. This marks the southern end of Dao Pa Shi Jie, possibly the most fascinating street in the whole city. This long narrow pedestrian-only (*bu xing jie*) lane is lined with seemingly modern dress shops on the ground floor. However, look up at the second floor of the two-story buildings and you'll be surprised to see genuine Qing Dynasty half-timber construction, with lattice work windows and roofs supported by intricately carved wooden beams decorated with beautiful artwork. One of the most beautiful examples is known as the Yue Yan Jia.

At No. 61 is a historic two-beam stone gate still standing beside a dress shop entrance. Slightly damaged stone sculptures

Top and above: Dao Pa Shi Jie in Anqing's old town.

Left: Dao Pa Shi Jie in Anqing's old town. *Right*: The new stone gate (pai fang) of Dao Pa Shi Jie, facing Long Shan Lu, in Anqing.

are still visible at the top of the gate and look like those you would find at a temple. A modern-day Chinese language plaque marks the site. Locals refer to the ruined remains of this gate as the **Dao Pa Shi Pai Fang**. The northern end of the lane is marked by a modern reproduction of a stone beam gate. Here the lane exits out onto the east-west street **Long Shan Lu**, constructed fairly recently in 1992.

Long Men Kou Jie (Old City Gate)

Heading north on Long Men Kou Jie takes you to the summit of the hill where you will find, on your right, a small park in front of a Ming Dynasty fortress gate. The stone block gate has a single-arched tunnel which passes through its center, and a ramshackle

Left: Memorial to a local revolutionary martyr at Long Men Kou in Anqing. *Right*: The derelict Long Men Kou fortress gate in Anqing.

Roman Catholic Cathedral (Tian Zhu Jiao Tang)

Located down a narrow side lane that branches off of Renmin Lu, this is the biggest church in Anqing. Its exact year of construction is uncertain, but it clearly dates from the Min Guo era or possibly even the Qing Dynasty. The cathedral's architecture is an impressive combination of Western and Chinese styles. It stands inside a walled compound with a large arched gateway, over the top of which are three large Chinese characters.

The main hall has a fascinating stone block façade that ascends to a bell tower in the center with three step-like levels on both sides. This tends to give it somewhat the appearance of a giant Chinese *pai lou*, or memorial gate. There are three entrances in front of the main hall's ground floor, with a stone balustrade around a low terrace and three short flights of steps up to each doorway. Above the three doorways are three vertical rectangular stone inscriptions of Chinese characters. Eight traditional Chinese-style stone fish, similar to those often seen on Chinese temples, also decorate the main hall's façade. Two stone dragon statues in front of the center entrance with their heads broken off are the only signs of damage. The dragons' stone heads lay on the ground in a corner of the courtyard. Otherwise, the cathedral is in perfect condition. Although the gate to the compound was open, the entrances to the main hall were locked shut, despite the fact that it was a Sunday.

Opposite the main hall, a statue of Saint Mary is dated 1986, showing that the church had reopened by this time, following the Cultural Revolution of 1966–1976 when all churches were closed. On the east side of the courtyard is a second arched gateway leading to another lane, but this gate is kept closed.

The back of the church's buildings opens out onto Xiao Su Lu, and partial views of their back sides can be had

Top and above: The Roman Catholic Cathedral (Tian Zhu Jiao Tang) of Anqing.

Broken stone statue outside the Roman Catholic Cathedral (Tian Zhu Jiao Tang) of Anqing.

---

two-story wooden pavilion on top of it. Two stone lions stand guard just outside the gate's entrance, and a modern statue of some revolutionary hero stands in the park. Unfortunately, some Communist Party institution is housed inside the grounds on the other side of the gate, so visitors are not allowed to actually enter the gate.

from here. Entrances that once existed into the compound from here are now kept closed.

Address: 58 Xi Lin Jie,
in between Renmin Lu to the south
and Xiao Su Lu to the north

The Yangzi Waterfront

The Yangzi River waterfront in Anqing.

The Feng Yan Ting marks the western end of Anqing's waterfront. Although the small open-air pavilion is an unimpressive modern construction, the location itself provides a panoramic view of the Yangzi River. Here you can ascend to the promenade atop the new flood wall. From this spot you can clearly see how Anqing once commanded the Yangzi River. All ships sailing downstream can be seen from miles away because of a large bend in the river to the southwest which forces ships to sail straight towards the city. During the Taiping Rebellion, when the Taipings occupied Anqing for eight years, cannons such as those now in the Anqing museum, would have been able to easily hit ships sailing downstream from this spot on the waterfront before they could reach or pass by the city. The Da Guan Lou across the street is an authentic two-story Qing Dynasty pavilion which is unfortunately now in a sad state of disrepair. The waterfront road running between the Feng Yan Ting and Da Guan Lou is called Xi Da Di Lu, but heading east the road soon changes to Yan Jiang Lu.

Waterfront Promenade
It is possible to walk along the top of the flood wall promenade all the way to Yi Jiang Si at its eastern end. Every few yards, there is a small pavilion providing shade from the sun or cover from the summer rainstorms. Along the way, you pass half a

The new pedestrian promenade atop the Yangzi River flood wall in Anqing.

dozen floating passenger ferry docks (*matou*) providing cross-river transportation to the Yangzi's southern shore. One of the ships is emblazoned with the words "Wan Dong Zhi Ke Du." It is fascinating to watch how the small ferry boats slowly struggle against the Yangzi's powerful downstream current on their return trip to the northern shore. Looking across the river at its opposite shore, it seems that the southern bank is lined with a forest of trees from east to west, without a single building or town in sight. Walking eastward, you pass a branch of the Bank of China. Next to it the Jiang Hai Bin Guan, the only hotel located directly on the waterfront, but one which has seen better days. At the east end of the promenade, the magnificent Zhen Feng Ta comes into view and it is from here that you will be able to get the best views and photographs of the entire enormous structure.

Anqing Yangzi River Bridge (Changjiang Da Qiao)

From the eastern end of the promenade you can also see the two triangular shaped concrete uprights of the new Changjiang Da Qiao highway bridge being constructed across the Yangzi River. Work started in 2001, but by October 2003, it was still only half completed. When it is finished, National Highway 206 will cross to the other side, and for the first time in its history, Anqing will be connected directly to the Jiangnan region south of the Yangzi River. After the bridge opens it may put the many cross-river passenger ferry services out of business. The biggest impact could be that Anqing may become the gateway to Jiuhua Shan on the other side of the river. This is because Anqing has, by far, the closest airport to the mountain, an advantage it has not been able to exploit until now due to the absence of a bridge here. The few airlines that fly there have been scheduling a decreasing number of flights to Anqing so long as it is a dead end destination. Once it becomes the gateway to Jiuhua Shan, the number of flights to the city will undoubtedly increase. It will also be much easier to reach Anqing by long-distance bus from Shanghai or from the railway stations at Wuhu and Tongling, without the current hassle of having to travel through the distant transportation hub of Hefei.

Renmin Lu

This is the main business street running through the center of Anqing's modern downtown area. It is here that you will find nearly all the hotels, the best restaurants, branches of the Bank of China and all other major Chinese banks, the post office, and stores. However, it is a very long street, so it is a good idea to know the exact address or at least the cross street for the place you are looking for.

If you have just arrived in town and need a place to stay, simply ask a taxi driver to take you up and down Renmin Lu until you find a hotel that fits your budget and meets your requirements. Even a city as isolated as Anqing now has a McDonalds and a KFC. If you are adventurous enough to try the local food, you will be pleasantly surprised. A delicious five-course meal of tasty local dishes can be had for as little as 35 Rmb, making the fast food joints seem ridiculously overpriced by comparison.

Ling Hu Gongyuan

Located on the northeastern edge of the city are three lakes grouped close together, the most beautiful of which is **Ling Hu**. Established in 1911, Ling Hu Gongyuan covers 438,000 sq m (4,714,590 sq ft), of which 30 percent is water. The park very much has an air of authentic antiquity about it, which distinguishes it from Lian Hu, its newer neighbor. Ling Hu has several temple-like complexes of buildings in traditional Chinese style architecture. The **Deng Shi Ru Stele Museum** (Deng Shi Ru Bei Guan) is a traditional courtyard compound built in 1925 in honor

Ling Hu Gongyuan in Anqing.

This page: Ling Hu Gongyuan in Anqing.

of Deng Shi Ru (1743–1805), a noted local calligrapher who lived during the Qing Dynasty. The Potted Landscape Research Institute also seems like it could date from the park's founding, and looks as if it may have once been a temple. Just outside the wall of the institute's garden is the small **Bloody Clothes Pavilion** (Xie Yi Ting), behind which is a domed tomb of some martyr. The park is full of many other beautiful pavilions, lotus ponds, weeping willow plants, cypress trees, pedestrian paths, and causeways that cross from the shore of one lake to another. There is also the **Yan Feng Ying Memorial Hall** (Yan Feng Ying Ji Nian Guan), a pavilion containing a small museum devoted to Yan Feng Ying (1930–1968), a local celebrity who was a performer of Huang Mei Opera, Anqing's variant of the Peking Opera.

Address: Yi Cheng Lu
intersection with Ling Hu Nan Lu

POINT OF INTEREST

On the author's last visit to Anqing in October 2003, he discovered a wonderful traditional lantern festival going on at Ling Hu Gongyuan late into the night. The dark night night was lit up with handmade paper lanterns of many elaborate designs and bright colors that were strung along the lantern posts of all the park's walkways. In the middle of the park's lakes were colorful mechanical dragons, swinging their heads and tails back and forth, and spouting streams of water from their mouths.

The park grounds were the backdrop of a number of different activities. These included moving mannequins dressed in traditional costumes, a wedding sedan chair procession, and a five-piece orchestra playing their instruments on a lawn stage looking very much like Sgt. Pepper's Band. One whole area of the park was devoted to Buddhist images. The colors were a kaleidoscope, but since all the images were handmade and covered with paper, there was a traditional feel to the whole carnival. At the front entrance to the park, outside the permanent gate, an enormous temporary colored paper gate had been set up, lit up inside by electric lights like a giant lantern.

One blinding display was a series of flashing round arches set up in a long series along the main walkway. Walking through these flashing arches was like passing through a time tunnel, which was appropriate given the traditional nature of the rest of the festival. One garish sight was the exhibition of color photos of nude Chinese women inside the Deng Shi Ru Museum. On reflection, the festival was held to celebrate the 1 October 1949 Communist Revolution. However, the displays of traditional Chinese images, Buddhist deities, and nude women, all represented aspects of Chinese life that the Communist Party (Gong Chang Dang) spent the first 30 years of their rule trying to destroy and eliminate, with great success, until the reform process began in 1979.

Entrance to the Bloody Clothes Pavilion at Ling Hu Gongyuan in Anqing.

Memorial to the Jing Fu Shu Yuan on the campus of Anqing Teachers College.

Lian Hu Gongyuan

Ling Hu is divided from a newer lake, known as Lian Hu, by the street Hu Xing Zhong Lu which runs in between them on a narrow strip of land. Lian Hu was finished in about 1992 and also features a park with pavilions. However, its modern appearance lacks the same charm as the quaint antiquated feel of Ling Hu Gongyuan. Following Hu Xing Zhong Lu to the north, you reach a third even larger lake known as Anqing Da Hu.

Anqing Teachers' College (Anqing Shi Fang Xueyuan)

Site of the original Anhui Provincial University (Shengli Anhui Daxue), with Western and traditional Chinese style buildings dating from the Min Guo era when Anqing was still the provincial capital city. This is still a university today, and at first sight its historical importance may not be immediately apparent. After entering the deceptively modern new gate facing the street, you pass a long row of traditional one-story wooden beam halls along your right. At the end of this row is an inscribed tablet tracing the history of the university from 2000 all the way back to its founding in 1652 as the Jing Fu Shu Yuan. Crossing the main tree-lined avenue of the campus, if you follow the lane known as Hong Lou Lu, you will come to the school's most impressive historic building. According to an inscribed stone tablet standing beside its entrance, the two-story, horseshoe shaped Hong Lou was built between July 1934 and August 1935. The Western style architecture includes a front façade resembling a Roman Catholic church. At the top is a round clock face, below which extends a veranda. This is one of the few monumental Min Guo structures left in the city. In front of the building is a round circle of trees and two square forested gardens, hiding the building from view from the main campus avenue and entrance gate.

Address: 128 Ling Hu Nan Lu, one block west of the main gate to Ling Hu Gongyuan

The Hong Lou of Anqing Teachers' College.

Chen Du Xiu's new tomb in Anqing.

Sights Outside the City
The Tomb of Chen Du Xiu (Chen Du Xiu Mu)

Drive out of the city towards Da Long Shan Village, past the toll gate, and onto National Highway 206 (Guo Dao Er Ling Liu). On the left side, you will soon see a new colorful sign labeled in English, "The Tomb of Chen Du Xiu" ("Chen Du Xiu Mu".) However, from this point reaching the actual site of the tomb becomes more of a challenge. The access road immediately becomes a muddy one-lane dirt track through the countryside. It passes a cement factory and encounters several unmarked intersections of dirt roads where it is not clear which way you should turn. Upon reaching the site, you find a shiny clean, brand new monument which was obviously erected very recently. Stone

PERSONALITIES

Chen Du Xiu (1879–1942) was the original founder of the Chinese Communist Party (Gong Chang Dang) in 1921. He was also the founder of the crucial literary magazine, *New Youth* (known in Chinese as *Xin Qingnian* and in French as *La Jeunesse*, both of which appeared on its cover), published in Shanghai starting in 1915. It was this magazine which first published such budding new authors as Hu Shi and Lu Xun.

However, Chen was blamed for the party's April 1927 debacle, in which its urban organizations were crushed throughout China's cities by the rival Guomindang, with whom Chen had supported a United Front policy. On 5 April 1927, Chen had issued a joint statement with Wang Jingwei in Shanghai expressing continued support for the Guomindang-CCP United Front, just one week before Chiang Kai Shek's (Jiang Jieshi's) 12 April bloody coup and suppression of the Communist Party (Gong Chang Dang). This is still known as his "big mistake." Chen was forced to resign as the Party leader at a special party conference held in Wuhan on 7 August 1927, in favor of a new leadership dominated by Li Li San. Later Chen was even expelled from the party by the Central Committee on 15 November 1929. On 15 October 1932, he was arrested in Shanghai and sent to the Guomindang capital in Nanjing where he was put on trial. On 26 April 1933, he was sentenced to 13 years in prison. Apparently, he was released early and died in obscurity in Sichuan Province on 27 May 1942, after notably spending the wartime years in Guomindang territory rather than in the Communist base area of Yanan. As recently as the 1980s, he was still being villified by party historians, and today, Chinese schoolchildren are told about the "big mistake" he made in April 1927.

steps lead up two tiers of stone terraces with white marble balustrades to a 1.5-meter-high white marble dome, in front of which stands a black stele tablet inscribed with red characters. Flowers beside the tomb show that Chen is still remembered fondly by a few people.

This new tomb was erected on 4 May 1998, and its construction could be a sign of his political rehabilitation. The inscription on the tablet refers to it respectfully as, "Chen Du Xiu Xian Sheng Zhi Mu," meaning, "The Tomb of Mr. Chen Du Xiu." However, the main reason for its existence is that Huai Ning County of Anqing Prefecture was the location of Chen's home town. According to some locals, this is his second tomb, an earlier one having been constructed elsewhere in the Anqing municpality at a place called Xiu Shan.

A new memorial tablet at Chen Du Xiu's new tomb in Anqing.

Great Dragon Mountain (Da Long Shan)
Many local legends have been recorded throughout history about Great Dragon Mountain (Da Long shan) which lies 16 km (10 miles) north of Anqing. Most of the stories surround the

POINT OF INTEREST

Several stories and poems about the Great Dragon Mountain (Da Long Shan) are found in the 1915 edition of the local county history (Huai Ling Xian Zhi):

"Thirty li north of Anqing there is a Dragon Mountain, on whose western slopes lies a spring, clear and deep, which has never failed. It flows down the mountain and waters several thousand mu of good land. In time of drought and famine the people pray there, and their prayers are always heard. Sometimes remarkable clouds are seen above the spring and around the top of the mountain. The custom of worshipping there began long ago."

There is also an undated poem that reads:
"There is a dragon mountain in Hsu (Anqing)
With a spring which waters the fields.
On the mountain is the spring
And upon the hillsides are tilled fields.
From the earliest ages the men of Hsu (Anqing) have received this help.
In time of trouble all heads are turned toward the mountain.
High above the hills float the clouds
And within them is a spirit who changes their shapes continually.
The people wondered who the spirit was
Until they found that it was the Long Wang (Dragon King).
Hence they rebuilt the temple (Long Wang Miao)
So that sacrifices might be made for a thousand years.
These sacrifices are still continued
And the people reap the reward."

POINT OF INTEREST

In 1824, the Provincial Governor of Anhui recorded the following story about the rebuilding of the Dragon King Temple, the fourth year of the Dao Guang reign:

> "Thirty li from the city of Wan (Anqing) there is a mountain, whose grandeur is like a painted screen with panels set at angles. It is called the Dragon Mountain. On the western side in a valley between two peaks lies a spring, called the Well of Heaven, where the Dragon God lives. In the time of Ming Tai Zu (about 1380AD), the god was given the rank of Tien Chin Hsun Chi, ... To the west of the spring there is a temple, which was first built in the time of Ming Chen Hua, (1465AD) and down to the present dynasty it was kept in good repair. Whenever a famine came the people would pray there.
>
> In the summer of the 4th year of Dao Guang, it did not rain for a long time ... so on the 11th day of the 6th month, I and my officials went to the side of the spring and prayed ... [The temple] was in ruins. Among the tiles and the moss I knelt in prayer ... just as I reached the city rain began to fall, and by the time I reached my yamen, the roads were full of mud ... The rain came as an echo to our prayers ... so I chose a site to the right of the spring for his temple. On top of the cliff I built a pavilion ... in order to show my gratitude to the god."

In 1824, the Provincial Governor of Anhui composed the following poem about Da Long Shan:

> "So impressive is the Dragon Mountain,
> So marvelous are its rocks and cliffs,
> They rise high into the heaven.
> The King of the Dragons abides there,
> Wrapped in fog in the morning,
> And in the evening clothed with smoke.
> Here is the Well of Heaven,
> With its strange stone cliffs.
> The water keeps down the dust.
> When the god rests,
> The water creatures rest also,
> And the mouths of great fish are closed.
> When the god goes forth,
> There go with him the golden snake,
> And the three-legged, marble-like Chi.
> In the morning he can traverse the rivers Huai and Pu,
> And in the evening he rests by their side.
> The servants of the god are many;
> Their numbers are like a field of flax.
> The spirits of the clouds stand in awe,
> When the god passes.
> The people hope for rain,
> And the god hears their prayer.
> He changes the river water into showers,
> Which fill the vessels of the people.
> The farmers also are glad,
> For the crops are doubled at harvest.
> Long life to the god;
> May he receive continual sacrifices,
> That the jars may be full of water,
> And the barns rich with grain."

Dragon Spring (Long Shan Chi) located in a valley between peaks on the western slopes of the mountain, and the worship of the mythical **Dragon King** (Long Wang). Stone stele inscribed with poems, temples, pavilions, and stories dedicated to the Dragon Spring and Dragon King have been erected on the mountain since the beginning of the Ming Dynasty.

The Hong Wu emperor Ming Tai Zu (1368–1398) officially recognized the god of the dragon spring as the Long Wang in 1380. During the Ming Cheng Hua reign (1465–1487), a **Dragon King Temple** (Long Wang Miao) and a stone monument were erected beside the spring. In 1465, people began to come to make sacrifices and pray to the Dragon King, especially in times of drought or famine. The Dragon King was considered as a kind of rain god. The original temple had fallen into ruins by the Dao Guang reign (1821–1850) of the Qing Dynasty, but was rebuilt in 1824 by the provincial governor of Anhui, who also wrote a poem about it. The reason the temple was reconstructed was because the residents of the area believed the Dragon King had been responsible for ending a severe drought that year.

Unfortunately, the Long Wang Miao apparently no longer exists. However, there is still an area on the mountain known as the Dragon Pool Scenic Area (Long Qiu Chi Jing Qu). A new Buddhist Temple was spotted at the foot of the mountain while traveling out of town on National Highway 206.

Little Orphan Island (Xiao Gu Shan)

Up the Yangzi River, shortly before reaching Hukou, is **Little Orphan Island** (Xiao Gu Shan). In 1925, Elizabeth Crump Enders described it as "rising, tall and like a mountain's summit, springing suddenly from out of the middle of the stream. A ghostly little

Little Orphan Island (Xiao Gu Shan) viewed from the west with the halls of Qi Xiu Si perched on a cliff-side terrace.

Little Orphan Island (Xiao Gu Shan) viewed from the north, with steps leading up to the tunnel-like Yi Tian Men entrance to the halls of Qi Xiu Si up on the terrace above.

temple gleamed in the darkening twilight halfway up its thickly wooded sides…" Although Little Orphan Island (Xiao Gu Shan) is seen by every ship passing up or down the river, its isolated location far from any port or town has meant that few foreigners have ever visited it or its hillside Buddhist temple, Qi Xiu Si, built up against the island's mountain slopes. The author is unaware of any previous English language account of the island by a foreigner who actually set foot on it.

The island is located in Anqing municipality's most western county of **Susong** (Susong Xian) on the border of eastern Jiangxi and western Anhui. The closest town in Anhui Province is Fu Xing Zhen. It seems a bus can be taken from Anqing city to a site where you can then go by boat. Across the Yangzi River from Fu Xing Zhen is the town of Pengze in Jiangxi Province, which can be reached by driving from Hukou and Jiujiang further upriver. The island can also be reached by boat from Pengze. Recent photos confrm that a hillside temple, **Xiao Gu Temple**, is built up against the island mountain's slopes, and another pavilion is on the summit. However, all of these appear to be new reconstructions.

Little Orphan Island (Xiao Gu Shan) has been the subject of hundreds of Chinese poems throughout its history. It has also been given many lyrical nicknames, including "the Only Island in the Yangzi River" (Changjiang Jue Dao), "The First Sea Gate" (Hai Men Di Yi Guan), and "Eye of the Sea" (Hai Yan). Rising out of the water at an elevation of 100 m (328.1 ft), the island stands on the Yangzi River's north bank in Susong County of Anhui Province, with the mountainous southern shore in Pengze County of Jiangxi Province. Ancient poets have described the island's shape as having a different appearance from each direction. They say it looks like a pen from the south, a bell from the west, a chair from the east, and a dragon from the north.

The Island's Buddhist temple, Qi Xiu Si, was established in the Tang Dynasty by the monk Ma Dao Yi. However, in the Northern Song (Bei Song) Dynasty (960–1126 AD) the temple's name was changed to Hui Ji Miao, and it became a place to worship the goddess Mazu rather than Buddha. During the Kang Xi reign (1661–1722) of the Qing Dynasty, the emperor renamed the temple Tian Hou Sheng Mu. In the Qian Long reign (1736–

1795), it was renamed again as Tian Shang Sheng Mu. Both imperial edicts show that in the Qing Dynasty, the purpose of the temple was more for worshipping Mazu than Buddha, although the two practices may have coexisted. When Commander F.H.E. Skyrme published his guide book to the Yangzi River in 1937, he reported that there was a Buddhist temple on Xiao Gu Shan.

On 30 December 1984, the island's Buddhist temple was reopened under its original name of Qi Xiu Si, and given provincial protection by the Anhui government as one of the 52 most important Buddhist temples in the province. The five main temple halls now include a Guan Sheng Dian or Guan Gong dedicated to the War God Guandi, a Da Xiong Bao Dian, a Tian Fei Dian, and a Mi Tuo Ge.

Although the emphasis is now once again decidedly on Buddhism, the temple has also reestablished a hall dedicated to Mazu (Tian Fei Dian).

POINT OF INTEREST

Mazu is a goddess who protects fishermen and sailors. Traditionally temples dedicated to her worship have been more popular in the coastal areas of China, such as Fujian, Hong Kong, and Taiwan. In those places she is variously known as Mazu, Tian Hou, or Tian Fei. On Xiao Gu Shan her local name is Xiao Gu Niang Niang.

The 365 steps to the mountain's summit begin at the bottom by entering the First Gate of Heaven (Yi Tian Men), which is more like the mouth of a cave or a tunnel than a gate. It leads visitors into a winding ascent through a subterranean corridor up the cliff face. This suddenly emerges on the first and lowest of a succession of four outdoor terraces at the Xian Yue Lou. Steps lead up to the second terrace where the temple halls actually begin. Here you will find two temple halls, the Guan Gong on the right and the Da Xiong Bao Dian on the left.

One of the small shrine halls of Qi Xiu Si on Little Orphan Island (Xiao Gu Shan).

Inside the Guan Gong is a statue of a Guan Yu, the Three Kingdoms general who was later deified as the God of War. Embedded in the right wall is a genuine stone inscription. Along the left wall is the gift shop with a fabulous selection of photographs and Chinese language books about the island. Behind the Guan Gong is the small Mi Tuo Ge.

The Precious Hall of the Great Hero (Da Xiong Bao Dian) appears

The Ban Bian Ta built right into the cliffs of Little Orphan Island (Xiao Gu Shan).

to be a genuine historical structure dating from the late Qing Dynasty, although its interior furnishings are obviously new. It has new gilded statues of Three Buddhas (San Fo) in the center of the back wall. In the middle is Sakyamuni (Shijiamouni), on his left side is Amitabha (O-Mi-Tuo-Fo), and on the right side is Yao Shi Fo. To the left of Amitabha are gilded statues of the Maitreya Buddha (Mi Le Fo), and Pu Xian seated on an elephant. To the right of Yao Shi Fo is a gilded statue of Wenshu seated on the back of some mythical animal. In front of the San Fo is an intricately carved ornate gilded wooden altar. Along both the left and right sides of the hall are gilded statues of the 18 Arhats (Shi Ba Luohan). In October 2003, five of the Arhats were missing, with only six on the left side, and seven on the right. It was said that the other five statues would arrive later. This is probably a sign that the hall was only recently refurbished.

The original temple halls, which all appear to date from the Qing Dynasty, are now sandwhiched in between two new wings constructed sometime after 1983. Down the corridor, running past the Da Xiong Bao Dian, is the temple's business office in the new south wing. The new north wing at the opposite end of the second terrace contains the monks Dining Hall (Zhai Fang) and kitchen. A golden wooden carved armchair is set up at the head of the hall for the temple's master. The two new wings also contain living quarters for the resident monks, of which there seem to be eight.

Steps lead up to a third terrace where you find a third temple hall containing another set of San Fo. This hall is also obviously a genuine historical structure dating from the late Qing Dynasty.

On the fourth and last terrace is a fourth temple hall, the Tian Fei Dian. The interior of this hall is by far the most impressive of all. Outside the Tian Fei Dian is a five-story brick pagoda built into the cliff side. It is known as Ban Bian Ta because only half (*ban*) the pagoda can be seen. However, because offerings are made here to Mazu (Tian Fei) by those praying to have children, it is sometimes also known as Song Zi Ta.

Taking the trail up the mountain from the Ban Bian Ta, you come first to the Guan Tao Ting, a relatively new pavilion erected in 1989. Near the summit is the Imperial Stone Tablet (Yu Shi Bei) inscribed with a poem about Xiao Gu Shan written by the emperor in 1547 during the Jia Jing reign of the Ming Dynasty.

On the summit of the island is a two-story, hexagonal pavilion known as the Shu Zhuang Ting. The first pavilion on this site was built in 1226 and was named the Mu Yang Ting. It was given its present name in 1529 when the pavilion was rebuilt.

Getting There:
Little Orphan Island (Xiao Gu Shan) is 90 km (56 miles) away from the nearest city of Anqing by road. To drive, it takes two-and-a-half hours one-way, and five hours both ways. The taxi fare will cost approximately 250 Rmb for a round-trip. A narrow neck of land now connects the island to the Anhui shore, allowing a vehicle to drive right up to the base of the Yi Tian Men steps. However, the road there from Anqing follows the top of the Yangzi River's north bank flood wall, which is guarded by a series of no less than four military check points manned by armed soldiers who wave a red flag for every vehicle to stop for inspection. Be sure to have your papers in order and be on your best behavior. The driver will be asked to get out of the car, the trunk will be opened, and any foreign passengers will be quizzically examined.

At the base of the island is a ferry dock for boats crossing the Yangzi River over to Pengze on the Jiangxi side. From there, it would be possible to drive to the next major upstream port of Jiujiang, but the distance and time spent would be about the same or more as to Anqing. Given the unreliability of the ferry service, Anqing definitely makes a safer choice as a base of operations.

Phone: 781-1066
Ticket: 5 Rmb

Anqing Practical Information

Anqing Area Code: (0556)

Hotels

Almost all of Anqing's hotels are located along Renmin Lu, the main east-west street.

Golden Phoenix Hotel (Jin Feng Huang Da Jiudian)
Best price to quality ratio in town. Clean, comfortable, quiet rooms recently redecorated for as low as 144 Rmb per night. Helpful staff. Some rooms have a view of the Zhen Feng Ta pagoda.

136 Renmin Lu
Phone: 552-8608, 552-8607

Feng Yun Hotel

Address: 170 Renmin Lu
Phone: 554-3322

Jiu Zhou Da Jiudian

Address: Renmin Lu

Anqing Hotel

Address: Renmin Lu

Jiang Hai Bin Guan

Address: 65 Yan Jiang Zhong Lu

Restaurants
Xin Wuxi Da Jiudian

Address: 320 Renmin Lu
Phone: 551-5963, 13955618188

Transportation
Anqing Long-Distance Bus Station (Gong Gong Chiche Zhan)

Address: Ling Hu Nan Lu
Phone: 558-3775, 551-4730.

Anqing Train Station (Huoche Zhan)
The spur line connecting Anqing to the Hefei-Jiujiang line was only constructed in 1992. Before than Anqing had never had a train station. This is a dead-end line, meaning you can only reach Anqing by train from either Hefei or Jiujiang.

Phone: 553-5198, 533-3666

Anqing Airport (Feiji Chang)
China Eastern Airlines provides flights two days a week between Shanghai and Anqing, using small propeller airplanes. The Anqing airport was completed in 1992.

Phone: 554-3848, 551-3973.

Anqing Yangzi River Boat Dock (Ma Tou)

Phone: 551-3306

Jiangxi Province

Hukou

Today, most people reach Hukou by traveling overland from the much larger city of Jiujiang just upriver. Driving down the new super highway eastward from Jiujiang, you travel through open fields dotted with many old structures resembling temples or ancestral halls, then over a range of small foothills. Suddenly the waters of the enormous ocean-like Poyang Lake (Poyang Hu) appears on the other side. This section of Poyang Lake (Poyang Hu) is known appropriately as the Lake Mouth (Hukou) because it forms a narrow neck of water connecting the much wider expanse of the lake proper to the south with the Yangzi River to the north. Hukou is also the name of the town placed strategically at the confluence of the Yangzi and Poyang Lake (Poyang Hu), on the eastern shore of the lake and southern shore of the river. It used to be necessary to take a ferry boat across from the Jiujiang side of the lake to the mountainous eastern shore, but a new suspension bridge with two H-shaped upright supports has now replaced the ferries. Many cargo ships can be seen sailing in and out of the lake here, most of them on their way to or from the provincial capital of Nanchang. Upon reaching the other shore, the highway travels through a series of two very long tunnels bored through the mountains. An off-ramp then takes you to the small town of Hukou.

Hukou's Historical Importance

Hukou has played an important strategic role in China's military history. In 1355, Zhu Yuanzhang, the founder of the Ming Dynasty, crossed the Yangzi River from Jiang Bei to Jiang Nan. The Ming capture of the south bank town of Taiping marked Zhu's rise to power. A year later, in March 1356, Zhu seized control of Nanjing and made the city his stronghold. His energies were then directed against Chen Yu Liang, a major rival who was based up the Yangzi River in Wuhan. The two competing naval fleets spent ten years fighting battles over the river towns between Nanjing and Wuhan, including Anqing and Jiujiang, as well as the freshwater sea of Poyang Lake (Poyang Hu).

The turning point of this decade-old war came on 4 October 1363. Zhu Yuanzhang won a decisive victory in a naval battle fought on the Yangzi River, at the town of Hukou which marks the mouth of Poyang Lake (Poyang Hu). Control of Hukou and Poyang Lake (Poyang Hu) meant that the Ming capital of Nanjing would never be seriously threatened by naval invasions from the west.

During the Taiping Heavenly Kingdom (Taiping Tian Guo), the Taiping rebels made Hukou a major military base. Unfortunately, the town was totally destroyed in 1858 when the Taiping rebels were defeated here.

On 8 July 1938 the Japanese captured Hukou on their way westward towards the Guomindang's temporary national capital at Wuhan. As a result, the town does not really have a historic old district.

Hukou Sights

There is a new waterside pedestrian promenade which runs all the way from the foot of Shi Zhong Shan to a spot near the Hukou Bridge. From the Hukou boat dock (*matou*), small ferries (*da chuan*) and fishing boats (*yu chuan*) can be taken for short voyages into Poyang Lake (Poyang Hu).

Up on the hillsides above Hukou town can be seen the buildings of two temples. One looks like a Confucius Temple (Kong Miao) or City God Temple (Cheng Huang Miao) from a distance, and has an impressive white three-arch memorial gate out in front. The other is a Buddhist temple hidden in the trees, with just its rooftops barely visible from down below.

Longevity Buddhist Temple (Song Shou Si)

The Song Shou Si Buddhist temple can be reached by following the paved road at the southern end of town, crossing a bridge over a stream and following a dirt road until you reach a shop on the left with the address No. 18. From here, a stone-step foot trail ascends the hillside through a poor residential district of semi-hostile local inhabitants who are not accustomed to seeing foreigners walking through their backyards. Be sure to be polite and friendly to them and they might not stone you to death. There is no way to drive a vehicle all the way in, and the final leg up the hillside can only be done on foot. The trail passes an enormous round dry stone well before finally reaching the temple.

A small four-story pagoda at Song Shou Si Buddhist Temple in the hills above Hukou town.

The small Song Shou Si Buddhist temple is impressive for its authentic simplicity. A small four-story solid white pagoda stands near the edge of the plateau, with a bird's eye view of Hukou town below. Beside this is a curious small shrine with an unusual stone god inside. Although the simple one-story halls look as though they were recently constructed, older stone relics scattered about the grounds testify to the existence of an earlier temple here. One lone monk was observed chanting to himself and repeatedly beating a wooden fish (*mu yu*) with a rhythm stick. This faithful act of devotion by someone hidden on a forested hilltop is powerful evidence that Buddhist temples in China today do not simply exist for the entertainment of tourists.

A small side hall of Song Shou Si Buddhist Temple in the hills above Hukou town.

Although a dirt foot trail continues through the thick forest, the only trail back to Hukou town is to return the same way you came. Hopefully you did not irritate any of the villagers on your way up.

POINT OF INTEREST

Stone Bell Hill (Shi Zhong Shan) gets its name from a mysterious bell-like sound that it somehow naturally produces. For centuries, Chinese scholars have sought to explain how the hill creates this sound. As early as the Northern Wei Dynasty (385–531 AD), Li Dao Yun (Li Yuan) (d. 527) wrote a commentary to a Han Dynasty work known as the *Water Classic* (*Shui Jing Ju*) in which he said, "If you stand over the deep pools and a faint breeze agitates the waves, then water and stone will smack against one another, giving the sound of a huge bell." During the Tang Dynasty, the Confucian scholar Li Bo (773–831 AD), who later founded the Bai Lu Dong Shu Yuan in 805 and then became the governor of Jiujiang in 825, visited Stone Bell Hill (Shi Zhong Shan) and wrote an essay about it in 798AD, in which he explained his theory that the sound was made by rocks with different tones being struck with a hammer. Neither of these first two theories fully satisfied the curious.

When the poet and Jinshi scholar Su Dong Po (Su Shi) (1037–1101) made the first of his three visits to Stone Bell Hill (Shi Zhong Shan) in 1084, during the seventh year of the Yuan Feng reign of the Northern Song (Bei Song) Dynasty, he was treated to a demonstration of Li Bo's theory by several temple monks, who proceeded to strike various rocks with hammers to produce ringing tones. Unconvinced that this was the real source of the sound, Su set off in a small boat that night and sailed around the shores of the hill in search of the answer. Shortly after this first visit, he wrote a famous essay known as the, "Shi Zhong Shan Ji," in which he claimed to have solved the mystery. Here are two variant translations of the key parts of Su's essay:

> "As the night came on and the moon grew bright, Mai and I got in a small boat and went off all by ourselves to a spot below the sheer cliff. The huge rock stood leaning a thousand feet above us, when a huge sound came out over the waters, booming like a bell being struck continuously. The boatman was quite frightened. But, when I took the time to examine the phenomenon closely, I found that there were crevices in the rocks at the foot of the mountain, whose depth I couldn't tell. When a small wave entered them, it heaved and sloshed about, producing this sound."
>
> Stephen Owen, 1996

> "That night there was a bright moon, so I, alone with Mai, took a small boat to the foot of the precipice where the mighty rock rose to a height of a thousand feet. Suddenly a loud continuous sound like the clang of bells and the roll of drums arose from the surface of the water. The boatman was terror stricken. Careful investigation, however, showed that the foot of the rock was full of cavities and fissures of unknown depth, and that when small waves penetrated them, the deep subterranean waters became roaring billows resulting in this clangour."
>
> Cyril Drummond Les Gros Clark, 1931

Stone Bell Hill (Shi Zhong Shan)

A drive down Hukou's one main street leads you to the base of the small hilltop promontory known as Stone Bell Hill (Shi Zhong Shan), which is undoubtedly the town's main attraction. A 32 Rmb ticket gives you entrance to this hilltop peninsula, which juts out into the water and separates the mouth of Poyang Lake (Poyang Hu) from the Yangzi River. This is an enormous scenic area overlooking the Yangzi River which is criss-crossed by a network of foot trails and features an incredible number of pavilions, pagodas, monuments, gardens, and ancient ruins.

Entering the gate today, you are first greeted by a new statue of the poet **Su Dong Po** (Su Shi) (1037–1101), who three visits to Stone Bell Hill (Shi Zhong Shan) during his lifetime. The first was in 1084, the later two in 1094 and 1101.

Next comes the **Stone Bell Pavilion** (Shi Zhong Ting), a small open-air stone beam structure inside which sits a weathered rock inscribed with characters. Although it appears to be older, the pavilion was built in 1984 in honor of both Da Yu and Li Bai. According to legend, the Tang dynasty poet **Li Bai** (Li Tai Po) (701–762 AD) visited this spot in search of evidence to prove the myth that the Great Yu (Da Yu), the mythical founder of the

The Lin Jiang Ta pagoda balanced on a cliff face of Stone Bell Hill (Shi Zhong Shan).

The Stone Bell Pavilion (Shi Zhong Ting).

Xia Dynasty, had supposedly dredged the nine rivers (*jiu jiang*) from this spot. The town of Jiujiang gets its name from this myth. The pavilion stands atop a natural rock outcropping with evidence of stone steps and flat platforms having previously been cut into it, signs that much earlier structures once stood on this spot. Beside the stone pavilion is a large billboard map of the area.

Just a few steps uphill from the stone pavilion is a newer wooden pavilion containing an iron bell which can be rung for a fee, the sound echoing out across the mountain. Continuing up the path climbing the hill, one comes to the unimpressive **Su Shi Pavilion** (Su Shi Ting). It is here that the trail forks into two paths, eastern and western corridors, that form a circular route around the mountain's summit. Approaching the Su Shi Pavilion, one can see from far down below an enormous stone block fortress looming in the forested hillside. Within its red walls stand many pavilions and halls. The enclosure can be reached from the Su Shi Pavilion by leaving the main trail, which continues straight ahead and entering through a gate in the wall to your right.

Once inside, pass beneath two enormous round brick structures and you will find yourself wandering through a beautiful landscape garden. On the southern edge of the garden overlooking the outer wall is the impressive two-story **Taiping Tower** (Taiping Lou). A seemingly genuine Qing Dynasty artifact, the wooden hall's walls, doors, beams, and posts are all decorated with intricate wood carvings of unusual animals and the windows are covered with lattice work. A terrace behind the hall looks directly down upon the Iron Bell and Stone Bell Pavilions below.

A large new statue of the Song Dynasty poet-traveler Su Shi (Su Dong Po) greets visitors to Stone Bell Hill (Shi Zhong Shan) just inside the entrance gate.

An iron bell hangs in another small pavilion near the entrance gate of Stone Bell Hill (Shi Zhong Shan).

The Taiping Tower was built by Ding Yi Wan, in the third year of the Tongzhi reign during the Qing Dynasty. Ding was one of the commanders of Zeng Guofan's Hunan Army, after Zeng's troops had defeated the Taiping garrison stationed here. **Peng Yu Lin**, a key lieutenant of Zeng Guofan's, originally named the hall the Fei Jie Tower. However, when the hall was restored in 1978, it was renamed by the Communist authorities in honor of the Taiping rebels, whom Communist historiography now praises as their ideological predecessors.

Crossing a footbridge over a pond takes you up a stone pathway through the landscape garden towards the hilltop **Plum Blossom Hall** (Mei Hua Dian). Along the way, many stone inscriptions, which seem to be authentic relics, can be seen in the rocks embedded in the hillside. The two-story wooden Mei Hua Dian is a much newer construction than the Taiping Dian. On occasion, an old man hits rocks with steel hammers in an attempt to give some sort of musical performance. Be warned that this can be rather annoying and may give you a migraine.

The covered corridor from Taiping Dian along the eastern edge of the summit leads to the rear entrance of the **Peach Blossom Cave** (Tao Hua Dong), a seldom visited section of the hilltop. By

The covered corridor from Taiping Lou to Tao Hua Dong at Stone Bell Hill (Shi Zhong Shan).

The Taiping Tower
(Taiping Lou) at
Stone Bell Hill
(Shi Zhong Shan).

Entrance to the
Peach Blossom Cave
(Tao Hua Dong).

Above: A stone foot bridge over a stream in front of the Taiping Tower (Taiping Lou).
Below: A natural rock outcropping with ancient steps cut into it behind the Stone Bell Pavilion (Shi Zhong Ting).

passing through the cave you will find yourself inside the garden of the Huan Xiang Villa. This villa is connected to two of the other most important historic structures on the hilltop, the Loyal Martyr Temple and the Bao Ci Temple. By exiting the front door of Huan Xiang Villa, you will find yourself on the main viewing terrace on the northern end of the hill overlooking the spectacular Yangzi River.

Alternatively, you could return to the Su Shi Pavilion from the Taiping Lou and resume following the main trail. This eventually reaches the Yangzi River viewing terrace but it tends to be more crowded. This main trail passes the gate of the Dark Purple Garden and then enters a long winding covered corridor which runs along a precipitous cliff top overlooking the mouth of Poyang Lake (Poyang Hu) down below.

To the left of the main corridor stands the **Boat Hall** (Chuan Ting), overlooking the lake's mouth. The Chuan Ting was built by county magistrate Chen Lian Yi during the Xian Feng reign of the Qing Dynasty. When the Japanese occupied Hukou on 8 July 1938, on their way up the Yangzi River towards Wuhan, they massacred many innocent Chinese civilians here by throwing them into the water and destroyed the original buildings. The Chuan Ting was rebuilt in 1979.

The real attraction of the Chuan Ting is that it points the way to two of the mountains most famous sights, the **Lin Jiang Pagoda** (Lin Jiang Ta) and the Stone Bell Cave itself. The old red brick pagoda is perched right on the cliff face. It is a solid structure and too small to enter inside, but still fascinating to look at and wonder how it could have been built where it stands. From the Chuan Ting terrace, one flight of stone steps leads down to the pagoda on the left, while a second flight of slippery stone steps leads down the cliff face to the Stone Bell Cave at the water's edge. A round hole cut in the

Above: The Loyalties Ancestral Temple (Zhao Zhong Ci) at Stone Bell Hill (Shi Zhong Shan).
Below: The Lin Jiang Ta pagoda at Stone Bell Hill (Shi Zhong Shan).

floor of the terrace reveals a view of the frighteningly dangerous stone steps spiraling down to the cliff below. Over the portal is the three-character inscription, "Yi Zhou Yan." The terrace offers good views of Hukou town, set in a kind of small natural harbor between two mountainous outcroppings, and the new suspension highway bridge crossing the lake mouth.

Back on the main trail, you will pass an entrance into the Guanyin Hall (Guanyin Dian) of Returning Kindness Buddhist Temple (Bao Ci Chan Lin) on your right. However, following the main corridor straight ahead all the way to its end leads you to the **Qing Zhuo Ting**. This is an uninteresting modern pavilion built in 1984 which nonetheless offers incredible views of the confluence where the mouth of Poyang Lake (Poyang Hu) meets the Yangzi River. The Yangzi is to your right and Poyang Lake (Poyang Hu) to your left.

On the west side of the Qing Zhuo Ting is another flight of dangerous stone steps leading down the cliff face of the Fan Zhou Precipice to the Stone Bell Cave at the water's edge. From the top of the steps, you can look back and see the pagoda. One can see why Su Dong Po (Su Shi) chose to approach the cave by boat from Hukou, rather than by descending downward from the hilltop. Sadly this method is not available to visitors today, even though approaching byboat would be easier and safer given the cave's location.

On the east side of the Qing Zhuo Ting is the main Yangzi River viewing terrace, a large open plaza at the northern end of the hill with some tables and chairs. Here, you will find the main entrances to the three most important historic buildings on the mountain: Bao Ci Temple, the Loyal Martyr Temple, and Huan Xiang Villa. These three structures are actually built side by side within the same outer enclosure wall, although they each have their own monumental entrance gates, interior courtyards, and internal halls.

The entrance to Huan Xiang Villa at Stone Bell Hill (Shi Zhong Shan).

The **Returning Kindness Buddhist Temple** (Bao Ci Chan Lin) was built by **Peng Yu Lin** in dedication to his mother during the Xian Feng reign of the Qing Dynasty. It was later rebuilt in 1903, during the Kang Xi reign of the Qing Dynasty. At some unspecified time in the 20th century, possibly during the Sino-Japanese War or the Cultural Revolution, all the original Buddha statues and those of the 18 Arhat (Shi Ba Luohan) were all destroyed. In 1980, the temple was restored again. However, the temple's main hall, the **Guanyin Dian**, currently has an odd array of deitieis, not all of whom are Buddhist. The Buddhist Guanyin deity in the center is flanked by other images of Confucian scholars, including one of the God of Fortune (Fu) holding a golden shoe.

The garden of Huan Xiang Villa viewed from the Qie Xian Ting pavilion.

Steps up the hillside, from the Stone Bell Pavilion (Shi Zhong Ting) to the Su Shi Pavilion (Su Shi Ting), lead past two round stone towers.

The entrance gate to the **Loyalties Ancestral Temple** (Zhao Zhong Ci) is by far the most impressive of the three, and is situated in the center of the other two gates. Its stone block and brick structure resembles those still found in the San Xia. Rising up three levels, this mountain gate was obviously once quite colorful, but its formerly bright red and yellow colors have now faded. The Loyalties Temple was once the site of a Taiping rebel army fortress and barracks. After the defeat of the Taiping army by Zeng Guofan, Peng Yu Lin built the temple here in 1858. Although the main courtyard was open, the main hall of the temple seemed to be padlocked shut. Old photographs show that there was once a statue of a Qing official, possibly Zeng Guofan, which stood immediately in front of the Loyalties Temple but is now missing. Modern signs refer to the temple as the Loyalties Ancestral Temple (Zhao Zhong Ci), but the original three-character inscription on the temple's front gate calls it the **Loyal Martyr Ancestral Temple** (Zhong Lie Ci). The identity of the loyal martyrs has since been revised. Before 1949, the temple was devoted to Qing Dynasty loyalists who died fighting against the Taiping rebels. After 1949, the temple was rededicated to the rebels themselves, who in the Communist version of history are now seen as having been the good guys.

On the east side of the Loyalties Temple is the **Huan Xiang Villa** (Huan Xiang Zhuang), built in 1858, the eighth year of the Xian Feng reign of the Qing Dynasty, as the home of **Peng Yu Lin**. The villa was restored in 1982. Behind the main halls of the villa is the octagonal wooden **Qie Xian Pavilion** (Qie Xian Ting), which faces a small walled landscaped garden. In the center of the garden is a pond stocked with jumping fish, and around its edges natural rocks engraved with inscriptions. A zigzag bridge across the pond leads to the **Peach Blossom Cave** (Tao Hua Dong) and the eastern corridor leading back to the Taiping Lou.

Address: Hukou Town
Phone: (0792) 633-1963, 633-2398

Poyang Lake (Poyang Hu)

With a total area of 4,070 sq km (1,571.4 sq miles), Poyang Lake is the largest freshwater lake in China. In 1947, the Yangzi River Inspector, G.R.G. Worcester measured the lake as being 144.8 km (90 miles) long and 32.2 km (20 miles) wide.

Fallen-Star Boulder (Luo Xing Shi) stands in the southwestern end of the lake, off the coast of Xing Zi County (Xing Zi Xian). The rock was said to be a star fallen from the Heaven, and may have actually been a meteorite. Legend has it that no matter how high the waters have risen, the boulder has never been submerged.

Near the Wu Cheng township in Yong Xiu county, Jiangxi Province, is the **Poyang Hu Migratory Bird Nature Reserve**. Here endless marshes, ponds, streams, and branching lakes form a vast swamp. Abounding with grass, waters, and aquatic products, this area, covering an area of some 90 sq km (34.7 sq miles), becomes the largest natural habit for thousands of migratory birds. Among those spending their winters here are white cranes, young swans, white storks, and whitehead cranes. Hawks, falcons, cormorants and other birds also make Poyang Lake (Poyang Hu) their home. In the Waterfowls Park, visitors can use the telescopes in the for bird watching.

Phone: (0792) 328-0111

New highway suspension bridge over the mouth of Poyang Hu connects Jiujiang with Hukou.

View of the confluence of the Yangzi River and Poyang Hu's lake mouth from the Qing Zhuo Pavilion (Qing Zhuo Ting) at Stone Bell Hill (Shi Zhong Shan).

The new Big Orphan Pagoda (Da Gu Ta) atop Shoe Island (Xie Shan) in the middle of Poyang Hu.

Shoe Island (Xie Shan)

Xie Shan is a small island located in the eastern end of Poyang Lake (Poyang Hu) and reachable only by boat. It is part of Hukou County of Jiujiang Municipality. True to its name, the island is shaped like a shoe (*xie*) and is dominated by a 304-m-high (1,000-ft-high) mountain (*shan*). Because it is also the only island in Poyang Lake, it has sometimes been called the **Big Orphan Island** (Da Gu Shan), to distinguish it from another island nearby in the Yangzi River known as the Little Orphan (Xiao Gu Shan). The shores of the island are characterized by sharp cliffs broken by one small harbor. In 1921, a visitor reported that from the harbor, a narrow trail leads up to the mountain summit occupied by the **Heavenly Empress Temple** (Tian Hou Gong). There was a Taoist priest in residence at the temple, and Tian Hou was still regarded by local people as the protector of sailors and fishermen. In the middle of the island stood the **Glistening Cloud Pagoda** (Ling Yun Bao Ta) built during the Kang Xi reign of Qing Dynasty in 1681. The original pagoda and temple were still intact when G.R.G. Worcester mentioned them in 1947, but were sadly destroyed during the Cultural Revolution (Wenhua Da Geming) of 1966–1976. Today they have been replaced by recently constructed replicas.

On the edge of the Stone Bell Hill (Shi Zhong Shan) parking lot is a small ticket office where seats for cruises out to the picturesque Shoe Island (Xie Shan) can be purchased. Look for the photos of the island on the windows. Tickets range in price from 22 to 60 Rmb, depending on the size of boat you take and the number of passengers in your group. Negotiating the ticket price can be an exhausting battle of the wills, so be sure to arrive with lots of patience. Furthermore, the larger ships do not follow any set departure schedule but simply wait until they have

The new Shoe Island Entrance Gate (Xie Shan Da Men).

The cliffside foot trail to the summit of Shoe Island (Xie Shan) hangs perilously over the water.

sold enough tickets before deciding to leave for the island. You may want to budget several hours of time just for buying the tickets and waiting for the boat to finally leave. Since it is impossible to see the island after dark, it is important to depart Hukou town with enough daylight to make the trip worthwhile.

The boat travels past the rock outcropping on the southern end of Hukou Town, passes under the Hukou Bridge, and enters the enormous expanse of Poyang Lake (Poyang Hu). An endless single line of barges can be seen traveling through the center of the lake. The eastern shore of Poyang Lake (Poyang Hu) is wild, uninhabited, low foothills. The western shore at the foot of Mount Lushan is more mountainous, and also more industrial, with occasional towns and factories. Mount Lushan is visible, shrouded in fog and clouds, towering over the lake. The foot of the mountain approaches right up to the lake's western shore.

The island of Xie Shan is visible for a long distance before it is reached, but unless you are standing right on the bow of the ship, it is difficult to get a good view of it during the approach.

Perpendicular rock cliffs form the entire shore of the island, which has no sandy beaches, not even a proper harbor. The boat drops anchor at a spot on the island where there is nothing but a small concrete terrace to greet visitors. A few modern imitation iron cannons fire off gunshots. Be forewarned that there is no town, village, or shelter of any kind on this island. There are no facilities such as restaurants, stores, shops, or hotels. Bring some refreshments with you if you think you might get hungry or thirsty during the trip.

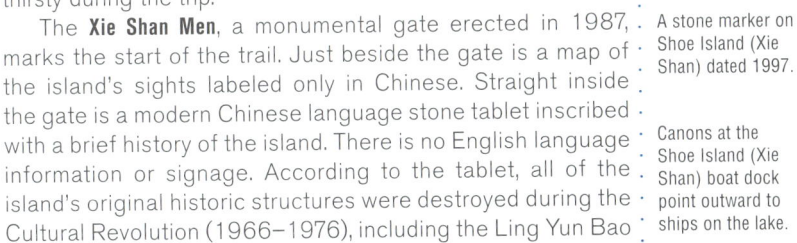

The **Xie Shan Men**, a monumental gate erected in 1987, marks the start of the trail. Just beside the gate is a map of the island's sights labeled only in Chinese. Straight inside the gate is a modern Chinese language stone tablet inscribed with a brief history of the island. There is no English language information or signage. According to the tablet, all of the island's original historic structures were destroyed during the Cultural Revolution (1966–1976), including the Ling Yun Bao Ta pagoda and Tian Hou Gong temple. However, at the beginning of 1985, the Hukou Xian county government decided to rebuild the pagoda, temple, terraces, and pavilions that had previously stood on the island. Reconstruction was well under way when the Mayor of the Jiujiang Municipality, Jiang Guozhen, paid an inspection visit on 26 October 1986 to check on the progress. By the end of 1987, all the current structures on the island had been completed.

The trail turns to your right and ascends sharply up along a narrow ledge blasted into the side of vertical rock cliffs that drop off straight into the waters of the Poyang Lake (Poyang Hu) below. About halfway up a second stone gate, the **Yi Tian Men**. The trail finally

A stone marker on Shoe Island (Xie Shan) dated 1997.

Canons at the Shoe Island (Xie Shan) boat dock point outward to ships on the lake.

reaches a relatively flat plateau at the summit, where a ring trail circles around the island in a loop allowing you to head in either of two directions and still return to the downward trail when it is time to make your descent. Turning to your right will take you first to the **Da Gu Temple** (Da Gu Miao), which has replaced the Tian Hou Gong, and then the **Watching Lushan Pavilion** (Guan Lu Ting) on the western tip of the island, from where you can catch views of Mount Lushan. Following the loop trail around to the southwestern corner of the island brings you to the newly built **Da Gu Pagoda** (Da Gu Ta), which has replaced the earlier Ling Yun Bao Ta. Continuing down the trail along the island's southern shore towards its eastern tip, you reach the **Confucius Pavilion** (Kong Sheng Ting).

At the island's eastern tip is the **Ancient Gun Terrace** (Gu Pao Tai), after which you can return to your starting point via the northern summit trail along the so-called **Ancient City Wall** (Gu Cheng Qiang).

The return boat trip makes the entire journey worth the effort. On the way back, the ship sails a complete circle around the island, giving a complete view of it and the pagoda perched on its summit. It is on this return trip that you definitely want to have your camera ready and fully loaded with film. Sit on the side of the boat facing the island and you will be able to get great pictures and views of the island just by looking out the side windows, without having to risk falling overboard by fighting the mobs at the bow and stern of the ship.

The cliffside foot trail to the summit of Shoe Island (Xie Shan).

Jiangxi Province

Jiujiang

Historical Background

The name "Jiujiang" means Nine Rivers. It has its basis in the legend of the **Great Yu** (Da Yu), the mythical founder of the Xia Dynasty who, according to legend, lived from 2205–2198 BC, and is said to have come to the Jiujiang area to survey the nine rivers here as part of his flood control efforts.

During the Tang Dynasty (618–907 AD), Jiujiang was also known as Jiang Zhou and **Xun Yang**. It is this latter name which is commemmorated by the main east-west avenue along the north end of Gangtang Hu, as well as by a recently constructed pavilion on the Yangzi River waterfront.

The Tang Dynasty bohemian traveler and poet **Li Bai** (Li Tai Po) (701–762 AD) lived in Jiujiang for several years from 756 to 758 AD, not counting two brief excursions to Susong in Anhui and Yangzhou in Jiangsu. Li Bai had fled to the safety of Jiujiang in response to the disorder caused by the An Lushan Rebellion (755–763 AD) against the Xuan Zong emperor (712–756 AD), in which both the Tang capitals of Luoyang and Changan (Xian) were captured by the rebels. He seems to have spent his time here visiting the Buddhist monks at the East Grove Temple (Dong Lin Si), writing poems about climbing Mount Lushan, and visiting one of his many wives who lived in nearby Nankang (Xing Zi). Although his purpose in coming to Jiujiang had been to escape the rebellion, he was accused of being a traitor to the Tang Dynasty in 758 AD. Subsequently, he was banished to Yunnan, which started him on a lengthy boat journey up the Yangzi River through the Three Gorges (San Xia). As an unofficial resident who held no government post, and being somewhat of a vagabond, Li Bai left only the poems written during his stay there.

Jiujiang's most famous official resident was probably the Tang Dynasty poet **Bai Ju Yi** (772–846 AD). He was stationed here as the local Sub-Prefect from 815AD to the spring of 819AD during the Yuan He (Xian Zong) reign (805–820 AD) of the Tang Dynasty, when the town was known as Jiang Zhou. Bai was a scholar-official of the Jinshi degree, and member of the Hanlin Academy. He had held the high position of Imperial Censor at the Tang capital at Changan (Xian), but was banished to Jiujiang in 1815 after being involved in a scandal. Although his assignment to govern Jiujiang was a demotion in rank intended as a punishment, he made good use of his time there by contributing to the town's development. According to local legend, Bai was responsible for building the first predecessor to the Cloud Water Pavilion (Yun Shui Ting) in Gangtang Hu, the lake in the center of the town. He also found time to visit nearby Mount Lushan and built a thatched cottage as a retreat in between the West Grove Temple (Xi Lin Si) and the East Grove Temple (Dong Lin Si). A reproduction of his cottage has been built on the shores of Ruqin Lake, on the summit of Mount Lushan. A new statue of Bai Ju Yi now stands in front of the Lute Pavilion (Pipa Ting) on Jiujiang's Yangzi River waterfront.

It was also in the Tang Dynasty when the town's lake was divided in half – Gangtang Hu to the north and Nan Hu to the south – by the cross-lake causeway and Xi Xian Bridge (Xi Xian Qiao). This causeway seems to have been built by **Li Bo** (773–831 AD), the founder of the White Deer Cave Academy (Bai Lu Dong Shu Yuan) on Lushan, during his term as governor of this city in the Jing Zong reign (825–827 AD) of Tang Li Zhan. The old walled city was entirely east of these two lakes, wedged between their shores and that of the Yangzi. In 1929, the walls were torn down.

Jiujiang changed hands several times from 1360 to 1363, during the time when Zhu Yuanzhang, the founder of the Ming Dynasty, rose to power. However, the critical battles in this campaign were fought on the nearby Poyang Lake (Poyang Hu) and at Hukou.

It was during the Taiping Rebellion (Taiping Tian Guo) of 1850–1864 that Jiujiang once again played a prominent role in Chinese history. The Taiping Rebels sailed down the Yangzi River, from Wuhan toward Jiangxi Province, and captured Jiujiang on 18 February 1853. On 11 February 1855, a Taiping fleet commanded by Shi Da Kai defeated a Qing naval force on the Yangzi River near Jiujiang. The commander of the Qing Dynasty forces, Zeng Guofan, lost his flagship to the Taiping garrison at Jiujiang. All his archives were lost, although he himself escaped. On 14 January 1857, Qing forces retreated from Jiujiang after a failed attempt to capture the city from its Taiping defenders. After occupying the city for five years, the Taipings finally lost control of Jiujiang to the Qing Dynasty forces of Zeng Guofan on 19 May 1858.

Jiujiang was opened as a treaty port in January 1862 in accordance with the **Treaty of Tientsin** (Tianjin) signed with Britain in 1858. The terms of this treaty were not executed until after the Great Powers military occupation of Beijing in 1860, thus delaying the opening of Jiujiang until later. A British concession was established in 1861, a year earlier than the port's actual opening to foreign trade. According to R.A. Villard's map, the British concession was located west of the old walled city, and east of a small tributary flowing into the Yangzi, wedged in between Gangtang Hu to the south and the Yangzi River to the north, roughly where the center of downtown Jiujiang is today. By 1863, the foreign community had established its own municipal council and begun construction of a Bund along the Yangzi. A horse racing course was established in 1864.

In the 1860s and 1870s, Jiujiang was a center of the British tea trade, complete with tea tasters, warehouses full of tea, and steamships arriving to carry shiploads of Chinese tea off to London, particularly during the April–July tea season. However, economic recession set in by the 1880s with greater competition from tea produced in India and Ceylon.

Nonetheless, the foreign presence continued to expand. The Jiujiang Club was founded in 1881, and in the same year Methodist missionaries established the William Nast College here. In 1883, a large Roman Catholic church was built, and this building can still be seen today. In 1885, the British firm of Butterfield & Swire opened an office here for their steamship line, the China Navigation Co. By 1889, the town supported a foreign population of 50 full-time residents, supplemented by half a dozen tea buyers who visited only during the three-month tea season. As a port of call for the Yangzi steamship lines, Jiujiang experienced a resurgence from 1895, and became the jumping off point for China's foreign residents, and later the upper-class Chinese, traveling to the newly established summer holiday resort of Kuling, located on the nearby mountain of Lushan.

Before the 1911 Revolution (Xin Hai Geming), Jiujiang was a walled city, with a 6.1-m-high (20-foot-high), 3.7-m-wide (12-foot-wide) city wall stretching 6.4–8 km (4–5 miles) in circumference around the town. After the revolution, this wall was gradually torn down, and by 1947, no remainders of it survived.

The 128-km (80-mile) railway between the Jiangxi provincial capital of Nanchang and Jiujiang was completed on 3 February 1915, having been financed with Japanese capital. Later, after the rise of Communist guerrilla bands in much of rural Jiangxi province from 1927 to 1934, this railway served as an umbilical cord that managed to keep both Jiujiang and Nanchang under Guomindang control.

The fate of Jiujiang's foreign community began to decline by the mid-1920s. Immediately after the May 30 Incident in 1925, the British consulate in Jiujiang was attacked by demonstrators who tried to burn it down. At the same time the Japanese Consulate was looted and a Japanese bank was burned down. A temporary calm set in for a year and a half, but with the military occupation of Jiujiang by the Guomindang's Northern Expedition (Bei Fa) on November 5, 1926, the British Concession was under a state of siege. After months of tense encirclement, it was finally overrun by a mob of Chinese protesters in January 1927, who were imitating similar events that had already occured in Wuhan. Although the British Consul Sir Alwyne Ogden (1889–1981) had been given orders to defend the concession, no shots were fired in its defense, and instead the remaining foreign community fled on British and American warships, which took them down river to the safety of Shanghai, never to return. Britain officially surrendered its Jiujiang concession on March 15, 1927 as part of the Chen-O'Malley Agreement of 19–20 February 1927 which also surrendered the British concession at Wuhan. The British Concession in Jiujiang officially became the Sixth District of the Jiujiang Municipality.

With the establishment of the new Guomindang national government in Nanjing, urban development came to Jiujiang in 1929 when the old city walls were torn down. In the same year, an 12.8 km (8 mile) road was built from the Jiujiang city center to Lianhua Dong, at the northwestern foot of Mount Lushan, from where flights of stone steps led up the mountain to the resort town of Kuling on the summit.

POINT OF INTEREST

Writing in 1905, B.L. Putname Weale described a trip upriver to Jiujiang:

> "... another little port separated from the outer world and sunk in the middle of vast inland China. A few miles below the town the river opens out on the right bank into the vast and shallow Poyang Lake, which native steam-launches and miniature steamers are beginning to furrow, displacing the junk of yore. A red bluff of land pushes up at you, you round the bend of the river, and Kiukiang (Jiujiang), one of the earliest ports settled by the white man after the Taipings had been crushed, is before you. There is the same little foreign settlement, pressed in between the water and the Chinese city walls; the same line of hulks, the same little bund; and withal a heat more crushing than any you have yet experienced along the river. Kiukiang (Jiujiang) has the questionable reputation of possessing the hottest summer in the whole of China."

B.L. Putnam Weale,
The Reshaping of the Far East, London: 1905.

By 1931, there was neither a British nor an American consulate at Jiujiang, the former British Consulate having been taken over by the Asiatic Petroleum Company. However, the Jiujiang Club was still functioning with 18 members housed in the former Municipal Building with a small library, ball room, tennis courts, and billiard room. There was also a British Naval Club housed in one of the former British Consulate's residential buildings.

Jiujiang's local economy was also changing in the 1930s. Once it had been a center of the tea industry, with two Russian-owned brick tea factories, and annual visits during the tea season by foreign tea buyers. However, by 1931, this trade had disappeared. It was also once the major export point for Chinese porcelain made in the inland town of Jingdezhen, and had numerous porcelain shops, although none of these shops are to be seen today. By 1931, Jiujiang had telephone services but electricity was available in the evenings only after 6:00PM. Private motor vehicles were nearly non-existent but there was a public bus service.

The 1930s also saw tourism begin to become an important part of Jiujiang's local economy, thanks to its role as the Yangzi River port for the moutain top resort of Kuling on the summit of Mount Lushan. On 20 October 1930, the China National Aviation Corporation (CNAC) established an air route from Shanghai to Hankou, with stops at Nanjing, Anqing, and Jiujiang. Even today, Jiujiang does not enjoy such good transportation connections, its airport having been closed down in 1999. In 1930, the China Travel Service began managing tourist facilities at Kuling. Automobiles and buses were available to transport visitors from Jiujiang to the foothills of the mountain, from where the rest of the journey was still made by chair bearers even as late as 1931. The entire journey took two-and-a-half hours one way. By 1931, telephone services had been established between Jiujiang and Kuling.

Until the Japanese occupation of 1938, Jiujiang continued to be a transit point for foreign and Chinese travelers visiting Lushan. After first capturing the town of Hukou, near Shi Zhong Shan, on 8 July 1938, Japanese naval vessels entered Poyang Lake (Poyang Hu) and landed troops on its western shore near the town of Xing Zi. This allowed them to advance on Jiujiang from the rear, in a surprise move that resulted in the capture of the city from a Guomindang garrison of 45,000 troops on 26 July 1938, causing a great deal of destruction in the process.

Hukou Sights: The Old Town
Following Gangtang Nan Lu from the cross-lake causeway, one comes to Yu Liang Lu, a street known for housing both an old colonial era Catholic church and an ancient Buddhist temple complex.

Roman Catholic Church
(Jiujiang Tian Zhu Jiao Tang)

The three-story red brick Catholic Church sits right at the intersection of Gangtang Nan Lu and Yu Liang Lu. Dating from treaty port days, it was closed during the Cultural Revolution (Wenhua De Geming), but reopened in 1984. This Catholic Church, with its tall steeple, still has the "JHS" inscription at the top. The base exterior seems to have been modified, covering up any foundation stone that would have shown the date of construction and original name.

Nengren Buddhist Temple
(Nengren Chan Si)

This functioning Buddhist temple has a resident monk population. Its main feature is an impressive seven-story pagoda, which stands in the middle of a beautiful garden compound. The history of this temple can be traced back to the sixth century Southern Dynasty (503–528 AD). It was renamed Nengren Si (Temple of Benevolence) during the Ming Dynasty (1368–1644). During the Qing Dynasty (1644–1911), the temple compound was expanded to cover a total area of 3,000 sq m (32,291.7 sq ft). As its modern name implies, the monks belong to the Chan Zong meditative sect of Chinese Buddhism.

Although the temple's origins date from the sixth century, it has suffered almost total destruction on two occasions: once during the Taiping Rebellion, and again during the Cultural

Jiujiang's Roman Catholic Church (Tian Zhu Tang).

Major sites in Jiujiang

Revolution (1966–1976). In September 1966, foreign visitors commented that all the religious icons had then been removed from the halls. The temple was later restored and reopened in 1988. Although it once had 200–300 resident monks before 1949, there are an estimated number of 30 monks living there now. This is still a fairly large number by today's standards.

A new monumental gateway (Shan Men) was built in 2002. A long tree-lined corridor passes the Book Shop (Shu Dian) and other Buddhist trinket shops selling items such as twin red wax candles shaped like the temple's pagoda for 10 Rmb a pair.

The temple has traditionally been thought to have had the following Eight Beautiful Scenes: The Great Victory Pagoda (Da Sheng Ta), the Stone Fishing Boat (Yu Chuan Shi), the Iron Buddha (Tie Fo), Twin Sun Bridge (Shuang Taiyang Qiao), the Animal Releasing Pool (Fang Sheng Chi), Hui Er Spring, Icy Hill, and Snow Cave. Unfortunately, the last three of these sights no longer exist, while some of the others are reproductions of the destroyed originals.

The entrance to the Heng Ha Dian of Neng Ren Si Buddhist Temple in Jiujiang.

Heng Ha Dian

The path leads directly to the first hall on the central west-east axis, the Heng Ha Dian. Its west entrance faces the temple's entrance gate on Yu Liang Lu. Inside the Heng Ha Dian are two enormous statues of the temple guardians, Heng and Ha. They are fierce-looking, black-faced warriors, similar to those found in the Heavenly Kings Hall (Tian Wang Dian).

Twin-Sun Bridge (Shuang Tai Yang Qiao)

Exiting the east side of the Heng Ha Dian, you come to an ancient three-arched stone bridge, which crosses the **Animal Releasing Pool** (Fang Sheng Chi), and is sometimes called the **Fang Sheng Qiao**. It connects the Heng Ha Dian with the Heavenly King Hall (Tian Wang Dian) on the east side of the pool. Legend has it that if you stand at the east end of the bridge, you can see two reflections of the sun in the surface of the pool, one on either side of the bridge. That is why the Fang Sheng Qiao is also known as the **Twin Sun Bridge** (Shuang Tai Yang Qiao). Turtles swim in the pool.

The **Heavenly Kings Hall** (Tian Wang Dian) is a new structure made from concrete all the way from its roof down to its floor. Inside, it contains impressively large and expressive statues of the four heavenly kings. One has a golden face with a smiling

The Qing Dynasty wooden Da Xiong Bao Dian of Neng Ren Si Buddhist Temple in Jiujiang.

A stone relic behind the Da Xiong Bao Dian of Neng Ren Si has had a hole worn through the center by years of dripping water, one drop at a time.

expression and holds a guitar; the second has a black face and holds a sword; the third also has a black face but holds a snake; and the fourth has a golden face with a staff in his hands. Two gilded golden Buddha images sit in the center of the hall inside a glass case. One is a Maitreya Buddha (Mi Le Fo), and on the back side is the warrior bodhisattva Wei Tuo, who is the protector of all Buddhist temples.

East of the Tian Wang Dian is a wide courtyard area that was undergoing reconstruction in May 2003, followed by the main hall of the temple, the **Precious Hall of the Great Hero** (Da Xiong Bao Dian). This hall's dusty wooden log structure with intricate wood carving decorations seems to be a genuine historic relic. It is flanked on either side by a new Bell Tower (Zhong Lou) and Drum Tower (Gu Lou), both apparently completed during the 2002–2003 renovations. Immediately behind the Da Xiong Bao Dian can be seen some genuine stone relics, including a square stone block with a smooth hole that has been worn through the top by dripping water.

On the south side of the Da Xiong Bao Dian is the **Scripture Pavilion** (Cang Jing Lou), and south

A wooden fish in front of the dining hall of Neng Ren Si is used to call meal times.

of that is the Dining Hall. The **Dining Hall** (Zhai Tang) has eleven long tables each laid out with 11 sets of two dishes and chopsticks, for a total of 121 sets of dishes. An older monk said that there are now 30 monks living here, but that there used to be 200 or 300. This story was later confirmed by an old lady selling candles near the front gate. It is not clear why 30 monks would need 121 sets of dishes, unless many lay visitors were expected. A large wooden fish and iron gong hung from the rafters just outside the dining hall.

The thousand-armed Guanyin statue inside the Guanyin Dian of Neng Ren Si in Jiujiang.

Behind the east side of the Da Xiong Bao Dian, a gateway through a wall leads into another courtyard lined with halls on three sides. To the right is the **Guanyin Dian** with a thousand armed Guanyin statue. To the left is the **San Sheng Dian** with statues of three Buddhist deities, including Amitabha (O-Mi-Tuo-Fo) Buddha in the center, the bodhisattva Guanyin on his right, and the bodhisattva Da Shi Zhi on his left. Da Shi Zhi is a bodhisattva thought to correspond with the Sanskrit name Mahasthanaparapta, the son of Amitabha.

The Great Victory Pagoda (Da Sheng Bao Ta) of Neng Ren Si Buddhist Temple.

The Great Victory Pagoda (Da Sheng Bao Ta)

The Nengren Buddhist Temple is actually a complex of many temple buildings covering an enormous forested garden compound, so not all of the structures fall into the central axis line. In the garden area, to the south of the Heavenly Kings Hall (Tian Wang Dian), is the **Great Victory Pagoda** (Da Sheng Bao Ta). The terrace in front of the Precious Hall of the Great Hero (Da Xiong Bao Dian) offers the best view of this pagoda.

The Great Victory Pagoda (Da Sheng Bao Ta) is a seven-story, octagonal pagoda dating from the Song Dynasty (960–1279). Local legend has it that this pagoda was originally built by local scholars seeking good luck in passing the imperial civil service examinations. After the pagoda was built, the scholars were more successful in passing the examinations than before. Today, the first floor of this pagoda houses a chapel dedicated to the Buddhist Goddess of Mercy (Guanyin). It is the custom to never let the candles in this chapel go out, and they are kept burning throughout the night. An exterior flight of steps leads up to the second floor of the Da Sheng Bao Ta, but a locked metal gate prevents entry. The interior steps obviously continue on upward.

Immediately behind the Da Sheng Bao Ta to the south is the **Dizang Dian**, dedicated to the bodhisattva Dizang (Kshitigarbha) who rescues departed souls from Hell.

Iron Buddha (Tie Fo)

Legend has it that during the Song Dynasty (960–1279), the abbot of the temple had a dream in which Buddha told him to expect the arrival in Jiujiang of a divine god who was traveling down the Yangzi River in a stone boat. The dream soon came true and the abbot and his priests met the living god as the latter approached the Jiujiang river bank in his stone boat, just as it has been foretold. Later, a life-size image of the god was made out of iron and placed inside a hall of the temple, while the god's stone boat was placed in the temple's courtyard. When the whole temple was destroyed during the Taiping Rebellion, the Iron Buddha temporarily disappeared, although its broken remains were soon discovered and restored to their previous state. When the temple suffered destruction again during the Cultural Revolution, the original Iron Buddha was finally destroyed forever.

South of the Fang Sheng Chi is a second pool of water with a long narrow stone dugout canoe, inside of which is seated a stone god wearing a golden yellow silk robe. This seems to be the reconstructed **Stone Fishing Boat** (Shi Yu Chuan) and the mythical **Iron Buddha** (Tie Fo) who supposedly rode it down the Yangzi River to Jiujiang.

The temple is located near the corner of Yu Liang Lu and Gangtang Nan Lu. Turn right at this intersection, go past the Catholic Church, and head up Yu Liang Lu. Within a block you will come to the entrance gate of Nengren Si on the left side of the street.

Address: Yu Liang Lu
Tickets: 10 Rmb

Entrance to the Guanyin shrine inside the base of the Da Sheng Bao Ta of Neng Ren Si.

Gangtang Gongyuan viewed from Lushan Lu in Jiujiang.

Gangtang Hu Scenic Area
Gangtang Hu and Nanmen Hu

These two lakes in the center of the city are divided only by a narrow causeway, which was built during the Tang Dynasty by Li Bo (773–831 AD). Li was the founder of the White Deer Cave Academy (Bai Lu Dong Shu Yuan) on Lushan, during his term as governor of Jiujiang, then known as Jiang Zhou, in the Jing Zong reign (825–827 AD) of Tang Li Zhan. It still carries traffic from one side of the lakes to the other via Gangtang Nan Lu and the ancient Xi Xian Bridge (Xi Xian Qiao). Gangtang Hu is more the center of life in the city than the Yangzi watefront. It is along the shores of the lake that people go for a stroll, groups of amateur Peking opera performers put on outdoor shows for free, and fortune tellers ply their trade with geomancers' spiritual diagrams.

The Lushan Lu waterfront along Gangtang Hu in Jiujiang.

A newly built man-made island and causeway in Gang Tang Hu viewed from Lushan Lu.

Gangtang Gongyuan

Take Lushan Lu, following the lake shore of Gangtang Hu, to Gangtang Gongyuan. This park has a small forested hill covered with a succession of weathered statues and monuments to forgotten past heroes of China's many 20th century wars, battles, and revolutions. Entering the park from Lushan Lu, the first one you encounter is an old Min Guo era stone pavilion built in classical European style with Greco-Roman columns. It has a four-character Chinese inscription still visible on it, which calls it the **Zhong Lie Chang Pavilion**. The name means that it is a memorial to the martyred heroes of a revolution, but fails to state which one. Possibly it was either the 1911 Revolution or the 1927 Northern Expedition. The inscription reads from right to left, proving that it was written before 1949.

Walking up to the top of the hill you find a bleak zoo with monkeys and peacocks housed in an unpleasant environment. Following the ridge you come along another martyrs' monument, a plain and uninspiring obelisk labeled as the **Memorial Tower**, commemorating all the heroes who died in the 1949 Revolution.

Following the ridge down to the base of the hill, the next surprise is a bust of **Cai Gong Shi**, a former Guomindang military officer shown in full uniform with his party's telltale blue and white star symbol clearly present on his cap. Although it is clear from the inscription who he is, it is a mystery as to exactly why he is honored here in this park by a fairly impressive statue.

The Zhong Lie Chang Pavilion in Gang Tang Gongyuan in Jiujiang.

1949 revolutionary martyrs memorial tower in Gang Tang Gongyuan in Jiujiang.

Statue of the Min Guo military officer Cai Gong Shi in Gang Tang Gongyuan in Jiujiang.

Tian Hua Gong Buddhist Nunnery

Across the causeway dividing the two lakes is a very narrow barely-two-lane road. Here, you will stumble across the Buddhist nunnery of Tian Hua Gong. This historic sight is not mentioned in any of the other guidebooks but is actually quite interesting.

The nunnery's red outer dragon wall and traditional buildings are visible from the lake shore. Its double red gate may be closed when you arrive but if you ask, they will be opened by friendly attendants and you will be allowed to enter. Inside the first courtyard is an incense burner. Aged wood carvings decorate the roof beams, and stone lotus pedestals standing in the courtyard add to the temple's authenticity. Straight ahead, in the main chapel, are new gilded Buddha statues with prayer cushions placed on the floor in front of them. Pass through the main hall and exit to find a three-story wooden pagoda tower with a chapel inside its first floor. This chapel has two gilded statues of women who obviously have played an important role in the nunnery's history. The second and third floors are closed to visitors.

Entrance gate to Tian Hua Gong.

Shrine at Tian Hua Gong containing a gilded mumr

The overall design of the temple is one of three courtyards linked together with various chapels off to the sides. Some of the chapels are devoted to unusual statues, such as the one of the two women in the pagoda, and another of a man that looks almost lifelike, as if it had actually been made by gilding his dead body. Behind the temple, near the dragon wall facing the lake, is an interesting model of a mountain criss-crossed with trails. This may be

A scale model of Mt. Lushan behind Tian Hua Gong.

meant to represent Lushan or some mythical place in Buddhist cosmology.

Exactly when the temple was built is a mystery, but from its appearance it must be a Qing Dynasty construction at least. No ticket is required, but a shop at the entrance is well stocked with candles, incense sticks, and even firecrackers.

The Misty Water Pavilion (Yan Shui Ting) on an island in Gang Tang Hu in Jiujiang.

Misty Water Pavilion (Yan Shui Ting)

The earliest record of this island comes from 208 AD, the 13th year of the Jian An reign during the Han Dynasty, when General Zhou Yu supposedly trained his maritime forces on Gangtang Hu and commanded his ships from a drum platform on this island.

Entrance gate to the Misty Water Pavilion (Yan Shui Ting).

According to local legend, the Tang poet and Jinshi scholar Bai Ju Yi (772–846 AD) had a pavilion built on an earthen mound in the lake here during the Yuan He era (806–820 AD) in the Xian Zong reign (805–820 AD) of the Tang Dynasty. This was when he served as the local Sub-Prefect of Jiujiang from 815 to 819 AD. In his writings from this time, Bai does mention visiting "the island in the lake." However, there seems to be no definite evidence of his building a pavilion there, although this would match with his behavior as governor of Hangzhou when he did build the Bai Causeway (Bai Di) in West

Lake (Xi Hu). Later, a structure on the island was named the Submerging Moon Pavilion (Jin Yue Ting). During the Song Dynasty (960–1279), Zhou Dun Yi built a causeway out to the island. After it had been destroyed, a local official named Huang Ten Chun rebuilt the pavilion during the Wan Li reign (1573–1620) of the Ming Dynasty. It was renamed the Misty Water Pavilion (Yan Shui Ting) at this time.

Over the years, the site was expanded until it became a complex of buildings including several halls and pavilions. During the Taiping Rebellion, in the Xian Feng reign of the Qing Dynasty, the entire complex was destroyed in 1853. The existing buildings were reconstructed after the rebellion was over, during the late Qing Dynasty.

In 1972, an overall renovation was conducted, and the existing zigzag bridge was built to connect the island with the lake shore. In 1978, the drum platform (*gu tai*) of General Zhou Yu was added to the front of the island facing the lake. A collection of traditional pavilions completely cover this small island.

The **Jiujiang Museum** (Jiujiang Bowuguan) is now housed inside the Qing Dynasty halls on the island. It offers a few old black and white photographs and some relics unearthed from a tomb somewhere nearby. Overall it is unremarkable and there is little English language information available. However, a shop here sells the only English language maps in the whole city, and these feature Jiujiang city on one side with a very detailed map of Lushan on the other, complete with roads, trails, and historic sites.

Another entrance gate to the Misty Water Pavilion (Yan Shui Ting).

The foot bridge connecting the Misty Water Pavilion (Yan Shui Ting) to the lake shore.

The Jiujiang Yangzi River waterfront.

The island is located at the north end of Gangtang Hu. Approach the causeway to the island from the intersection of Jiao Tong Lu and Xun Yang Lu.

Phone: 822-3190
Tickets: 5 Rmb

The Yangzi River Waterfront

From Yan Shui Ting, follow Xun Yang Lu to its intersection with Lushan Bei Lu. Turn right down the latter street, following it all the way to Bin Jiang Lu which runs along the length of the city's Changjiang waterfront area. The entire waterfront area is currently under reconstruction, with a new breakwater and raised promenade being built to replace the old one. It was this old breakwater which burst open during the floods of 1998, allowing river water to pour into the city.

The former British Consulate in Jiujiang, on Bin Jiang Lu along the Yangzi River waterfront.

Former British Consulate

One block to the left of the Lushan Bei Lu and Bin Jiang Lu intersection is the only genuine colonial era building still standing on the watefront. This is a two-story yellow structure with Greco-Roman columns and wrought iron balconies on the second floor. It currently houses some company offices but it was formerly the British Consulate from the

1860s to 1927, and stood at one corner of the British Concession. After the concession was abolished in 1927, the building was used by the British-owned Asiatic Petroleum Company (APC) into the 1930s. You can enter the building and explore it if you like.

Jiujiang Port Ferry Terminal (Jiujiang Matou)

Walk along Bin Jiang Lu and you will pass by the **Jiujiang Port Ferry Terminal** (Jiujiang Matou), which supposedly has ships traveling upriver to Wuhan and downriver to Shanghai, but seems to be abandoned inside. A new shopping center shaped like an ocean liner now sits on the Yangzi waterfront next to the Jiujiang Port Terminal

The Jiujiang Yangzi River Ferry Terminal.

A floating boat dock on the Yangzi River waterfront at Jiujiang.

The Xun Yang Ta on the Yangzi River waterfront at Jiujiang.

Xun Yang Tower (Xun Yang Ta)

After a very long walk, you will finally arrive at the first in a series of main attractions, starting with the recently reconstructed Xun Yang Ta. This tower is named after the Tang Dynasty name for Jiujiang city.

Although there is no historical record of the tower being built or destroyed, poems about it were written as early as the 8th century in the Tang Dynasty, and as late as the Kang Xi reign (1661–1722) of the Qing Dynasty, convincing at least the local residents that it must have existed in reality at one time.

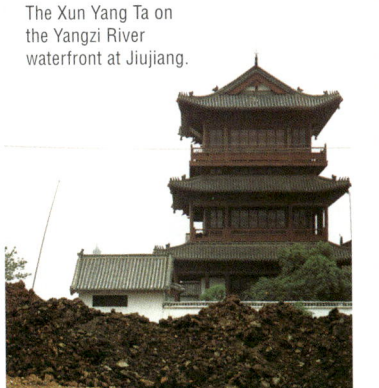

POINT OF INTEREST

In the Ming Dynasty novel, *The Water Margin* also known as *Outlaws of the Marshes* (*Shui Hu Zhuan*) — supposedly written by Luo Guan Zhong — the Song Dynasty (960–1279) rebel, Song Jiang, is described as composing a poem while drinking wine in the Xun Yang Tower.

The present structure was built iin 1986. This is a low, wide, rectangular shaped wooden structure, and would be better described as a pavilion (*ting*) rather than a tower (*ta*), despite its official name.

It sits on Bin Jiang Lu facing the Yangzi River, just west of Suo Jiang Ta. The admission price is 6 Rmb, and on the back of the ticket is a detailed description of the building's story, written in Chinese.

Phone: 857-7298
Admission: 6 Rmb

Entrance to the Xun Yang Ta in Jiujiang.

Suo Jiang Pagoda (Suo Jiang Ta)

The new Yangzi waterfront sea wall and pedestrian promenade had been completed along Bin Jiang Lu as far as the **Suo Jiang Ta** in May 2003. However, the waterfront promenade in the immediate vicinity of the Suo Jiang Ta had not yet been completed, which meant the pagoda was still fenced off and closed to the public. One can only hope for the reopening of Jiujiang's oldest genuine historical relic.

This pagoda is an octagonal seven-story red brick tower built in 1585. It sits on top of a small hill known as the Jiong Long Rock on Bin Jiang Lu, facing the Yangzi River. It is within sight of the Xun Yang Ta, which stands just a few yards away to the west.

The Suo Jiang Ta pagoda on the Yangzi River waterfront at Jiujiang.

The Suo Jiang Ta pagoda with the new Jiujiang Yangzi River highway bridge behind it.

Yangzi River Bridge (Changjiang Da Qiao)

Just past the Suo Jiang Ta is the Yangzi River Bridge (Changjiang Da Qiao) which crosses the river over to Hubei province on the opposite shore. This bridge was completed in 1973 and, as such, was one of the first to cross the Yangzi after those completed earlier in Wuhan and Nanjing. It is 7,676 km (4,769.7 miles) long, and carries both road and rail traffic. It was last renovated in August 2003. If you continue down Bin Jiang Lu, you will have the bridge on your left, and a new unimpressive lake called **Bai Shui Hu** on your right, wedged between the elevated bridge onramps.

The Lute Pavilion (Pipa Ting)

Continue past the Yangzi River Bridge (Changjiang Da Qiao) on the Jiangxi side and you will come to the lake shores of Bai Shui Hu and eventually to the Lute Pavilion (Pipa Ting). The pavilion sits on the left between the river and the lake. Here, the Yangzi waterfront has been renovated with a new sea wall and promenade.

The **Pipa Ting** is pleasant looking, although unspectacular. It is supposedly a reconstruction of an earlier pavilion first built in the Tang Dynsty. The octagonal pavilion has double roof eaves. Before the pavilion stands a white marble statue of **Bai Ju Yi** (772–846 AD), famous Tang poet and former Sub-Prefect of Jiujiang from 815 to 819 AD.

Amateur Peking Opera performance outdoors in the park along Gangtang Hu in Jiujiang.

POINT OF INTEREST

Although he was governor of Jiujiang, Bai Ju Yi was, in reality, living in exile from the capital at Changan (Xian). In 816AD, during his second year in Jiujiang, Bai recorded a chance encounter on the river's edge with a talented pipa player. Like him, this woman had also been exiled to this place from the capital. The beauty of her music and the coincidence of their tragic fates caused Bai to write a lengthy poem about the experience. It was called "Song of the Lute" ("Pipa Xing"), part of which is reproduced below:

> "Xun Yang (Jiujiang) on the Yangzi, seeing off a guest at night;
> maple leaves, reed flowers, autumn somber and sad.
> The host had dismounted, the guest already aboard the boat.
> We raised our wine, prepared to drink, though we lacked flutes and strings.
> But drunkenness brought no pleasure, we grieved at the imminent parting.
> At parting time, vague and vast the river lay drenched in moonlight.
> Suddenly we heard the sound of a lute out on the water;
> The host forgot about going home, the guest failed to start on his way.
> We traced the sound, discreetly inquired who the player might be.
> The lute sounds ceased, but words were slow in coming.
> We edged our boat closer, inviting the player to join us;
> Poured more wine, turned the lamps around, began our revels again.
> A thousand pleas, ten thousand calls, and at last she appeared;
> But even then she held the lute so it half covered her face."

> "Since last year when I left the capital,
> I've lived in exile, sick in bed, in Xun Yang town (Jiujiang).
> Xun Yang (Jiujiang) is a far off region — there's no music here.
> All year long I never hear the sound of strings or woodwinds.
> I live near the Pen River, an area low and damp;
> With yellow reeds and bitter bamboo growing all around my house.
> And there, morning and evening, what do I hear?
> The cuckoo singing his heart out, the mournful cry of monkeys.
> Blossom-filled mornings by the spring river, nights with an autumn moon.
> Sometimes I fetch wine and tip the cup alone.
> To be sure, there's no lack of mountain songs and village pipes;
> But their wails and bawls, squeaks and squawks are a trial to listen to.
> Tonight, though, I've heard the words of your lute;
> Like hearing immortal music — for a moment my ears are clear.
> Do not refuse me, sit and play one more piece;
> And I'll fashion these things into a lute song for you."

Burton Watson, 1984.

The Road to Hukou

From Jiujiang, you can keep heading east to the town of Hukou. Unfortunately, east of the Lute Pavilion (Pipa Ting) is an unpleasant industrial area, forested with smoke stacks belching black clouds. The road is a maze of potholes, until one finally leaves this armpit at a toll gate, which opens up onto a new super highway.

This highway runs through open fields dotted with many old structures resembling temples or ancestral halls. Driving over a range of small foothills, Poyang Hu suddenly appears on the other side, with a new suspension bridge that has two H-shaped upright supports crossing the lake mouth (*hukou*) to the mountainous eastern shore. Many cargo ships can be seen sailing in and out of the lake here, most of them on their way to or from the provincial capital of Nanchang. Upon reaching the other shore, the highway travels through a series of two very long tunnels bored through the mountains. An off-ramp then takes you to the small town of Hukou.

Amateur musicians perform outdoors in the park along Gangtang Hu in Jiujiang.

Jiujiang Practical Information

Jiujiang Area Code: (0792)

Jiujiang Hotels
Jiujiang Binguan
Known as the best hotel in town, but also the most expensive. Located on the Nan Hu lake shore, next to the Nan Hu Binguan.

Address: 30 Nan Hu Lu
Phone: 856-0018
Fax: 856-6677
Prices: 380–500 Rmb with a 100 Rmb surcharge for foreigners

White Deer Hotel (Bai Lu Binguan)
This is a Chinese-style luxury hotel. One-day organized tours of Lushan start from here. The hotel is located on the main street away from either the river or the lakes.

Address: 133 Xun Yang Lu
Phone: 822-2818
Fax: 822-1915
Prices: 245–285 Rmb

Xun Yang Da Jiudian
This establishment has rooms facing Gangtang Hu.

Phone: 898-6333
Fax: 898-6999
Address: 118 Xun Yang Lu
Prices: Average 200 Rmb

Jiu Long Binguan

Address: 75 Lushan Lu, across from the Gangtang Hu lakeshore
Phone: 823-6779
Fax: 822-8634
Prices: 220 Rmb

Wu Zhou Fandian

Address: 86 Xun Yang Lu
Phone: 811-3796
Prices: 180–200 Rmb

Bei Gang Binguan

Address: Bin Jiang Lu
Phone: 822-5582
Prices: 180 Rmb

Kuang Lu Binguan

Address: 88 Xun Yang Lu
Phone: 822-8893
Fax: 822-1249
Prices: 150–180 Rmb

Nan Hu Binguan

Address: 28 Nan Hu Lu, on the lake shore.
Phone: 858-5042
Prices: 140–180 Rmb

Jiujiang Transportation
Air Travel
Jiujiang's old airport was closed in 1999. For several years after this, the closest airport was the new Chang Bei Feijichang outside Jiangxi's provincial capital of Nanchang, which itself opened in October 1999. However, in 2002, the first phase of the new Jiujiang Mahiuling airport was completed, allowing limited direct domestic flights to Jiujiang to begin once again.

Train Travel
Jiujiang has a train station on Da Zhong Lu, which offers direct rail links to the nearby provincial capitals of Nanchang, Wuhan, and Hefei. Jiujiang is also now the place where the new Kowloon-Beijing express train crosses the Yangzi over a new bridge. A new rail line is currently under construction which will link Jiujiang with the town of Tongling in Anhui Province when finished.

River Travel
Jiujiang Ferry Terminal
Yangzi River Ferries stop at the Port of Jiujiang Ferry Terminal on Bin Jiang Lu at its intersection with Jiao Tong Lu. Jiujiang is 752 km (470 miles) upriver from the mouth of the Yangzi.

Travel Agents
CITS (China International Travel Service)
Nan Hua Binguan, Second Floor
28 Nan Hu Lu
Phone: 858-1974

Jiangxi Province
Lushan

Historical Background

As far back as 4,000 years ago, Da Yu, the reputed founder of the Xia Dynasty, visited the mountain out of the admiration for its beautiful scenery. Other emperors such as Shi Huangdi (221–210 BC) of the Qin Dynasty and Liu Che, Emperor Wu Di (141–87 BC) of the Western Han Dynasty, supposedly set foot here.

Sima Qian (145–90 BC), historian of the Western Han Dynasty (206BC–23AD), travelled to the mountain and included a description of the trip in his book, *Historical Records (Shi Ji)*.

Although not included as one of the Four Sacred Buddhist mountains or Taoist mountains, Lushan has served as a spiritual retreat and haven for hermits and scholars belonging to various philosophies for nearly 2,000 years. At one time, there were 360 Buddhist temples and more than 200 Taoist temples on Lushan. It was here, at Dong Lin Temple, that the Pure Land school (Jing Tu Zong) of Buddhism had its origins during the Eastern Jin Dynasty in the 4th century AD. It was also here, at Bai Lu Dong, that the first Chinese university was founded. Due to the ravages of the Taiping rebellion, the Sino-Japanese War and the Cultural Revolution, only a handful of the temples which once stood here are still active today. However, one can still find the weathered, romantic ruins of thousands of former Buddhist and Taoist temples scattered throughout Lushan's forested hills. Sometimes the crumbling stone walls of a former shrine suddenly appear in the dark shadows of the trees as you hike along a mountain trail, but in other cases only the place name survives.

Before the destructive waves of first the Taiping Rebellion and then the Cultural Revolution occured, the temple bells resounded day and night in Dong Lin

Si, Xi Lin Si, and Da Lin Si, and armies of monks gathered in Gui Zong Si, Hui Hai Si, and many other temples. The mountain was populated with so many Buddhist monks, whose heads were all shaved, that it was said you would rarely see people with hair on Lushan. In 1899, Edward Selby Little wrote that when he first arrived on the summit of Lushan in 1895, "Ruined temples could be traced in all directions; there having been nearly 400 destroyed by the Taipings." According to Little, **Yellow Dragon Temple** (Huang Long Si) was the sole remaining functioning Buddhist temple on the summit at that time.

White Deer Cave Academy (Bai Lu Dong Shuyuan) was first built in the Tang Dynasty by the reclusive Confucian scholar Li Bo. It was revived in the Southern Song (Nan Song) Dynasty by the neo-Confucian philosopher **Zhu Xi**. The academy prospered and experienced renovations throughout the Southern Song, Yuan, Ming, and Qing Dynasties. Many Confucian masters came to gave their lectures here. It was the oldest, largest, and most influential Confucian Academy (Shuyuan) of imperial China, and occupies an important place in the history of Chinese education.

The natural beauty of the mountain surpasses that of Huang Shan or any other place in China. Waterfalls, some hundreds of feet high, come cascading down from the peaks into dragon pools. The mountain consists of 99 peaks, 22 waterfalls, 18 streams, and 14 lakes or ponds. Of all the peaks, Da Han Yang Feng is the highest, rising 1,474 m (4,836 ft) above sea level. It is said that on a clear night, you can see the lights of Wuhan from the top of the peak, even though the city is hundreds of miles away.

Lushan's natural wonders have been celebrated by Chinese poets and travelers for centuries. **Tao Yuan Ming** (365–427 AD), a noted poet of the Eastern Jin (Dong Jin) Dynasty (317–419 AD), once led an idyllic life on the mountain, living and farming here in seclusion. **Li Bai** (Li Tai Po) (701–762 AD) visited the mountain five times and set up a "reading house" here in which to live and study. **Bai Ju Yi** (772–846 AD) was so fascinated by the beautiful scenery of the mountain that in the 9th century, he built a thatched cottage here to view the picturesque landscape and listen to the trickling springs. **Su Dong Po** (Su Shi) (1037–1101), a famous poet of the Northern Song (Bei Song) Dynasty, drew his inspiration from Lushan's natural beauty and wrote many of his poems about it. **Zhu Xi** (1130–1200), a noted educator of the Southern Song (Nan Song) Dynasty, gave many lectures to students at the White Deer Cave Academy (Bai Lu Dong Shuyuan), expounding his ideas of neo-Confucianism. **Xu Xia Ke** (1586–1641), a famous traveler of the Ming Dynasty, reportedly climbed up to the summit of Wu Lao Feng to survey the surrounding area. All told, at least 500 famous Chinese poets, writers, scholars, and travelers have visited the mountain throughout its history and left behind them more than 4,000 poems, 400 rock inscriptions chiseled into its stone cliffs, and countless other writings, paintings, and calligraphy.

The first foreigner to visit Lushan was undoubtedly the Italian Jesuit Matteo Ricci (1552–1616), who became friends with the Confucian scholars at the White Deer Cave Academy (Bai Lu Dong Shuyuan) in 1596. Ricci aptly described Lushan as "always covered with clouds and fog," so thick that it could never be seen even from the nearby lake of Poyang Hu.

It was the summer heat of nearby Jiujiang that first prompted China's resident foreign community to construct a mountaintop retreat at Lushan in the late 19th century.

Lushan was established as a summer resort community for Westerners in 1895 under the name Kuling. Its original purpose was to provide a cool sanctuary for foreign residents of the Yangzi River treaty ports, which were all known for their intense summer heat. The town was built by an enterprising developer named Edward Selby Little. He managed to acquire the land under the pretext of a haven for Christian missionaries, who under the unequal treaties, were permitted to buy land and build houses anywhere in China. However, his true aim was the creation of a real estate development in which he sold lots and villas to any foreigner who could afford to buy one. In 1903, an Estates Council was formed as a self-governing body for the community. This council was responsible for the taxation and land sales, as well as public health and public works. The Council continued to govern Kuling until the Japanese occupation of 1937.

Although legally not a treaty port or a concession, Lushan was run just like one, with its own municipal council, police force, hospital, churches, schools, library, post office, and hotels. The town overlooks the Yangzi valley below and is not far from the former treaty port of Jiujiang. However, in the beginning it was accessible only by sedan chairs carried up a steep trail consisting of thousands of stone steps. Only recently was it connected to the outside world with a paved road.

In 1921, Kuling consisted of 500 houses, two churches, a hospital, and two boarding schools for the children of expats, one American and the other British. However, by then it had begun to become a favorite holiday resort of the rich and famous Chinese, as well as foreigners. As a result, the community experienced a dramatic expansion over the next two decades. Despite the development of Kuling during this time, there was never a road for vehicles to drive to the summit during the Min Guo period (1911–1949). When Emil S. Fischer visited Lushan in August 1935, he was able to fly into Jiujiang. After taking a bus from the city to Lianhua Dong, he had to be carried up the mountain to Kuling in a sedan chair balanced on the shoulders of four chair bearers. The climb up to the summit via "several thousands of steps," took four hours. When Commander F.H.E.

Skyrme published his travel guide to the Yangzi River in April 1937, Kuling could still only be reached from Jiujiang by a two-stage combination of motor vehicle and sedan chair.

Much of the old Kuling resort still exists today, including an estimated 1,000 historic villas built in the style of 15 different countries. Many of the original houses have become guest villas, and the old hospital has been turned into a posh new hotel. The summer homes of many historic figures, including Chiang Kai Shek (Jiang Jieshi) and Mao Zedong, are now open to public visitors. On 6 December 1996, the United Nations Educational, Scientific and Cultural Organization (UNESCO) included Lushan as one of the world's cultural treasures on the World Heritage List.

During the 20th century, China's political parties have always been attracted to Lushan as a retreat for important party meetings. In December 1926, the Guomindang held an important party conference here to mediate between its rival Wuhan and Nanjing factions. On 20 May 1927, a second Guomindang conference was held here, with the rival Wuhan and Nanjing regimes represented by Wang Jingwei and Li Zong Ren respectively. From 24 to 28 September 1930, the Third Plenum of the Chinese Communist Party (CCP) Sixth Central Committee was held on Lushan. Wang Ming (Chen Shaoyu), head of the Returned Students Clique who had spent several years in the Soviet Union, attacked the policies of the current party leader Li Li San, while Zhou En Lai played his typical role of a neutral mediator. After the Communists had successfully been driven out of Jiangxi province in 1934, Lushan became known as the Guomindang's unofficial summer capital, with many high-ranking party officials having summer homes here, and the party setting up an officers training center. Later the Communist Party also held three important party conferences on Lushan in 1959, 1961, and 1970. More details on these political events can be found on page 338 under the entry for the People's Assembly Hall (Renmin Ju Yuan).

Lushan Sights: Summit Area

The summit area within the boundaries of the national park lies in between the park's two entrances at the **North Gate** (Lushan Bei Men) and **South Gate** (Lushan Nan Men). It costs 85 Rmb to enter this area. Most of the main attractions are to be found in this area. However, a large number of famous Lushan sights are actually located outside the park boundaries on the lower slopes or at the foot of the mountain.

Northern Summit Area
Guling Town

Modern day Guling is on the same site as the original Kuling town but lacks any remaining historical atmosphere at all. The current town is a noisy, hectic place full of recently built shops, restaurants, banks, and hotels. However, by passing through the town center to the municipal park one gets a terrific view. Facing north from the city park, you see the enormous deep **Scissors Gorge** (Jiandao Xia) down below and the surrounding rocky mountain peaks above. If you turn around and face south, towards the **East Valley** (Dong Gu), you can understand how the town got its original nickname of "The Gap," as it is situated right in the saddle of a mountain pass.

Small Heavenly Pool Peak (Xiao Tian Chi Feng)

To the east of Guling Town is Small Heavenly Pool Peak (Xiao Tian Chi Feng), so named as to dinstinguish it from the Great Heavenly Pool Peak (Da Tian Chi Feng) on the southern rim of Lushan's summit.

Nuona Pagoda (Nuona Ta)

The Small Heavenly Pool Peak (Xiao Tian Chi Feng) is topped by the conical, white Buddhist stupa-shaped Nuona Pagoda (Nuona Ta). This 21-m-high (68.9-ft-high) pagoda and its adjoining temple were built in 1934, in honor of the Tibetan Buddhist monk Hutuktu Nuona, who is buried here. Nuona was the 32nd successor of the Rnying-ma-pa of Tibetan Buddhism

The Scissors Gorge filled with clouds viewed from Guling Town atop Mount Lushan.

and the 5th successor of the Yuanjue Sect. The pagoda is visible from Guling Town and can be reached by taking Shan Bei Lu towards the Lushan North Gate (Lushan Bei Men). This same site was previously the location of a 16th century Buddhist temple known as Xiao Tian Chi Si, which was erected by the Ming Emperor Wan Li. By 1921, the temple had already decayed into ruins which were then still visible.

River Viewing Pavilion (Wang Jiang Ting)
The small pavilion is situated on the precipice of Xiao Tian Chi Feng, just north of Guling Town. Despite its small size, the pavilion offers an impressive view over the immense void of the Scissor's Gorge (Jiandao Xia), with the Yangzi River visible in the distance.

Lotus Flower Valley (Lianhua Gu)
This valley was opened up for development with the construction of a road around 1920. It was then the site of a large YMCA camp, as well as the summer homes of wealthy Chinese who were not yet allowed to live inside the Kuling Estates area.

The **Green Dragon Pool** (Bi Long Tan), also called the **Wang Jia Po** twin waterfall, lies deep in the seldom visited Lianhua Valley near the Lushan North Gate (Lushan Bei Men). The rushing twin waterfalls are wonderful and the green pool is lovely. Wang Jia Po gets its name after the home of the Wang family who once lived here.

Big Forest Peak (Da Lin Feng)
To the west of Guling is Big Forest Peak (Da Lin Feng), the site of **Fairy Glen** (Xianren Wu) and an old Chinese cemetery. At an elevation of 1,005.8 m (3,300 ft), Da Lin Feng is famous for its spectacular view in all directions. From here, a foot trail begins its long descent to the **Dong Lin Valley** (Dong Lin Gu) towards Dong Lin Temple (Dong Lin Si), which is actually located at the northwestern foot of the mountain.

Old Western villa in the Mount Lushan summit area.

From Guling town, two main valleys branch off to the South. The East Valley (Dong Gu) descends down He Dong Lu and He Xi Lu to Lulin Hu and features most of the old historic villas. West Valley (Xi Gu) descends down Da Lin Lu to Ruqin Hu. Da Lin Lu and Da Lin Feng are both named after the Buddhist **Big Forest Temple** (Da Lin Si), which once stood in the West Valley. When Bai Ju Yi visited Da Lin Si in 818AD, after having climbed up **Big Forest Peak** (Da

Old Western villa in the Mount Lushan summit area.

Lin Feng), he reported that the "mountain temple" was no more than "a log hut," although it was inhabited by monks who had come from all over China. Bai discovered that he was the first non-monastic visitor to the temple since the Confucian scholar and former governor of Jiujiang, Li Bo (773–831 AD) visited 20 years earlier, showing just how isolated the summit area was then. Although the temple had long since disappeared, the First Conference of the World Buddhist Federation was held at the site of the Da Lin Temple ruins on Lushan, hosted by the Chinese Buddhist monk **Tai Xu**, from 13–15 July 1924.

Russian Valley (Lulin Gu)
The Lulin Hotel (Lulin Binguan)

This is a fascinating place in a quiet isolated part of the mountain, far from the hustle and bustle of Guling town, but strategically situated near many of the key sights to see. It is surrounded by thickly forested hills on all sides, with a view of the Lulin Hu from the third floor. There are no other shops, restaurants, hotels, or large buildings nearby, but the hotel itself offers a fine restaurant, store, and even a KTV bar. The hotel

The Lulin Hotel in the former Russian Valley, an area that is now mostly flooded by Lulin Hu.

is a genuine artifact of the colonial era. It consists of three floors with outer walls built entirely of stone blocks which are a foot thick. It has also stone arched windows, wooden floors, and a tin-covered sloped roof. It almost feels as if you are staying in a medieval European castle fortress.

It has two towers on either end, which extend out from the main body of the structure, giving you windows with views in three different directions. In addition to the main building, the hotel has two other similar buildings, giving a total of 150 rooms or 300 beds.

Fog shrouds some of the hill tops from view, and rain falls in intermittent torrents making a relaxing sound. For the most part, the hotel seems like an earthly paradise, except on Chinese national holidays, such as May 1st, when hoards of people rampage through.

Top: Forested hills around the Lulin Hotel in the former Russian Valley.
Above: The historic Lulin Hotel in the former Russian Valley.

Mao Zedong's Villa (Mao Zedong Bieshu)

The Lushan Museum (Lushan Bowuguan) is just up the road along the shore of Lulin Hu. This building was originally built in 1960 and served as Mao Zedong's private villa during the Communist Party conferences held on Lushan in 1961 and 1970. It is a one-story structure which is spread out over a large area with a courtyard in the center, giving it four separate wings. One room is still equipped with Mao's original furniture, including a gigantic bed, a gigantic office desk the width of two normal ones, and two doors allowing for secret entrances or emergency

Entrance gate to Mao Zedong's former villa on Mount Lushan, now the Lushan Museum.

escapes. Both doors are heavily padded on each side with stuffed leather cushions, soundproofing the room from any eavesdropping.

There is one room dedicated to black and white photos of Lushan's ancient historical sights, such as temples. Another is dedicated to photos of its colonial era villas, and a third to the Communist Party conferences which took place there in 1959, 1961, and 1970.

Phone: 828-2341

Lulin Hu now fills most of the former Russian Valley. A road crosses the reservoir dam.

Lulin Lake (Lulin Hu)

Walking around the other side of Lulin Hu, you cross what at first seems to be just a normal bridge, but turns out to be the top of a dam built in 1955. On the left side is the lake, but on the right side is a deep valley, the remaining lower half of Lulin Gu. Lulin Hu is, in fact, an artificial reservoir created in 1955. This was the time when the dam flooded the original head, located southeast of the East Valley (Dong Gu). In the colonial days, this head was known as the Russian Valley, but the Chinese have always referred to is as Lulin Gu. At the south end of the dam is a very steep set of stone steps leading down to the floor of the remaining unflooded portion of the valley below.

Lulin Hu and the unflooded portions of the former Russian Valley.

Han Po Pass (Han Po Kou)

It is possible to hike up to Han Po Pass from Lulin Hu by following a steeply inclined paved road which passes the gate marking the turnoff to the **Botanical Gardens** (Zhiwu Yuan). This continues up a final sharp ascent to the parking lot. Han Po Kou lies 1,210 m (3969.8 ft) above sea level, in the middle of the Han Po Ling ridge in the southeast part of Mount Lushan, with the peaks of Wu Lao Feng to the north and Jiu Qi Feng to the south. From Han Po Kou, it is possible to enjoy the scenes of the neighboring mountain peaks and Poyang Lake, as well as a beautiful sunrise if you can get there early enough. Unfortunately, the area directly in front of the trademark three-arch brick gateway tends to be full of people spilling out of tour buses that it is difficult to get a good view.

Heading back down to Lulin Hu on foot, one is in constant danger of being run over by the horn-honking flood of vehicles choking the entire width of the road. The only alternative is to join the vehicular crowd by becoming a bus passenger yourself. However, by doing so, you miss the hiker's ground-level perspective.

East Valley (Dong Gu)

This valley is where most of the oldest villas, hotels, and other historic 20th century sights are located. It was originally known as Kuling Valley or Cow Valley, and was the first part of Lushan to have foreign settlers during the colonial era. In later years, as Russian Valley and West Valley were developed, the East Valley continued to be considered the most prestigious location to live, and residents of the other valleys were looked down upon as low-class newcomers.

Left: A rushing stream flows through the East Valley (Dong Gu) of the Mount Lushan summit area.
Right: The East Valley (Dong Gu) of the Mount Lushan summit area is criss-crossed by a network of stone-paved pedestrian lanes.

Kuling American School (Villa No. 381)

The school was founded in 1916 with the aim of providing the children of missionaries and expatriate businessmen with an American curriculum. The old Kuling American School is now the Yee Yuan Guest House and has been designated as Villa No. 381. The large building is fairly unremarkable looking on the inside where it resembles a dormitory. Its outside stone façade resembles an Oxford college. It is located down on the floor of the East Valley, near a rushing stream, well below the Huan Shan highway.

Phone: 828-3647, 828-1964

This page: The former Kuling American School, now open to the public as a hotel.

The People's Assembly Hall (Renmin Ju Yuan)

Just a short walk up the valley floor from the old Kuling American School is the People's Assembly Hall (Renmin Ju Yuan). This was where important Communist Party congresses, conferences, and central committee meetings were held in 1959, 1961, and 1970. At the 2–16 August 1959 **Lushan Conference** of the Communist Party's Eighth Central Committee, moderates led by Liu Shaoqi and Deng Xiaoping scored a major victory against Mao Zedong's ultra-leftist economic policies and cultural intolerance. Liu Shaoqi, who had replaced Mao as Chairman of the People's Republic of China in December 1958, blamed the predecessor for the "man-made problems" of the 1958 Great Leap Forward. Mao was forced to publicly accept the blame for his mistakes and after the conference was over, he went into early retirement as an honorary but powerless figurehead. Although Mao scored one small victory by having the moderate Defense Minister Peng De Huai replaced with his ally Lin Biao, the 1959 Lushan Conference ushered in a five-year period of relative stability and moderation in all fields, including culture and economics, before Mao returned from retirement and launched the 1966–1976 Cultural Revolution. Eleven years later, the Second Plenum of the Ninth Central Committee was also held here from 6–23 September 1970.

The hall is reached by crossing a bridge over a small rushing stream. The building is now open to visitors and seems to be popular with Chinese tourists, as the parking lot out front is packed with vehicles. Despite the important party decisions made there, the interior is fairly unimpressive, resembling a high school auditorium. Nonetheless, it was the site of some historic events in modern Chinese political history. Although it seems more Communist in style, according to some sources the meeting hall was formerly a theater built during the Guomindang era, when other nearby buildings were used as a military officers training academy.

Phone: 828-2584

The People's Assembly Hall (Renmin Ju Yuan) on Mount Lushan.

Guomindang Party Institute (Lushan Dasha)

Right beside the People's Assembly Hall is a row of slightly older buildings that played an important role in the history of their political rival, the Guomindang or Nationalists. This complex includes a row of three connected two-story stone block buildings with traditional upturned eave roofs, balustrade-lined steps, and plazas. Beside these traditional looking buildings is a three-story yellow concrete structure at the top of a long flight of wide steps. This complex of buildings was built in 1934 as the Guomindang Central Committee Party Institute with the main function of training Guomindang military officers. It was the site of an important 16 July 1937 Guomindang Party Conference at which Chiang Kai Shek (Jiang Jieshi) gave his first public speech in favor of national defense against the Japanese invasion, which had just started with the Marco Polo bridge incident in Beijing a few days earlier. Photos of this speech, showing Chiang (Jiang) striking a defiant pose in military uniform in front of a radio microphone with his fist raised in the air, are on display at Mei Lu Bieshu. After 1949, the Guomindang Party Institute was renamed The Lushan Mansion (Lushan Dasha). Since 1983, it has functioned as a two-star hotel and restaurant.

Former Guomindang party training center beside the Renmin Ju Yuan.

Sign on the Lushan Mansion (Lushan Dasha).

The Lushan Mansion (Lushan Dasha), former Guomindang military officers school.

Sitting at this spot, it is striking how each new Chinese regime in history has sought political legitimacy by building its government and political party structures either right beside or even on top of those of the previous regime which they overthrew. Chiang Kai Shek (Jiang Jieshi) put the Guomindang's central government headquarters in Nanjing right in the same compound as the Ming, Qing, and Taiping Tian Guo rulers had done before. Later the Communist Party put its provincial party headquarters in the exact same place, now known as the Tushuo Zongtongfu. The Lushan Guomindang Party Institute was obviously considered to be a war trophy of sorts, as it was chosen as the site for the Communist Party's conference hall. Even today the spot is heavily patrolled by teams of

Zhu De's former villa on Mount Lushan.

The former Church of the Ascension (Sheng Gong Hui) in the Mount Lushan summit area.

Steps leading up to Zhu De's former villa on Mount Lushan.

blue-uniformed military guards and party secret police in plain clothes.

Zhu De Villa (Villa No. 359)

Back on the main highway, just above Lushan Dasha and Renmin Ju Yuan, Villa No. 359 is located at No. 8 Middle Road (Zhong Lu). This lovely two-story stone block villa has had a fascinating series of occupants illustrating the waves of change during China's 20th century history. It was first built in 1902 by an American, Reverend John Elias Williams, at a time when Guling was mainly a foreign Christian missionary community. In 1932, it was bought by **Xiong Shi Hui**, who was then the Guomindang Party Chairman for Jiangxi province. During the era of Guomindang political rule, Chiang Kai Shek (Jiang Jieshi) held several meetings in this house. Later, after the 1949 revolution, the same villa served as the home of Red Army founder **Zhu De**, who lived there during the Communist Party's Lushan conferences of 1959 and 1961. A large collection of old black and white photos of Zhu De visiting the sights on Lushan are displayed on the walls of both floors of the villa. Among these photos are one of him visiting Xianren Dong (Immortal's Cavern) and another at Nuona Pagoda. The villa is now used as a luxury hotel, and the large suites are all furnished with a private jacuzzi and sauna as well as beds with telephones built into the headboards.

The Church of the Ascension (Sheng Gong Hui)

Off the main highway is Middle Two Road (Zhong Er Lu), which was called "Central Avenue" in colonial days. Along this road are a string of historic buildings. The first is the Church of the Ascension, now known as Villa No. 283 and renamed the "Sheng Gong Hui." This Gothic style stone church was built in 1910 by American missionaries. During the 1959 Communist Party conference, the church was turned into a "dancing hall," and visited by the likes of Mao Zedong and Liu Shaoqi. Today, the inside houses a tacky souvenir shop and faux museum.

Lushan Library (Lushan Tushuguan)

The Kuling Estates Library once stood in a stone walled, one-story building on Middle Two Road (Zhong Er Lu), just north of the Church of the Ascension. Before, it was clearly labeled with a stone inscription in the wall over the front entrance, which read in English, "Kuling Library." As one of the main Western residential communities in China before 1949, Kuling had an immense library of English language publications. Many of these were rare studies of Chinese history, geography, religion, and politics published in China by resident foreign-owned publishing companies that no longer exist. Amazingly enough, the old Kuling Library's valuable collection initially survived the 1949 revolution intact. When the collection was absorbed into the new Jiangxi Provincial Library system in 1949, it numbered over 60,000 volumes. In 1964, the Jiangxi Provincial Library published a catalog of 31,126 of the titles, the remainder being excluded for unspecified reasons. The titles ranged in date of publication from as early as 1853 and as late as 1947. However, the fate of the collection since the 1966–1976 Cultural Revolution is unclear.

The Kuling Hotel (Villa No. 246)

Farther uphill along Middle Two Road (Zhong Er Lu) is a derelict old building which is still labeled the "Kuling Hotel" in faded painted English letters using the old spelling for the town's name. The fact that it is spelled this way shows that this is probably the original sign dating from the colonial era. Back then, this was the five-star place to stay. Today, it is terribly run down, although still open to guests as the **Dong Guo Binguan**. It still has a small stone pavilion in its front yard. Inside the main lobby is a framed, water-stained Chinese language document describing the original Kuling Hotel's history. Sadly, the current staff know nothing about it.

Phone: 828-5073

The historic Kuling Hotel, amazingly still open for business, but a bit worse for wear.

The Lushan Hotel (Lushan Dajiudian)

Formerly known as Dr. Barrie's Hospital, the now luxurious and expensive Lushan Hotel is a few yards up the road from the Kuling Hotel. It is located where the Middle Two Road (Zhong Er Lu) rejoins the main highway, now designated as He Xi Lu. This is the same intersection where He Dong Lu (East He Road) also begins, separated from He Xi Lu (West He Road) by a small rushing stream in between. Along the stream is a nice, green, forested parkland. Several old stone footbridges cross the stream, one of them dated as having been built in 1918.

Chiang Kai Shek's Villa (Mei Lu Bieshu)

Following He Dong Lu along the east side of the stream, you encounter a whole string of old colonial villas, including most importantly **Mei Lu Villa** (Mei Lu Bieshu). This is the former summer home of Chiang Kai Shek (Jiang Jieshi) and his wife Song Meiling, which you can enter for a 15 Rmb ticket. Mei Lu Villa was built in 1903 by Lord S.O. Reynolds and acquired by Song Meiling in 1933. It served as the couple's summer home from 1934 to 1949, during which Chiang (Jiang) stayed here more than twenty times. The two-story stone and wood house sits on a sloping hillside inside a large walled and gated compound. A large stone in the front yard is inscribed with the two Chinese characters for "Mei Lu," which were supposedly written by Chiang (Jiang) himself.

Mei Lu Villa (Mei Lu Bieshu), the former vacation home of Chiang Kai Shek (Jiang Jieshi).

Inside, the walls of the house are decorated with a large collection of fascinating old black and white photos of Chiang Kai Shek (Jiang Jieshi). Many of the photos seem to be unique to this exhibit, as they are not displayed at either of his former residences in Nanjing or Chongqing. The photos are clear original copies. However, no photography is allowed inside, nor are any good copies of these unique pictures available for sale in the souvenir shop. This photo collection is even more amazing for the favorable image it presents of Chiang (Jiang). It shows him dressed as a Mandarin scholar studying books, happily playing chess with his wife, giving rousing anti-Japanese speeches in favor of national defense, and heroically leading the war effort against the Japanese invasion.

After the 1949 revolution, Mei Lu Bieshu was treated as a war trophy, just like the Guomindang Party Institute. Even though there was nothing really outstanding about the house, the mere fact it had previously been the home of Chiang Kai Shek (Jiang Jieshi) made Mao Zedong choose it as his residence during the Communist Party's Lushan Conferences of 1959 and 1961, until his new much larger villa down on the shores of Lulin Hu was completed. This later became the residence of Mao's wife, Jiang Qing, during the Communist Party's Lushan Conference of 1970. There is a well-stocked souvenir shop on the way out of the house which offers books and VCDs unavailable elsewhere.

Phone: 828-1855

Another view of Mei Lu Villa (Mei Lu Bieshu), the former vacation home of Chiang Kai Shek (Jiang Jieshi).

West Valley (Xi Gu)

Following Da Lin Lu downhill from Guling Town, it becomes apparent that there are far fewer old villas in this valley compared to Dong Gu. There are also more modern-day shops and residents. On the left side of the road, you will pass an enormous three-story rectangular stone structure in an abandoned condition. It has the year, "1922," inscribed on it but there is no name or sign designating what it once was or is today.

Zhi Pu Hotel (Zhi Pu Binguan)

Near the bottom of the hillside on your right is an original stone gate marking the entrance to the modern-day Zhi Pu Hotel. On one gatepost is inscribed the information, "1929, Lot 24, West Valley." However, up the hillside, behind the first modern building is the original Zhi Pu Hotel structure, which may have originally had a different name. This 1929 structure is quite impressive, with half oval casement windows, wood paneled interior walls, wood-carved staircase balustrades. The interior was redecorated in May 2002. The hotel's terrace has an attractive view of the valley. From here, a flight of stone steps lead down to the Ruqin Hu lakeshore below.

The historic Zhi Pu Hotel on Mount Lushan, recently redecorated and reopened for business.

Ruqin Lake (Ruqin Hu)

Continue down the main road of Da Lin Lu, pass the modern Ruqin Hu Hotel on the left before reaching the mouth of Ruqin Lake.

This page: Two historic stone villas with their foundations now submerged by the rising waters of the man-made reservoir Ru Qin Hu. The former wealthy tenants have been replaced by several families of local peasants in each house.

At this point, the paved road continues along the eastern shore of the lake, passing by many modern-day resort buildings on its way to the disappointing Hua Jing Park and the Flower Path at the opposite end of the lake.

A much better choice is to turn right at this juncture and follow a dirt trail through some wetlands and around the western shore of the lake. Standing in the wetlands, you get an excellent view of three old stone villas standing right on the lake shore, one to the right and two to the left. The two on the left are the most impressive and can be approached by following the western shore trail.

Passing by the foot of the stone steps leading up to the Zhi Pu Hotel, you come to the first two-story stone villa, which seems abandoned. Continue and you will reach the second and more impressive one. This second two-story stone villa was built on top of stone arches placed right in the water so that the house stands as if on stilts over the lake itself. The first floor has no rooms and serves only to support the second floor, which is reached via a gangway connecting to it from the hillside. A Chinese peasant family is now living inside the second floor and they are, unfortunately, not too welcoming of visitors snooping around the interior.

Hua Jing Park

The main attraction in Hua Jing Park is the replica of Bai Ju Yi's thatched cottage. The cottage originally stood at

Ru Qin Lu crosses the Ru Qin Hu reservoir dam, below which is the Jing Xiu Gu valley.

The entrance gate to Hua Jing Park near Ru Qin Hu on Mount Lushan.

the northwest foot of Mount Lushan, between Xi Lin Si and Dong Lin Si, below Da Lin Feng. It was first built by Bai Ju Yi in 816AD when he was serving a four-year term as governor of Jiujiang.

In 1986, the cottage was moved to or rebuilt at its present location on the Flower Path in Hua Jing Park. Its architectural style is supposedly the same as the former cottage. Built of wood with a grass roof, it has two rooms and four windows, and faces south. In front of the cottage stands a 20 m (65.6 ft) stone statue of Bai Ju Yi.

Brocade Valley (Jingxiu Gu)

Continue around the western shore of the lake, and the trail eventually connects with the main north-south highway, called Ruqin Lu at this portion. The highway crosses what seems to be a bridge over the lake, but is in fact a reservoir dam. The lake on the left side is an artificial man-made creation. On the right side, a giant chasm opens up into the Brocade Valley (Jingxiu Gu). A extremely steep flight of stone steps leads down from the dam to the Heavenly Bridge. This trail continues to wind a long distance and finally reaches the ancient Taoist shrine inside Immortals' Cavern (Xianren Dong).

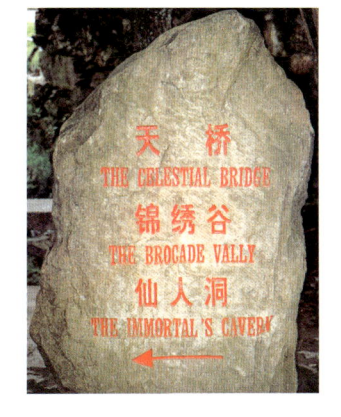

An inscribed stone points the way to the trail down the Jing Xiu Gu valley.

Heavenly Bridge (Tian Qiao)

Tian Qiao is a finger of stone which extends far out over the Jing Xiu Valley just below the Ruqin Lake reservoir dam bridge. From this bridge, you can often see people standing precariously on the rock ledge suspended in mid-air over the deep chasm. Although the rock formation does not cross the canyon all the way to the other side, it does extend out quite far, and is said to resemble the remains of a broken bridge. According to a popular legend, the first Ming Emperor **Zhu Yuanzhang** was able to use the Tian Qiao to escape from a persuing Yuan Dynasty general. The bridge still connected to the other side when Zhu crossed it, but as soon as he reached safety, half the bridge was destroyed by a thunderbolt, thus preventing his pursuers from capturing him.

Immortals' Cavern (Xianren Dong)

This can be reached most easily by continuing to follow the highway down the southern side of the mountain from Ruqin Lake, until you reach the Xianren Dong parking lot. To the right is the trail leading to the Ming Dynasty Imperial Tablet Pavilion (Yu Bei Ting), Immortals' Cavern (Xianren Dong), and Tai Sheng Lao Jun Taoist Temple (Lao Jun Dao Guan), all of which are just a short walk away, albeit over a dangerous trail of stone steps that drops off into empty space with no guard rails. A second trail at the far end of the Xianren Dong parking lot leads down to the Great Heavenly Pool (Da Tian Chi) Scenic Region.

The natural stone cave Xianren Dong is also sometimes known by the less respectful and somewhat mocking name of "Fairy Cave". According to legend, the Taoist monk **Lu Dongbin** lived in this cave during the Tang Dynasty and later became an immortal, hence the name of the cavern. Inside the cave, there is a spring called **One Drop Spring** (Yi Di Quan). Carved on the cave wall beside the spring are inscriptions such as, "Heavenly Spring Cave," and "Sweet Spring in Immortal's Cave." In the middle of the back wall stands a stone shrine named **Chun Yang Palace** (Chun Yang Gong), which is devoted to the worship of Lu Dongbin. Natural sunlight streams into the cave through its wide mouth. Taoist monks inhabited this place until 1949, and it was then a scene of active worship and ritual. John J. Espey recorded a visit there when he was a student at the Kuling American School. Just outside the cave is the **Lao Jun Taoist Temple** (Lao Jun Dao Guan).

Brave visitors stand on the Heavenly Bridge (Tian Qiao), which hangs out in mid-air over the deep Jing Xiu Gu valley below.

Nearby is the **Cliff of Buddha's Hand** (Fo Shou Yan), which is inscribed with those three characters. The presence of this inscription, together with another on the cave wall which reads "Zhu Lin Si" meaning **"Buddhist Temple of the Bamboo Grove"**, seems to imply that this was, a one time, a Buddhist religious site as well as a Taoist one. The inscription on the stele inside the nearby Yu Bei Ting would seem to date the Buddhist temple to the beginning of the Ming Dynasty. This means that the two temples either coexisted or the Taoist one was set up later, even though the story of its patron saint dates back earlier to the Tang Dynasty.

Imperial Tablet Pavilion (Yu Bei Ting)

This small, square, stone-walled pavilion with a tiled roof of upturned eaves was built by **Zhu Yuanzhang**, the first emperor of the Ming Dynasty, in 1394 during the 26th year of his reign. It stands on the Sheng Xian Tai (Immortalizing Terrace), beside the Xianren Dong, and was renovated in 1917. Doors open on three sides, but the north side is kept closed due to a myth that Jiujiang will be destroyed if that side of the pavilion is ever opened. Housed inside the pavilion is a stone stele inscribed with the biography of **Zhou Dian**, a native of Nanchang whom Zhu Yuanzhang had encountered many times, always under bizarre circumstances. The lengthy inscription of 2,340 characters was written by the emperor himself, recording his respect for Zhou Dian. During most of his lifetime, Zhou was considered to be an insane madman, and Zhu Yuanzhang actually tried to have him executed on numerous times. Eventually, the emperor recognized him as a true prophet.

Legend has it that once the Zhu Yuanzhang realized the truth of Zhou's prophecies, he travelled to Lushan and visited him at Xianren Dong where the latter was then living. At that time Xianren Dong was known as the **Buddhist Temple of the Bamboo Grove** (Zhu Lin Si), and an inscription bearing this name is still engraved in the stone cliff face of the cave, giving some credence to the story. Western visitors reported having seen this inscription in 1921, at which time it appeared quite old, so it is by no means a new invention.

One of the 99 mountain peaks of the Mount Lushan range.

Great Heavenly Pool Peak (Da Tian Chi Feng)

The Great Heavenly Pool Scenic Region is situated on a ridge protruding from Great Heavenly Pool Peak (Da Tian Chi Feng). The latter should not be confused with the Small Heavenly Pool Peak (Xiao Tian Chi Feng) which is located on the northern summit of the mountain.

The Great Heavenly Pool Scenic Region can be reached by car or by hiking down a fairly easy

Map labels:
- Circular Buddha Hall
- Great Heavenly Pool Pagoda
- Manjusri Terrace
- Great Heavenly Pool
- Dragon Head Precipice
- Stone Gate Valley

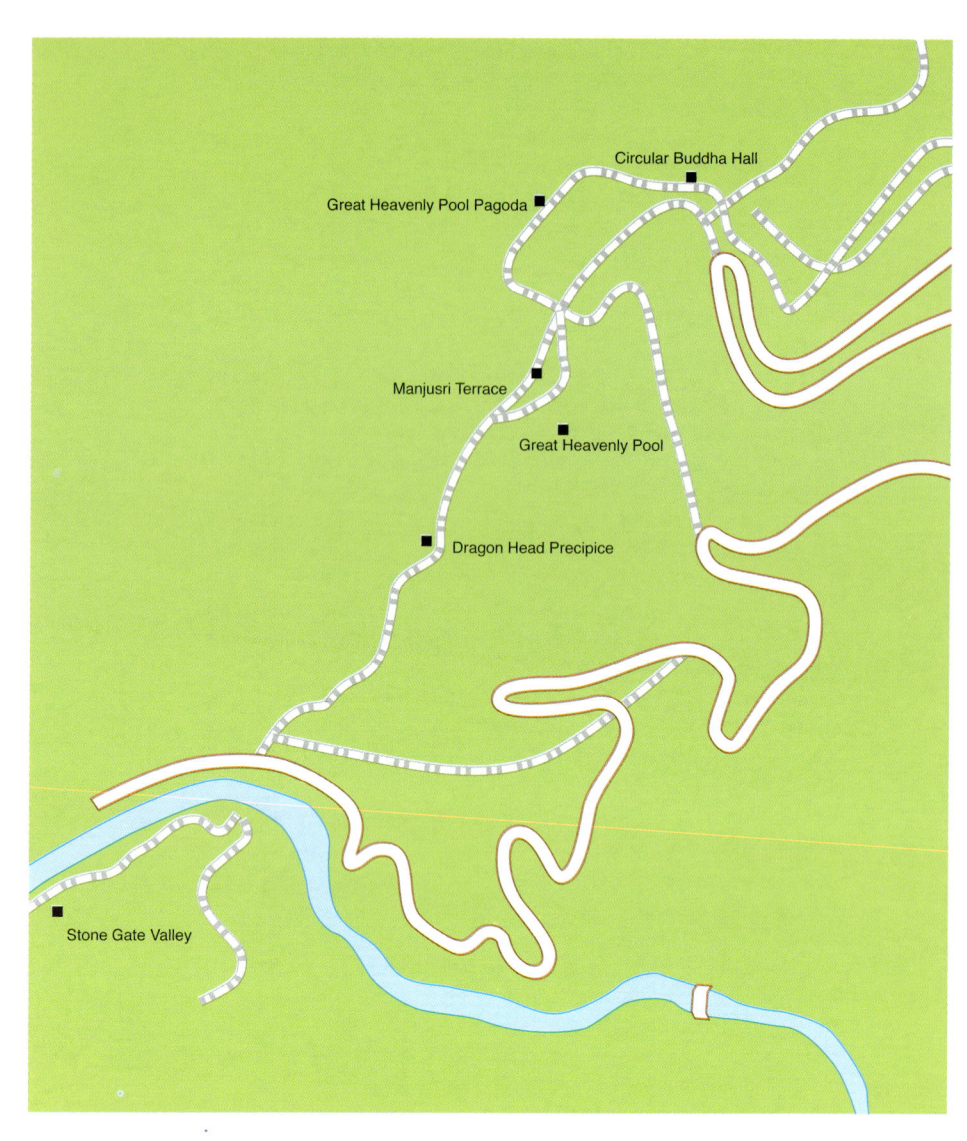

Great Heavenly Pool Scenic Region

trail from the Xianren Dong parking lot, along a forested ridge, past a two-story ancient stone watch tower.

From the parking lot, two trails follow different paths along the ridge. The newer trail is much easier to follow but it is, of course, much more crowded with tour groups. Moreover, the new trail bypasses several of the older and more interesting sights which can only be reached by taking the original trail.

This area features a fascinating network of historic sights, as well as spectacular views of the surrounding mountain peaks. This area was once the location of a Buddhist temple complex spread out over a fairly wide mountainous terrain.

High mountain peaks of the Mount Lushan range, with cloud filled valleys below.

The Circular Buddha Hall (Yuan Fo Dian)

The old trail, seemingly ignored by most modern-day visitors, leads to the Circular Buddha Hall (Yuan Fo Dian). The site offers heart-stopping views of the rock cliffs and mountain peaks of the Brocade Valley (Jinxui Gu). The hall sits on a promontory, which drops off into a 762 m (2,500 ft) chasm on one side with no handrails to prevent a nasty fall. This is a two-story stone structure, which is completely round and has a conical roof that comes to a point in the center. The building was originally named the Five Buddha Garden (Wu Fo Yuan) because each of its five entrances had a Buddha image, none of which remain today. The building is closed and abandoned now, with no monks in attendance, but it is fascinating to look at from the outside. It has a three character sign over the main entrance labeling it as the "Yuan Fo Dian." The round shape of the structure is quite unusual for a Buddhist building, and possibly unique. On one side of the hall is a curious square drinking well with small gold fish swimming in it.

Entrance to the Circular Buddha Hall (Yuan Fo Dian) on Mount Lushan.

According to an inscription on a stone tablet lying on the ground nearby, the Yuan Fo Dian was built in 1933 by **Tang Shengzhi** (1889–1970) for his mother, who was a devout Buddhist.

The Circular Buddha Hall (Yuan Fo Dian) on Mount Lushan.

The Great Heavenly Pool Pagoda (Da Tian Chi Ta)

Continuing from the Yuan Fu Dian, the old trail drops down a flight of steps and then ascends up another flight of steps up a second hill on the ridge of the Tian Chi Peak, at the top of which is the Great Heavenly Pool Pagoda (Da Tian Chi Ta). The 20-m (65.6-ft) stone pagoda has five stories and six sides. It supposedly dates from the Song Dynasty (960–1279), when it

PERSONALITIES

Tang Shengzhi, who also rebuilt the Da Tian Chi Ta, played an important role in the Northern Expedition (Bei Fa) of 1926–1927 as a Guomindang military commander. Subsequently, he held high level military posts in Nanjing throughout the 1930s. Tang had been a Hunan province warlord allied with Wu Pei Fu before he joined the Northern Expedition on 2 June 1926 and was placed in command of the Nationalists Fourth Army Group. He was responsible for the Guomindang's capture of the key cities of Changsha and Wuhan. However, having mistakenly aligned himself with the left-Guomindang regime in Wuhan, Tang was forced into early retirement in 1927 after the victory of the party's right wing led by Chiang Kai Shek (Jiang Jieshi). However, by 1929, Tang was recalled by Chiang (Jiang) to help recapture the Wuhan area from the Guangxi Clique generals, Bai Chongxi and Li Zong Ren.

After gaining this victory in support of Chiang's (Jiang's) leadership, Tang was rewarded with a series of high level posts at the national capital in Nanjing. From 1931 to 1935, Tang served simultaneously as Chairman of the Military Council and Inspector General of Military Training. On 12 November 1937, Tang was placed in command of the 100,000-man army defending Nanjing against the invading Japanese, but fled the city just before its fall on 13 December. Tang resurfaced in a prominent role for the last time in July 1949, when he handed over Hunan province to the Communists without a fight.

was built by Prime Minister Han Fuzhou in 1127–1130, and bears an inscription that it was visited by a high official in the year 1527. It was partly destroyed during the Taiping Rebellion (1850–1864), during which the top part collapsed. Visitors in 1921 described it as being "ruined" and called it the "Broken Pagoda." However, it was rebuilt by Tang Shengzhi (1889-1970) in 1927 and is now in perfect condition. It can be seen even from a long distance away, the top of the pagoda emerging from the trees. However, the section of the trail leading up to the hilltop where it stands is quite dangerous as the edge drops off into a 762 m (2,500 ft) chasm.

Dragon Fish Pool (Long Yu Tan)
After reaching the pagoda, the old trail drops down again and briefly rejoins the new trail. At this junction, an older side trail turns right and leads to an ancient rectangular stone pool full of live gold fish. The site is surrounded by a stone wall with an iron gate. According to modern day signs, this pool is known as the Dragon Fish Pool (Long Yu Tan). However an older inscription chiseled into the stone gate of the wall surrounding the wall says "Yun Shan Guan" meaning Cloud Mountain House.

Lao Mu Qin Ting
Somewhere in between the pagoda and the temple there was once a small stone pavilion known as the **Lao Mu Qin Ting** at a spot known as **Qing Liang Yan**. It was still there when visitors saw it in 1921, noting that it had recently been restored and that it bore an inscription dating from the year 1522 of the Jia Jing reign of the Ming Dynasty.

Left: Stone gate for the trail from Tian Xin Tai down to Long Shou Yan.
Right: The Dragon Fish Pool (Long Yu Tan).

Great Heavenly Pool Temple (Da Tian Chi Si)

Back at the junction, the new trail travels around the eastern slope of a third hill, past some new buildings, while the old trail heads up a flight of steps to the top of this third promontory. Passing through an ancient stone gate, the top block of which is inscribed with the three characters for "Tian Chi Si," you enter the former grounds of the Great Heavenly Pool Temple (Da Tian Chi Si). This temple was supposedly founded by the monk **Hui Chi** during the Eastern Jin (Dong Jin) Dynasty (317–419 AD), and was later expanded and restored by a succession of emperors. The first Ming emperor Zhu Yuanzhang (1368–1398) gave it the name Tian Chi Hu Guo Temple. Later the Yongle emperor, Ming Cheng Zu (1403–1424) changed the name to Tian Chi Wan Shou Temple. The restoration of 1432 by the Xuan De emperor (1426–1435) was the last one, although the Tai Chang emperor, Ming Guang Zong, (1620) had just enough time in his brief reign to change the temple's name once again to Tian Chi Miao Ji Temple. In 1921, visitors described the temple as already being in a "dilapidated" and "feeble" condition, although it still had two stone lions. Any remaining original temple buildings were destroyed by the Japanese during World War II. A few authentic relics remain, but virtually all the standing structures are post-WWII reconstructions.

What you find today is a small one-story single hall modern day replica of the original temple, inside of which is now a tacky souvenir shop. There are no monks in attendance and no actual worshipping or ceremonies. It is not a functioning temple in any sense nowadays. Even the sign on the outside of the building bears the five character inscription for Old Address of Heavenly Pool Temple (Tian Chi Si Jiu Zhi).

The Manjusri Terrace (Wen Shu Tai).

Upon closer inspection, the site does reveal itself to be the original location of a real temple. Ancient flagstones with surfaces worn down smooth by generations of pilgrims' feet line the plaza out in front of the current temple hall. An ancient stone bridge approaching the temple hall crosses over a rectangular water pool. Looking from either the left or right angle, some original decorations are visible on the sides of the stone bridge's arches, and a few ancient inscriptions can be found carved into the bridge's surface, including the two characters for Lushan.

Manjusri Terrace (Wenshu Tai)
A short distance away from the temple hall is a one-story rectangular stone building with three arched doorways and a viewing platform up on its roof. The platform above is now known as the Manjusri Terrace (Wenshu Tai), the historic name for this spot. The building itself is neither new nor ancient, and appears to be a Min Guo era construction. Inside the ground floor is the **Lushan Tian Chi Cha Chang**, a tea house serving genuine Lushan Cloud Tea made from freshly picked and roasted leaves.

Despite the shortage of genuine historic relics, this promontory is well worth a visit for its incredible views of the surrounding mountain peaks and valleys in three directions. A sea of white clouds is visible in the valley below.

To the west of the former site of Tian Chi Temple there is a square stone terrace called the **Tian Xin Tai**, which means that it is a place for watching the sky. It was built by Lin Sen, the former President of the Guomindang government in the 1930s.

Dragon Head Precipice (Long Shou Yan)
From near the Da Tian Chi Si, you can find two more stone gates with trails leading down the mountain. The main trail to your right leads to **Dragon Head Precipice** (Long Shou Yan). Along the way it passes the Manjusri Cave (Wenshu Dong). The cave apparently has a history going back to the year 841 AD of the Tang Dynasty and in 1921, it was still being inhabited by resident Buddhist monks. The trail then continues its steep descent to the **Stone Gate Valley** (Shi Men Jian Gu) and its newly built suspension bridge, which stretches across the valley. Be careful because the trail down consists of very steep stone steps.

Stone Gate Valley (Shi Men Jian Gu)
This valley can also be reached by an easy walk down the main highway from the Heavenly Pool parking lot to the turnoff onto a narrow one-lane road called Shen Long Gong Lu. This road is named after a temple that once was there but is now long gone. It was a "Pusa Miao," meaning a Buddhist temple, according to one local old lady, but no visible traces of it could be found after a search of the area. The temple had already disappeared when

visitors passed through the area in 1921, but they recorded seeing a stone inscription at the site which read, "Palace of the Divine Dragon Named by Wenshu," (Wenshu Shuo Fa Shen Long Chih Gong). Wenshu is the Chinese name for the Buddhist deity Manjusri, but dragon temples were a form of popular religion commonly found before 1949 but banned ever since then.

A road sign marking the turn off says that it is 2.4 km (1.5 miles) to the Stone Gate Calley (Shi Men Jian Gu) and 2.8 km (1.7 miles) to the suspension bridge. You can choose a long descent to the valley floor by following the road which switchbacks back and forth across the mountainside at a gentle slope, or you can drop straight down in a vertical descent via a slippery long flight of stone steps. Full-sized tour buses are prohibited from using this road, so it is a comparatively quiet walk. However, the peacefulness was disturbed by KTV music blasting from somewhere on the valley floor below.

On the valley floor, a rushing stream flows through a series of small waterfalls and pools. Unfortunately, the fog is so thick in this pocket that it is hard to see more than a few feet. The road continues past an abandoned 1950s era hotel down the right side of the stream.

A footbridge crosses to the left side in front of a beautiful waterfall that roars over four horizontal bands of rock that cut across underneath it. The valley here is similar to Jiu Long Gu on Huang Shan except for the pervasive litter everywhere. You can climb down from the trail to a sand bar below and walk right up to the waterfall.

Following the trail down the left bank of the stream, you come to a second larger concrete footbridge balanced on top of a single giant arch over the growing chasm below. It is large enough for cars to pass over to the tea house on the left side. Just past the tea house, a steep flight of slippery stone steps

The boulder strewn stream of Stone Gate Valley (Shi Men Jian).

Stone remains of the former Incense Mills at Stone Gate Valley (Shi Men Jian).

which ascend the cliff face hanging over a deep chasm is, apparently, the only access from the valley floor to the suspension bridge located somewhere above but hidden from view by the thick white clouds of fog.

Crossing over the second footbridge back over to the right bank, and following the road further down the valley, one comes to what at first seems to be a third footbridge. However upon closer inspection, this bridge is actually the top of a small concrete dam connected to a hydroelectric power station on the left bank. Looking upstream, one sees a much larger and older two-tiered stone dam that has created a beautiful, although man-made, waterfall.

Just downhill from the dam, the right bank road suddenly dead ends in a cul-de-sac which seemingly provides no access to any foot trails leading to either the suspension bridge or the Dragon Head Precipice trail, contrary to the impression given by most maps of the area. Likewise, there was no sign of any trail leading up the valley to the Reservoir Dam bridge.

Hiking back up out of the valley to the main highway proves surprisingly easy if you take the short cut. Simply follow the long vertical flight of stone steps cutting across the repeated switchbacks in the road. At the top of the steps, you emerge from the valley's sea of fog and back into the sunshine.

This foot trail exits out of the valley at a farm with an amazing amount of stone work, including a subterranean river that emerges from a stone water gate allowing the stream to actually flow underneath the farm. It may once have been one of the many incense mills visitors reported seeing on Lushan in the 1920s, where incense sticks were made for use in temples. Rest here for a while and watch the ocean of fog in the Stone Gate Valley (Shi Men Jian Gu) below flow in and out like the tide, clearing up and then sucking in again. The surrounding mountains are at first hidden from view, then reappear, and again suddenly disappear behind the white clouds.

Waves of fog roll in over the Lushan mountains.

The narrow deep canyone of Stone Gate Valley (Shi Men Jian Gu).

Jiong Long Lu

From where the main highway, here known as Jiong Long Lu, crosses the Lushan Reservoir Bridge, built in 1953, a trail leads off along the shore of the reservoir towards the Yellow Dragon Pool area. At this point it is impossible to take a vehicle up the highway back to either Heavenly Pool or Xianren Dong as traffic is only permitted to travel one-way downhill. This means those sites can only be reached from here by driving all the way around the mountain, up the East Valley, through Guling Town and back down the West Valley again. The main highway continues to snake up the mountainside through uninhabited forest until it reaches a four-way junction. To the right, the Huan Shan highway exits out of the Lushan National Park through the South Gate and heads down the mountain toward Nanchang. To the left, a gated dirt road takes a long roundabout way to Yellow Dragon Pool Temple. Also on the left is the paved two-lane Huan Shan highway heading back to the Lulin Hu area. At this point, traffic becomes two-way again, but a diligent old woman gatekeeper armed with a large bamboo stick makes sure than no one drives down to the reservoir on the one-way-only Jiong Long Lu.

Golden Bamboo Terrace (Jin Zhu Ping)

Located just off the main Huan Shan highway, in between the Lushan South Gate and Lulin Hu, is the small farming community of Golden Bamboo Terrace (Jin Zhu Ping). This village is situated in a small basin reached only by an unmarked foot trail leading off the highway near the 28 km stone marker. The trail leads up over a small ridge and drops down into the basin below that is surrounded by hills on three sides and open only at the lower end. At first glance, it is just a peasant farming community growing tea, but at closer inspection it turns out to be a Shangri-la of authentic hidden archeological treasures. Best of all, despite being labeled on maps, its attractions are a well-kept secret unknown to virtually all holiday visitors. There is no road in and no signs of outside life such as parking lots, tour buses, taxis, tour guides, billboard signs, and no tourists.

Xuan Miao Guan Taoist Temple

The first archeological site to appear is the stone and wood ruins of a temple, designated as "Xuan Miao" on local maps, but called by the locals "Xuan Miao Guan". This seems rather strange as a "Miao" is normally a Confucian temple, while a "Guan" is a Taoist temple. Three high walls made of massive uncut stones

The former entrance gate to the Taoist Temple of Mystery (Xuan Miao Guan) at Golden Bamboo Terrace (Jin Zhu Ping) in the Lushan summit area.

The stone and wood ruins of the rear of the Taoist Temple of Mystery (Xuan Miao Guan) at Golden Bamboo Terrace (Jin Zhu Ping) in the Lushan summit area.

are still standing, connected together at two corners, with the wall on the fourth side now collapsed into piles of rubble. In the middle section of wall, facing south, is the original arched stone gate still intact with a pair of closed wooden doors. The inscription stone is still in place above the arched doorway and two of its three large horizontal characters are clearly legible, reading "Xuan" on the left and "Guan" on the right, with the middle character now illegible. The smaller vertical inscription on the left records the author's name, while that on the right records the date of construction as "Min Guo Bing Yin," seemingly dating it to the Republican era of 1912–1949. The ruins seem to be much older and a visitor's description of the site published in 1921 states that it was already abandoned then. A row of four cedar trees along the front of the gate wall look old enough to have been planted by the original Taoist monks. A flight of broken stone steps lead up to the gate. There is no roof remaining and the three walls are open to the sky. Piles of broken stone blocks lie around the walls.

According to maps, the trail makes a loop through this place. The northern end is fairly short, but there is supposed to be a longer southern end that connects with the main highway in another place downhill. However, this section of the trail seems to have been obliterated by terraces of modern-day tea fields.

Gong Qian's Stone Tomb Pagoda (Gong Qian Chan Shi Mu Ta)

Temple complexes like Xuan Miao Guan often have other holy sites nearby, such as the graves of the monks who once lived there. Walk through the tea fields and explore the forested hillside opposite the peasants' houses — you will be rewarded with the discovery of more incredible historic sites.

A fairly recent memorial marker at Gong Qian's Stone Tomb Pagoda (Gong Qian Shi Mu Ta) near the Golden Bamboo Terrace (Jin Zhu Ping) in the Lushan summit area.

Gong Qian's Stone Tomb Pagoda (Gong Qian Shi Mu Ta) near the Golden Bamboo Terrace (Jin Zhu Ping) in the Lushan summit area.

Gong Qian's Stone Tomb Pagoda (Gong Qian Chan Shi Mu Ta) is possibly one of the most remarkable religious monuments in all of China, as well as one of the most intact and well preserved genuine relics. This is a late Ming Dynasty site dating from 1619, the 46th year of the reign of Ming Emperor Wan Li. The name of the site reflects its main feature: a stone (*shi*) pagoda tower (*ta*) marking the tomb (*mu*) of a Zen (Chan) Buddhist monk named Gong Qian. Chan (Zen) Master Gong Qian was the founder of the **Buddhist Temple of the Thousand Buddhas** (Qian Fo Si), which was established in Jin Zhu Ping in the year 1579. It is unclear whether the Buddhist temple site was the same as where the ruins of the Taoist Xuan Miao Guan now stand.

A low stone wall encloses a diamond-shaped space within which are many stone tablet inscriptions, stone balustrades, stone carvings of lions and dragons, and Buddhist-looking stone lotus pedestals. Just outside the entrance gate are two stone tablets, each with lengthy inscriptions carved into them.

The entrance into the enclosure is a gate formed by two stone posts topped with stone lion statues. Next come a pair of large stone tablets, one on each side but facing each other, each of which is topped by a stone dragon statues. Each of the stone tablets have lengthy inscriptions written on them, but the one on the right has been defaced with characters written in black spray paint. Past the two stone tablets are long stone balustrades on either side, decorated with scenes of animals and flowers. At the tip of the diamond-shaped enclosure stands a fairly tall stone lotus pedestal which is covered with legible inscriptions on all eight sides of its hexagonal section. One of the inscriptions seems to be written in Tibetan characters. Finally, behind the stone lotus pedestal is another stone tablet covered with inscriptions. Clearly there is a wealth of written historical records here, which if fully translated into English, could reveal the secrets behind the history of this mysterious place.

A short distance away from this site, hidden in the trees, is another monument dedicated to the Buddhist Chan (Zen) master Gong Qian. This one consists of a small stone pagoda and a large stone inscription. Part of the inscription is still legible and reads as "Ming Gong Chan Shi Mu Dao," meaning "The Way to the Ming Dynasty Tomb of Eminent Monk Gong." The octagonal stone pagoda has three storys and is perched on top of a boulder, which itself is balanced on top of yet another boulder. It seems so carefully balanced there that it could fall over at any moment and it is hard to believe that it has, in fact, been standing in place for hundreds of years. The top third of the pagoda is covered with inscriptions on all eight sides, but these are barely legible. Right beside the pagoda is a large stone boulder covered with a very big, long inscription carved into its full length. This inscription is still quite legible.

Stone animal on the gate post of Gong Qian's Stone Tomb Pagoda (Gong Qian Shi Mu Ta).

A close up shot of Gong Qian's Stone Tomb Pagoda (Gong Qian Shi Mu Ta).

Yellow Dragon Valley (Huang Long Gu)

The Yellow Dragon Valley (Huang Long Gu) encompasses several main sights including the Yellow Dragon Pool (Huang Long Tan), the Black Dragon Pool (Wu Long Tan), the Three Precious Trees (San Bao Shu), the Yellow Dragon Buddhist Temple (Huang Long Si), and the Buddhist Scripture Pavilion (Ci Jing Ting). It was formerly situated in a peaceful, isolated, forested valley accessible only by foot. However, the construction of a long dirt road that runs all the way in from the Lushan South Gate has paved the way for mobs of tourists to disturb the tranquility that used to exist here.

For those who prefer a hike in the woods, the valley can still be reached on foot from several different directions. The original trail starts in the East Valley (Dong Gu), near the bridge crossing the stream over to the People's Assembly Hall. It follows the stream down to the East Valley until it crosses a footbridge over the Russian Valley below the Lulin Lake Dam. From here, the trail crosses over a northern ridge of Yu Ping Peak and drops down into the Yellow Dragon Valley. Before reaching the temple itself, a side trail branches off and goes up to the late Ming Dynasty Buddhist Scripture Pavilion (Ci Jing Ting) built in 1587. A newer trail starts from near the Tai Ji Hotel on the Huan Shan highway, just south of Lulin Lake. This trail climbs a steep flight of stone steps up a southern ridge of Yu Ping Peak. It then descends long vertical flights of stone steps down the sharp back side of the forested mountain.

Yellow Dragon Temple (Huang Long Si)

This temple was originally a late Ming Dynasty construction, built in 1585. Its main hall is open to worshippers and visitors. Inside, it has a pretty standard Buddhist temple configuration. Three large gilded Buddha statues are seated inside the front entrance, and 18 gilded Arhat (*Luohan*) statues line the walls, with nine on each side. In the back, facing the rear exit, is a gilded statue of Guanyin (Goddess of Mercy) riding on top of an alligator's head emerging from the ocean waves. All of the statues and ornaments seem brand new, but the building itself may be an authentic restoration of an original structure. Old worn down flagstones line the surrounding plazas.

A second smaller yellow chapel behind the main hall features a bizarre collection of assorted new Buddhist statutes piled together. In reality, this is a monument to brazen commercialism, as a TV monitor in the corner blasts VCDs and shop clerks sell cheap trinkets displayed in glass cases. There are a few Buddhist monks wandering about dressed in their habits, but somehow the whole atmosphere seemed more touristy and fake than genuinely spiritual.

In the day, annoying tour guides with throngs of tourists in tow infiltrate the grounds and turn the whole place into a circus. However, if you visit at night when all the crowds are gone, it is almost possible to have a real spiritual experience. After the sun

Left: The Great Hall of the Precious Hero (Da Xiong Bao Dian) of Yellow Dragon Buddhist Temple (Huang Long Si) in the Yellow Dragon Valley (Huang Long Gu) of the Lushan summit area.
Right: The smaller rear hall of Yellow Dragon Buddhist Temple (Huang Long Si).

Two of the three gilded Buddha statues inside the The Great Hall of the Precious Hero (Da Xiong Bao Dian) of Yellow Dragon Buddhist Temple (Huang Long Si).

has set, the main temple hall glows eerliy in the surrounding darkness from the forests of red candles burning inside the chapel and outside on the plaza. The evening temple bell chimes several times as the sun sets and echoes out in the pitch black darkness.

Edward Selby Little wrote that when he first visited the summit of Lushan in 1895, Huang Long Si was then the only functioning Buddhist temple left on the mountain. Today, the situation seems be oddly the same, with other temple sites in ruins or devoid of any resident monks.

A four-story iron incense burner, shaped like a pagoda at Yellow Dragon Buddhist Temple (Huang Long Si).

A statue of Guanyin at Yellow Dragon Buddhist Temple (Huang Long Si).

Scripture Bestowing Pavilion (Ci Jing Ting)

This small but beautiful stone pavilion was erected by the Ming Emperor Wan Li in the year 1587. Inside is a 1.8 m (6 ft) marble stele inscribed with a dedication to Wan Li's mother, in gratitude for her gift of 41 volumes of Buddhist scriptures presented to the Huang Long Si. This pavilion is located on the forested hillside behind the temple, on the trail leading to the lower Lulin Valley.

The Three Precious Trees (San Bao Shu)
Further downhill from the front of the temple stand the Three Precious Trees (San Bai Shu), which are undoubtedly very old, although their exact age is debatable. From here, the old trail continues downhill along a flight of stone steps, for a considerable distance through the forest, to the Yellow Dragon Pool (Huang Long Tan). From the trees to the pool, there are a number of stone inscriptions carved into natural rocks.

Yellow Dragon Pool (Huang Long Tan)
A large stone inscription on a rock marks the turnoff onto a short side trail leading to Yellow Dragon Pool, which is in a small tributary leading into the main stream below. A beautiful high waterfall pours directly into this pool, making this an ideal background for picture-taking. Nearby, there was a woman with two copper kettles of water with handles. For some unkown reason, she was selling tickets to touch them.

Black Dragon Pool (Wu Long Tan)
Back on the main trail, you have a choice of two trails once you cross a footbridge over a larger stream. The trail to the right leads to Black Dragon Pool (Wu Long Tan). This is a much larger pool with several waterfalls flowing into it. The stream has a small island in the middle of it, which is a perfect place for taking pictures of the waterfall. Commercial photographers have set up shop here and will take your picture for a fee.

Back at the footbridge, the trail to the left leads around the Lushan Reservoir and down to the Jiong Long Lu reservoir dam bridge. From here, it is possible to catch a taxi back to Lulin Lake. Alternatively, you can choose to walk back out the way you came, as long as you do not mind climbing long flights of seemingly endless vertical stone steps up the perpendicular slope to the summit of the ridge before dropping back down to the trail head on the Huan Shan highway.

Qing Lian Valley (Qing Lian Gu)
It's possible to take a minibus to Qing Lian Gu, which will cost 50 Rmb each way. The route will take you past the turnoff to **Han Po Kou**, through the Botanical Gardens main gate, past the **Da Kou Waterfall** trailhead, along a torturous winding mountain road, past the **Wu Lao Peak** trailhead, and down into the beautiful but isolated Qing Lian Valley. The first half of the valley is a broad, wide, level area of green fields. You will then pass by the dirt road turnoff to the former site of **Qing Lian Temple**, then continue through the large parking lot area, through a modern gateway, until the paved road ends at an old stone resort building. There are shops and places to eat here.

Lushan Botanical Gardens (Lushan Zhi Wu Yuan)

The Lushan Botanical Garden was established in 1934. It has more than 3,400 varieties of plants, at least 94 of which are rare species protected by law and are valuable for botanical research. The whole garden covers an area of 300 hectares (741.3 acres), including forests of pine and cypress trees.

Phone: 828-2223

Above: Lushan tea fields produce the famous Lushan Cloud Tea.

Stone entrance gate to the Lushan Botanical Gardens.

Below: The forested narrow road to Five Old Men Peak (Wu Lao Feng) and Qing Liang Valley.

Wu Lao Peak (Wu Lao Feng)

The trailhead to the summit of Wu Lao Peak (Wu Lao Feng) starts from the Qing Lian Gu road. This peak rises 1,358 m (4,455.4 ft) above sea level and stands in the southeastern corner of Lushan overlooking Poyang Lake below. It gets its name from the legend that the mountain's five peaks look like five old men. Beside the trail, as it approaches the summit of Wu Lao Peak, is a lengthy English language inscription chiseled into a stone tablet by Western visitors to the mountain back in the 1920s. Standing on the summit of the peak, you can see the rolling ridges of the mountain and the vast water of Poyang Lake or enjoy the wonderful scene of the sunrise and the seas of clouds. However, better views of the mountain itself can be had from the area of Hai Hui Temple (Hai Hui Si) at the southeastern foot of Lushan on the ring road. The side facing the lake is the one most photographed, and it is from this vantage point that you can truly appreciate the mountain's peculiar shape. After ascending the summit of Wu Lao Feng, the trail descends a ridge towards the Qing Lian Valley and the San Die Quan waterfall.

Qing Lian Si

The dirt turnoff to Qing Lian Si is marked by an enormous rectangular stone boulder covered with many stone inscriptions, including a very large one and several other smaller ones. Following the dirt road, you cross a footbridge over a stream and find yourself in a farming village with no temple in sight. If, by chance, you ask the local women, who wash their clothes in the stream by beating them against rocks, about the temple, they are likely to say "xianzai meio," meaning "now we don't have." They may also say "tamen qu la, tamen hui jia la," meaning that the temple monks have all gone away and gone home.

In fact, the temple no longer exists. Not even a trace of the original buildings or a single relic remains, save for the stone inscriptions at the road head. However, on the edge of the village, you will find a beautiful forested side valley with a rushing stream. This is a great place to have a picnic lunch, especially after a long hike from San Die Quan. It is a completely unspoilt site, with no signs of modern civilization in view. Birds with long black and white tail feathers chirp and land on rocks in the stream to drink water. You may find yourself wishing that you could live in a

This page: These mammoth inscribed stone relics, lying in a field beside the road, are all that remains of the former Qing Liang Si Buddhist Temple.

place like this forever, but be sure you catch the last minibus out of the valley before it gets dark. Remember, this place is a very long way from civilization as we know it.

Three Step Waterfall (San Die Quan)

This waterfall is often referred to as "the first wonder of Mount Lushan" and regularly appears in landscape paintings of the mountain. The waterfall rushes from the ravine in Qing Lian Valley, behind Wu Lao Peak and tumbles into the deep valley through three stages, over a cliff which drops 155 m (508.5 ft) down to a pool at its base. The waterfall gets its name from the three separate waterfalls which together make up the whole. Unfortunately, it is quite difficult to reach, even today. Many poets

A farmer's pigs enjoy their dinner at a farm near the former site of Qing Liang Si.

A rushing mountain stream cascades down into the Qing Liang Valley near the former site of Qing Liang Si.

The Qing Liang Valley.

and scholars throughout Chinese history lamented their misfortune at never having been able to see it in person and had to content themselves with paintings of it instead.

To the right of the parking lot at the end of the Qing Lian Valley road, a dirt road continues a distance up, through the forest, to the Wu Lao Peak trailhead. Here, stone steps lead in two directions — one goes up the mountainside to Wu Lao Peak and the other down to the electric train station and foot trail to Three Step Waterfall (San Die Quan). It is also possible to reach the waterfall via a branch of the Wu Lao Peak trail, but this is a very long hike up to the top of the summit and then down endless switchbacks.

From the parking lot at the end of the Qing Lian Valley road, the main trail to the waterfall follows a narrow canyon along a roaring stream and is all downhill on the way in. There are several sections of white water rapids, dragon pools, and waterfalls. Two footbridges cross the stream. The trail follows a gradual gradient and unlike most trails in China, it never becomes too dangerous or precariously placed along the edge of a precipice. After a rather pleasant walk, you will finally reach the train station at the far end of the line. By taking the path least followed, you can be

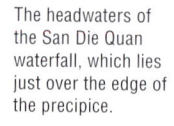

The headwaters of the San Die Quan waterfall, which lies just over the edge of the precipice.

The Qing Liang Valley trail down to the Three Step Waterfall (San Die Quan).

rewarded by discovering the very head of the Three Step Waterfall (San Die Quan), where the stream flows through a narrow rock mouth and over the edge of a precipice, dropping more than 300 m (about 1,000 ft) into the next valley below. There are usually no people at all in this spot and you can take some incredible pictures.

Now that you have seen the head, the next thing is to get a good view of the waterfall proper. For this, one would need to be at the bottom, somewhere in front or off to the side. Unfortunately, most maps do not really prepare you for this situation. The trail leading down from Wu Lao Peak might offer better views, as would one that comes in from near Guling Town, but both of these involve a full day's hike. There is also another trail that starts below the waterfalls and heads uphill from Lushan East Gate (Lushan Dong Men). This can be reached by a separate road from Jiujiang, and is covered in the section on Lushan East Gate (Lushan Dong Men).

When you have finished exploring the Three Step Waterfall (San Die Quan) area, you can take the train back uphill. The cost is 50 Rmb to go back up and 30 Rmb to go downhill. The German engineer operating the train's onboard computer system may be the only foreigner you see in this area. From the train station, follow a wooded trail along the rushing stream with many swimming-hole-type stone pools. The whole canyon is reminiscent of Jiu Long Gu on Huang Shan.

The Qing Liang Valley trail pas many smaller waterfalls on th way down to th Three Step Waterfall (San Die Quan).

End of the Qing Liang Valley trail with a modern pavilion for viewing the Three-Step Waterfall.

Lushan Sights: Northwestern Slopes

Lushan has a circumference of 314 km (195 miles), which means that many of its historic and natural sights are not actually at the summit area, but spread far apart around the foot of the mountain's slopes. The northwestern slope area is full of historic sites, but lies well outside the boundaries of the park, at the northwestern foot of the mountain. It is probably best reached by driving from Jiujiang, as you cannot drive

A man-made waterfall on Mount Lushan.

Railroad tracks for the Qing Liang Valley train down to the Three Step Waterfall (San Die Quan).

there directly from Guling Town or the summit area. It is possible to walk there from Guling, taking a trail that begins from Da Lin Peak, but this involves a very long, steep descent.

It is also possible to take a taxi minibus from downtown Jiujiang out to the fabled Dong Lin Si at the northwestern foot of Lushan for a cost of 100 Rmb. Although public buses travel the same route for 2 or 3 Rmb, it may be worth the added cost to have the flexibility of your own driver if you wish to explore the many scenic detours available. The main highway passes through an old gateway that still says "Jiujiang Airport," a reference to the old site that has been closed since 1999, and then follows a bumpy, patchwork asphalt road through green countryside. These northwestern foothills at the base of Lushan are rich in cultural and historical sites well worth visiting. Several other temple sites can be reached by side roads and trails branching off this main one and heading up into the western foothills of Mount Lushan.

Lianhua Town

Turn off the main highway onto a side road at the small village known as Lianhua Town (Lianhua Zhen). From here, you can drive up into the Lushan foothills to **Gui Yuan Si**, a 90-year old, single-halled Buddhist temple with half a dozen extremely elderly monks and nuns still living there.

Return to Lianhua Town and resume traveling south on the main highway. Within a short distance, on the left side of the

The Lotus Flower Cave (Lianhua Dong) Buddhist Temple complex on the slopes of Mount Lushan.

road, one comes to the turnoff to **Lianhua Cave** (Lianhua Dong), a large Buddhist temple complex built into the steep western hillside of Mount Lushan. A well paved road goes all the way to the destination. In fact, the original road to the summit of Lushan, built by Edward Selby Little in 1895, traveled this same route. Walking is not suggested as the distance is quite far, and the final approach to the temple becomes extremely steep. Once at the temple, generous amounts of walking are required to climb the steep flights of steps from one hall to another, each of which is built on terraces at dramatically different elevations.

Taiping Gong Temple

Traveling on the main highway, from the village of Taiping, a rocky dirt road branches off into the Lushan foothills to the former site of the **Taiping Gong** temple. This road is paved with broken fragments of ancient square flagstones. Scattered along the sides are broken stone fragments with decorative carvings. These probably belonged to the original temple buildings.

The new much smaller Taiping Miao ancestral temple on the site of the former Taiping Gong.

The present-day Taiping Miao is a one-hall wooden beam and brick wall structure. A vertical three-character sign board on the right side of the entrance reads "Taiping Gong," although local residents seem to call it Taiping Miao nowadays. The horizontal four-character sign board over the entrance reads, "Jiu Tian Yun He," roughly translated as "Nine Heaven Cloud Crane." Inside are statues of three strange gods, including one of an old man carrying an umbrella while riding an ox. The worn stone steps leading up to the hall seem to be the original ones, but the hall itself is obviously a reconstruction dating from after the Cultural Revolution. An exhaustive search of the surrounding area revealed no sign of the famed twin stone pagodas known as the Bo Xi Ta, which visitors had still found standing in the 1920s. No monks or priests reside at the temple now, but an elderly woman serves as its attendant. Local villagers were seen parading their children inside the temple and coaxing them to

A curious statue inside the new Taiping Miao ancestral temple.

kneel and prayer before the gods, as well as offer monetary contributions to the donation box.

The original Taiping Gong was a Taoist temple built on this same site during the Tang Dynasty by Emperor Kai Yuan (Xuan Zong) in either 731 AD or 732 AD, after he had a dream about this spot. At its peak there were 1,500 Taoist monks living here. In 970 AD, the name was changed to **Taiping Miao** (Temple of Heavenly Peace). During the Yuan Dynasty, the original temple was destroyed by the Mongols in 1350. However, in the Ming Dynasty, the temple was restored during the Jia Jing reign (1522–1566).

Past Taiping Miao, the dirt road continues up through the fields, with increasingly impressive views of Lushan's peaks. This road passes some old stone tombs of local people, a few small ancestral halls, circular rock haystacks, and homes decorated with pairs of colorful door gods. It then crosses over a stone bridge, where a stone foot trail can be followed through farmers' fields until it connects with the paved road leading to the large Buddhist temple complex at **Lianhua Cave** (Lianhua Dong). Although views of the temple complex can be seen from this point, it is still a long hike up the mountainside to get there, even after reaching the paved access road. As such, it may be better to hire a taxi from the main road at either the villages of Taiping or Lianhua.

West Grove Buddhist Temple (Xi Lin Si)

No road signs pointed the way as we reached a fork and turned left up to the sites of West Grove Buddhist Temple (Xi Lin Si) and East Grove Temple (Dong Lin Si) in the western foothills. Oddly enough, the temple buildings of the West Grove Temple (Xi Lin Si) can be see from the new Jiujiang-Nanchang expressway, but cannot be reached from it. Access is only possible from the two narrow lanes round the mountain highway, which is in great disrepair.

POINT OF INTEREST

As late as 1921, visitors could still see the ruins of two 12.2-m (40-ft) square towers near the main temple courtyard. Each tower had an external staircase of 32 steps. Their Arabesque architectural style was considered quite unusual. These towers were built during the Jia Jing restoration. One served as the Bell Tower (Zhong Lou) for the Taiping Miao temple and the other as the Drum Tower (Gu Lou). They were known collectively as the Bo Xi Ta or Mother-in-Law and Daughter-in-Law towers.

When Johannes Prip-Moller visited the site in 1929, the Bell Tower was still standing in its entirety. However, the top half of the Drum Tower had already collapsed. All the original Taiping Gong structures were destroyed during the Cultural Revolution (1966–1976). The temple's current hall is a fairly recent construction opened on 8 October 1998.

The original flag stone paved road to the former site of Taiping Gong.

The red entrance gate to the West Grove Buddhist Temple (Xi Lin Si).

The first sight one sees is of the white, new-looking **West Grove Pagoda** (Xi Lin Ta) and the walled West Grove Temple (Xi Lin Si) complex, which is below that of East Grove Temple (Dong Lin Si). The compound of the West Grove Temple (Xi Lin Si) is surrounded by a red dragon wall, with an undulating top. The temple was founded around 379 AD. Although visitors in 1921 found that little remained of the temple, the entire site was obviously in a state of good repair in May 2003. It would seem that it had been recently renovated or reconstructed.

West Grove Pagoda (Xi Lin Ta) has an unusual Bavarian appearance, painted white with a sloping conical top, it gradually narrows in width from the base to the summit. Each side of the octagonal pagoda has four niches filled with small statues of Buddha. This appears to be a brick and mortar structure with a white plaster layer over the bricks. A traditional tripod roof bracket design decorates the exterior. Supposedly, the seven-story octagonal tower was originally built in the Tang Dynasty reign of Xuan Zong (712–756 AD), and last rebuilt in 1702 during the Qing Dynasty reign of Kang Xi (1661–1722). In 1921, visitors found the structure covered with bushes and grass, testifying to its age.

The West Grove Buddhist Temple's pagoda (Xi Lin Ta).

Although nowadays it is commonly referred to simply as Xi Lin Ta, two earlier names are inscribed on its northern base. These names are **Pagoda of a Thousand Buddhas** (Qian Fo Ta), and **Pagoda of Hui Yuan** (Hui Yuan Ta). The latter name shows that this pagoda was originally dedicated to the memory of the monk who founded the nearby East Grove Temple (Dong Lin Si).

Bai Ju Yi's Thatched Cottage

The cottage of the Tang Dynasty poet and Jinshi scholar Bai Ju Yi (772–846 AD) originally stood somewhere in between the West and East Grove temples, below the Big Forest Peak (Da Lin Feng). It was first built by Bai in 816 AD while he was serving a four-year term as the Sub-Prefect of Jiujiang from 815 to 819 AD.

POINT OF INTEREST

During the Tang and Song dynasties, the West Grove Temple (Xi Lin Si) received visits from some of the most famous poets of the day. During his four years as Sub-Prefect of Jiujiang from 815 to 819 AD, Bai Ju Yi (772–846 AD) often visited this site. He wrote a poem about it entitled "Visiting the Xi Lin Temple," in which he said:

"I dismount from my horse at Xi Lin Temple;
I throw the porter my slender riding whip.
In the morning I work at a government office desk;
In the evening I become a dweller in the Sacred Hills."

Arthur Waley, 1945

Later, in the Northern Song Dynasty (960–1126), Su Dong Po (Su Shi) wrote his most famous poem about Lushan on the walls of the West Grove Temple (Xi Lin Si) during a visit of several days to the mountain in 1084. Later, the poem appeared in a published volume of Su's works called *The Forest of Records*. Here are two variant translations of what Su said in this poem:

"From the side, a whole range;
From the end, a single peak.
Far, near, high, low, no two parts are alike.
Why can't I tell the true shape of Lushan?
Because I myself am in the mountain."

Burton Watson, 1966

"See it stretched before you in a ridge;
from the side it becomes a peak,
no matter from where I look at the mountain
it is never exactly the same.
I cannot tell the true face
of Lushan
which is simply because I myself
am here within the mountain."

Stephen Owen, 1996

In letters to his friends, Bai often mentioned that he was living "in a hut on the Lushan" and spoke of seeing Buddhist monks when he looked out his windows. Although Bai was never able to return here after his departure in 818 AD, he maintained a written correspondence with the monks of Xi Lin Si and Dong Lin Si for the next 30 years, asking them to look after his cottage until he could come back. In 1986, the cottage was either moved to or rebuilt at its present location on the Flower Path in Hua Jing Park, beside Ruqin Lake on Lushan's summit. Its architectural style is supposedly the same as the former cottage. Built of wood with a grass roof, it has two rooms and four windows, and faces south. In front of the cottage stands a 20 m (65.6 ft) stone statue of Bai Ju Yi.

POINT OF INTEREST

Although he had been forcibly exiled to Jiujiang from the Tang capital at Changan (Xian) as a punishment, Bai Ju Yi seems to have enjoyed himself here once he arrived and discovered the natural beauty of his new surroundings. Here are two variant translations, both oddly enough by the same person, of how he described in a letter to his friend Yuan Zhen (779–831 AD):

"In the autumn of last year I visited Lushan for the first time. Reaching a point between the Eastern Forest (Dong Lin) and Western Forest (Xi Lin) Temples, beneath the Incense Burner Peak (Xiang Lu Feng), I was enamored by the unequalled prospect of cloud-girt waters and spray-clad rocks. Unable to leave this place, I built a cottage here. Before it stand ten tall pines and a thousand tapering bamboos. With green creepers I fenced my garden; with white stones I made bridge and path. Flowing waters encircle my home; flying spray falls between the eaves. Red pomegranate and white lotus cluster on the steps of the pond. All is after this pattern, although I cannot name each delight. Whenever I come here alone, I am moved to prolong my stay to ten days ... not only do I forget to go back, but would gladly end my days here."

Arthur Waley, 1945

"In the autumn of last year I began making excursions into the Lushan and found a spot between the two Forest Monasteries (Xi Lin Si and Dong Lin Si), just under the Incense Burner Peak (Xiang Lu Feng), where the clouds and waters, fountains and rocks were more lovely than at any other place on the mountain. The situation delighted me so much that I built myself a cottage there. There is a group of high pine trees in front of it and a fine cluster of tall bamboos. I have covered all the walls with green creepers and made paved paths of white rock. A stream almost encircles it and I have a waterfall at my very eaves. There is a white lotus in my pool and red pomegranite on its banks ... Every time that I go to be alone here for a few hours the visit tends to prolong itself into one many days ... I forget all about going home and would be content to stay here till the end of my days."

Arthur Waley, 1949

[Note: In all his accounts of Lushan, Bai Ju Yi seems to have confused Incense Burner Peak (Xiang Lu Feng) with Big Forest Peak (Da Lin Feng).]

East Grove Temple (Dong Lin Si)

Driving past West Grove Temple (Xi Lin Si), one next sees the much larger East Grove Temple (Dong Lin Si) complex come into view. The latter is a very large, rectangular, walled compound, positioned on a north-south axis, with a forested hill at the northern end. On top of the hill stands another very new-looking pagoda that somewhat resembles the Ling Gu Ta on Zijin Shan in Nanjing.

A gurgling stream flows beside the road to the South of both the West and East Grove Temples (Dong Lin Si and Xi Lin Si). A legend that is immortalised in the East Grove Temple's (Dong Lin Si's) **Three Laughing Hall** speaks of how the monk, Hui Yuan, had a rule never to cross the stream to the outside world. It is possible that this could be the stream in question. A bridge crosses the stream and follows another road southward, supposedly heading to **Shi Men Jian Gu**. An ancient three-character stone tablet stands just outside the temple's gate, which faces a parking lot, lined with shops, and a small village.

The East Grove Temple (Dong Lin Xi) was originally built in 384AD, the ninth year of the Tai Yuan reign during the Eastern Jin Dynasty, by Hui Yuan, an eminent Buddhist monk. Hui Yuan lived in the temple for over 30 years and founded the Pure Land sect (Jing Tu Zong) of Chinese Buddhism there. This sect was later exported to Japan and is indisputably the most popular form of Buddhism in China today. In the 5th century AD, the temple erected a 3-m (10-ft) **Bronze Pagoda** (Tie Ta), covered with Sanskrit inscriptions from the Diamond Sutra on top of the North Mountain (Bei Shan) behind the temple. The temple was restored in 732AD, during 19th year of the Kai Yuan era (713–741 AD) of the Xuan Zong reign (712–756 AD) of the Tang Dynasty. The original Dong Ling Pagoda (Dong Lin Ta) was built on the top of Bei Shan in the same year. However, this tower was destroyed during the Taiping Rebellion (1850–1864) and later rebuilt in the late Qing Dynasty (1644–1911).

A side view of the new entrance gate, bell and drum tower of East Grove Buddhist Temple (Dong Lin Si) at the foot of Mount Lushan.

The East Grove Temple (Dong Lin Si) seems to have had a close relationship with the chief poets of the Tang and Song dynasties. **Li Bai** (Li Tai Po) (701–762 AD) is recorded as having paid several visits during his 756–758 AD residence in Jiujiang. **Bai Ju Yi** (772–846 AD) continued to exchange correspondence with the monks of the temple for nearly 30 years after he left Jiujiang in 819AD. In 845AD, just one year before his death, he presented one of only a half dozen copies of his complete written works to the temple's library. The Northern Song poet, **Su Dong Po** (Su Shi) (1037–1101) paid a celebrated visit to the area in 1084, and exchanged poems with the Abbot of the East Grove Temple (Dong Lin Si) on later occasions.

Throughout its more than 1,600 years of history, the temple has experienced repeated cycles of construction, destruction, and renovation. After the 1949 Revolution, the first cycle of renovations began when **Master Guo Yi** took over as abbot of the temple in 1961. He spent the next four years repairing it. Repairs had just been finished in 1965 when Master Guo was forced to leave the temple in 1966, for the duration of the Cultural Revolution (1966–1976). It was not until 12 years later that he was able to return to The East Grove Temple (Dong Lin Si) in June 1978. By that time, the temple had been reduced to less than 10 percent of its former size, and consisted of only one small building of three connected halls inside a round walled compound at the foot of the North Mountain (Bei Shan). Small scale repairs began in 1978, but major reconstruction to replace buildings destroyed during the Cultural Revolution did not begin on a full scale until the summer of 1981. The new **Tomb Pagoda of Ancestor Hui Yuan** (Hui Yuan Zu Shi She Li Ta) was completed in 1984, and the new **Precious Hall of the Great Hero** (Da Xiong Bao Dian) was built between 1987 and 1990. The **Jiangxi Provincial Buddhist College** was opened in February 1993, and it seems some buildings must have been added as facilities for this institute. After Master Guo's death in March 1994, his own tomb was added to the Bei Shan hilltop under the name **Master Guo Tomb Pagoda** (Guo Yi Lao He Shang Ta). Because Bei Shan now had several pagodas, its name was then changed to the **East Grove Temple Pagoda Garden** (Dong Lin Si Ta Yuan).

The entrance to the East Grove Temple (Dong Lin Si) is now marked by a new three-portal stone entrance gate, which leads across an open plaza to a much larger new gatehouse built like a fortress with three red, double gates. After this is a courtyard

The new pagoda of East Grove Buddhist Temple (Dong Lin Si) atop the North Hill (Bei Shan).

with two new-looking three-story Drum and Bell Towers, followed by the main halls and finally the pagoda on the hilltop.

Inside the inner walled compound, there are eight main halls. Through the recently built **Heavenly King Hall** (Tian Wang Dian) is a **Lotus Pond** (Lianhua Chi) set in a large courtyard. To the east of the pond are three halls along the eastern wall of the compound, starting with the **Tea House** (Cha Ting). Just north of this is the **Guest House** (Ke Tang), behind which is the **Chan Zhao Hall**. On the north side of the Lotus Pond is the main building, the **Precious Hall of the Great Hero** (Da Xiong Bao Dian), whose last rebuilding started in 1987 and was completed in the summer of 1990. Next to the Precious Hall of the Great Hero (Da Xiong Bao Dian), on its east side, is the **Arhat Hall** (Luohan Tang) with rows of new golden statues of Buddhist saints. Behind the these two halls is a courtyard followed by another row of three halls. These three halls include the **Hu Fa Dian** immediately behind the Precious Hall of the Great Hero (Da Xiong Bao Dian), the **Shen Yun Dian** on the east side of the Hu Fa Dian and immediately behind the Arhat Hall (Luohan Tang), and then the **Three Laughing Hall** (San Xiao Tang) on the east side of the Shen Yu Dian.

Preserved in front of the Three Laughing Hall (San Xiao Tang) is a stone carving portrait depicting the story "The Three Laughing by Tiger Stream (Hu Xi)." According to this story, the temple's founder Hui Yuan had a rule that he would never cross the Tiger Stream (Hu Xi) near the temple. One day, while saying goodbye to his good friends **Tao Yuanming** (365–427 AD) and **Lu Xiujing**, he was so absorbed in his talk with them that he forgot his discipline and went farther than Tiger Stream (Hu Xi). As soon as he crossed the bridge, a tiger roared to warn him. The three were startled out of their talk, but burst into laughter at the realization of what the tiger meant. Hui Yuan hurriedly bid farewell to his friends and returned to the temple, having learned his lesson to never again go farther than Tiger Stream (Hu Xi).

Immediately behind the Shen Yun Dian is the small **Buddhist Reading Hall** (Lian Fo Tang). In the northwest corner is the old **Bell and Drum Tower** (Zhong Gu Lou). Also in the compound is the new three-story **Jade Buddha House** (Yu Fo Lou).

Behind the rear wall of the compound is a large hill known as the **North Mountain** (Bei Shan). At the foot of the hill is the **Yi Jing Terrace** (Yi Jing Tai). On the path leading up to the hilltop are several springs and pools, including the **Old Dragon Spring** (Gu Long Qian) and a small pond called **Chu Mo Chi**. Legend has it that a tunnel once connected the East Grove

An ancient stone marker at the entrance gate to East Grove Buddhist Temple (Dong Lin Si).

Temple (Dong Lin Si) with Nanjing through the Chu Mo Chi. Behind the temple grounds, at the foot of Bei Shan, is the **Bright and Clever Spring** (Chong Ming Quan), sometimes called the Well of Intelligence. At the top of the forested hill is the **Wenshu Pavilion** (Wenshu Ge).

Bei Shan once housed the original **Tomb of Hui Yuan** (Yuan Gong Mu), the founder of the East Grove Temple (Dong Lin Si) who lived on the temple grounds for over 30 years during the 4th century AD. Outside the entrance to the tomb was a Qing Dynasty memorial tablet erected in 1817. As late as 1921, visitors were still able to enter the interior of the tomb. It was then described as having had an octagonal shape, stone walls, and a ceiling supported by pillars. Inside the tomb were two tablets with inscriptions dating from 1244, the fourth year of the reign of Emperor Shun Yu. According to these inscriptions, the personal belongings and writings of Hui Yuan were walled inside his tomb. Unfortunately, it seems that this tomb was later destroyed sometime between 1921 and 1984.

Since 1994, Bei Shan has also been known as the **Dong Lin Temple Pagoda Garden** (Dong Lin Si Ta Yuan) and the **Hui Yuan Tomb Pagoda Garden** (Hui Yuan Gong Ta Yuan). The hilltop area includes the **Tomb Pagoda of Master Guo** (Guo Yi Lao He Shang Ta), which is shaped like a Tibetan stupa and was erected after his death in March 1994. There is also the **Tomb Pagoda of Ancestor Hui Yuan** (Hui Yuan Zu Shi She Li Ta), reconstructed in the summer of 1984. An earlier pagoda known as the **She Li Ta** was "destroyed during the war," leaving only a few scattered stone blocks as remains.

From the small village outside the gate of the East Grove Temple (Dong Lin Si), a three-portal memorial archway (*pai lou*) can be seen in the distance, on a forested slope to the south. From the village, a road veers off, up the southern hillside to the site of this memorial gateway. Local people simply say that the road goes to Lushan, a rather imprecise statement considering the mountain's size. Two Chinese language billboards at the parking lot provide more detailed maps of the area. The road up the hillside passes through an inscribed stone gate, then after a

The famous Tiger Stream (Hu Xi) that the Buddhist monk Hui Yuan refused to ever cross.

short walk, reaches a modern cemetery (*ling yuan*). A dirt road continues to wind up the hillside around the cemetery to the memorial archway above. It is from the bends in this road that you get the most spectacular bird's eye views of the two temples in the valley below. Finally you reach the three-portal stone memorial gate, a rather recent construction, which marks the transformation of the dirt road into a narrow muddy foot trail. If followed, this trail may eventually lead the hiker to Guling Town atop Mount Lushan's summit.

Jiangxi Provincial Buddhism Association

Headquarters phone: 889-2865

Lushan Eastern Slopes (Lushan Dong Men)

The eastern slopes and foothills of Mount Lushan along the shores of Poyang Lake (Poyang Hu) are collectively known as the East Gate of Mount Lushan (Lushan Dong Men). This fascinating area is full of natural wonders such as immense waterfalls, gorges, and rushing mountain streams. It was also once home to the largest number of Buddhist temples in the Lushan area, some of which are still functioning today, while the ruins and remains of many others can still be found. The hunt for the sites of these many small functioning and ruined temples scattered along a network of trails in the eastern foot hills is an exhilarating experience that could make anyone feel like a true explorer. However, one reason the area receives few visitors is that access is limited to one two-lane highway that is in extreme disrepair. Be prepared for an extremely bumpy axle-breaking ride, which nonetheless will be worth the effort. The journey from downtown Jiujiang to Lushan's eastern slopes begins on a new six-lane highway known as Jiu Wei Dadao, which unfortunately soon turns into a narrow two-lane chuck-holed asphalt road. At a small fork in the road at the first village, veer to the left. After that, the road becomes dirt in some places.

The Mount Lushan East Gate (Lushan Dong Men).

The first sight you come across is a sign pointing towards the **Blue Dragon Pool** (Bi Long Tan) to the right, where a side road branches off to this destination. After passing under a gate over the main road, you come to **Hai Hui Zhen**, a small village named after a nearby historic temple.

This is an important intersection, where the road straight ahead continues in the direction of Xing Zi, while a side road to the right heads toward the **Three-Step Waterfall** (San Die Quan) trail head.

Three-Step Waterfall (San Die Quan)

The side road to the waterfall is a new concrete two-lane highway that is in a better condition than the main road around the mountain. Good views of **Wu Lao Peak** (Wu Lao Feng) can be had to your left as you are driving up the road. The road reaches a gate where you must purchase a ticket for 33 Rmb to enter the **Lushan San Die Quan Scenic Area**. A map of the area is conveniently printed on the back of the ticket. Stretch your legs here to enjoy the scenery. A natural rock ampitheater encloses the area on three sides, with the Wu Lao Peak (Wu Lao Feng) to your left.

A rushing stream flows down Lushan's eastern slopes from the Three-Step Waterfall (San Die Quan).

Lushan's east peaks loom over the Three-Step Waterfal Hotel (San Di Quan Binguar

Lushan San Die Quan Scenic Area Management Committee
Phone: 879-2557, 879-2558, 879-2518
Fax: 879-2559
Web site: http://www.lssdq.126.com

The road continues up a narrowing forested canyon with high mountains on both sides until it finally arrives at a parking lot near the trailhead. Here you will find a conveniently located restaurant and a well-stocked store selling all manner of food and drink including packets of Lushan Cloud Tea (Lushan Yun Cha), camera film, cold beer, cold ice tea, and frozen ice cream — all items that you would not find in any of the small towns along Lushan's eastern rim. There is usually a shuttle bus parked here that can take you back to Hai Hui Zhen. The trailhead begins where a footbridge crosses a rushing stream across the road. Once you are across the footbridge, the endless flights of steep stone steps begin ascending sharply.

The road does continue a very short distance up to the separate parking lot and front entrance of the Lushan Three Step Waterfall Hotel (Lushan San Die Quan Binguan), a wonderfully clean hotel with good facilities and spectacular views of the surrounding scenery. From the hotel's comfortable lobby you can sit at a table, drink tea, and gaze out the windows at the surrounding mountain peaks. The hotel store sells bars of soap, guidebooks, instant noodles, and Lushan Cloud Tea. Spotlessly clean pubic restrooms are available for the dusty traveler to wash up, even if you are not a guest. However, if you do decide to stay, room rates range from 198 to 258 Rmb. When compared to the other mountain resorts in the eastern Lushan area, such as at Guanyin Qiao and Taiyi Cun, this is definitely the best choice for the quality of facilities and beauty of the natural surroundings.

Phone: 879-2203, 879-2205, 879-2255

The outside of the Three Step Waterfall Hotel (San Die Quan Binguan).

The inside of the Three Step Waterfall Hotel (San Die Quan Binguan).

The Three Step Waterfall Hotel (San Die Quan Binguan) sandwiched in between mountain peaks.

Natural rock formations at the Three Step Waterfall Hotel (San Die Quan Binguan).

Hai Hui Buddhist Temple (Hai Hui Si)

Shortly after leaving the small village of Hai Hui and driving south in the direction of Xing Zi, you will suddenly come across a road branching off to the right. Across the road is a modern new blue and white gate bearing a bilingual sign reading "Zhong Guo Lushan Hai Hui Youlan Qu" which means "Hai Hui Excursion District of Lushan China". Just behind this is a second gate over the same road bearing the Chinese inscription, "Lushan Wu Lao Feng Fengjing Qu," roughly translated as, "Lushan Five Old Men Peak Scenic Sights Area." These two signs mark the new access road leading to the fabled Buddhist temple, Hai Hui Si. Drive up this paved access road, past the waterworks, a few old stone houses, and through another incomplete white gate until the paved road ends at an old resort area with a large number of stone dormitory style buildings nestled in the pine tree forest. From the parking lot, the original cobblestoned road to the temple ascends up the forested hillside. If you would like to take a longer walk, this original road actually runs parallel to the modern new paved road as far downhill as the white gate posts.

The entrance gate to the Hai Hui Excursion District (Hai Hui You Lan Qu).

The entrance gate to the Five Old Men Peak Scenic Area (Wu Lao Feng Jing Qu).

Hiking through the forest, the sound of rushing water heralds a stream, on the other side of which is an abandoned four-story building. If you turn right up a cobblestone side trail at the stream, you will find an ancient Buddhist shrine cave hidden under a large boulder with a stone wall surrounding it. Inside the cave is a brick altar with a small, new, porcelain Guanyin statue on it. The cave entrance has a metal gate that is kept locked. Beside the cave is a modern inscribed sign. For lack of a better name, we can call it the Guanyin Cave (Guanyin Dong).

The former Animal Releasing Pool (Fang Sheng Chi) of Hai Hui Si Buddhist Temple.

Back on the main trail, cross the stream to the temple's outer entrance gate which bears a three-character inscription reading, "Hai Hui Si." Inside this gate appears the Hai Hui Temple halls and grounds, with the five massive peaks of Wu Lao Feng shrouded in fog behind it. A half-oval stone pool, just below the main terrace, bears carved images along the sides of its walls. The first hall has a curious three-character inscription over its entrance reading "Zhen Mian Mu," roughly translated as "Two-Face Tomb." A disused incense burner sits inside the first hall. Non-monastic families of people seem to be living inside the first row of halls.

A short walk up the hill, behind the first row of buildings, is a side gate through a wall leading into another enclosure containing two halls separated by a courtyard. The gate is kept locked but upon knocking, the door is opened by a lone elderly Buddhist nun who is happy to permit entry to visitors. The nun appears to be the only monastic resident of the temple, although a child monk — no older than 12, with a shaved head and dressed in robes — has been spotted on the grounds. The rear of these two halls is now furnished with all the paraphernalia of a Buddhist temple, including one brand new golden Buddha statue. However, shoes must be removed before entering the hall, and the resident nun will not permit any photographs of the statue to be taken.

Two smaller temples which used to be nearby were the **Golden Bamboo Nunnery** (Jing Zhu An), and the **Beautiful Cliff Temple** (Hua Ya Si). A stone, stepped foot trail enticingly ascends the forested mountain slopes from the site of Hai Hui Temple, with the mystery of these other lost temples beckoning to the adventurous traveler. The trail forks into upper and lower branches. Following the upper branch, the hunt for the Golden Bamboo Nunnery (Jin Zhu An),

The Five Old Men Peak (Wu Lao Feng), shrouded in clouds, looms over the site of Hai Hui Si Buddhist Temple.

Above, left: Entrance to the Zhen Mian Mu hall of Hai Hui Si Buddhist Temple.
Above, right: The new entrance gate to Hai Hui Si Buddhist Temple, at the end of the trail.

Below: Ruins of an old mountain resort now burned to the ground near Hai Hui Si.

POINT OF INTEREST

The name "Hai Hui" was given to this temple in the Qing Dynasty during the reign of Emperor Kang Xi (1661–1722), replacing the earlier name of Hua Yen Si. The existing temple buildings were reconstructed in 1903, making them just 100 years old. The original entrance gate, which no longer exists, was inscribed with the phrase "Lian Pang Hai Yu," meaning "The Sea Gate of the Lotus Country." Visitors in 1921 found 20 monks of the Chan (Zen) sect still living there.

which used to be nearby, ends at what was probably the site, a plateau up the mountainside surrounded by an overgrown stone wall with a gate. Inside are many stone walls, scattered broken bricks and pottery, and the remains of what may have been a fruit orchard — plum trees, peach trees, and palm trees. However, there are no inscriptions or tablets. The upper trail eventually reaches a small stream in a gully but becomes too overgrown to follow further.

The lower branch trail passes two small tombs, crosses a stream, and then opens out onto a clearing of tea fields from where you can see the **Bai Lu Dong Pagoda** in the distance, albeit at a much lower elevation. Hike through the tea fields and you will eventually reach a small village of tea roasters hard at work. Past this village is another small stream with an inscription on a small rock. Local people say that the trail continues on to another temple, but after this stream the route ascends upward sharply with no temple in sight. If you have the time, these hills are full of functioning and ruined temples worth hunting for. On the return trip back down, take in a bird's eye view of Hai Hui Temple.

The main hall of Hai Hui Si Buddhist Temple with its attendant Buddhist nun.

White Deer Cave Academy (Bai Lu Dong Shu Yuan)

Located on the southeast side of Wu Lao Peak (Wu Lao Feng), the White Deer Cave Academy (Bai Lu Dong Shu Yuan) covers a mountainous area of 200 hectares (494.2 acres), with a building area of 3,800 sq m (40,902.9 sq ft). It is circled by mountains and waters in a peaceful atmosphere. From the main road, if you can call it that, you turn right onto the Bai Lu Dong side road, go through a new gate and past a new pagoda up on a hill on the left. The twisting, winding side road snakes downhill into a forested canyon until it comes to a gate house where you must stop to buy a 20 Rmb ticket, which allows you to proceed to the parking lot.

To the right of the parking lot is a rushing stream, while a walled compound nestled in the thickly forested deep valley lies in front.

The environment is beautiful and serene, and it is easy to see how it would have been an appropriate place for quiet study and learning.

A Confucian academy (*shu yuan*) was first opened here in the year 805 AD, in the Xian Zong reign (805–820 AD) of Emperor Li Chun during the Tang Dynasty, when the scholar Li Bo (773–831 AD) fled from the city of Luoyang with his brother seeking the quiet seclusion of the mountains. When Li Bo was appointed the governor of nearby Jiang Zhou (Jiujiang) in 825 AD, during the Jing Zong reign (825–827 AD) of Tang Li Zhan, he had some of the first pavilions built here. In 940 AD, during the Southern Tang (Nan Tang) Dynasty, the imperial government established the Mount Lushan Imperial College here, also known as the White Deer Imperial College. It was then considered equal in status with the Jinling National University in the Nantang capital of Nanjing. In 960 AD, during the Taizu reign (960–976 AD) of the Northern Song (Bei Song) Dynasty, Emperor Zhao Kuangyin upgraded the academy to the rank of a university by imperial decree, and it is sometimes still referred to as the oldest continuously functioning university in China.

The academy flourished during the Southern Song (Nan Song) Dynasty when it ranked first among the four largest classic learning academies of China. The most famous director of the Bai Lu Dong Academy was **Zhu Xi** (1130-1200), who restored the college during his three-year tenure as Prefect of Nankang from 1179 to 1181, during the Xiao Zong reign (1162–1189). Zhu Xi was a famous Southern Song idealist philosopher who founded neo-Confucianism under the rubric of "Dao Xue," and developed his new educational policies here. His ideas later formed the basis of the imperial examination system (*keju*) for centuries, and his rules for the White Deer Academy, "Bai Lu Shu Yuan Chiao Kuei," were adopted by other Confucian academies all over China. Today he is best known for his work, *Reflections on Things at Hand*, published in an English translation by Chan Wing-Tsit in 1967. The Confucian revival

The Lin Xin Men stone gateway of White Deer Cave Academy (Bai Lu Dong Shu Yuan).

More internal gates and courtyards of White Deer Cave Academy (Bai Lu Dong Shu Yuan).

The main gate (Da Men) of White Deer Cave Academy (Bai Lu Dong Shu Yuan).

of the Southern Song has been heavily analyzed by modern scholars, but the two best studies of Zhu Xi's ideas are probably still the 1923 work by J. Percy Bruce, *Chu Hsi (Zhu Xi) and His Masters*, and Carson Chang's 1957 monograph, *The Development of Neo-Confucian Thought*.

The academy derives its current name from when the Tang Dynasty Confucian scholar **Li Bo** (773–831 AD) lived here as a reclusive hermit for 20 years, from 805 to 825 AD. It is said that he had a tame white deer (*bai lu*) which accompanied him wherever he went. In 1530, to commemorate this story, a stone statue of the deer was placed inside a small man-made cave (*dong*) of arched stone blocks behind the **Confucius Hall** (Da Cheng Dian) here in 1530. It is said that the existing stone sculptured deer is an authentic cultural relic of the Ming Dynasty, and first-hand observations of it seem to support this.

The Academy fell into a state of dormant abandonment in the late Yuan Dynasty. According to a visiting prefect in 1366, barely any of the previous structures survived. Thankfully, it received several waves of state investment in the early Ming Dynasty. Bai Lu Dong experienced a major reconstruction from 1436 to 1438, under the direction of the Nankang Prefect Qu Fu (Chai Pu Fu). During these two brief years, four major new halls were added, including the Da Cheng Dian, Bao Gong Ci, Zhu Xi Ci, and the Ming Lun Tang. At least two new gates were built, including the Da Cheng Men (Li Sheng Men) and Lin Xin Men. In 1495, the Academy was given 1,000 *mu* of land to support itself, and published the first edition of its institutional history, the *Bai Lu Dong Shu Yuan Zhi*. By 1497, in the Hong Zhi reign (1488–1505), it had more than 500 resident students. More land and buildings were added in 1501 and 1511, and a second edition of its institutional history was published. By the middle of the 16th century the academy owned 2,300 *mu* of land.

In the late Ming Dynasty, the Academy was still illustrious enough to warrant a visit in 1595 by the Jesuit **Matteo Ricci** (1552-1616). He engaged in lengthy philosophical debates and

A Republican Era (Min Guo) hall of White Deer Cave Academy (Bai Lu Dong Shu Yuan).

discussions with the students and faculty, including the headmaster Zhang Huang. Ricci wrote in his letters to his friends and colleagues about how impressed he was with the level of scholarship at Bai Lu Dong, and Zhang Huang reciprocated the compliment by publishing Ricci's map of the world for the first time in China in his encyclopedic work, *Tu Shu Pian*. The quality of the Academy's instruction was so highly regarded in the 17th century that its graduates could receive the coveted Juren degree without taking the otherwise required provincial examinations.

During the change of dynasties from Ming to Qing, the Academy seems to have been abandoned once more for a period of time. It was rebuilt again between 1655 and 1657. However, during the late Qing Dynasty, the Academy suffered a gradual irreversible decline. At the time of Carl F. Kupfer's visit in 1913, he described it as "an institution without a recognized president or faculty, without a Board of Trustees, or even a janitor. The students seem to be a law unto themselves. This explains the dilapidated condition of the buildings; whole sections of the wooden partition being broken out and used for fuel. Over some parts the roof is crushed in, and weeds are flourishing in the rooms. The memorial tablets, of which there are many, have sagged in all directions, and many have fallen down and are broken. It is now nothing more than a quiet place for students to hide away from the disturbances of home life, and so be better able to prosecute their private studies."

The shrine inside the Confucius Hall (Da Cheng Dian) of White Deer Cave Academy (Bai Lu Dong Shu Yuan).

In 1988, the site was declared a key cultural relic of China. The buildings are now in a much better condition than when Kupfer saw them, although all the students are long gone and it is no longer a functioning educational institution of any kind.

The present building complex of the Academy stands from east to west along the Guan Dao stream. All these buildings face south with their backs towards the north, and are built of stone, brick, or wood. The Academy gate, at the entrance, to the walled compound is about 6 m (19.7 ft) high, constructed of bricks and wood. Square brick pillars support the roof. The Academy's main entrance gate (*Shu Yuan Da Men*) bears a horizontal tablet with the inscription, "The White Deer Cave Academy" (Bai Lu Dong Shu Yuan) written by Li Meng Yang, the Education Intendant who oversaw the academy's restoration in 1511. Enter the Academy Gate and follow the path beside the Guan Dao stream. You will reach a crossroad marked by a sign. Straight ahead is the **Lin Xin Gate** (Lin Xin Men), while immediately to the left is the **Worshipping Saints Gate** (Li Sheng

Men), the entrance to a courtyard containing the **Reporting Merits Ancestral Temple** (Bao Gong Ci), the **Zhu Xi Ancestral Temple** (Zhu Xi Ci), and the **Western Tablets Gallery** (Xi Bei Lang).

The Worshipping Saints Gate (Li Sheng Men) was formerly called the **Da Cheng Men**. It was first built in 1182, during the Xiao Zong reign (1162–1189) of the Southern Song Dynasty, and rebuilt during the Ming Dynasty in 1436. It has four pillars, and measures 22.1 m (72.5 ft) in length by 7.3 m (24 ft) in height. A tablet inscribed, "Zhan Xue Men," hangs on the lintel.

The **Reporting Merits Ancestral Temple** (Bao Gong Ci) was originally called the Ancestral Sages Temple. It was first built in 1438, during the Ming Dynasty, by the Nankang Prefect Qu Fuxing to offer sacrifices to Li Bo, Zhu Xi, and other scholars who had contributed to the Academy in its early years. In 1497, the name was changed to the Zhou Duen Yi Zhu Xi Temple, and the Ancestral Saint Temple was moved elsewhere. **Bao Gong Ci** lies to the west of the present-day Temple of Zhu Xi and has the same architectural style, and is made of brick and wood.

The **Temple of Zhu Xi** (Zhu Xi Ci) was first built during the Ming Dynasty in 1438 as a hall to offer sacrifices to the scholar, Zhu Xi. The rectangular temple is built of brick and wood. In the hall stands a self-portrait stone inscription of Zhu Xi. On its left is placed a stele about the record of the Temple of Zhu Xi. On its right side is the stele of the rules of the White Deer Cave Academy written by Zhu Xi. Above it hangs a tablet with the words "Xue Da Xin Tan," inscribed by the Qing Emperor Kang Xi.

The **Confucius Hall** (Da Cheng Dian), originally called Li Sheng Hall (Li Sheng Dian), was first built during the the Xiao Zong reign (1162–1189) of the Southern Song Dynasty in 1182 as a place to hold memorial ceremonies for Confucius and his disciples. It was rebuilt in 1438 during the Ming Dynasty. Three impressive granite altars face each other, and 12 disciple tablets line the walls, with six on each side. The hall's wooden tripod-shaped roof brackets supporting its double eaves make it appear to be an authentic structure. The hall was previously described as featuring a large statue of Confucius (Kong Fuzi) surrounded

A stone tablet paivilion (Shi Bei Ting) inside White Deer Cave Academy (Bai Lu Dong Shu Yuan).

by smaller statues of his disciples, including **Mencius** (Meng Ze) and Zhu Xi (1130–1200). Currently, however, there is no sign of these statues in the hall, only the memorial tablets.

The **Imperial Book Pavilion** was first built in 1811, during the Xiao Zong reign (1162–1189) of the Southern Song Dynasty and was formerly called the Imperial Edict Building. It was built for collecting the Confucian classics, commentaries on them, dynastic histories, ancient Chinese prose, and the collected works of Zhu Xi. The square, two-story pavilion is made of wood. In the middle there is a tablet inscribed "Imperial Book Pavilion." The posts outside the pavilion bear an antithetical couplet which reads "The spring is so clean that it can wash stone, the mountain is so beautiful that it can collect books."

The **Orange Osmanthus Pavilion** lies in the center of the Academy on a rectangular platform. It is a wooden structure. Inside the pavilion stands a stone stele inscribed with the Orange Osmanthus planted by Zhi Yan. Outside the front of the pavilion are two fragrant orange osmanthus trees.

The **Hall of Expounding Ethics** (Ming Lun Tang) was first built in 1436, during the Ming Dynasty, by the Nankang Prefect Qu Fu (Chai Pu Fu), and then rebuilt three times in 1497, 1614, and 1657. In the past, it was also called the Zheng Lan Hall.

Past the Ming Lun Tang, a narrow corridor turns to your left, passing in between the high walls of adjoining courtyards, and leads to the **White Deer Cave** (Bai Lu Dong) in the hillside behind the Confucius Hall (Da Cheng Dian). White Deer Cave is like a Ming fortress. It is a stone-block square structure, with an arched entrance leading into a vaulted chamber containing a white deer statue and a large inscribed tablet. Behind the tablet is a stone incense burner. The structure's stone blocks are a darkened color, covered with red and green moss. The tablet is mossy, weathered, and worn. Likewise, the deer statue does not appear new either. The White Deer Cave is definitely a man-made creation, and was most likely never a natural cave. In 1530, during the Ming Dynasty,the Nankang Prefect Wang Zhen had a hole dug into the hillside behind the Da Cheng Hall. By 1535, the hole had been turned into an arched vault of granite blocks measuring 4 m (13.1 ft) in height, 4.15 m (13.6 ft) in width, and 6.35 m (20.8 ft) in depth. The last renovations were made in 1672, during the early Qing Dynasty.

To the left of the entrance to White Deer Cave, there are stone steps that climb up to the **Missing Sages Terrace** atop the cave's stone block structure. It was first built during the Ming Dynasty in 1530, at the same time as the cave beneath it. It is a colorful but

The famous stone statue of the white deer (Bai Lu) inside the White Deer Cave (Bai Lu Dong) at White Deer Cave Academy (Bai Lu Dong Shu Yuan).

obviously new reproduction of a traditional style pavilion, with a square, wooden structure, and double-layered roof eaves supported by sets of brackets. This is the **Missing Sages Pavilion**, originally built in 1551 by the Jiangxi Imperial Inspector Cao Bian. This marks the highest point on the Academy grounds.

The **East and West Tablet Galleries** (Dong Bei Lang and Xi Bei Lang) contain many stone stele inscriptions, including the "Record of the White Deer Cave Academy," and the "Poem of the White Deer Cave," both written by Li Meng Yang, the Ming Dynasty Education Intendant of Nankang Prefecture who was responsible for the restoration of Bai Lu Dong in 1511. Another tablet bears the 1442 "Record of Bai Lu Dong Academy's Reconstruction" (Chong Jian Bai Lu Dong Shu Yuan Ji). Near the East Tablet Gallery is the **Worshipping Virtue Temple** built in 1838. It supposedly contains a wax figure museum, but was closed when the author visited.

Walking farther up the streamside path, one comes to a Min Guo era compound on the left, with a two-story arcade structure in the courtyard. Passing through the ground floor of this building leads you, surprisingly, into another large hidden compound behind it containing the **Hall for Welcoming Guests** and a large bronze statue of **Zhu Xi** (1130–1200). Beside the Welcoming Guests Hall is a simple restaurant where you can eat lunch or dinner.

Back on the streamside path, the trail passes the small Du Dui Pavilion (Du Dui Ting) and continues on into the thick forest

Statue of the Song Dynasty Confucian scholar Zhu Xi stands in a courtyard in front of the Welcoming Guests Hall (Ke Tang) at White Deer Cave (Bai Lu Dong) at White Deer Cave Academy (Bai Lu Dong Shu Yuan).

of cedar and pine trees, eventually crossing a mossy stone footbridge over a waterfall and a small gorge full of rushing white water of the Guan Dao Xi. This seems to be the **Zhen Liu Bridge** (Zhen Liu Qiao). Under the bridge, in the rushing stream, is a big stone on which is carved two Chinese characters "Zhen Liu," written by Zhu Xi himself. The bridge is 3.2 m (10.5 ft) wide, 12.5 m (41 ft) long and 10 m (32.8 ft) high. In 1181, Zhu Xi built the original bridge out of wood. In 1813, Yang Shu Ji, the Prefect of Nankang, changed it into a stone bridge. Beyond this point, the trail continues an unknown distance through the forest, up into the Lushan foothills.

Another ancient stone relic inside the White Deer Cave (Bai Lu Dong) at White Deer Cave Academy (Bai Lu Dong Shu Yuan).

Turning around and following the streamside trail back to the parking lot, one passes the **Lin Xin Gate** (Lin Xin Men). This is an impressive three-portal stone beam gate that was first built by the Nankang Prefect, He Jun, during the Ming Dynasty in 1438, and was originally constructed out of wood. It was changed into a stone memorial arch by the Nankang Prefect, Zhou Zu Yao, in 1469. The stone gate has six vertical posts connected by two horizontal stone beams. Although the original inscription tablets seem to have been removed, Lin Xin means "Culture Stars," implying that many talented intellectuals have passed through this gate to study and teach here. The gate faces the Guan Dao stream. Just inside the Lin Xin Men is the Zhuang Yuan Bridge (Zhuang Yuan Qiao), a small stone footbridge crossing the square-shaped **Pan Pool** (Pan Chi). "Pan" means being enlightened by education.

In addition to Carl F. Kupfer's 1913 account, *Sacred Places in China*, the best description of Bai Lu Dong available in English is contained in John Meskill's, *Academies in Ming China*, published by the University of Arizona Press in 1982.

Bai Lu Dong is located on the southeastern ring road around the foot of Lushan, in between Hai Hui Temple to the north and Guanyin Qiao to the south. The nearest major town is Xing Zi, the former Nankang, about five miles to the south.

Phone: 879-2291

Qi Xian Valley (Qi Xian Gu)

Back on the main highway, the poorly maintained road continues on to the small town of Bai He Zhen (White Crane Town), whose major purpose is to serve as a crossroads. Straight ahead on the main road is Xing Zi, the largest city on Lushan's eastern slopes. Turn left at the statue of two silver aluminum deer and you will head up Taiyi Lu to another intersection where a white gate on the left marks the access road to the famed Qi Xian Valley (Qi Xian Gu). Arriving at the end of the pavement, a giant new gate shaped like a fortress marks the beginning of the valley where no vehicles are allowed.

Fields and peaks of Mount Lushan with waves of clouds rolling in like the ocean tide.

Goddess of Mercy Bridge (Guanyin Qiao)

After paying 18 Rmb to enter the area, the attendants will open the fortress gate and allow you inside. Mountain peaks of Lushan hover above you while rice fields surround you. You pass an antiquated wooden waterwheel still in use, and then the deep **San Xia Jian** gorge begins to appear to your left. Just before reaching the gorge, you will pass the **Sixth Spring under Heaven** (Zhao Yin Quan) hidden inside a small stone pavilion (Liu Quan Ting). Although it may not look that appealing to drink from today, it supposedly received its designation from Lu Yu, known as the "Tea Sage" of China.

An ancient wooden water wheel on the trail to Zhao Yin Quan and Guanyin Qiao.

The San Xia Jian near Guanyin Qiao.

The ancient stone Guanyin Bridge (Guanyin Qiao) over the San Xia Jian canyon.

Suddenly, the single arch, stone block **Goddess of Mercy Bridge** (Guanyin Qiao) appears, perched 18.3 m (60 ft) above the depths of the Three Gorges Canyon (San Xia Jian). The stream's white water pours and roars through the rock crevices of the deep gorge down below. This bridge is sometimes said to have been built in the Jin Dynasty (265–420 AD), although other sources date its construction later, in the Zhen Zong reign (998–1022) of the Northern Song (Bei Song) Dynasty, between 1011–1014. We know that the Northern Song poet Su Dong Po (Su Shi) (1037–1101) saw the bridge during his ten-day vist to Lushan in 1084. In his journal known as the *Forest of Records*, Su described what he called the "Three Gorges Bridge (San Xia Qiao)" as being "beyond comparison" and one of "the two most entrancing spots" he saw during his visit. Still in good condition after at least 1,000 years, it continues to carry travelers across the stream. The bridge is crafted from seven parallel rows of arched stone blocks interlocked in a mortise and tenon pattern. Each one of the 105 granite blocks is 24.4 m (80.1 ft) long, 4.1 m (13.5 ft) wide, 10.7 m (35.1 ft) high, and weighs 1 tonne. On a boulder near the bridge are the characters "Jin Jing," meaning "Golden Well," the name for this part of the gorge.

A shrine with wooden statues inside the Ci Hong Si temple.

Immediately on the other side of the bridge is the single hall of the **Ci Hong Si** Buddhist temple with new, as yet ungilded, sandal wood images.

Turning left at the Ci Hong Si and heading downstream along the edge of the gorge takes you to the **Guanyin Qiao Hotel and Restaurant**. This place has clean, well-furnished rooms for just

The terrace in front of the Ci Hong Si temple.

Steps lead down to the San Xia Jian canyon near Guanyin Qiao.

150 Rmb, but amenities are few. Peace and quiet is in abundance, but there are no telephones, hot water, or bath towels, and the nearest store or taxi cab is far away in the town of Xing Zi. All electricity seems to be solar powered. The restaurant serves simple but affordable Chinese-style food, and its window seats have great views of the San Xia Jian gorge. However, this is the only food available anywhere in the valley, and it can get old fast. There are no cold drinks since the restaurant has no refrigeration. When this restaurant is closed, you go hungry.

Guanyin Qiao Hotel
Phone: 265-1888
Fax: 265-2912
Web site: http://www.china.lssn.com

The Qi Xian Valley above Guanyin Qiao.

The **Couple Tree** (Fuqi Shu), still standing near the hotel, is actually a pair of intertwined trees originally planted by Chiang Kai Shek (Jiang Jieshi) and his wife Song Meiling during one of their many visits to Lushan sometime in the Min Guo era.

Guanyin Qiao used to mark the end of a trail that descended all the way from Han Po Kou on the summit of Mount Lushan. Part of the original foot trail can still be followed as far as the Qi Xian Si Buddhist temple. Hiking up a gradual incline through a forest of pine trees, you find none of the infuriating endless flights of stone steps so typical of trails in China. After reaching an unmarked fork in a trail, you turn to the right and continue following the course of the stream rushing in the gorge down below.

The first sight on your left is the small **Lu Duan Spring** (Lu Duan Quan), followed immediately by an overhead view of the much more impressive **Wo Waterfall** (Wo Pu) and **Jade Pool** (Yu Yuan Tan) on your right. At this spot, the stream rushes over a rock cliff into a deep water pool surrounded by natural rock on all sides. In 1907, two Christian missionaries, including a faculty member of St. John's University in Shanghai, drowned while swimming here.

A little further up the trail, a rock terrace opens up to the right, and you can walk out to the edge of the stream and stand at the top of the Wo Waterfall where it plunges down into the Jade Pool below. This rock terrace is covered with aged inscriptions that have been chiseled into the rock. In one corner of this rock terrace is a massive square inscription protected by a low stone railing. This is the **Feng Yu Xiang Shou Shu Shi Ke Mo Zi Pian**, a very lengthy essay about the Confucian philosopher Mo Zi (470–391 BC) written by the Min Guo warlord, **Feng Yu Xiang** (1882–1948), in his own handwriting during one of his visits to Lushan.

The Wo Pu Waterfall drops dramatically down into the Jade Pool (Yu Yuan Tan) in the Qi Xian Valley just below Qi Xian Si Buddhist Temple.

The treacherou Jade Pool (Yu Yuan Tan) whe a teacher of St. John's University was found, drowne

PERSONALITIES

Feng Yu Xiang once commanded his own army of followers known as the National People's Army (Guo Min Jun). His most famous act was undoubtedly his eviction of the last Qing Dynasty emperor, Pu Yi, from the Forbidden City in Beijing on 5 November 1924. He is usually known to Westerners somewhat naively as the "Christian General."

Feng began his military career as an officer in the Bei Yang Jun. He was a loyal supporter of the Qing Dynasty until shortly before the 1911 Revolution (Xin Hai Geming), after which he became a warlord associated with the conservative Zhili Clique. This was a group he had affiliations with untill he suddenly launched the Peking coup that ousted the emperor from the capital in 1924. After achieving notoriety from this radical action, Feng's Guo Min Jun in 1925 acquired control over Inner Mongolia and the Yellow River valley provinces of Gansu, Shaanxi, and Henan. He was able to maintain his hold on these territories with brief interruptions until 1930.

During the height of his power from 1925 to 1930, Feng was approached by virtually all Chinese political groups seeking his support. However, he displayed the traits of an ideological chameleon. From 1914 to 1925, Feng had been promoted as the so-called "Christian General" by Western missionaries in China. From 1925, they became disillusioned with him and began calling him the "Red General" instead. It was only after the death of Sun Yat Sen (Sun Zhongsun) in 1925 that Feng began to support Sun's program and join the Guomindang party. In 1926, Feng visited the Soviet Union for six months. After his return to China, he sided briefly with the left Guomindang regime based at Wuhan in 1926–1927, before choosing to side with the party's right-wing led by Chiang Kai Shek (Jiang Jieshi) in 1927. Finally, Feng launched a rebellion against Chiang (Jiang) from 1 April to 31 October 1930.

After this failed rebellion, Feng retired from politics and lived as a recluse in isolated rural areas for several years. In December 1935, he decided to join the Guomindang government and moved to the capital at Nanjing, where he lived until October 1937. He actively supported the Guomindang regime during the Sino-Japanese War (1937–1945), even retreating with them to Chongqing. However, after Japan was defeated, Feng went to the United States where he spent two years leading a publicity campaign against the Guomindang regime. When he died mysteriously in September 1948, he was rumored to be shifting towards supporting the Communist Party. In 1949, his wife even joined the new regime as a government minister. Feng was buried on Tai Shan in Shandong where he had spent many of his years in retirement after 1930.

The mammoth rock inscription of warlord Feng Yu Xiang dedicated to the philosopher Mo Zi.

The best English source on Feng's life is still James E. Sheridan's 1966 biography *Chinese Warlord*. However, many new Chinese language sources not available to Sheridan have recently been published including *Patriotic General Feng Yu Xiang (Ai Guo Jiang Jun Feng Yu Xiang)* by Guo Xu Yin published in Zhengzhou, Henan in 1987; *The Biography of Feng Yu Xiang (Feng Yu Xiang Zhuan)* edited by Gu Li Juan and published in Harbin in 1997; five volumes of *Feng Yu Xiang's Diaries (Feng Yu Xiang Ji Ri)* published in 1992 by the Second National Archives in Nanjing; and *Feng Yu Xiang Nian Pu* edited by Jiang Tie Sheng and published in Jinan in 2003 by the Qi Lu Shu She.

Stone ruins at Qi Xian Si Buddhist Temple.

Qi Xian Buddhist Temple (Qi Xian Si)

Beyond this spot, the trail bends to the right through a terraced clearing of rice fields, buttressed by stone retaining walls. Suddenly the Qi Xian Buddhist Temple (Qi Xian Si) appears in front of you. When the author visited the site in May 2003 the temple was in the process of being rebuilt, with rows of concrete pillars for a new hall sticking up out of the ground. Beside this stood the remains of one small original wooden-beam hall, with only three walls still standing. The side missing a wall exposed the interior of the hall, which contained three large golden Buddhist effigies. On the right stood Guanyin, and beside her two other incarnations of Buddha, all wearing golden silk robes. Beside this main hall was a one-story barrack-like structure containing

Above: Stone Buddhist Tomb Pagoda on the trail from Guanyin Qiao to Qi Xian Si Buddhist Temple.

The old temple halls of Qi Xian Si Buddhist Temple under reconstruction.

Buddhist statues inside the old temple halls of Qi Xian Si Buddhist Temple.

two small shrines, one of them devoted to Guanyu. A few stone relics littered the ground, including some broken tablets and stone pillar pedestals. There were no resident monks visible, and the place seemed abandoned, although one two-story barrack hall had obviously once been a residence. In the center of the dirt courtyard stood one large tree that may have been there since the original temple was founded.

The name Qi Xian Si means **Temple of Seven Sages**. The original temple grounds were surrounded by a red wall. The main entrance gate was inscribed with the phrase "Bu Er Fa Men" or "The Gate of the Only Teaching." Directly inside the gate was a statue of the Maitreya Buddha (Mi Le Fo). Visitors in 1921 found that a few monks of the Chan (Zen) sect were still living here at that time. The temple was founded during the Jin Dynasty (265–420 AD). However, it seems to have been given its present name in 825AD by the Tang Dynasty Confucian scholar Li Bo (773–831). The surrounding valley gets its name from this temple.

A statue of the War God Guan Yu at Qi Xian Si Buddhist Temple.

The old trail to Han Po Kou continues past the temple to a small village, which is named after the temple, but which the locals pronounce as Xi Xian Si. You can continue up the trail to a second smaller nameless village, but here the old trail disappears. There is a stone bridge across the stream here, and if you cross it to the other side it is possible to climb up the terraced fields to Taiyi Lu. However there aren't really any more interesting sights within walking distance, with the exception of the small, hard to find, and currently closed **Taiping Buddhist Temple** (Tai Ping Si). Distance and terrain make it impossible to walk to Han Po Kou from here since the old trail has not been maintained.

The Qi Xian Valley near Qi Xian Si Buddhist Temple.

The hair-raising road to Taiyi Peak crosses this stream without a bridge. Beside the crossing is a rock inscribed with the words "White Crane Canyon" (Bai He Jian). The author saw a car plummet headlong into the river and capsize at this very spot.

Taiyi Village (Taiyi Cun)

You can hire a minibus in Xing Zi or Bai Lu Zhen to make the trip up Taiyi Lu to Taiyi Village on the top of Taiyi Peak (Taiyi Feng) of Mount Lushan. The road is extremely long, and although it makes a gradual ascent initially, it reaches a ford across the river where there is no bridge, and which is difficult to cross on foot. A large rock beside the stream here is inscribed with the three characters for "Bai He Jian" which means "White Crane Canyon." After this ford, the road begins to switch back up the mountainside in a series of terrifying hairpin corners that drop off into space. At the last hairpin corner, there is a terrific view of a large waterfall cascading down the mountainside.

The closed entrance to the small Tai Ping Si Buddhist Temple. It is in a very isolated spot that can be reached from the Taiyi Peak Road.

Above: A modern pavilion at the top of Taiyi Peak looks down on the Qi Xian Valley below.
Below, left: The Taiyi Peak Hotel stands isolated, alone, and abandoned on a windy mountain top.
Below, right: A stone villa atop Taiyi Peak that once belonged to the Guomindang military leaders.

A rickety flight of bamboo steps leads up to a platform for looking at the enormous inscribed Taiyi Stone (Taiyi Shi).

Eventually the road reaches a false summit where you will find the recently built three-story **Taiyi Hotel** (Taiyi Binguan), standing in the middle of nowhere. If the Guanyin Qiao Hotel seems isolated, the Taiyi Hotel might as well be on the moon. Here, there is no village or town of any kind and the nearest stores or restaurants are miles away at the bottom of the mountain, down a suicidal one-lane road. The hotel does not do a lot of business and seems abandoned from the outside. However, a knock on the locked door reveals a few caretakers hiding inside who are willing to let you in upon request. The wind here is incredibly strong, and feels as if it could blow you off the mountain.

Phone: 255-0888

Above: A small pavilion atop Taiyi Peak (Taiyi Feng).
Left: The stone swimming pool atop Taiyi Peak (Tai Yi Feng) where Guomindang military leaders once swam during their relaxing holidays here.

A powerful waterfall rushes down into White Crane Canyon (Bai He Jian) below, viewed from the precipitous edge of a hairpin corner on the frighteningly steep and narrow road up to Taiyi Peak (Taiyi Feng).

Nearby is the Jiujiang Lushan Jiu Qi Lu You Xian Gongsi, which has a small garden and pavilion with spectacular views of the Qi Xian Valley below. There is also a terminal for the cable car line (*suo dao*) that runs up to Han Po Kou, but it was not operating when the author visited.

From the hotel, the road continues a short distance further uphill. It ends at the **Taiyi Village** (Taiyi Cun) parking lot, from where a network of stone paved foot trails wander through a thick bamboo forest. Here you will find hidden a number of stone walled villas, built by a group of 18 high-ranking Guomindang military officers as a private holiday resort during the Min Guo period. Each villa has a sign, written in Chinese, describing its brief history. The stone swimming pool used by the officers still exists today. Stone inscriptions left by the original occupants can be found in several places, most notably in the enormous

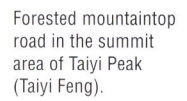

Forested mountaintop road in the summit area of Taiyi Peak (Taiyi Feng).

Taiyi Stone (Taiyi Shi), a huge boulder with two massive characters chiseled into it. Stone carvings were also inlaid in the wall of the former blockhouse at the entrance of the village. The name "village" is somewhat misleading as there do not seem to be any permanent residents here, and there are no facilities of any kind outside of the semi-abandoned hotel.

A round moon gate (*yue men*) on Taiyi Peak (Taiyi Feng).

Han Po Kou Trail
A steep descent of 3,500 stone steps leads down from an elevation of 975.4 m (3,200 ft) at Han Po Kou, through the Qi Xian Valley until it arrives at the southeastern foot of Lushan. Here, it connects with the southern ring road leading to other historic sights in either direction. Along the way down, or up, the Qi Xian Valley trail passes many fascinating natural and historical sights. A number of small pavilions serve as rest stops along this extremely difficult trail. Descending 243.8 m (800 ft), the first rest stop comes at the **Pavilion of Joy** (Huan Xi Ting). A short distance down is the stone **Shoulder Resting Pavilion** (Xi Jian Ting). The name of this place dates from the time when chair bearers traveled up and down the path, carrying passengers who were seated in compartments balanced on bamboo poles stretched over the shoulders of several men. The Han Yang and Wu Lao Peaks can both be seen from here. At 304.8 m (1,000 ft), the steps finally end and the trail passes through a gateway into rolling foothills.

Lushan Southern Slopes (Lushan Nan Shan)
Xing Zi
The town of Xing Zi, situated on the shores of Poyang Lake and at the foot of Beautiful Peak (Xiu Feng), is the biggest city on the eastern slopes of Lushan, although technically it is in the

area known as Lushan Shan Nan, or Lushan South Mountain. This town has a lot of modern conveniences not found elsewhere outside of Jiujiang. Unfortunately the area has suffered an immense amount of environmental damage, spoiling much of its natural beauty. Nonetheless, it is a relief to find stores that actually sell cold drinks and other necessities.

There is also a decent and affordable hotel here, the **Nankang Binguan**, although it is far from new. Nankang was Xing Zi's previous name, and it is this name that appears on maps and in books published before 1949.

Phone: 266-6560

Beautiful Peak (Xiu Feng)

The main highway passing through Xing Zi to the **Beautiful Peak (Xiu Feng) Scenic Site** travels through acres of stone quarries on both sides of the road where the deafening sound of rock saws and choking dust of white powder fills the air. It seems this is where all the stone sculptures of ornamental lions and dragons are mass produced for all of China. You have to pass through this unpleasant area to get to Beautiful Peak (Xiu Feng), so roll up your windows, plug your nose, hold your breath, and cover your ears.

An impressive old gate tower in Xing Zi town. Inside the pavilion on top sits a man whose full-time job is to scare visitors away with threats of imminent arrest.

Although it was once considered one of the most beautiful sights on Lushan, nowadays **Beautiful Peak** (Xiu Feng) is a bit of a disappointment, and may not be worth the day-long expedition it takes to get there from Jiujiang. Admission tickets are an exorbitant 50 Rmb per person, and there are no maps available in any language to help guide visitors through the area. Inside, the atmosphere is somewhat like an amusement park, including an incredibly fake one-hall Buddhist temple with a single actor pretending to be a monk. Many of the historic sights shown on earlier maps and described by earlier travelers seem to have disappeared. Furthermore, local touts seem to wander about attempting to prey on innocent foreign visitors.

Past the fake temple is a 1940s era resort consisting of a row of several red brick buildings.

Phone 255-1957

Follow the single trail beyond the hotel and you will come to a small stone pagoda beside the trail, before finally reaching a dragon pool at the bottom of the falls. Around the pool are many inscriptions chiseled into the rocks, some of which are reputed to be poems written by famous visitors over the years. This spot tends to be extremely crowded, and not very peaceful. From here the trail heads straight up endless flights of vertical stone steps if you care to get closer looks at the two waterfalls. A lower trail crosses a bridge over the stream, below the dragon pool, and heads over to the bottom station of the cable car (*suo dao*), which can take you higher up the mountainside for views of the two waterfalls. However, when the author was there the cable car was not operating, just like the one on Taiyi Peak. Many tourist services in this area seem to operate on an extremely casual and random schedule, so do not count on them being available.

This scenic area was once the site of an ancient Buddhist temple and now includes many natural wonders as well as historic monuments and relics. The name "Xiu Feng" means "beautiful peak", and in this case the name fits. Historic structures and relics include the **Number One Hill Stone Inscription** (Di Yi Shan), the **Guanyin Pavilion** (Guanyin Ting) with its 16th century stone inscription of the bodhisattva Guanyin (Guanyin Shi Ke), **Shuang Gui Hall** (Shuang Gui Dian), **Yan Zheng Qing Tablet** (Yan Zheng Qing Bei), **Huo Lang Pavilion** (Huo Lang Ting), **Imperial Tablet** (Yu Bei), **Shu Yu Pavilion** (Shu Yu Ting), and the **Tomb Tower** (Mu Ta). The Di Yi Shan inscription used to mark the gateway to a Buddhist Temple, **Xiu Feng Si**, which belonged to the Chan (Zen) sect and was built by an emperor during the Southern Tang (Nan Tang) Dynasty. However, this temple was destroyed during the Taiping Rebellion and still had not been rebuilt when visitors explored the site in 1921. Only scattered ruins remain today. Two other historic structures which were still standing in 1921 were the **Xiu Feng Pagoda** (Xiu Feng Ta), a seven-story, hexagonal, granite structure above Double Sword Peak, and the **Yellow Cliff Temple** (Huang Ya Si)

The iron bell on top of the Xing Zi gate tower. Taking this photo caused the author to be chased by an angry guard for half an hour before he gave up.

Stone Buddhist Tomb Pagoda (Mu Ta) near the Dragon Pool (Long Chi) at Beautiful Peak (Xiu Feng) near the town of Xing Zi.

This is the Dragon Pool (Long Chi) at Beautiful Peak (Xiu Feng) near the town of Xing Zi.

located at the base of the Double Sword Peak. These two sites no longer appear on maps but you can enjoy searching for them anyway.

The two main natural wonders to see are the fan-shaped **Horse Tail Falls** (Ma Wei Pubu), and the **Yellow Cliff Falls** (Huang Ya Pubu), both located just beneath **Double Sword Peak** (Shuang Jian Feng). The two immense waterfalls come roaring down the mountain side and converge in a single narrow gorge, the **Qing Yu Xia**, that flows into the **Dragon Pool** (Long Chi). All along the gorge are numerous inscriptions carved into the rocks by previous visitors over hundreds of years. One of the oldest inscriptions is by the 5th century poet-scholar **Tao Yuanming** (365–427 AD). Some examples of some of the inscriptions include, "Winds, Springs, Clouds and Gorges all unite here," and, "A sight not to be missed." Pavilions have been built all along the gorge to permit a better view of the inscriptions and the falls, most notably the **Ting Tao Pavilion** (Ting Tao Ting) located beside the Dragon Pool, and the **Waterfall Watching Pavilion** (Guan Pu Ting), located further up the gorge. A cable car now runs from near Ting Tao Pavilion to the top of **Manjusri Peak**, the summit of which looks down on the Lushan Waterfall. Other natural sights in the area include the **Arhat Pine** (Luohan Song) and **Bright Spring** (Chong Ming Quan). Like the Bright Spring at Dong Lin Si, a better translation for this might be Intelligent Spring or Wisdom Spring as drinking its water is supposed to make you smarter.

The **Xiu Feng Hotel** (Xiu Feng Binguan) serves visitors to this relatively isolated part of the mountain.

Phone: 266-6422, 266-6266

Temple of Ten Thousand Pines (Yi Wan Song Si)

Half an hour's walk away from Beautiful Peak (Xiu Feng) is where the Temple of Ten Thousand Pines (Yi Wan Song Si) once stood. Supposedly, the temple dated from the Liang Dynasty (502–555 AD). Although it too was destroyed during the Taiping Rebellion, some significant ruins were still visible to visitors in 1921. Four stone tablets from the 6th century still bore the characters "Dragon, Tiger, and Clouds bless you." The mountain behind the temple is **Cloud Blessing Peak** (Yun Chin Feng). Sadly, the location of this temple is no longer shown on maps.

Temple of Conversion (Gui Zong Si)

Continuing southward on the around-the-mountain highway from the Beautiful Peak (Xiu Feng) Scenic Area, you pass through the town of **Gui Zong Zhen**, named after a famous Buddhist temple (Gui Zong Si), which locals say no longer exists. However, exploration of the foothills nearby could reveal some traces of the ruins. Unfortunately the author did not have time to do this during his several trips to Lushan.

The name "Gui Zong Si" means "Temple of Conversion." The temple was founded in the year 341 AD during the Eastern Jin (Dong Jin) Dynasty (317–419 AD). According to the story about how the temple got its name, it was originally a **Confucius Temple** (Fuzi Miao) until the abbot donated the site to Buddhist monks who had come "from the Far West," possibly meaning Tibet. When visitors inspected the site in 1921, the temple was still actively in use, with an estimated 300 monks living there. They belonged to the Chan (Zen) sect.

The yellow exterior walls enclosing the temple grounds were inscribed with records of many past emperors having come here. Upon entering the grounds, the first hall encountered was the **Heavenly King Hall** (Tian Wang Dian) containing statues of the Four Heavenly Kings (Si Tian Wang). Two other images in the hall are of the Maitreya Buddha of the Future (Mi Le Fo), and Wai Tuo Pusa.

The main hall had a roof decorated with "spiral ornaments" as a Tibetan temple would. Inside was a giant gilded statue of Buddha, and another of the bodhisattva Guanyin, crafted in Indian style with 48 arms. There was also a **Buddhist Sutras Library** (Cang Jing Ge) containing some sutras given by an emperor. Across the courtyard from the **Guest Hall** (Ke Tang) was the **Ancestors Hall** (Zu Tang) containing a figure of the temple's founder and patron saint. In the middle of the courtyard was the **Black Ink Pond** (Shui Mo Chi) around which were several inscribed tablets from the Li Zong reign (1224–1264) of the Southern Song Dynasty dated 1237.

Lushan Hot Springs (Wen Quan)

The town of Wen Quan, named after the natural hot springs (*wen quan*) in this area, is another disappointment. It is a dirty little town without a single paved street, the main highway having turned to mud. From Wen Quan Town, it is possible to cross a mountain pass over the southern foothills of Lushan and then circle around to the road along Lushan's western slopes and follow it all the way back to Jiujiang, passing the sites of Dong Lin Si and so on along the way.

Getting There

Either a tense hair-raising white-knuckle ride in a taxi (80 Rmb) or a public bus (7 Rmb) from Jiujiang takes you up to the top of Lushan mountain. This goes via the narrow ribbon of seemingly endless blind hairpin corners dropping off into thin air, almost worse and certainly longer than the Yun Gu Si road up Huang Shan. As frightening as the ascent may seem today, before 1949 there was no road to the summit, and visitors had to walk or be carried in sedan chairs up thousands of stone steps.

Today visitors arrive by bus or taxi at the Lushan North Gate (Lushan Bei Men), where it is necessary to buy an 85 Rmb admission ticket into the mountain top area. (You will have to pay a 20 Rmb fee for your taxi if this how you got there.) The white fog can be so thick here at the mountain pass that you cannot see the ticket booth from the taxi. After passing through a tunnel and driving through Guling Town, the main road — known as the Huan Shan Highway here — proceeds down the East Valley (Dong Gu). After this, it runs along the shore of Lulin Lake, and then eventually exits out the Lushan South Gate (Nan Men). The road then heads in the direction of Nanchang, from where you can also approach the mountain, albeit for a much higher taxi or bus fare.

Lushan Practical Information

Lushan Area Code: (0792)

Lushan's Hotels

150 star guesthouses, ordinary hotels, sanatoriums, and resthouses which can offer over 20,000 beds.

Lushan Hotel (Lushan Binguan)

This is the most luxurious and expensive hotel on Lushan. In the East Valley, just below Guling Town.

Address: 446 He Xi Lu
Phone: 828-2060
Fax: 828-2843
Prices: 120–580 Rmb

Guling Fandian

Address: 104 He Dong Lu
Phone: 828-2200
Fax: 828-2209
Prices: 200–400 Rmb

Lushan Dasha
This is the former Guomindang officers' training school in the East Valley.

Address: 506 He Xi Lu
Phone: 828-2178

Lulin Hotel
This hotel is a complex of old, stone-walled summer resort buildings near Lulin Hu.

Address: No. 1347
Phone: 828-2424, 828-2120
Fax: 828-1262
Prices: 160 Rmb normal rate / 280 Rmb holiday rate

Lushan Xiao Xia Hotel
A modern three-story hotel near the People's Assembly Hall in the East Valley.

Address: No. 511
Phone: 828-9950, 829-4588, 829-4589
Fax: 828-1301

Lushan Xing Run Mansion (Lushan Xing Run Dasha)
Set in the midst of pine trees, this is a three-story, stone-walled, old villa in the East Valley.

Address: No. 361
Phone: 828-8721, 828-8720
Fax: 828-8725

Lushan San He Hotel
A modern hotel, west of Guling town, on Da Lin Peak.

Address: No. 809 Hui Yuan Lu
Phone: 829-9966, 829-5555
Fax: 829-9977

Xing Long Hotel
Another modern hotel on Da Lin Peak, also west of Guling Town.

Address: No. 1168 Hui Yuan Lu
Phone: 828-9220, 828-9221, 828-9222

XDT Hotel
Also located on Da Lin Peak, this modern hotel lies west of Guling Town.

Phone: 828-8858
Fax: 828-8857

Lushan Travel Agents:

Lushan Tour Bureau
Address: Guling Lu
Phone: 828-2998

Lushan Scenic Area Administrative Bureau
Phone: 828-2998

Lushan Tour Service Co.
Phone: 828-1083

Lushan Tour Co.
Address: 443 He Xi Lu
Phone: 828-2482

Lushan China Travel Service (CTS)
Address: 1042 Guling Lu
Phone: 828-2427

Lushan China International Travel Service (CITS)
Phone: 828-2497

China Travel Tickets Booking Center
Address: 1042 Guling Lu
Phone: 828-1862
Fax: 828-7783

Jinye Tickets Center
Address: Bai Yun Restaurant on Zheng Lu
Phone: 828-5343

Part 2:

Topics of Interest

The Treaty Ports

D uring the Ming Dynasty, Nanjing served as China's ocean port, and the fleet of Admiral **Zheng He** (1371–1435) sailed up and down the Yangzi headed to and from expeditions around the world. According to recent historical research, China actually dominated the world's oceans from this Nanjing seaport, from 1405 to 1433. This was long before the first oceanic voyages of European explorers such as Vasco de Gama, Columbus, or Captain Cook.

Establishing the Treaty Port System

In a stunning reversal of fortunes, the First Opium War, which had started in Guangzhou in December 1839, ended with the 29 August 1842 **Treaty of Nanking**. The treaty, which was negotiated at the Jing Hai Temple in Nanjing and signed on board the British warship HMS Cornwallis anchored in the Yangzi River, ceded Hong Kong to the British and opened up five coastal treaty ports in the cities of Guangzhou, Xiamen, Fuzhou, Ningbo, and Shanghai. There is a new museum at **Jing Hai Temple** in Nanjing devoted to this treaty.

Subsequent treaties, such as the 1858 **Treaty of Tientsin** (Tianjin) – which was ratified and implemented only after the foreign armies occupied Beijing in 1860, and which ended the Second Opium War of 1856–1860 – and the 1876 Chefoo (Yantai) Convention, opened up a whole series of treaty ports up and down the Yangzi River, including Chongqing, Yichang, Wuhan, Jiujiang, Wuhu, Nanjing, and Zhenjiang. When China lost the First Sino-Japanese War of 1894-1895, the **Treaty of Shimonseki** added Japan to the list of foreign powers entitled to the same treaty port rights as Great Britain, France, and the United States.

As a result of these treaties, foreigners set up thriving colonial communities up and down the Yangzi River from Chongqing to Shanghai. Within these concessions, they enjoyed extraterritoriality, meaning they were not subject to Chinese law. They had their own municipal governments, police forces, fire departments, etc. In addition, foreign troops could be stationed there, and foreign warships could sail up and down the Yangzi River.

Consuls and Commissioners

In any Yangzi River treaty port, the two most important men were usually the British Consul and the Customs Commissioner, who was British even though he was a Chinese government employee. The Chinese maritime customs had first been taken over by the British Consul at Shanghai in 1854, when the rebellion of the Small Sword Society occupied the Chinese districts of Shanghai and burned down the original customs house. This later led to creation of a new Imperial Chinese Customs Service in 1861. Each treaty port had a Customs House which was located in a prominent spot on the waterfront Bund and was often the most impressive-looking structure of the town. The Customs Houses in Wuhan and Shanghai still stand today. The customs commissioners of each treaty port reported to the Inspector General of Customs, who was also British.

Sir **Robert Hart** (1835–1911) was by far the longest serving Inspector General and the early history of the service is thus nearly inseparable from his biography. Hart came to China in 1854 and served in the British Consular Service until 1859 when he resigned to join the Chinese Imperial Maritime Customs Service. At that time, the Customs Service was in the process of formation, and was not finally established until 1861, after the October 1860 Convention of Peking had ended the Second Opium War. During the first two years (1861–1863) of the new customs service, the nominal head was the rather peculiar Horatio N. Lay, who spent nearly his entire term as Inspector General on leave in Europe. During Lay's two-year absence from China, Hart served as acting Inspector General. When Lay resigned in 1863 due to the scandal surrounding his attempt to operate his own private fleet of warships in Chinese waters, the infamous Lay-Osbourne Flotilla, Hart officially became Inspector General. He held this post for the next 48 years until his death in September 1911, just before the fall of the Qing Dynasty he served so faithfully. Hart was actually considered to be too biased in favor of the Chinese viewpoint by some Westerners, and after the 1900 siege of the foreign legations in Beijing, he tried to explain it as all a misunderstanding in his book, *These From the Land of Sinim*, published in 1901. A famous statue of Hart once stood on the Bund opposite the Custom House in Shanghai, but this is now gone.

The customs service did much more than just collect trade tariffs. It expanded its role to the point that it completely controlled Chinese inland and coastal navigation. In addition to the customs commissioner at each treaty port, its staff included harbor masters, river inspectors, coastal inspectors, harbor and river pilots, engineers, and lighthouse staff, a large percentage of whom were foreigners. By 1896, the customs service had even taken over the Chinese postal service, so that the Inspector General of Customs was now concurrently the Inspector General of Posts. In 1901, the customs service began collecting taxes on domestic trade within China, in addition to the foreign trade it had exclusively taxed before. This was the cause of much local discontent amongst the Chinese merchants at the treaty ports.

After the 1911 Revolution, the postal service became an independent agency run by the Chinese government, but the Maritime Customs Service continued to function as a British-dominated extra-governmental institution as it had before. The only change was that the Inspector General and his headquarters were now based in Shanghai rather than Beijing as they had been before.

The customs service also became quite active in publishing English language volumes about China's inland and coastal navigation, including many useful studies of the Yangzi River region's geography, economy, politics, history, and culture. By 1937, it was issuing nine different series of daily, monthly, annual, and decennial trade reports. In addition to these trade reports, it published 44 volumes in its Special Series; 51 volumes in its Miscellaneous Series; 75 in its Service Series; 132 in its Office Series; and 10 in its Inspectorate Series.

Sir **Frederick Maze** (1874–1959) was the most illustrious of Hart's successors. He had had a long career in the Customs Service with postings throughout the Yangzi River treaty ports. He served as Customs Commissioner at Yichang (1900), Wuhan (1921–1925), and Shanghai (1925–1929), before finally becoming Inspector General of Customs in 1929. This was a post he held until he was interned by the Japanese in December 1941. He was later released in 1943.

One of the most prominent British Consuls on the Yangzi River was Sir **Alwyne Ogden** (1889–1981), who had the knack for repeatedly finding himself in hotspots during the phase of China's rising nationalism and Britain's declining imperial power. Ogden served as Consul in Wuhan in 1925, during a period of strikes and protests. He went on to be Consul at Jiujiang from February 1926 to January 1927, when he was responsible for organizing the evacuation of all British residents in the face of the concession's forcible occupation by military forces of the leftist Guomindang. From 1937 to 1939, he was Consul at Shanghai, where he organized the evacuation of British civilians who wished to flee the city after it was encircled and gradually strangled by the Japanese in November 1937. From the frying pan of besieged Shanghai, he jumped into the fire of Japanese-occupied Nanjing, where he served as Consul from February 1940 to April 1941.

Western Commerce on the Yangzi

Although the Customs Commissioner and the British Consul were usually the first foreign representatives to arrive in a newly-opened port, they were soon followed by the agents of British shipping and trading firms such as Butterfield and Swire (Taiku) and Jardine Matheson (Ewo). By 1891, **Butterfield and Swire** had opened up offices in the Yangzi River ports of Zhenjiang (1890), Wuhu (1884), Jiujiang (1885), Hankou (1885), and Yichang (1891). Their fleet, sailing under the name of the **China Navigation Co.**, numbered 80 steamships by 1925. This had increased to 87 ships by 1929, making it the largest fleet on the Yangzi. They made regular runs from Shanghai as far up river as Chongqing. The names of the ships reflected the river ports they visited, such as Zhenjiang, Anqing, Jiujiang, Poyang, Shashi, Yichang, Wanxian, and Chongqing.

The oil business in China was dominated by two foreign companies, both of which relied on the Yangzi River as their distribution channel. The **Asiatic Petroleum Co.** (APC) was a British-owned oil company which had extensive shipping and tank farm facilities over in Pudong. They ran their own fleet of steamships up and down the Yangzi River. In 1929, the APC fleet numbered nine vessels. The American oil company **Standard Oil Co. of New York** (Socony) had its own fleet of nine ships sailing the Yangzi by 1925, and this increased to 11 by 1929. As part of their business operations, both APC and Socony supported resident communities of foreign employees at most of the Yangzi River treaty ports.

The **Dollar Line** (Da Lai Gongsi) was an American-owned shipping company based in San Francisco and founded by Robert Dollar (1844–1932). Dollar used his last name as a marketing tool, making the U.S. dollar sign the company logo, which was painted on all the smoke stacks and hulls of the company's ships. After Dollar's first visit to China in 1902, the Robert Dollar Co. began running its fleet of steamships up and down the Yangzi River in 1903. After 12 years of operating their China shipping business from the company's headquarters in San Francisco, they opened a branch office in Hankou in 1915, and followed this with another in Shanghai two years later. In the summer of 1919, American architect Henry K. Murphy designed a new seven-story office building for the company in Shanghai. The new offices were to be erected on a piece of property at 51 Canton Road, just behind the Union Insurance Building, and half a block from the Bund. Construction started in 1920 but completion of the building only came about in early 1922. When it was finished, the company's logo flew on the company's flag from a two-story flagpole on the roof.

Another American-owned passenger shipping line on the Yangzi was the **Yangstze Rapids Steamship Co.** They had a fleet of eight ships on the river by 1929, but mainly focused on the Three Gorges section of the Yangzi River between Yichang and Chongqing.

Although not a Western country, Japan enjoyed the same benefits as the other treaty powers after 1896. The Japanese shipping company Nishin Kisen Kabushiki Kaisha had a fleet of 26 steamships sailing between China's coastal cities and Yangzi River ports in 1929. Many of the company's ships were named after Yangzi River ports, including the Fuling Maru, the Yunyang Maru, and the Lushan Maru.

The Missionaries

According to the treaties, Christian missionaries were allowed to propagate their faith freely, a right which was interpreted to mean that the missionaries could purchase property and build churches wherever they liked. Many former treaty ports along the Yangzi still have large churches and cathedrals. Jiujiang and Yichang, for example, both have notably large Catholic cathedrals.

B.L. Putnam Weale described this phenomenon as it appeared to him on a trip he took up the Yangzi River in the year 1905:

> "In full view of everything and occupying the best site, a Roman Catholic church, massive and calculated to impress the Chinese mind, rears itself high above everything else. All along the river you notice these Roman Catholic churches, either crowning the crests of hills or pushing into the front rank at the water's edge, every site carefully chosen by the master priests of the mother Church, so that the power and dignity of the See of Rome shall be properly impressed on Chinese minds."
>
> B.L. Putname Weale, *The Reshaping of the Far East*, London: 1905.

In addition to churches and cathedrals, the missionaries were responsible for establishing a network of 16 colleges and universities in China before 1949, many of which were in the Yangzi River ports. Some of the smaller ones, such as Griffith John College in Hankou and William Nast College in Jiujiang, have disappeared. However, others such as St. John's University in Shanghai, the University of Nanking, and Ginling College in Nanjing continue to educate students to this day, albeit under new names and the new management of the Chinese government. Jessie G. Lutz has estimated that in 1936, the Christian missionary colleges in China were educating 12 percent of all Chinese college students, and that by 1947, this number had risen to as high as 20 percent. Furthermore, a study of publications such as *Who's Who in China* show that graduates of these Christian colleges formed the political and economic elite of Min Guo China.

Many of the homes and buildings the Europeans and Americans constructed still stand as one of the main attractions when visiting these places. Wuhan's five foreign concessions were known for their waterside Bund promenade, similar to Shanghai's Waitan. The entire town of Lushan, near Jiujiang, is a museum of Western architecture built between 1895 and 1937. Even in Nanjing you can still find pre-war European style buildings along its old Yangzi River waterfront promenade.

Beginning of the End

The "years that were fat" lasted a relatively short time for most treaty ports. After 1925, China began experiencing a wave of rising nationalism that gradually succeeded in reducing the presence of foreigners in the country.

In October 1926, the left wing of the Guomindang party captured Wuhan, where they set up their new central government. A few weeks later, they captured the treaty port of Jiujiang on 4 November 1926. The Wuhan regime included many famous individuals including Song Qingling, T.V. Soong (Soong Ziwen) as Finance Minister, Sun Ke (Sun Fo) as Communications Minister, Eugene Chen (Chen Yuren) as Foreign Minister, and Wang Jingwei as Head of State.

On 5 January 1927, they took over the British concessions at Hankou at Jiujiang by force. Negotiations between the Wuhan Guomindang regime and the British government resulted in the 19 February 1927 **Chen-O'Malley Agreement** whereby Britain had to surrender its concessions at Hankou and Jiujiang effective 15 March 1927. Meanwhile, the Guomindang army advanced progressively down the Yangzi River, occupying first Anqing and then Wuhu. Each time the army captured another town, anti-foreign riots broke out and the foreign communities had to be evacuated by British and American warships patrolling the river.

In Nanjing, the resident foreign community was terrorized during the Guomindang's 24 March 1927 occupation of the city and forced to flee for their lives, suffering numerous casualties along the way. Several first-hand accounts have been published describing their perilous escape from the city by climbing over the Ming city wall.

Jessie G. Lutz has estimated that by July 1927, out of the 8,000 Christian missionaries who had been living and working in inland China at the start of the year, only 500 remained. This exodus led to the appointment of the first Chinese presidents of Christian colleges in 1928, and the registration of these institutions with the new Chinese central government in Nanjing starting in 1929.

Foreign Gunboats on the Yangzi

As part of the treaty port system, foreign warships sailed up and down the river between Shanghai and Chongqing on a daily basis. Britain and the United States had special fleets based in Shanghai which served just this purpose.

The U.S. Navy's squadron of ships known as the **Yangtze River Patrol** existed in various forms from 1854 to 1941. It was this squadron which was immortalized in the book and movie, *Sand Pebbles*. In 1874, the USS Ashuelot became the first U.S. naval vessel to reach Yichang from Shanghai, but was unable to get upstream through the gorges. Forty years later, in 1914, two U.S. Navy gunboats, the USS Palos and the USS Monocacy, became the first ships of the Yangtze River Patrol able to navigate the gorges and reach Chongqing. Six new gunboats were added to the Yangtze River Patrol in 1926–1927, including the infamous USS Panay, all of which were capable of reaching Chongqing. These ships were responsible for protecting the lives and property of foreign missionaries, merchants, and diplomats. On more than one occasion, they had to be called upon to evacuate foreign residents of the treaty ports and move them out of harm's way, most notably during the events of 1927 when foreigners fled from the Yangzi River towns of Wuhan, Jiujiang, Nanjing, and Zhenjiang.

Although all the Yangzi treaty ports between Chongqing and Shanghai were lost in 1927, it was not until the Japanese invasion ten years later that the foreign naval presence on the river finally disappeared. The penultimate sign of the changing times came with the 12 December 1937 **Panay Incident** in which the U.S. naval vessel evacuating the American embassy staff from Nanjing was attacked and sunk by repeated waves of Japanese bombers and fighter planes, despite the fact that it was flying the American flag on a clear sunny day. After the Japanese occupation of the surrounding area, the Shanghai

International Settlement continued to exist from 1937 to 1941 as an isolated island cut off from the Yangzi River trade that once made it an economic center. The surviving ships of the Yangtze River Patrol were bottled up in Shanghai until just before the attack on Pearl Harbor, when they were evacuated to the Philippines just in time to be captured by the Japanese there.

The Sun Sets on Empire

In January 1943, a treaty was signed in Chongqing between China, Britain, and the United States which formally eliminated all the Yangzi River treaty ports, Shanghai's foreign concessions, the U.S. Navy's Yangtze River Patrol, and British control over the Chinese Maritime Customs Service. Nonetheless, the position of British Consul was retained for some major cities.

After the Japanese surrender, Alwyne Ogden returned to Shanghai to serve as Consul again from 1945 to 1948. During this time, he was responsible for organizing the rescue and repatriaion of the 7,000 Britons who had been held in Japanese internment camps in China during the war.

A final humiliating end to the foreign naval presence on the Yangzi was sounded on 20 April 1949 with the crisis over the British naval vessel, the **HMS Amethyst**, which was attacked and captured by Communist forces while attempting to resupply the British embassy in Nanjing. Although the ship eventually escaped, this was only after weeks of being held hostage and with a great loss of life among the officers and crew. Today, the **Zhenjiang Museum** commemorates the Amethyst incident with some artifacts taken from the ship, including its anchor.

Departure of the Missionaries

Even after the establishment of the People's Republic in October 1949, many Christian missionaries tried to remain in China. This was particularly true of those serving as faculty and administrators at the 13 foreign-funded Christian universities which then existed in China, such as the **University of Nanking** and **Ginling College** in Nanjing, and **St. John's University** in Shanghai. Although they had previously been criticized often for supposedly hiding behind the protection of foreign gunboats and diplomats, the fact that so many were willing to stay on even after the rest of the foreign presence had departed shows that they had some guts after all.

As late as the fall of 1950, some universities' faculty still included foreign missionaries. However, new regulations governing religious organizations were issued in January 1951. These regulations prohibited any financial support from foreign countries, thus cutting the universities and their missionary staff off from their overseas organizations and sources of funds. A national conference of Protestant church leaders held in Beijing in April 1951 resulted in the expulsion of the final remaining foreign missionaries from China. The foreign presence in China was then back to where it had been in 1839.

Navigation of the Lower Yangzi River

Exploration and Opening

In the First Opium War (1839–1842), British ships were never able to get any further upriver than Nanjing. However, after the signing of the 1858 Treaty of Tianjin, Lord Elgin reached Hankou on 6 December 1858 in the first foreign warship to sail past Nanjing.

In early 1861, Admiral Sir James Hope led a second naval expedition from Shanghai to establish new British consulates at Zhenjiang, Jiujiang, and Hankou. However, Hope only reached Yuezhou (Yueyang), 253 km (158 miles) west of Hankou, before turning back. Captain Blakiston disembarked at Yozhou and managed to become the first European to travel all the way through the gorges to Chongqing by native river craft, even continuing westward as far as Ping Shan on the border of Yunan.

Anglo-American Rivalry

Following hot on the heels of Admiral Hope's opening up of the lower Yangzi to foreign trade as far west as Hankou, the American trading firm Russell & Co. formed the Shanghai Steam Navigation Co. in 1862, which quickly established a monopoly on Yangzi River passenger and cargo shipping. By 1872, the Shanghai Steam Navigation Co. had a fleet of 17 steamships on the river. However, new competition began to appear the same year when, in 1872, John Swire formed the China Navigation Co. as the Yangzi River arm of Alfred Holt's ocean-going Blue Funnel Line. In 1873, the China Merchants Steam Navigation Co. was formed. Four years later, in 1877, they were able to purchase the entire river fleet of the American-owned Shanghai Steam Navigation Co., which had dominated Yangzi River commerce over the previous years. After having been forcibly driven off the river by the Shanghai Steam Navigation Co. back in 1867, Jardine Matheson returned to the Yangzi in 1881 with the establishment of their Indo-China Steam Navigation Co.

The China Tea Races

In the 19th century, one fascinating aspect of the shipping scene along the lower Yangzi was the annual

Tea Races which were held every May when the high-water season began. In these races, the fastest ocean-going steamers competed to be the first to sail up the Yangzi as far as Hankou, pick up a load of fresh Chinese tea, and sail back to London with their cargo. The fastest ships would command the highest freight rates and were the first to sell their cargo of tea in London at the highest prices. The race would also attract wagers, in the form of a lottery, on which ship would be first. As many as 17 ships would compete each year, with the main competitors being the red-funnel Glen Line, owned by McGregor, Gow & Co., and the Blue Funnel Line, owned by Alfred Holt. Although races between ships visiting China's coastal ports had been going on for some years, the Yangzi River Tea Races did not really get started until the opening of the Suez Canal in 1869. From then on, the time required to visit Hankou and return to London with a cargo of tea continued to experience an annual decrease over the next 14 years. In 1870, the fastest ships took 61 days to travel from Hankou to London, but by 1883, they had reached their peak speed of only 31 days, having cut the required time nearly in half. The trip downriver from Hankou to Wusong could, by itself, take as little as 36 hours by steaming non-stop without halting at any ports along the way. However, after 1883, increased competition from tea grown in British India and the great cost of building fast ocean-going steamers caused the China Tea Races to effectively be discontinued. Thereafter, the annual time spent transporting tea from Hankou to London actually increased and in 1885, the time required to travel the distance returned to that clocked nearly a decade earlier in 1876.

Buddhism in China

Historical Development

Although most Westerners seem to associate Buddhism with neighboring Tibet, China, in fact, has a much older Buddhist tradition. Its origins date back about 800 years, even before Buddhism became the dominant religion in Tibet in the 9th Century AD.

Eastern Han Dynasty (25–220AD)

Buddhism was reportedly first introduced into China during the reign of **Emperor Ming Ti** (58–76 AD) of the **Eastern Han Dynasty** (25–220 AD). It was in the year 67 AD that **White Horse Temple** (Bai Ma Si), the very first Buddhist temple in China, was constructed in Henan Province near the Han capital city of Luoyang. Construction of the temple was prompted by the arrival of two monks from India who came riding on the backs of white horses. The temple still exists, along with the graves of the two monks.

Eastern Jin Dynasty (317–420AD)

During the Eastern Jin Dynasty (317–420 AD), important events in the development of Chinese Buddhism included the founding of Lingyin Si in Hangzhou in 326 AD; the founding of Dong Lin Si at Lushan in 384 AD; the beginning of the translation of Buddhist texts by the Indian **Kumarajiva** (Jiu Mo Luo Shi) in Changan (Xian) in 401 AD; the founding of the Pure Land Sect (Jing Tu Zong) by the monk Hui Yuan at Dong Lin Si in Lushan; and the return to China in 414 AD of the Chinese monk **Fa Xian**, who had spent the six years since 399 AD in India collecting Buddhist texts.

Hui Yuan (334–417 AD) played an important role in shaping early Buddhist doctrine in China during the Eastern Jin Dynasty (317–420 AD). For this reason, he is known as the father of the main interpretation of the faith still practiced in the country today. Buddhism originally had two main schools of thought, the older **Theravada** or Minayana (Lesser Vehicle or Xiao Cheng) and the later **Mahayana** (Greater Vehicle or Da Cheng). The earlier Theravada school was a more monastic and scholastic faith which emphasized the need to achieve personal spiritual salvation through the rigorous study of Buddhist scriptures or **Tripitaka** (San Zang). This was best achieved by committing oneself to an austere life within a monastery. The monks in these monastaries lived off the support of the community but cared little about the spiritual salvation of the public at large. The Mahayana school, on the other hand, promoted the idea that anyone could achieve Nirvana simply by praying to a **bodhisattva** for salvation. Bodhisattva's were those Arhats or Buddhist disciples who had forsaken the opportunity to enter Nirvana in order to help save others.

Taking the Mahayana school as his starting point, Hui Yuan founded the **Pure Land** sect (Jing Tu Zong). The main purpose of the Pure Land sect was to make Buddhism appealing to a wider audience and not simply to those willing to dedicate their lives to full-time study of the scriptures in a monastery. According to Pure Land doctrines, any individual could achieve rebirth in the western paradise if they simply carried out the rituals of occasionally visiting temples to pray, chant the mantra "O-Mi-Tuo-Fo," burn incense, and do good deeds. Neither expert knowledge of the scriptures nor life in a monastery were necessary. Key parts of this school were the veneration of the **Amitabha Buddha** (O-Mi-Tuo-Fo), the **Maitreya Buddha** of the future (Mi Le Fo), and the bodhisattva **Avalokitesvara** (Guanyin), sometimes referred to as the Goddess of Mercy. In a way, this made Chinese Buddhism more like Christianity. This is the reason why it is wrong to use the word monastery, instead of temple, for most Buddhist houses of worship in China. The Jing Tu sect was incredibly successful and is today the most popular in China, with the more monastic **Chan** sect (Chan Zong; known in Japan and the West as Zen) coming in second place. Although there was once a wider variety of sects, most Buddhist temples in China today belong to either the Jing Tu or Chan schools. During the Tang Dynasty, the Jing Tu sect was exported to Japan where it still has followers.

In 402AD, Hui Yuan postulated what might be considered a doctrine that called for the separation of church and state. His treatise entitled, "A Monk Does Not Bow Down Before a King," ("*Shamen bu jing wang zhe lun*"), argued that Buddhist monks need not show any outward signs of respect to any representatives of secular authority, including the emperor. Incredibly enough, this doctrine was accepted by the Prime Minister Huan Xuan and decreed to the public as state policy. Nowadays, all religious institutions in China are closely regulated by the state, which is also their main source of financial support.

Northern & Southern Dynasties (420–589AD)

During the **Northern Wei** Dynasty (Bei Wei), imperial patronage of Buddhism caused a massive expansion in the number of Buddhist temples in China, many of which remain today. The Dunhuang Buddhist Cave Temples were begun in Gansu in 440AD, when the Northern Wei (Bei Wei) Dynasty capital city was still at Lanzhou in Gansu. The Yungang Buddhist Cave Temples were constructed at Datong on Wuzhou Shan in Shanxi from 460–494 AD, after the Northern Wei capital had moved to Pingcheng in Shanxi. The Buddhist rock carvings at Qi Xia Si outside Nanjing, in Jiangsu, were begun in 483AD. The Longmen Caves were begun in Luoyang, Henan, in 494AD. Shao Lin Si on Mount Songshan, outside Luoyang in Henan, was founded in 496AD. Huashan Si in Suzhou, Jiangsu, was founded in 503AD. It is estimated that by the 6th century AD there were 30,000 Buddhist temples in the territory governed by the Northern Wei (Bei Wei) Dynasty.

The anti-scholastic and iconoclastic Chan sect traces its origins to their First Patriarch, the Indian monk **Bodhi Dharma** (Pu Ti Da Mo). Bodhi Dharma is sometimes described as the last patriarch of Indian Buddhism and the first patriarch of Chinese Buddhism. He is said to have arrived in China sometime between 520 and 526 AD during the reign of Wu Di, the first Emperor of the Liang Dynasty, who had his capital in Nanjing. He criticized Liang Wu Di's construction of Buddhist temples, and also minimized the need for studying the Buddhist scriptures. Instead, he emphasized the importance of meditation and supposedly illustrated this by spending nine years staring at a wall.

The **Tian Tai** sect (Tian Tai Zong), was founded by Chih Yi (538–597 AD) on Tien Tai Shan in Zhejiang Province near the city of Ningbo. Chih Yi devised a new system for classifying the life and teachings of the historical Sakyamuni Buddha into five chronological periods. The sect began to receive imperial patronage in 577AD, after which Chih Yi made several trips to the imperial capital in Changan (Xian). In contrast to both the Jing Tu Zong and Chan Zong, the Tian Tai Zong emphasized the importance of seriously studying the Buddhist scriptures. Their main inspiration came from the White Lotus Sutra (Fa Hua Jing). Although it has attracted much attention from historical scholars, the Tian Tai Zong, as a living faith, has essentially died out in modern day China.

Tang Dynasty (618–907 AD)

During the Tang dynasty, the most positive event in the development of Buddhism was undoubtedly the return of the monk **Xuan Zang** (596–664 AD). In 645AD, Xuan Zang came back to the capital city of Changan (Xian) after being away for 16 years in India. Having left China in 629AD, against the explicit orders of the Tang Emperor Tai Zong (626–649 AD), he brought back with him some 657 Buddhist texts, which were later translated from Sanskrit into Chinese. Xuan Zang recorded his travels in his own work, *Record of the Western Regions*, which was published in 646AD. However, the best known version of his story is the one contained in one of Chinese literature's four greatest novels, *The Journey to the West* (Xi You Ji). This is a Ming Dynasty work written by Wu Cheng En (1500–1582) during the Jiajing reign, although the earliest printed edition dates from 1592, the 20th year of the Wan Li reign. Nonetheless, it should be emphasized that much knowledge of Buddhist doctrines had already been brought to China centuries earlier by Kumarajiva (Jiu Mo Luo Shi), Fa Xian, and Bodhi Dharma (Pu Ti Da Mo).

Several important developments occurred within the Chan sect during the early Tang Dynasty. The Sixth Patriarch of the Chan school, **Hui Neng** (638–713 AD), wrote the "Platform Sutra" (Fa Bao Tan Jing). Hui Hai (720–814 AD) introduced the practice of Chan monks performing manual labor.

In 772AD, the Tang emperor Dai Zong (762–779 AD) ordered the construction of a Manjusri Hall (Wen Shu Dian) in every Buddhist temple in China. This was the beginning of the **Wen Shu** (Manjusri) cult, which is still prevalent in Chinese Buddhism today.

However, these positive developments in Chinese Buddhism early in the Tang Dynasty were largely erased by the destruction caused when Tang Emperor Wu Zong (840–846 AD) allowed his Taoist advisers to talk him into a publicly declared campaign to completely eliminate Buddhism from China. In 844AD, he began a series of steps that slowly strangled and ultimately destroyed Buddhism in China.

First he cut off the temples' sources of financial support by forbidding laypeople to contribute or donate funds. He also banned all pilgrimages to sacred sites. Some temples in isolated mountaintop locations such as on Jiuhua Shan, Wutai Shan, and Lushan depended on pilgrimage traffic in order to survive. Much like during the years between the 1949 revolution and 1966 start of the Cultural Revolution, this elimination of outside support caused the monks residing at the temples to slowly starve and forced many to abandon their temple abodes in search of food and livelihood elsewhere.

In the same year, Wu Zong ordered the closure of all small Buddhist shrines and temples, hermitages, and hostels. Since small temples formed the majority of all temples in China, and played an important role of recruiting and training younger monks who would then move up to the larger temples later in life, this move essentially destroyed the next generation of monks who would have replaced the older generation when the latter passed away. Wu Zong also commanded that all gravestones of Buddhist monks be destroyed. Temple bells were confiscated, and monks living in the smaller temples were forced to return to lay life in their home towns. Again, this step was quite similar to that taken immediately after the 1949 Revolution.

Finally, in 845AD, after two years of increasing restrictions, Wu Zong ordered all Buddhist monks in China under the age of 50 to return to lay life, and the seizure of all property owned by Buddhist temples, including the landed estates that provided the financial income and food the temples' monks needed to survive. The Japanese Buddhist traveler Enin, who was in Xian at the time, reported that in this one city alone, 300 Buddhist monks were defrocked each day for over two weeks, until only those over the age of 50 remained. Even these remaining monks could be forcibly returned to lay life if they did not possess a valid ordination certificate issued by the government. According to Enin, these documents were often stolen from the monks by state officials eager to reduce the number of monks by any means.

Wu Zong very nearly achieved his publicly declared goal of destroying Buddhism in China. By the end of 845AD, he had issued regulations that permitted a maximum of 49 Buddhist temples staffed by no more than 800 monks to exist in all of China. By the emperor's own accounting, during his reign, he had succeeded in destroying a total of 4,600 Buddhist temples and 40,000 smaller Buddhist shrines and hermitages; and had forcibly secularized 260,500 Buddhist monks and nuns who were returned to lay life and sent back to their home towns. Finally, all Buddhist monks visiting China from foreign countries were expelled, including the Japanese monk Enin, who is the historian's main source for this time period.

Wu Zong's most destructive act may have been when he ordered all Buddhist scriptures in China to be burned in the first month of 846AD. This was followed by the nine-year Huang Chao rebellion, which resulted in nearly all monastic libraries and Buddhist scriptures in China being destroyed during the 9th century. Even finding a complete copy of the basic **Tripitaka** (San Zang) Buddhist canon apparently became quite difficult for Chinese monks.

This massive loss of Buddhist texts in turn caused the demise of the Chinese Buddhist sects that relied on scriptures and commentaries of previous eminent monks in order to explain their complicated belief systems. In particular, the Tian Tai and

Hua Yen schools of Chinese Buddhism virtually disappeared because no one could explain their doctrines without access to the missing texts written by their founders and early leaders.

Centuries later, copies of the Tian Tai and Hua Yen Zong scriptures were discovered in Korea and Japan, but by that time, it was much too late to restore the sects to life and was only of interest to historians. As a result, the Tian Tai and Hua Yen sects never really recovered.

The disappearance of these rival Buddhist schools of thought left the surviving Chan and Pure Land sects in a much stronger position. Both of these schools of thought were much less affected by Wu Zong's destruction of the libraries since their belief systems had always minimized the necessity of scholarly study and instead promoted meditation and chanting of mantra-like phrases. As a result of Wu Zong's elimination of their rivals, Chan and Pure Land have continued to be the dominant sects in China to this day. In fact, even the differences between Pure Land and Chan doctrines have become blurred as most present-day temples practice a mixed combination of both.

Wu Zong's successor, Xuan Zong (846–859AD), was a believer in Buddhism who slowly reversed the religious policies of his predecessor, but he moved gradually in order not to offend the Taoists and Confucian scholars. In fact, the new emperor began promoting the doctrine of Three Teachings (San Chiao), a belief that Taoism, Confucianism, and Buddhism could peacefully coexist, and which is still a dominant attitude in China today.

Xuan Zong allowed Buddhist temples to reopen, but continued to restrict their number and size. Initially, he only permitted two temples to function in each prefecture, with each temple limited to a maximum population of 50 monks, all of whom had to be over 50 years of age. Since there was still a shortage of metal, Xuan Zong continued to prohibit the use of gold, silver, copper, or iron for the creation of Buddhist sculptures, and instead required that only wood, stone, or clay be used. This policy was not too different from his predecessor, who had previously seized and melted down all metal Buddhist statues. It was not until 851AD, six years into his reign, that Xuan Zong lifted the restrictions on the construction and staffing of Buddhist temples and finally permitted the unlimited building of temples and ordination of new monks.

Xuan Zong seems to have favored the Pure Land sect, as he ordered the reconstruction of **Dong Lin Si**, the former home of the sect's founder Hui Yuan, at the foot of Mount Lushan in 852AD.

Song Dynasty (960-1279)

By the Song Dynasty (960–1279), the Pure Land and Chan schools were the two main Buddhist sects to have survived the years of persecution and decline. During the Song Dynasty, the image of the **Maitreya** Buddha (Mi Le Fo) evolved into the "grinning, pot-bellied hedonist" known as the "Laughing Buddha," or **Pu Tai Ho Shang** (Bu Dai), the "Hemp Sack Monk." Bu Dai was previously a mythical figure in Chinese tradition whose identity was somehow merged with that of the Maitreya. One of the earliest existing examples of this representation of Mi Le Fo as the "Laughing Buddha" is probably the stone sculpture of him found at **Fei Lai Feng** near Ling Yin Si in Hangzhou, the capital of the Southern Song Dynasty. The bodhisattva **Avalokitesvara** (Guanyin) was originally depicted as a man, as seen in early stone carvings and paintings found in India and Central Asia, but in China the image had evolved into that of a beautiful woman by the 12th century AD. One significant contribution to Buddhist doctrine made during the Song Dynasty was the compilation by **Wu Men Hui Kai** (1184–1260) of the volume of Chan writings known as "The Gateless Gate," or "Wu Men Guan."

Yuan Dynasty (1271-1368)

After briefly flirting with supporting Taoism, the Mongol **Yuan Dynasty** (1271–1368) established Buddhism as the official state religion, but they chose the Lamaist variant practiced in Tibet, which had little popular support in Han China.

The Republican (Min Guo) Period (1911-1949)

After the fall of the Qing Dynasty in 1911, Buddhist temples in China were cut off from state support and remained dependent on their own sources of financial support for the duration of the Min Guo era. Nonetheless, they achieved an unprecedented amount of freedom from state control which allowed them to ordain monks and expand temples almost without restriction. As a result, both Karl L. Reichelt and Holmes Welch have described this 38-year period as one of "Buddhist Revival."

In 1934, Karl L. Reichelt estimated that there was one million Buddhist monks and nuns in China, with possibly many more wandering monks who went uncounted. However, Holmes Welch was a little more conservatve in his later studies of the same period. According to Welch, China had 500,000 Buddhist monks and nuns living in 100,000 Buddhist temples and monasteries in 1930. Jiangsu Province alone had 7,000 Buddhist temples housing 20,000 monks and nuns in the 1930s. Shanghai municipality reportedly had 6,000 Buddhist monks and nuns in 1930.

By the eve of the Communist takeover in 1949, Welch estimates the total number of resident monks and nuns for all of China had increased to 800,000 residing at 230,000 temples and monasteries. Obviously many of these were small shrines and hermitages with only a few monks, but the larger temples had as many as 300 residents. Some of the popularity associated with being a Buddhist monk may have been a result of the exemptions monks enjoyed from taxation, military conscription, and police investigation. Interestingly, the numbers also reflect the temples' possession of sufficient wealth to support large resident populations, and this wealth came largely from the donations of devout lay believers.

Era of Destruction (1949–1976)

The popular perception is that Buddhism in China suffered little persecution after the 1949 revolution, and remained that way until the Cultural Revolution (Wenhua Da Geming) began in 1966. Contrary to this, research by Holmes Welch has shown that Buddhist temples began to suffer persecution by the new Communist regime almost immediately.

The sources of financial support from lay believers, which the temples had depended on during the Min Guo era, were cut off in the 1950s. Donations and pilgrimages were banned; religious ceremonies which lay believers had previously paid to have performed were considered superstitious and prohibited; and all farmland belonging to temples, monasteries, and shrines which had been providing rental income and food supplies were seized by the state under the Agrarian Reform Law of June 1950. Smaller temples were closed, flooding the larger ones with an influx of now homeless monks, until the traditional practice of wandering monks visiting other temples was itself banned.

The general result was one of near starvation conditions for monks living in some temples, particularly those such as Jiuhua Shan in Anhui which were in isolated locations and dependent upon the income formerly received from pilgrims. However, even if the practices of making donations to temples had not been banned, the economic foundation of the middle class lay believers was eliminated by 1957 when all private businesses were nationalized. The end result was that many temples became abandoned or depopulated as monks were forced to leave in search of food or livelihood elsewhere.

In Shanghai alone, the number of Buddhist monks fell from an all time high of 6,200 in 1930 to only 1,500 by February 1950. In 1952, a government official confidentially disclosed that the total number of monks in China had already been reduced from 800,000 in 1949 to only 300,000, a reduction of

62 percent within just three years of the revolution. A Buddhist official in Jiangsu Province stated in 1957 that there were 7,000 Buddhist temples housing 20,000 monks and nuns in his province, compared to 79,000 temples with 171,000 resident monks and nuns in the 1930s. This represented an 88 percent reduction in the resident population and a 91 percent reduction in number of temples. Holmes Welch estimated that by 1957, the total number of Buddhist monks and nuns in China had been reduced by 90 percent compared to that before 1949. Nonetheless, at this stage the temple buildings themselves continued to physically survive.

In 1960, a more relaxed government policy towards Buddhism coincided with the ascendancy of the moderate political faction within the Communist Party led by Liu Shiaoqi and Deng Xiaoping. Making financial donations to temples, and payment of fees for the performance of Buddhist religious ceremonies by monks were once again permitted. However, most evidence suggests that this new domestic policy towards religion was closely linked with foreign policy, and was applied mainly to those temples in cities such as Beijing, Shanghai, and Hangzhou, which were more likely to be visited by foreign tourists. The policy was that each major city should have one "monastic showplace" in good repair for tourists to visit. Many of the Buddhist temples that remained open were no longer living institutions but cultural museums.

This moderate policy continued until the Cultural Revolution began in 1966, when even the structures themselves were burned down and all religious icons inside them were destroyed. A massive campaign of attacks by the Red Guards started in August 1966, and by September every Buddhist temple in China had been closed down for the first time since 845AD, along with every Taoist temple, church, and mosque. In August 1967, an overseas Buddhist visitor to Shanghai found that the Fa Zang, Yu Fo, and Jing An temples had all been closed, the monks had been sent home, and the religious icons inside had been removed. As Holmes Welch says, "Buddhism disappeared from sight in August 1966."

Buddhism in China Today

After having been closed and looted for ten years during the Cultural Revolution (1966–1976), Buddhist temples all over the country have not only been progressively reopened since about 1980, but have been restored and even expanded. Two common myths in the West are that the Buddhist and Taoist temples in China today are only museum pieces for tourists, and that only little old ladies still attend them to perform acts of worship. In reality, both these myths are completely false.

Many temples now have large populations of resident monks who study the scriptures and perform ceremonies. The author can attest to having found religious ceremonies being performed in isolated places where no foreign visitors could have ever been expected, and in many places where the author was the only foreigner present. Likewise, the author has seen worshippers of all ages actively participating in religious activities, including successful businessmen wearing pinstripe suits and youths who looked as if they were dressed for a visit to the disco. The streets approaching most temple entrances are lined with shops selling religious articles, including incense sticks, red candles, stacks of paper money meant to be burnt as offerings, Buddha statues, as well as cassette tapes of Buddhist chants and songs. It is quite common today to see men and women of all ages wearing wrist bracelets made of wooden beads inscribed with the characters "O-Mi-Tuo-Fo," as well as taxi drivers with an image of Buddha dangling from their rear view mirror.

Pure Land and Chan temples both have active congregations of lay worshippers. Shanghai's **Fa Zang Jiang Si** is packed with worshippers every week, who spend hours praying, chanting, and singing songs of praise to Amitabha Buddha and the bodhisattva Guanyin. After they leave, the temple is inundated with gifts of fruit and other food, left behind as donations for the resident monks. On Jiao Shan Island near the town of Zhenjiang, Jiangsu, the Chan sect **Ding Hui Si** holds regular conferences attended by hundreds of laypeople who spend the day actively studying volumes of Buddhist scriptures.

The lifestyle of today's Buddhist monks is a mixture of the sacred and profane, with standards of behavior seemingly less strict than before 1949. In the past, monks took a vow of poverty. Today, monks are commonly seen waiting to get on board expensive flights at China's airport, buying a 25 Rmb cappucino at Starbucks coffee shops, and owning the latest model of mobile phones. Former restrictions on leaving the temple grounds seem to be unenforced, as monks and nuns can often be seen wandering up and down the shopping streets of towns. On several occasion, monks have been seen smoking cigarettes. Likewise, the author has not been able to find any genuine functioning meditation halls (*chan tang*), where monks used to sit day and night meditating and chanting according to a rigid ceremonial procedure. Nonetheless, the author has observed the shaved heads of monks bearing the round burn marks of having been branded when they took their vows, a practice that scars one for life and which was initially banned after the establishment of the People's Republic of China (PRC) in 1949.

Buddhism in China has survived the persecution of the mid-9th century Tang Dynasty, the competition from Confucianism and Taoism, the destruction of many of its temples during the Taiping Rebellion, the competition for China's hearts and minds from the Christian missionaries of Treaty Port days, and finally the Cultural Revolution followed by China's economic modernization. It has proven to be a resilient and enduring faith.

Nonetheless, the temporary closure of most temples and churches during the height of the SARS epidemic in May 2003 illustrates that the state still has the power to eradicate religion in China if and when it chooses.

Buddhist Temple Architecture

Contrary to some Western sources, Buddhist temples in China do not all follow an identical floor plan. However, there are some patterns which typically appear with occasional unique variations diverting from the norm.

Temples are usually composed of a collection of buildings within a walled compound, with the main entrance gate facing south and leading into a central axis along which the main halls are aligned. East and west of the main gate, there may be a **Drum Tower** (Gu Lou) and a **Bell Tower** (Zhong Lou).

Some temples have a single large **Pagoda** (Ta) outside the compound in front of the main gate, while others may have a set of two **Twin Pagodas** (Shuang Ta) on either side of the gate. Another design is for a single large pagoda to stand in the center of the temple's compound. Pagodas are also sometimes found standing all alone on a hilltop or in a forest. The latter is especially true if it is a **Tomb Pagoda** (Mu Ta), meant to mark the grave of a monk or the temple's founder. These types of tombs are often found in forested hillsides outside temple compounds. Pagodas are nearly always seven stories high, although nine-story pagodas may also be seen occasionally. They can be square with four sides (Si Fang Ta), round, or octagonal in shape. Materials used to construct these pagodas could be bricks, wood, stone, or even iron. It is the **Iron Pagoda** (Tie Ta) that tends to be the oldest and most rare. These are followed in age by stone, then brick and finally wood. Usually the wooden ones are of the most recent construction, dating from the Qing Dynasty. Usually, every pagoda had an interior ladder or stairway leading all the way up to the top, but in recent years access to the upper floors of many pagodas has been disallowed because the climb was hazardous.

Entering the main gate, the first significant building of a temple may be **Heng Ha Dian,** which houses the two fierce warrior guardians Heng and Ha. More commonly though, it may be the **Hall of the Four Heavenly Kings** (Tian Wang Dian). Writing in 1932, C.A.S. Williams described the four heavenly kings as such: The Guardian of the East, Mo Li Ching, has a white face and a magical sword inscribed with the characters for Earth (Ti), Water (Shui), Fire (Huo), and Wind (Feng). When he swings his sword, it causes a black wind, fire, and thick smoke, which in turn unleashes thousands of spears. The Guardian of the West, Mo Li Hai, has a blue face and carries a "four-string guitar." The Guardian of the South, Mo Li Hung, has a red face and carries the "Umbrella of Chaos," which if opened causes "universal darkness," thunderstorms, and earthquakes. The Guardian of the North, Mo Li Shou, has a black face. He carries two whips and a snake.

In the 1934 edition of his classic study, *Truth and Tradition in Chinese Buddhism*, Karl L. Reichelt described the four heavenly kings this way: "Tseng Chang is red and carries an umbrella in his hand. He represents the South. Chih Kuo is blue and holds a guitar in his hand. He represents the West. Kuang Mu is white and has a sword. He represents the East. To Wen is black and carries a snake and a pearl in his hand. He represents the North."

However, Albert H. Stone and J. Hammond Reed described their 1921 visit to a Tian Wang Dian this way: "Upon entering the grounds, the first hall encountered is the **Heavenly Kings Hall** (Tian Wang Dian) containing statues of the Four Heavenly Kings (Si Tian Wang), with their faces painted red, green, black, and white. Yang Ying Chung has a red face and holds an umbrella, which, if opened, could cause the destruction of the world; Huang Bao has a green face and holds a zither which, if played, could cause a storm; Hong Biao has a black face and holds a snake; Chao Yun Ting has a white face and holds a sword."

In addition to the statues of the Four Heavenly Kings, the Tian Wang Dian may contain a statue of the **Maitreya Buddha** of the future (Mi Le Fo), or this deity may reside in a separate hall of its own (Mi Le Fo Dian). C.A.S. Williams describes Mi Le Fo as appearing thus: "very stout, with the breast and upper abdomen exposed to view. His face has a laughing expression, and he is also known as the Laughing Buddha. He stands in the first hall...."

Behind Mi Le Fo, on the other side of a partition, is usually found **Wei Tuo**. He is dressed in martial armor and holds a sword. Wei Tuo is considered the guardian protector of the temple and always faces the northern exit of a hall towards the temple's inner courtyard.

This is usually followed by the second main building on the central axis, the **Precious Hall of the Great Hero** (Da Xiong Bao Dian). Situated in the center of this hall, facing the southern entrance, are usually three large gilded Buddha statues (San Fo) seated side by side. The one in the center is virtually always the historical Prince Siddartha, represented as **Sakyamuni Buddha** (Shi Jia Mou Ni Pusa). Although the identities of the other two may vary, the

Sakyamuni is typically joined by the Amitabha Buddha (O-Mi-Tuo-Fo) on one side and the bodhisattva Manjusri (Wen Shu) on the other. Sometimes Sakyamuni Buddha (Shi Jia Mou Ni Pusa) appears alone, flanked by smaller figures of his two main disciples, **Ananda** (A Nan Tuo) and **Kasyapa** (She Mo Teng or Mo He Jia Ye).

Sakyamuni (Shi Jia Mou Ni) can be depicted in many forms. In fact, his image has evolved over time and has varied significantly among the different countries where Buddhism spread to. In China, he is normally shown with a wisdom bump on the top of his head, his hair illustrated by spiral curls sometimes compared to snails, elongated earlobes split at the ends to illustrate his removal of the heavy golden jewelry worn when he was an earthly prince. On rare occasions, Sakyamuni Buddha is shown wearing a royal crown like that of a king. He is most often shown cross-legged with the soles of his bare feet exposed upward, seated on an enormous blue lotus flower blossom. However, he can sometimes be shown standing or even reclining on a couch. His hands can be positioned in a variety of different gestures, each one having special significance to the expert devotee. The most commonly seen hand gesture is the one known as "the blessing," in which his right arm is raised up with an open palm hand and three fingers extended, while the left arm hangs downward with the palm of his hand in his lap.

Amitabha (O-Mi-Tuo-Fo), the Buddha of Infinite Light who governs the Pure Land of the Western Paradise, is also depicted with a wisdom bump on his head, snail-curled hair, and elongated split earlobes. One hand is raised to chest level holding a lotus blossom, while the other arm hangs downward with an open palm.

The bodhisattva **Manjusri** (Wen Shu) is usually depicted holding a flaming sword in his right hand and the long stem of a blue lotus flower in his left hand. Originally, he was depicted as riding a lion, but this is rarely seen in Chinese temples today. Wen Shu is the patron deity of Wu Tai Shan.

Behind the **Three Buddhas** (San Fo), separated by a wall, is usually a shrine to the Goddess of Mercy, the bodhisattva **Guanyin**, whose statue faces the northern exit of the hall. She is the patron deity of Putuo Shan island in Zhejiang Province.

Along both sides of the Bao Dian are often found statues of the **Eighteen Arhats** (Shi Ba Luohan), with nine on each side. Sometimes there is a separate **Arhat Hall** (Luohan Dian), especially when the number of Arhats depicted is as many as 100 or even 500. A hall with 500 arhats is known as a **Wu Bai Luohan Tang** (Five Hundred Arhats Hall).

POINT OF INTEREST

One set of dieties who had disappeared from most temples but seem to be making a comeback is the 24 Devas (Zhu Tian), who were described by Reichelt as frequently appearing in Chinese Buddhist Temples during the Min Guo era. According to him, they included such non-Buddhist figures from Chinese tradition Confucius (Kong Fu Zi), the War God (Guandi), the God of Literature (Wen Chang), and the Kitchen God (Zao Shen); Hindu gods such as Brahma, Indra, and Yama (Yen Lo); as well as Buddhist dieties such as the Four Heavenly Kings (Si Tian Wang) and the bodhisattva Wei Tuo. Nowadays, it is extremely rare to see this group of Devas with its many non-Buddhist gods, kings, and judges in Chinese Buddhist temples. Today, the Guang Ji Si in Wuhu, Anhui has a full set of 24 Devas, with 12 colorful standing figures lining both sides of the Yao Shi Fo Hall. Some of them have long flowing black beards and are dressed like Confucian scholars, while others are women. The only other example is at the Ying Jiang Si in Anqing, which for some reason only has 20 figures. However, the Longhua Si in Shanghai displayed a new set of 20 Deva statues in its Da Xiong Bao Dian in 2003.

The third main hall behind the Da Xiong Bao Dian is usually the **Da Bei Dian** (Great Sadness Hall), but great variations occur in this case.

Temples also typically had residential quarters for the monks who lived there, as well as a **Library** or **Scripture Storage Pavilion** (Ci Jing Ting, Cang Jing Ge, Cang Jing Lou, or Cang Shu Lou) housing the Tripitaka (San Zang), Buddhist sutras and other religious books. Sometimes there is an **Ancestor Hall** (Zu Shi Dian) containing a life-like effigy of the monk or abbot who first founded the temple.

As these temples were more than just monastic retreats for the resident monks, the public was welcome to visit. As such, several buildings were set aside to serve visiting guests. These facilities usually included a **Guest House** (Ke Tang) and a **Vegetarian Restaurant** (Su Cai Guan) or **Dining Hall** (Zhai Tang). The Dining Hall may sometimes be called the **Hall of Five Reflections** (Wu Guang Dian) as a token of thanks to those who had provided the food. Outside the Dining Hall, there is normally a wooden fish (*pang*) and an iron gong shaped like a ship's anchor, which are struck to announce meal times. In the days before modern hotels existed outside of China's big cities, many foreign travelers made regular use of the guest facilities at Buddhist temples. Today this is less common, although it can still be done at places such as Jiuhua Shan.

Other typical structures include the **Fang Zhang Shi Fangzi** (the Abbot or Temple Master's Room), the **San Sheng Dian** (The Three Saints Hall), and the **Da Fo Dian** (Big Buddha Hall).

A large number of other bodhisattvas and Buddhist deities may appear in Chinese Buddist temples, sometimes with halls (*dian*) dedicated to them, even though they were originally unknown in Indian Buddhism or have been dramatically transformed since being imported to China. **Dizang** (Kshitigarbha) is the patron deity of Nine Flower Mountain (Jiuhua Shan) in Anhui, and many temples in this province have halls dedicated to him. Di Zang has the special ability to rescue departed souls even after they've already gone to Hell and bring them back to Heaven. Because of this power, he plays an important role in Buddhist funeral ceremonies.

In Anhui province, separate halls are sometimes dedicated to **Yao Shi Fo**. Even though Yao Shi Fo cannot be directly connected with the Sanskrit name of any of the original Buddhist deities known in India, in China he is considered a heavenly Buddha who has the power to heal all diseases without the aid of any medicine. Occasionally appearing with Guanyin is the bodhisattva **Da Shi Zhi** who is thought to correspond with the Sanskrit name Mahahasthanaparapta, the son of Amitabha. Da Shi Zhi has the power to actually implement the compassionate wishes of Guanyin. Although previously of greater importance, the bodhisattva Samantabhadra, known in China as **Pu Xian**, is less seen today. The one exception is on Emei Mountain in Sichuan province, where Pu Xian is the patron deity. Traditionally depicted riding an elephant, Pu Xian is now more commonly shown seated on a lotus flower.

Vairocana, known in China as **Pi Lu Zhe Na** or **Pi Lu Fo** for short, represents the Buddhist law or doctrine. In some Anhui temples, Pi Lu Dian are halls dedicated to the Pi Lu Zhe Na and are the places where lectures and education on Buddhist doctrine take place. The War God (Guandi), modeled after the historical figure **Guanyu** of the Three Kingdoms (San Guo). is also often venerated at Buddhist temples, sometimes in his own hall (Guandi Dian).

At least before 1949, Chan Zong temples in particular might also have had a **Meditation Hall** (Chan Tang), Buddha Recitation Hall, and Buddhist Dharma Law Hall (Fa Tang).

Bibliography

Nanjing
Recent Guidebooks
Administration Bureau of Dr. Sun Yat-sen's (Sun Zhongshan's) Mausoleum. *The National Park of Dr. Sun Yat-sen*. Hong Kong: Hong Kong International Publishing House, 1998. [Hardcover coffee table book full of color photos.]

China: Nanjing. Beijing: China Travel & Tourism Press, 1983. [A small paperback travel guide. The first one published after China's opening to the West.]

Nanjing Municipal Government. *Nanjing China: A Tourist Guide*. Beijing: Five Continent Publicity Publishing House, 1999.

Sun Yat-sen (Sun Zhongshan) Memorial Hall. *The National Park of Dr. Sun Yat-sen's Mausoleum*. Nanjing: 2000. [Small brochure-sized booklet with photos and a useful sketch map.]

Xu, Huping. *The Treasures of the Nanjing Museum*. Hong Kong: London Editions, 2001.

Southern Dynasties Nanjing
Bryant, Daniel Joseph. *Lyric Poets of the Southern Tang (Nan Tang)*. Vancouver: University of British Columbia, 1982.

Marney, John. *Liang Chien Wen Ti*. Boston: Twayne Publishers/G.K. Hall & Co., 1976.

Ming Nanjing
Farmer, Edward L. *Early Ming Government: The Evolution of Dual Capitals*. Cambridge, Mass.: Harvard University Press, 1976.

Gallagher, Louis J. (tr.) *China in the Sixteenth Century: Mathew Ricci's Diary*. New York: Random House, 1953.

Levathes, Louise. *When China Ruled the Seas:1405–1433*. New York: Oxford University Press, 1996. [The story of Admiral Zheng He.]

Mote, Frederick W., and Denis Twitchett (ed). *The Cambridge History of China Vol. 7: The Ming Dynasty, 1368–1644*. Cambridge: Cambridge University Press, 1988.

Mote, Frederick W., "The Transformation of Nanking, 1350–1400" in *The City in Late Imperial China* by G. William Skinner (ed). Stanford University Press, 1977.

Prip-Moller, Johannes. "The Hall of Lin Ku Ssu Nanking" in Artes Monuments, Vol. III. Copenhagen, 1935.

Qing Nanjing
Miyazaki, Ichisada. *China's Examination Hell: The Civil Service Examinations of Imperial China*. New Haven: Yale University Press, 1981.

Wu, Wo-yao. *Vignettes from the Late Chi'ing (Qing): Bizarre Happenings Eyewitnessed Over Two Decades*. Hong Kong: Chinese University of Hong Kong, 1975. [Includes stories of officialdom in Qing Dynasty Nanjing.]

Republican (Min Guo) Nanjing

Chen, Jimin (ed). *Jinling Zhan Gu*. 1991.

Chen, Jimin (ed). *Min Guo Guan Fu*. 1993.

China Travel Service. *Nanking*. Shanghai: n.d, circa 1920s. [16 pp travel guide including Nanking city, Purple Mountain, Sun Yat-sen (Sun Zhongshan) Mausoleum, Ming Tombs, Spirit Valley, Tomb of Tan Yan Kai, Confucian Temple & Bazaar, Pei Chi Ko North Pole Tower, and Lotus Lake. Includes photos and a map.]

Eigner, Julius. "The Rise and Fall of Nanking" in *National Geographic*, Vol. LXXIII, No. 2, February, 1938, pp 189–224.

Hobart, Alice Tisdale. *Within the Walls of Nanking*. New York: MacMillan Co., 1927. [First-hand story of the siege of Nanking by the Guomindang army in 1927 as told by a member of the resident foreign community there.]

Kwok, K. W. *The Splendours of Historic Nanking: Eighty Photographic Studies, with Descriptive Notes, of Ancient and Modern Nanking*. Shanghai: Kelly & Walsh, 1933.

Ma, Chao Chun (Ma Chao Jun). *Nanking's Development, 1927–1937: Report on the Activities of the Municipality of Nanking*. Nanking: Municipality of Nanking, 1937. [Ma was the mayor of Nanjing.]

Musgrove, Charles D. "Constructing a National Capital in Nanjing, 1927-1937" in *Remaking the Chinese City, 1900-1950* by Joseph W. Esherick (ed). University of Hawaii Press, 2000.

Tushuo Zongtongfu. Nanjing: 2000. [55 pp booklet on the former Presidential Palace. All the text is in Chinese. Old and new photos with no English captions.]

Tyau, T.Z. *Two Years of Nationalist China*. Shanghai: Kelly & Walsh, 1930. [Includes a chapter called "Planning the New National Capital," i.e. Nanjing, pp 379–399.]

Uchiyama, Kiyoshi. *Guide to Nanking*. Shanghai: Commercial Press, 1910. [Uchiyama was Chancellor of the Japanese Consulate in Nanjing.]

Ward, Ralph A. *Nanking: The Capital, Symbol of the New Life of China*. Peiping (Beijing): California College in China, n.d. (ca. 1935).

Wartime Nanjing (1937-1945):

Boyle, John Hunter. *China and Japan at War, 1937–1945: The Politics of Collaboration*. Stanford, 1972.

Bunker, Gerald E. *The Peace Conspiracy: Wang Ching-Wei and the China War, 1937–1941*. Cambridge, Mass.: Harvard University Press, 1972.

Noessler, Max. *Nanking*. Shanghai: 1945. [In German, but with excellent photos of the city.]

U.S. Office of Strategic Services, Research and Analysis Branch. *Structure and Personnel of the Nanking Puppet Government and Hong Kong Administration*. Washington, D.C.: U.S. Department of State, Office of Intelligence Research, 1945.

General Histories of Nanjing

Chen, Ping. *Nanjing De Wen Wu*. Nanjing: Nanjing Chubanshe, 1998.

Nanking Woman's Club. *Sketches of Nanking*. Nanking: 1933. [Revised and enlarged version of 1923 first edition.]

Till, Barry and Pula Swart. *In Search of Old Nanking*. Hong Kong: Hong Kong and Shanghai Joint Publishing Company, 1982.

Wang, Neng Wei (ed). *Nanjing Jiu Ying, (Old Photos of Nanjing a.k.a. Old Fashions of Nanjing)*. Preface by Qu Wu. Nanjing: People's Fine Arts Publishing House, 1998.

Ye, Zhao Yan. *Old Nanjing: Reflections of Scenes on the Qinhuai River (Lao Nanjing: Jiu Ying Qinhuai)*. Beijing: Foreign Languages Press, 2003. [The Chinese first edition was published in Nanjing in 1998 by the China Second National Archives (Zhongguo Di Er Lishi Dang An Guan).]

Zhenjiang

Jingkou Qu Zhi, 1992.

Li, Tian Gang (ed). *Impressions of 19th Century Chinese Cities: Allom's Paintings (Da Qing Di Guo Cheng Shi Yin Xiang)*. Shanghai: Guji Chubanshe, 2002. [Contains a chapter on Zhenjiang, with engravings of Jiao Shan (Silver Island). Chinese text with English table of contents and chapter headings.]

Qi Li De Jin Shan, 1990.

Zhongguo Zhenjiang Fengjing Mingsheng, September 2001.

Ma An Shan

Dangtu Xian Zhi. 1996.

Ma An Shan Shi Zhi. 1992.

Zhang, Guobao, and Yang Guo. *Ma' An Shan*. Beijing: New World Press, 1989.

Wuhu

La Mission de Wuhu. Wuhu: Catholic Mission, 1940.

Prager, Emily. *Wuhu Diary*. New York: Random House, 2001. [Prager spent three months in Wuhu in 1999.]

Wuhu Shi Zhi. 1995.

Wuhu Xian Zhi. 1993

Jiuhua Shan

Chizhou Di Qu Zhi. 1996

Fang, Zheng Quan, et al. *Jiu Hua Mountain: A Buddhist Sanctuary in China (Jiuhua Shan: Zhongguo Fojiao Sheng Di)*. Hefei: Scenery Area Administration of Jiu Hua Mount, n.d. (ca. 1997).

Kupfer, Carl F. *Sacred Places in China*. Cincinnati: Press of the Western Methodist Book Concern, 1913.

Johnston, Reginald Fleming. *Buddhist China*. London: John Murray, 1913. [Contains three chapters on Jiuhua Shan.]

Prip-Moller, Johannes. *Chinese Buddhist Monasteries: Their Plan and Its Function as a Setting for Buddhist Monastic Life*. London: Oxford University Press, 1937.

Qingyang Xian Zhi. 1992.

Anqing

Anqing Di Qu Zhi. 1995.

Directorium el Vicariato Apostolico de Anking. Anking: 1935.

Directorium Missionale Archidioecesis de Anking. Anking: 1947.

Directorium Missionarium Vicariatus de Anking. Anking: 1940.

Fang, Ji Ren (ed). *Xiao Gu Shan Gu Jin Shi Lian Xuan (Selections of Ancient and Modern Poetry About Xiao Gu Shan)*. Hong Kong: Tian Ma Tu Shu Co. Ltd., 1998. [Includes some color photos and a historical/geographical introduction by the editor.]

Geil, William Edgar. *Eighteen Capitals of China*. London: Constable & Co., 1911 (2 volumes).

Shryock, John Knight. *The Temples of Anking and Their Cults; a study of modern Chinese religion*. Paris: Librairie Orientaliste P. Geuthner, 1931. Reprinted in 1973 by AMS Press in New York. Originally a Ph.D. Thesis, University of Pennsylvania: 1927.

Tongcheng Xian Zhi. 1995.

Xia, Kun and Song Lian (ed). *The Look of Anqing (Anqing Feng Mao)*. Anqing: Xiang Gang Ming Cai, 1992.

Jiujiang

Dreyer, Edward L. "The Poyang Campaign, 1363" in *Chinese Ways in Warfare* by Kierman and Fairbank (ed). Cambridge, 1974.

Kupfer, Carl F. *Sacred Places in China*. Cincinnati: Press of the Western Methodist Book Concern, 1913. [Kupfer was president of the William Nast College in Jiujiang. Despite the book's somewhat misleading title, it focuses mainly on historic sites in the Jiujiang area, on Lushan, and on Jiuhua Shan in nearby Anhui. The one exception is a chapter on Putuo Shan in Zhejiang.]

Munro-Faure, Paul Hector. "The Kiukiang Incident of 1927" in *Journal of the Hong Kong Branch of the Royal Asiatic Society*, Vol. 29, 1989, c.1991, pp 61–76. [Munro-Faure worked for the Asiatic Petroleum Co. and was in Jiujiang in 1927 when the British Concession fell to the Guomindang.]

Lushan

Archibald, John, and Edward S. Little. *The Fight for Kuling in 1892–1895*. Hankow (Hankou): The Central China Post, 1924. [Section I contains a series of articles from Hankou's *Central China Post* written by Kuling co-founder John Archibald in August 1923 and entitled, "The Fight for Kuling." Section II consists of the text of a speech given by Kuling co-founder Edward S. Little to the Chinkiang (Zhenjiang) Literary Association in Yangzhou in June 1899, and published as a pamphlet later that same year under title "The Story of Kuling."]

Espey, John J. *Tales Out of School: More Delightful, Humorous Stories of a Boyhood in China*. New York: Knopf., 1947. [Espey attended Kuling American School in 1924.]

Fischer, Emil S. *From Tientsin to Kuling*. Shanghai: Sunday Times, 1935.

Jiangxi Provincial Lushan Library English Catalogue. Lushan: 1964.

Johnston, Tess, and Deke Erh. *Near to Heaven: Western Architecture in China's Old Summer Resorts*. Hong Kong: Old China Hand Press, 1994. [Contains one chapter on Lushan.]

Lao Bieshu Congshu Dao Lushan Kan Lao Bieshu. HBA Press, 2001.

Li, Hua, and Li Ke You. *Bai Lu Dong Shu Yuan (White Deer Cave Academy)*. Zhongguo She Hui Chubanshe, 2000.

Lu Shan She Ying Dao You. 2000.

Meskill, John. *Academies in Ming China*. Tucson: University of Arizona Press, 1982.

Sherertz, Paul (ed.) *Lushan Memories*. San Diego: 1988. [Edited volume of memoirs by various former foreign residents of Lushan during Min Guo era.]

Shi, You Yi, and Cui Lin (ed). *Mount Lushan*. Fuzhou, Fujian: Hai Feng Publishing House, 1996.

Stone, Albert H. and J. Hammond Reed. *Historic Lushan, The Kuling Mountains*. Hankow: Arthington Press/Religious Tract Society, 1921.

Wang, Ching-chun. *Japan's Continental Adventure*. London: G. Allen & Unwin, 1941. [Appendix: A. "Why China Resorts to Armed Resistance," a speech delivered by Generalissimo Chiang Kai Shek (Jiang Jieshi) at a gathering of Chinese leaders at Kuling on 17 July 1937.]

The Opium War on the Yangzi (1839-1842)

Bingham, John Elliot. *Narrative of the Expedition to China*. London: 1842. [2 volumes.]

Cunynghame, Captain Arthur. *The Opium War: Being Recollections of Service in China*. Wilmington, Del.: Scholarly Resources, 1972. [Reprint of 1845 edition.]

Fay, Peter Ward. *The Opium War, 1840-1842*. Chapel Hill: University of North Carolina Press, 1975.

Holt, Edgar. *The Opium Wars in China*. London: 1964.

Loch, Granville Gower. *The Closing Events of the Campaign in China: The Operations in the Yang-Tze-Kiang and the Treaty of Nanking*. London: Murray, 1843.

Ouchterlony, John. *The Chinese War: An Account of All the Operations of the British Forces from the Commencement to the Treaty of Nanking*. London: Saunders and Otley, 1844.

Teng Ssu Yu. *Chang Hsi and the Treaty of Nanking, 1842*. Chicago University Press, 1944. (Translation of Chang Xi's diary.)

Waley, Arthur. *The Opium War Through Chinese Eyes*. London: Allen & Unwin, 1958.

Wei, Yan. Translated by Edward H. Parker. *Chinese Account of the Opium War (Sheng Wu-Chi)*. Wilmington, Del.: Scholarly Resources, 1972. Reprint of the 1888 ed. published by Kelly & Walsh, Shanghai.

The Taiping Rebellion

Bales, W.L. *Tso Tsungtang (Zuo Zongtang): Soldier and Statesman of Old China*. Shanghai: Kelly & Walsh, 1937.

Brine, Lindesay. *The Taeping Rebellion in China*. London: 1862. [A secondary source, but based on Taiping documents, some of which are reproduced.]

Curwen, Charles A. *Taiping Rebel: the Deposition of Li Hsiu-Cheng (the Zhong Wang, Li Xiucheng)*. Cambridge: Cambridge University Press, 1977.

Edkins, Jane R. *Chinese Scenes and People*. London: 1863. [Contains a description of a visit to the Taiping capital in Nanjing by her husband, Rev. Joseph Edkins.]

Fishbourne, Captain Edmund G. *Impressions of China, and the Present Revolution*. London: 1855. (Fishbourne was the Commander of the HMS Hermes, which in 1853 transported Sir George Bonham and Thomas Taylor Meadows on their visit to the Taiping capital in Nanjing.)

Fortune, Robert. *A Residence Among the Chinese*. London: 1857.

Gregory, J.S. (ed). *Western Reports on the Taipings: A Selection of Documents*. 1982.

Hail, William James. *Tseng Kuo Fan (Zeng Guofan) and the Taiping Rebellion*. New Haven: Yale University Press, 1927.

John, Rev. Griffith. *The Rev. Griffith John's Experience of the Insurgents*. Canton: 1861.

Lane-Poole, Stanley. *The Life of Sir Harry Parkes*. (2 Volumes.) London: 1894. [Parkes was on Admiral Hope's voyage up the Yangzi to Hankou in 1861.]

Lay, Walter T. (tr.) *The Autobiography of the Chungwang, Li Hsiu Cheng Kung Chuang (the Zhong Wang, Li Xiucheng)*. Shanghai: Presbyterian Mission Press, 1865.

Lay, Walter T. (tr.) *The Kan Wang's Sketch of the Rebellion*. Shanghai: 1865.

Lindley, A.F. (Lin Li). *Ti-Ping Tien-Kwoh: The History of the Ti-Ping Revolution*. (2 volumes.) London: 1866. [Lindley lived in Nanjing as an active supporter of the Taiping cause.]

Meadows, Thomas Taylor. *The Chinese and Their Rebellion*. London, 1856. [Meadows was the British Consul who acted as interpreter for Sir George Bonham on the 1853 HMS Hermes mission to the Taiping capital in Nanjing.]

Medhurst, W.H. (tr) *Books of the Thae-Ping-Wang Dynasty*. Shanghai: 1853. [Medhurst was a member of the 1853 HMS Hermes mission to the Taiping capital in Nanjing. He later translated a treasure trove of Taiping documents and publications that he had brought back with him to Shanghai.]

Michael, Franz. *The Taiping Rebellion: History and Documents*. Seattle: University of Washington Press, 1972. [3 volumes.]

Spector, Stanley. *Li Hung Chang (Li Hongzhang) and the Huai Army*. Seattle: University of Washington Press, 1964.

Williams, S.W. *The Middle Kingdom*. 1882. [Contains an account of the battle for control of Anqing based on the Zhong Wang's testament.]

The Treaty Port System

Abend, Hallett Edward. *Treaty Ports*. New York: Doubleday, 1944.

Coates, P.D. *The China Consuls: British Consular Officer, 1843-1943*. Hong Kong: Oxford University Press, 1988.

Elder, Chris (ed). *China's Treaty Ports*. Hong Kong: Oxford University Press, 1999. [An anthology of first hand historical accounts. Includes chapters on Chongqing, Yichang, Wuhan, Jiujiang, and Nanjing.]

Feuerwerker, Albert. *The Foreign Establishment in China in the Early Twentieth Century.* Ann Arbor: University of Michigan, 1976.

Hart, Robert. *The I. G. in Peking: Letters of Robert Hart, Chinese Maritime Customs, 1868–1907.* Edited by John King Fairbank, Katherine Frost Bruner, and Elizabeth MacLeod Matheson; with an introd. by L. K. Little. Cambridge, Mass.: Belknap Press of Harvard University Press, 1975.

Hart, Robert. *These From the Land of Sinim: Essays on the Chinese Question.* London: Chapman & Hall, 1901.

Murphy, Rhoades. *Treaty Ports and China's Modernization.* Ann Arbor: University of Michigan, 1970.

Tai, E.S. *Treaty Ports in China.* New York: Columbia University, 1918.

The Maritime Customs, China. *Documents Illustrative of the Origin, Development, and Activities of the Chinese Customs Service.* 7 vols. Shanghai: Inspectorate General of Customs, 1937. [568.8/M387 at the Shanghai Library. 7 vols — Vol. 1: Inspector General's Circulars, 1861–1892; Vol. 2: 1893–1910; Vol. 3: 1911–1923; Vol. 4: 1924–1931; Vol. 5: 1932–1938; Vol. 6: Despatches, Letters, Memoranda, etc., 1842–1901; Vol. 7: Index. "Sir Robert Hart: A Biographical Sketch" by Sir Charles P. Lucas, pp 375–388; "The Chinese Post Office," by H. Kirkhope, pp 276–293; "List of Treaty Ports" pp 646–648.]

Wright, Stanley F. *China's Customs Revenue Since the Revolution of 1911.* Shanghai: Statistical Department of the Inspectorate General of Customs, 1935 (3rd ed, revised and enlarged). [Compiled by order of the Inspectorate General of Customs, 1935. With the assistance of John H. Cubbon. No. 41 in the *China: Maritime Customs, Special Series.*]

Wright, Stanley F. *China's Struggle for Tariff Autonomy.* Shanghai: Kelly & Walsh, 1938.

Wright, Stanley F. *Hart and the Chinese Customs.* Belfast, Northern Ireland: William Mullan & Son Ltd, 1950.

Foreign Gunboats on the Yangzi

Earl, Lawrence. *Yangtse Incident: the Story of HMS Amethyst.* New York: Knopf, 1951.

Icenhower, Joseph Bryan. *The Panay Incident.* New York: F. Watts, 1971.

Koginos, Manny T. *The Panay Incident: Prelude to War.* Lafayette: Purdue University, 1967.

McKenna, Richard. *The Sand Pebbles.* Annapolis: Naval Institute Press, 2000.

Murfett, Malcolm H. *Hostage on the Yangtze: Britain, China, and the Amethyst Crisis of 1949.* Annapolis: Naval Institute Press, 1991.

Perry, Hamilton Darby. *The Panay Incident: Prelude to Pearl Harbor.* New York: Macmillan, 1969.

Phillips, C.E. Lucas. *Escape of the Amethyst.* New York: Coward-McCann, 1958.

Sawyer, Frederick Lewis. *Sons of Gunboats.* Annapolis: U.S. Naval Institute, 1946.

St. John, Jeffrey. *Voices from the Yangtze: Recollections of America's Maritime Frontier in China.* Napa: Western Maritime Press, 1993.

Tolley, Kemp. *Yangtze Patrol: the U.S. Navy in China.* Annapolis: Naval Institute Press, 1971.

Woodrooffe, Thomas. *Yangtze Skipper.* New York: 1937.

Missionaries on the Yangzi

Cartwright, Frank T. *A River of Living Water: A Historical Sketch of Nanking Theological Seminary (1911–61).* Singapore: Board of Founders, 1963.

Garst, Laura D. *In the Shadow of the Drum Tower.* Cincinatti: 1911.

Jubilee Papers of the Central China Presbyterian Mission, 1844–1894: Comprising Historical Sketches of the Mission Stations at Ningpo, Shanghai, Hangchow, Soochow, and Nanking, with a Sketch of the Presbyterian Mission Press. Shanghai : American Presbyterian Mission Press, 1895.

Latourette, Kenneth S. *A History of Christian Missions in China*. New York: Macmillan, 1929.

Lyall, Leslie. *A Passion for the Impossible: The China Inland Mission, 1865–1965*. Hodder & Stoughton, 1965.

Stuart, John Leighton. *Fifty Years in China: The Memoirs of John Leighton Stuart, Missionary and Ambassador*. New York: Random House, 1954.

Varg, Paul. *Missionaries, Chinese and Diplomats: The American Protestant Missionary Movement in China, 1890–1952*. 1958.

Yu, Rev. Paul. *Eyes East*. New Jersey: St. Anthony Guild Press, 1948.

Republican China (Min Guo) 1911-1949

Bergere, Marie-Claire. *Sun Yat-sen (Sun Zhongsun)*. Stanford: Stanford University Press, 1998.

Chang, Jung with Jon Halliday. *Madame Sun Yat-Sen (Soong Ching-ling)*. Middlesex, England: Penguin Books, 1986. [About Song Qingling.]

Chao, T.K. *Highway Construction and Transport in China*. Nanking: 1937.

Duiker, William J. *Tsai Yuan-pei (Cai Yuan Pei): Educator of Modern China*. 1977.

Eastman, Lloyd E. (ed). *Chiang Kai-shek's (Jiang Jieshi's) Secret Past: The Memoir of his Second Wife, Ch'en Chieh-ju*. Boulder: Westview Press, 1993.

Eastman, Lloyd E. *Seeds of Destruction: Nationalist China in War and Revolution, 1937–1949*. Stanford, Calif.: Stanford University Press, 1984.

Eastman, Lloyd E. (ed). *The Nationalist Era in China, 1927–1949*. Cambridge: Cambridge University Press, 1991. [Contents of this book were previously published as part of volume 13 of The Cambridge History of China.]

Eastman, Lloyd E. *The Abortive Revolution: China Under Nationalist Rule, 1927–1937*. Cambridge, Mass.: Harvard University Press, 1974.

Epstein, Israel. *Woman in World History: Soong Ching Ling (Madame Sun Yat-sen)*. Beijing: New World Press, 1995, Second Edition. [About Song Qingling.]

Li, Tsung-jen (Li Zong Ren), and Tong Te-kong. *The Memoirs of Li Tsung-jen (Li Zong Ren)*. Boulder: Westview Press, 1979.

Linebarger, Paul. *Government in Republican China*. New York, 1938.

Linebarger, Paul. *The China of Chiang Kai Shek (Jiang Jieshi) : A Political Study*. Boston, 1941.

Martin, Wilbur C. *Sun Yat-sen (Sun Zhongshan): Frustrated Patriot*. New York: Columbia University Press, 1976.

Pepper, Suzanne. *Civil War in China: the Political Struggle, 1945–1949*. 1978.

Schiffrin, Harold Z. *Sun Yat-sen (Sun Zhonghsn): Reluctant Revolutionary*. Boston: Little, Brown & Co., 1980.

Sih, Paul K.T. *The Strenuous Decade: China's Nation-Building Efforts, 1927–1937*. New York, 1970.

Sun, Yat-sen (Sun Zhongshan). *The International Development of China*. New York: Putnam, 1922.

Rea, Kenneth W., and John C. Brewer (ed). *The Forgotten Ambassador: The Reports of John Leighton Stuart, 1946–1949*. Colorado: Westview Press, 1981.

Wei, Julie Lee, et al (ed & tr). *Prescriptions for Saving China: Selected Writings of Sun Yat-sen (Sun Zhongshan)*. Stanford, Calif.: Hoover Institution Press, 1994.

Historic Universities on the Yangzi

Ayers, William. *Chang Chih-Tung (Zhang Zhi Dong) and Educational Reform in China*. Harvard University Press, 1971.

Chyne, W. Y. *Handbook of Cultural Institutions in China*. Shanghai: Chinese National Committee on Intellectual Cooperation, 1936.

Deng, Peng. *Private Education in Modern China*. Connecticut: Praeger, 1997.

Forster, Lancelot. *The Universities Along the Yangtze*. Hong Kong: South China Morning Post, 1932.

Gregg, Alicia H. *China and Educational Autonomy: The Changing Role of the Protestant Educational Missionary in China, 1807–1937.* 1946.

Hartnett, Richard A. *The Saga of Chinese Higher Education from the Tongzhi Restoration to Tiananmen Square: Revolution and Reform.* Lewiston, New York: E. Mellen Press, 1998.

Hayhoe, Ruth. *China's Universities, 1895–1995: A Century of Cultural Conflict.* New York: Garland Publishing, 1996.

Israel, John. *Rebels and Bureaucrats: China's December 9ers.* Berkeley: University of California, 1976. [Traces the evolution of Chinese student nationalism forward from the December 9, 1935 protests onward.]

Israel, John. *Student Nationalism in China, 1927–1937.* Stanford: Stanford University Press, 1966.

Kirk, Florence A. *Sunshine and Storm: A Canadian Teacher in China, 1932–1950.* Victoria, British Columbia, 1991.

Lutz, Jessie Gregory. *China and the Christian Colleges, 1850–1950.* Ithaca: Cornell University Press, 1971.

Smalley, Martha L., and Karen Jordan. *Guide to the Arichives of the United Board for Christian Higher Education in Asia (Record Group No. 11).* Yale University Divinity Library Special Collections, 1982. http://webtext.library.yale.edu/xml2html/divinity.011.con.html Yale University Divinity Library. *China Christian Colleges and Universities Image Database.* From the United Board for Christian Higher Education in Asia (UBCHEA) Online Archives. http://research.yale.edu:8084/ydlchina/index.jsp

Smalley, Martha L., Tess Johnston, and Deke Erh. *Hallowed Halls: Protestant Colleges in Old China.* Hong Kong: Old China Hand Press, 1998.

The Educational Directory of China. Shanghai. Volumes for 1917 and 1920.

Thurston, Mrs. Lawrence (Matilda), and Ruth M. Chester, *Ginling College.* New York: United Board for Christian Colleges in China, 1955.

Wheeler, Reginald W. *John E. Williams of Nanking.* New York: Fleming H. Revell Co., 1937. [Biography of the vice-president of Nanking University, 1910–1927, who was killed during the Guomindang occupation of the city in March 1927.]

Yeh, Wen-Hsin. *The Alienated Academy: Culture and Politics in Republican China, 1919–1937.* Cambridge, Mass.: Council on East Asian Studies, Harvard University Press, 1990.

Chinese Buddhism

Chen, Kenneth K.S. *Buddhism in China: A Historical Survey.* Princeton University Press, 1964.

Chung Fang Yu. *The Renewal of Buddhism in China: Chu Hung and the Late Ming Synthesis.* NY: Columbia University Press, 1981. [Chu Hung was a Pure Land monk who debated Matteo Ricci in a series of correspondence.]

Edkins, Joseph. *Chinese Buddhism.* London: Kegan Paul, Trench, Trubner, & Co., 1879. London: 1883, 2nd ed.

Prip-Moller, Johannes. *Chinese Buddhist Monasteries: Their Plan and Its Function as a Setting for Buddhist Monastic Life.* London: Oxford University Press, 1937.

Reichelt, Karl Ludvig. *Truth and Tradition in Chinese Buddhism: a Study of Chinese Mahayana Buddhism.* Shanghai: Commercial Press, 1934. (4th ed, revised and enlarged)

Ren, Ji Yu (ed). *Fojiao Da Cidian (Dictionary of Buddhism).* Nanjing: Jiangsu Gu Ji Chubanshe, 2002.

Soothill, William E. *A Dictionary of Chinese Buddhist Terms.* London, 1937.

Weinstein, Stanley. *Buddhism Under the Tang.* Cambridge University Press, 1987.

Welch, Holmes. *Buddhism Under Mao.* Cambridge, Mass.: Harvard University Press, 1972.

Welch, Holmes. *The Buddhist Revival in China.* Cambridge, Mass.: Harvard University Press, 1968.

Welch, Holmes. *The Practice of Chinese Buddhism, 1900–1950.* Cambridge, Mass.: Harvard University Press, 1967.

Wright, Arthur F. *Studies in Chinese Buddhism*. New Haven: Yale University Press, 1990.

Xing, Ge. *Fo Bao (Buddhist Treasure)*. Shanghai: Shanghai Wen Yi Chubanshe, 2003.

Zurcher, E. *The Buddhist Conquest of China: The Spread and Adaptation of Buddhism in Early Medieval China*. Leiden: E.J. Brill, 1959.

Yangzi Travel & Exploration

Bird, Isabella L. *Yangtze Valley and Beyond*. Boston: Beacon Press, 1987. [Reprint of 1899 edition recording trip taken in 1898.]

Blakiston, Thomas Wright. *Five Months on the Yang-Tsze; and Notices of the Present Rebellions in China*. London: John Murray, 1862. [Blakiston traveled in 1861 and was the first foreigner to make the complete journey up the Yangzi River from Shanghai to Chongqing, including a lengthy investigation of the Taiping capital at Nanjing. His intrerpreter was Bishop Samuel I. Schereschewsky, later founder of St. John's Unversity in Shanghai. Some of the information concerning the Taiping rebels was collected by R. J. Forrest, and was originally published in the *North China Herald* in two articles entitled, "Nanking and the Inhabitants Thereof," and "The Taipings at Home."]

Enders, Elizabeth Crump. *Temple Bells and Silver Sails*. New York: Appleton, 1925.

Fitkin, Gretchen Mae. *The Great River: The Story of a Voyage on the Yangtze Kiang*. Shanghai: North-China Daily News & Herald, 1922. Introduction by Arthur C. Sowerby.

Great Britain, Admiralty, Hydrographic Dept. *The Yangtze Kiang Pilot: Comprising the Yangtze Kiang from Woosung Bar to the Head of Navigation, also Poyang Lake and Rivers Flowing into It, Han Kiang, Tungting Lake and Rivers Flowing into It, Chialing Kiang, and Min Kiang*. London: H.M.S.O., 1928 2nd ed.

Little, Archibald. *The Far East*. Oxford: Clarendon Press, 1905.

Oliphant, Laurence. *Narrative of the Earl of Elgin's Mission to China*. London: William Blackwood and Sons, 1860.

Putnam Weale, B.L. *The Reshaping of the Far East*. London: MacMillan & Co., 1905.

Skyrme, Commander F.H.E. *The Yangtsze-Kiang*. Shanghai: North China Daily News and Herald, 1937. [Skyrme was a ship captain for the Indo-China Steam Navigation Co.Ltd.,which was owned by Jardine Matheson & Co. The preface by Arthur C. Sowerby is dated 27 April 1937. Skyrme's description of his journey upriver from Shanghai to Chongqing was the last travel account published before the Sino-Japanese War started in July 1937.]

Villard, R.A. *Map of the Yangtse-Kiang...From its Mouth to Chungking, and General Chart from Mouth to Source, with Plans of Shanghai, Chinkiang, Nanking, Wuhu, Kuikiang, Hankow, Ichang and Chungking...* Shanghai: 1895. [Map of the Yangtse-Kiang with plans of treaty ports.]

Woodhead, H.G.W. *The Yang-tzse and its Problems*. Shanghai: Mercury Press, 1931.

Worcester, G.R.G. *The History of the Yangtze: Its Trade and Ships*. n.p, n.d., ca. 1940. [Unpublished 504 pp typed manuscript, held by Xujiahui Cang Shu Lou in Shanghai. Worcester covers in detail the history of European exploration and navigation of the Yangzi from 1839 to 1940.]

Western Commerce on the Yangzi

Anderson, Irvine H. *The Standard-Vacuum Oil Co. and U.S. East Asian Policy, 1933–1941*. Princeton University Press, 1975.

Blue, A.D. "European Navigation on the Yangtse" in *Journal of the Hong Kong Branch of the Royal Asiatic Society*, Volume 3, 1963, pp 107–130. [Blue was employed by the China Navigation Co., operated by Butterfield & Swire, from 1928 to 1938.]

Grover, David Hubert. *American Merchant Ships on the Yangtze, 1920–1941*. Westport, Conn.: Praeger, 1992.

Hobart, Alice Tisdale. *Oil for the Lamps of China*. New York, 1933.

Lindsay, T.J. "The Hankow Steamer Tea Races" in *Journal of the Hong Kong Branch of the*

Royal Asiatic Society, Vol. 8, 1968, pp 44–55. [Lindsay worked for Butterfield & Swire from1933 to 1966.]

Lubbock, Basil. *The China Clippers*. n.d.

Torrible, Captain Graham. *Yangtze Reminiscences: Some Notes and Recollections of Service with the China Navigation Company Ltd. 1925–1939*. Hong Kong: Swire & Sons, 1975.

The Sino-Japanese War (1937-1945)

Dreyer, Edward L. *China at War: 1901-1949*. New York: Longman, 1995.

Five Months of War. Shanghai: North China Daily News & Herald, 1938. [22 pp of text, followed by 133 pp of photos with detailed captions.]

Japan's War in China. Shanghai: China Weekly Review, n.d. [A series of small volumes published between 1937 and 1939 summarizing daily news accounts of the Sino-Japanese War in booklet form with maps. Extensive coverage of the 1938 Yangzi campaign.]

Lee, Edward Bing-Shuey. *One Year of the Japan-China Undeclared War*. Shanghai, 1935.

Munro-Faure, Paul Hector. "China on the Brink of War" in *Journal of the Hong Kong Branch of the Royal Asiatic Society*, Vol. 30, 1990, c.1993, pp 89–145. [Munro-Faure worked for the British-owned Asiatic Petroleum Co. and was in Nanjing in 1937 for several months just before the city fell to the Japanese.]

China's Poet Travelers
Anthologies

Bynner, Witter, and Kiang Kang-hu. *The Jade Mountain*. New York: Knopf, 1929.

Liu, Wu-chi, and Irving Yucheng Lo. *Sunflower Splendour: Three Thousand Years of Chinese Poetry*. New York: Anchor Books, 1975.

Minford, John. *Classical Chinese Literature*. 1996. [A compilation of previously published English translations from over the previous century.]

Owen, Stephen. *An Anthology of Chinese Literature: Beginnings to 1911*. Norton, 1996. [Includes studies of both the Tang and the Song Dynasties.]

Owen, Stephen. *The Great Age of Chinese Poetry, the High Tang*. New Haven: Yale University Press, 1981.

Waley, Arthur. *Translations from the Chinese*. New York: Knopf, 1945. [Includes his two earlier works, "170 Chinese Poems" and "More Translations from the Chinese" published in 1918 and 1919 respectively. About half the content covers Bai Ju Yi.]

Watson, Burton. *The Columbia Book of Chinese Poetry: From Early Times to the 13th Century*. New York: Columbia University Press, 1984.

Bai Ju Yi

Feifel, Eugen. *Po Chu-I (Bai Ju Yi) As a Censor: Memorials to Emperor Xian Zong, 808–810*. Mouton, 1961.

Levy, Howard S. *Translation's From Po Chu-I's (Bai Ju Yi's) Collected Works*. New York: Paragon, 1971-1978. [4 volumes.]

Watson, Burton. *Po Chu-I (Bai Ju Yi): Selected Poems*. New York: Columbia University Press, 2000.

Waley, Arthur. *The Life and Times of Po Chu-I (Bai Ju Yi)*. London: George Allen and Unwin, 1949.

Li Bai

Hamill, Sam. *Banished Immortal: Li Tai Po (Li Bai)*. 1987.

Obata, Shigeyoshi. *The Works of Li Po (Li Bai)*. London: J.M. Dent, 1922.

Waley, Arthur. *The Poetry and Career of Li Po (Li Bai), 701–762 AD*. London: George Allen and Unwin, 1950.

Su Dong Po (Su Shi)

Clark, Cyril Drummond Le Gros. *Selections from the Work of Su Tung-Po (Su Shi)*. London: Jonathan Cape, 1931. [Contains a brief biography of Su, plus his essays on Stone Bell Hill (Shi Zhong Shan) at Hukou, the Temple of Qu Yuan at Zigui, and the Yen Yu Rock in Qutang Gorge, with extremely well researched historical and explanatory footnotes.]

Clark, Cyril Drummond Le Gros. *The Prose Poetry of Su Tung-Po (Su Shi)*. Shanghai: Kelly & Walsh, 1935. Foreward by Chien Chung-shu. [Contains a much expanded biography of the poet compared to Clark's earlier volume, once again with extremely well researched historical and explanatory footnotes.]

Lin Yu Tang. *The Gay Genius: The Life and Times of Su Tungpo (Su Shi)*. New York: John Day, 1947. [A biography with few reproductions of the poets actual work. Focuses heavily on his Hangzhou years.]

Watson, Burton. *Su Tung-Po (Su Shi): Selections From a Sung (Song) Dynasty Poet*. New York: Columbia University Press, 1965.

General Reference Sources

Couling, Samuel. *Encyclopedia Sinica*. Shanghai: Kelly & Walsh, 1917.

Goodrich, L. Carrington. *Dictionary of Ming Biography, 1368–1644*. 1976. [In 2 volumes.]

Hummel, Arthur W. *Eminent Chinese of the Ching (Qing) Period*. Washington, D.C.: Government Printing Office, 1944. [2 volumes.]

Hsu, Immanuel. *The Rise of Modern China*. New York: Oxford University Press, 1983.

Mote, Frederick W. *Imperial China: 900–1800*. Cambridge: Harvard University Press, 1999.

Moule, A.C., and Percival W. Yetts. *The Rulers of China, 221BC–1949AD: Chronological Tables*. New York: Praeger, 1957.

Paludan, Ann. *Chronicle of the Chinese Emperors*. London: Thames & Hudson, 1998.

Twitchett, Denis, et al (ed). *Cambridge History of China, 1978–1992*. [15 volumes.]

Watson, Burton, (tr). *Records of the Grand Historian of China: Translated from the Shih-chi (Shi Ji) of Ssu-ma Chien (Si Ma Qian)*. New York: 1961. [2 volumes.]

Who's Who In China: Biographies of Chinese Leaders. Shanghai: China Weekly Review, 1936.

Woodhead, H.G.W. *China Year Book (26 volumes)*. Shanghai and Tianjin: 1913–1939.

Appendices

Appendix A: Notes on Chinese Nomenclature

Chinese orthography is an extremely complicated topic with many questions for which there are no official right or wrong answers. Choosing the "correct" orthography is often a judgement call.

Chinese normally write their language using characters that are pictographic ideograms or symbols resembling Egyptian hieroglyphics, rather than with letters or an alphabet.

Each character usually represents on syllable with its own phonetic sound. However it takes at least two characters, and sometimes more, to make a complete name of a person, place or thing. One character by itself usually cannot be a name

Phonetic Systems

Before 1949, foreigners devised many ways of writing Chinese characters phonetically, with the most popular being the Wade-Giles system. This system is the one still most recognized by most Westerners today, and is still used in the majority of books on China printed in the West. Examples of this older phonetic system include Nanking (Nanjing), Peking (Beijing), Sun Yat Sen (Sun Zhongshan), Chiang Kai Shek (Jiang Jieshi), Kuomintang (Guomindang), and Mao Tse Tung (Mao Zedong).

After 1949, the People's Republic of China established the new Pinyin phonetic system, along with the Putonghua standardization of the oral language. Because it is the Pinyin phonetic system which is exclusively used in China today, foreign visitors need to become familiar with it in order to communicate with people here, ask for directions, and read street signs. However, because most foreign readers still only recognize certain well-known names in their Wade-Giles form, it is still necessary to occasionally use the Wade-Giles system in books written for a foreign audience. For example, Jiang Jieshi is the correct Pinyin spelling of the Guomindang's former leader, but most foreigners only recognize the Wade-Giles form of his name, Chiang Kai Shek. The Wade-Giles form may be important to identify the person to the foreign reader, but the Pinyin form is important for the traveler to use once they actually arrive in China.

A major issue of debate regarding the Pinyin system is whether the syllables or phonetic sounds of multi-syllable, multi-character names should be written all together as one block of text, or if spaces should

The Four Tones

Standard Mandarin Chinese has four tones, although other local dialects have more. Most pinyin phonemes can represent more than one Chinese character, some as many as four different chracters, each with a different meaning. Being sure to get the right meaning requires pronouncing the pinyin phoneme with the correct tone. However, people will probably guess what you mean based on the context of the situation if your tone is wrong. Unfortunately, space does not permit us to go into this complicated part of the language in any further detail.

Hotel Vocabulary

A hotel can be called any one of three names: *fandian*, *binguan*, or *dajiudian*. It is probably safest to go with *binguan*, as this is the most common, as a *fandian* can also be a restaurant.

hotel room	fang jie
floor	lou
which floor?	shenme lou? or nage lou?
quiet	anjing
quiet room	anjing fang jie
too loud	tai da sheng!
new	xinde
old	laode
new room	xinde feng jie
telephone	dian hua
television	dian shi
electricity	dian
light/lamp	deng
reservation	yu ding
how much does it cost?	duo shao chien
	or ji dia (Shanghai Hua)
that's too expensive!	tai gui le!
that's very cheap!	hen pieni!
how many days?	duo shao tian?
one day	yige tian
two days	liange tian
tomorrow	ming tian
the day after tomorrow	xiage xinqi
passport	hu zhao
residence permit	ju liu zheng
I'm going home now	wo hui jia le
receipt	fa piao
deposit	ya jing*

*Chinese hotels will often insist that foreigners pay an absurdly huge deposit even for a night's stay. The best strategy is to stand your ground and simply refuse to pay it. [Impossible – *bu xing*!] One argument that usually works is to tell them you don't want telephone service. [*Wo bu yao nimende dianhua.*] Often times their reasoning is that as a foreigner you may make a bunch of long distance phone calls. Tell them you have a mobile phone. [*Wo yo wode shoji.*]

Food Vocabulary

restaurant	*canguan* or *canting* or *fandian*
coffee shop	*kaffei guan* or *kaffei ting*
breakfast	*zao fan*
lunch	*wu fan*
dinner	*wan fan*
cold	*bing de*
hot	*re de*
spicy	*la de*
not spicy	*bu la de*
chicken	*ji*
beef	*niu rou*
pork	*ju rou*
fish	*yu*
noodles	*mien* or *mian tiao*
rice	*fan*
vegetables	*qingcai*
tea	*cha*
water	*shui*
beer	*pijou*
wine	*huzhou*
red	*hong de*
white	*bai de*
glass	*bei ze*
bottle	*ping*
take out	*dai zou*
eat here	*zai zheli*
check please!	*ma dan!*

Emergency Vocabulary

police	*jin cha*
public security bureau	*gong an ju*
security guard	*bao an*
help	*bang*
help me!	*ni bang wo, hao ma?*
	or *wo yao ni bang wo.*
I have a problem/question.	*Wo yo wenti.*
He/she is a bad man/woman.	*Ta shi bu hao ren.*
I don't like him/her.	*Wo bu xihuan ta.*
I don't want to.	*Wo bu yao le.*

Roads

expressway	*gao jia*
avenue	*da dao* or *ma lu*
road	*lu*
lane	*jie* or *xiang*
alley	*longtan* or *hutong*
public square	*guang chang*
bridge	*qiao*

Administrative Divisions

province	*sheng*
municipality	*shi*
city	*cheng*
county	*xian*
town	*zhen*
district	*qu*
village	*cun*
new village	*xin cun*
old village	*lao cun*

Appendix C: Transportation in China
Types of Trains in China

In China, there are three kinds of trains and four types of seats in them.

- The slowest and most uncomfortable trains are denoted by all numbers with no letters, for example, No. 45232. These trains are usually standing room only, and filled with cigarette smoke and drunken peasants with their live chickens. The trains are sometimes old, steam-powered, coal-burning locomotives that stop at almost every village with along the way. There is no air conditioning but the windows can be opened.

- The faster and more comfortable trains are called "K-Trains" and are denoted by a letter and number, for example, No. K4542. Typically these are faster and more comfortable than a slow train, but not as good or as fast as a T-train. However, K-Trains can be a hit or miss as far as comfort and quality is concerned. Sometimes there is little visible difference between a K- and a T-Train, but other times it may be the other way around. Technically, smoking is not allowed on K-Trains, so people will have a puff in the connecting corridor between cars.

- The fastest and most comfortable trains in China are the T-Trains. These are supposed to be express trains with limited stops, and they are the newest. Of course this also means they are the most expensive. T-Trains only have "soft seats" (*ruan xi*), and smoking is not allowed. However, this also means the windows are all sealed shut.

- "Hard seats" (*ying zuo*) are the cheapest seats on the K-Trains, which also offer soft seats (*ruan xi*). A hard seat may actually be a wooden bench or may, instead, be a cushioned seat despite its name.

- A "hard sleeper" (*ying wo*) is a cheap bed, and smoking is allowed on trains that have these.

- A "soft sleeper" (*ruan wo*) is a soft bed on T-Trains, so smoking is not allowed. This is the most expensive form of train available, sometimes costing close to the same as a plane ticket. What is puzzling is why anyone would choose to pay the same price and travel two days by train instead of two hours by air.

Train Vocabulary

train	*huoche*
train station	*huoche jia* or *huoche zhan*
train ticket	*huoche piao*
K-Train	*kuai yidian huoche*
T-Train	*te kuai huoche*
seat	*zuo wei*
seat number	*zuo hao*
soft seat	*ruan xi* or *ruan zuo*
hard seat	*ying zuo*
soft sleeper	*ruan wo*
hard sleeper	*ying wo*

Getting a Taxi

Taxi drivers are not allowed to stop and pick up passengers just anywhere along the street as there are officially designated taxi stations that look identical to bus stops. You must wait at a taxi station until a taxi comes along and picks you up. The good news is that the standard minimum taxi fare in a city like Nanjing is still only 7 Rmb, compared to Shanghai's 10 Rmb.

Taxi Vocabulary

car/automobile	*jiao che*
go	*chu* or *guo chu*
turn left	*zuo guai*
turn right	*you guai*
go straight	*yi zhi zou*
hurry up!	*kuai yidian!*
stop here!	*ting zai zheli!*
now!	*xianzai!*
Where do you want to go?	*Ni yao chu shenme difang?*
Please give me a receipt.	*Ni gai wo fa piao, hao ma?*

Long-Distance Bus Transportation
The long-distance bus service is becoming a comfortable alternative to traveling by train. The buses are usually air-conditioned or heated, and feature soft seats that can recline. Prices tend to be a little higher than for trains, and the journeys usually take longer. The advantage is that buses may leave more frequently, or leave at times when trains are not available. The biggest disadvantage is no restroom on the bus and no food is served, and passengers will have to wait for the infrequent 15 minute stops at roadside rest areas to relieve themselves or get food.;

Bus Vocabulary
bus	*qiche* or *gong gong qiche*
bus station	*qiche zhan*
bus ticket	*qiche piao*

Airplane Vocabulary
airplane	*feiji*
airplane ticket	*fei ji piao*
airport	*feiji chang*

Index

18 Arhats *see* Shi Ba Luohan
1911 Revolution (Xin Hai Geming)
  28, 50, 60, 69, 76, 106, 143, 148,
  303, 313, 403

A

Academica Sinica 109, 112
Air Force Memorial
  see Hang Kong Lie Shi Gong Mu
Amitabha *see* O-Mi-Tuo-Fo
Ancient Buddhist Scripture Reading
  Terrace *see* Gu Bai Jing Tai
Anhui 10, 40–41, 43, 47, 51, 89,
  112, 190, 193–195, 221, 223,
  247, 250–251, 262, 275–277,
  279, 301, 326
Anqing 46–47, 147, 193–194, 200,
  209, 222, 249–280, 282, 305
Anqing Museum
  see Anqing Shi Bowuguan
Anqing Shi Bowuguan (Anqing
  Museum) 257, 258–259, 265
Anqing Shi Fang Xueyuan (Anqing
  Teachers' College) 271
Anqing Teachers' College
  see Anqing Shi Fang Xueyuan
Asiatic Petroleum Company 305, 319

B

Bai Chong Xi Gu Ju 88
Bai, Ju Yi 190, 302, 316, 322–323,
  328, 332, 345, 374–378
Bai Lu Dong Shuyuan (White Deer
  Cave Academy) 284, 302, 312,
  328–329, 388–396
Bai Lu Zhou (White Egret Isle)
  39, 111
Bai Ma Gongyuan (White Horse Park)
  114
Bai Sui Gong (One Hundred Year Old
  Palace) 225, 238–242, 246, 248
Bao En Ta (Porcelain Pagoda)
  46, 48, 138, 146
Bao Gong Pagoda *see* Bao Gong Ta
Bao Gong Ta (Bao Gong Pagoda)
  139–140
Bao Zhi Gong 39, 139–140
Beamless Hall *see* Wu Liang Dian
Beautiful Peak *see* Xiu Feng
Bei Fa *see* Northern Expedition
Bei Gu Shan 6–9, 11, 17–19, 21, 34

Bei Ji Ge (North Pole Tower)
  50, 109, 112, 114
Bell and Drum Tower (Zhong Gu Lou)
  377, 379
Bell Tower (Zhong Lou)
  22, 166, 199, 248, 264, 308, 372
Big Forest Peak *see* Da Lin Feng
Black Dragon Pool *see* Wu Long Tan
Black Dragon Pool Park
  see Wu Long Tan Gongyuan
Blakiston, Thomas 3, 46, 194, 250
Bo Xian 27
Bo Xian Park (Bo Xian Gongyuan)
  7, 8, 27–29
Bodhi Dharma *see* Pu Ti Da Mo
Brocade Valley *see* Jingxiu Gu
Building No. 1 *see* Yi Hao Lou
Building No. 2 *see* Er Hao Lou
Butterfly & Swire 7, 194, 303

C

Cai Shi Ji 181–182, 184–185, 187
Cai Shi Ji National Park *see* Cai Shi Ji
Cai Shi Ji Scenic Area *see* Cai Shi Ji
Cai, Yuan Pei 50–51, 84, 109
Central Party Headquarters 57, 93
Chan Zong (Chan Sect) 15, 24–25,
  150, 152, 241, 306
Changan (Xian) 39, 112, 181, 189,
  301–302, 323, 377
Chao Yang Men *see* Zhongshan Men
Chaotian Gong (Chaotian Palace)
  48, 84, 87, 118–119, 179
Chaotian Palace *see* Chaotian Gong
Chen, Du Xiu 272
Cheng Qiang Bowuguan (City Wall
  Museum) 79, 80, 113
Chiang, Kai Shek (Jiang, Jieshi)
  21, 30, 51, 56, 61–63, 65,
  88, 90, 92–94, 98, 130, 132,
  141–144, 166, 330, 339–340,
  342–343, 350, 402–403
Chiang Kai Shek's Villa
  see Mei Lu Bieshu
China Navigation Co. 7, 194, 303
Chu Hsi *see* Zhu Xi
Church of the Ascension
  see Sheng Gong Hui
Ci Jing Ting (Scripture Bestowing
  Pavilion) 359, 361
Ci Shou Pagoda *see* Ci Shou Ta

Ci Shou Ta (Ci Shou Pagoda)
  13, 15–16
Circular Buddha Hall
  see Yuan Fo Dian
City Wall Museum
  see Cheng Qiang Bowuguan
Communications Ministry
  see Jiaotong Bu
Communist Party
  see Gong Chan Dang
Confucius Temple (Fuzi Miao) 48, 57,
  85, 111, 117–119, 250, 282, 415
Cui Zhou 106, 108
Cultural Revolution (Wenhua Da
  Geming) 13–14, 102, 116,
  166, 234, 239, 247, 251, 264,
  292, 297, 299, 306–307, 311,
  327, 338, 341, 371–372, 378
Customs House *see* Hai Guan

D

Da Huang Jia (Royal Hotel) 30, 35
Da Lin Feng (Big Forest Peak)
  332, 345, 375, 377
Da Long Shan (Great Dragon
  Mountain) 249, 273, 275
Da Sheng Bao Ta (Great Victory
  Pagoda) 307, 310, 311
Da Tian Chi Feng (Great Heavenly
  Pool Peak) 331, 347
Da Tian Chi Si (Great Heavenly
  Pool Temple) 352–353
Da Tian Chi Ta (Great Heavenly
  Pool Pagoda) 350
Da Tian Tai Chan Si (Great Heavenly
  Terrace Buddhist Temple) 246
Da Xiong Bao Dian (Precious Hall of
  the Great Hero) 14–15, 23,
  136, 167, 199–200, 230–231,
  233–234, 239, 241–242, 246,
  253, 255, 277–278, 308–310,
  360–361, 378–379
Da Yu (Great Yu) 285, 301, 327
Da Yun He *see* Grand Canal
Dang Shi Shi Liao Chen Lie Guan
  (Guomindang Historical Relics
  Exhibition Building) 55, 89, 121
Dao Pa Shi Jie 262–263
Deng, Yan Da 141–142
Devas *see* Zhu Tian
Ding Hui Si (Ding Hui Temple)
  20, 22–25

Ding Hui Temple see Ding Hui Si
Ding Shan 51, 69, 78, 105–106, 153
Dizang (Kshitigarbha) 157, 193, 198, 200, 224, 232, 237, 239, 247, 310
Dizang Dian (Kshitigarbha Hall) 200–201, 235, 237, 310
Dong Gu (East Valley) 331–337, 343, 356, 359, 416–417
Dong Lin Si (East Grove Buddhist Temple) 301–302, 372, 374–375, 377–380
Dong Nan Daxue (Southeast University) 49, 88, 103–104
Dong Shui Guan (East Water Gate) 68, 76
Dragon Fish Pool see Long Yu Tan
Dragon Head Precipice
  see Long Shou Yan
Drum Tower (Gu Lou) 22, 49, 53, 93, 113–114, 132, 166, 199, 308, 372

E

East Grove Buddhist Temple
  see Dong Lin Si
East Valley see Dong Gu
East Water Gate see Dong Shui Guan
Elephant Hill see Xiang Shan
Elgin, Lord 45, 193, 250
Er Hao Lou (Building No. 2) 57
Examination Yuan see Kaoshi Yuan
Executive Yuan see Xing Zheng Yuan

F

Fa Hai Cave see Fa Hai Dong
Fa Hai Dong (Fa Hai Dong) 15–17
Fei Caihong Qiao (Flying Rainbow Bridge) 86
Feng Huang Song (Phoenix Pine) 223, 238, 243–245, 248
Feng Run Men see Xuan Wu Men
Feng, Yu Xiang 61, 402–403
First Opium War 5–6, 24, 114, 147, 259
Five Old Men Peak see Wu Lao Feng
Flying Rainbow Bridge see Fei Caihong Qiao
Foreign Ministry see Wai Jiao Bu
Former British Consulate 8, 31, 105, 305, 318
Former Presidential Palace
  see Tushuo Zongtong Fu
Four Heavenly Kings see Si Tian Wang
Fu Gui Shan 48, 50
Fuzi Miao see Confucius Temple

G

Gan Lu Buddhist Temple
  see Gan Lu Si
Gan Lu Si (Sweet Dew Temple/Gan Lu Buddhist Temple) 19, 34
Gangtang Gongyuan 312–313
Gangtang Hu 301–303, 312–314, 316–317, 322, 324–325
Ghost Face see Gui Lian
Ginling College see Jinling Nuzi Daxue
Goddess of Mercy see Guanyin

Goddess of Mercy Bridge
  see Guanyin Qiao
Golden Bamboo Terrace
  see Jin Zhu Ping
Golden Island see Jin Shan
Gong Chan Dang (Communist Party) 66, 87, 164, 258, 268, 272, 330, 339, 403
Gong Qian Chan Shi Mu Ta (Gong Qian's Stone Tomb Pagoda) 357–359
Gong Qian's Stone Tomb Pagoda
  see Gong Qian Chan Shi Mu Ta
Grand Canal (Da Yun He) 5–7, 9, 21, 27, 36
Great Dragon Mountain
  see Da Long Shan
Great Heavenly Pool Pagoda
  see Da Tian Chi Ta
Great Heavenly Pool Peak
  see Da Tian Chi Feng
Great Heavenly Pool Temple
  see Da Tian Chi Si
Great Heavenly Terrace Buddhist Temple see Da Tian Tai Chan Si
Great Victory Pagoda
  see Da Sheng Bao Ta
Great Yu see Da Yu
Green Hill see Qing Shan
Gu Bai Jing Tai (Ancient Buddhist Scripture Reading Terrace) 246
Gu Lou see Drum Tower
Guandi Miao (War God Temple) 57, 121
Guang Ji Buddhist Temple
  see Guang Ji Si
Guang Ji Si (Guang Ji Buddhist Temple) 182–183, 193, 198–201
Guanyin (Goddess of Mercy) 15, 116, 157–158, 161–162, 168, 192, 230, 235, 242, 255, 257, 292, 309–310, 360–361, 385, 404, 415
Guanyin Cave see Guanyin Dong
Guanyin Dong (Guanyin Cave) 157–158, 385
Guanyin Qiao (Goddess of Mercy Bridge) 383, 396–402, 404
Gui Lian (Ghost Face) 68, 73, 83
Gui Zong Si (Temple of Conversion) 328, 415
Guilin Shi Lou (Guilin Stone House) 140–141
Guilin Stone House see Guilin Shi Lou
Guling Town 330–333, 343, 356, 368, 370, 381, 416
Guo Fang Yuan (National Defense Park) 83
Guomindang 8, 21, 51–53, 59, 62–63, 87, 90, 93, 109, 129, 132, 141–142, 145, 163–164, 330, 339
Guomindang Central Supervisory Committee see Zhongyang Jian Cha Wei Yuan Hui
Guomindang Historical Relics Exhibition Building see Dang Shi Shi Liao Chen Lie Guan

Guomindang Party Institute
  see Lushan Dasha

H

Hai Guan (Customs House) 194, 209
Hai Hui Buddhist Temple
  see Hai Hui Si
Hai Hui Si (Hai Hui Buddhist Temple) 364, 385–388, 396
Hai Jun Bu (Ministry of the Navy) 54
Hai Ling Men see Yi Jiang Men
Han Po Kou (Han Po Pass) 336, 362, 402, 405, 410–411
Han Po Pass see Han Po Kou
Han Xi Men see Hang Zhong Men
Han Zhong Men (Han Xi Men) 68, 77
Hang Kong Lie Shi Gong Mu
  (Air Force Memorial) 163–164
He Ping Men (Shen Ce Men) 64, 68–69, 73–74, 76, 122
He Ping Ta (Peace Pagoda) 112–113
He, Xiang Ning 144–145
Heavenly Bridge see Tian Qiao
Heavenly Kings Hall
  see Tian Wang Dian
Hefei 195–196, 222, 247, 251, 267, 280, 326
Heng Ha Dian 136, 165, 230, 307
Hong Jue Pagoda see Hong Jue Ta
Hong Jue Ta (Hong Jue Pagoda) 150
Hu, Han Min 50–51, 141
Hua Cheng Si (Transformation Temple / Hua Cheng Temple) 225, 232–234
Hua Cheng Temple see Hua Cheng Si
Hua Jing Park 344–345, 376
Huan Zhou 77, 106–107
Huang He (Yellow River) 39–40, 149, 403
Huang Long Gu (Yellow Dragon Valley) 359–360
Huang Long Si (Yellow Dragon Buddhist Temple) 328, 359–361
Huang Long Tan (Yellow Dragon Pool) 355, 359, 362
Huang Shan (Yellow Mountain) 186, 195, 200–201, 223, 244, 247, 250, 328, 354, 368, 416
Huang Shan Bao Ta 186
Huangpu Tongxue Hui Li Zhi She
  (Lizhi Association of Huangpu Classmates Society) 55–56, 89
Hui Ju Buddhist Temple
  see Hui Ju Chan Si
Hui Ju Chan Si (Hui Ju Buddhist Temple) 245–246, 328
Hukou 46, 275–276, 281–300, 302, 305, 324

I

Immortals Cavern see Xianren Dong
Imperial Examination Museum
  see Jiangnan Gong Yuan
Imperial Stele Pavilion
  see Yu Bei Ting
Iron Buddha see Tie Fo
Iron Pagoda see Tie Ta

J

Jiang, Jieshi see Chiang, Kai Shek
Jiang Jieshi Guan Gong 88
Jiang Tian Si 13–15, 17
Jiangnan Gong Yuan (Imperial Examination Museum) 57, 85
Jiangsu 2–3, 8, 40, 43, 47, 49–51, 63, 84, 89, 92, 301
Jiangsu Provincial Assembly (Jiangsu Zi Yi Ju) 50, 57, 93, 122
Jiangxi 40, 43, 47, 51, 89, 108, 221, 276, 279, 295, 302–303, 330, 340
Jiangxi Provincial Buddhism Association 381
Jiangyin 2–4, 58
Jiao Guang Ji Nian Guan (Jiao Guang Memorial Hall) 23, 25
Jiao Guang Memorial Hall see Jiao Guang Ji Nian Guan
Jiao Shan (Silver Island) 6, 9, 11, 17, 20, 22–27, 33, 35
Jiaotong Bu (Ministry of Communications) 53–54, 122
Jie Fang Men 70, 79, 80, 107, 109, 113, 117
Jie Yin An (Jie Yin Buddhist Nunnery) 238, 242–243
Jie Yin Buddhist Nunnery see Jie Yin Buddhist Nunnery
Jiming Si (Rooster Crow Temple) 57, 79–80, 109, 112, 114, 116, 121
Jin, Qiao Jue see Kim Gio Gak
Jin Shan (Goldern Island) 6, 9–17, 21, 23, 28, 35–36
Jin Zhu Ping (Golden Bamboo Terrace) 356-358
Jin Zhu Ta 191–192
Jing Hai Si (Quiet Sea Temple) 70, 114–115, 153–154
Jing Hu (Mirror Lake) 204–206, 209, 218–221
Jing Tu Zong (Pure Land Sect) 15, 24, 231, 241, 327, 377
Jingxiu Gu (Brocade Valley) 345, 349
Jinling see Nanjing
Jinling Daxue (University of Nanking) 51, 60, 93–98
Jinling Nuzi Daxue (Ginling College) 60, 94–95, 97–100
Jinling Xie He Sheng Xueyuan (Nanjing Theological Seminary) 53, 101
Jiong Long Lu 355–356, 362
Jiuhua Cun see Jiuhua Village
Jiuhua Jie Qu see Jiuhua Village
Jiuhua Shan 80, 184, 193, 195, 198, 221–248, 266
Jiuhua Village (Jiuhua Cun/Jiuhua Jie Qu) 225–227, 230–231, 233, 235, 239, 244, 248
Jiujiang 46–47, 189, 209, 221, 224, 276, 279–282, 287, 295, 301–326, 329–330, 333, 345, 347, 368, 370, 377–378, 381, 389, 412, 415–416
Johns Hopkins Center 105

Johnston, Reginald F. 224–2 25, 231–234, 246
Ju Bao Men see Zhong Hua Men
Junshi Dang An Guan (Military History Archives) 54–55, 89, 122

K

Kaoshi Yuan (Examination Yuan) 56–57, 94, 121
Kim Gio Gak (Jin, Qiao Jue) 193, 198, 224, 232, 237, 246–247
Kshitigarbha see Dizang
Kshitigarbha Hall see Dizang Dian
Kuling American School see Villa No. 381
Kuling Hotel see Villa No. 246
Kupfer, Carl F. 224–226, 237, 392

L

Lan, Yong 150
Lan Yong Cave see Lan Yong Dong
Lan Yong Dong (Lan Yong Cave) 149–150
Li Bai (Li Tai Po) 38–39, 140, 181–183, 187–191, 223, 285, 301, 328, 378
Li Bai Tomb see Li Bai Wen Hua Yuan
Li Bai Wen Hua Yuan (Li Bai Tomb) 187–189, 190
Li, Bo 284, 302, 312, 328, 333, 389, 391, 393, 405
Li, Hong Zhang 49, 52, 210
Li, Li San 272, 330
Li Zong Ren 61–63, 99, 330, 350
Lian Hu Gongyuan 268
Liang Dynasty Tombs 164, 170
Liang Wu Di 19, 38, 39, 136, 139, 161, 165,168
Liang Zhou 106–108
Lianhua Dong (Lotus Flower Cave) 304, 329, 370–372
Lianhua Gu (Lotus Flower Valley) 332
Lianhua Town 370–371
Liao, Zhong Kai 144
Lin, Sen 51–52, 56, 140–141, 166, 353
Ling Gu Buddhist Temple (Ling Gu Si) 39, 112, 134, 136–139
Ling Gu Gongyuan (Spirit Valley Park) 136–137, 140, 146, 152, 164
Ling Gu Pagoda see Ling Gu Ta
Ling Gu Ta (Spirit Valley Pagoda/ Ling Gu Pagoda) 135, 137–140, 145–146, 377
Ling Hu Gongyuan 267–269, 271
Ling Zhou 106–107
Lion Hill see Shizi Shan in Wuhu
Lion Peak see Shizi Shan
Little, Edward Selby 328–329, 361, 371
Little Orphan Island see Xiao Gu Shan
Lizhi Association of Huangpu Classmates Society see Huangpu Tongxue Li Zhi She
Long An Nunnery 234–235
Long Men Kou Jie (Old City Gate) 263

Long Shou Yan (Dragon Head Precipice) 351, 353, 355
Long Yu Tan (Dragon Fish Pool) 351
Longevity Buddhist Temple see Song Shou Si
Lotus Flower Cave see Lianhua Dong
Lotus Flower Valley see Lianhua Gu
Lu, Xun 54, 272
Lulin Bin Guan (Lulin Hotel) 333–334
Lulin Gu (Russian Valley) 333–336, 359
Lulin Hotel see Lulin Bin Guan
Lulin Hu (Lulin Lake) 332–336, 343, 356, 359, 416–417
Lulin Lake see Lulin Hu
Lushan 17, 108, 189, 298, 300–305, 312, 316–317, 325, 327–418
Lushan Botanical Gardens see Lushan Zhi Wu Yuan
Lushan Dajuidian (Lushan Hotel) 342, 416
Lushan Dasha (Guomindang Party Institute/Lushan Mansion) 339–340, 342, 417
Lushan Dong Men 368, 381
Lushan Hot Springs see Wen Quan
Lushan Hotel see Lushan Dajuidian
Lushan Library see Lushan Tushuguan
Lushan Mansion see Lushan Mansion
Lushan Nan Shan 411
Lushan Tushuguan (Lushan Library) 341
Lushan Zhi Wu Yuan (Lushan Botanical Gardens) 363
Lute Pavilion see Pipa Ting

M

Ma An Shan 2, 181–192
Maitreya Buddha of the Future see Mi Le Fo
Manjusri Terrace see Wenshu Tai
Mao, Zedong 133, 202, 204, 330, 340, 343
Mao Zedong Bieshu (Mao Zedong's Villa) 334
Mao Zedong's Villa see Mao Zedong Bieshu
Mei Lu Bieshu (Chiang Kai Shek's Villa /Mei Lu Villa) 339, 342–343
Mei Lu Villa see Mei Lu Bieshu
Mei Yuan Xin Cun (Plum Blossom New Village) 65, 87
Meiling Bieshu (Song Meiling Villa) 143
Meridian Gate see Wu Chao Men
Mi Le Fo (Maitreya Buddha of the Future) 15, 159, 166, 200, 239, 246, 253–254, 278, 308, 405, 415
Middle River Pagoda see Zhong Jiang Ta
Military History Archives see Junshi Dang An Guan
Ming Cheng Qiang (Ming Dynasty City Wall) 59, 67, 68
Ming Dynasty City Wall see Ming Cheng Qiang

Index

Ming Gu Gong (Ming Palace) 42, 67, 76, 81, 119, 122
Ming Gu Gong Gongyuan (Ming Palace Park) 67, 81, 82
Ming Palace Park
  see Ming Gu Gong Gongyuan
Ming Palace *see* Ming Gu Gong
Ming Tombs (Ming Xiao Ling) 74–75, 122–123, 126–130, 137–141, 146, 163, 225
Ming Xiao Ling *see* Ming Tombs
Ming Yuan Lou (Ming Yuan Tower) 57, 85–87
Ming Yuan Tower *see* Ming Yuan Lou
Ministry of Communications
  see Jiaotong Bu
Ministry of Foreign Affairs
  see Wai Jiao Bu
Ministry of Railways *see* Tie Dao Bu
Ministry of the Navy *see* Hai Jun Bu
Mirror Lake *see* Jing Hu
Misty Water Pavilion
  see Yan Shui Ting
Mo Chou Hu (Mo Chou Hu) 111
Mo Chou Lake *see* Mo Chou Hu
Mosque *see* Qingzhen Si
Mu Fu Shan 155–156, 163
Murphy, Henry K. 52, 57, 89, 97, 100, 132, 137–138

N

Nan Tang Er Ling (Two Southern Tang Dynasty Tombs) 40, 150–152
Nanchang 281, 303, 324, 326, 347, 356, 416
Nanjing (Jinling) 3–9, 11, 21, 35, 37–180, 181, 189, 191, 193, 195, 202, 221, 225, 247, 250–251, 259, 272, 282, 304–305, 322, 339, 342, 350, 377, 380, 389, 403
Nanjing Bowuguan (Nanjing Museum) 74, 84
Nanjing Catholic Church
  see Nanjing Tian Zhu Jiao Tang
Nanjing Changjiang Da Qiao (Nanjing Yangzi River Bridge) 65, 154
Nanjing Jiao Tang (Nanjing Protestant Church) 120
Nanjing Mosque
  see Nanjing Qingzhen Si
Nanjing Municipal Government 121
Nanjing Municipal Museum 87, 119
Nanjing Museum
  see Nanjing Bowuguan
Nanjing Protestant Church
  see Nanjing Jiao Tang
Nanjing Qingzhen Si (Nanjing Mosque) 120
Nanjing Theological Seminary
  see Jinling Xie He Sheng Xueyuan
Nanjing Tian Zhu Jiao Tang (Nanjing Catholic Church) 120
Nanjing Yangzi River Bridge
  see Nanjing Changjiang Da Qiao
Nankang *see* Xing Zi
Nanmen Hu 312
Nantong 2–3

National Defense Park
  see Guo Fang Yuan
Nengren Buddhist Temple
  see Nengren Si
Nengren Si (Nengren Buddhist Temple) 306–311
North Pole Tower *see* Bei Ji Ge
Northern Expedition (Bei Fa) 8, 51, 63, 137, 142, 194, 304, 313, 350
Nuona Pagoda *see* Nuona Ta
Nuona Si 107–108
Nuona Ta (Nuona Pagoda) 107–108, 331, 340

O

O-Mi-Tuo-Fo (Amitabha) 15, 168, 230, 239, 242, 253, 278, 309
Old City Gate *see* Long Men Kou Jie
One Hundred Year Old Palace
  see Bai Sui Gong
Overseas Chinese Hotel 57–58

P

Peace Pagoda *see* He Ping Ta
Peach Blossom Hill *see* Tao Hua Shan
Peng, Yu Lin 47, 182, 288, 292, 294
People's Assembly Hall
  see Renmin Ju Yuan
Phoenix Pine *see* Feng Huang Song
Pipa Ting (Lute Pavilion) 302, 322, 324
Plum Blossom New Village
  see Mei Yuan Xin Cun
Porcelain Pagoda *see* Bao En Ta
Poyang Lake (Poyang Hu) 46, 281–282, 285, 291–292, 295–299, 302, 305, 324, 329, 336, 363–364, 381, 411
Precious Hall of the Great Hero
  see Da Xiong Bao Dian
Precious Hall of the Sacred Body
  see Rou Shen Bao Dian
Presidential Palace
  see Tushuo Zongtong Fu
Prip-Moller, Johannes 136, 139, 150, 152, 224, 371
Pu Ti Da Mo (Bodhi Dharma) 161, 162, 230
Pure Land Sect *see* Jing Tu Zong
Purple and Gold Mountain
  see Zijin Shan

Q

Qi Xia Buddhist Temple *see* Qi Xia Si
Qi Xia Si (Qi Xia Buddhist Temple) 165–167, 169
Qi Xian Buddhist Temple
  see Qi Xian Si
Qi Xian Gu (Qi Xian Valley) 396, 401, 402, 406, 408, 410–411
Qi Xian Si (Qian Si Buddhist Temple) 402, 404–406
Qi Xian Valley *see* Qi Xian Gu
Qi Yuan Si (Tending Garden Temple) 225, 227, 230–231, 241, 248
Qian Fo Ta (Thousand Buddha Pagoda) 25–26, 375

Qing Lian Gu (Qing Lian Valley) 362, 364–366
Qing Lian Si 364
Qing Lian Valley *see* Qing Lian Gu
Qing Liang Men 68, 73, 83
Qing Liang Shan 73, 97, 110
Qing Liang Si 110, 364–365
Qing Shan (Green Hill) 184, 190–191
Qing Yang 221–222, 226, 232
Qing Zhen Si (Mosque) 64, 120, 208–209, 260–261
Qinhuai River 47–48, 58, 67–68, 71, 73, 76–77, 82, 85, 118
Quiet Sea Temple *see* Jing Hai Si

R

Railways Ministry *see* Tie Dao Bu
Rainflower Terrace *see* Yuhua Tai
Ren Jia Po Jie 262
Renmin Ju Yuan (People's Assembly Hall) 330, 338–340, 359
Ricci, Matteo 42, 329, 391–392
River Viewing Pavilion
  see Wang Jiang Ting
Roman Catholic Church/ Cathedral
  see Tian Zhu Jiao Tang
Rooster Crow Temple *see* Jiming Si
Rou Shen Bao Dian (Precious Hall of the Sacred Body) 225, 235–239
Royal Hotel *see* Da Huang Jia
Ruqin Hu (Ruqin Lake) 302, 332, 343, 345–346, 376
Ruqin Lake *see* Ruqin Hu
Russian Valley *see* Lulin Gu

S

Sacred Way (Shen Dao) 84, 122–123, 127–129, 1 51–152, 163, 165, 184, 225
Sakyamuni *see* Shijianmouni
San Bao Bei (Three Treasures Tablet) 140
San Bao Shu (Three Precious Trees) 359, 362
San Die Quan (Three Step Waterfall) 364–369, 382
San Fo 15, 23, 230, 233, 239, 278
San Guo *see* Three Kingdoms
San Tai Dong (Three Terrace Cave) 157, 160–163
San Xia *see* Three Gorges
San Zang *see* Tripitaka
San Zhao Dong 23, 27
Sanjiang Normal College 49, 96, 100, 103
Scripture Bestowing Pavilion
  see Ci Jing Ting
Second National History Archives
  see Zhongguo Di Er Lishi Dang An Guan
Shan Men 20, 22, 201, 307
Shanghai 2–4, 6, 8–9, 21, 35, 45, 50, 58–59, 61, 88, 97, 118, 120, 132, 138, 142, 154, 178, 180, 195, 198, 206, 221–222, 247–249, 267, 272, 280, 304–305, 319, 402
Shen Ce Men *see* He Ping Men

Shen Dao see Sacred Way
Sheng Gong Hui (Church of the Ascension) 340-341
Shi Ba Luohan (18 Arhats) 15, 23
Shi, Da Kai 44, 46, 250, 302
Shi Men Jian Gu (Stone Gate Valley) 353-355, 377
Shi Men Kou (Stone Gate Mouth) 206-207
Shi Tou Cheng (Stone City) 68, 83
Shi Tou Cheng Gongyuan (Stone City Park) 68, 70, 73, 82-83
Shi Wang Dian (Ten Kings Hall) 236-238
Shi Zhong Shan (Stone Bell Hill) 182-183, 282, 284-285, 287-289, 291-292, 295, 297, 305
Shijiamouni (Sakyamuni) 15, 157, 159, 200, 230, 239, 242, 278
Shizi Shan (Lion Peak) 70, 78-79, 114, 153
Shizi Shan in Wuhu (Lion Hill) 1 94-195, 210-212
Shoe Island see Xie Shan
Shuang Jing Lu 27
Shuang Taiyang Qiao (Twin Sun Bridge) 307
Si Tian Wang (Four Heavenly Kings) 157, 166, 199-200, 230, 233, 253, 307, 415
Silver Island see Jiao Shan
Sino-Japanese War 8, 63, 101, 104, 133, 292, 327, 403
Skyrme, F.H.E. 3, 12, 195, 277, 329
Small Heavenly Pool Peak
   see Xiao Tian Chi Feng
Small Nine Flower Hill
   see Xiao Jiuhua Shan
Song, Meiling 98, 143-144, 342, 402
Song Meiling Villa see Meiling Bieshu
Song, Qingling 52, 132, 145
Song Shou Si (Longevity Buddhist Temple) 282-283, 305
Southeast University
   see Dong Nan Daxue
Spirit Valley Buddhist Temple
   see Ling Gu Buddhist Temple
Spirit Valley Pagoda see Ling Gu Ta
Spirit Valley Park
   see Ling Gu Gongyuan
Stone Bell Hill see Shi Zhong Shan
Stone City see Shi Tou Cheng
Stone City Park
   see Shi Tou Cheng Gongyuan
Stone Gate Mouth see Shi Men Kou
Stone Gate Valley
   see Shi Men Jian Gu
Stuart, John Leighton 94-95, 101
Su Dong Po (Su Shi) 16, 284-285, 287, 292, 328, 374, 378, 399
Su Shi see Su Dong Po
Sun, Fo 94, 99
Sun, Ke 129-130, 135
Sun Ke Lou 135, 146
Sun, Quan 5, 37, 68, 83
Sun, Yat Sen see Sun, Zhongshan

Sun Yat Sen Mausoleum
   see Zhongshan Ling
Sun Yat Sen Memorial Hall s
   ee Sun Zhongshan Ji Nian Guan
Sun Yat Sen Museum
   see Sun Zhongshan Ji Nian Guan
Sun, Zhongshan (Sun, Yat Sen) 28, 50, 57, 60, 69, 74, 90, 93-94, 99, 126, 129, 131-132, 134-135, 137, 142, 144-145, 171
Sun Zhongshan Ji Nian Guan (Sun Yat Sen Memorial Hall) 134-135
Suo Jiang Pagoda see Suo Jiang Ta
Suo Jiang Ta (Suo Jiang Pagoda) 320-322
Supreme Court see Zuigao Fayuan
Susong 189, 276, 301
Swallows Crag see Yanzi Ji
Sweet Dew Temple see Gan Lu Si

T

Tai Cheng (Tai City) 79-80, 116-117
Tai City see Tai Cheng
Taiping Bowuguan (Taiping Museum) 87
Taiping Gong Temple 371
Taiping Heavenly Kingdom
   see Taiping Tian Guo
Taiping Museum
   see Taiping Bowuguan
Taiping Rebellion 49, 90, 127, 136, 138, 166, 168, 182, 193, 259, 265, 302, 307, 311, 317, 327, 351, 377, 413-414
Taiping Tian Guo (Taiping Heavenly Kingdom) 7, 43, 169, 282, 302, 339
Taiyi Cun (Taiyi Village) 383, 407, 410
Taiyi Village see Taiyi Cun
Tan, Yan Kai 141-143, 174
Tang, Shengzhi 349-351
Tao Hua Shan (Peach Blossom Hill) 129
Temple of Conversion see Gui Zong Si
Temple of Ten Thousand Pines
   see Yi Wan Song Si
Ten Kings Hall see Shi Wang Dian
Tending Garden Temple see Qi Yuan Si
Three Gorges (San Xia) 1, 294, 301
Three Kingdoms (San Guo) 5, 37-40, 83, 183
Three Precious Halls see Zhan Tan Chan Ling San Da Bao Dian
Three Precious Trees
   see San Bao Shu
Three Step Waterfall
   see San Die Quan
Three Terrace Cave see San Tai Dong
Three Treasures Tablet
   see San Bao Bei
Tian Hua Gong Buddhist Nunnery 314
Tian Jiang Si 14, 17
Tian Qiao (Heavenly Bridge) 345-346
Tian Wang Dian (Heavenly Kings Hall) 14-15, 23, 136, 166, 230, 232-233, 252, 255, 257, 307-308, 310, 379, 415

Tian Zhu Jiao Tang (Roman Catholic Church/Cathedral) 120, 194, 197-198, 209, 218, 222, 264, 306
Tie Dao Bu (Ministry of Railways) 53-54
Tie Fo (Iron Buddha) 307, 310-311
Tie Ta (Iron Pagoda) 19
Ting Tang Gongyuan (Ting Tang Park) 216-217
Ting Tang Park
   see Ting Tang Gongyuan
Tongling 10, 195, 221, 223, 247, 267, 326
Tou Tai Dong 157-160
Transformation Temple
   see Hua Cheng Si
Treaty of Tientsin (Tianjin) 7, 45, 49, 250, 303
Teaty port 7, 43, 49, 84, 114, 194, 303, 329
Tripitaka (San Zang) 39, 224, 232
Tushuo Zongtong Fu (Former Presidential Palace) 48, 54, 62, 64, 87, 89, 90, 92, 122, 339
Twin Sun Bridge
   see Shuang Taiyang Qiao
Two Southern Tang Dynasty Tombs
   see Nan Tang Er Ling

U

University of Nanking
   see Jinling Daxue
Urban Development Exhibition Hall 87

V

Villa No. 246 (Kuling Hotel) 341-342
Villa No. 359 (Zhu De Villa) 340-341
Villa No. 381 (Kuling American School) 337-338, 346

W

Wai Jiao Bu (Ministry of Foreign Affairs) 53, 122
Wang Jiang Ting (River Viewing Pavilion) 162, 332
Wang, Jingwei 52, 56, 60, 66, 85, 90, 95, 129, 133, 272, 330
War God Temple see Guandi Miao
Welch , Holmes 13-14, 224
Welcome the River Temple
   see Ying Jiang Si
Wen Quan (Lushan Hot Springs) 415
Wenhua Da Geming
   see Cultural Revolution
Wenshu Tai (Manjusri Terrace) 352-353
West Flower Hall see Xi Hua Dian
West Grove Buddhist Temple
   see Xi Lin Si
West Valley see Xi Gu
White Deer Cave Academy
   see Bai Lu Dong Shuyuan
White Egret Isle see Bai Lu Zhou
White Horse Park
   see Bai Ma Gongyuan

Index

Wu Chao Men (Meridian Gate) 67, 76, 81
Wu Lao Feng (Five Old Men Peak/Wu Lao Peak) 328, 336, 362–366, 368, 382, 386, 388
Wu Lao Peak see Wu Lao Feng
Wu Liang Dian (Beamless Hall) 136–140, 152
Wu Long Tan (Black Dragon Pool) 359, 362
Wu Long Tan Gongyuan (Black Dragon Pool Park) 109–110
Wuhan 10, 43, 49–50, 59, 61–62, 133, 142, 154, 189, 272, 282, 291, 302, 304, 319, 322, 326, 328, 330, 350, 403
Wuhu 43, 46–47, 181, 183, 187–188, 193–222, 223, 247, 267

X

Xi Gu (West Valley) 332, 336, 343, 356
Xi Hua Dian (West Flower Hall) 89–90
Xi Jing Du Jia (Xi Jing Ferry Lane) 31–34
Xi Jing Ferry Lane see Xi Jing Du Jia
Xi Lin Si (West Grove Buddhist Temple) 302, 328, 345, 372, 374, 376–377
Xian see Changan
Xiang Shan (Elephant Shan) 8, 27
Xianren Dong (Immortals Cavern) 160, 340, 345–348, 356
Xiao Gu Shan (Little Orphan Island) 275–279, 297
Xiao Jiuhua Shan (Small Nine Flower Hill) 112
Xiao Tian Chi Feng (Small Heavenly Pool Peak) 331–332, 347
Xie Shan (Shoe Island) 281, 295–300
Xin Hai Geming see 1911 Revolution
Xin Ming Men 79
Xing Zheng Yuan (Executive Yuan) 61–62, 92–93, 143
Xing Zi (Nankang) 301, 305, 382, 385–396, 401, 407, 411–414
Xiu Feng (Beautiful Peak) 411–415
Xu, Da 111, 163
Xuan Miao Guan Taoist Temple 356
Xuan Wu Hu Gongyuan (Xuan Wu hu Park) 79, 106, 109
Xuan Wu Hu Park see Xuan Wu Hu Gongyuan
Xuan Wu Men (Feng Run Men) 76–77, 106–107, 109
Xuan, Zang 111–112, 139
Xun Yang Ta (Xun Yang Tower) 319–321
Xun Yang Tower see Xun Yang Ta

Y

Yan Shui Ting (Misty Water Pavilion) 316–318
Yang, Ting Bao 54–57, 65, 88–89, 104
Yangzhou 10, 21, 63, 289
Yangzi River 1–13, 17–18, 20–22, 24, 26, 30, 33, 34–35, 37, 39–41, 43–47, 49, 51, 58, 63, 65–66, 78, 83–84, 105, 114, 132–133, 149, 161, 164, 180–184, 186–189, 191, 193–195, 197–198, 201–202, 204, 212–215, 218, 221, 223, 247, 249–253, 265–266, 275–277, 279, 281–282, 285, 291–292, 295, 297, 301–303, 305, 310–311, 318–321, 323, 326, 329–330, 332
Yangzi River Runyang Highway Bridge (Runyang Changjiang Gonglu Da Qiao) 9
Yanzi Ji (Swallows Crag) 68, 84, 155–157, 163, 181–182
Yao, Shi Fo 15, 116, 200, 230, 241–242, 278
Yellow Dragon Pool see Huang Long Tan
Yellow Dragon Buddhist Temple see Huang Long Si
Yellow Dragon Valley see Huang Long Gu
Yellow Mountain see Huang Shan
Yellow River see Huang He
Yi Hao Lou (Building No. 1) 56
Yi Ji Shan 194, 212–215
Yi Jiang Men (Hai Ling Men) 53–54, 69, 78–79, 153
Yi Wan Song Si (Temple of Ten Thousand Pines) 414
Ying Jiang Si (Welcome the River Temple) 200, 252–253, 255–258
Ying Zhou 106–107, 115
Yong Mu Lou 135
Yu Bei Ting (Imperial Stele Pavilion) 21
Yu Qi Buddhist Temple see Yu Qi Si
Yu Qi Si (Yu Qi Buddhist Temple) 149–150
Yuan Fo Dian (Circular Buddha Hall) 349–350
Yuan, Shi Kai 50–51
Yue Fei 40, 149
Yuhua Tai (Rainflower Terrace) 47, 59, 71, 148

Z

Zen Sect see Chan Zong
Zeng, Guofan 44, 47–49, 52, 85, 108, 117, 121, 138, 251, 294, 302–303
Zeng, Guoquan 47, 49, 59, 250–251
Zhan Tan Chan Ling San Da Bao Dian (Three Precious Halls) 235
Zhang, Xun 50–51
Zhang, Zhi Dong 49, 96, 103, 105
Zhe Shan Gongyuan (Zhe Shan Park) 202–203
Zhe Shan Park see Zhe Shan Gongyuan
Zheng, He 87, 111, 114, 120, 146, 149–150, 152–153
Zheng He Bowuguan (Zheng He Museum) 87
Zheng He Gongyuan (Zheng He Park) 87, 111

Zheng He Museum see Zheng He Bowuguan
Zheng He Park see Zheng He Gongyuan
Zheng Qi Pavilion see Zheng Qi Ting
Zheng Qi Ting (Zheng Qi Pavilion) 130–131
Zhenjiang 3, 5–36, 44–46, 84, 178
Zhenjiang Lieshi Lingyuan 34
Zhenjiang Museum (Zhenjiang Bowuguan) 8, 30
Zhi Gong Dian (Zhi Gong Hall) 139–140
Zhi Gong Hall see Zhi Gon Dian
Zhi Pu Bin Guan (Zhi Pu Hotel) 343–344
Zhi Pu Hotel see Zhi Pu Bin Guan
Zhong Gu Lou see Bell and Drum Tower
Zhong Hua Men (Ju Bao Men) 59, 69, 71–73, 148
Zhong Jiang Ta (Middle River Pagoda) 194, 197–198, 218
Zhong Lou see Bell Tower
Zhongguo Di Er Lishi Dang An Guan (Second National History Archives) 55, 89, 121–122
Zhongshan Ling (Sun Yat Sen Mausoleum) 129–134
Zhongshan Lu Shang Ye Bu Xing Jie (Zhongshan Road Pedestrian Mall) 196, 206, 218, 220
Zhongshan Men (Chao Yang Men) 54, 59, 67–68, 74–75, 84, 1 28–129, 132
Zhongshan Road Pedestrian Mall see Zhongshan Lu Shang Ye Bu Xing Jie
Zhongyang Jian Cha Wei Yuan Hui (Guomindang Central Supervisory Committee) 54, 89
Zhou, En Lai 65, 87, 330
Zhu De Villa see Villa No. 359
Zhu Tian (Devas) 200, 242, 255
Zhu Xi (Chu Hsi) 328, 389, 391, 393–396
Zhu, Yuanzhang 40, 67, 81, 111, 116, 119, 122, 126, 138, 153, 157, 159, 183, 249, 281–282, 302, 346–347, 352
Zi Xia Hu (Zi Xia Hu) 130
Zi Xia Lake see Zi Xia Hu
Zijin Shan (Purple and Gold Mountain) 39, 42, 50, 59, 74–75, 82, 94, 111–112, 114, 116, 122, 129–132, 140–141, 143, 146, 152, 163–164, 377
Zijin Shan Cable Car see Zijin Shan Suo Dao
Zijin Shan Observatory (Zijin Shan Tian Wen Tai) 42, 145–146
Zijin Shan Suo Dao (Zijin Shan Cable Car) 145
Zongtong Fu see Tushuo Zongtong Fu
Zu Tang Shan 150, 152
Zuigao Fayuan (Supreme Court) 53, 101

About the Author

Eric. N Danielson's understanding and knowledge of China first started to develop when he was a college student back in the 1980s. He studied modern Chinese history under the guidance of Professor Kent Guy at the University of Washington in Seattle, where he earned a B.A. in History in 1988. In 1994, Eric earned his M.A. in History from George Washington University in Washington, D.C. He has published works on Kurdistan, Yugoslavia, and China.

Eric has lived and worked in Shanghai for he past five years. He is an education consultant and academic manager in China's rapidly growing private education industry. He welcomes reader comments and feedback, and may be reached at ShangConsultant@netscape.net.